D0761005

*Fact and Fantasy in
Freudian Theory*

Fact and Fantasy in Freudian Theory

Second Edition

PAUL KLINE

METHUEN
London & New York

First published in 1972 by
Methuen & Co. Ltd
11 New Fetter Lane, London EC4P 4EE
Second Edition 1981
Published in the USA by
Methuen & Co.
in association with Methuen, Inc.
733 Third Avenue, New York, NY 10017
© 1972 & 1981 Paul Kline
Printed in Great Britain at the University Press, Cambridge

All rights reserved. No part of this book may be reprinted
or reproduced or utilized in any form or by any electronic,
mechanical or other means, now known or hereafter invented,
including photocopying and recording, or in any information
storage or retrieval system, without permission in writing
from the publishers.

British Library Cataloguing in Publication Data

Kline, Paul
Fact and Fantasy in Freudian theory. — 2nd ed.
1. Psychoanalysis
I. Title
150.19′52   BF173.F85

ISBN 0-416-72640-2

Contents

Contents

Preface

The first edition of *Fact and Fantasy in Freudian Theory* proved a useful guide as to what aspects of Freudian theory had been and could be subjected to the Popperean scientific test of refutability. It was there concluded that Freudian theory was not a single coherent theory but rather a collection of theories, some of which were supported by objective quantified evidence, so that any blanket rejection of Freudian theory was unjustified.

This first edition provoked an immediate response from Eysenck (1972) and Eysenck and Wilson (1973), who not unexpectedly attempted to refute the positive claims made on behalf of Freudian concepts. More recently Fisher and Greenberg (1977, 1978) have essentially repeated the exercise in *Fact and Fantasy in Freudian Theory* but on a huge scale, where up to that date almost all relevant papers and theses have been cited.

In our second edition of *Fact and Fantasy in Freudian Theory* we have several aims which can be succinctly listed.

1. We want to answer some of the criticisms, raised by critics hostile to psychoanalysis, of the first edition. Many of their points, as we have argued briefly elsewhere (Kline, 1978), do not stand. Some of the arguments however, for example that in some cases alternative hypotheses were not considered, were reasonable and these we shall be taking account of.

2. Since 1972 a large amount of new evidence relevant to psychoanalytic theory has accumulated. Some of this has been summarized in Fisher and Greenberg (1977), a summary we shall be adopting.

However, this will be no act of plagiarism because, as will become clear from the discussion, in our view Fisher and Greenberg are quite uncritical: they accept results at their face value with almost no consideration of methodological adequacy. Their book reads like a bibliographic listing of results. Furthermore, Fisher and Greenberg's survey stopped well before 1977.

In addition, the present author has recently carried out some extensive studies of psychoanalytic theory which need reporting and placing in the context of other findings and these investigations will be analysed. Some of these studies use principles and methods developed on the continent of Europe and are little known in Great Britain and America. No mention or reference to them can be found in Fisher and Greenberg (1977), for example, yet these offer, in our view, perhaps the most powerful objective method of investigating psychoanalytic theories.

3. Finally, over the eight years since the writing of the first edition, some of our ideas concerning the nature of psychoanalytic theory and its place relative to other psychological theories have not unnaturally changed. These new views on the

significance of various psychoanalytic concepts will be incorporated into our second edition.

With these additions and alterations the second edition of *Fact and Fantasy in Freudian Theory* will, we hope, remain the standard reference for the objective study of psychoanalytic theory.

Introduction

The aim of this book is relatively simple — to establish what parts of Freudian theory have been confirmed or, at least, could be confirmed by objective, scientific, psychological research. In short, to establish psychoanalysis as a true science. This is necessary because Freudian theory, so far as it is dependent on data at all, rests on data which by the criteria of scientific methodology are totally inadequate. These data are, for the most part, the free associations of patients undergoing therapy and their dream reports, and both of these sources lack quantification and are riddled with subjective interpretation. The achievement of such an aim seems worthwhile if only because the influence of Freud's ideas has been so pervasive. Art and literature as well as psychiatry and other fields associated with mental health have been radically affected. Yet academic psychology has tended to disregard psychoanalytic theory or even to consider it a positively baleful influence on precise scientific thought.

Thus the first chapter of the book is devoted to a brief statement of what the scientific method is and how it may be applied to a study of psychoanalytic theory. It is not intended to be a comprehensive study of scientific methodology or the philosophy of science, subjects demanding books to themselves. It does, however, deal with the particular problems of validating Freudian hypotheses.

Based on this analysis the rest of the book is devoted to a study of specific hypotheses to be found in the writings of Freud. It would be idle to pretend that every empirical proposition in his voluminous output (twenty-four volumes of collected papers) has been examined. What has been attempted, however, is a careful scrutiny of the scientific evidence, as defined in our opening chapter, which bears upon his major hypotheses. Thus, for example, chapters are devoted to the Oedipus and castration complexes, to psychosexual personality syndromes and to defence mechanisms.

Further, unlike Fisher and Greenberg (1977), we have not attempted to include a description of every experiment reported in the journals which is or purports to be relevant to psychoanalytic theory. This because, as we make clear in Chapter 1, we have adopted rigorous standards of experimentation such that the results should be acceptable to unbiased psychologists of whatever persuasion, and on such criteria many experimental investigations of Freudian theory are weak in the extreme. Many use tests and measures of unproven validity or in some cases of proven invalidity (as for example is the case with many of the variables from the Rorschach test). To describe such experiments only to argue in conclusion that no inferences can be drawn from them is pointless. Such experiments are discussed only where their findings have been taken by others in the field as confirmation or refutation of Freudian theory. In this instance it is obviously relevant to demonstrate the weaknesses of the investigations.

A serious difficulty in the study of psychoanalysis lies in the emotional attitudes it arouses in both its adherents and its opponents — feelings which are not conducive to a rational appraisal of its value. Psychoanalysts, at the earliest stages in the development of the theory, frequently argued that any opposition to the ideas was a form of resistance — a mechanism of defence against the unpalatable truths it contained. As Medawar (1969) has pointed out, this is contrary to all the canons of scientific investigation and he consequently tries to dismiss the *whole* theory as entirely unscientific, a rejection with which Eysenck would thoroughly agree. A further barrier is the psychoanalytic claim that only those who have undergone an analysis themselves can understand the ideas. These arguments have been entirely ignored thoughout this book.

In accord with the concept of psychoanalysis as many theories rather than one, each chapter is devoted to a study of the objective scientific evidence relevant to one of the basic postulates in psychoanalytic theory. For many such postulates the amount of good evidence is small. This has enabled us to discuss the researches at greater length than is often found in surveys of this type. Great attention has been paid to the quality of the measurements and the experimental design of the investigations. This is of vital importance since a mere description of an investigation and a statement of results can be totally misleading in areas where the methodology is complex and there is no single agreed procedure among psychologists. Our discussion of the research has therefore been designed to allow the reader to judge for himself the extent to which the Freudian theory has been confirmed and to enable him, if he wishes, to disagree with our interpretation. Without this discussion, however, the book would consist of dogmatic assertions of necessarily little weight.

In some cases, however, the amount of experimental evidence is enormous. To review all this in detail would be impossible in a book of this size and equally arduous for both writer and reader. Here the method used has been to review first the methodological problems involved in testing the theory and then to examine only those studies which meet these criteria.

This approach where each chapter is concerned with the evidence relevant to one of the major Freudian postulates is interrupted only at one point where two broad methods are described, methods which are so powerful that they are applicable to a wide range of psychoanalytic hypotheses, although as yet they are little used outside the laboratories where they were developed. We refer here to Scandanavian work on percept-genetics (Kragh and Smith, 1970) and the experimental studies by Silverman and his colleagues in New York (e.g. Silverman, 1971).

The subject matter of the chapters follows a logical developmental sequence: the first chapters are concerned with the Freudian hypotheses concerning child development which lead to his structured hypotheses of mental provinces, defence mechanisms and the contents of the unconscious as revealed in dreams. This in turn leads on to the hypotheses concerning neuroses, the success of psychoanalytic therapy and a brief study of neo-Freudian theories in the light of the experimental evidence. Lastly, in the final chapter, we review those parts of psychoanalytic theory which have been supported and assess the status of the theory. Nevertheless, despite this sequential arrangement of chapters, each is self-contained and can be read on its own by readers interested in one particular part of Freudian theory.

Psychoanalytic theory has never been drab or uninteresting. It is our hope and fantasy that this book will help to put psychoanalysis back among the sciences and encourage imaginative researchers to investigate with methodological precision those areas of human thought and behaviour that Freudian theory has attempted to illuminate and which behaviouristic psychologies seem unwilling to study or even to contemplate.

1

Freudian theory and scientific method

Eysenck (1953a) answering his own question — 'What is wrong with psycho-analysis?' — claims that the answer is simple: 'Psychoanalysis is unscientific.' First, therefore, it is necessary to clarify the meaning of the term scientific as applied to a theory.

THE MEANING OF SCIENTIFIC

Marx (1963) in a definition that would seem agreeable to the majority of philosophers of science argues that there are three fundamental elements of all scientific-theory construction:

1. Observations — which must be under *controlled* conditions (that is eliminate the role of extraneous variables).
2. Constructs — which must be *operational* (that is have clearly specified and identifiable empirical referents).
3. Hypotheses — which must be *testable* (that is clearly disconfirmable).

It is certainly true to say that on all these criteria much of Freudian theory is open to criticism.

OBSERVATIONS

The observations on which Freudian theory rests are made by psychoanalysts during therapy. The raw data of psychoanalytic theory consist of the free associ-ations of the patient and the reports of dreams to which further free associations are elicited. These raw data are not even recorded as spoken but are recalled later by the analyst. Thus there is no quantification, no control group, nor indeed any check on the reliability of the analyst's memory.

CONSTRUCTS

Many of the constructs in psychoanalytic theory are vague and difficult to relate to any external referent: for example, the concepts of eros and thanatos, the life and death instincts. Thus Freud (1920) in 'Beyond the pleasure principle' writes that there are two kinds of instinct: 'Those which seek to lead what is living to death and others, the sensual instincts, which are perpetually attempting and achieving a renewal of life'. It is, obviously, no simple matter to operationalize these terms.

HYPOTHESES

It is inevitably the case that if the constructs of a theory are themselves unclear, any hypotheses of which they form a part must be difficult to refute. Even worse, they may be impossible to test. For example, the anal character (Freud, 1908a) is considered to be, in psychoanalytic theory, the result of repressed anal erotism. Although at present this hypothesis is not testable because there are no adequate measures of anal erotism (an example of a vague construct) or repression, it may be tested in principle at least. Until recently the back of the moon could not be observed, yet the statement or hypothesis that the back of the moon was made of cheese was testable and refutable in principle and hence scientific. However, the Freudian theory of the anal character cannot easily be refuted. Thus if parsimony, a sublimation of the retentive desire, were not found to be part of the anal character, the Freudian theorist can point to Jones (1923) and argue that generosity too may be included, being a reaction-formation against the retentive desire.

These examples make it clear that on these criteria of scientific theories Eysenck (1953a) is correct. Psychoanalytic theory is open to serious criticism. However, psychoanalytic theory is of such a kind that these criticisms are not necessarily entirely destructive.

THE NATURE OF PSYCHOANALYTIC THEORY

Rapaport and Gill (1959) have attempted to impose a four-fold hierarchical structure onto psychoanalytic theory which is exceedingly useful for the clarification of the theory. This structure with the examples given by the authors is set out below.

1. *Empirical proposition*. Around the fourth year of life boys regard their fathers as rivals.
2. *Specific psychoanalytic proposition*. The solution of the Oedipal situation is a decisive determinant of character formation and pathology.
3. *General psychoanalytic proposition*. Structure formation by means of identifications and anti-cathexes explains theoretically the consequences of the 'decline of the Oedipus complex'.
4. *Metapsychological proposition*. The propositions of the general psychoanalytic theory which explain the Oedipal situation and the decline of the Oedipus complex involve dynamic, economic, structural, genetic and adaptive assumptions.

This taxonomy is the basis for the argument, suggested above, that the failure of psychoanalytic theory to stand scrutiny against the normal criteria of science is not necessarily destructive. The criticisms raised by Eysenck (1953a) are directed against the top of the hierarchical structure — general psychoanalytic propositions and metapsychological propositions; they do not apply with the same force to the empirical basis — empirical and specific psychoanalytic propositions. Indeed, the problem of the scientific validity of psychoanalysis in terms of this structure turns about this question. Are the empirical propositions and specific psychoanalytic propositions true? In other words, the first concern is with the observations. Indeed it seems pointless to criticize the metapsychology of psycho-analytic theory on the grounds of internal inconsistency, or untestability of the hypotheses, before establishing whether or not the empirical data, which the metapsychology seeks to subsume, are well founded or not. This is the approach adopted in this book. Psychoanalytic theory has been carefully examined in order to set out as precisely as possible the empirical or specific psychoanalytic propositions. The psychological literature has then been reviewed to see whether or not these propositions may be regarded as true. This procedure, it should be noted, has been objected to by Martin (1964), who argues that to restate the theory in this way is to alter it. Nevertheless, if one proceeds with care, this need not be the case.

There is a further characteristic of psychoanalytic theory which is relevant to its viability as a scientific theory. This is that it is not a unified theory but a collection of parts (Farrell, 1961). This means that even if certain psychoanalytic hypotheses are shown to be false it does not destroy the whole of psychoanalysis. Thus, for example, even if dreams do not express wishes, the castration complex might well lie behind homosexuality. Farrell (1951, 1961, 1964) has, of course, long been interested in the problem under discussion — the scientific validity of Freudian theory — and he makes a number of points which deserve mention.

1. He agrees with Eysenck (1953a) that psychoanalytic theory cannot be called scientific because the evidence on which it is based is not of established validity. In addition its terms are not clearly enough defined. These criticisms relate to the observation and constructs of Marx (1963).

2. However, he refuses (1964) to consider psychoanalytic theory as a myth, as suggested by Popper (1959), on the grounds that it is not considered to be, even by its most hostile opponents, purely fictitious, it invokes no supernatural persons and does not make use of 'popular' ideas. Nor indeed is it a pre-scientific theory in that unlike, for example, *De Rerum Natura* it can be used for something — psychotherapy.

3. He thus concludes (1964) that psychoanalytic theory cannot be said to be true; for the data on which it is based are not well established. On the other hand it cannot be said to be false — because no collection of evidence has, as yet, falsified the entire complex. Finally there is no acceptable alternative to the theory. This last argument has been much stressed by Conant (1947), who argues that theories are not deposed by facts that do not fit them, but by alternative superior theories. In summary, Farrell describes psychoanalytic theory as a premature empirical synthesis offered in advance of the evidence.

This is the view of psychoanalytic theory accepted in this book. The theory is regarded as a huge collection of empirical hypotheses and propositions some of which may be true. Certainly the metapsychology is unscientific but equally certainly the implicit empirical propositions, in the sense that they are testable, are not. Because the theory is not unified, the disproof of some or even most of the propositions is not fatal to the whole theory — a view also proposed strongly by Sherwood (1969).

SOME OTHER VIEWS OF PSYCHOANALYTIC THEORY

It must be made clear that the view of psychoanalysis and its scientific status adopted in this book, the logical positivist viewpoint advocated by Popper (1959) and Kuhn (1970), is only one of many. Thus Cheshire (1975), for example, has shown that many of the apparent inconsistencies within psychoanalytic theory are in fact more apparent than real and that it is not as incoherent or meaningless as its critics would have us believe. This viewpoint is fully accepted by the present writer but is irrelevant to the purpose of this book, which is to establish the empirical foundations of the theory. However, even if the claims of Cioffi (1970) that the theory is formally defective were accepted (refuted in our view by Cheshire, 1975), this would still not be relevant to this book.

However, as Eysenck and Wilson (1973) stress, Ricoeur's (1970) argument that what is important in psychoanalytic theory is the phenomenology of environmental variables, how they appear to the subject rather than to the observer, seems relevant. For on this view the positivist approach adopted in this book just will not do. Scientific, publicly verifiable quantification can never deal with the subjective constructs claimed by Ricoeur to be central to the psychoanalytic position. Our position here is, however, clear. It may well be the case that Ricoeur is correct. If he is then in our terms psychoanalytic theory is not scientific. Its study becomes not science but philosophy or hermeneutics. If he is correct then all the experiments to be cited in this book will prove negative. The theory will not be supported. It can be argued, then, that psychoanalysis is not scientific. Our approach implicitly puts Ricoeur's argument to the test. Thus Ricoeur's claims do not *per se* invalidate the positivist empirical approach adopted here, although, of course, they could well explain negative findings.

In summary, therefore, it is not argued that the empirical approach to the testing of psychoanalytic theory is the only method of studying that theory. However, it is claimed that this approach is the only one that is capable, in the view of most philosophers of science, of examining the scientific status of psychoanalytic theory and that, of course, is the purpose of this book.

THE TESTING OF THE EMPIRICAL PROPOSITIONS

As Eysenck (1965a) says, the reason why psychoanalysis 'has never been taken very seriously by people with some regard for the principles of scientific method' resides in the nature of the data on which psychoanalytic theory is based. The fact is that the psychoanalytic method is not the scientific method (Farrell, 1964).

This means that the effort to establish the empirical propositions of psychoanalysis scientifically must largely depend on the work of psychologists. The data from psychoanalytic sessions have not done this, nor are they likely to do so for some time. Thus Crown (1968), a psychoanalyst writing on psychoanalysis and the scientific method, categorically states that analysts are not prepared to use the methods appropriate to the sciences because these distort the data.

ACCEPTABLE DATA FOR PSYCHOANALYTIC THEORY

In this book the objective evidence for psychoanalytic theory is reviewed and discussed. Only investigations where the data had any claims to scientific respectability have been examined. Thus, for example, if tests were used they had to be tests with some evidence for their validity. This has meant that the majority of studies with the Rorschach have not been considered. Eysenck (1961) succinctly puts the case against the Rorschach technique, namely that in studies of its validity there is an inverse correlation between positive results and methodological excellence! Other projective techniques are open to similar criticisms but their results have been used where evidence for the validity of the particular score was presented.

If Freudian hypotheses concerning special groups were under examination, then control groups were regarded as essential. After all, the Freudian claim that paranoid schizophrenia is caused by repressed homosexuality is not proven by demonstrating that homosexuality is repressed in paranoids unless it also be shown that such homosexuality does not occur in non-paranoid schizophrenics. This is a matter of simple logic.

A third constraint on the types of study examined was that there has to be some form of statistical analysis of results so that non-significant fluctuations of scores would not be seized on as evidence for or against the theory. The judgement of the statistical excellence of the analysis naturally involved a consideration of the sampling techniques.

The final consideration given to all studies was whether the results were in fact relevant to psychoanalytic theory. This to some extent constitutes a value judgement but where the empirical propositions were clear the problem was not so difficult. Where they are not, then the results of objective studies can be used to clarify the theory itself. This difficulty of deciding the relevance of an investigation to Freudian theory was partly overcome by examining only those studies where the hypothesis tested was clearly stated and deliberately related by the author to Freudian theory. Alternative and perhaps more parsimonious explanations of the results were also discussed. In summary, for the type of data that can put psychoanalytic propositions onto a scientific basis, the following criteria were considered important:

1. Sampling procedures and use of adequate control groups.
2. Validity of tests used.

3. Quality of the statistical analysis of results.
4. Relevance of the conclusions to psychoanalytic theory and possible alternative hypotheses.

At this point it should strike the reader that such studies are not different from the normal procedures of respectable scientific disciplines. If, therefore, the results of any such studies support psychoanalytic theory, there is no reason at all why that part of it that is supported should not be scientifically acceptable.

THE PROBLEM OF REFUTATION

As has been stated earlier, refutability is essential if a theory is to be regarded as scientific. This raises a peculiar difficulty in the objective study of psychoanalysis. If the theory is supported and there is no other viable explanation of the results, it seems fair to argue that this is evidence in favour of psychoanalysis. If, on the other hand, the theory is not supported, the results do not necessarily refute the theory. This is simply because in many cases the validity of the tests is not perfect. This means that if the results are positive they can be accepted, since error is random and likely to spoil rather than to improve the results in any systematic way. If they are negative it *may* be because the tests are faulty. Thus refutation of psychoanalytic theory is not easy.

2

The Freudian theory of
psychosexual development

OUTLINE OF THE THEORY

'Sexual life does not begin only at puberty but starts with clear manifestations soon after birth' (Freud, 1940). 'Sexual life comprises the function of obtaining pleasure from zones of the body — a function which is subsequently brought into the service of that of reproduction' (ibid.). This sexual drive first manifests itself through the mouth during the first year of the infant's life. This is the *oral phase*. Around the third year the erotogenic zone of the anus comes to the fore — the *anal phase*. Third comes the *phallic phase*, around the age of four, where the chief erotogenic zone is the penis (in the case of the girl — the clitoris). The final phase of sexual organization is the *genital phase* established after puberty. At this stage all the previous phases are organized and subordinated to the adult sexual aim of pleasure in the reproductive function (Freud, 1933 and 1940). The pleasure derived from stimulation of the erotogenic zones, which plays a part in mature sexual behaviour, is known as oral erotism, anal erotism and phallic erotism respectively.

According to psychosexual theory this infantile sexuality is crucial to the personality development of the individual because it cannot always be directly expressed. The clearest example of this is the adult anal character — a triad of traits: parsimony, orderliness and obstinacy — which is derived from repressed anal erotism (Freud, 1908a). In the concluding paragraph of this paper, Freud states that 'The permanent character traits are either unchanging perpetuations of the original impulse, sublimations of them or reaction-formations against them.' As an example of the process, kissing may be regarded as a perpetuation of oral erotism, orderliness a reaction-formation against anal erotism (the desire to smear the faeces) and parsimony as a sublimation of anal erotism (desire to retain the faeces). From this outline of the theory it is clear that character traits can be derived from all these infantile pregenital stages of sexuality. Indeed Fenichel (1945) points out that such correlations of personality and infantile sexual development were the first discovery of psychoanalytic characterology.

Adult personality is therefore related to infantile sexuality. The extent to which oral erotism, for example, is directly expressed or sublimated in any individual depends upon two further factors. One is constitutional — each zone is differentially capable of excitation (Freud, 1905a). The other is environmental — in this

7

example, the duration and nature of the feeding and weaning process. Excessive satisfaction at feeding means that the individual is loth to renounce oral erotism. Similarly excessive frustration (e.g. too rapid and early weaning) produces the same effect. This refusal to renounce the pleasure from a particular erotogenic zone is known as fixation. Freud (1916-17) likens fixation and regression to an advancing army in enemy territory leaving occupation troops at all important points. The stronger the occupation troops left behind (fixation) the weaker is the army that marches on. If the latter meets a too powerful enemy force (e.g. toilet-training) it may retreat to those points (regression) where it had previously left the strongest occupation troops. The stronger a fixation the more easily will regression take place if difficulties arise. Fixations most frequently are rooted, according to Fenichel (1945), in satisfactions which simultaneously gave reassurances against some anxiety or helped in the repression of some feared impulse. Variations in adult personality, therefore, are linked, according to this theory, to fixations at and regressions to these psychosexual stages. Such fixations are themselves related to child-rearing procedures as well as to constitutional factors.

IMPORTANCE OF THE THEORY

There can be no doubt that this is an important theory in psychoanalysis: much has been made of its implications. Berkley-Hill (1921), for example, attributed the character and behaviour of Hindus to repressed anal erotism, a factor which was employed by Spitzer (1947) and Gorer (1943) in the clarification of Japanese culture. Freud (1913b) regarded fixation at the anal phase as important in the development of obsessional neurosis while Abraham (1916) related depression to the oral phase. Sexual repressions also are considered to spring from fixations at various phases. If this be insufficient evidence, Roheim (1934) regarded the whole of western culture as anal and Menninger (1943) considered the anal phase as 'without doubt the most important period in the development of not only individuals but whole cultures as well'. Freudian psychosexual theory gives insight into the nature and causes of personality development and implicitly suggests how desired behaviour patterns might be produced. It implies, also, possible alleviation of disorders in that the conflicts resulting in fixation may be resolvable under psychoanalytic therapy. It is from this theory that the first five years of life are considered crucial for adult behaviour. For, as has been indicated, normal personality variations, neuroses, cultural differences and sexual anomalies are based upon psychosexual development within this period.

THE HYPOTHESES

At this point it should be evident that within this theory there are implied three independent sets of hypotheses of which two, at least, are open to empirical validation. These hypotheses may be thus expressed:

1. that there exist in mature adults certain constellations of personality traits,
2. that certain constellations of personality traits are related to child-rearing procedures,
3. that the mouth, the anus and the phallus are erotogenic zones in early childhood.

The first hypothesis is basic to the whole theory. If, for example, it could be shown that the anal traits of obstinacy, parsimony and orderliness do not in fact occur together (to a greater extent than would be expected by chance), i.e. that no such syndrome as the anal character exists, then psychosexual theory breaks down. Thus the first empirical test must be to discover whether such constellations of traits as the oral, the anal and the phallic character do occur. If they do not, Freudian theory is refuted. If they do, a small part, and perhaps the most interesting part, of psychosexual theory is supported. Clearly it could well be the case that such syndromes do exist but that they are unrelated to infantile sexuality and child-rearing procedures.

If it can be shown that such syndromes exist, the second hypothesis becomes crucial. Are such syndromes related, as the theory implies, to child-rearing procedures? Clearly longitudinal child-studies and cross-cultural investigations will be necessary to confirm or refute this second hypothesis. However, such empirical tests, although difficult to execute, are conceptually clear.

The third hypothesis, on the other hand, is more difficult to confirm. The problem is to know what observations would confirm or refute the theory. Does, for example, frequent thumb-sucking, as Freud (1905a) supposes, constitute evidence for the mouth being an erotogenic zone? These problems will be fully considered in the relevant chapter.

Before any examination of the evidence relevant to these three hypotheses, it is necessary to define the theory more precisely. The remaining section of this chapter will be concerned, therefore, with the psychoanalytic descriptions of the character syndromes and the child-rearing procedures and erotogenic zones implicated in their development.

SOURCES

Whereas the original psychosexual theory may be found in Freud, as is evident from the outline, the detailed descriptions of the personalities are to be found elsewhere. These sources will now be quoted, since what follows is a summary of their texts.

1. Oral character — Abraham (1924) and Glover (1924a, 1924b).
2. Anal character — Freud (1908a, 1917a), Abraham (1921), E. Jones (1923) and Menninger (1943).
3. Urethral traits — E. Jones (1933).
4. Phallic traits — Reich (1945) and E. Jones (1915).

Fenichel (1945) contains useful information on all these stages.

THE ORAL CHARACTER

Most authorities distinguish between traits derived from the first phase — sucking — and the later oral sadistic stage — biting. A distinction is drawn, too, between traits derived from over-indulgence and frustration. It is to be noted that more direct expression of oral erotism is permissible in western society than of anal erotism. All agree that oral characteristics are to some extent mixed with later anal influences (Fenichel, 1945).

TABLE 2.1. *Summary of descriptions of the oral character*

Trait	Source — sucking or biting	Frustration or satisfaction (where clearly stated)
(a) Found in Abraham (1924)		
Optimism	S	Satis.
Dependency and inactivity: feeling that people will do things for them	S	Satis.
Pessimism	S	F
Desire for a regular income	S	Satis.
Dependency = Demanding attitudes: 'clinging like a leech'	S	F
Impatience	S	F
Hostility and cruelty: 'clinging like vampires'	S	F
Need to give (often by way of mouth)	S	—
Talkativeness	S	—
Feeling of an inexhaustible flow of ideas	S	—
High valuation on own ideas	S	—
Hostile, sarcastic, biting speech patterns	B	—
Generosity	S	Satis.
Envy, hostility	B	F
Jealousy	B	F
Cheerfulness, sociability	S	Satis.
Malice	B	F
Accessibility to new ideas	S	—
Ambition	—	—
Love of soft foods	S	—
Love of hard foods	B	—
Curiosity and delight in observation	—	—

Trait	Source — sucking 'or biting	Frustration or satisfaction (where clearly stated)
(b) Found in Glover (1924a and 1924b) but not in Abraham		
Rhythmic character of oral reactions	—	—
Quick motor movements	—	—
Buying drinks to produce intoxication in others	B	—
Generous presents of advice	S	F
Tooth-grinding	—	—
(c) Found in Fenichel (1945)		
Voracious reading	—	—

Glover (1924a) summarized oral characteristics under the oral triad of impatience, envy and ambition. 'He hankers after the plums and yet behind it all is a feeling that the silver spoon is, or ought to have been, in the mouth.'

THE ANAL CHARACTER

The anal triad — obstinacy, parsimony and orderliness — was the first discovery (Freud, 1905a) in Freudian psychosexual theory. It has been the most extensively studied both by psychoanalysts and by academic psychologists. Part of its interest lies in the prima-facie absurdity of linking such traits to anal erotism repressed by pot-training. As has been indicated, anal erotism is regarded as a very powerful influence on personality in psychoanalysis because almost none of it can be directly expressed in western society. It therefore emerges in the character as reaction-formations or sublimations.

TABLE 2.2.   *Summary of descriptions of the anal character; orderliness, parsimony and obstinacy (Freud, 1908a)*

(a) Found in Jones (1923)
  Procrastination followed by intense concentration, boring persistence, self-willed independence — a belief that nobody can do anything as well as oneself
  Inability to depute work
  Minute attention to detail
  Intolerant insistence in doing things one way
  Strong drive to clean things (routine chores)
  Profound interest in handwriting
  Opposition to any attempt to guide one's conduct
  Resentment of any thwarting
  Resentment of advice
  Standing on rights and dignity
  Strong feelings at any injustice

Dislike of time being used up against one's will
Irritability and vindictive desires of revenge (symptoms of above)
Highly individualistic
Pleasure spoiled by small things out of place
Love of self-control
Interest in the backs of things

(All the above derive from interest in the act itself. Those below derive from interest in the product of the act.)

(i)   Sublimation of retaining tendency
      Parsimony: avarice and meanness, especially copro-symbols — money, time, food, books — 'all collectors are anal erotic'
      Pleasure in finding things
      Tenderness to children
      Tendency to domineer

(ii) Reaction-formation to retaining tendency
      Orderliness — love of symmetry
      Pedantry, love of exactitude, delight in organizing
      Reliability
      Hatred of waste

(iii) Sublimation of the impulse to give (not part of the anal character but useful for finding what anals are not)

(iv) Reaction-formation of the impulse to give (strictly not part of the anal character but having certain traits in the triad already mentioned above)

(These last two sections represent fixation at the anal expulsive level and are outside the strictly Freudian concept of the anal character.)

(b)   Found in Abraham (1921) but not in Jones
      Pleasure in possessing something rare or unusual
      Pleasure in statistics and tables — Bradshaws, etc.
      Critical of others, generally malcontent
      Dislike of spending money on perishable things
      Simultaneous performance of more than one activity
      Pleasure in looking at one's own mental creations
      Dislike of new subjects
      Delight in meticulous planning, orderly rooms but untidy cupboards
      Dislike of feeling obliged to anyone, love of doing the opposite of most, e.g. curious tastes in food, clothes

---

CHARACTERS DERIVED FROM FIXATION AT OTHER PSYCHOSEXUAL LEVELS

Oral and anal characteristics are far more important in psychoanalytic personality theory than characteristics derived from fixation at other levels. Jones (1915 and 1933) has described urethral and phallic characters, and Reich (1945) has discussed the phallic personality. However there are far less detailed pictures of these available than is the case with the oral and anal character. Consequently, a very brief description of each will be given below. Such brevity is also due to the fact that very few objective studies of these characters exist, so that a lengthy description would be irrelevant.

The urethral character

Ambition is the dominant trait, derived from infantile competition in respect of urination (Fenichel, 1945). Indeed, Glover (1924a) refers to the urinary character. Unnatural pleasure in fire is also claimed to be a related trait (Freud, 1932).

The phallic character

Typical traits are recklessness, self-assurance and resolute courage. There is often intense pride and vanity.

Such then are the descriptions of the personality characteristics considered by psychoanalysis to be derived from fixation at various psychosexual levels. It will be clear that these descriptions and theories enable the first two hypotheses to be put to the empirical test — do such constellations of traits in fact occur and, if they do, are they related to child-rearing procedures and psychosexual stages? In the next chapter the objective evidence bearing on the first hypothesis will be considered — the evidence from personality measurement.

3

The objective evidence concerning psychosexual personality syndromes

INTRODUCTION

In this chapter investigations of the first of the hypotheses implicit in Freudian psychosexual theory will be discussed: are constellations of personality traits, as described in psychoanalytic theory, in fact observable? Only those studies *deliberately* aimed at defining these syndromes will be examined. More general studies of personality which incidentally confirm or refute these hypotheses will be reviewed in a later chapter.

THE NATURE OF THE EVIDENCE

Clinical studies of small numbers of individuals are inherently irrelevant to the Freudian hypotheses. By the laws of probability certain traits would be found occurring together in certain individuals. What is required therefore are investigations of large populations such that the magnitude of observed correlations can be reliably estimated. It is also essential that reliable and valid measuring instruments be used. Thus clinical impressions and rating scales in general carry less weight as evidence than personality inventories and, best of all, objective personality tests. Consequently, as befits the problem, the majority of the researches discussed below will be psychometric studies of these personality syndromes. Generally, the review will be arranged chronologically except where a particular investigation bears directly on the problem under discussion and is therefore better discussed out of sequence.

THE GOLDMAN-EISLER STUDIES OF THE ORAL CHARACTER

Goldman-Eisler reported in three papers (1948, 1950 and 1951) an investigation into the oral character. Her first study (1948) sought to establish the existence of two typical oral personality patterns — the oral pessimist and the oral optimist. Her other two papers investigated the aetiology of such characteristics and will be discussed in the chapter devoted to the aetiological hypotheses in Freudian psychosexual theory, although the 1951 paper gives further details of the tests used. The relevant parts of these papers will be discussed together since they represent one investigation.

Brief description of the study

A sample of 115 middle-class adults, age-range 18-35, completed rating scales for the nineteen traits, mentioned in the psychoanalytic literature under the titles of oral optimist and oral pessimist. Profiles based on the top twenty and bottom twenty subjects closely fitted the psychoanalytic descriptions and a factor-analysis of the scores (Burt's simple summation method) revealed a factor of oral pessimism which was similar to the Freudian picture except that it did not load on compulsion, aggression or autonomy. From this Goldman-Eisler concluded that there was a syndrome of oral pessimism but that the psychoanalytic description which emphasizes aggression and compulsion should be modified. She suggested tentatively that there were two kinds of oral pessimists: (a) the placid kind, and (b) the impulsive and aggressive kind who would go to psychoanalysts for treatment, whereas the others would not. This speculation would account for the inclusion of aggression and impulsion as oral characteristics.

Comments and conclusions

Although the sample was somewhat homogeneous, this cannot be held to invalidate the results for it would tend to depress not raise the correlations. The rating scales were reliable (mean split-half r was 0.56) but the only evidence for their validity was face-validity — the items appeared to refer to oral traits. Face-validity is not considered to be satisfactory for personality tests (Cattell and Warburton, 1967), especially since in this study there was no check on the major response-sets of acquiescence or social desirability which Cronbach (1946, 1950) and Jackson and Messick (1961) regard as an important source of variance in personality testing.

Another point to be noted is that the factor-analysis was not rotated to simple structure and another more elegant solution, not fitting Freudian theory, might be possible.

In view of these points the claim that there are two oral syndromes of optimism and pessimism must be treated with caution. These results give tentative rather than definitive support for psychoanalytic theory although the profiles based on extreme scorers were strikingly clear. The second part of this study relating oral characteristics to weaning will be reviewed in Chapter 5.

BARNES' (1952) STUDY OF PSYCHOSEXUAL THEORY

Barnes (1952) examined the whole Freudian theory of psychosexual development in a factor-analytic study of questionnaire items. Items apparently pertaining to various levels of psychosexuality were given to a sample of 266 male students, median age twenty-three years. These subjects had also completed the Guilford—Zimmerman Temperament Survey, the scores from which were used as markers to identify the factors emerging from the tetrachoric inter-correlations of the Freudian scales. Were the Freudian theory correct, oral, anal and phallic factors would be expected to emerge as well as, perhaps, a general genital factor. Since the Guilford factors were not intended to measure any such variables and since there is nothing from their description which suggests any congruence with these Freudian concepts, these factors ought to be independent of the hypothesized Freudian factors. It is of course possible, as Barnes points out, that even more Freudian factors might be predicted, e.g. oral dependent and oral sadistic, anal expulsive and anal retentive, and, if the item writing were sufficiently sensitive, urethral and phallic factors. From the orthogonal rotation of the centroid analysis, however, eleven factors emerged, none of which could reasonably be identified with the predicted psychosexual factors. The first factor Barnes claimed was meticulousness, which might possibly be identified as anal in that all its loadings were on anal tests although not all the anal tests loaded on it. Of the other factors only one, factor 6, independent self-sufficiency, even faintly resembled a Freudian factor, in this case orality, although factor 11, masculine dominance, could possibly be regarded as phallic. The other factors emerging were: externalized aggression, impatient exhibitionism, a factor with loadings on tests at all levels of psychosexual development, puritanical anti-feminism, optimistic self-confidence (identified as very similar to Guilford's I), flexible ascendance (very similar to Guilford's S), mild anti-feminism and liking for routine together with two factors which could not be identified from the pattern of their loadings.

Comments and conclusions

These results cannot be considered to refute the psychoanalytic theory for a number of reasons. The original correlations were tetrachoric. Guilford (1958) has shown that these have a standard error about twice as large as that of product—moment correlations and that they are unduly affected by the evenness of the dichotomy. This means that the reliability of the factor-analysis must be in doubt.

As with the previous investigation, there is no evidence for the validity of the scales except face-validity and no checks against response-sets. Furthermore, the reliability of the scales cannot have been high since they contained either five or ten items and reliability is related to length. Thus this study neither refutes psychoanalytic theory nor supports it.

STUDIES WITH THE KROUT PERSONAL PREFERENCE SCALE (KPPS)

Krout and Krout (1954), Stagner, Lawson and Moffit (1955) and Stagner and Moffit (1956) have conducted studies of Freudian psychosexual personality syndromes, using the KPPS as their instrument of measurement. The test itself has also been investigated by Snider (1959) and Littman, Nidorf and Sundberg (1961), whose findings must be considered in the appraisal of results achieved with these scales.

THE KPPS

This scale purports to measure (Krout and Krout, 1954) ten developmental levels of personality growth — infantile passive, prenatal, oral sucking, oral sadistic, anal retentive, anal expulsive, narcissistic, feminine, masculine, intro-familial sublimation and social sublimation. From this it can be seen that the test goes beyond orthodox Freudian psychosexual theory, although if valid it would still be useful for testing classical psychosexual theory. Each scale contains ten items to which subjects indicate like or dislike.

Validity

Krout and Krout were not content to rely on face-validity for these scales. First they demonstrated that the scales were independent of the Bell Adjustment Inventory (Bell, 1938), as they ought to be from the nature of the variables in both tests. This alone is not sufficient evidence of course since, for example, intelligence would be equally unrelated to the Bell Inventory. In addition small samples of normals and neurotics were compared. Although there were differences on certain scales — e.g. normals were higher on the anal retentive scale — it is difficult to substantiate the validity of the test by this method without knowing the nosological category of the neurotics. Thus, for example, obsessional neurotics would not be hypothesized to be lower on an anal scale, and depressives ought to be more oral than normals. Finally the scores from fourteen pairs of twins were examined, together with ratings by observers. Although little more than anecdotal the differences observed do support the validity of the scales. In general these validity studies support the validity of the KPPS and thus the existence of the psychosexual personality syndromes.

Reliability

Split-half reliabilities for such short scales were very high — all between 0.89 and 0.98. Inter-scale correlations were low, showing that the sub-tests were independent and that acquiescence could not be a major factor in the results. There appears to have been no check on the effects of social desirability.

Conclusions

From this paper it is clear that the KPPS is a reliable measure of ten independent variables. The face-validity of the items is good and the validity studies presented, although not definitive, strongly suggest that the scales are valid and thus by implication that the Freudian personality syndromes in fact exist.

STUDIES USING THE KPPS

The work of Stagner, Lawson and Moffit (1955) and Stagner and Moffit (1956)

Stagner et al. selected the three best items (by item-analysis) from each scale of KPPS and then subjected the inter-item correlation to an oblique (Quartimax) factor-analysis on a sample of 200 male and 200 female students. Although ten factors emerged, as would be expected from the low inter-correlations of the scales, the pregenital scales, which are of closest relevance to this chapter, did not form clear factors, although the later scales (extension of psychoanalytic theory) did.

With only three items per factor and with the size of inter-item correlations being dependent on item-splits, the rather poor results of this factor-analysis are not unexpected. Indeed, that there were ten factors is in itself encouraging. In fact, in 1956 Stagner and Moffit investigated the problem further.

In this more rigorous study of Freudian psychosexual theory with the KPPS these authors argued that if a type is a functional, organized unity, then individuals classified into one type should show greater similarities to one another than to persons classified into other types. To test this hypothesis, three men were chosen on the basis of KPPS scores to represent each of the ten types.

The inter-correlations between all the thirty subjects selected were calculated and an analysis of variance was computed to compare the mean within-type correlation with the mean between-type correlation. If the theory were correct, within-type correlations should be greater than between-type correlations. In fact, there were no significant differences. From these results Stagner and Moffit (1956) argued that a typological organization of personality is not the best way of representing the functional relationships of these particular responses. They cast doubt on the general Freudian psychosexual theory. To the argument that only rare cases exemplify the types and that these are probably neurotics, these authors reply that such rare instances may be only those special combinations of varying trends which must be expected to occur occasionally in any population in accordance with probability theory. Such cases would not justify a 'type' theory of personality organization. Oral, phallic and anal types are only extremes of a continuum. They conclude by arguing that even if a subject is high on oral erotism this knowledge does not provide a good basis for predicting other personality traits.

Comments

1. The typology suggested by Stagner does not seem implicit in Freudian theory. The anal character may be legitimately regarded, in theory, as the extreme of a continuum — just as is the extravert and introvert as measured by the EPI (Eysenck and Eysenck, 1964). Severe pot-training of a person with strong anal erotism produces the full range of anal characteristics. A less severe training produces fewer traits. At the other extreme is the person of weak anal erotism and gentle training. He shows very few anal characteristics.

2. The last point, that knowledge that a person is high on oral erotism provides no basis for predicting other features of his personality is in fact a denial that syndromes of traits are derived from fixation at psychosexual phases. Stagner and Moffitt (1956) claim that the behaviour due to fixation is extremely restricted in nature with little generalization. However, the weakness of the argument is in the data.

Since the scales are uncorrelated, individuals chosen to represent one type would not be expected to be more alike than those representing another on these scales. What should have been done was to find degrees of similarity on other variables. Then it would be possible to argue about predicting other traits of personality.

Conclusions

It does not appear that the conclusions drawn by Stagner are supported by the data. On the other hand these findings do not support psychosexual theory but are, rather, irrelevant to it. In fact Stagner and Moffit (1956) were not really testing Freudian theory at all — despite their intentions.

The work of Snider (1959) and Littman et al. (1961)

As part of a research into marriage Snider gave the KPPS to 152 stable married couples. The men scored more highly than the neurotic groups in the manual to the test, and the women were more like neurotics than normals.

Comments on Snider

This throws doubt on the validity of the scales in the test and the adequacy of the normative data reported by Krout and Krout (1954) on which the validity of the test was based.

Littman et al. investigated the patterns of norms and the correlations between the KPPS scales on a sample of around 300 Oregon students. They found sex-differences on six of the scales and concluded that the unities postulated by Krout and Krout did not exist. Although they used a later revision of the test with a trichotomous response (the earlier studies used a dichotomous response-scale), so that the results are not entirely comparable, they concluded that the earlier findings did not apply to the Oregon sample. They considered the test to be invalid rather than the Freudian theory at fault.

Comments on Littman et al.

With a test of this sort it is impossible to tell whether the theory or the test is at fault. If the test results are not in accord with theory the test cannot be valid for this is its only criterion of validity. If however the theory is untrue, a valid test cannot be constructed. Consequently in examining the evidence for psycho-analytic personality-theory, it is necessary to consider the results of researches simultaneously rather than each research in isolation. If tests of the syndromes can be constructed in accord with theory, this is good evidence for the validity of the theory. But if large numbers of tests fail to show themselves valid with no technical, psychometric reasons for failure, the theory must be rejected.

CONCLUSIONS FROM THE STUDIES WITH THE KPPS

One of the apparent advantages of the KPPS was that Krout and Krout (1954) had offered some evidence for its validity. The work of Snider (1959) and Littman et al. (1961) suggests, however, that much of this evidence is of dubious value and that the test is invalid. If this be the case the studies of Stagner are not useful. In any case, it has been shown that Stagner's conclusions (Stagner and Moffit, 1956) are not supported by his data. What may be concluded from these studies, therefore, is that they failed to support Freudian theory probably because the KPPS is not a valid measuring instrument for psychosexual personality levels. The results may certainly not be used to refute the theory.

THE DYNAMIC PERSONALITY INVENTORY (DPI) (GRYGIER, 1961a)

This test was developed from the KPPS which, as has been shown, is not a satisfactory instrument for the measurement of psychosexual personality constellations. The DPI, according to the first test manual (Grygier, 1961a), purports to measure 'tendencies, sublimations, reaction-formations and defence mechanisms associated with the various patterns of psychosexual development'. If therefore the scales could be shown to be valid, the psychosexual personality syndromes would be shown to exist and the first set of hypotheses in the theory would be supported. As with the KPPS, therefore, this test deserves most careful scrutiny.

DESCRIPTION OF THE DPI

There are thirty-three scales in the DPI so that it goes very far beyond orthodox psychosexual theory. This is because Freudian theory was regarded as a stimulus for the construction of this test rather than a rigid framework. Nevertheless, as is to be expected all the classical Freudian psychosexual patterns have scales purporting to measure them — five oral scales, six anal scales and several relevant to fixation at the phallic level. A descriptive list of the thirty-three variables is set out in Table 3.1.

TABLE 3.1. *The DPI scales*

H	Hypocrisy: self-satisfaction with own moral standards, lack of insight
Wp	Passivity: liking for comfort, warmth and mild sensual impression
Ws	Seclusion and introspection as a defence against social anxiety
O	Orality: interest in food; liking for sweet, creamy food
Oa	Oral aggression: pleasure in biting and crunching, liking for strong drinks and savoury foods; suggestion of free floating aggression and anxiety about its control
Od	Oral dependence, especially on parents and parental substitutes
Om	Need for freedom of movement and emotional independence: a reaction-formation against oral dependence
Ov	Verbal aggression: verbally and/or intellectually aggressive behaviour
Oi	Impulsiveness, changeability, spontaneity, reactive speed, emotional expressiveness

Ou   Unconventionality of outlook

Ah   Hoarding behaviour: anxious possessiveness, stubborn, clinging persistence

Ad   Attention to details: orderliness, conscientiousness and perfectionism

Ac   Conservatism, rigidity and tendency to stick to routine.

Aa   Submissiveness to authority and order

As   Anal sadism: emphasis on strong authority, cruel laws and discipline

Ai   Insularity: reserve and mistrust, social and racial prejudice

These 'A' scales from their description appear to be the anal scales of the DPI. Only the last of these, Ai, does not seem relevant to the psychoanalytic picture.

P   Interest in objects of phallic-symbol significance

Pn   Narcissism: concern with clothes and appearance; sensuous enjoyment of luxury

Pe   Exhibitionism: conscious enjoyment of attention and admiration

Pa   Active Icarus complex: psycho-physical drive, drive for achievement

Ph   Fascination by height, space and distance: aspirations at the fantasy level

Pf   Fascination by fire, winds, storms and explosions: vivid imagination

Pi   Icarian exploits: interest in active exploration, a love of adventure

S   Sexuality: conscious acceptance of sexual impulses

Ti   Enjoyment of tactile impressions, interest in handicrafts and creative manipulation of objects

Ci   Creative, intellectual and artistic interests

M   Masculine sexual identification, masculine interests, attitudes and roles

     [*or*]

F   Femine sexual identification, feminine interests, attitudes and roles

MF   Tendency to seek roles regardless of their sexual identification

Sa   Interest in social activities

C   Interest in children, need to give affection

EP   Ego-defensive persistence: tendency to act wth renewed effort in the face of difficulties

Ei   Initiative, self-reliance and a tendency to plan, manage and organize

---

EVIDENCE FOR THE VALIDITY OF THE DPI

There are three manuals to this test — those of Grygier (1961b and 1970) and the most recent edition by Grygier and Grygier (1976) which collates most of the evidence relevant (in Grygier's view) to the validity of this test. As we have argued, unequivocal support for the validity of the DPI scales is *ipso facto* unequivocal support for the constructs of oral and anal character as well as a number of other psychoanalytic concepts.

We shall first examine the evidence for the validity of the oral and anal scales adduced by Grygier and Grygier (1976). This consists of correlations with various external criteria (in Chapter 4 of the manual) and in Chapter 5 a series of factor-analyses.

CORRELATIONS WITH EXTERNAL CRITERIA (GRYGIER AND GRYGIER, 1976)

The first study quoted in sufficient detail by Grygier and Grygier (1976) for a proper evaluation of the validity of the oral and anal scales was selection procedures for positions of leadership in a government organization. Unfortunately, even here no actual coefficients are quoted, only levels of significance. Furthermore, the validity and reliability of the ratings of personality used as external criteria are unknown, so that no firm conclusions can be drawn. At most it could be argued that some of the correlations (e.g. independence and 'strong personality') are sensible.

Grygier and Grygier (1976) cite the thesis work of Bishop (1965). With a small sample of sixty-seven subjects she found that high scorers on the Ah (anal hoarding scale) were more affected than low scorers by losing money, in that in the losing condition high scorers found boring tasks more hateful than did low scorers: the converse was true in non-losing condition.

This may be tenuous support for the validity of the Ah scale as a measure of parsimony but it is a long way from demonstrating the concept of the anal character.

Grygier himself carried out a series of studies of homosexuals and paedophiles (studies which we discuss in Chapter 10 for their bearing on psychoanalytic theories of sexual disturbances). Their relevance to the validity of the oral and anal scales is that the paedophile turned out to be 'oral dependent', to quote Grygier and Grygier (1976): he was high O and Od. This certainly supports clinical appraisals of such sexual offenders, as the manual points out. These findings then give some support for the notion of the oral character.

The other studies quoted in Chapter 4 of the manual, although relevant to the DPI as a whole, are not pertinent to our purpose of assessing the validity of the O and A scales. Our conclusions from the correlations with external criteria must be modest. There is slight support for the validity of some of the oral and anal scales but it is no more than that. In fact such validity studies would not be powerful unless ratings were made (needless to say of known reliability and validity) of the various oral and anal traits. In brief the correlations with external criteria give slight support for the validity of the O and A scales. There is certainly insufficient evidence to warrant making substantive inferences from the O and A scale scores.

FACTORIAL STUDIES (GRYGIER AND GRYGIER, 1976)

While the previous external criterion studies are in principle difficult to use as strong evidence for the validity of the O and A scales, factorial studies of the DPI should be most powerful.

DESIGN OF ADEQUATE FACTOR STUDIES

As we have previously pointed out in some considerable detail (Kline, 1979a; Cattell and Kline, 1977), since many factor-analysts seem unaware of the fact in utilizing factor-analysis as a method validating test-variables, it is always necessary to identify the factors emerging from the analysis other than by their item or scale loadings. For example, a factor could prove common to a set of items purporting to measure authoritarianism. However, such a factor is not support for the validity of the test. Some other evidence that the common factor is authoritarianism is necessary. Such evidence could be adduced from external criterion studies or it could emerge from further factorial studies in which the location of the common factor in factor-space was determined. This is best done by factoring the test with a wide variety of other tests. Thus in the case of the DPI all factors should be identified by external criterion relations and/or factored with the other most well-established personality tests.

Lest readers think this merely quixotic, it must be remembered that common factors could be due to response-sets such as acquiescence — saying yes regardless of item content — (Cronbach, 1946, 1950), social desirability (Edwards, 1957) or could be simply specific to a set of items.

Thus then the logical demands of satisfactory validity studies of the DPI are such that factoring with other scales is really essential unless superlative external evidence for the identification of the factors is provided. However, even if these logical criteria are met there are further technical necessities for adequate factor-analytic studies and these must now be briefly discussed. Our discussion will be short because this subject is so complex that a summary is all that can be attempted. Despite the contentious nature of factor-analysis, there is now general agreement among experts in the field as to what are the technical demands of adequate factor-analyses. For further reading, Nunnally (1978) and Cattell (1978) are helpful. Kline (1979a) and Cattell and Kline (1977) also offer simple accounts of the matter.

TECHNICAL DEMANDS FOR ADEQUATE FACTOR-ANALYSES

The basic problem with factor-analysis, a difficulty that has in fact led many psychologists inexperienced in the technique to condemn it, is the indeterminacy of any solution. An infinity of mathematically equivalent solutions is possible. However, Cattell and his colleagues at Illinois, utilizing the principles of Thurstone's multifactor solutions (see Cattell, 1966b, especially), have overcome this problem. They demonstrate that if simple structure is reached, replicable factor-analyses can be carried out, this replicability effectively solving the indeterminacy problem. The problem therefore becomes one of obtaining simple structure. It is to this end of ensuring that simple structure is reached that Cattell has set out a number of technical demands for adequate factor-analyses. If these technical demands are met, it is highly probable, although not inevitable, that simple structure will be reached. If they are breached, simple structure will be reached only by some fortunate chance.

Before briefly summarizing the most important of these technical points (they are set out in detail in Cattell and Kline, 1977), we shall justify the aim of obtaining simple structure.

The importance of simple structure

There are two reasons, above all, why simple structure should be aimed at in factor-analyses. Firstly, given that there are infinities of solutions, then according to the law of parsimony, Occam's razor, the simplest solution is the one to choose. Thus simple structure, defined as obtaining factors each with a few high loadings and the majority of loadings around zero (the number of these zero loadings is the hyperplane count) is the specific way of applying the law of parsimony in factor-analysis.

Secondly, as Cattell has pointed out (Cattell and Kline, 1977; Cattell, 1978), when simple structure is obtained, factor-analytic results are replicable. In other words, from studies with common variables the same factors emerge, a finding which gives one confidence in the status of the emerging factors. In addition the extensive factorial studies of Cattell, Eysenck and to a lesser extent Guilford in the field of personality have shown that these simple structure factors have useful predictive power of real-life criterion behaviours in both education and the clinical and occupational fields.

For these reasons, therefore, simple structure should be obtained and this, according to Cattell (1973), demands that the following rules are adhered to in the execution of factor-analyses.

1. Strategic choice of variables.
2. Proper sampling of subjects.
3. Objective tests for the number of factors.
4. Iteration of communalities.
5. Maximizing of simple structure (the purpose of the first four rules) in oblique rotation.
6. Bargmann (1953) test of simple structure.
7. Invariance of factor-pattern across researches.
8. Invariance of higher-order factor-pattern.

Let us now briefly discuss these requirements from the viewpoint of our problem of trying to validate the oral and anal scales of the DPI. The strategic choice of variables implies that there must be sufficient tests for each factor such that a factor can emerge. This usually means three or four relevant variables to each factor. In this respect the DPI does have sufficient O and A scales. If a proper simple replicable structure is to be obtained, then a wide variety of subjects with as much relevant variance as possible should be sampled. Homogeneous samples can give misleading results. These first two requirements although important are little more than commonsensical as regards sound research-design.

The third requirement is highly important. After the initial principal components-analysis, we have to decide how many factors go into the rotation.

This is a critical decision since too few factors can lead to the emergence of higher-order factors at the first order, while too many factors leads to an untidy and by no means replicable result. What therefore is needed is some objective test of how many factors to rotate.

Often the custom of rotating factors with eigen values greater than one was adopted (the Harris—Kaiser criterion). However, Cattell (1966a) has argued that this leads to an overestimate of the number of factors, especially in a matrix with a large numbers of variables. Cattell favours his Scree Test (Cattell, 1966a), which is essentially a graphical method for selecting the factors. Certainly with artificial examples this works well, although with real data the number of factors is more problematic and Cattell (1978) admits that much experience and skill is necessary. Nevertheless, experienced workers can achieve reliable results. Recently Velicer (1976) has introduced a new method which is more objective than the Scree Test and this appears highly promising, although further research is needed to ensure that it is satisfactory in all conditions.

The interation of communalities (rather than putting unities in the diagonal thus making the common factor-analysis into a principal components-analysis) is done to avoid mixing common and specific variance. However, Barrett and Kline (in press) have shown that in practice this makes little difference to the results.

If we follow Cattell, then these four requirements should ensure that simple structure can be reached. An oblique rotation is suggested to avoid the restriction of the orthogonal position (i.e. unrelated, uncorrelated factors). It must be remembered that in an oblique rotation, if the orthogonal position is the best fit, then it can be adopted. For an orthogonal rotation the converse is not true.

Two further points need to be made about the rotation to simple structure. Even if the first four requirements have been meticulously observed, a poor rotation procedure can fail to reach simple structure. Indeed, it can be argued that of all the points mentioned in the technical requirements, this one concerning the rotation itself is the most essential. How then can we ensure an adequate rotation? The simplest approach is to follow that of Thurstone (1947) and aim for factors with a few high loadings and a large number of nil loadings. Cattell (e.g. 1966a) refers to this process as maximizing the hyperplane count and most adequate modern rotations aim to achieve this. Generally, a figure around 80 per cent would be considered good. Thus in any adequate oblique rotation the hyperplane count should be given and it should fall around this figure. Maxplane (Cattell and Muerle, 1960) is the rotation favoured by Cattell. Direct Oblimin (Jennrich and Sampson, 1966) is, when properly used, another powerful procedure.

The second point concerns the very definition of simple structure. Our definition and the oblique methods of rotation designed to reach it follow essentially the precepts of Thurstone and the procedures of Cattell. Guilford and his colleagues (e.g. Guilford, 1977), however, prefer a different argument. They reason thus. An orthogonal set of factors (i.e. an uncorrelated set of factors) is *per se* more simple than an oblique correlated set, even though the orthogonal position may mean (and usually does) that each individual factor is more complex than it would be if an oblique rotation were used. This argument is, of course, one of scientific judgement.

Two counter arguments lead us to adopt our position.

(a) It seems unlikely that, in the real world, the major dimensions of personality are in fact uncorrelated.

(b) As we have indicated, the test of a factor, that it reflects a real influence and is not a mathematical artefact only, lies in its capacity to predict external life-critera.

On these grounds as the handbook to his tests and the whole corpus of Cattell's work indicates (summarized in Cattell and Kline, 1977) Cattell's factors do meet these criteria. Guilford's factors are less impressive (Guilford et al., 1976). Thus we feel that the argument for oblique simple structure cannot be dismissed.

One further point concerning the technicalities of factor-analysis remains — the ratio of subjects to variables and its influence on the stability of factors. Nunnally (1978) argues that for reliable results ten times the number of subjects to variables is necessary. This is the most conservative view. Guilford (1956) on the other hand claims that twice the number is sufficient. Most other writers of repute in the field, e.g. Harman (1976), Cattell (1978) and Gorsuch (1974), are intermediate. What is clear, however, in this dispute is the lack of (a) empirical evidence where the effects of varying these ratios can be observed, and (b) mathematical justification for the claims. Most of these writers rely on their experience in the field. In fact Kline has produced clear and well-replicated factor-structures where the ratio was less even than two to one (e.g. Kline and Storey. 1978a).

All these technical demands for adequate factor-analyses have been discussed so that the factor-analyses of the DPI scales can be properly evaluated. These statistical requirements on their own, of course, are not sufficient to ensure that a study is acceptable, even if they are entirely met. The actual research-design especially the selection of relevant variables, as we have previously discussed, is also critical.

THE FACTOR-ANALYSES IN GRYGIER AND GRYGIER (1976)

I. The first study was carried out on 438 male architectural students. Orthogonal Varimax and oblique Direct Oblimin rotations were performed using different numbers of factors in the rotations to compare the different results. Technically, it can be seen, this first study meets many of the criteria suggested in the previous study. However, it must be noted that (a) no test of simple structure was made, and (b) Direct Oblimin was used without varying the parameters affecting the position the vectors can take up. This severely limits the possibilities of this technique reaching simple structure. Furthermore, no other measures were used. Thus the only way the anal or oral factors could be identified is through internal consistency with other DPI factors — a circuitous and manifestly unsatisfactory method of demonstrating scale-validity.

In fact in this investigation some of the factors emerge as anal or oral factors, and the validity of the oral and anal scales while not refuted is not supported by this first investigation.

It must be made clear that this is not to criticize the DPI as a worthless personality test. Indeed as Kline and Storey (1978a) — a paper which we discuss later — showed, the DPI is a highly interesting test. However, it is as a measure of oral and anal character that we question it.

II and III. Studies two and three, carried out with large samples (around 10:1 ratio of subjects to variables), we shall say little about because all the comments concerning the first study are relevant to these. It is useful to note here that the factors emerging were in the main similar but not identical to those in the first study.

IV and V. These two investigations factored the responses of samples of 271 homosexuals and 165 Canadian offenders. Again similar technical deficiencies apply to these studies as previously discussed. These two broadly similar researches showed an authoritarian personality factor which, loading on the anal scales, was in fact confirmation of an anal or obsessional personality, as far as is possible without other marker variables to support the identification. There was little support for the oral character. It is further noteworthy that the factors in these studies were, some of them, identifiable as similar to those found previously. Others, however, were clearly different.

Generally, then, it may be argued that the four factor-analytic studies quoted in the test manual do little to support the validity of the oral and anal scales and hence do little to confirm the psychoanalytic psychosexual hypotheses of the anal or oral character. The best that may be adduced is the emergence in two of the researches of the authoritarian factors which are certainly similar to descriptions of the anal character.

Before we leave this first section of Grygier's manual, a final point deserves comment. A worrying feature of all these analyses taken together is the lack of agreement between results. Ideally we should expect to find a stable factor-structure underlying the correlations of the scales. In our view the instability of these factors can be attributed to the failure to reach simple structure and with proper rotation it is likely that more reliable results would be achieved. Grygier (1979) however argues that a stable structure should not be expected, a view which we examine in detail below. Suffice it to say here that this position is not tenable. In brief, these studies offer slight support for the anal character.

OTHER FACTORIAL STUDIES

Grygier and Grygier (1976) examine other published factorial studies and we shall now scrutinize these together with some investigations not discussed in their manual. These include two by the present author, Kline (1968a, 1978a) and Kline and Storey (1978a).

The work of Glasberg et al. (1969)

These authors factored the DPI in two samples, one male and one female, of asthmatics, allergic but non-asthmatic patients and controls of chronic in-patients. For each sample eight factors were rotated to the Varimax orthogonal criterion. Despite the failure to reach simple structure, among the males an anal factor was found (listed as conservatism). Among the females no such factor was found although that of submission to authority was not dissimilar.

The problem with this research is that the differences between males and females may be due to the technical deficiencies of the analyses — notably in the number of factors extracted as significant and in the orthogonal rotation. This makes firm conclusions difficult to draw. However, in both samples some support emerges for the construct of anal character.

The work of Stringer (1970)

Stringer (1970) subjected Kline's (1968b) factor-analysis of the Dynamic Personality Inventory (see p. 30 for the discussion) to an oblique factor-analysis followed by the extraction of second-order factors. However, the eleven oblique factors emerging from this study were still not a close fit to psychoanalytic psychosexual theory. Stringer described the four second-order factors as being consistent with the theory. He identified a factor of masculine identification ('despite the intrusions of elements of orality'), a bipolar oral—anal factor, feminine identification and a phallic factor (with unexpected loadings on anal scales). It seems to us that this second-order analysis of the Dynamic Personality Inventory is still a long way short of confirming psychosexual theory. We should expect oral, anal and phallic factors as was hypothesized by Barnes (1952) in his early study.

Stringer argues that one of the difficulties in the original study by Kline (1968b) was the small size of his sample; he therefore subjected to another oblique rotation the scores on the DPI of 357 male students. Eleven factors were again extracted. Again Stringer claims that these results support psychosexual theory: three bipolar oral—anal factors, an anal singlet, three phallic factors, two factors of feminine identification, a postgenital social-sublimation factor and a prenatal early-oral factor. Reference to our outline of psychosexual theory must make it clear that these results cannot be regarded as confirmatory. Two oral factors, erotism and sadism, two anal factors, expulsive and retentive, can be predicted from the theory. There seems to be no room for three. Nor is the bipolarity of orality and anality expected since, as Abraham (1921) points out, oral and anal fixations are often related. To argue that this factor-analysis supports psycho-sexual theory is to make that theory so vague as to be entirely worthless.

Comments and conclusions

We conclude from this study by Stringer (1970), which certainly overcomes the technical shortcomings of the study by Kline (1968b), that the Dynamic Personality Inventory is not a valid measure of Freudian psychosexual theory. Its scales are not related in accordance with prediction. Whether this be due to the invalidity of the scales or the theory cannot be settled from studies of this type. Stringer thus supports the previous findings by Kline (1968b).

The work of Freeman (1970)

A study by Freeman of samples of university students is examined in some detail in the test manual. However, since he used unrotated components, his findings are of no relevance to our search for the oral and anal character in that a components-analysis is simply descriptive and is not a unique solution.

Finally the manual quotes the work of Salce who in a thesis for the University of Paris gave the French version of the DPI to a sample of professional men. Since no evidence is presented for the equivalence of the French and British versions, the factor-analysis of the French scales (without marker variables) is virtually uninterpretable. This study is best ignored (for our purposes).

Conclusions from the factor-analyses quoted in the manual

The only conclusion to be drawn from these analyses is that there is some evidence for an anal character because some factors in the studies do show the A scales clustering together. There is however little factorial support for the oral character. Much of the instability in the results may be due to the failure in most of the studies to reach simple structure, despite the claim in the manual that factor-stability is not of paramount importance (a claim to be discussed later in this section)!

FACTOR STUDIES NOT IN THE MANUAL

The work of Bromley and Lewis (1976)

Bromley and Lewis subjected the responses of a sample of psychiatric patients (100 female and 75 male) to the DPI to an orthogonal Varimax analysis. Despite the limitations of this work, the orthogonal rotation being unlikely to reach simple structure, and the lack of any variables other than those in the DPI itself, the results are relevant to this chapter because the authors identified three factors: an anal, an oral and a phallic factor. The anal factor was highly similar to that found by Kline (1968a) (see p. 30) loading on all the anal factors other than Ah. The oral factor was much less clearly defined by the O scales and also loaded on C, while the phallic factor loaded on the P factors other than Pe and PN.

This analysis suggests that an anal syndrome can be found among psychiatric patients but the evidence for the other psychosexual factors is less clear. Too much should not be made of this study because there is no external validation of the factors nor is their position in personality factor-space made clear. In brief, there is here some support for the anal character.

A pilot study of the DPI (Kline, 1968b)

Kline (1968a) subjected the scores on the DPI of students at two colleges of education to a Varimax orthogonal rotation of a principal components-analysis. The rationale for this validity study was simple. Since the construction of thirty-three scales is an extension of psychoanalytic theory, for those scales which have no obvious theoretical basis there ought to be strong statistical justification — in terms of clear factorial pattern. For the scales relevant to psychosexual theory factor loadings may be predicted, e.g. an oral factor with loadings on the oral scales, an anal factor and a phallic factor with loadings on phallic interest, Icarus complex, fascination by heights, fascination by fire, liking for adventure and narcissism (see the description of the phallic character in Fenichel, 1945).

Results

Eleven factors emerged from the Varimax analysis. However, only the first was in accordance with psychosexual theory — it was clearly an anal or a super-ego factor. The second factor appeared to be masculine interests and was perhaps interpretable in Freudian terms as a phallic factor. The third was feminine interests but was not in accord with the psychoanalytic theory. None of the other factors was interpretable in terms of psychosexual theory. Indeed three factors could not be meaningfully named in relation to the scales loading on them. It was concluded from these results that the construct validity of the DPI was not high. Only the anal scales *could* be valid in that they were measuring a common factor. The difficulty of naming the factors, even in non-Freudian terms, suggests that the scales are not valid.

Comments and conclusions

This was very much a pilot study. The N of 70 was too small to produce highly reliable results and the Varimax analysis, being orthogonal, probably failed to reach simple structure. As Stringer (1970) indicated this study demanded replication, which Stringer (1970) attempted to do (see p. 28). However, worse than the technical defects mentioned above is the design flaw such that no variables were included in the study to enable the emerging factors to be located in factor-space, without which factorial identification is little better than guessing.

To remedy these deficiencies, Kline and Storey (1978a) carried out a further study of the DPI.

The work of Kline and Storey (1978a)

In a study which meets most of the criteria of technical efficiency, the DPI was administered to 128 subjects (61 male) of whom the majority were students. In addition the 16PF test and the EPI were given to enable the relation of the DPI factors to be elucidated against those which are best established. Further, since it was clear that some of the Grygier factors if valid would not load on the Cattell and Eysenck factors, all other psychosexual scales with any claim to validity were inserted into the study — the Gottheil oral scale (Gottheil, 1965b), the Lazare oral scales (Lazare et al., 1966), Ai3Q, the measure of the anal character (Kline, 1971) and OPQ and OOQ, two new scales to measure oral optimistic and oral pessimistic personalities (Kline, 1978b). All these scales are discussed in later sections of this chapter.

The correlations between all these factors were subjected to a Promax rotated factor-analysis, in which there were fifteen significant factors. Although the Promax (Hendrickson and White, 1966) rotation does not always reach simple structure, in this case the factor-structure is unlikely to be awry since the Cattell and Eysenck factors load up as they normally do. Furthermore, as evidence of the stability of the results, the first factor closely resembles the first factor found in the previous study.

Results

Of the fifteen factors only one was as expected from psychosexual theory. This was the first factor which, loading on the DPI A factors, Ai3Q (the anal measure devised by Kline (1971)) and H (hypocrisy) together with negative weightings on Si (sexuality) and OU (unconventionality), is clearly to be identified as an anal or obsessional factor.

This identification is further supported by its loading on Cattell's G (super-ego) and Q3 (control). This factor is, in our view, strong support for the existence of a syndrome of personality traits similar to that described in psychoanalysis under the term anal character. Of course these findings are not pertinent to the aetiology (and hence the term anal) of the factor, merely its existence. It is noteworthy that this factor is highly similar to the anal factor found in the previous study of the DPI (Kline, 1968b) and to other work, to be discussed in later sections of this chapter, reported in Kline (1968a).

None of the other factors supported Freudian psychosexual theory (no oral factor or factors) although factor 15 was interesting since it linked creativity with phallic symbolism.

CONCLUSIONS FROM THE STUDIES WITH THE DPI

Our conclusions from all validity studies of the DPI are simple.

(a) This test offers some support for the construct of the anal character.
(b) There is very little confirmation for other psychosexual syndromes.

We must stress, however, that this is not a condemnation of the DPI. As Kline and Storey (1978a) pointed out, this test is clearly measuring variance quite separate from that measured by some of the best established factored tests such as those of Cattell and Eysenck. However, equally clearly the labels on some of the scales are misleading, so that research is required to identify the DPI variance with greater accuracy than has yet been done. This however is not relevant to this chapter. The critical conclusion is that the DPI confirms the existence of the anal character but not the other psychosexual syndromes.

Before leaving the DPI to examine investigations with other tests, mention should be made of a paper by Grygier (1979) commenting on the studies by Bromley and Lewis (1976) and Kline and Storey (1978a). He asserts, without substantiation, that since factor-analysis deals with responses to test-items, it is inevitable that factorial results will differ from occasion to occasion. No theoretical reason is given for this statement and empirically it is nonsensical since on many different occasions the same factor structure does appear with tests such as the EPQ and the Cattell 16PF tests, as has been extensively documented by many authors including Cattell and Kline (1977) and Kline (1979). Indeed, as is clear from the classical test model and the factor model described in Nunnally (1978), it is to be expected in tests that factors would not change, for the reliability of a set of items is its correlation with the population of items of which it is a subset. Hence changes in factor structure indicate errors of measurement. The argument that it is the responses to items not items that are factored is not powerful since this is true of every factor-analysis of tests *per se*.

Thus Grygier's (1979) comments cannot impugn the conclusions concerning the DPI, that it supports the concept of the anal character but no other sexual syndrome.

FURTHER STUDIES OF THE ORAL AND ANAL CHARACTER

Studies of the anal character by Farber (1955) and Rabinowitz (1957)

Farber and Rabinowitz published two papers on the anal character which, owing to methodological imperfections, will receive the briefest description. Farber examined the relationship between anal characteristics and political aggression in a sample of 130 students; he found a positive significant relationship between the variables of 0.37. Such a finding of course implies the existence of the anal syndrome.

Comments

His scale to measure the anal character consisted of five items all keyed 'Yes'. The only evidence for their validity other than item content was the fact that each item correlated with the total score. This, of course, indicates only that the scale was measuring a common factor, not what that factor was. Furthermore, two of the items referred to professors, e.g. 'I get terribly annoyed with the professor who . . .' No evidence was presented concerning the reliability of this scale. The political-aggression scale was equally short and again keyed 'Yes'. Rabinowitz (1957) argued that the scales probably measured acquiescence rather than anal characteristics — hence the positive correlation. He therefore wrote five anal items keyed 'No' and five political-aggression items keyed 'No'. The new ten-item scales failed to correlate significantly. However when they were scored for acquiescence the correlation again became significant — 0.27. From this Rabinowitz concluded that the anal scale was a measure of acquiescence. Farber (1958) attempted to answer the criticism by criticizing the anal items of Rabinowitz in terms of content. Certainly item 2 of the new scale (concerned with sleeping habits) did not seem particularly relevant to the anal triad. Indeed Rabinowitz stated that his concept of anality was taken from the summary of Farber's (1955) original paper!

Conclusions

It seems highly unlikely, both in terms of item content and test length, that either of these two anal scales was valid. Certainly no evidence for validity was presented. These findings are probably best ignored as they clearly cannot be regarded as sound evidence for the existence of an anal syndrome.

The Beloff study (1957)

Beloff investigated the structure and origin of the anal character in a study which therefore dealt with two of the hypotheses implicit in psychosexual theory. In this chapter only the first part of the investigation — concerned with the syndrome of anal characteristics — will be considered.

Summary

Questionnaire items were constructed from a search of the psychoanalytic descriptions of the anal character and administered to a sample of just over 100 students. The item inter-correlations were factor-analysed and a general factor appeared — considered by Beloff to be an anal factor. From the emergence of this factor, it was argued that anality was a meaningful dimension of personality. An examination of the factor loadings of the individual items persuaded Beloff that the emphasis given in the literature to certain traits, notably cleanliness and parsimony, was perhaps wrong — they had small loadngs on the general factor. Two attempts were made to demonstrate the validity of the scale. First, self-report responses were correlated with ratings by peers. In this way an estimate of how self-reports corresponded to observed behaviour was obtained. The correlation was satisfactory (0.48). Furthermore, scores on the anal test were correlated with the Guilford personality factors. Here the results were inconclusive. There was a small but significant correlation with T (thinking introversion) of 0.34, which fits the hypothesis that the anal character is due to over-learning, which itself is typical of introverts (Eysenck, 1953b). However, contrary to hypothesis, there was no correlation with S (social introversion) or R (freedom from care). From this first part of her paper Beloff concluded that the anal character does exist — the first hypothesis was supported.

Comments and conclusions

Of the studies so far reviewed this one offers by far the best evidence for the psychoanalytic theory, so it deserves careful examination. There are a number of points that must be made.

The emergence of a general factor among the items is not *ipso facto* evidence for the anal character. It is still necessary to demonstrate what this general factor is. The content of the items, i.e. the face-validity, suggests that it is the anal character, and the fact that the scale fails to correlate with the Guilford scales is further indirect support for its validity. Furthermore, the correlation between self and peer ratings indicates that the test reflects observed behaviour and this eliminates the possible influence of response-sets. Nevertheless the only positive evidence for the validity of the scale lies in its item content.

As with the study by Barnes (1952), the correlations were tetrachoric. As was pointed out in the discussion of that study, these are not reliable and if they are to be factored Guilford (1958) suggests that a sample size of 300 or more is desirable. Beloff's small sample size would not have been a serious defect if she had not *compared* item loadings on her general factor, and then attempted to argue from their values that the emphasis in the literature was wrong. This interpretation is far too precise bearing in mind the unreliability of these factor loadings which only accounted, anyway, for 43 per cent of the variance.

However, despite these statistical caveats which limit the possible interpretations and the lack of clear evidence of validity, this study by Beloff may be regarded as sound evidence for the anal character.

The Gottheil studies

Gottheil (1965b) conducted an empirical study of oral and anal characteristics on a group of 200 soldiers. Personality questionnaire items were written from a study of the psychoanalytic literature and subjected to item-analysis. Item-analysis revealed that items tended to form a scale in the hypothesized manner. The correlation between the two scales was −0.22. From this it was concluded that oral and anal syndromes did in fact occur.

The validity of the scales

To a certain extent the validity of these scales had been endorsed in a previous study by the author (Gottheil, 1965a). Fifteen psychiatrists and five psychologists had been asked to predict the responses of oral and anal characters to these questionnaires. There was good agreement in both cases, especially so for the anal character. This study at least demonstrated beyond reasonable doubt that the item content of the scales was relevant to the syndromes concerned.

Comments and conclusions

Apart from this demonstration of face-validity and homogeneity (item-analysis) there was no further attempt to demonstrate the validity of these scales. Without this the identification of common factors as oral and anal must remain doubtful.

Although these studies appear to support Freudian theory, before the results can be accepted more convincing evidence for the validity of the scales must be forthcoming.

The work of Gottheil and Stone (1968)

This study, which examined the relationship between scores on the Gottheil anal and oral tests and mouth and bowel habits, is truly an investigation of the aetiology of the psychosexual syndromes and is fully examined in Chapter 5, which is devoted to that subject. However, part of the findings is relevant to this chapter in that a factor-analysis of the items, a Quartimax oblique analysis, failed to yield a clear oral or anal character.

Comments

While this result is clearly no confirmation of the oral or anal character, a few points concerning the factor-analytic techniques must be made. First the matrix of items and subjects was less than square: 179 subjects, 186 items. As Nunnally (1978) demonstrates, this leads to factor-analyses of dubious meaning. His suggested ratio of 10:1 is perhaps excessive but a square or less than square matrix is not satisfactory.

This alone casts doubt on the results. Furthermore, item inter-correlations almost always lead to factors of slight variance, hence clear factors were unlikely. Finally, there was no check on whether simple structure was obtained in the Quartimax analysis. In brief, as regards the oral and anal factors this study by Gottheil and Stone (1968) was inadequate to test the hypothesis.

The work of Kline with the Gottheil tests

Kline (1973b) administered the oral scale of the Gottheil test to a sample 294 students and submitted the results to a standard item-analysis. Only eighteen of the items formed a scale (biserial correlations with total score of items 0.30 or greater being the criterion). From this it was concluded that in Great Britain at least this scale could not be valid, for the items were not all measuring the same factor.

Andrich and Kline (1981) reanalysed these data and compared them with responses of 600 Australian students, using instead of the classical psychometric techniques Rasch (1960) scaling. Rasch scaling enables items to be evaluated for difficulty regardless of the sample taking the test and similarly provides scores for subjects taking into account (or independent of) item difficulty. It is thus especially useful for cross-cultural studies or for developmental investigations where subjects have to be retested, since once the Rasch calibration of items has been carried out, any subset of items should yield the same scores for subjects as any other. According to the Rasch model, the Gottheil oral items were satisfactory. However, this by no means demonstrates that the test is valid and on the strength of these two studies the oral scale developed by Gottheil could not be used for substantive investigations of orality.

The Kline and Storey (1977) investigation

Kline and Storey carried out an extensive research into many aspects of orality, which resulted in the publication of a number of papers which will be discussed as they bear upon the particular point under examination. As part of this work, the Gottheil oral scale was factored together with other psychosexual scales (including the Dynamic Personality Inventory) and the 16PF and EPI tests. Thus, it was hoped, an oral factor or factors could be properly located in factor-space.

The full results of this factorial investigation will be discussed later in this chapter, as they bear strongly on the construct of the oral character. However, the Gottheil oral scale did load on the emerging oral factor (oral optimism) but it also loaded on two other factors highly, on a factor of confidence and on impulsiveness. This lack of factor-purity could account for the failure of the item-analysis in Kline (1973b).

Technically the study was not perfect, since an oblique Promax rotation was used which may not have reached simple structure. However, most of the factors emerged as predicted and it is unlikely that this was the cause of the lack of validity of the Gottheil oral scale.

In brief, Kline's work with the Gottheil oral scale suggests that it measures the oral optimistic syndrome but is not factor-pure and it should not be used without considerable reservations.

The work of Lazare, Klerman and Armor (1966): the Lazare scales

Lazare, Klerman Armor (1966) carried out a factor-analytic study of the oral, obsessive and hysterical personality patterns. In this study a 200-item, 20-trait personality questionnaire was constructed. The oral items were mostly the same as those used by Goldman-Eisler (1948, 1950 and 1951). The oral character was measured by seven traits — pessimism, passivity, oral aggression, rejection of others, aggression dependence and parsimony. The obsessive character was measured by orderliness, obstinacy, parsimony, rejection of others, emotional constriction, self-doubt, severe super-ego, rigidity and perseverance. This description makes it clear that the obsessive character as defined here is identical with that of the anal character. In a later chapter in this book, concerned with the bearing of more general personality studies on Freudian psychosexual theory, the similarity between these two concepts will be examined. A major source of information on this point is the paper by Delay, Pichot and Perse (1962). The hysterical character is not relevant to the theory and will not be discussed here. These tests were then given to ninety female neurotic patients and the results were subjected to an orthogonal Varimax rotated factor-analysis.

Results

Three clear factors emerged. Factor 1 was identified as hysterical. Factor 3 was identified as anal and was very clear with loadings on orderliness (0.74), severe super-ego (0.62) and perseverance and obstinacy (0.54). The second factor was more tentatively labelled oral, but did not so closely fit the psychoanalytic picture with loadings of dependence (0.66), pessimism (0.65) and passivity (0.61). Parsimony and aggression failed to load on this factor. Nevertheless it was concluded that oral and anal syndromes did occur in accordance with psychoanalytic theory.

Comments

Although the Varimax analysis is far from ideal and the sample was somewhat restricted, being female neurotics and smaller than desirable, this factor-analysis is some support for the oral and anal syndromes although it is plain that the oral constellation is not clear-cut. The evidence of three factors rather rules out response-sets as accounting for the results since these would have tended to produce a general factor. Although there are no external studies of validity relating these scales to other tests, the fact that the scales load on factors, as expected, is good evidence for their validity — a different matter from illustrating that items in one scale load on *one* common factor — which fails to show what that factor is. It is noteworthy that these authors claim that their results are similar to those of Goldman-Eisler (1948, 1950 and 1951). This, however, is hardly surprising since they used the same items.

These same authors (1970) replicated these findings in a further sample of ninety patients. All the strictures that applied to the first study are again pertinent to this one. However, the similarity of the emerging factors is important since error tends to be uncorrelated unless, obviously, systematic.

Conclusions

The conclusion from these two investigations is that the Lazare scales certainly deserve further investigation. What is needed is to locate the factors in personality-space and to relate them to other putative scales.

In fact two recent studies have attempted to do this and these will now be examined.

The work of Paykel and Prusoff (1973)

Paykel and Prusoff (1973) administered the Lazare scales and the Maudsley Personality Inventory (Eysenck, 1959b) to around 150 depressed patients of whom 131 completed all the testing. Thus, in this study, the relation of oral and anal character to extraversion and neuroticism, two of the personality factors with the largest variance, can be assessed.

Results

The principal components-analysis was hand-rotated (*sic*) such that the obsessive (anal) character was characterized as stable and slightly introverted while the oral character was neurotic and introverted.

Comments

Since this study was with depressed patients, great caution must be shown in extrapolating the results to non-depressive populations. Even then great care must be taken in interpretation since hand-rotation is unlikely to reach simple structure unless carried out by factorists of considerable experience.

Conclusions

This study despite its excellent rationale is hindered by grossly inadequate execution of the factor-analysis. At best it is further support for the anal and oral syndromes.

The work of Kline and Storey (1977)

Kline and Storey (1977) in the paper referred to in our evaluation of the Gottheil scales also examined the Lazare scales. The rationale of the investigation was to scrutinize the relation of these scales to other putative measure of psychosexuality and to establish their location within the personality sphere.

In this study only the oral scales were used. The Lazare scales did not come out well in the rotated factor-analysis. Four of them, D, E, F and Pe dependence, egocentricity, fear of sexuality and pessimism, loaded on the Neuroticism factor (Eysenck's N). Thus the oral pessimist tends to be neurotic. This is certainly in accord with psychoanalytic theory in that the subject fixated at the biting level who has not had sufficient breast-feeding would be expected to be unstable. However, the other loadings of these factors were on a specific factor (no other variables loaded on it, despite the fact that OOQ (Kline, 1978b) and the Gottheil scales were included in the analyses). This looks very much as if the Lazare scales measure neuroticism together with a certain amount of specific variance.

Conclusions

These further studies of the Lazare scales do not strongly support their validity. The oral scales would appear largely to measure Eysenck's Neuroticism. The Paykel and Prusoff study cannot be treated seriously because it used hand-rotation. In our view better scales are needed for the measurement of psychosexual variables.

THE WORK OF KLINE

From 1968 Kline has carried out extensive psychometric studies of psychosexual syndromes, first of the anal character and more recently of the oral character. We shall proceed chronologically and first examine the studies of the anal character.

THE WORK OF KLINE ON THE ANAL CHARACTER

Kline (e.g. 1967c, 1968b, 1969a) has made several studies of the anal character using a thirty-item personality test, Ai3, as a measure of anal characteristics. The paper relevant to this chapter is Kline (1969a) where the evidence for the validity of the scale is summarized This paper claims to demonstrate the existence of an anal syndrome within a normal population.

The validity of Ai3 as a measure of the anal character

   (a) *Construction of Ai3.* As with many of the scales discussed in this chapter, the items for Ai3 were written from a search of the psychoanalytic descriptions of the anal character. Items were submitted to item-analysis and to checks for acquiescence (the percentage of anal responses keyed 'Yes' endorsed by subjects was compared with the percentage keyed 'No': clearly these ought to be the same). Social desirability was checked upon by examining the proportions of the sample responding 'Yes' to each item. An item with an even split can hardly be said to be socially desirable. In the light of these three checks items were rewritten and again submitted to item-analysis. The thirty best items were selected covering the whole range of the anal triad in respect of content. These items were then submitted to further item-analyses on different samples. The majority of items had a correlation with the total scale beyond 0.4.

(b) *Reliability of Ai3*. In three separate studies the internal consistency of Ai3 was 0.67.

(c) *Discriminatory power*. The discriminatory power of the test was very high — Ferguson Delta 0.97 (Ferguson, 1949).

At this point the study reported in Kline (1969a) diverged from those previously reviewed in this chapter in that attempts were made to validate the scale. Face-validity and homogeneity of items were not regarded as proof of validity. Three factor-analytic construct-validity studies were carried out and one concurrent validity study was made.

Construct validity study 1

A Varimax rotation of Ai3 with the Cattell 16PF test and Eysenck's EPI was computed on a sample of Ghanaian students. This study strongly supported the validity of Ai3 in that it was independent of all the personality scales in terms of correlation yet loaded on the Cattell second-order super-ego factor. This factor may be better identified as one of defence mechanisms since id-pressure (Q4) has a negative loading on it. This result is in accord with psychoanalytic theory of defence mechanisms against anal erotism repressed into the id.

Construct validity study 2

A Varimax rotation of Ai3 with the MMPI and the Beloff (1957) and Hazari (1957) scales was computed on a further sample of students. Again the validity of Ai3 was supported. It did not correlate with any of the MMPI scales but had positive correlations with the Beloff measure of the anal character and the Hazari scale of obsessional traits. In addition it did not load on the first general factor of emotionality, which runs through the MMPI scales, but loaded on the second factor identified as obsessional traits. This analysis, therefore, supported the symptom—trait dichotomy in obsessional disorder (Foulds, 1965; Sandler and Hazari, 1960).

Construct validity study 3

Ai3 was given together with the DPI to a sample of students. The results were subjected to a Varimax rotation. Here the validity of Ai3 was again supported since a clear anal or super-ego factor emerged (see Kline, 1968b) on which Ai3 and the DPI anal scales loaded. However Ai3 appeared superior to the anal scales of the DPI in that it was more factor-pure.

Concurrent validity study

Ai3 was given to a sample of students who were rated by their tutors for anal characteristics. An analysis of variance of the scores on Ai3 of those rated high and those rated low was significant at the 0.01 level. This fourth study was regarded as important, despite the crudity of the five-point rating scale, because it indicated that responses to Ai3 were related to observed behaviour.

From these studies Kline (1969a) concluded that Ai3 was a valid measure of the anal character and that the anal character was a meaningful dimension of personality within a normal population.

Kline (1971) carried out a further study with this test in which it was administered to a large sample (around 2000) of sixth-formers. The scores on Ai3 of arts and science specialists were then compared and the correlation of the test with academic performance was computed.

Results and discussion

As is implicit in psychoanalytic psychosexual theory, arts students scored significantly lower than their science colleagues (the attraction of science being the need for control, the precision of measurement, the certainty of results). Interestingly there was a small but significant negative correlation between success in GCE 'A' level and Ai3 scores among the science students. In other words scientists attracted to science because of its outlet for obsessionality are not the best scientists. In brief this study gave modest support for the validity of Ai3.

The work of Kline and Storey (1978a)

In this investigation of the Dynamic Personality Inventory referred to earlier in this chapter, Ai3 was also administered. As we saw it loaded up on what was clearly an obsessional or super-ego factor and was independent of the other main personality factors. Its only other loading was a negative one on an impulsivity factor. This first anal factor was a close replica of the one previously found in the 1968 investigation of the DPI. Certainly this replication must stand as powerful evidence for the validity of Ai3 and hence the concept of anal character.

Conclusions concerning Ai3

All this evidence, especially the last study, when taken together is strong support for the validity of Ai3 and thus of the anal character, as a syndrome of traits as described by Freud. Ai3 would appear to be a reliable and discriminating test with a reasonable construct-validity, a view endorsed by Eysenck (1978) and Lorr (1978). If it is required to measure anal characteristics, then Ai3 is probably the test best equipped for the purpose. Thus these studies by Kline do support the psychoanalytic hypotheses of the anal or obsessional character.

Conclusions concerning the anal character based on Ai3

That Ai3 is valid is *ipso facto* support for the construct of anal character, as we have argued. However, one interesting aspect of the findings is that the anal character seems to be a syndrome of traits not only in Great Britain but also among the Ghanaians. Our Ghanaian study showed clearly that only a few items failed to work in Ghana. Since the cross-cultural study of Freudian hypotheses is particularly pertinent to their scientific status, and since Freud frequently made statements of universal applicability, Kline and Mohan carried out a study of Ai3 in India (Kline and Mohan, 1974). Here, however, there were numerous items that failed to work properly. For example items about smoking were overlaid by the Sikh prohibition of the habit, our testing being in a predominantly Sikh area. However, although the test was not usable in its current form in this part of India, the majority of items did still form a scale and there was every indication that the anal character was a dimension of personality in that culture as indeed was claimed by Berkley-Hill (1921).

Thus our small-scale cross-cultural studies suggest that the anal character is a syndrome of traits not restricted to the west. Possibly Rasch scaling (see p. 35) might yield a proper cross-cultural comparison on Ai3Q.

Finally, mention should be made of a paper by Hill (1978) who claimed that the factor-analytic studies cited above provided no evidence for the anal character. He claimed that unless a scale is factor-pure it cannot be used as evidence for the existence of a dimension (a claim that is easily refuted; for example, a test can load on both fluid-ability and verbal reasoning) and that problems of factor-analysis, such as we discussed in our study of the technique, invalidate the findings. Kline (1978a) has rejected both these arguments and demonstrated that our most recent study of the DPI (Kline and Storey, 1978a) strongly confirms these putative artefactual results. This paper by Hill does not stand critical scrutiny since he has an imperfect conception of the nature of a factor, which is hardly surprising since this is not a field in which this author publishes widely.

THE WORK OF KLINE ON THE ORAL CHARACTER

Kline has recently carried out an extensive series of studies of orality. Two of the publications (Kline and Storey, 1977; Kline and Storey, 1978a) have already been discussed because they are relevant to the Dynamic Personality Inventory and the work of Paykel and Prusoff (1973).

The overall strategy of our study of orality was similar to that of our earlier studies of the anal character. In essence two tests of the oral syndrome — OOQ and OPQ — were developed and validated, thus testing the first of the psychosexual premises (that an oral character or characters exist), and then the aetiology of the syndrome was examined (work to be discussed in Chapter 5).

Construction of OOQ and OPQ

A preliminary examination of the current tests used in the study of orality (the

Goldman-Eisler scales, the Gottheil test and the Lazare scales) revealed that all were psychometrically far from ideal. In most cases reliability was not particularly high and there was almost no evidence of validity. Indeed, authors had been content, in the main, to rely on the face-validity of the items. It was therefore decided to construct and validate new tests of orality.

Item-writing and rationale of items

The psychoanalytic literature was searched for descriptions of oral personality traits. The table of oral traits to be found in Chapter 2 (Table 2.1 p. 10) serves as a useful summary of the best descriptive adjectives.

Items were written of the 'Yes'/'No' variety, hopefully tapping the traits, care being taken to avoid items to which one response was clearly going to be affected by social desirability, and to write items with oral responses keyed 'Yes' and keyed 'No' in equal numbers.

Study of the traits designated as oral in the psychoanalytic literature suggested that two tests would be necessary: one measuring oral optimistic traits, the other pessimistic traits. This meant that the item pool was subjected to two separate analyses.

Test-construction method

Fifty-eight pessimistic and sixty-seven optimistic items (approximately half keyed 'No') were administered to four samples for item trials, each sample being analysed separately to obviate the problem of item unreliability. These samples were:

1. 100 female sixth-formers from two schools.
2. 83 male sixth-formers.
3. 110 college-of-education students (mainly male).
4. 164 college-of-education students (mainly female).

The item-analytic method used was to compute the biserial correlation of each item with its total scale score (either OOQ or OPQ). Items were selected if they reached the criteria of at least a 0.3 correlation with the total score and were within the 20-80 per cent endorsement rate, in all samples. In fact twenty items in each scale reached these criteria, and these selected items were inserted into the tests for a final trial with a new sample of 100 students. These items proved satisfactory in this cross-validating study.

Reliability of OOQ and OPQ

Internal consistency

OOQ corrected split-half 0.46

OPQ corrected split-half 0.71

(These figures are derived from a sample of 100 students.)

Although the reliability of OOQ is less than desirable, especially for individual use, this is partly due to the fact that the oral optimistic syndrome is so diverse, thus making its internal consistency inevitably low.

Test—retest reliability

For practical usage of a test, the test—retest reliability is probably more significant than the internal-consistency reliability. Here both tests are satisfactory.

OOQ 0.64

OPQ 0.765

(These figures were derived from a sample of fifty-four students. The time interval was one year.)

From this we can conclude that OOQ and OPQ are sufficiently reliable to justify their use.

Validity of OOQ and OPQ

Since we could not establish criterion groups of high and low oral characters, it was decided to investigate the construct validity of OOQ and OPQ by locating these variables within personality-space. The study already discussed (Kline and Storey, 1977) was designed for this purpose. 126 subjects were administered the Gottheil scale, the Lazare scales, the Dynamic Personality Inventory (all psychosexual tests which we have fully examined) together with Eysenck's EPI, the 16PF test of Cattell (Cattell, Eber and Tatsuoka, 1970) and Ai3Q, our test of anal character. This study enabled us to see how OOQ and OPQ are related to other putative psychosexual scales and to the main personality factors. Obviously if OPQ and OOQ simply loaded on one of the Cattell factors, which are not intended to be measures of oral personality, they could not be valid.

Statistical analysis

The test scores were correlated and subjected to principal components-analysis followed by an oblique Promax rotation. The clear emergence of the Cattell and Eysenck factors suggested that simple structure had been obtained.

Results

The results strongly supported the validity of these tests and hence the existence of oral personality syndromes. These findings can be succinctly summarized.

1. The oral pessimistic character and oral optimistic character are not, as the descriptions hinted, simply opposite ends of a continuum. This is attested by the correlation of −0.269 between the two tests. Clearly both tests are necessary and generally orally fixated subjects did fall into one or the other categories. However, many subjects scored around the mean for each test.

2. The Promax analysis clearly demonstrated the construct-validity of the two tests.

(a) *OOQ* loaded on two factors (3 and 8). Factor 3 was the anxiety factor, loading on Eysenck's N and Cattell's Q4, O and C (see Chapter 4 for a full discussion of these factors). Since OOQ loaded negatively it means that the oral optimist tends to be stable. Factor 8 was the sociability factor, loading on extraversion and interest in social activities.

This means that the oral optimist as measured by OOQ is the stable social extravert. This fits well with the description of the oral characters and demonstrates the validity of OOQ.

(b) *OPQ* loaded positively on factor 3, the anxiety factor. Thus the oral pessimist is anxious. It further loaded on factor 2 which was Cattell's L, protension factor. This factor is described by Cattell (Cattell et al., 1970) as a factor associated with the defence by projection of inner tensions. Since oral traits are conceived of as defences against oral erotism, this factor-analysis is again good support for the validity of OPQ.

Summary

This validity study suggests that the oral optimist is a stable extravert while the oral pessimist is an anxious, tense and projecting individual. Since the two tests, OOQ and OPQ, do seem to measure variables in accord with their item content and since this content fits the descriptions of the oral characters, and since the items form homogeneous scales, it must be concluded that:

1. there is evidence for a personality constellation similar to that described in the psychoanalytic literature as the oral optimist, and

2. there is evidence for a personality constellation similar to that described in the literature as the oral pessimist.

Whether these syndromes should be described as oral, i.e. whether they are related to orality or oral erotism, will be discussed in Chapter 5.

OTHER RESEARCH INTO THE ORAL AND ANAL CHARACTER

Fisher and Greenberg (1977) cite a long list of researches attempting to isolate oral and anal syndromes. Most of these we have fully examined. Some which they cite are unpublished dissertations. We prefer to omit these as evidence since almost all competent research reported in theses appears later as papers. In fact the only research listed there that we have not discussed is a paper by Robinson and Hendrix (1966) relating to the oral character. The citation of this paper highlights the weakness of Fisher and Greenberg's uncritical approach. Thus each study is summarized in a table and all in all the results are held to support these psychosexual syndromes. However, no mention is made of methodological problems, e.g. sampling, the validity of tests used or the adequacy of factor-analyses. Without this, bad research carries equal weight with good. This paper by Robinson and Hendrix (1966) reports the results of a factor-analysis of the Blacky Pictures. The Blacky Pictures (Blum, 1949) portray a family of dogs in various family situations relevant to Freudian psychosexual theory. The oral pictures, for example, show Blacky biting his mother's collar, and Blacky being suckled. Subjects are required to describe the pictures and are (in these examples) designated as orally fixated or not, depending upon their responses.

From this description, a few points concerning the status of this research by Hendrix and Robinson can now be made:

1. The Blacky Pictures constitute a projective test. Based upon psychoanalytic theory, responses can be interpreted as showing fixation at various psychosexual stages. However, such interpretation cannot constitute objective evidence for psychoanalytic theory, since the interpretation is precisely of the kind we are trying to investigate.

2. The responses do not indicate oral traits. Thus any factors emerging are of a quite different kind from those based upon trait questionnaires. Any such factors are relevant to the aetiology of traits not the traits themselves. As such the Blacky Pictures are fully discussed in Chapter 5 on the aetiology of these psychosexual syndromes.

3. As we pointed out previously (Kline, 1973a) there is little evidence to support the validity of the Blacky Pictures. Since that date there has been no further research to reverse that view. Thus this study by Robinson and Hendrix (1966) cannot be held to validate the concept of the oral personality.

CONCLUSIONS FROM ALL THE STUDIES

As must now be clear, the methodology of many of these studies is flawed. It seems that the investigators of this problem view their results with hope rather than precision. Indeed the flaws may be easily summarized:

1. There has been far too much reliance on item-content, i.e. face-validity. Barnes (1952) and Krout and Krout (1954) are examples of this.

2. There has been little effort made to overcome the problems of response-sets. Edwards (1957) has shown in detail the influence of social desirability, and acquiescence has been recognized as a source of error since Cronbach (1946). Beloff (1957) and Grygier (1961a), as well as the two authors already cited, exemplify this fault.

3. Related to this there has been correspondingly little attempt to demonstrate the validity of the scales used.

4. The fourth error is the assumption that the demonstration of a common factor accounting for item-variance, either by factor-analysis or item-analysis, is evidence of validity. As has been pointed out it is not: the factor must still be identified.

The studies by the present author have attempted to overcome these problems and it is more difficult to impugn these investigations on these counts. Hence perhaps more weight should be attached to these results.

Nevertheless, when all these studies are considered together, despite their collective shortcomings, the weight of the evidence enables certain conclusions to be drawn.

There does appear to be an anal character

A syndrome of traits similar to that described by psychoanalysis is discernible in normal and abnormal populations. Beloff (1957), Grygier (1961a) and Kline (1969a) have produced measures of this with significant positive correlations between each other. Kline's scale, Ai3, has also been shown to have construct-validity. The investigation by Kline and Storey (1978a) was particularly strong support for the syndrome. In an abnormal population the study of Lazare et al. (1966) lends confirmation to this syndrome. Lesser support comes from the work of Gottheil (1965a, b) and from Barnes (1952) — the meticulousness factor.

The oral character, although less well-vindicated, has reasonable support

Goldman-Eisler (1948, 1950, 1951) in a normal population, and Lazare et al. (1966) with an abnormal sample, used a scale which they identified as oral. Goldman-Eisler found extreme scorers closely resembled the psychoanalytic picture of the oral optimist and the oral pessimist. The factorization of the scale by Lazare was not so clear-cut. On the other hand Barnes (1952), Krout and Krout (1954) and Grygier (1961a) have produced little firm evidence for the oral character.

The Gottheil (1965b) scale was at least homogeneous, although only face-valid. OOQ and OPQ (Kline, 1979) do further confirm the concept of oral optimists and oral pessimists.

There is no evidence in favour of other psychosexual personality syndromes

The complex scales of Barnes (1952), Krout and Krout (1954) and Grygier (1961a) have entirely failed to support the psychoanalytic hypotheses.

LIMITS OF THE CHAPTER

Theoretical

It must be stressed that this chapter is concerned only with the evidence for the existence of the hypothesized psychosexual personality syndromes. It is not concerned with their relationship to psychosexual phases of childhood and child-rearing procedures, which was the second of the hypotheses implicit in Freudian psychosexual theory. Thus in the conclusions above the claim that there is an anal character refers only to the existence of the syndrome. The term anal is used because it is the Freudian term not because it is implied that the syndrome is related to or stems from anal erotism.

Empirical

Furthermore, the evidence from more general personality studies must be reviewed — evidence which incidentally confirms or refutes these hypotheses.

SUMMARY

1. This chapter has reviewed those studies aimed at verifying the first set of hypotheses implicit in psychosexual theory, namely that certain personality patterns are observable in adults.
2. The relevant studies have been summarized and discussed in the light of Freudian theory and experimental procedures.
3. It was concluded that there is firm evidence for the anal character and more moderate support for the oral character. The other syndromes were not confirmed.

TABLE 3.2. *Summary of results*

Syndrome	Result	Studies
The anal character	Strong support	Beloff (1957)
		Grygier (1961a)
		Kline (1969a)
		Lazare et al. (1966)
The oral character	Support	Goldman-Eisler (1948, 1950, 1951)
		Lazare et al. (1966), Kline and Storey (1978a)
Other syndromes	No support	Barnes (1952)
		Krout and Krout (1954)
		Grygier (1961a)

4

Psychometric studies of personality

The psychometric study of personality has usually involved the factor-analyses of measures of personality. The results of this work have been fully examined in *Psychometrics and Psychology* (Kline, 1979a), where all the most important personality factors to have emerged from this research are set out and described.

RELEVANCE TO PSYCHOSEXUAL PERSONALITY SYNDROMES

Most of the work in the psychometrics of personality is frankly empirical. Thus its aim has been to uncover the dimensions accounting for the largest amounts of personality variance. The relevance to Freudian theory lies in the answer to this question. Are the personality dimensions uncovered by the objective statistical procedure of factor-analysis the same as the psychoanalytic personality dimensions? Or do they resemble them to any degree? Obviously, if they do, then this is sound support for psychoanalytic theory, albeit one not intended by the researcher.

Thus in this chapter we shall set out the personality factors that have been found by the most important workers in the field, notably Cattell, Eysenck, Guilford, Comrey, Jackson and Howarth. This work has been designated important because to a considerable extent the technical demands of adequate factor-analyses (see Chapter 3) have been met and some effort has been made to validate the identification of the factors.

Why so many factors? Before setting out the various factors identified by these researchers, the question of why so many factors have been isolated demands some explanation. As we discussed in our section on factor-analysis, the differences often turn on technical matters, whether the factors are oblique or orthogonal, whether simple structure was properly obtained and to a less extent on the type of samples employed. Although we have demonstrated (Kline, 1979a) that many of these apparently different factors overlap on re-rotation, it is simplest in the context of our aim — the isolation of psychosexual syndromes in the purely empirical search for factors (in contrast to the deliberate searching of our previous chapter) — to treat them as separate subsets of factors. Nevertheless, readers should bear in mind that these sets are not totally independent.

THE WORK OF CATTELL

Cattell has made the most sustained attack on the factor-analysis of personality over the last forty years. Cattell originally claimed (Cattell, 1957) that sixteen personality factors (those in his 16PF test) could account for the major part of personality variance. More recently Cattell (1973, and Cattell and Kline, 1977) has increased the number of factors: twenty-three normal and twelve abnormal factors, these last accounting for psychiatric personality disturbances. If Cattell's arguments were correct, then it would be reasonable to expect psychosexual personality syndromes, if such exist, to overlap with his factors.

THE BASIC DATA OF CATTELL'S WORK

There are three sources of data for the factorial studies of Cattell:

(a) *L data*: these are based on correlations of ratings made by trained observers of subjects in life-situations. These correlations have then been subjected to factor-analysis.

(b) *Q data*: these are based on the factorization of responses to personality questionnaires designed, as far as possible, to tap the traits and factors found in L data.

(c) *T data*: these derive from the factor-analysis of objective test devices. Although at an early stage of development and beset by the low reliability of the tests in their present form, Cattell regards these data as potentially the best in personality assessment. This is because they are free from distortion both deliberate and accidental, such as that caused by response-sets.

Nevertheless, since the compendium of objective test devices (Cattell and Warburton, 1967), which contains the most complete list of such tests, clearly indicates that as yet most of the factors emerging from T data cannot be clearly identified (despite their advantages) much of the discussion in this section must centre on the more clearly defined and closely studied L and Q factors. As will be seen these two sets of factors are well matched.

DESCRIPTION OF FACTORS

Since, as has been stated, most of the factors emerging from objective tests have not been clearly identified, although Cattell and Schuerger (1978) have produced a published test for ten of the factors (and a high-school version is also available), only those factors which appear relevant to the psychosexual syndromes will be discussed. The descriptions are to be found in Cattell and Warburton (1967), except where the factor exists in the OA battery (Cattell and Schuerger, 1978).

UI19. Independence *v.* subduedness. This is characterized by conscientiousness, exacting criticalness, reliability, restraint, control, concern for accuracy and standards, independence and refusal to make errors. The high UI19 person is better with machines and ideas than people, is perfectionist and does not relax easily.

Descriptively, there is a considerable resemblance in this factor to the anal character. Indeed if parsimony were present, the identification would be complete. Since, as yet, none of the 800 objective tests contain such a measure this lack is easily explicable. As it stands, however, this factor supports the Freudian claim for an anal character.

UI33. Reactive dismay (pessimism) *v.* sanguine poise. The person high on UI33 is pessimistic, believes that most events will affect him unfavourably, is slow in warming to new tasks, is inhibited, compulsive but tends to have good intellectual achievement.

Although not as obvious as UI19, the resemblance to oral pessimism, the claimed result of frustration at the oral level, is clear. Particularly interesting, in view of the claims of Fenichel (1945) that anal and oral influences are linked, is the presence of certain anal components, e.g. compulsion. This factor may be regarded with great caution, as tenuous support for an oral syndrome. None of the other T factors appears relevant to psychosexual syndromes.

Despite the difficulties with T factors, mainly because they are not yet fully developed, UI19 and UI33 do offer some support for the existence of oral and anal syndromes. It is noteworthy that UI19 and UI33 are both in the OA battery.

TABLE 4.1. *Q Factors*

Source trait index	Low-score description	High-score description
A	SIZIA Reserved, detached, critical, aloof, stiff	AFFECTIA Outgoing, warmhearted, easygoing, participating
B	LOW INTELLIGENCE Dull	HIGH INTELLIGENCE Bright
C	LOW EGO STRENGTH At mercy of feelings, emotionally less stable, easily upset, changeable	HIGHER EGO STRENGTH Emotionally stable, mature, faces reality, calm
E	SUBMISSIVENESS Humble, mild, easily led, docile, accommodating	DOMINANCE Assertive, aggressive, competitive, stubborn
F	DESURGENCY Sober, taciturn, serious	SURGENCY happy-go-lucky, gay, enthusiastic
G	WEAKER SUPER-EGO STRENGTH Expedient, disregards rules	STRONGER SUPER-EGO STRENGTH Conscientious, persistent, moralistic, staid
H	THRECTIA Shy, timid, threat-sensitive	PARMIA Venturesome, uninhibited, socially bold

Source trait index	Low-score description	High-score description
I	HARRIA Tough-minded, self-reliant	PREMSIA Tender-minded, sensitive, clinging, overprotected
L	ALAXIA Trusting, accepting conditions	PROTENSION Suspicious, hard to fool
M	PRAXERNIA Practical, 'down-to-earth', concerned	AUTIA Imaginative, bohemian, absent-minded
N	ARTLESSNESS Forthright, unpretentious, genuine, but socially clumsy	SHREWDNESS Astute, polished, socially aware
O	UNTROUBLED ADEQUACY Self-assured, placid, secure, complacent, serene	GUILT PRONENESS Apprehensive, self-reproaching, insecure, worrying, troubled
Q1	CONSERVATISM OF TEMPERAMENT Conservative, respecting traditional ideas	RADICALISM Experimenting, liberal, free-thinking
Q2	GROUP ADHERENCE Group-dependent, a 'joiner' and sound follower	SELF-SUFFICIENCY Self-sufficient, resourceful, prefers own decisions
Q3	LOW SELF-SENTIMENT INTEGRATION Undisciplined, self-conflict, follows own urges, careless of social rules	HIGHER STRENGTH OF SELF-SENTIMENT Controlled, exacting will-power, socially precise, compulsive, following self-image
Q4	LOW ERGIC TENSION Relaxed, tranquil, torpid, unfrustrated, composed	HIGH ERGIC TENSION Tense, frustrated, driven, overwrought

These are the original sixteen factors of the 16PF test. In addition seven further factors have been found:

D	Insecure excitability
J	Coasthenia *v.* Zeppia (active *v.* controlled)
K	Mature socialization *v.* boorishness
P	Sanguine casualness
Q5	Group dedication with feelings of inadequacy
Q6	Social panache
Q7	Explicit self-expression

The list in Table 4.1 constitutes Cattell's twenty-three normal factors, which are fully described in Cattell and Kline (1977). It is important to note that all these factors have been found in both L and Q data, other than the Q factors (1-7), hence their nomenclature, which belong to the questionnaire realm.

It is clear from the description of each of these factors that none of them is measuring any of the psychosexual personality syndromes. Nevertheless Q2, F and E could well be related to orality and G, Q3 and Q4 and J might be related to the anal character. In brief, as it stands the 16PF does not appear to provide a measure of the psychosexual syndromes but it is possible that measures might be developed from it if clear criterion groups were available.

In fact the studies by Kline and Storey (1977 and 1978a) support this view based upon the description of the factors. Thus the OOQ (optimistic) scale had modest but significant correlations with A, H, Q2 and E, while Ai3 loaded on the anal or super-ego factor together with Q3 and G. Factor J which occurs in L data is not included in the 16PF test so that we have no empirical results relevant to it. This factor is discussed on p. 53.

Thus from both factor descriptions and our own empirical studies it can be concluded that none of the Cattell primary factors is the same as or highly similar to the psychosexual syndromes. However, it might be possible from combinations of factor scores to approximate psychosexual measurement.

CATTELL SECOND-ORDER FACTORS

Because these primary factors are themselves inter-correlated it is possible to factor the correlations and obtain second-order factors from them. The main second-order factors are:

Anxiety. This factor is concerned with anxiety in the generally accepted sense — worry over problems and difficulties, feelings of guilt and tenseness.

Extraversion. A high score indicates an outgoing, uninhibited person, a good mixer. The introvert on the other hand is shy and self-contained.

These first two are much the most important second-order factors.

Radicalism. The high scorer is aggressive, independent, self-directing.

Tender-mindedness. Sensitivity, liability to frustration and emotionally controlled conduct.

Super-ego. This second-order factor loads alone on factor G which has already been described. This factor is implicated in the anal syndrome.

It is clear that only the second-order factor G is at all related to any of the psychosexual syndromes. The relationship of G, as has already been discussed, is not sufficient to allow that it be used as a measure of and evidence for the anal character. These second-order factors, therefore, may not be regarded as evidence for the existence of psychosexual personality syndromes.

In his more recent work (e.g. Cattell and Kline, 1977) some other second-order factors have emerged — discreetness, subjectivity, good upbringing, humanistic involvement and tough stability. Again it must be said that none of these new factors resemble any psychosexual syndrome.

Before leaving the factors we must return briefly to factor J since Cattell (1957) claims that it is heavily implicated in the anal character. The particular point of interest here is, of course, the fact that Cattell recognizes the existence of the syndrome. Indeed he goes on to argue that 'the anal erotic pattern is a syndrome of two or more factors (maybe J, A and G)' (1957, p. 138). This 'maybe' indicates, of course, that Cattell was unable to measure it.

Since this is the case the question must arise as to the grounds for Cattell's belief that the anal character exists. After all the whole basis of Cattell's enormous output has been the faith that measurement is essential to a scientific psychology. This question involves two points:

   (a) the nature of these Cattellian factors,
   (b) the nature of the original data on which they were based.

THE FACTORS AS SOURCE TRAITS

The factors which have been described are regarded by Cattell as source traits. These source traits are defined as structures responsible for a pattern of behaviour appearing as a factor. This is in contrast to surface traits which may not be due to single sources of variance. Surface traits consist of syndromes of trait elements of descriptive value, as in psychiatric syndromes, for example, but accountable in terms of factors. According to Cattell, surface traits are not as useful for personality measurement as source traits because they are very numerous and not clearly separated. It is to be noted, however, that if, as is the case with the anal character, source traits cannot adequately measure surface traits or syndromes, they cannot be regarded as substitutes for them as regards measurement.

THE NATURE OF THE ORIGINAL DATA: SURFACE TRAITS

The original data from which all factors — source traits — and surface traits were derived were ratings for trait elements in normal populations. These trait elements were themselves defined after searching the dictionary for words describing behaviour and after synonyms had been eliminated. The fact that all these terms were in the analysis thus enables Cattell to claim that his sixteen factors (now twenty-three), which account for the variance among these ratings, account for the major variance of personality. This is also the reason that Cattell (1946, 1957) can state categorically that there are fifty surface traits that may be reliably defined. Cluster-analysis of the correlations between these ratings for trait elements defined fifty surface traits or syndromes among them. To form a surface trait, the elements must correlate at least 0.4 with each other. It is these surface traits that the factors underlie. Therefore, since it has been shown that the factors do not, in all cases, adequately measure the surface traits, it is necessary to examine these empirically defined surface traits to see to what extent any of them correspond to the hypothesized Freudian psychosexual syndromes.

Surface traits

Of the fifty surface traits defined in normal populations those set out in Table 4.2 appear relevant to psychosexual syndromes

TABLE 4.2. *Surface traits relevant to psychosexual syndromes*

AA2	Conscientious effort *v.* quitting, incoherence. This embraces nuclear traits, persevering, pedantic, painstaking, conscientious, thoughtful
AB4	Infantile, demanding *v.* emotional maturity, frustration tolerance
CB3	Lack of restraint, adventurousness *v.* general inhibition, fearfulness. This includes the traits bold, enterprising, assertive, sociable, incontinent
D2	Sociability, sentimentalism, warmth *v.* independence, hostility, aloofness. This includes the traits responsive, affectionate, sentimental, social interests, family interests, dependent, friendly, frank, genial, tough
D5	Cheerful, enthusiastic, witty *v.* coldhearted, sour, mirthless. This embraces the traits, cheerful, enthusiastic, optimistic, laughterful, witty
F1	Gratefulness, geniality *v.* hardness, vindictiveness, coldheartedness
F2	Gratefulness, kindness *v.* hostility, cynicism. This includes the traits grateful, idealistic, self-denying, friendly
F3	Friendliness, generosity, co-operativeness *v.* hostility, meanness, obstructiveness
H1	Thrift, tidiness, obstinacy *v.* lability, curiosity, intuition. The following descriptions are included — habit-bound, thrifty, logical, pedantic

AA2 and H1 are clearly implicated in the anal character. Cattell indeed identifies H1 as the anal erotic complex. The oral character would appear to be caught by the surface traits AB4, D4, F1, 2 and 3. The surface trait CB3 resembles the phallic character. It is encouraging for Freudian theory that these surface traits based on the inter-correlation of ratings should thus appear. As with the studies reported in the previous chapter, the clearest syndrome is that of the anal character.

Recently, however, Howarth (1976) has called into question the number and nature of the original L factors, the basis of all Cattell's work. Howarth reanalysed the original data matrix and emerged with six factors only (not twelve as in Cattell's early work, work of course that had to be done without recourse to modern computer programs). According to Howarth, seven factors describe this original personality sphere — co-operativeness, phlegmatic *v.* surgent, emotional maturity, extraversion, conscientiousness and emotional stability.

While the import of these results for the psychological importance of Cattell's work is indubitable (albeit not altogether clear), for our purpose of examining Cattell's findings *vis-à-vis* psychosexual theory, the inferences remain unchanged, since none of these new factors overlaps to any important extent with psychosexual syndromes.

CATTELL ABNORMAL FACTORS

The normal personality factors, although excellent for discriminating neurotics from normals, did not show themselves as effective in the differentiation of psychotics. For this reason Cattell and colleagues developed from a study of the psychiatric terms and personality items used in measures of the abnormal personality the abnormal personality sphere. Factor-analyses of these abnormal sphere items revealed a set of special abnormal factors. Their provenance and validity is fully discussed in Cattell (1973) and Cattell and Kline (1977). It is arguable that perhaps psychosexual personality syndromes might overlap more with abnormal than normal factors, hence this list is of particular interest (see Table 4.3).

TABLE 4.3. *Cattell abnormal factors*

D1	Hypochondriasis
D2	Zestfulness
D3	Brooding discontent
D4	Anxious depression
D5	Euphoria
D6	Guilt and resentment
D7	Bored depression
Pa	Paranoia
Pp	Psychopathic deviation
Sc	Schizophrenia
As	Psychasthenia
Ps	General psychosis

From this list it is clear that none of these abnormal factors could be identified with any of the psychosexual personality traits.

CONCLUSIONS FROM THE WORK OF CATTELL

T factor source traits, UI19 and UI33, offer some evidence for the existence of oral and anal syndromes. Factors F, E and Q2 and J, from questionnaire data, could well be implicated in the oral character and from this same realm factors G, Q3 and Q4 may be related to the anal character. Factor H, adventurousness, is related to the phallic character. However, it is clear from this that none of the source traits is able on its own to provide a measure of and thus evidence for psychosexual syndromes. Surface traits, on the other hand, representing observable syndromes, are more likely to provide such evidence and in fact the anal character is clearly supported by H1 and AA2 while there is less clear support for the oral character (AB4, D5 and F1, 2, 3) and the phallic syndrome (CB3).

Indeed, in summary, within Cattell's system, psychosexual personality syndromes are to be thought of as surface traits.

THE WORK OF EYSENCK

Eysenck argues that the main variance in the personality sphere can be most elegantly encompassed by three factors; Extraversion, Neuroticism and (a more recent innovation) Psychoticism, E, N and P. An individual's behaviour, therefore, is determined by his position on these three dimensions which can be measured by the Eysenck Personality Questionnaire, the EPQ (Eysenck and Eysenck, 1975). Kline (1979a) and Cattell and Kline (1977) have demonstrated beyond reasonable doubt that Eysenck's E is essentially the same as Cattell's second-order Exvia factor and that N is virtually identical with Cattell's Anxiety. In the Cattell normal factors, P has no obvious equivalent. Empirical work (e.g. Kline, 1967a) confirms the identity of N and E with the Cattell second-order factors.

Since we have shown that the Cattell second-order factors do not overlap, in themselves, the psychosexual syndromes of psychoanalytic theory (although Kline and Storey (1978a) showed, it will be recalled, that the oral optimist was the stable extravert), it follows that only P could in fact be relevant to psychoanalytic psychosexual theory. In fact as our brief description of P indicates this is not the case. The descriptions of the Eysenck variables are based upon the manual to the EPQ.

Extraversion — The typical high scorer is sociable, gay, expressive and fond of excitement whereas the introvert is quiet, retiring, calm, controlled and a lover of books rather than people.

Neuroticism — This is defined in terms of worry, anxiety, instability and moodiness.

Psychoticism — This is tough-mindedness. The high scorer is insensitive, inhumane, sensation-seeking and cruel.

There can be no doubt that these variables are not to be confused with psychosexual syndromes.

THE GUILFORD FACTORS

Guilford is a pioneer in the factorial analysis of personality tests. His first papers indeed factored face-valid items (Guilford and Guilford, 1934, 1936) although inevitably by modern statistical standards they were not fully adequate.

However, over the years the tests have been gradually developed and expanded and in 1976 a full manual to all the scales appeared (Guilford et al., 1976). Owing to the long time-span of test development, it is by no means simple to draw up a definitive list of these Guilford factors. The one to appear below consists of those factors that have been the most thoroughly investigated not only by Guilford and colleagues (e.g. Guilford and Zimmerman, 1956) but by independent investigators wishing to locate them within the wider personality sphere (e.g. Eysenck and Eysenck, 1969).

Before examining the list of Guilford's factors for any resemblance to psychosexual syndromes, two points deserve note. First Guilford is the only major worker in the field of personality to favour orthogonal rotation of primary factors, i.e. he prefers to see uncorrelated sets of relatively complex variables. This leads us to the second point that there is some overlap with the Cattell set of factors if the Guilford factors are allowed to take up an oblique position (Cattell and Gibbons, 1968). However, as Eysenck and Eysenck (1969) demonstrated in their large-scale study of the Cattell, Guilford and Eysenck (EPI not EPQ) items, these Guilford primaries do not emerge with the clarity one might hope for. This last result has to be treated with some caution, however, since relatively few Guilford items went into the analysis, thus increasing the likelihood that higher-order factors such as E and N would be found. Despite these caveats the Guilford factors deserve scrutiny and are set out in Table 4.4.

TABLE 4.4. *The Guilford factors*

G	General activity
R	Restraint
A	Ascendance
S	Sociability
E	Emotional stability
O	Objectivity
F	Friendliness
T	Thinking introversion
P	Personal relations
M	Masculine emotions

It is clear, as we found with the Eysenck and Cattell factors, that none of the Guilford factors supports the existence of any psychosexual personality syndromes. It is however possible that a combination of F, S and G might approximate the oral optimistic personality.

Conclusions

As was the case with the Cattell factors, there is no clear identification with psychosexual personality syndromes. In Guilford's terms these syndromes would be special combinations of factors. Thus we can argue that Guilford's work does not confirm (although it does not refute) psychoanalytic psychosexual theory.

COMREY'S FACTORS

Comrey (1970) has supplied eight further factors in his Comrey Personality Inventory. This is an interesting test because it uses clusters of items as the correlational base rather than individual items and because there are multipoint response-scales rather than dichotomies, both features which should increase the reliability of the correlations.

Barton (1973) has shown that with proper rotation to simple structure many of these Comrey factors can be identified as the Cattell second-order factors. Nevertheless these factors are widely used and it is interesting to see to what extent they overlap the psychosexual personality syndromes.

TABLE 4.5.   *The Comrey factors*

T	Trust
O	Orderliness
C	Social conformity
A	Activity
S	Stability
E	Extraversion
M	Masculinity
P	Empathy

The descriptions of these factors make it clear that one, O (orderliness), to some extent resembles a psychosexual syndrome — in this case the anal character, orderliness being one of the triad of traits. However the fact that each syndrome is made up of a collection of traits suggests that the best factor-analysis can hope for is to uncover the separate elements.

Browne and Howarth (1977) factored a large matrix of items from a vast selection of factored tests in a sample of more than 1000 students. There are some technical problems in this study — especially those concerned with the number of factors rotated, the provenance of the items and the fact that some of the items were changed (in respect of phraseology) to produce a greater uniformity of style within the whole questionnaire — so that the results cannot be regarded as the definitive list of personality factors. Kline (1979a) has discussed this research in considerable detail and it is clear that these factors are worthy of consideration. For our purposes, to see whether psychosexual syndromes have been uncovered or not, the technical difficulties can be ignored, especially since we shall concern ourselves with the largest factors, i.e. those least likely to be affected by any technical deficiencies.

TABLE 4.6 *Browne and Howarth factors*

1	Social shyness
2	Sociability
3	Mood swings
4	Adjustment — emotionally
5	Impulsiveness
6	Persistence
7	Hypochondriac — medical
8	Dominance
9	General activity
10	Trust
11	Super-ego

In this list of robust factors, two of them are clearly related to the anal character, as some example items will show, and one is more tendentiously connected.

(a) Super-ego — I am not overconscientious: I think I am more easy-going about right and wrong than most people.
(b) Persistence — I give up easily: I have no difficulty in finishing a task.
(c) Impulsiveness — I seldom stop to think things over before I act. I am sometimes slow to make up my mind.

These three factors contain some items relevant to anal characteristics, although by no means all items fit the descriptions.

Conclusions

This study gave only slight support for the syndrome of the anal character. Possibly a combination of the three factors discussed above might crudely measure it.

CONCLUSIONS FROM THE FACTORIAL STUDIES OF PERSONALITY

We cannot survey all the factored scales that have been developed. This would be pointless since many of them are technically inadequate and propose factors whose validity is attested only by the content of their items. Instead we have scrutinized the factors that emerged from the large-scale factorial studies of personality questionnaires, work by authorities in the field — Cattell, Eysenck, Guilford and Comrey.

It is clear that broadly no psychosexual personality syndromes have been isolated in their work, although in some cases combinations of factors might be able to encapsulate these variables. Generally, however, it must be concluded that the massive factorial personality studies have not thrown up psychosexual personality syndromes. Their work cannot, therefore, be used to support this concept of psychoanalytic theory.

OTHER NON-FACTORIAL PERSONALITY VARIABLES

Although, as we have argued in Kline (1979), the factorial analysis of various fields leads to the identification of major dimensions of fundamental importance, if only in terms of variance accounted for, it is possible to construct tests by other methods. One method is to select test items in terms of their ability to discriminate criterion groups. The MMPI (Hathaway and Mackinley, 1951) is the outstanding personality test of this type. The second method is to correlate each item, in the item trials, with the total test score. This essentially is a simplified form of factoring the items. We shall briefly consider certain tests, if well-known, constructed by this method or by analagous methods of item-analysis.

THE MMPI

Unlike the personality inventories previously discussed in this chapter, which were developed by factor-analysis, the MMPI was developed by criterion-keying. Items were selected for scales because they were able to discriminate criterion groups from a control group of normals. The criterion groups consisted of patients classified by psychiatrists into the well-known Kraepelinian categories. If, therefore, oral, anal, and phallic characteristics formed important syndromes of personality, the MMPI scales might be expected to cover these, especially since these Freudian categories were originally discovered in clinical patients. The nine MMPI standard clinical scales are set out in Table 4.7 so that it is possible to see to what extent these variables are related to the Freudian psychosexual syndromes.

TABLE 4.7.   *The MMPI standard clinical scales*

Hs	The hypochondriasis scale is a measure of the amount of abnormal concern over bodily function
D	The depression scale measures the depth of the clinically recognized symptom complex, depression
Hy	The hysteria scale measures the degree of resemblance to patients who have developed conversion symptoms
Pd	The psychopathic deviate scale measures the similarity of the subject to a group of persons whose main difficulty lies in their absence of deep emotional response, their inability to profit from experience and their disregard for social mores
Mf	The masculinity scale measures the tendency towards masculinity or femininity of interest pattern
Pa	The paranoia scale measures the paranoid (suspicious, brooding, with delusional persecutory feelings) tendencies in the subjects

Pt   The psychasthenia scale measures the similarity of the subject to psychiatric patients who are troubled by phobias or compulsions — the obsessional neurotics

Sc   The schizophrenia scale measures the similarity of the subject to those diagnosed as schizophrenic

Ma   The hypomania scale measures the personality factor characteristic of persons with marked overproductivity of thought and action

In addition there is the Si, social introversion, scale, which measures the tendency to withdraw from others and is thus similar to the Eysenckian introversion variable.

Even that brief description of the standard clinical scales of MMPI is sufficient to indicate that they do not directly measure under another name any of the Freudian psychosexual syndromes. Nevertheless it is possible that the D depression scale is related to the oral pessimism syndrome. Although the Pt scale, psychasthenia, is frequently referred to as an obsessional symptom scale, this does not imply that it is a measure of the anal or obsessional character. Apart from the fact that Ai3 — a measure of the anal character (Kline, 1969a) — was shown to be independent of the Pt scale, there is a distinction drawn between obsessional symptoms and obsessional traits. Foulds (1965) and Sandler and Hazari (1960) make this point explicit: traits are ego-syntonic, often a source of pride to the subject and relatively enduring. Symptoms, on the other hand, are ego-dystonic, a source of misery to the subject and his relatives and friends, and are frequently transient. From this it is clear that none of the standard MMPI scales could be used as a measure of psychosexual level and thus they do not support the existence of the syndromes.

OTHER MMPI SCALES

Hathaway and McKinley (1951) are careful to point out that in addition to the standard clinical scales many other scales may be empirically derived from the MMPI. Indeed the MMPI may be regarded as an item pool. In fact over 200 scales may have been constructed from the MMPI items (Dahlstrom and Welsh, 1960). The majority of these are not relevant to psychosexual syndromes so that it would be pointless even to list their names. Those that are relevant however will be discussed in the next section when further investigations with other tests are reviewed.

It must also be pointed out that over the years the MMPI has been subjected to factor-analysis (some of the results we discuss below) despite the problems of response-sets (social desirability and acquiescence especially) and the fact that some items contribute to more than one scale thus rendering the scales non-independent and making them, strictly, unsuitable for factor-analysis.

One way around the problem of scale-dependence is to factor items or item-parcels. This was done by Cattell and Bolton (1969) and the end result was the set of abnormal factors which we have already discussed. Generally, factoring the

MMPI tends to produce, as might be expected, a general factor of emotionality or the admission of neurotic symptoms (see Orme, 1965).

Despite all these difficulties of factoring the MMPI, various investigators have used the items as a pool for scale-construction and factored their scales. The number of such studies is huge and we shall review here only those that seem in fact to have thrown up evidence relevant to the existence of psychosexual personality syndromes. In this section we shall also include investigations which have used scales other than the MMPI and which, of course, bear upon psychosexual character formation.

OTHER INVESTIGATIONS

THE WORK OF FINNEY

Finney (e.g. 1961a, 1963, 1966) has produced a number of papers on the structure of personality and its childhood antecedents. Thus he has provided evidence relevant to two of the empirical hypotheses implicit in Freudian psychosexual theory. Naturally only the work on character structure will be discussed in this chapter.

The 1961a study

Finney administered a 600-item inventory, composed of items from the MMPI, the Gough scale (Gough, 1957) and the F scale of the Authoritarian personality (Adorno et al., 1950) to a sample of fifty men and fifty women, mainly neurotics. The scores were subjected to a centroid factor-analysis and then to an objective, oblique simple structure-rotation. From this oblique rotation Finney identified the following factors:

1. *Anal compulsive character or reaction-formation.* On this factor there were substantial loadings on orderliness (0.61), stinginess (0.41) and stubbornness (0.30). Gough's (1957) rigidity scale loaded 0.70 on this factor, while a score comprised of all these scales loaded 0.78. The authoritarian F scale loaded 0.24. It should be observed at this point that the loadings quoted refer to the combined oblique analysis on 100 subjects. Finney identifies this factor confidently as the anal character and suggests from the loadings that its most prominent feature is rigidity. This factor accounted for the largest portion of the variance.

From the face-validity of the scales there is little doubt that this factor is an anal factor. Although each scale has no proven validity, the fact that they fall together as suggested by theory is in itself some evidence for their validity. The Gough scale of rigidity has some construct-validity in the work of Rokeach (1960). This factor must be regarded as sound evidence for the existence of an anal dimension within an abnormal population.

Other factors in this study were:

2. *Hysterical character or repression.*

3. *Paranoid character or projection.*

4. *Conversion.*

5. *Oral aggression and delinquency.* This factor had loadings on the following scales, Pd (MMPI) 0.58, Gough-Petersen delinquency 0.52. High scorers on this last scale were described by Gough (1957) as demanding and exhibitionistic. Finney admits that his identification was only tentative and that it is not a well-defined factor. It cannot be regarded on the evidence of these loadings as firm support for the oral character.

6. *Obsessive worrying.*

These six factors were the ones that appeared in all three analyses — men alone, women alone and combined. The other factors, which were not replicated, will not be considered since the factorization of fifty-nine variables on fifty subjects leads to loadings of considerable unreliability.

Conclusions

From the viewpoint of psychosexual theory this study provides firm evidence for the existence of the anal character as a dimension of personality in abnormal populations. It also provides interesting evidence concerning defence mechanisms and will, therefore, be again considered from that point of view in Chapter 8.

It should be pointed out that this work by Finney does not truly meet the requirements for adequate factor-analyses which we have previously discussed. Thus the ratio of subjects to variables is small, the absolute number of subjects is not as large as is desirable and there is no evidence that simple structure was reached. Furthermore, the centroid solution only approximates the principal components solution. Despite this, the results can be used because these defects contribute to random not systematic error. Here the emergence of an anal factor at all, in conditions of such noise, is impressive. Not, therefore, an ideal study but one whose results can stand.

THE WORK OF PICHOT AND PERSE (1967)

Pichot and Perse (1967) carried out a factorial study of the concept of sub-validité on a sample of 260 male neurotics. The concept of sub-validité has been identified by Sjobring (1963) and is closely related to what has been called asthenia, neurasthenia and psychasthenia. The subject high on the dimension of sub-validité is characterized by doubt and difficulty in making decisions as well as other obsessional symptoms. In this study the following tests were used and subjected to a Varimax orthogonal rotation of a principal components analysis:

Hazari obsessional trait scale (Hazari, 1957).
Hazari obsessional symptom scale.
Finney An scale (Finney, 1961b). A measure of the anal character.
Finney Rep scale. A measure of repression or hysterical character.

Sub-validité scale of Marke and Nyman (1960).

MMPI scales, Hy, Pa and Pd both subtle and obvious scales (Wiener, 1948).

Three significant factors emerged:

(a) Clear pathology. This is not relevant to this chapter.
(b) Anal character. The loadings on this factor were: 0.883 An, 0.844 Hazari traits, 0.552 Rep, and —0.565 MMPI Pd.
(c) Defensive tendency. Again this factor is not relevant to the chapter.

Comments and conclusions

Factor (b) is yet again evidence for the existence of an anal syndrome in an abnormal population. In the previous study examined, that of Finney (1961b), the An scale loaded on an anal factor and provided evidence of an anal syndrome. This study reinforces that conclusion. It also suggests that the Hazari A scale of obsessional traits is measuring the anal character which is further evidence for its existence. The negative loading on Pd is impressive, since psychopathy can be regarded in psychoanalytic theory as due to defective super-ego. Super-ego is, of course, important in the development of the anal character. Only the loading on the Rep scale is unexpected.

This study is good support for the existence of the anal syndrome in an abnormal male population. It also supports the validity of the An scale and the Hazari trait scale with an abnormal population.

It is now clear that the work of Hazari on obsessional traits and symptoms must be reviewed.

THE WORK OF HAZARI (1957) AND SANDLER AND HAZARI (1960)

Hazari (1957) in his doctoral thesis and Sandler and Hazari (1960) in the paper derived from that study, investigated the distinction between obsessional symptoms and obsessional traits among fifty male and fifty female neurotics. To this end, items from the Tavistock Self-Assessment Inventory (Sandler, 1954) were selected if they appeared to be relevant to either obsessional traits or obsessional symptoms. Traits were regarded as ego-syntonic and enduring features of the personality whereas symptoms were considered to be ego-dystonic and of a more transient nature. A factor-analysis of the item inter-correlations revealed two factors, one loading on items pertaining to traits, the other on items pertaining to symptoms. This first factor identified as obsessional character was regarded by the authors as evidence for the existence of an obsessional character among this population.

Comments

The interest of this investigation, from the viewpoint of this chapter, lies in the identification of the obsessional character. This is because many writers regard the obsessional character as identical to the anal character. Thus Delay, Pichot and Perse (1962), for example, in a truly excellent study of the relation of obsessional symptoms and obsessional traits, argue that the obsessional character is the psychiatric term for the anal character. Such a term allows the existence of the syndrome but makes no reference to the exclusively Freudian aetiology of repressed anal erotism. Nevertheless examination of psychiatric as distinct from psychoanalytic texts, e.g. Mayer-Gross, Slater and Roth (1961), Henderson and Gillespie (1956), reveals one major difference between the obsessional and the anal character. Parsimony, part of the anal triad, is not part of the obsessional character. Nevertheless there is a considerable similiarity between the two syndromes.

Examination of the item content of the Hazari scale reveals that there are no items relevant to parsimony. However, if the anal character is a true syndrome the scale could still be used as a valid measure of the anal character.

Evidence for the validity of the scale

Apart from item content and homogeneity there is no evidence presented for the validity of this scale. Indeed since all items are keyed 'Yes' acquiescence could well play a part in the variance. So too could social desirability since many of the items appear liable to this form of bias. For example:

I am a punctual sort of person.
I have a higher standard of cleanliness than the average person.

However, in his thesis Hazari (1957) presented case studies of the subjects and these showed, to some extent at least, that the scale was valid. If the evidence presented by Hazari (1957) and Sandler and Hazari (1960) as regards validity is not entirely convincing, the work of Pichot and Perse (1967) where it loaded on the same factor as the An scale of Finney (1961b) and the validity study of Kline (1969a) where it correlated with the Beloff scale (Beloff, 1957) and Ai3 (Kline, 1969a) provide further empirical evidence.

Fontana (1978) carried out extensive investigations of the Sandler—Hazari scale on a total of 736 subjects. He found that in normal non-clinical populations both obsessional traits and obsessional symptoms could be observed. From the viewpoint of this thesis, the important point is that once again an obsessional syndrome was clearly demonstrated, a finding which supports the existence of the anal character. Generally, in all samples, the correlation of traits and symptoms was small, only rarely reaching statistical significance.

As Kline (1967b) also found, there was no significant correlation between measures of traits and extraversion or neuroticism as measured by the EPI, thus further confirming the independence of the obsessional trait factor.

It may be concluded from Fontana's studies that there is a syndrome of traits resembling the description of the anal character and independent of E and N which the Sandler and Hazari questionnaire does measure.

Conclusions

The work of Sandler and Hazari shows that in an abnormal population an obsessional syndrome of traits appears to be a dimension of personality. Further empirical work with their scale gives some evidence for its validity, while the theoretical approach of Delay, Pichot and Perse (1962) indicates that essentially the obsessional and the anal character are the same. The Sandler and Hazari studies, therefore, must be regarded as support for the existence of an anal syndrome. This is especially true when further studies with the Hazari scale are taken into account.

OTHER POSSIBLY RELEVANT SCALES

Great care must be taken in examining personality scales not designed to measure psychosexual syndromes, to see whether in fact they do so under another name. Thus any scale of neatness (part of the anal character) should not be used as evidence for the anal character whose significance lies in the syndrome neatness and obstinacy and parsimony. However, as Dixon (1971) has pointed out, and as we have repeatedly found in small-scale unpublished studies, there is *some* similarity to the anal character in concepts such as: Dogmatism (Rokeach, 1960), Authoritarianism (Adorno et al., 1950), Rigidity (Gough, 1957) and Conservatism (Wilson and Patterson, 1970). However, none of these variables can be identified as the anal character.

Recently, some psychiatric personality questionnaires for use with clinical patients have been developed which include measures of obsessional symptoms and traits, e.g. the scales of Cooper (1970) and Barret et al. (1966). Although these have little more than face-validity, the very fact of their existence shows that some practical value is still placed on the concept of obsessional personality — a notion similar to that of the anal character.

CONCLUSIONS FROM ALL THE STUDIES

There is little support for the existence of these psychosexual syndromes from the major questionnaire studies of personality. The scales of Guilford and Eysenck and the clinical scales of the MMPI do not appear to measure similar variables. The basic source traits of Cattell are also not relevant although it is possible that certain combinations of these might be developed to provide measures of them. T, objective test, factors however are more promising: UI19 is, descriptively, not unlike the anal character. Cattell's surface traits do resemble psychosexual syndromes to some extent and H1 is identified by him as being the anal character. This must be regarded as good evidence for its existence. It is to be noted that it is a failing of his source traits that, as yet, they are unable to account for all the surface traits.

Finney (1961a) and Pichot and Perse (1967) together provide further good evidence for the existence of an anal syndrome, this time within abnormal populations. Hazari (1957) and Sandler and Hazari (1960) also support the existence of the anal character with their obsessional trait scale. Comrey, in his studies, provides support for both the anal character, his compulsion factor, and the oral character, the dependence factor, although it must be admitted that further evidence is needed concerning the validity of these scales.

In the previous chapter concerning studies deliberately aimed at providing objective evidence for psychosexual personality theory, it was concluded that there was good evidence for the anal character and some less clear evidence for the oral character. The evidence for more general studies of personality points the same way.

The conclusions may be thus summarized:

1. *There is good evidence for the anal character.* This is supported by Cattell (surface trait, H1), Finney (1961b), Pichot and Perse (1967) with the An scale, and Hazari (1957), Sandler and Hazari (1960) and Fontana (1978). To a lesser extent Comrey's studies provide evidence.

2. *There is some evidence for the oral character.* This is supported, to some extent at least, by the surface traits of Cattell and by the work of Comrey. It is by no means as clear as the anal character.

3. *There is almost no support for other psychosexual syndromes.* Cattell's factor H and surface trait CB3 are the only evidence that can be offered.

5

The relation of psychosexual personality syndromes to infantile experiences

As was pointed out in the opening chapter, psychosexual theory has implicit in it three basic empirical propositions:

1. that certain adult personality syndromes may be observed,
2. that these are related to infant-rearing procedures, and
3. that pregenital erotism may be observed in infants.

Since the effects of child-rearing procedures are created through repression or frustration of this pregenital erotism, propositions two and three are related. The two previous chapters have considered the evidence for the first proposition. In this chapter we shall examine the objective studies of the last two hypotheses. That this is a worthwhile procedure has been demonstrated by the findings already discussed — that some of these hypothesized personality syndromes do seem to exist.

A study of the objective evidence reveals that four different approaches have been used by the investigators, and these, which are set out below, will be discussed and evaluated in separate sections in this chapter. The five methods are:

1. Retrospective studies of the infantile experiences of adults.
2. Cross-cultural studies.
3. Current and longitudinal studies of children.
4. Studies with the Blacky Pictures (Blum, 1949).
5. Other techniques.

These five methods have been used because each method has certain specific problems (or indeed faults).

PROBLEMS OF THE DIFFERENT METHODS

1. Retrospective studies of adults

The difficulty here is simple — recollection. The fact is that the majority of adults are unable to recollect with any accuracy early childhood events. Freud, of course, used the fact of infantile amnesia as one of his arguments to support the concept of repression of infantile sexuality and the Oedipus complex. L. C. Robbins (1963), in a most interesting investigation, showed that parents' recollections of the details of how they had weaned and pot-trained their children were not closely related to records of these events made at the time as part of a longitudinal study. Newson and Newson (1963) in Nottingham found, in their study of parental child-rearing practices and attitudes, that recall of training milestones became inaccurate after an interval of more than a year. This means that the child-rearing data in such studies is likely to be of dubious validity. The advantage of this approach lies in the fact that adult personality tests of the psychosexual syndromes have been developed so that criterion populations can be compared.

2. Cross-cultural studies

This approach involves severe problems of measurement in alien cultures. Biesheuvel (1962) has discussed these difficulties which may be insuperable in some societies. On the other hand the attraction of cross-cultural studies resides in the opportunities to study the effects of truly diverse child-training procedures.

3. Current and longitudinal studies of children

Current studies of children are beset with the difficulty of obtaining adequate measures of personality. Eysenck and Eysenck (1969) show clearly, for example, that their junior EPI is not viable below the age of nine. Furthermore, interpretative measures such as doll-play do not have high validity. On the other hand, child-training data can be accurate. However, it must be observed that very often such current studies still use retrospective data concerning infant experience. These studies may well have the disadvantages, therefore, of both this and the first method.

4. The Blacky Pictures (Blum, 1949)

Some investigators have used this projective technique, specifically designed to test Freudian psychosexual hypotheses, in an attempt to measure infantile experiences indirectly and thus overcome the problems discussed above. Their validity is not obvious however, and evidence for the validity of this technique and the results achieved with it are discussed in the relevant section. Corman (1969) has developed a similar test, the PN test, using pigs rather than dogs. This too will be discussed.

1. RETROSPECTIVE STUDIES OF CHILD-REARING PROCEDURES AND ADULT PERSONALITY

INTRODUCTION

Despite the problems of the validity of the data on child-rearing procedures when these are recalled by adults (remember that in the study by Newson and Newson (1963) a gap of one year was sufficient to blur the memory), a number of such studies has been conducted. The general plan of these investigations is to select subjects, typical of the personality syndrome claimed to be derived from oral or anal fixation in childhood (usually by means of psychometric tests), and then to investigate how they were weaned or pot-trained. In this section those investigations where fixation was measured by the Blacky Pictures (Blum, 1949) will not be considered. The validity and reliability of the Blacky Pictures and the work done with them are separately examined (see p. 109). It should now be obvious that many of these investigations have already been discussed in the previous chapter — for the support they bring to the first of the empirical propositions implicit in Freudian psychosexual theory that the hypothesized personality syndromes do in fact exist. These studies will now be examined again but this time in relation to the second empirical proposition of the theory — are these personality syndromes related to repressed pregenital erotism and specific child-rearing procedures?

THE WORK OF GOLDMAN-EISLER ON THE ORAL CHARACTER

Goldman-Eisler (1950, 1951) attempted to relate the scores on a personality questionnaire designed to measure oral optimism and oral pessimism to the weaning procedures of the subjects taking the test.

Sample and validity of scales. In Chapter 2 the validity of these scales for selecting oral optimists and oral pessimists was fully discussed. It was concluded that although these scales had face-validity and were reliable, further evidence for their validity was necessary before the results of this study could be regarded as definitive evidence for the existence of the syndromes. The samples, too, were considered somewhat homogeneous but this was not a serious fault in that correlations would tend to be depressed rather than boosted. Positive results, therefore, would hardly be likely to be artifactual.

Feeding data. The feeding data were obtained from the subjects themselves — many of whom were students. It was thus retrospective data at least fifteen years old. Furthermore, as Hoffman and Hoffman (1964) point out, no data were obtained concerning feeding procedures after weaning from the breast. This is important since bottle-feeding of orange juice after weaning on to solid food gives sucking gratification which is clearly relevant to the repression of oral erotism. Similarly whether milk was fed by cup or bottle is another relevant factor.

Results. In the 1951 study early weaning was related to oral pessimism but in this oral factor it was noted that there was little impulsion aggression or autonomy. These traits tended to cluster together and were not related to early weaning.

Comments

The fact that early weaning was related to oral pessimism, even though this factor did not embrace the whole gamut of oral characteristics as portrayed in the psychoanalytic delineation (see p. 10), does support Freudian theory. When the dubious nature of both the feeding data and the validity of the scales is taken into account the fact that any correlation at all was observed is remarkable.

It must remembered in these studies that when the data is not ideal, unless it can be shown that the measures are not only in error but actually measuring some other factor, any correlation is still support for the theory. Error would lead to no correlation by definition (being randomly distributed). No correlation, on the other hand, for this same reason of error variance, cannot necessarily by held to refute the theory.

Conclusions

The unproven validity of the scales and the fact that the oral factor, related to early weaning, was not a precise match to the Freudian description means that this study cannot be regarded as convincing evidence for the hypothesized aetiology of the oral character. In addition it must be pointed out that the design of this study does not constitute a true test of psychoanalytic psychosexual theory. In the delineation of psychosexual theory (pp 7-8), it will be remembered, Freud (1905a) drew attention to the genetic aspects of the psychosexual constitution: that is oral, anal and phallic erotism is of differing intensity in each individual. This means that the same weaning process or toilet-training procedure will produce differing degrees of fixation in each individual — quite a mild weaning might severely traumatize an infant whose oral erotism was intense.

For all these reasons, therefore, this correlation between a factor of oral pessimism and early weaning is considered to be some support for the Freudian position. It cannot be considered as proof or as very strong evidence. On the other hand, and this is most important, these Goldman-Eisler studies cannot, by any stretch of the imagination, be used to refute Freudian theory. To the present writer it seems that Goldman-Eisler has better supported the existence of the oral syndrome than its hypothesized aetiology.

THE WORK OF THURSTON AND MUSSEN (1951)

Thurston and Mussen investigated the relationship between infant feeding-gratification and adult personality. This study was not discussed in the previous chapter because no measure of the oral character was used.

Tests. The group form of the TAT was used from which measures of oral traits were derived.

Infant-feeding data. These were gathered from questionnaires sent to the mothers of the subjects in the sample.

Sample. Ninety-one male undergraduates (students of psychology).

Results. No significant relationship was found between infant feeding-gratification and oral traits. Freudian psychosexual theory was not considered to be supported.

Comments

The first point to be discussed concerns the validity of the TAT, as a measure of oral traits. There appears to be no sound evidence that the TAT is a valid measure of these traits. As with many projective techniques, it is relatively easy to derive face-valid indices from the responses. Nevertheless firm evidence must be supplied before the score is used. Without this it thus seems highly doubtful whether in fact orality was being measured in the study. In addition, again in common with many other projective techniques, the reliability of such oral scores (not only test—retest but also repeated marking by the same markers) must be dubious. Such unreliability would again lead to low validity. It is therefore concluded that without good evidence of validity TAT measures cannot be accepted.

The second point is similar to that raised in the discussion of the work of Goldman-Eisler (1951) — the validity of the data on infant feeding. The discussion will not be repeated. Suffice it to say that it is most unlikely that such retrospective data is valid.

Conclusions

Since in this investigation both the test of oral personality and the measure of infant feeding-gratification are of dubious value, the final result of no significant correlations is not unexpected. Again the design of the investigation fails to take into account the psychosexual constitution of the subjects and this must be regarded as a weakness. Consequently it is concluded that while the results of this study in no way support psychoanalytic theory, equally they do not refute it.

THE WORK OF BELOFF (1957)

This study by Beloff of the anal character has been fully discussed in the previous chapter. There it was concluded that her scale was in all probability a valid measure of the anal factor, although the emergence of a general factor running through the items and a high face-validity are not of themselves sufficient to demonstrate validity.

Sample. 120 college students.

Infant-training data. Interview material from the mothers of the subjects.

Tests. Guilford scales and the Beloff anal scale.

Results. There was no correlation between the severity of pot-training as judged by the age of completion (the earlier the more severe it was held to be) and scores on the anal questionnaire. There was, however, a correlation between the scores on the anal scale of mothers and their children. Beloff concluded from these results that the psychoanalytic aetiology was not valid.

Comments and conclusions

In common with the other studies, using retrospective data on child-rearing procedures, no account was taken of the psychosexual constitution of the subject. Inevitably, too, for reasons that have already been discussed the validity of this pot-training data cannot be considered high simply because it was gathered so long after toilet-training was completed. The anal test however does appear to be valid. Thus it is possible to argue that the failure to obtain positive correlations was due to the inadequacy of the pot-training data. This view is, perhaps, supported by the fact that Beloff identified early completion of training with severity — an arguable but not necessarily correct identification.

The conclusion from this study therefore must be that it fails to support the Freudian theory. It cannot, however, be held to refute it.

FURTHER STUDIES

In respect of the oral character, Fisher and Greenberg (1977) cite two further retrospective studies. One of these, an unpublished thesis by Stein (1958) seems to us irrelevant to orality since it was concerned with the relation of age of completion of weaning and how it was done with the manner in which theories of moral transgression were handled as part of projective testing. Even if the validity of these projective measures were taken on trust, this is a long way off from the concept of the oral character as described in psychoanalysis.

The work of Miller and Swanson (1966) on defences is also cited as a carefully designed and thoughtful study. However, the variables related to the severity of weaning retrospectively obtained from the mothers of a large sample in this study were not oral traits but guilt and other indices of defence mechanisms measured by projective tests.

Apart from the problem of the validity of projective test data (unless specific evidence is adduced that they are valid), it is not relevant to the concept of the oral character to relate any variable to weaning; the critical issue is whether specific oral traits are or are not related to weaning and feeding.

As regards the anal character, Fisher and Greenberg (1977) cite no other retrospective studies of any importance. Most such investigations do not properly fall into our first category since they were concerned with children.

The reason that there are no more recent researches of the retrospective type is probably that the problem of the accuracy of mothers' recall of weaning and pot-training is so dubious. Attractive and clear-cut as this method is in logic, in practice it is difficult.

CONCLUSIONS FROM THE RETROSPECTIVE STUDIES

Owing to the doubts concerning the validity of the data on child-rearing in all these investigations, the fact that two of them failed to support Freudian theory cannot be regarded as a refutation of it. Since, too, in all these studies the personality measures are of unproven validity (although there is some evidence for the Beloff anal scale) there is further cause for confusion. The theoretical weakness of the design, in that no account was taken of the psychosexual constitution of the subjects, can also be used to explain the failure of these studies to corroborate psychoanalytic theory. In all fairness to these researchers it should be said that as yet there is no measure of psychosexual constitution which they might have used and it could be argued that any such differences would be randomly distributed throughout a sample so that the effects would be cancelled out. Actually this argument is unlikely in terms of psychoanalytic theory in that it is probable that intensity of oral or anal erotism is an important factor in causing fixation since it increases the *perceived* severity of the weaning or toilet-training.

In short, therefore, two of these investigations, Thurston and Mussen (1951) and Beloff (1957), fail to support Freudian theory. The work of Goldman-Eisler (1951) gives some support. None of them, however, refutes psychoanalytic psychosexual theory.

2. CROSS-CULTURAL STUDIES

INTRODUCTION

If we disregard the difficulty of the individual's psychosexual constitution, cross-cultural studies of child-rearing practices and adult personality are clearly of great interest in the elucidation of these psychoanalytic aetiological hypotheses. For in cultures different from our own, diverse infant-training procedures can be observed such that a real test of the Freudian hypotheses may be made. An additional advantage, especially in more traditional cultures than that of Europe, lies in the homogeneity of many customs due to the fact that deviation from the cultural norm is regarded as bad. Psychoanalysts and psychoanalytically oriented anthropologists have not failed to see the implications of these different culture patterns for their theories. Thus Berkley-Hill (1921) attributed much of the religion, philosophy and character of the Hindus to repressed anal erotism and similar arguments have been invoked concerning the Japanese personality by Gorer (1943), La Barre (1945) and Spitzer (1947). Devereux (e.g. 1947 and 1951) has written a series of papers linking the personality of the Mohave Indians to oral and anal erotism repressed and fostered by their child-rearing practices. None of these studies was, however, quantitative or experimental. They were, on the contrary, speculative and impressionistic and as such they fall outside the scope of this book.

However, Whiting and Child (1953), in the course of their reading of the relevant anthropological literature for their classic investigation of child training and personality, rated seventy-five primitive societies for a large number of child-training procedures. They were thus able to use quantitative methods for relating these procedures to personality traits similarly quantified from the literature. Their findings, therefore, in so much as they bear on the aetiological hypotheses, will be examined below.

Yet another approach in the study of cross-cultural psychological variables is to use tests and measures standardized in the west (including America) and to make statistical comparisons of the results. This method, unfortunately, is beset with problems, especially where measures of personality are involved. Nevertheless cross-cultural studies have been carried out with, for example, the Cattell 16PF personality test (see p. 50) in France (Cattell, Pichot and Rennes, 1961),

Germany (Cattell and Nesselroade, 1965), Japan (Tsujioka and Cattell, 1965) and Ghana (Kline, 1967a).

PROBLEMS OF USING TESTS IN CULTURES DIFFERENT FROM THOSE WHERE THEY WERE DEVELOPED AND STANDARDIZED

Cattell (1957) distinguishes, in the study of personality, culture-free and culture-bound personal characteristics. Intelligence and anxiety level, for example, might be included among the former; among the latter sentiment for sport or science. This same distinction may also be applied to items within scales. In the MMPI can be found an item concerned with the enjoyment of Drop the Handkerchief (item 70). This is certainly a culture-bound item, whereas the item in Eysenck's MMQ, 'Have you ever been made unconscious for two hours or more by an accident or blow?' appears to be virtually culture-free. Such items are extreme instances of a distinction which is often difficult to draw. In addition there is the problem of whether in two different cultures the same behaviour has the same motivation. Indeed Biesheuvel (1962) argues that the relevance of items in different cultures constitutes the main problem in the cross-cultural testing of personality. Therefore before any tests can be satisfactorily used, the items must be subjected to item-analysis in the new population and the validity of the test must also be demonstrated. Needless to say, in addition to the problem of item content there are the difficulties of translation and the administration of tests to non-literate non-English-speaking samples. It must be concluded, therefore, that the problems of the validity of self-report tests in non-western cultures, together with the difficulties of administration, make the interpretation of results extremely complex. Obviously good evidence that such tests are working as designed must be advanced before results may be taken at their face value.

Recently Kline (1977) has devoted considerable effort to elucidating the precise bearing that cross-cultural studies have for the scientific evaluation of Freudian theory together with the particular problems associated with the various methods. In fact various general conclusions concerning the demands of good cross-cultural testing can be made. What is presented here is essentially a summary of the more detailed presentation quoted above.

The emic—etic dilemma (e.g. Berry and Dasen, 1974)

Any cross-cultural comparison of a variable implies that the variable is an etic construct, i.e. one that is culture-free and has a meaning in the cultures concerned. However in cross-cultural psychology it can be argued that few if any constructs are in fact cross-culturally applicable. The emic view is that only variables which are significant for a particular culture should be studied. Hence cross-cultural studies are by definition impossible (other than for a few gross variables).

Our solution to this dilemma is first to demonstrate that our tests are working effectively and equivalently in the two or more cultures before making comparisons. In this way we are measuring etic constructs with emic measures. As we indicated above, the demonstration of cultural equivalence is best done by item factor-analyses and item-analyses. Rasch analysis (Rasch, 1960) which is claimed to be sample-free and to yield measures of ability independent of item difficulty might seem ideal for cross-cultural demonstrations of cultural equivalence. However, we have found severe problems utilizing Rasch analysis with the EPQ both in Great Britain and in Thailand owing to the fact that the latent-trait dimensionality of the Rasch model is very different from factor-analytic dimensions (Barrett and Kline, 1980; Kline et al., 1980).

Sampling difficulties

Since a certain sophistication is necessary to complete personality questionnaires in cultures where a high level of education is restricted to a small minority, samples are necessarily homogeneous and unrepresentative of the whole population. Interpretations must be duly cautious. This problem is further exacerbated if the test is left in English. Translations obviously prevent certain difficulties and inappropriate items remain so even when translated. The best, although imperfect, solution is back-translation. Here the translated version is rendered back into the original by one ignorant of the test. Resulting differences highlight any translation difficulties which can usually be resolved.

The use of projective tests

Projective tests appear to overcome many of the objections that can be raised against the use of personality questionnaires in cross-cultural studies, and extensive reviews of their cross-cultural use have been provided by Spain (1972) and Lindzey (1961). The objections to projective tests on grounds of lack of scientific rigour have been so powerfully put by Eysenck (1959a) and less spectacularly by Vernon (1964) that we can list them as virtually accepted views. These objections are: poor reliability, both between occasions and between examiners; poor validity in the vast majority of cases, especially for the Rorschach Test; the fact that the test scores have been shown to reflect transitory moods of the subject although they are claimed to measure 'deep' layers of the personality; and the fact that methods of test administration as well as how the subjects conceive the test also affect results as can response-sets such as social desirability.

This is why for the purposes of the scientific study of personality projective tests have been widely eschewed. The cross-cultural use of projective tests does not nullify these points, it adds further difficulties. As we wrote in 1977, views with which we still agree, it is clear that for example the TAT pictures are culture-bound — to a middle-class America of the 1930s. Lee (1953) produced an Africanized version but this would suit only certain tribes there, and would not be useful elsewhere. In addition culture influences affect picture-recognition and depth-perception as shown in the work of Hudson (1960, 1967) in South Africa, Deregowski (1966) in Zambia and Kilbride and Robbins (1969) in Uganda. Kline (1975) indeed, working with the Pin-Men Test with Indian students, found some similar perceptual problems. In fact Wober (1967) suggested that some cultures are not visually oriented but are keyed to other perceptual modes, a hypothesis that has profound implications for cross-cultural testing. From all this it must be concluded that the cross-cultural use of projective tests with visual stimuli is unlikely to yield data of high scientific integrity.

Of course it is possible to construct projective tests that do not employ visual stimuli, thus avoiding the special cross-cultural perceptual problems. Sentence-completion techniques are well-known non-visual tests and Phillips (1965) has produced an example which may be suitable in a wide variety of cultures. However, it demands literacy (if used as a group test), some familiarity with the conventions of test-taking, and translation. Thus if used in a large number of different samples the similarity of one version to another is by no means obvious. Furthermore there is little evidence of validity so that at best it could be regarded as a measure worth further investigation.

Despite all these objections to the cross-cultural use of projective tests, which we regard as overwhelming, as the extensive bibliographies in Lindzey (1961) and Spain (1972) indicate, they have been widely used. Are we then to write off all this work as valueless? As scientific evidence, as we have argued, it is really unsatisfactory. However, the best of it provides marvellous insights into the societies studied which can then be tested in a more rigorous fashion. Thus it may well be the case that the brilliant investigator can use a projective test to useful effect whereas the Grub Street tester can produce nothing. An outstanding example of this sensitive use of tests and procedures which are far from scientific is to be found in Carstairs' (1957) study of the Rajputs in central India. Sampling was not random in that Carstairs set himself up in a village and sought volunteers. The data themselves were biographies, interviews and Rorschach responses, yet so deft is the handling of this material that there can be few readers who do not feel that they have reached a good understanding of the personalities of these subjects. Nevertheless this does not mean that these data-gathering techniques are suited for scientific investigation. The value of scientific tests lies in their objectivity — their ability to give the same result regardless of tester.

However, we do not propose to abandon the use of projective techniques in the cross-cultural study of personality. What we propose for the research use of projective tests in alien cultures is the procedure used by Holley, in numerous investigations and fully described in Holley (1973), with the Rorschach test. In this Holley scored the Rorschach dichotomously for the presence or absence of various schizophrenic signs, whose scoring was highly reliable. The protocols from depressives, schizophrenics and normals were then subjected to G correlational analysis (Holley and Guilford, 1964) in which correlations between people were computed, followed by Q factor analysis and a Varimax rotation. These investigations revealed that depressives could be separated from normals with a validity of 1 (i.e. perfectly), a result which Holley (1973) attributed to error-free statistical analysis. There seems little doubt that the most significant feature of these results from the viewpoint of the scientific utility of projective tests lies in the reliable scoring procedure although the G index is a useful correlational index in the study of groups. That the method is useful with other projective tests is revealed by ongoing studies of criminal psychiatric subjects by Hampson and Kline (1977) where these were clearly separated from controls and fell into meaningful groups using this form of statistical analysis with the TAT, House—Tree—Person Test and Family Relations Indicator. Of course to interpret the nature of the discriminating test factor needs considerable further study which is why, at present, the method is suggested as for research use only. Certainly it would be highly interesting to administer a battery of projective tests to samples from a wide variety of different societies and attempt to see empirically by the use of G methodology how they might be discriminated. Thus, to take a concrete example, if we thought that two societies offered particularly good chances for different Freudian defences to develop, this method with the right projective tests, free enough to allow such mechanisms to be observed, could put the theory to a rigorous test. The same procedure could be adopted with typically anal and oral cultures.

From this it is clear that for the cross-cultural testing of psychoanalytic psychosexual theory there is no one projective test that can be recommended. Rather it is a method of statistical analysis that could prove viable. Thus it is true that the majority, if not all, of projective cross-cultural studies cannot be regarded as scientific evidence for psychoanalytic theory, however interesting the results. On the other hand, projective tests still offer considerable possibilities for cross-cultural research.

At this juncture a little more needs to be said about the Yale studies (Whiting and Child, 1953) in which ethnographic reports of various societies are subjected to statistical analysis — the hologeistic method.

THE HOLOGEISTIC METHOD

Advantages

The obvious advantage of the hologeistic method for the validation of Freudian theory (and indeed any theory of child development) is that it puts to the test its generality over cultures. This is particularly important with respect to Freudian theory because this claims to have discovered universal truths about human beings despite the fact that the majority of Freud's patients were Viennese Jews.

The second advantage is that the method allows the maximum variance for child-rearing procedures, hence any relation of personality to child-rearing will be observed unattenuated by homogeneity of variance. In Great Britain, for example, as Newson and Newson (1963) demonstrate, there is relatively little variation in weaning or pot-training — the result of health education in the culture — and any extremes are *per se* abnormal. Thus there is a confounding of variables. If a wide variety of cultures is sampled, very considerable variations, yet all normal, can be found.

These advantages, as claimed by Whiting (1968), make the hologeistic method in our view extremely powerful as a test of the scientific validity of psychoanalytic theory. However, before the results can be properly interpreted, it is important to realize that the hologeistic method has a number of technical problems which, if they are not overcome, can considerably weaken the force of the findings. It is certainly insufficient, in the study of psychoanalytic theory, simply to quote uncritically the results of hologeistic studies as evidence for or against the theory as do Fisher and Greenberg (1977).

Technical problems

Campbell and Naroll (1972) have an excellent survey of the problems involved in the hologeistic method, a survey which we have previously discussed (Kline, 1977). The relevant parts of this discussion follow here since, as was the case with projective tests, our views have not substantially changed. Campbell and Naroll (1972) examine eleven problems associated with the hologeistic method, of which the most pertinent to the testing of psychoanalytic theory are scrutinized.

The first difficulty concerns sampling societies. Thus there is no way of extracting a probability sample of existing societies simply because so many of them have not been described. Since there are in the region of 5000 societies of which only one-fifth have been sufficiently documented for study (and that not for all variables), sampling bias is obviously a factor in any investigation. However from the viewpoint of the validation of Freudian theory this problem is not important, because if Freudian hypotheses are or are not upheld in what at worst is a wider sample than that found in the consulting rooms of Vienna, the finding is significant. Thus if the hypotheses are confirmed, it is weak to argue that there are still societies of which we are ignorant. Similarly if the hypotheses are not supported it is unlikely that they would be in these other societies. However, it remains true that complete generalization to all human beings is not possible. Another important problem related to that of sampling concerns the definition of a tribe or society. Although language, political organization and territorial occupancy have been used to define societal boundaries, there is no agreed definition among anthropologists. Nevertheless it is possible to draw up a world-wide cross-cultural sample of societies such that there is no problem in discriminating any one society from any other. Since in such a sample of societies we can be sure that all the societies are different it makes sense to use this sample or draw from it in our cross-cultural studies of Freudian theory, as was done by Whiting et al. (1958) in their investigation of the Oedipus complex, where societies were chosen to represent as many as possible of the culture areas designated by this method (Murdock, 1957).

Data accuracy is the third point raised by Campbell and Naroll (1972) and is in our view the most critical of the problems. How accurate are anthropological data? Random errors tend to lower correlations so that the fact that significant correlations are obtained with these methods suggests that this is not an important feature. However, there may be systematic sources of error which could produce artefactual correlations. While this could be the case it must be noticed that it must be a systematic tendency among anthropologists in general since Whiting and Child (1953) used seventy-five different societies involving a very large number of anthropologists. Bias among one or two would not have had this effect. Now this systematic biasing is very important in the elucidation of Freudian theory, because it is possible that the anthropologist was aware of Freudian theory so that critical Freudian variables, such as weaning and pot-training and subsequent personality patterns, might become the objects of subjective perception. In some cases of course the anthropologist may have been a committed Freudian, for example Roheim or Muensterberger, although as we have pointed out one or two instances of bias in a large sample of reports should not grossly affect the results. Campbell and Naroll (1972) suggest that there are certain quality controls that can be used in the evaluation of anthropological reports — familiarity with the native language, length of stay among natives and the degree of participation in the culture. Related to these quality controls are such points as how many of the behaviours reported were actually observed. How many subjects actually responded in this way? How normal is such behaviour in the society — i.e. baseline rates need to be set up. How reliable, between observers, are these reports? However it should be noted that errors such as these are not systematic but random and would tend, therefore, to reduce the size of correlations. Our view of this problem of the reliability of the anthropological report is that it may be riddled with error especially where the information is obtained from informants. However it will be random error and the systematic sources of bias do not seem likely to be so important over a wide range of anthropologists. Thus we would argue that the fact that significant results can be obtained with this method, against all the possibilities of confounding error, means that the hologeistic method is still useful in the elucidation of Freudian theory.

Campbell and Naroll (1972) are, quite rightly, concerned over the interpretations of the correlations resulting from this approach, especially the problem of the causal analysis of correlations. They suggest, in view of the fact that there are often data on these societies which are relevant to cultural change, that cross-lagged correlations might be useful. However, with reference to the notion of causality, if we can accept Cattell's (1973) concept of factors, when rotated to simple structure — an important proviso, which the majority of factor-analytic researches fail to grasp (Cattell and Kline, 1977) — as causal agencies, the factor-analysis of these correlation matrices is the obvious solution.

Another serious problem lies in the fact that there is a paucity of data relevant to certain problems in the published monographs which form the basis of these investigations. Obviously one solution is to attempt to collect the data specifically for the investigation but if a good sample of societies is to be included, then this is a lengthy procedure.

A final problem which Campbell and Naroll (1972) discuss is a general one with large matrices of correlations — namely that a number of correlations will be significant only by chance. However if we split the sample up into meaningful parts, for example, by region, this both tests the real significance of correlations (for true correlations will be significant in both samples), and looks at the interesting question of regional differences. Important here are the correlations that occur in both samples. If we have more than two samples failure to correlate in one of them may indicate genuine regional variation.

Galton raised a difficulty with this method — do cross-cultural correlations reflect functional association or cultural diffusion, owing to borrowing or migration? If the latter is the case then the problem of the independence of the samples arises and hence the statistical basis of the whole method. This problem is related to that of adequate sampling of cultures which we have already discussed. If however a sample is chosen such that no pair of the societies has contiguous borders, the effect of cultural diffusion is clearly minimized. But if our interest lies in the testing of particular hypotheses concerning child training and personality, as is the case in our concern for Freudian theory, the Galton problem is not serious since the personality patterns are unlikely to have spread via such cultural diffusion. For further discussion of this problem readers are referred to Naroll and Cohen (1970) and Whiting (1968).

These problems, although serious, do not seem to infirm the hologeistic method as a powerful means of verifying psychoanalytic theory, at least those parts of it which implicate environmental factors as important determinants of personality.

With all these problems in cross-cultural investigations in mind, both of testing and of ethnographic study, we shall now turn to an examination of the results that have been obtained.

THE WORKS OF WHITING AND CHILD (1953)

Kardiner (1945), in *The Psychological Frontiers of Society*, makes a distinction between Primary and Secondary Institutions. *Primary Institutions* comprise those aspects of culture, especially child-training practices, which in his opinion produce the basic personality structure of members of a society and have an important influence on other aspects of culture — the *Secondary Institutions*. Whiting and Child (1953) claim that this is their basic approach. Whereas, for example, Gorer (1943) and La Barre (1945) assumed that toilet-training affected personality and interpreted the Japanese personality in the light of this assumption, Kardiner claims that his approach allows the hypotheses to be tested as they arise. Consequently, following Kardiner, Whiting and Child do attempt to put the Freudian hypotheses to the test. It should be clear that the concepts themselves of Primary and Secondary Institutions are, if not derived from, certainly influenced by psychoanalytic psychosexual theory.

Sample. Seventy-five primitive societies, and an American middle-class reference group (N = 50) as used by Davis and Havighurst (1946, 1947).

Raw data. Ethnographic reports of these societies.

Dimensions of measurement. Five dimensions: oral, anal, sexual, dependent and aggressive. For the sexual dimension sub-systems were used: immodesty, masturbation, heterosexual play and homosexual play. For the aggressive dimension, the sub-systems were: temper trantrums, physical aggression, verbal aggression, property damage and disobedience.

For all these dimensions the child-training practices of each society were examined for:

1. Initial satisfaction.
2. Socialization anxiety.
3. Age of socialization.

Method of measurement. Three independent judges rated the literature on a seven-point scale (e.g. degree of anxiety). Then within each society the five dimensions were ranked. The reliability of these judgements ran from 0.55-0.95.

Reliability of ratings. The median r of the ratings for the three judges was 0.85 (confident ratings). For their doubtful ratings it fell to 0.61.

This rater reliability is very satisfactory — as high as the reliability of many psychological tests. But no matter how skilful the ratings, all is wasted if the original ethnographic material is inaccurate. Without extensive and precise observation of the individual societies it is clearly impossible to say how accurate each of these reports is. It is to be noted that a dimension was not rated if the particular report contained no relevant information. Although only distinguished reports were used, the validity of these rating scales must remain enigmatic and interpretation of the results must be accordingly cautious. Such were the measures of child-training procedures.

The personality measures

Whiting and Child (1953) argue from a combination of what they describe as Psychoanalytic and Hullian drive theory that fixation due to excessive indulgence is positive fixation whereas negative fixation is derived from excessive severity. In the anal sphere, for example, a love of defaecation would be regarded as positive fixation and extreme modesty about secretion as negative fixation (Fenichel, 1945). So the personality measures were resolved into indices of positive and negative fixation based on the ethnographic report.

Explanations of illness and disease will concentrate around areas of negative fixation. Thus the index is the occurrence of this kind of explanation. If therapeutic value is attached to responses in any area, this is regarded as an index of positive fixation.

Both these indices are related to the generalization of anxiety. Thus the belief that kissing is a source of infection is considered to be anxiety derived from oral anxiety and the belief that it is a cure for toothache is considered to be euphoria derived from general oral euphoria. It is clear that such arguments are not so easily applicable in a society where the causes and treatments of illness are more thoroughly understood.

Thus the Freudian hypothesis that negative fixation is produced by excessive severity of socialization and positive fixation by excessive indulgence can now be put to the test.

A. Negative fixation

The greater the *socialization anxiety* in any area, the more will *explanations of illness concentrate* round that area, in any society.

Results

> *Oral* and *aggressive* dimensions strongly confirmed (t sig. 0.0005 and 0.005).
> *Dependence* dimension confirmed (t sig. 0.05).
> *Anal* dimension slight confirmation (t sig. 0.03).
> *Sexual* dimension no confirmation.

Curiously enough it was also found that negative fixation in the *dependent and aggressive* dimensions was related to initial satisfaction in these areas. These findings demonstrate that, except in the last two areas, positive and negative fixation are indeed different.

B. Positive fixation

The greater the *initial satisfaction* in any area, the greater will be deemed the *therapeutic value of the responses* related to that area, in any society.

Results

No significant differences in any area except the *sexual dimension* (t sig. 0.01 level). *Progressive satisfaction* was then substituted for initial satisfaction. Then positive fixation in the oral dimensions was related (0.05 sig.) but the anal dimension was related in the wrong direction. Whiting and Child (1953) conclude from this that there is no evidence for positive fixation.

Comments

As the results stand, the position is that Whiting and Child have provided evidence from the study of these seventy-five primitive societies that negative fixation is related to severity of socialization-training, at least in some areas (supporting Freudian theory). They have failed to find evidence that positive fixation is related to indulgence and they thus refute Freudian theory. However, the question of the validity of these most ingenious personality measures must be examined. First, it must be said that there is no evidence that they are valid. Their validity depends on the chain of reasoning mentioned above concerning the generalization of anxiety. All that can be said is that the reasoning appears sound (in fact brilliant); however, it must have empirical support. The only empirical support these measures could have would be if they correlated with the child-training procedures, because they would thus fit their (Freudian) constructs, i.e. have construct-validity. When they fail to fit, as do the measures of positive fixation, it is impossible to tell whether the measure or the theory is at fault.

Whiting and Child themselves admit this point in their discussion of the negative results of their positive-identification hypothesis. In addition, the point raised in discussion of the child-rearing data must not be forgotten — that the validity of those measures depends upon the accuracy of the ethnographic literature. It is interesting to note than in further studies not relevant to the problem of the childhood origins of the oral and anal personality, no correlations whatever were established with the anal dimension. This fact strongly suggests that in this sphere the reports may have been faulty — with random error no correlations would have been expected. In addition it would be peculiarly ironic if the anal dimension, so strongly stressed in psychoanalysis and certainly the first (Freud, 1908) to be developed into the implicit psychosexual theory, were in fact the dimension of child-rearing which had no effect on adult personality. What then of Menninger's claim (1943) that the anal phase of childhood was undoubtedly the most important not only in the development of individual personality but of cultures as well, and Roheim's claim (1934) that the whole of western culture was anal? To substantiate this on the basis of indirect measures such as those of Whiting and Child would be possible, since on no other theory could such results be understood, but to refute them on such measures without demonstrated validity is hardly possible.

There is one other point. Some readers may perhaps be wondering what relationship these personality measures have with the oral and anal syndromes. In fact the oral pessimist and the anal character are the results of negative fixation at the oral and anal phase respectively; the oral optimist the result of positive fixation.

Conclusions

The main conclusions have in effect been made clear in the discussion. Despite the problems of measurement and the possible faults in the original material, Whiting and Child (1953) have provided good evidence for the concept of negative fixation. There seems no other convincing explanation of the results. They have, on the other hand, failed to support positive fixation. This may be due to faults in psychoanalytic theory or it could be due to errors of measurement. Thus this finding does not refute psychosexual theory.

Perhaps even more important than these results are the possibilities this quantitative method of analysis opens up in the cross-cultural elucidation of psychoanalytic hypotheses (and indeed in the study of many other hypotheses). From this point of view, *Child Training and Personality* is a most impressive and brilliant work. Later in this book some of their other findings, as well as further work by their colleagues, will be discussed.

In summary, Whiting and Child (1953) have provided impressive support for negative fixation but failed to confirm positive fixation among a large number of primitive societies.

THE STUDY BY KERLINGER (1953)

Kerlinger wrote a brief critique of the studies of Japanese personality by Gorer

(1943) and La Barre (1945). As has been made clear, these investigations were not considered to be within the scope of this section because of their impressionistic approach and the lack of any precisely defined data. Kerlinger makes the point that many of the so-called facts assumed by these writers concerning child-rearing practices are simply not true. This severely underlines the danger of studies not empirically based on precise observation. It does, however, support the fact that these and similar highly interesting and speculative investigators have not been seriously considered.

THE WORK OF STRAUSS (1957)

Strauss examined the relationship between anal and oral fixation and personality among a Sinhalese sample. Before examining this study in further detail one point needs to be emphasized. The sample consisted of third-grade children (around 9-10 years). These were, therefore, in the latency period according to the Freudian theory. Now the oral and anal characters were observed in adults, not children, and the fact that sexual strivings tend to die down in the latency period may well mean that in children of this age the typical personality traits do not appear. This argument will be further discussed later in this chapter when the empirical work with children is scrutinized (see p. 90).

Sample. Thirty-four children in grade 3 of a highland village school (all in the grade). Thirty-nine children in grade 3 of a city school (one-third of the grade). (Both these rural and urban schools were, of course, in Ceylon.)

Tests

(a) Personality — the California Test of Personality and the Rorschach. A Sinhalese translation was used for the Californian Test.
(b) Oral and anal frustration indices — based on interviews with the mothers of the subjects as to their infant-training procedures.

Statistical analysis. A Chi-square method was used: the children were split into three groups on the oral and anal frustration index, and two groups on the personality tests.

Results. There were no significant associations between infant-training and personality traits in this study and Freudian psychosexual theory was not supported.

Comments

The methodology of this study is beset with problems. The validity of the Rorschach test is by no means agreed upon, even when used in the west. Eysenck (1959a) has made a severe attack upon it, which still remains to be answered. The Sinhalese version of the California Personality Test has not been validated either, so that the two measures of personality cannot be regarded as trustworthy. Furthermore, as was pointed out in the discussion of the problems of obtaining satisfactory data on child-rearing procedures, interviewing of parents some years after the completion of the training in question is not likely to produce accurate recall. The fact that data for both personality and child-rearing processes are so liable to error obviates the need for a more subtle statistical analysis than that chosen for this study. Finally the sample, although both urban and rural, is probably too small to be truly representative.

Conclusions

Although conducted in a non-western culture, this study is in fact hardly cross-cultural in that no use of the cultural differences was made. Indeed being in Ceylon may well have hindered the results. It does become cross-cultural, however, if the argument is then produced that Freudian theory does not work in Ceylon!

The conclusion to be drawn from this study is that *Freudian theory was not confirmed*, a finding which may have been due to the methodological problems involved in testing in Ceylon. On account of these problems the negative findings cannot be considered to refute psychosexual theory.

THE WORK OF SCOFIELD AND SUN (1960)

Scofield and Sun studied the effect on personality of Chinese and American child-training practices.

Sample. Forty Chinese students at Oklahoma University.

Tests. Cattell 16PF test.

Infant-training. The system of Whiting Child (1953) was followed. Oral, anal, sexual, dependent and aggressive dimensions were rated as more or less severe than American middle-class norms by three graduate students.

Results. The 16PF test was able to discriminate the Chinese from American students since the coefficient of pattern similarity (rp) was only 0.11 which was not significant. Since, according to the ratings of infant-training, the Chinese were *not* more severe on the anal dimension it was hypothesized that there would be no difference on the anal traits of compulsivity and rigidity of control. This was confirmed. Scofield and Sun (1960) consider this finding to confirm Freudian psychosexual theory.

Comments

This is not a convincing study for a number of reasons. First, forty Chinese students at an American university can only, at best, be a representative sample of Chinese students studying in America. These may have very different backgrounds from other Chinese. Even more important is the claim that there were no differences in compulsivity or rigidity of control on the 16PF test. The fact is that the 16PF has no real measures of this. Q3, self-control, is the nearest factor to it but, as Cattell (1957) himself makes clear, the 16PF contains no scale for anal traits. This was empirically demonstrated by Kline (1969a). A full discussion of the relation of the 16PF factors to Freudian psychosexual syndromes may be found in Chapter 4. Finally, mention must be made of the use of Whiting and Child's (1953) rating system. To use it on seventy-five societies, where in effect seventy-five measurements are made, does much to obviate errors. To use it on one society as was done in this study is probably to exceed its capacity. Reliability strongly affects the use of the tests with individuals on account of the standard error of measurement being related to it. Thus the use of this scale on one society is not likely to yield a valid result.

Conclusions

The size and homogeneity of the sample, the nature of both the personality test and the measure of infant-training used, all mean that the results of this study must be treated with great caution. It can only be regarded as but the most tenuous support for psychoanalytic theory.

THE WORK OF KLINE (1969a)

Kline carried out a cross-cultural study of the anal character in Ghana, using a sample of Ghanaian students.

Sample. 123 Ghanaian students at the University of Cape Coast, Ghana. Mean age 30 years.

Tests. Ai3, a measure of the anal character, the EPI and the 16PF test (Cattell).

Statistical analysis. T test, between Ghanaian sample and comparable British samples, of scores on Ai3.

Results. The Ghanaians were significantly more anal than their British counterparts (t = 5.06 sig. beyond the 0.01 level).

Discussion and comments

There can be little doubt that the sample was representative of Ghanaian students since Wyllie (1966) has shown that there are few social differences between students at Cape Coast and those at Legon — the largest of the three Ghanaian universities. The high mean age is also typical of Ghanaian students. This is almost certainly due to the fact that many Ghanaian students have to study on their own in the evenings to reach the entrance standard of the universities (Peil, 1965).

The validity of Ai3 has already been discussed in Chapter 3. It appears to be a valid measure in Britain. In Ghana too, somewhat surprisingly, it still works efficiently. In an earlier study (Kline, 1967a) the EPI and the 16PF test were shown to be valid with this Ghanaian sample. Ai3 factored out as predicted with these tests — good evidence for its validity. Furthermore an item-analysis showed only a few items in the scale to be inefficient so that it can be concluded that Ai3 was valid in Ghana.

Thus, from the point of view of sample and test, this cross-cultural study is satisfactory even if limited to students. The result, therefore, that Ghanaian students were more anal than their British contemporaries must imply, if Freudian theory be correct, that Ghanaian pot-training is more severe than British.

Studies of Ghanaian pot-training

Pot-training data were derived, in this investigation, from the relevant literature. It was not considered feasible to question the subjects, who were unused to psychological research and whose first glimpse of a psychometric test occurred in the present study. Furthermore the ordinary problems of retrospective data on child-rearing procedures were considered sufficiently overwhelming.

Unfortunately the evidence concerning Ghanaian pot-training was scanty and untrustworthy. Field (1940, 1960), Lystad (1958) and Tait (1961) make no mention of it. Kaye (1962) devotes a chapter to it in his book on child development in Ghana. The data, however, were collected by students untrained in the social sciences and give the impression of referring to ideal rather than actual behaviour. The general conclusion to emerge from Kaye is that throughout Ghana there may be found a considerable variety of pot-training methods, as regards age of starting, severity of training and expected age of completion of training. Whiting and Child (1953) rated the Ghanaian Ashanti tribe, some of whose members are included in the sample in the present investigation, as severe in their pot-training as their middle-class American reference group. Since it could be argued from the work of Sears, Maccoby and Levin (1957) in America and of Newson and Newson (1963) in this country that British and American methods are similar, it follows that the anal training of the Ashanti, at least, and Nottingham mothers is similar.

From these tenuous arguments, if anal training is related to the anal personality, a greater variance might be expected among the Ghanaians than among the British and the mean scores should be the same. These can only be tentative hypotheses because, as should be clear, not enough is known about Ghanaian pot-training. Indeed, the same could also be said of British child-rearing practices. Thus, as a cross-cultural study designed to elucidate the aetiology of the anal character, this investigation by Kline (1969a) must be regarded as a failure.

However, the result that the Ghanaian sample was significantly more anal than the British one, even if it failed to elucidate the aetiology of the anal character, did support the concept of the anal character. For, as was mentioned earlier, many of these Ghanaian students had been forced to study in the evenings after work, often for many years, to obtain entrance qualifications. Such efforts undoubtedly demand considerable persistence — one of the anal triad of characteristics. Orderliness, too, over such a long period of study and planning would all enter into such an effort so that the result, in terms of this special sample, makes good psychological sense and confirms the validity of Ai3 in Ghana.

Conclusions

This study by Kline (1969a) underlines the problems involved in the cross-cultural study of these Freudian hypotheses. Although the validity of the personality test, Ai3, was established, the study floundered through the paucity of accurate data on toilet-training practices.

It must be concluded, therefore, that this study fails either to support or to refute the aetiology of the anal character, although it does support its existence.

FURTHER STUDIES OF THE ORAL AND ANAL CHARACTER BY KLINE

Despite the failure of the Ghanaian study to provide conclusive evidence, Kline carried out further studies of both the anal and oral character in India with the hope of elucidating their aetiology.

Study by Kline and Mohan (1974)

This research deserves only the briefest mention. Ai3 (fully described on p. 39) was administered to a large sample of around 150 Indian students in Amritsar, in the Punjab. The rationale was the psychoanalytic claim made by Berkley-Hill (1921) that the Indian culture was anal. However an item-analysis of Ai3, before examining the mean differences in score between the Indian and British samples, unfortunately revealed that the test had failed to work properly in the new culture, despite the fact that it had proved viable in Ghana. Examination of the failing items showed that there were good cultural reasons to account for the failure. For example in Amritsar, which is the centre of the Sikh religion, any item concerned with smoking (as in Ai3) was bound to fail, smoking being forbidden for Sikhs. Similarly, any item concerned with revolutionaries was doomed since at the time of testing bombs were dropping in Amritsar; it borders on Pakistan. Indeed, the test was clearly not valid in India. Hence any comparisons of means with other cultures could be simply misleading. This was particularly unfortunate because an examination of the differences between Muslim, Hindu and Sikh subjects on Ai3 would have been an interesting test of Berkley-Hill's (1921) hypothesis. In brief this research was a total failure.

The work of Kline and Storey (1980)

As part of an extensive research into the aetiology of the oral character which will be reported in more detail in a later section of this chapter, Kline and Storey (1980) attempted a study of the oral character similar to that described above. This time the tests used where OOQ and OPQ (see p. 42 for a description). Only the results with OPQ will be described since OOQ was destroyed in transit from India.

Sample. 122 female students in the colleges constituting a large university in Amritsar. The rationale of the research was that a comparison of vegetarians and non-vegetarians should prove fruitful since such food-preferences are related to fixation at the oral level. Indian samples were used because of the crankiness attached to vegetarianism in the west (sandals, shorts, healthy living and Hampstead socialism).

Results. OPQ worked well in this culture, as determined by classical item-analysis. However, there were no differences between vegetarians and non-vegetarians, either overall or within religious affiliations such as Hindu, Sikh and Muslim. Nor were there any differences between the religious groups.

Conclusions

This small-scale study failed to confirm Freudian hypotheses linking oral personality traits with vegetarianism, at least among this Indian sample.

Fisher and Greenberg (1977) cite four other cross-cultural studies which we have not discussed. However, in our view they are irrelevant to a chapter on psychosexual personality traits — one being concerned with religion, one with drinking, one with romantic love and one with transference.

CONCLUSIONS FROM ALL THESE CROSS-CULTURAL STUDIES

In terms of results these cross-cultural studies have yielded little concerning the aetiological hypotheses of psychosexual theory. Indeed all that has been demonstrated is the phenomenon of negative fixation (Whiting and Child, 1953). In terms of methodology however the position is different. Here the work of Whiting and Child offers enormous possibilities in the hands of imaginative researchers. In other chapters of this book we shall examine some of the fruits of their work.

Nevertheless an appraisal of the results, as far as psychosexual aetiological theory is concerned, strongly suggests that cross-cultural studies are, alas, the sirens of the researcher into psychoanalysis.

3. CURRENT AND LONGITUDINAL STUDIES OF CHILDREN

INTRODUCTION

As we have seen, the problem in retrospective studies of adults, aimed at elucidating Freudian psychosexual hypotheses, lies in the dubious validity of recollections about infant-training procedures. Obviously current and longitudinal studies avoid this pitfall. Nevertheless these too are beset with difficulties. These problems will be briefly discussed below so that the investigations to be discussed in this section may be usefully evaluated.

Infant-rearing data

Although more accuracy can be established when the data are collected at the time of the events than in retrospective studies, it would be mistaken to assume that information is necessarily valid. To use Newson and Newson (1963) as an example, these authors found that data collected by the university research worker were not in close agreement with those obtained by the health visitor whose results appeared to be distorted by social desirability: others were telling her what they thought they *ought* to do.

The actual method of obtaining weaning and toilet-training information is also important — as stressed by Caldwell (1964). A superficial questionnaire, a structured interview and a long series of depth-interviews are likely, for example, to yield different results depending on the degree of rapport than can be achieved with the parent. The interviews, if well conducted, ought to be able to avoid obvious distortion from social desirability. On the other hand, if the interviewer is also conducting the research, he may unwittingly reinforce the responses he would like to hear (the Greenspoon effect). Again, observation in the home may well produce distortion — e.g. inhibition of paternal aggression (see Lytton, 1969). Nevertheless the high reliability of the rating scales used in the study by Sears, Maccoby and Levin (1957) does suggest that, with care, reasonable validity of data can be attained. What must be stressed, however, is that current data are not *necessarily* more valid than retrospective.

Age of subjects

This constitutes the most important objection to this approach to the study of Freudian psychosexual theory. The oral, anal and phallic characters (see p. 9) are *adult* personality patterns considered to be derived from infant-training experiences. Thus to attempt to observe these characteristics in children or even adolescents is not an adequate test of psychoanalytic theory. This is especially true in the case of pre-pubertal children. Thus in Freudian theory, after the Oedipus complex has been repressed and the super-ego comes into being around the age of five, the child enters the latency period. Until puberty, repression is relatively successful and there are few signs of conflict. Since the personality traits, subsumed under the various psychosexual syndromes, are in fact defences against repressed pregenital erotism — sublimations and reaction-formations (see p. 196) — it is not to be expected that such configurations would show up in childhood. This means, therefore, that only studies of infant-training procedures which are followed up to adulthood constitute proper tests of Freudian theory. Investigations of childhood disturbances in behaviour are not relevant.

Measures

Even if we were to admit into the discussion studies of the effects of weaning or pot-training on children's behaviour, we run into the further problem of adequate measures for children of this age. Projective techniques such as the Rorschach and the TAT are not considered suitable (see p. 5) for reasons of validity and reliability, and Eysenck and Eysenck (1969) have clearly demonstrated that personality questionnaires for children younger than nine are of dubious validity.

Finally a problem will be discussed which, though relevant to other approaches (adult and cross-cultural studies), is of particular importance in investigations of children. For obvious reasons it is usually ignored in the other approaches.

The terminology

Caldwell (1964) makes the point that even in an area of study as apparently simple as child-rearing, the concepts (if that is not too grand a term) are not clear. For example, weaning can mean the withdrawal of the breast but the continuation of the bottle, the introduction of solid food into the diet, or the abrupt transition to solid food followed by milk, sufficient only for thirst and fed by cup. In tropical countries, indeed, weaning may mean an abrupt change to solid food only. Again the terms early or late, applied to weaning or toilet-training, are purely subjective judgements in the absence of accurate up-to-date normative data (which still do not exist). Indeed the meaningfulness of 'weaned' or 'toilet-trained' can be questioned. Most children, for dietary reasons, continue to drink milk long after weaning (even if from a cup) and many children who are considered to be toilet-trained continue occasionally to soil or wet the bed. The vagueness of the terms means that precise investigation is difficult and that investigations may not be strictly comparable.

One further point remains to be noted about researches of this type. Some studies of children still use retrospective data about infant-training procedures. This means, in this writer's opinion, that they have the faults of retrospective as well as current and longitudinal studies with the merits of none.

Summary of points

Current and longitudinal studies overcome the inadequacy of recollected data about infant-training, although such data are still often imprecise. In addition they pose their own problems of measurement and are often irrelevant to psycho-analytic theory. Some studies indeed are retrospective.

In the discussion below, only those investigations which have successfully overcome the problems inherent in the method will be examined.

THE ORAL CHARACTER

Most of the investigations are seriously deficient as tests of psychoanalytic hypotheses mainly because the personality measures are of unproven validity and the children too young. Thus Rogerson and Rogerson (1939) might be held to support Freudian theory in that, compared with breast-fed children, bottle-fed children suffered more from enuresis and sibling jealousy and were considered to be more nervous. However the data consisted of observations made in visits to the home and school. In addition, the children were but seven years old. This study cannot constitute objective evidence for Freudian theory. Peterson and Spano (1941) investigated a large sample of normal children in a research that is often seized on by opponents of psychoanalytic theory as disproving Freud (e.g. O'Connor and Franks, 1961). Certainly the result that there were no correlations between length of breast-feeding and indices of personality development does appear to refute Freudian theory. However the measures used — Fels rating scales, the Joel Behaviour Maturity scale and the Vineland Maturity scale together with the Brown Personality Inventory — are not of proven validity. This study, therefore, cannot refute the theory. These two investigations have been

mentioned because they highlight the problems, discussed above, in the verification of this part of psychosexual theory and because they suffer from being too
general. Neither of these researches set out to investigate specifically the
psychoanalytic hypotheses concerning breast-feeding and its effects on personality. These were empirical studies of the broad effects in terms of personality
development and disturbance. What is needed to test the Freudian theory are
investigations aimed at the *oral traits* — dependency, optimism and typical oral
euphoria.

In fact only one study (Hernstein, 1963) follows up the sample until subjects are
old enough to put the psychoanalytic hypotheses to the test. Of the studies with
children, only that of Sewell and Mussen (1952) used measures with known
validity, although the work of Sears, Maccoby and Levin (1957) did use carefully
developed and reliable rating scales. It is to be noted, however, that both these last
two investigations based their feeding data on maternal recollection. The results
of these three studies will now be considered, together with an earlier study by
Sears et al. (1953).

The work of Sewell and Mussen (1952) and Sewell (1952)

Sample. 162 farm children of 'old American stock'. They were aged 5-6 years
and from unbroken homes.

Child-training data. Obtained from interviews with mother — and, therefore,
retrospective.

Personality data. Interviews and tests were used. The California Test of
Personality, the Haggerty—Olson—Wick behaviour rating scale and the
Wisconsin Test of Personality (a projective technique) were administered to the
sample. From the interview ratings an adjustment index for each child was
calculated.

Statistical analysis. X^2 was used to test associations between various infant-
training practices and scores.

Results. There was no association between personality test scores and breast-or
bottle-feeding, demand or schedule feeding, gradual or sudden weaning, or
finally, favourable (as judged by the authors) feeding practices. In addition oral
symptoms, as rated by observers, were not associated with any of the feeding
variables.

Conclusions and comments

Sewell (1952) and Sewell and Mussen (1952) concluded from these results that
there was no support for the psychoanalytic claim that infant-feeding practices
affected personality development.

This conclusion cannot, of course, be disputed. Nevertheless the findings
cannot be regarded as a refutation of Freudian theory because of the methodological imperfections in the study, although it is undoubtedly one of the better
investigations into this problem. These imperfections will be briefly discussed.

(a) *The statistical analysis*. To dichotomize the scores for analysis by Chi-square is inevitably to lose an immense amount of information — a twenty-point scale is far more discriminating than a two-point scale. Furthermore the dichotomies imposed on the weaning data may well have been artificial — some children are *both* breast- and bottle-fed.

(b) *The weaning data.* The retrospective data may have been of dubious accuracy.

(c) *The personality data.* Personality scales such as the California test are notoriously unreliable and thus invalid with such very young children. Similarly the validity of the other scales is not fully established.

Thus then these data are so likely to be compounded with error that failure to demonstrate any significant associations is not unexpected.

The work of Sears et al. (1953)

This study examined the childhood antecedents of aggression in forty pre-school children. Although a less popular study than their later work on patterns of child-rearing, probably because it was written up with greater emphasis on the technicalities of the research, it is in some ways superior to the later work.

Sample. Twenty boys and twenty girls.

Feeding data. Obtained from interviews with the mother — retrospective.

Personality data. Observations of dependent and aggressive behaviour in the nursery school.

Results. Dependency was positively correlated with severity of weaning and rigid schedule feeding.

Comments and conclusions

Dependency, is of course, one aspect of the oral character, so that this result appears to give some support to Freudian theory. However the sample size is small, probably too small to accept conclusions opposed to the results of most of the other studies. Furthermore, the feeding data were retrospective — although the age of the children was such as to minimize errors due to loss of memory. The personality data, based on observations of specific behaviours at specific times in the nursery school, are probably about as good of their kind as is possible. Certainly they are far superior to teachers' ratings, maternal reports or Rorschach protocols. Although this study supports the theory, Sears et al. (1957), discussed below, with a far larger sample but with inferior data based on maternal interviews, were not able to confirm the findings.

This investigation does support psychoanalytic theory. However the sample size was small so that the results must be accepted with caution.

The work of Sears, Maccoby and Levin (1957)

Their investigations into the effects of child-rearing procedures on the personality development of children described in *Patterns of Child Rearing* are monumental in size and effort. Nevertheless their conclusions must be cautiously considered because the original data are by no means ideal.

Sample. 379 mothers in the Boston area. Their children were five years old.

Data. The data were obtained by interviews with the mother. These data were concerned with child-rearing procedures and child variables — aggression, dependency and conscience developments were among those studied. Again, therefore, the feeding procedures had to be recollected by the mother.

Statistical analysis. Correlation between rating scales.

Results. Bottle-and breast-feeding had no effects on aggression, dependency or conscience development. Indeed the only relationship found significant was that late-weaned children were more upset when weaning did occur.

Comments and conclusions

As with the Sewell (1952) study, no effects on personality from either breast-feeding or bottle-feeding have been noted. Nevertheless the nature of the data, especially the retrospective feeding data, does not inspire confidence in the results. Nor indeed do the high reliabilities of the rating scales necessarily mean high validity. If a mother incorrectly recalls her methods on one occasion, on the second occasion she is likely to repeat what she said. Thus unless it were maintained that the error of recall was due to *deliberate* distortion, these high reliabilities are not altogether convincing. The most that can be said for them is that they are better than low reliabilities.

Although *Patterns of Child Rearing* is a well-known work on the effects of training procedures, its results cannot be regarded as serious refutation of Freudian theory. The fact is that the data cannot stand careful scrutiny.

The work of Hernstein (1963)

This study will be briefly discussed because it is the only longitudinal study which follows up the sample into adulthood. It is also of interest because the work has been described by Caldwell (1964) as the 'best-designed' study of those that she reviewed and as an 'excellent' investigation.

Sample. Forty-seven boys and forty-seven girls, followed up to age 18.

Infant-training data. Taken from records made at the time: type of feeding and duration of sucking were recorded.

Personality data. TAT (age 12), Rorschach (aged 18), also incidence of personality problems.

Results. Bottle- or breast-feeding had no effect on the personality scores.

Comments and conclusions

As we have made clear throughout this book, projective tests are not regarded, in general, as valid measures of personality. The Rorschach especially is under suspicion in view of Eysenck's powerful indictment (Eysenck, 1959a), where he points out that validity studies of the Rorschach are positive in outcome in inverse relation to the statistical rigour with which they are conducted. Similar gloomy findings apply to the TAT. Thus this study cannot be regarded as either well-designed or excellent by this writer.

These studies have been singled out for examination because, despite their shortcomings, they are the best of their kind. Nevertheless, as has been shown they are not sufficient to support or refute the theory.

Other longitudinal studies of orality

Caldwell (1964) lists a large number of studies of the effects of breast-feeding which we have not discussed on account of their methodological imperfections. These are listed in Table 5.1 with the reasons for omission.

TABLE 5.1. *Further studies of the effects of breast-feeding*

Hoefer and Hardy (1929)	No measures of personality
Childers and Hamil (1932)	Data reported symptoms of disturbance: feeding data retrospective
Holway (1949)	Personality data based on doll-play sessions: sample very small
Newton (1951)	Teachers' rating of personality data
Hytten et al. (1958)	Sample only three months old
Durrett (1959)	Retrospective feeding data: personality data based on doll-play
Murphy (1962)	Personality measures not reliable
Bernstein (1955)	Oral behaviour not personality data examined

Fisher and Greenberg cite a long list of studies which include some not mentioned here (see Table 5.2). However, none of these deserve comment since some are irrelevant (as described by Fisher and Greenberg), so that one wonders why they were inserted into the list at all, and the rest use measures of dubious validity or worse, or use no statistical analysis.

TABLE 5.2. *Irrelevant studies of the effects of breast-feeding*

Stendler (1954)	No statistical tests
McArthur et al. (1958)	Irrelevant here but see Chapter 10
Kagan and Moss (1962)	No measures of oral traits Children young
Davis and Ruiz (1965)	Irrelevant

Thus Fisher and Greenberg (1977) despite their extensive citations add nothing in respect of the aetiology of the oral character. There papers seem to be included if the word dependency occurs in the abstract. Certainly these papers can be held neither to confirm nor to refute psychosexual theory.

THE ANAL CHARACTER

Needless to say, the problems discussed in connection with studies of the oral character are all pertinent to investigations of the anal character. Many of the studies are not truly relevant to the psychoanalytic theory of the anal character in that they have been concerned with aggression or disturbance rather than the postulated anal traits of parsimony, orderliness and obstinacy.

Thus Huschka (1942) studied, from case records, the effects of coercive bowel-training on emotional disturbances as noted in the clinic among a large sample of children who were aged from 1-13 years. Over half of this sample of emotionally disturbed children had been severely trained and most of these had reacted against the training. However, without a normal control group the results cannot be interpreted (it could be that the greater proportion of normal children receive a severe pot-training). In addition emotional disturbances are not predicted only by Freudian theory as the result of harsh training. This much quoted investigation, therefore, cannot be held to refute or confirm psychosexual theory. Nevertheless some studies are relevant to psychosexual theory and use measures which are acceptable, to some extent, as objective evidence. These will be considered in more detail after the three studies discussed in relation to the oral character have been briefly examined. These studies investigated pot-training but did not attempt to test the Freudian theory with any precision.

The work of Sewell (1952)

Sample, methods and analysis. These have all been fully described in the section on the oral character (see p. 93) and will not be repeated here.

Results. Sewell argued that, since only a small percentage of the Chi-squares were significant, there was really no evidence for a link between toilet-training and later personality in the child.

Comments and conclusions

Caldwell (1964) points out that most of the significant Chi-squares were those related to toilet-training. This suggested to her that there was a link and that better adjustment as measured by the California Personality Test was related to late training.

This study is cited because the dependent variables were measures with some kind of validity. Nevertheless to link late training to good adjustment (albeit tentatively) is a far cry from confirmation of the psychosexual aetiology of the anal character.

The work of Sears et al. (1953 and 1957)

These two investigation have been described in the previous section on the oral character. In addition, the effects of toilet-training on dependency and aggression (Sears et al., 1953) and the emotional reactions to training (Sears et al., 1957) were studied. Again, as was the case with Sewell (1952), this work is not relevant to the psychoanalytic theory of the anal character. It has been mentioned here only because it has been previously discussed.

The work of Alper, Blane and Abrams (1955)

Samples. Two small samples of middle-class children and two small samples of lower-class children in a nursery school.

Pot-training data. No data. It was assumed that middle-class children had a more severe pot-training.

Personality tests. Finger-painting and crayoning tasks, under observation.

Results. The middle-class children, compared with the working-class sample, appeared more concerned about the messiness of finger-painting and with cleanliness generally. There were no such differences on the crayon drawings.

Comments and conclusions

This study is entirely vitiated by the assumption that middle-class children have a more severe bowel-training than do their working-class contemporaries. Even if this were generally true, two small samples (eighteen and twenty) would be insufficient for the purposes of generalization. Thus the differences cannot be attributed to differences in pot-training (and hardly to social-class differences). However, the personality measure — finger-painting — is, in psychoanalytic theory, a good index of anal erotism. Thus Jones (1923) says that painting is a sublimation of smearing faeces. This means that those receiving a severe training should be less likely to sublimate than those who are gently trained, since sublimation, although a defence, is not as effective as reaction-formation, in this case being too like the original, unacceptable activity.

Thus the interpretation of the results can only be that middle-class children dislike finger-painting more than do working-class children. The reasons for this may be simply in terms of domestic habits. Bowel-training *cannot* be implicated in these findings.

The work of Bernstein (1955)

Sample. Forty-seven pre-school children.

Pot-training data. Based on maternal interview.

Personality data. Observations of child in test situation. Collecting and smearing tasks.

Results. Severity of training was not related to collecting objects or to playing with paint or cold-cream.

Comments and conclusions

The pot-training data were retrospective but the age of the children was such that the length of time was not excessive. The collecting and smearing tasks are relevant to Freudian theory. Nevertheless, the study needs to show whether tasks in an experimental situation are related to similar activities in real life. Do children who collect stamps, for example, collect more in the test situation than non-stamp-collectors? A more serious objection to the study lies in the age of the children. Repression of anal erotism is cultural as well as domestic. Modesty-training for example plays its part. In these children the full fruits of repression may not have emerged. Finally the subjective nature of the pot-training data based on interviews must be remembered.

This study clearly fails to confirm the psychosexual theory of the anal character. It cannot be held to refute it, however, without more evidence concerning the validity of the measures of personality and the accuracy of the pot-training data. In addition, the age of the children throws some doubt on the negative inter-pretation of the results with regard to psychoanalytic theory.

The work of Hetherington and Brackbill (1963)

This study of nursery-school children is certainly the best conducted of those investigations which use children as subjects.

Subjects. Thirty-five pre-school children — twenty boys and fifteen girls.

Pot-training data. Questionnaires were sent to the mothers.

Personality data. Obstinacy, parsimony and orderliness were assessed by several different behavioural indices for each of the three traits.

Analysis. Correlations for each sex separately.

Results. Obstinacy and orderliness were not, in these samples, found to be unitary traits, i.e. there were no correlations between the different observations of orderliness or of obstinacy. For girls the total scores for the three traits were correlated together, i.e. they formed a syndrome, but this was not the case for boys. None of these three total scores was related to severity of pot-training, but the scores were related to measures of the trait (by attitude questionnaire) in the dominant parent in the household.

The authors conclude from these results, as did Beloff (1957) (see p. 33), that the term 'anal character' should be dropped. If there is an anal character it is clearly unrelated to pot-training.

Comments and conclusions

The power of this study resides in the fact that more than one observational measure of each of the triad of anal traits was made. If, as it turned out, obstinacy and orderliness are not unitary traits it is impossible to say they originate in any kind of family attitude or child-rearing procedure. Nevertheless the fact that in girls the three traits cluster together to form a syndrome supports one part of Freudian theory. The derivation of the anal character from the attitudes of the dominant parent supports the concepts of Fromm and Horney (see p. 426), who regard the anal character as originating from family attitudes, not repressed anal erotism.

However, against the good points it must be remembered that the sample size is very small: correlations on samples of twenty and fifteen have a large standard error. Thus failure to correlate together could easily be due to the small size of the sample. In personality studies correlations of beyond 0.5 are rare and thus would not be significant with this sample. Furthermore the scales given to the parents to assess anal traits and pot-training are of unknown validity. This failure to establish correlations between pot-training and personality may again be due to the small size of the sample.

Finally we come to the question of the age of the sample. The anal character is an adult personality pattern and it is possible that in childhood repression of anal erotism produces different symptoms.

This study deserves replication on a larger sample. As it stands, it cannot be considered as refuting the Freudian theory of the anal character, although it is a powerful piece of evidence against it.

Conclusions from all the studies of the anal character

As was the case with the oral character, these studies provide no support for the Freudian theory of the aetiology of the anal character. On the other hand none of these investigations fulfils adequately the criteria of a good study. The best of them, that of Hetherington and Brackbill (1963), suffers from having far too small a sample.

THE PHALLIC CHARACTER

There appear to be no studies in the literature examining the origins of the phallic character. In the previous chapter, it will be remembered, there was no objective evidence for the phallic character as a syndrome (see p. 46). It might be thought that studies of bladder-training were related to phallic characteristics. However the studies of bladder-training, e.g. Despert (1944), have not attempted to relate this to personality development. One further point remains to be noted about the possible antecedents of the phallic character according to psychoanalytic theory. Weaning is important in the development of personality because it contributes to the repression of oral erotism at a time when the child is in the oral phase, when the mouth is the centre of excitation — the most important of the erotogenic zones. Similarly, in western society at least, anal training takes place when the anus has become the centre of excitation. Bladder-training on the other hand, characteristically takes place *before* the phallic stage has been reached. Thus it may not be the crucial variable, even theoretically, in the development of the phallic character. Rather, it may be the treatment of infantile masturbation. However the fact remains that no studies have been conducted.

THE CORRELATIONAL APPROACH

Dissatisfaction with the results of studies such as those reported above has led some investigators to approach the problem in a different way. Thus Triandis and Lambert (1961), for example, subjected interview data on child-rearing practices in six cultures to factor-analysis in an attempt to discover what were the basic variables in maternal behaviour. In the American sample, factors of maternal warmth and the control of aggression were shown to be important. In the less technological societies, a factor concerned with putting responsibility onto the child emerged. Finney (1961a and 1963) has used this method in an attempt to discover what child-rearing practices were related to personality development.

The work of Finney (1961a, 1963)

Since both these papers report different aspects of the same investigation they will be considered together. Finney (1961a) deals with the oral character, while the 1963 paper examines the anal syndrome.

1961a

Sample. Thirty-one male children and mothers. The children were all seen at a child-guidance clinic.

Child variables. Ratings by teachers and clinicians for the following variables: dependency, anxiety, pessimism, conscience, hostility — both overt and covert — and repression.

Maternal variables. Clinical ratings and ratings at interview of the following variables: nurturance, hostility, selective reinforcement of dependency, failure to be firm, rigidity and need achievement. In addition, the MMPI hysterical character scale was used.

Analysis. Correlations were computed between all variables.

Results

(a) A syndrome of oral traits was shown to occur in this sample of children.

(b) This oral character in children was related to lack of nurturance in mothers, though only the correlation with pessimism reached the 0.05 level of significance. An interesting finding was that the correlations with nurturance rose when selective reinforcement of dependency was partialled out.

Conclusions. Finney (1961a) concluded from this study that these results supported the work of Goldman-Eisler (1950, 1951), discussed earlier in this section and in Chapter 3 (see pp 14 and 70), who had argued that the oral character in adults was related not to feeding but to the general nurturance of the mother (of which feeding is a measure).

1963

Child variables

(a) General anal character,
(b) stubbornness,
(c) submissiveness as rated by teachers and clinicians.

Maternal variables. Rigidity — as rated in previous study. All the other variables of the previous study were available for analysis.

Hypotheses. Rigid mothers would have children above average in

1. stubbornness,
2. submissiveness,
3. anal character.
4. This maternal rigidity would be related more closely to the general concept — the anal character — than to either of its components.

These four hypotheses were derived from the results of Sears et al. (1957), who tentatively suggested that anal characteristics might be caused by direct training for orderliness — and that the relationship to toilet-training was therefore coincidental in that these mothers (who tend to be rigid in everything) are the ones who give strict training. In addition, it will be remembered (see p. 33), that Beloff (1957) found that her anal students had anal parents. This attempt to link the anal character not to repressed anal erotism but rather to more general parental antecedent behaviour is reminiscent of Horney and Fromm (especially the necrophilous character, Fromm, 1965), whose ideas are briefly discussed in the light of the evidence in Chapter 12 (see especially p. 421).

Results

(a) *Within-children correlations.* Stubbornness was correlated with submissiveness 0.60. The anal character correlated 0.25 with stubbornness and 0.44 with submissiveness.

(b) *Correlations between mothers and children.* Maternal rigidity correlated 0.59 with anal character, but only 0.23 and 0.18 (NS) with submissiveness and stubbornness. Maternal need achievment correlated 0.34, and over-protection (nurturance held constant) 0.46 with anal character.

(c) *Further correlations in the child.* In the child, further correlates of the anal character were: orderliness, rigidity, reaction-formation, obsessiveness and feelings of guilt.

Conclusions. Finney (1963) argued that these results demonstrated the utility of the Freudian concept of the anal character. Thus the anal character may be regarded as a source trait for two reasons:

(a) It has a high correlation with its antecedents while the surface traits of stubbornness and submission have a smaller one.

(b) It is less related to other source traits than its components. In fact anal character was not related to aggression, dependency or repression whereas submission was related to all of these.

Thus Finney (1963) concludes that anal character is a source trait related to rigidity in the mother.

Comments on both studies

Both these studies support the existence of an oral and an anal syndrome in children and relate them to maternal variables. The argument, that perhaps the oral character is related to nurturance in general (of which feeding is a measure), is not supported by these data. If breast-feeding is itself related to nurturance the correlation with nurturance may be equally due to the relation between nurturance and breast-feeding. The observed correlation, therefore, may be an artefact of the relation between nurturance and breast-feeding, just as much as the opposite suggested by Finney — that the Freudian claim was an artefact. Similarly with the anal character. It *may* be related to rigidity through pot-training or to pot-training through rigidity. Correlational studies cannot answer this problem unless feeding and toilet-training data are also inserted into the investigation.

Without such data, these results are predicted from Freudian theory if indeed rigid mothers do pot-train severely and nurturant ones indulge their hungry infants.

The sample of thirty-one mothers and children is not large and, in that the children were attending child-guidance clinic, cannot be regarded as representative of the general population. The data too — ratings by teachers and clinic staff — are of questionable validity. However the neat and psychologically meaningful pattern of the results suggests that the data are in fact valid.

Conclusions

These studies confirm the existence, even in children, of oral and anal personality syndromes. They link these to maternal attitudes which are associated with different kinds of child-rearing procedures. In that there are no measures of breast-feeding or pot-training, Freudian theory would have predicted these results along with Fromm and Horney. Without these extra data there is no way of deciding which hypotheses the results support.

PREGENITAL EROTISM

So far the work discussed in this section has been concerned with the effects of child-rearing procedures on psychosexual personality syndromes. As was made clear in the outline of psychoanalytic psychosexual theory, the hypothesis is that these procedures cause repression of pregenital erotism. It is clearly important to establish whether the concepts of oral and anal erotism can be demonstrated to be useful in understanding infant behaviour. Thus the work already examined has tended to the conclusion that these psychosexual syndromes are useful dimensions of personality but are related to child-rearing practices only in so far as these practices themselves reflect the personalities of the mothers (Goldman-Eisler, 1951; Beloff, 1957; Hetherington and Brackbill, 1963; and Finney, 1963). However this evidence is far from decisive. If the existence of pregenital erotism could be unequivocally demonstrated or refuted, a far better evaluation of Freudian psychosexual theory would be possible than from studies of the effects of infant-training alone.

Oral erotism

In his 'Three Essays on Sexuality' Freud makes it clear that the mouth becomes a focus of excitation partly because in feeding the warm flow of milk has caused pleasurable sensation there and partly because of a 'constitutional intensification of the erotogenic sensation of the labial region' (Freud, 1905a, p. 182). Such children, oral children, become epicures of kissing and inclined to smoking and drinking. What is the empirical evidence for oral erotism — the erotogenicity of the mouth and lips of the infant? Sears (1943), in his review of the early work on this problem, argues that generally the evidence supports the Freudian claim, implicit in the concept of oral erotism, that thumb-sucking is the result of oral deprivation.

Levy (1928), in an early study which is still extensively quoted, showed that finger-sucking was related to inadequate sucking while feeding. Sears (1943) elegantly summarizes his findings in a table which indicates that of ninety-four children who did not suck their fingers only one had experienced inadequate sucking while feeding, defined by withdrawal from feeding too quickly due to excess of milk or lack (as in breast-feeding), forced withdrawal due to time-regulated feeding, or feeding without sucking. Of the twenty-eight finger-suckers, twenty came from these 'unsatisfactory categories'. Furthermore children who used dummies did not suck their thumb. This category of dummy-suckers were included as non-finger-suckers, thus confusing the results. Nevertheless the main conclusion still holds — finger- or dummy-sucking seems to be a compensation for insufficient sucking during infancy. The Freudian concept of oral erotism is, therefore, supported. It must be pointed out, however, that the data were parents' recollections of infant behaviour. The dubious nature of such data has already been fully discussed earlier in this chapter.

Levy (1934) conducted a brilliant *experimental* investigation into sucking with puppies. The use of dogs enabled Levy to vary feeding conditions experimentally and thus provide a rigorous test of the hypothesis that insufficient sucking during feeding caused increased non-nutritive sucking — as the Freudian concept of oral erotism suggests. From a litter of six, two puppies were fed with a nipple with a small hole; in addition, after feeding they were allowed to suck a nipple to satiety. These *long feeders* averaged around one hour's sucking per day. Two puppies were *short feeders* — a large-holed nipple and no extra sucking. These averaged around twenty minutes' sucking per day. The *breast-feeders* were left with the bitch. The breast-feeders did no body-sucking and were uninterested if a finger was offered to them. The long feeders responded to the finger only before meals. The short feeders chewed and sucked each other's bodies between meals. This is impressive support for the claim that sucking is related to the amount of sucking during feeding. In this book we have eschewed experiments and studies with animals on the grounds that they were unlikely to be relevant to Freudian theory which is distinctively concerned with human motivation. However, this study by Levy has been included because it was done to provide experimental support for his previous finding with infants. The results may well only apply to dogs but they support his previous findings. Sears (1943) argues that the studies by Levy confirm Freudian views in that sucking appears to be, to some extent at least, independent of hunger.

However, as Caldwell (1964) points out, further studies of the effects of different lengths of feeding on oral behaviour have not supported the work of Levy (1928) and thus have run counter to Freudian theory. Roberts (1944) found, among two small groups of thumb-suckers and non-thumb-suckers, that thumb-sucking was related to length of feeding time. Klackenberg (1949) found that more sucking occurred after short feeds and did not occur at all in a group who used pacifiers. Levine and Bell (1950) also supported the findings of Levy (1928) in that a small group of children who were given dummies did not develop thumb-sucking, with the exception of two subjects who preferred their fingers. These three studies may be held to confirm the link between the amount of non-nutritive and nutritive sucking. These investigations support therefore, the concept of oral erotism. Simsarian (1947), however, made a careful investigation of five children breast-fed on demand. All these sucked their thumbs and Simsarian concluded from this that unlimited sucking opportunities did not necessarily preclude thumb-sucking. This is course implied that there were other reasons, as yet unknown, for the habit. This study appears to be the first to cast doubt on the work of Levy; although in fact Simsarian generally supported the findings while emphasizing that there were exceptions to the rule.

Davis et al. (1948) were the first investigators to challenge seriously the findings briefly reported in the previous paragraph. Sixty infants were studied from birth for ten days. There were three groups — breast-, bottle- and cup-fed. The measure of oral drive or oral erotism was the length of time the babies sucked a finger offered to them. Contrary to previous findings, over the ten days the breast-fed children increased their sucking time; there was no change in the others. Thus the very group which would have been expected to have shown the least deprivation and the least amount, therefore, of non-nutritive sucking, showed the most. However these children were very young. What would have been more interesting would have been the amount of sucking after three months. Furthermore, there was no check on the length of feeding time and if the breast-feeders were quick compared with the bottle-fed, this might have accounted for the difference. That the cup-fed showed no increase in sucking is not as opposed to Freudian theory as might appear. For Freud claimed that the erotogenicity of the mouth was due in part to the pleasurable experience of sucking during feeding which was denied this sample. Clearly, however, the whole study is contrary to previous results and since the sample was so young it was clear that further research was necessary.

Sears and Wise (1950) did this in a well-known investigation in which they studied the children from eighty families. These children, from 5-8 years, were divided into groups — breast-feeding, bottle-feeding and cup-feeding. These data were, as can be seen from the ages of the children, retrospective. Age of weaning was also studied to investigate the amount of nutritive sucking.

The results of this investigation were:

(a) The later the weaning, the greater the reaction to it. This result is contrary to the work of Levy and psychosexual hypotheses, in that these are the children who have had the most sucking, and who should, therefore, be less disturbed than early-weaned infants.

(b) More thumb-sucking among the late-weaned infants (difference not sig.). Again this is contrary to Freudian theory.

These results support a learning-theory (Skinnerian) model for thumb-sucking. Those chidren who have had the most experience of sucking and the most reinforcement will have the greater difficulty in renouncing the habit. Thumb-sucking by stimulus-generalization from the breast or teat will be equally hard to extinguish in satisfied infants. This interpretation would account, of course, for the finding of Davis et al. (1948) that cup-fed children whose sucking had minimal reinforcement did not suck their thumbs. Before the results are accepted as disproving Freud and supporting Skinner, it is necessary to explain the earlier findings and to scrutinize the data on which this study is based.

First the data are retrospective: the smallest gap between weaning and recollection was four years. As we stressed earlier in this section, such data are unreliable. Robbins (1963), who asked mothers who had taken part in a longitudinal study to recollect the same data a few years later, found differences between the two sources of data as great as the differences in child-rearing procedures between the social classes! Furthermore, the amount of nutritive sucking was estimated from the age of weaning. This takes no account of the speed or duration of individual feeding so that, in fact, early-weaned infants *could* have had more sucking than late-weaned infants. Furthermore, all weaning was completed by seven months — relatively early.

Caldwell (1964) attempts to reconcile the work of Levy (1928) and Sears and Wise (1950) on just this point by claiming that the two studies do not present data on the same issue (Sears and Wise being concerned with the effects of *the age of weaning*, Levy with the effects of *duration of feeds*). This rather facile explanation will not do however because Traisman and Traisman (1958), who studied over 2000 subjects, found that length of feeding was positively correlated with thumb-sucking although very long feeders (+ one hour) had the lowest incidence. This non-linearity of relationship may indicate that the relationship between feeding and thumb-sucking is very complex or, as Caldwell (1964) suggests, that the long-feeding infants drifted off to sleep and thus did not receive constant oral stimulation. This last explanation is most unconvincing in view of the commonplace of reinforcement learning that random schedules of reinforcement lead to responses more difficult to extinguish than those constantly reinforced. Thus this group, if the learning-theory model were correct, would be expected to show the greatest amounts of thumb-sucking. This study cannot really be held to support the findings of Sears and Wise (1950). Bernstein (1955), in a research that has already been discussed (see p. 98), found that feeding gratification, as estimated from time of weaning, and length and number of feeds per day, was positively correlated (although not significantly) with the choice of lollipops rather than chocolate. Thus if such a food choice is related to sucking, as Bernstein assumes, it supports Sears and Wise (1950) rather than Levy (1928).

Caldwell (1964) considers that the study by Yarrow (1954) solves the apparent contradiction in these two sets of findings — the one supporting Freudian theory, the other a reinforcement model.

Yarrow (1954) investigated the relationship in sixty-six children between thumb-sucking and length of breast-feeding, duration of individual feeds and the time during which breast-feeding lasted.

The results of this investigation were:

(a) Children who had no breast-feeding did no more thumb-sucking than children who had three months of such feeding, although the non-significant difference was in the direction that longer breast-feeding produced less thumb-sucking. This result therefore favours Levy and the Freudian hypothesis.

(b) Age of weaning from breast or bottle produced no significant difference in thumb-sucking. Here the non-significant difference was that late-weaned children showed more thumb-sucking and emotional disturbance. This result supports Sears and Wise and the reinforcement model.

(c) There was a significant relationship between short feeding in the first six months and thumb-sucking. This finding confirms Freudian theory.

Yarrow argues that reinforcement theory cannot account for the findings of his own research (or of the researches discussed here): that thumb-sucking is related to brief feeding during infancy *and* late weaning (i.e. long overall sucking time). He hypothesizes that in early infancy (the oral period) the oral drive is strongest. Then fast feeding can lead to deprivation of sucking, hence fixation and thumb-sucking. Prolonged satisfaction of this drive when it has begun to wane (the oral sadistic stage when biting is more important) can lead to fixation and hence thumb-sucking. This, therefore, is a critical period hypothesis but so, too, is Freudian psychosexual theory.

Conclusions from studies of oral erotism

Yarrow (1954) has certainly offered a plausible explanation of the empirical findings discussed in this section and his explanation closely fits Freudian theory in that the oral stage is precisely that period when the mouth is the centre of excitation; also, sucking would be expected to become less important as the oral sadistic stage was begun. In addition, as Fenichel (1945) emphasizes, fixation in psychoanalytic theory can be thus derived from deprivation or excessive satisfaction. These studies have indicated that at the oral phase early in infancy, failure to get enough nutritive sucking leads to other forms of oral activity. This is powerful support for the concept of oral erotism as it is described in Freud (1905a). It thus appears from these studies that it is a useful and meaningful concept.

Anal erotism

Freud (1908a) claimed that the repression of anal erotism in infancy produced the anal character. We have already reviewed studies demonstrating that there is a syndrome of traits or a dimension of personality that fits the Freudian description — obstinate, parsimonious and orderly. Studies relating this to pot-training and anal erotism have not been generally successful and Beloff (1957), Hetherington anal Brackbill (1963) and Finney (1963) all considered that the term 'anal' was a misnomer and should therefore be abandoned. The inference to be drawn from these findings is, perhaps, that there is no such thing as anal erotism.

We shall now turn, therefore, to an examination of those investigations which throw light on the concept of anal erotism. In psychosexual theory, anal erotism refers to the highly pleasurable sensations arising from stimulation of the anal canal (Freud, 1905a, p. 186).

Unfortunately the studies involving anal behaviour involve disorders of bowel function. Prugh (1954) found that colonic disorders were related to severe training. Anthony (1957) related various kinds of encopresis to types of toilet-training, while Woodmansey (1967), using careful clinical studies of sixty children and reviewing a large number of clinical studies, concludes that bowel-training is the most important circumstance leading to dyschezia and that 'the prevention and treatment of functional disorders of defaecation (including constipation, diarrhoea and incontinence) generally depends on avoiding toilet-training' (p. 221).

The reason for the lack of investigations relevant to the Freudian concept of anal erotism, compared to oral erotism, is of course relatively simple. In the case of the oral zone, evidence of oral stimulation, independent of hunger, is to be seen in sucking behaviour. In the case of anal erotism no such obvious evidence of stimulation is forthcoming: what perhaps might be regarded as relevant evidence would be anal masturbation or passive sodomy. No studies of these behaviours in fact exist, partly because, in western cultures at least, these responses are heavily discouraged. Anal erotism tends to be repressed. Furthermore, unless the concept of anal erotism be accepted, functional disorders of the bowel cannot be accepted as evidence for the concept. Indeed Woodmansey regards the effects of bowel-training on defaecation as evidence for the inhibition of the defaecatory reflex — hence the constipation.

From this it must be admitted, therefore, that in the investigations of the consequences of toilet-training on infant behaviour there exists no evidence relevant to the concept of anal erotism. One investigation of an entirely different type does deserve mention. Duthie and Gairns (1960) showed that the anal canal in man was exquisitely sensitive to pain, heat and cold. This study is evidence that the anus *could* be a centre of excitation unlike areas of the body not well endowed with sensory nerves.

Conclusions

There is no experimental evidence relevant to the concept of anal erotism.

CONCLUSIONS FROM ALL CURRENT STUDIES OF CHILDREN

The conclusions from these studies may be briefly stated. There is no strong evidence relating oral or anal characteristics in children to either weaning or pot-training. However, severe problems of methodology mean that this failure to support Freudian theory cannot be regarded as a refutation of the theory. There is some evidence, however, in respect of the anal character (Hetherington and Brackbill, 1963; and Finney, 1963) that it is associated perhaps not with pot-training but with maternal rigidity.

The concept of oral erotism in psychosexual theory does seem to be confirmed by the experimental studies of Levy (1928), if the interpretation of results which fit the reinforcement model of sucking behaviour (Yarrow, 1954) is accepted. Anal erotism however, which is in essence far harder to demonstrate, has no relevant experimental work.

From this summary of the conclusions it is clear that we have not advanced far since Orlansky (1949) wrote that there was no firm evidence showing that early infantile experiences had any effects on personality development.

4. THE BLACKY PICTURES

Because of the problems of measuring child-rearing procedures and parental attitudes to them, with both adults and children, indirect testing techniques such as are provided by projective tests are of great interest. Blum (1949) has developed a projective technique — the Blacky Pictures — for precisely the purpose of testing psychoanalytic hypotheses concerning personality development.

DESCRIPTION OF BLACKY PICTURES

The Blacky Pictures are a set of twelve cartoons portraying a family of dogs in situations which are peculiarly relevant to psychoanalytic theory. There are four dogs in this family — two parents, Blacky who can be of either sex (always the same as the subject taking the test) and Tippy, a sibling of Blacky. Subjects have to tell a little story about what they think is going on in each picture and how each of the characters is feeling. This spontaneous story is then scored for presence or absence of disturbance in the area concerned. In addition, after each story the subject is asked several multiple-choice questions about the cartoon. A further source of scoring is a spontaneous mention of a cartoon other than the one to which they are responding. A final task in this test is to sort the pictures into liked and disliked and choose the most liked and the most disliked. These two choices, according to the manual to the test, are symptomatic of disturbance in the relevant areas.

TABLE 5.3.   *The Blacky Pictures*

Variables measured	Relevant cartoon
1. Oral erotism	Blacky being suckled
2. Oral sadism	Blacky tearing his mother's collar
3. Anal expulsiveness	Blacky defaecating between his parents' kennels
4. Anal retentiveness	As above, with different scoring
5. Oedipal intensity	Blacky watching his parents making love
6. Masturbation guilt	Blacky licking his genitals
7. Castration anxiety (males) or penis envy (females)	Blacky watching Tippy, apparently about to have her tail cut off
8. Positive identification	Blacky playing with a toy dog
9. Sibling rivalry	Blacky watching parents fondle Tippy
10. Guilt feelings	Blacky having a vision of an angelic figure
11. Positive ego ideal and	
12. Love object	Variables 11 and 12 use two pictures differently scored for each sex, (a) vision of an ideal female dog, (b) vision of an ideal male dog.

The description in Table 5.3 of the variables makes it clear that if these measures were valid the Blacky Pictures is an ideal technique for examining the postulated relationship between child-rearing procedures and adult personality syndromes — the oral, anal and phallic characters. Variables 1, 2, 3, 4, and 7 are clearly of especial interest.

THE RELIABILITY OF THE BLACKY PICTURES

Since low reliability is a general fault with projective techniques as a whole (e.g. Jensen, 1958) — a fact which virtually precludes high validity — it is essential to ensure that the Blacky Pictures are not deficient in this respect. In considering the reliability of these pictures we must not ignore the point raised by Beck (1958) who claims that results with this test are not comparable from administration to administration except between examiners who have worked together, or for the same tester. Even if this view is too extreme we must realize that the fact that highly skilled testers can achieve reliable results does not mean that all testers will be able to do this.

Test—retest reliability

Charen (1956a, b) calculated test—retest reliabilities for the Blacky dimensions among a group of tuberculosis patients. All except for the castration-complex score were low or negative These poor reliabilities could not have been due to actual personality changes, it was argued by Charen, since other personality tests revealed no such differences. Blum (1956a) however has objected to this study on a number of counts, the main one being that Charen had not administered the test in full but had based his findings on the multiple-choice items alone. Actually this restriction to the multiple-choice items should have led to increased reliability since the rating of the stories is subjective and far more likely to differ from occasion to occasion as well as from marker to marker.

A further study of test—retest reliability by Berger and Everstine (1962) on a sample of college students was more promising. All the dimensions revealed significant reliabilities ranging from 0.2 to 0.54. It must be noted that these are scarcely high enough to justify the use of the Blacky Pictures with any confidence in an individual case. Thus as far as test—retest reliability goes, it may be concluded that although low it is high enough to support the use of the test with groups, as in most research.

Internal-consistency reliability and inter-marker reliability

Granick and Scheflin (1958) using a sample of forty children carried out a detailed study of inter-marker reliability of the Blacky Pictures. On all but two dimensions there was 68-95 per cent agreement in scoring the spontaneous stories among ten judges. Five judges were able to match test—retest protocols with between 72 per cent and 100 per cent accuracy. It is to be noted that this finding supports the contention made above concerning the importance of the marker's skill in projective tests. The internal consistency of response was high, as judged by the correlation (0.92) between structured and unstructured stories. It was discovered however that there was little consistency in thematic production in response to cartoons among this sample. From this study it is probably fair to conclude that considerable consensus of opinion regarding the marking of the stories can be reached and that an individual's test—retest protocols can be satisfactorily matched. This, of course, implies that the reliability of the test is not too low.

Conclusions from the studies of reliability

The general conclusion to be reached from these investigations is that there is some agreement between markers, between occasions and between different parts of the test. It is also fair to emphasize the fact that the multiple-choice items in the test, a very unusual feature for a projective technique, do not yield any inter-marker variance — a considerable advantage. Nevertheless the reliability is not as high as is desirable and it must be admitted, along with Sappenfield (1965), that the Blacky Pictures are best used with groups rather than individuals. However, it is clear that the Blacky Pictures are reliable enough to be valid. The evidence for their validity must now be examined.

THE VALIDITY OF THE BLACKY PICTURES

A basic problem in the validation of the Blacky Pictures lies in the difficulty of establishing a firm criterion. This is because the criterion, psychoanalytic theory, is itself being examined by the test. Thus failure of prediction, e.g. that ulcer patients will be oral, can be due to faults in the theory, the test or both. However some evidence for the validity of the Blacky Pictures has been adduced.

Thus Sappenfield (1965), reviewing the relevant evidence, argued that their validity was supported in that generally some theoretical predictions have been confirmed in each study and only rarely have results contradicted hypotheses. However, since precise prediction is difficult from psychoanalytic theory, such an argument does not carry much weight.

Blum (1949), in the first reported study with the Blacky Pictures, argued that sex differences and inter-correlations between the psychosexual dimensions strongly supported Freudian theory and hence the validity of the test. Seward (1950), however, and Zubin, Eron and Schumer (1965) have attacked this study on the grounds that Blum only studied the significant correlations, thus capitalizing on chance, and only looked for theories to test after he had obtained the results: a procedure involving the danger of fitting the data to theory and, in the case of psychoanalysis, theory to data.

Blum and Hunt (1952) reviewed a number of studies which had used the Blacky Pictures on the grounds that confirmation of Freudian theory clearly implied the validity of the technique. Thus Lindner (1953) found sexual offenders more disturbed than a control group of other prisoners on nine of the Blacky dimensions. Blum and Miller (1952) found that a nine-year-old girl who was extremely high on the Blacky oral-erotism dimensions was very high on other oral variables, for example, rate of ice-cream eating. Aronson (1953) was able to differentiate paranoid schizophrenics from non-paranoid cases on the two oral scales and the anal-retention dimension. From studies such as these it does appear that the Blacky Pictures have some sort of construct-validity.

A factor-analytic approach to the problem has also been tried. Neuman and Salvatore (1958) factored the responses and found that the internal structure of the scores generally supported the validity of the pictures in that the factors emerging were in accord with psychoanalytic theory. However, this was true only for the male sample and they concluded that the Blacky Test was best used with males alone. Apropos of this point Rossi and Solomon (1961) found that among a group of college females the words 'Blacky' and 'Dog' were regarded as significantly more masculine than the term 'Cat'. It must be pointed out here that this is scarcely surprising in that 'Dog' has a specifically masculine meaning. Nevertheless this may account for the fact that the technique appears to be more effective with male samples.

Blum (1962) also factored the responses of 210 male students to the pictures. Thirty factors emerged which, in effect, replace the old scoring manual to the test. Many of these were in accord with psychoanalytic theory although the study was based on data obtained from group administration. Great weight appears to be attached to the multiple-choice items in this marking scheme.

Conclusions concerning the validity of the Blacky Pictures

The general conclusion to be drawn from these studies of the validity of the Blacky Pictures is that they do have some kind of validity. The fact that in some cases the theory is supported in studies using these pictures must be adduced as evidence for their validity. After all, it is difficult to construct *ad hoc* hypotheses to relate, for example, the responses to a picture of a dog tearing its mother's collar to the possession of gastric ulcers. This means that it is possible to use the Blacky Pictures as a test of psychoanalytic theory. Where the results agree with theory, the theory may be regarded as supported — at least to some extent. Where the theory is refuted it will not be acceptable to impugn the validity of the Blacky Pictures. The only caveat concerns the sex of the sample. Clearly failure with female samples may be due to failure of the technique.

Since it appears that the reliability and validity of the Blacky Pictures is such that they may be used to test psychoanalytic theory (although the results must be interpreted with caution), in the next section the relevant investigations will be examined. Studies will be reviewed which examine the postulated relationship between adult personality traits and the child-rearing procedures which are regarded as bringing about the repression of pregenital erotism.

Before leaving the Blacky Pictures to discuss the substantive results obtained with them, we must mention a Gallic derivative of this test, the PN test (Corman, 1969), which uses a pig rather than a dog as its animal hero. There are more cards than in the Blacky pictures and subjects need only comment on those they wish. It is therefore a far less constrained technique than the Blacky Pictures and in addition is better drawn and less embarrassing to administer to adult educated subjects who find the aesthetic quality of the Blacky Pictures less than pleasing. This technique has been little used in Great Britain: indeed Kline and Cooper (1977) seem about the only workers to have essayed the test. It *could* be a useful test for the validation of Freudian theory, but much research needs to be done to demonstrate its validity before it could be used with any confidence.

THE ORAL CHARACTER

The work of Blum and Miller (1952)

This first study may be briefly considered because its sample consisted of nine-year-old children and it by no means follows, from psychosexual theory, that the adult character traits representative of fixation at various levels will, in fact, manifest themselves in childhood.

Tests. Measures used apart from the oral dimensions of the Blacky Pictures included teachers' ratings for oral behaviour and oral personality traits, sociometric studies and actual observations in the class-room.

Results. Rank—order correlations indicated that extreme interest in food was strongly related to oral erotism as measured on the Blacky Pictures: the need for approval and concern over giving and receiving were also significantly related.

Comments and conclusions

This study cannot be regarded as impressive support for the relationship between oral traits and oral erotism because the validity of the teachers' ratings is not known. Some of the observational data are better, e.g. the number of ice-creams consumed. However the interesting part of psychosexual character development does not lie in the 'unchanged perpetuation of oral erotism', as in eating, but in the sublimations and reaction-formations against it, as in the oral traits. The fact that the sample consists of children also weakens this investigation.

The conclusion to be drawn from this study is that the oral dimensions of the Blacky Pictures are related to eating behaviour in children. This is good evidence for the validity of the Blacky Pictures. This study, however, does not provide good support for the relationship between oral character traits and oral erotism.

Fisher and Greenberg (1977) point out in connection with this study that there was a significant relationship between observations of orality (defined as non-purposive mouth activities) and teachers' ratings for various oral traits. However, as we have argued, the validity of the teachers' ratings is unknown and the demonstration that mouth activities are related to these traits is a long way from demonstrating that a cluster of such traits is related to fixation at the oral phase. It would be important to know, for example, what variables were *not* related to such activity. For example, licking lips might be a fixation of anxiety.

We still argue that the small numbers in this study and the lack of evidence of validity for most of the measures make it impossible to draw any firm conclusions.

The work of Kline (1970)

Kline, in an investigation of the relationship between oral erotism and oral character traits, administered the oral dimensions of the Blacky Pictures and the oral scales of the Dynamic Personality Inventory to a sample of students.

Sample. Forty-two female students in a college of education.
Tests. DPI (see p. 20 for a discussion of its validity) and the Blacky Pictures.
Results. None of the oral scales of the DPI correlated significantly with the oral scales of the Blacky Pictures.

Freudian theory, therefore, was not supported. However, as we showed in our discussion of the DPI (see p. 32), it is by no means certain that these oral scales are valid.

Conclusions

If the oral scales of the DPI are not valid, it is difficult to account for this invalidity. As has been discussed in Chapters 3 and 4, there is some objective evidence for the existence of the oral character. This study, therefore, does not support the Freudian psychosexual aetiology.

Kline and Cooper (1977) carried out a study of defences against orality on a small group of students. Two slides (one using the oral stimulus of the test PN, the other a picture of a pig from an advertisement for bacon) were shown tachistoscopically, each in a series with gradually increasing exposure times. This is the percept-genetic method (Kragh and Smith, 1970), which is fully discussed and described in our chapter on defence mechanisms, in which subjects have to describe each exposure.

An analysis of this technique did show that typical Freudian defence mechanisms could be seen when the PN picture was shown but none were present in response to the bacon pig — evidence, therefore, for oral fixation in some subjects.

It would be wrong to make too much of this study which in any case will be discussed again in our chapter on defence mechanisms, but it suggests that the PN oral stimulus could be useful in psychoanalytic research.

THE ANAL CHARACTER

The work of Adelson and Redmond (1958)

Adelson and Redmond investigated personality differences in the capacity for verbal recall in a study which is of some relevance to the aetiology of the anal character.

Sample. Sixty-one female college students.

Tests. The anal retentive and anal expulsive dimensions of the Blacky Pictures.

Method. Thirty-two anal expulsives, eighteen anal retentives and eleven neutrals were selected by their Blacky Pictures scores. One disturbing passage of prose and one neutral passage was then given for the students to learn. It was hypothesized that retentives would recall verbal passages significantly better than expulsives.

Results. Retentives did recall both passages better than expulsives: the neutral group fell between them and there were no differences in non-verbal material.

Comments and conclusions

Adelson and Redmond are not clear as to how they derive their hypothesis from psychoanalytic theory. They quote Fenichel (1945) as a support but give no more detailed reference. It seems to the present writer that the hypothesis is based on little more than a generalization of the term 'retentive'. Clearly the non-verbal material in the experiment did not cover all the possibilities of what could constitute such material so that the comparison with verbal material must be limited.

The interest of the experiment as regards this chapter is that character traits related, even if tenuously, by psychoanalytic theory to the anal phase (thus supporting the anal aetiology of the anal character) are shown to be so related. In short this investigation may be regarded as slight support for psychosexual theory.

The work of Pedersen and Marlowe (1960)

These investigators attempted to replicate the findings of Adelson and Redmond (1958) which have been discussed above.

Sample. Seventy college students.

Results. In this study expulsives recalled more disturbing material than did the retentives, whereas the retentives recalled more neutral material.

Comments and conclusions

Pedersen and Marlowe have clearly failed to replicate the findings of Adelson and Redmond. As was pointed out in the discussion of the first study, the basic psychoanalytic hypothesis under investigation was not easily derived. The conclusion to be drawn from these two studies therefore is that despite appearances they have little relevance for classical psychoanalytic theory. They cannot support it on any grounds but they can hardly refute it either.

The work of Kline (1968b)

Kline (1968b) investigated the relationship between obsessional traits and symptoms and anal erotism by administering to a small sample the anal dimensions of the Blacky Pictures and a number of personality tests.

Sample. Forty-six university students.

Measures. Hazari obsessional-trait scale, Hazari obsessional-symptom scale, the Beloff scale and Ai3 (anal character) were the personality questionnaires used in this study. All have been fully discussed in previous chapters. The anal dimensions of the Blacky Pictures were also given.

Results. All the personality scales except the Hazari traits had correlations significant at the 1 per cent level with the anality score from the Blacky Pictures. This anality score was the total score on the two dimensions. The rationale for this addition comes from the factor-analytic study of the Blacky Pictures by Blum (1962), where a common anal factor seems to emerge. The highest of these correlations was 0.6 — with Ai3. The Beloff scale and Ai3 correlated significantly (1 per cent level) with the retentive score while only the Hazari symptom scale correlated with the expulsive score (0.05 level).

Comments and conclusions

The fact that two anal scales, the Beloff scale (Beloff, 1957) and Ai3 (Kline, 1967c), had positive correlations with the anal retentive dimension of the Blacky Pictures and the anality score must be regarded as positive evidence for Freudian psychosexual theory. This is particularly the case when the concept of the anal constitution (Freud, 1905a), the anal stamp, is also brought into consideration. This would account for the failure of studies attempting to find positive correlations between pot-training procedures and adult personality when this factor is ignored. A given type of pot-training would be of different severity for children whose anal erotism was of different strength.

The factor-analysis of Blum (1962) also suggests that it is best to ignore the expulsive—retentive distinction in the Blacky Pictures and regard both scores as measures of anal erotism. This means that the fact that the symptom scale correlated significantly with the expulsive dimension and not the retentive should not be stressed. However this correlation is again support for psychosexual theory since obsessional symptoms are regarded as intrusions of repressed material into consciousness — the result of unsuccessful defence against anal erotism.

Even if the validity of the Blacky Pictures in considered suspect it is still striking that responses to an anal situation, a picture of a defaecating dog, should be linked to the possession of anal traits and symptoms.

It must be concluded that this study offers support for the Freudian aetiology of the anal character, especially when the full theory including the anal constitution is taken into account.

Eysenck and Wilson (1973) have some pertinent criticisms of this paper, which they regard as no support for psychoanalytic theory. For example they question the validity of the Blacky Pictures as a measure of anal erotism. They write, somewhat coarsely, that this Blacky Picture is a rough index of attitudes to shitting dogs. However, even if this is correct then the correlations with the obsessional scales still support Freudian theory since we may fairly ask why attitudes to shitting dogs (and the anal scores are not just references to cleanliness) should so correlate.

They regard the reference to the anal stamp, the anal constitution, as a weakness in the logic of the paper. This is not so, since the anal stamp allows fixation (as measured by Blacky) to occur regardless of the severity of pot-training. Hence the correlations of Ai3Q and the Blacky Pictures are not contrary to the Freudian hypothesis as strictly the correlations between severity of pot-training and obsessional traits are.

Finally, Eysenck and Wilson (1973) consider that the whole investigation is not properly aimed at psychoanalytic theory since Freud never explicitly hypothesized that anal character would be an important dimension of behaviour on a non-psychiatric population. This is, frankly, nonsense. In the first place Freudian theory does not have to be explicit. It is quite permissible to deduce from it. Indeed the power of a theory is partly dependent on its implications. Secondly, Freud claims in his original paper on anal erotism (1908a) that character traits are sublimations, defences or direct expressions of repressed pregenital erotism. It is not, perhaps, for nothing that Eysenck and Wilson describe themselves as tyros in the field of psychoanalytic theory. Thus this objection is quite ill-founded.

Thus our original conclusions seem to us still sound, despite the rhetorical objections of these writers, objections stimulated by anything supporting Freudian theory. Indeed the only conclusion one can draw from Eysenck and

Wilson's (1973) book is that Freud, despite his enormous output, was always wrong. He never reached even the chance level of success.

COMBINED STUDIES OF THE ANAL AND ORAL CHARACTERS

Some studies have concerned themselves with differences between the oral and the anal personality as defined by the criterion of the Blacky Pictures. These investigations will now be examined. In fact almost all these studies have been done by Noblin, Timmons and associates.

The work of Noblin (1962)

In his doctoral dissertation Noblin investigated operant conditioning among oral and anal psychiatric patients. However, it would be incorrect to cite this work as evidence for the psychosexual aetiology of these character-types because they were selected not only on the criterion of the Blacky Pictures (measure of pregenital erotism) but also on the criteria of specific behaviours, related in psychoanalytic theory to fixation at these levels, and of the neurotic disorder from which they were suffering. These last two criteria confound the experiment since this section is devoted to the evidence for the relationship between the first criterion and these last.

The work of Noblin, Timmons and Kael (1963, 1966)

In this study, Noblin et al. (1963, 1966) investigated the differential effect of positive and negative verbal reinforcement on anal and oral characters, as defined by the Blacky Pictures alone, so that the results become relevant to the aetiological problem.

Sample. Undergraduates classified as oral or anal by the Blacky Pictures.

Hypotheses. Orals would show conditioning to positive reinforcement and worsening of performance with negative reinforcement whereas anals should show the opposite effect.

Basic psychoanalytic hypothesis. In psychoanalytic theory the oral character is depicted as dependent and compliant, the anal character negative, hostile and resistant.

Results. All hypotheses were supported.

Comments and conclusions

Although the experimental hypotheses were supported, it is difficult to estimate how closely these results bear on psychosexual theory. It is surely arguable that ease of conditioning by positive reinforcement is evidence for dependence and submissiveness and that the opposite result is evidence for hostility and obstinacy. Thus, although these findings do not run contrary to psychoanalytic theory, they may not be regarded as very positive support.

The work of Timmons and Noblin (1963)

In this investigation the same hypothesis as above was put to the test — that orals would condition more easily than anals in a verbal conditioning association. The hypothesis was supported.

Comments and conclusions

As with the previous study it is hard to be certain to what extent these findings are relevant to psychoanalytic theory. Indeed, Beloff (1957) predicted that anals would be easy, rather than difficult, to condition, if psychosexual theory were correct, on the grounds that anal traits are evidence of over-learning and stimulus-generalization of toilet-training. Thus again it must be concluded that this study cannot with justification be used to support Freudian psychosexual theory.

At this point it must be stated that in their review of these experiments, Fisher and Greenberg (1977) came to different conclusions from those above. They regard these studies as powerful support for psychoanalytic theorizing. Thus in the Noblin (1962) investigation in which psychiatric cases were used, anals were more easily conditioned by money (money being a faeces symbol) and orals by sweets. However, it is to be noted that the patients were selected by criteria additional to the Blacky Pictures. Thus patients were diagnosed as oral if they were impatient at meals. Hence it is not surprising that for this group sweets were potent reinforcers. As regards money, the hypothesis is odd in that the psychosexual symbolic value of money is not held to be the only determinant of liking for money.

The problem with these studies is that for us the relationship to condition-ability of psychosexual character types is so loose as to be little more than intuitive. Since, in addition, the replicative study of Cooperman and Child (1971) failed to confirm the findings, we cannot regard them as powerful support for psychosexual personality theory.

THE PHALLIC CHARACTER AND OTHER PERSONALITY SYNDROMES

No studies of these have been carried out with the Blacky Pictures.

CONCLUSIONS FROM ALL THE BLACKY STUDIES OF THE AETIOLOGICAL HYPOTHESES

The only studies which bear specifically on this problem are those of Kline (1968b, 1970). In the case of the oral character Freudian theory was not supported, while in the case of the anal character it was. However even optimistic Freudians could not regard correlations with the Blacky Pictures as definitive evidence. At best such studies offer positive evidence which must be considered alongside evidence from other sources.

The other studies of the oral and anal character discussed above are hard to interpret. In fact, despite their promising appearance they add very little relevant evidence to the problem. At least they do not run counter to psychosexual theory.

To sum up: one study contradicts the theory of the oral character (Kline, 1970); one study supports the theory of the anal character (Kline, 1968b); other studies are not relevant.

Further points about the Blacky Pictures

Since the Blacky Pictures appear to offer such good opportunities to examine the Freudian psychosexual aetiological hypotheses the paucity and the general irrelevance of the studies may, perhaps, have struck the reader as curious. However, the reasons for this are clear. Most of the investigations with the Blacky Pictures assume the validity of the Pictures and much of psychoanalytic theory and hence use them to test different hypotheses. These researches are, of course, extremely important in a study of Freudian theory and will be examined in the relevant chapters.

Summary

Studies of the relationship between repressed pregenital erotism and personality traits in which the Blacky Pictures were used have been reviewed. Most of the studies were found not to relate with any precision to the theory. Only two studies seemed to be truly relevant — those of Kline (1968b, 1970). One of these supported the theory (the anal character) the other failed to do so (the oral character). However it was stressed that, inherently, the Blacky Pictures can only provide interesting supportive, rather than definitive, evidence.

5. OTHER TECHNIQUES

THE WORK OF GOTTHEIL AND STONE (1968)

Gottheil and Stone carried out a most important study, relevant to the libidinal theory of the oral and anal characters, in which they used the oral and anal scales developed by Gottheil (1965b) (see p. 35 for a discussion of these tests).

Sample. 179 subjects. The age range was seventeen to twenty-six years and their mean intelligence was 112. They can be considered to be of normal personality in that none was receiving psychiatric treatment.

Measures. The Gottheil (1965b) forty-item oral and anal scales. In addition items were written enquiring into the mouth and bowel habits of the subjects. In all there were 186 items.

Method and analysis. The 186 items were treated each as a separate variable. Scale scores were also used as variables. The inter-correlations were subjected to an oblique (Quartimax) factor-analysis. In addition an inverse factor-analysis was carried out — of subjects, not items. Inter-correlations between subjects were also given a cluster-analysis.

Rationale. If the oral and anal characters are related to pregenital erotism, then mouth and bowel habits should also be related to these personality syndromes.

Results

A. *The first oblique factor analysis* of items yielded five factors:

1. Denial of difficulty of bowel function.
2. Oral traits, anal traits and one mouth habit.
3. Dullness and indifference.
4. Denial of anal trait items.
5. Oral optimism.

These last two factors accounted for but 5 per cent of the variance.

This first analysis, therefore, does not suggest that oral and anal character are important features of personality (their factors account for little variance). Furthermore neither is related to mouth or bowel habits.

B. *The sub-scale analysis* yielded three oral factors (dependency, passivity and pessimism) and a demanding factor, four anal factors (non-resilience, obsessive recrimination, perfectionism, parsimony) and a practical factor. However, all the loadings were low. Factor scores were calculated and the inter-correlations between factors were examined. There were no correlations between oral character and mouth habits, or anal character and bowel habits.

C. *The inverse factor-analysis.* This should show types of people. In fact three such types (factors) emerged:

1. Weak, worrying and complaining.
2. Shy, timid and constricted.
3. This factor was not meaningful.

D. *The cluster-analysis* or correlations between persons revealed similar factors to the inverse factor-analysis.

Gottheil and Stone concluded from these results that the existence of the oral and anal characters as syndromes of personality was supported but that they were relatively unimportant in the description of personality. The sub-scale analysis, too, reflected to some extent the psychoanalytic description and was thus a further confirmation. However there seemed to be no relationship between these syndromes and mouth or bowel habits and there was no evidence of types of people resembling the anal or oral character.

Comments and conclusions

As has been already pointed out, these oral and anal scales have no demonstrated validity other than the fact that, to experienced clinicians, the items appear pertinent to the personality syndromes, i.e. face-validity. The fact that items are discriminating and measure common factors in no way shows what those factors are. Thus the failure to relate mouth and bowel habits could be due to the invalidity of the scales. Social desirability and behaviour mediated by class — e.g. 'When you meet people do you notice whether their fingernails are clean?' (item 30, anal scale) — might be confounding factors.

These same objections can apply to the mouth and bowel habits items. Social desirability, to appear in a good light, could well be expected to apply to items relating to such personal behaviour. Thus the failure to relate such habits to these personality syndromes cannot be imputed to the fact that no such relationship exists.

A more serious objection lies in the size of the correlation matrix. It is generally accepted (e.g. Harman, 1976) that there should be far more subjects than variables to achieve a stable analysis. In this case it must be noted that there are almost equal numbers. This may well account for the meaningless factor 3 in the inverse analysis. Thus the large number of variables (or the small number of subjects) makes the factor-analysis of doubtful worth. Great caution must be shown in interpreting the loadings. The small amount of variance, therefore, accounted for by oral and anal factors may be a statistical artefact.

A further point related to the sample size should be considered in assessing the results of the inverse factor-analysis. If, for example, a person scoring one SD above the mean on the anal test were regarded as an anal character, we should expect about thirty anal characters in this sample, by definition. This we might expect to find using inverse factor-analysis. If, however, our criterion is more stringent, this number rapidly drops and with the imperfections of any testing devices inverse factor-analysis would be hard put to isolate so small a number. Clearly, as the authors point out, inverse analysis needs a far more heterogeneous sample including non-normal subjects.

From this study therefore, we cannot conclude that the oral and anal personalities are unimportant in the description of personality and unrelated to mouth or bowel habits. The technical problems discussed above and the limitations of the sample make this far too general. Nevertheless Gottheil and Stone (1968) do not provide any support for the Freudian aetiological theory. There is some confirmation of the personality syndromes.

THE WORK OF PETTIT (1969)

This investigation sought to test the psychoanalytic claim that the anal character over-values time.

Sample. Thirty-seven male and fifty-four female undergraduates.

Tests. A forty-item time scale, the DPI anal scales (see p. 20) and Schlesinger's (1963) anal scale.

Results. The time scale correlated significantly and positively with the Schlesinger scale (0.643) and the DPI scales (0.507). Pettit concluded that the psychoanalytic theory was supported.

Comments and conclusions

Although this result supports Freudian theory it does not constitute impressive evidence because of the contamination of anal and time scales. This is because the psychoanalytic writers stress the importance of time to the anal character and thus measures of the anal character tend to have time references in them. For example, item 1 of the Beloff (1957) scale is concerned with unpunctuality, as is item 15. The other items in the scale are by definition and method of scale-construction related to these. Thus a correlation with a time scale is inevitable. Similarly the time scale itself is concerned with more than time. For example, this item: 'I feel I am *more conscientious* about being on time than most people.' This conscientiousness is also part of the anal character. In addition the social desirability of time scale and anal items is often high for middle-class samples — a fact which could account for the correlations.

This positive correlation between time-scale scores and anal-character scores means little other than that the anal measures contained, as they ought, references to punctuality. Presumably it does support the validity of the anal scales in that the correlation would be predicted.

THE WORK OF SCODEL (1957) AND WIGGINS ET AL. (1968)

Two studies which produced results which confirmed Freudians would certainly regard as relevant to the aetiology of the oral and anal characters deserve a brief mention. Scodel (1957), in a study of the determinants of heterosexual preference in males, found that men who liked small breasts gave more dependent responses on the TAT. Dependency, of course, is a trait claimed to be part of the oral character, who, according to psychoanalytic theory, should be concerned with breasts. The fact that small rather than large breasts were preferred would have to be attributed to reaction-formation. If we ignore the question of the validity of the TAT we must admit that only psychoanalytic theory could have explained this observed relationship. This, then, could be regarded as support for the Freudian aetiology of the oral character.

Wiggins et al. (1968) carried out a further investigation of this same question. Their aim was to attempt to establish whether there was any truth in the popular belief often held by men themselves that there are leg-men, breast-men and buttock-men (to formalize the linguistic terms). The result relevant to Freudian theory was that preference for large buttocks was associated with a need for order, as measured by the Edwards Personal Preference Scale. Need for order is one of the anal triad of characteristics. The anal character prefers large buttocks. Certainly no other theory than Freudian psychosexual theory could have predicted this finding.

Clearly these two findings could not support Freudian psychosexual theory. Nevertheless it must be admitted, even by the most convinced Eysenckian, that these results are highly interesting in the light of the theory. Eysenck (e.g. 1972) has frequently cited this discussion of the study by Wiggins as evidence of our inability to interpret experimental results and of our eagerness to seize upon any result and claim it to support Freud. Thus we should like to stress here that we do not regard these findings as confirming psychoanalytic theory.

Beck et al. (1976) essentially replicated this study by Wiggins et al. but with a sample of 115 women students. Here the findings were in the opposite direction in that women who preferred males or females with large buttocks were low on orderliness. Such a finding is by no means readily explicable.

THE WORK OF FISHER AND GREENBERG (1977)

Fisher and Greenberg (1977) have an exhaustive list of studies linking oral and anal traits to various other scales and observations of behaviour. However, most of them are quite irrelevant to psychosexual theory. For example, one study found differing attitudes to success and failure among high and low orals (Lish, 1969). Many studies show that oral characters tend to wish not to be alone when anxious. Such claims support to some extent the validity of the tests by which oral subjects were designated oral, but they do not help to establish any links between psychosexual traits and child-rearing procedures or repressed pregenital erotism, so they will not be discussed in this chapter.

More relevant are the sections in Fisher and Greenberg (1977) devoted to the question of whether oral and anal characters (defined in terms of character traits) seek special oral and anal gratifications. Obviously if this turned out to be the case, then the aetiology of these syndromes would be supported.

However, few of the studies these authors cite are, as it turns out, relevant to our goal. For example, they discuss investigations showing that the obese produce more oral imagery (mention of food, etc.) in response to projective tests than do non-obese controls. Now, such work cannot ever support psychoanalytic theory. Since the problem of obese patients is that they eat too much, the fact that food is a more common response among them than normals requires no construct such as orality to explain it. What would constitute evidence would be the finding that obese patients had oral traits — a quite different research.

Similarly, studies of alcoholics and ulcer patients, also cited by Fisher and Greenberg, require not that these show food- or drink-responses to projective tests but that they possess oral personality traits. The same applies to studies of smokers and non-smokers.

Thus most of the studies which they cite, although relevant to orality, do not bear on the aetiology of the oral character. In fact studies such as these are discussed later in our book in Chapter 10 on neurosis and abnormal behaviours.

The evidence cited by Fisher and Greenberg (1977) in relation to anal traits has again to be treated with extreme caution. Rosenwald (1966, 1972) carried out a highly interesting study in which anal characters had to perform tasks with their hands in a faecal-like substance. However, to explain any findings again requires no construct such as anal erotism or anality. For if anal characters are neat and concerned with cleanliness it is obvious that they will not like getting their hands dirty. Thus all the experimental studies which they cite, indicating that subjects selected by anal questionnaries are critical or orderly or obstinate, show only that these particular traits are possessed by high scorers on the questionnaires. This is relevant to the validity of the scales but only in part. For what is really necessary to show validity is that the whole syndrome of traits is present.

Although, as we have argued, most of the investigations cited by Fisher and Greenberg (1977) are not pertinent to our question — the aetiology of the anal character — one study, an unpublished doctoral thesis by Lerner (1961), is highly relevant. This demonstrated that there were differences in the perception of words of anal and non-anal connotation presented on a tape-recorder among stamp-collectors, but not among non-collector controls. In other words collectors were different from non-collectors in respect of sensitivity to anal stimuli.

First a few words of caution: the samples were small, only fifteen in each group. Furthermore the differences in sensitivity involved both perceptual defence where there is delay in recognition and perceptual vigilance, its opposite. Nevertheless the fact that stamp-collectors did differ from controls is important evidence for the aetiology of the anal character because as Jones (1923) has claimed all collectors are anal erotic, and in a study such as this there is no contamination between the questionnaire measurement (with items on cleanliness and parsimony) and behavioural observation of these traits.

What has been shown is that, as predicted from theory, stamp-collectors are more sensitive to anal stimuli than controls. No other theory would seem to explain these results and they must be regarded as modest support for psychosexual theory, modest (a) because the sample is small and (b) because the interpretation assumes that sensitivity to anal stimuli is an index of anality.

Fisher and Greenberg cite studies showing that anal characters are specially concerned with time and money. Again, however, these cannot be said to bear on the aetiology of the anal character because interest in time and money (punctuality and parsimony) are both involved in the definition of the syndrome.

Fisher (1970) in his highly interesting study of the experience of one's body, the body image, claimed that anal characters were concerned with their backs. Fisher and Greenberg (1977) argue that this may be evidence for the aetiology of these traits since the anus 'is associated with back'. This really won't do, since what is required here is that the anal character is specially concerned with his buttocks or anus.

THE WORK OF KLINE (1979) AND KLINE AND STOREY (1980)

Finally, Kline and Storey (1980) and Kline (1979b) have carried out a series of studies of the aetiology, mainly of the oral character, which will be briefly described and discussed.

Kline and Storey (1980) using their oral tests, OOQ and OPQ, to measure oral personality traits, tests which have been fully described previously (see p. 41), derived a number of hypotheses from psychosexual theory relative to the aetiology of the oral character and put these to the test. These hypotheses were:

(a) Dentists are more oral sadistic than medical controls.
(b) Oral optimists like milky, warm foods: oral pessimists like hard, crispy, bitter foods.

(c) Vegetarians and non-vegetarians differ in respect of oral traits.

(d) Members of the Dracula society will show extreme scores on measures of oral personality traits.

(e) There will be greater perceptual defence to oral stimuli among high scorers on OPQ and OOQ than among controls.

(f) Wind instrument players will show more oral traits than other musician controls.

(g) Pen-chewers score more highly on OPQ than controls.

(h) Smokers score more highly on OPQ than controls.

It is to be noted that if confirmed none of these hypotheses simply demonstrate that the behaviour measured in the tests is observed in behaviour. There is a genuine aetiological link as hypothesized in the psychosexual theory of orality.

Although readers must be referred to the original paper (Kline and Storey, 1980) for full details of subjects in these studies (in which a total of 570 subjects was tested), the main results can be summarized.

1. Subjects who chewed their pen tops did score significantly higher on OPQ than controls. OPQ contains no questions about chewing or eating or anything concerned with the mouth.

2. In two studies, smoking was related to scores on OPQ. In the first there was a point biserial correlation of 0.38 between smoking and scores on OPQ. In the second, heavy smokers (twenty or more cigarettes a day) scored significantly higher than light smokers on OPQ. In each case the Ns were greater than 50.

3. Food preference was related to scores on OOQ and OPQ. High scorers on OOQ liked asparagus, bananas and cream, nuts, honey, tapioca, boiled fish and fruit fools. High scorers on OPQ liked hot pickles and disliked raw carrots and nuts. On neither OPQ nor OOQ are any of the items related to food preferences.

The other hypotheses were not supported. From this set of results it appears that oral personality traits as measured by OPQ and OOQ (two of the few oral tests that have any evidence for validity) are related to behaviours involving the mouth. It was the wider extrapolations of Freudian theory that were not confirmed in this study.

It must be stated that our study of vegetarianism and orality was carried out on Indian samples since we argued that vegetarianism in India was less compounded by the Hampstead vegetarian syndrome: shorts, sandals, socialism and sinless sex. However, OPQ was lost in transit and there were no significant differences on OOQ.

In brief, this study by Kline and Storey (1980) does not support the psychosexual aetiology of oral traits although the three confirmed hypotheses do perhaps confirm a limited aspect of the theory. Incidentally, this study counters the claim by Eysenck and Wilson (1973) that researchers in psychoanalysis never report negative findings.

Kline (1979b) carried out a further study of psychosexual fixation and neuroticism. Freud (1905a) claimed that psychosexual development resembled the onward march of troops. Fixation resembled the leaving of troops at certain points with the consequent weakening of the onward marching force. Hence psychosexual fixation leads to weakened ego-development and neuroticism. It follows from this that a *total* fixation score (at all levels) should be related to a measure of neuroticism and this was put to the empirical test.

The measure of total fixation was the sum of scores on OOQ −20, OPQ and Ai3Q, the author's tests of oral and anal character, all fully described in this book. Fixation at the oral erotic level was measured by low scores on OOQ, hence the −20. High scorers were compared with low scorers on Eysenck's N. In fact, as predicted from psychoanalytic theory, there was a large and significant mean difference in the predicted direction. Total fixation was related to neuroticism. Since only OPQ, of these tests, was significantly related to N on its own, it was ascertained that the observed relationship was not simply due to this variable.

This study demonstrates that total fixation (as measured by the possession of personality traits held to be due to fixation at three levels of development) is related to neuroticism. It is thus modest support for psychosexual theory.

CONCLUSIONS FROM THE FIVE METHODS

The number of investigations examined in this chapter is good evidence for the immense amount of research effort that has been expended in the study of the aetiology of psychosexual personality syndromes. Nevertheless Freudian theory is supported by only a few studies. Goldman-Eisler (1950, 1951) found some relationship between weaning and oral characteristics, and Kline (1968b), using the Blacky Pictures, linked anal characteristics to anal erotism. The concept of oral erotism does seem to be supported (Yarrow, 1954; Whiting and Child, 1953). Apart from this, the other studies failed to confirm the Freudian hypotheses, except for the recent investigations by Kline (1979b) and Kline and Storey (1980).

Should the weight of this negative evidence, therefore, compel us to reject the aetiology of these personality syndromes? Certainly the work of Beloff (1957), Finney (1963) and Hetherington and Brackbill (1963) on the anal character supplies a more commonsense developmental background — that orderly parents tend to produce orderly children — than does psychoanalytic theory. These findings, indeed, support the neo-Freudian views of Fromm and Horney (see p. 420).

It seems to us, however, that this heavy weight of negative evidence cannot be used to refute the theory. Rather it is a sign of the profound problems involved in testing psychological hypotheses involving infant behaviour and experience. As has been amply demonstrated, few of these studies are free from methodological difficulties. Certainly the few supporting studies cannot be used to demonstrate the truth of the Freudian theory. These too are beset with problems and the results, while reaching statistical significance, are not decisive enough to confirm the theory.

In brief, therefore, it must be concluded that Freudian psychosexual theory, as it relates personality syndromes to infantile experiences and repressed pregenital erotism, receives almost no support. On the other hand, methodological problems are more than sufficient to acount for such failures.

PSYCHOSEXUAL THEORY IN THE LIGHT OF THE EVIDENCE

As was shown in Chapter 2, devoted to the outline of Freudian psychosexual theory, there are implicit in the theory three distinct propositions:

(a) that certain constellations of personality traits may be seen in adults,
(b) that these syndromes are related to infant-rearing procedures, and
(c) that pregenital erotism is a feature of childhood. It is, of course, the repression of this pregenital erotism (c) by the infant-rearing procedures (b) that gives rise to the psychosexual personality syndromes (a).

Chapters 3 and 4 have examined the evidence for the first of these propositions while the evidence for the last two hypotheses has been scrutinized in Chapter 5. The studies of psychosexual theory as a whole, therefore, depend upon the conclusions reached in all these chapters. In this section, which will be of necessity extremely brief, all the evidence so far adduced will be brought together, so that the theory may be properly evaluated. All that will be presented will be the bare conclusions. Thus stated, they may appear as somewhat dogmatic assertions. The evidence, however, has been fully discussed in previous chapters and for corroborative details readers must look there.

SUMMARY OF FINDINGS

1. There is good evidence to support the existence of an *anal syndrome* (Beloff, 1957; Grygier, 1961b; Kline, 1969a; Lazare et al., 1966; Cattell, 1946; Finney, 1961a; Pichot and Perse, 1967; Kline and Storey, 1978a).

2. There is some evidence (not so strong as above) to support the existence of an *oral syndrome* (Goldman-Eisler, 1948, 1950, 1951; Lazare et al., 1966; Kline and Storey, 1978b).

3. There is no evidence for any other hypothesized psychosexual dimensions.

4. From the considerable number of studies attempting to relate infant-rearing procedures to personality development only four studies give even slight support to the Freudian theory:

(a) The oral character (Goldman-Eisler, 1950, 1951; Kline and Storey, 1980).
(b) The anal character (Kline, 1968b).
(c) The oral and anal character (Kline, 1979b).

The thesis by Lerner (1961) although on a small sample might also be considered as some confirmation for the aetiology of the anal character.

5. There is evidence for the concept of oral erotism (Yarrow, 1954; Whiting and Child, 1953).

6. Grave methodological problems have made it difficult to accept the weight of evidence — failing to show the effects of infant-rearing procedures on personality — as refutation of Freudian theory.

CONCLUSIONS

The obvious implication of these results, and one that would be eagerly seized on by opponents of psychoanalytic theory, is that psychosexual theory has not stood up to objective empirical testing and should therefore be abandoned. Freud, the argument would run, successfully observed two personality constellations but his aetiological hypotheses to account for them were totally wrong. Furthermore the great importance attached to weaning and toilet-training by psychoanalysts on account of this theory is unjustified, as is the nomenclature of these personality syndromes. If all this is abandoned the clinical observations of these oral and anal characters become less impressive. The anal character becomes the obsessional personality, a well-established syndrome in psychiatry (Mayer-Gross et al., 1961), or the anancastic psychopath of Schneider (1958). The oral character, which is not as clear-cut, could doubtless be accommodated somewhere in the concept of social extraversion.

This view is not entirely acceptable, however. In the first place, the studies attempting to relate these personality syndromes to infant-training procedures are methodologically deficient. This does not mean, however, that the theory should again be abandoned because it is untestable. Testability as a criterion for scientific theories applies to *logical* testability. The abundance of evidence cited already point to the fact that psychosexual theory meets this criterion. At present the theory is untestable for *technical* reasons — the difficulty of obtaining adequate training data for adults or personality data from children. Clearly we must await longitudinal studies.

A second reason for not abandoning psychosexual theory lies in the fact that it is relevant to other branches of psychology — notably in the understanding of sexual disturbances and neuroses. This side of the theory is discussed and the evidence examined in Chapter 10 (see pp. 342-53). If psychosexual theory is also found to be disconfirmed by this evidence, then there may well be good reason to reject it.

The conclusions that we draw from the evidence on psychosexual theory may be briefly stated. There is good evidence for the existence of personality dimensions resembling the anal and oral characters but these have not been linked to repressed pregenital erotism nor to infant-rearing procedures in an entirely convincing way. The aetiological hypotheses may not, however, be rejected until better techniques of investigation have been devised.

6

The Oedipus and castration complexes

In the boy

The Oedipus complex is described by Freud as a situation which every child is fated to pass through and which is the inevitable result of the length of his dependence in childhood and his life with his parents. At the phallic phase, the boy 'becomes his mother's lover'.

> He desires to possess her physically in the ways in which he has divined from his observations and intuitive surmises of sexual life . . . his early awakened masculinity makes him seek to assume, in relation to her, the place belonging to his father. . . . His father now becomes a rival who stands in his way and whom he would like to push aside.

This is Freud's description of the Oedipus complex. However in our civilization it is 'doomed to a terrible end' (Freud, 1940).

According to Freudian theory, the Oedipus complex is repressed into oblivion by fear of castration — the castration complex. The mother, in an effort to stop infantile masturbation, threatens that his father will cut his penis off.

> But if, when he is threatened, he is able to recall the appearance of female genitals or if, shortly afterwards, he has a glimpse of them — of genitals, that is to say, which really lack this valued part — then he takes what he has heard seriously and coming under the influence of the castration complex experiences the severest trauma of his youthful life. (ibid.)

From this description of the theory so far, it is clear that two brief definitions are possible:

Oedipus complex. Love of mother by boy, and jealous hatred of father.
Castration complex. Fear of castration by father.

In 'The dissolution of the Oedipus complex' Freud (1924a) claimed that the complex is 'smashed to pieces by the shock of threatened castration'. At the same time as this, the super-ego — the heir of the Oedipus complex — is developing by introjection or identification with the father (through this castration fear). This therefore brings about the end of the Oedipus complex and introduces the latency period.

In boys, therefore, the castration complex effectively destroys the Oedipus complex and brings about the development of the super-ego.

In the girl

With girls, the situation is clearly different. The castration complex for them consists in feelings about not having a penis; this is referred to by Freud (1927a) as penis envy. At the phallic phase the girl, finding her clitoris inferior to the penis as a source of pleasure, turns against her first object of love, the mother — whom she holds responsible for her lack of penis (Freud, 1933). Thus she turns towards her father and the Oedipus complex (called in the case of girls the Electra complex) has begun. In psychoanalytic theory the girl turns towards the father, first to have a penis at her command but later to have a baby (baby being a symbolic penis). As Fenichel (1945) points out, once the object change has been accomplished the girls' Oedipus complex is analagous to that of the boy. She loves the father and hates the mother. In girls, therefore, the castration complex effectively creates the Oedipus complex.

One further problem remains: in boys the castration complex brings about the end of the Oedipus complex and the development of the super-ego — identification through fear. What brings about the end of the Oedipus complex in girls and the development of the super-ego? In girls the identification is anaclitic, i.e. through fear of loss of love. This means that the super-ego is not so strongly developed in women (Freud, 1927a). In addition Oedipal attitudes are more likely to remain with women — they are not so strongly repressed — which (Freud, 1940) is not altogether harmful.

Thus because the Oedipus complex is the result of the castration complex in girls the development of the super-ego is different.

IMPORTANCE OF THE THEORY

Apart from the fact that the Oedipus and castration complexes are involved in the development of the super-ego and account for sex differences in that development, the Oedipus complex is crucial to an understanding of later behaviour. Thus at puberty when the repressed Oedipal feelings are reawakened the individual must 'Devote himself to the *great task of freeing himself from the parents*' (Freud, 1916-17). For the son it means freeing himself from his love of his mother and for his hatred of or domination by his father. Few achieve an ideal solution. 'In neurotics . . . this detachment is not accomplished at all. . . . In this sense the Oedipus complex is justifiably regarded as the kernel of the neuroses' (Freud, 1916-17).

Indeed, in his last work (1940), Freud said: 'if psychoanalysis could boast of no other achievement than the discovery of the repressed Oedipus complex, that alone would give it a claim to be counted among the precious new acquisitions of mankind.'

THE EMPIRICAL HYPOTHESES ARISING FROM THE THEORY

The outline of the Freudian concepts of the Oedipus and castration complexes ought to make it clear that this part of psychoanalytic theory contains propositions that can be put to the empirical test. In fact the following hypotheses have been constructed from the theory:

1. Boys at the phallic stage have an overt love for their mothers: later this is repressed.
2. Girls at the phallic stage have an overt love for their fathers: later this is repressed (not perhaps as entirely as with boys).
3. Boys at the phallic stage are afraid of castration.
4. Girls at the phallic stage greatly desire a penis and regret their lack of one.
5. Boys at the phallic stage are hostile towards their fathers.
6. Girls at the phallic stage are hostile towards their mothers.
7. In adults there should be sex differences in moral behaviour — justice, guilt, duty. This hypothesis is derived from the fact that the Oedipus complex is not surely resolved in women thus producing a less powerful super-ego.
8. Cultural factors should affect these findings, e.g. in cultures where the father does not live with the mother.
9. Different results would be expected in orphan children.

N.B. We have not considered the *genetic* hypothesis concerning the Oedipus complex stated in 'Totem and taboo' (Freud, 1913b). Here Freud suggested that in some unstated (presumably Lamarckian) fashion the Oedipus complex was inherited. Since this is entirely contrary to the findings of modern genetics, we have followed Fenichel (1945) in regarding it as a cultural phenomenon depending upon the family environment. This and similar apparently unacceptable notions in psychoanalytic theory are discussed in the final chapter of this book.

EMPIRICAL STUDIES OF THE OEDIPUS AND CASTRATION COMPLEXES

THE WORK OF KUPPUSWAMY (1949)

Kuppuswamy attempted to investigate the incidence of the Oedipus complex by sending questionnaires concerning which child parents preferred and which parent children preferred. This study merits only the briefest consideration since it is highly unlikely that a questionnaire could tap the Oedipus complex which was only discovered or inferred from lengthy free associations. In summary, Kuppuswamy found that fathers and mothers prefer sons and that boys and girls prefer mothers. This result was regarded as partial confirmation of the Oedipus complex.

Conclusions and comments

First of all, simple questions of preference are not relevant to the Oedipus complex. They ignore defence mechanisms such as reaction-formation and sublimation — also part of Freudian theory and not to be ignored since, according to the theory, the Oedipus complex in boys is 'broken upon the rocks' of the castration complex — that is it is repressed and unconscious. In addition problems of social desirability of responses are inherent in the questionnaire method. This study, therefore, may be dismissed as of little value. It is a good example of one of the reasons psychoanalysts ignore psychological research into psychoanalytic theory: the research concerns itself with psychoanalytic concepts so grossly distorted as to be unrecognizable.

THE WORK OF McELROY (1950)

McElroy discussed three methods of testing the Oedipus complex. Unfortunately he gives no report of the results thus obtained but the paper is worth brief examination because it provides a useful background to evaluate the methodology of empirical investigations. It indicates immediately, for example, the short-comings of the work of Kuppuswamy (1949). A short description of the methods is set out below.

1. A questionnaire is constructed to deal with all possible aspects of the physical appearance of women and this includes the use of drawings. Half a sample of young married men complete this questionnaire first concerning their mothers and then their wives. The other half reverse this order. The intensity of the Oedipus complex (or its presence) is measured by the correlation between the two profiles.

2. Photographs of mothers and wives are used. Three copies of the photograph of each wife are necessary. Then cards are constructed with four photographs. The mother of subject X is in the left hand corner. One of the other three pictures is the wife of subject X, the other two photographs are the wives of two other subjects selected at random. Subjects in the experiment are told the aim of this is to assess the likeness in appearance of mothers and daughters. Since selection of wife and mother will occur by chance on one-third of occasions, an index of Oedipal strength may easily be estimated.

3. Parent-preference in children. Children use pastel colours on grey paper. Then they draw their parents in pastel. Finally they are asked to name their favourite colour. The colour of each parent is then noted.

Comments

These methods may be easily elaborated. For example, a more accurate way to find the child's favourite colour would be by the psychophysical method of paired comparisons (see Woodworth and Schlosberg, 1955) where every colour is compared with each other. Again, in method 2, care would have to be taken that the photographs were of a similar quality. Nevertheless it is clear that these three methods are all viable ways of attempting to assess both the strength and the existence of the Oedipus complex as it is conceived in Freudian theory.

In respect of this work by McElroy, a brief paper by Miller (1968) is of some interest. In this study forty females rated pictures of male physiques for resemblance to their fathers. When asked which they would prefer as a lover, the picture chosen tended to that either most or least like their father. This finding is support for the Oedipus complex and also for the defence mechanism of reaction-formation or denial — where the opposite of the unconscious feeling appears in behaviour. Such an experiment, of course, can only be but modest confirmation of the importance of the Oedipus complex since choosing a picture of a lover is an adumbration of actually having one. Nevertheless these results do support Oedipal theory.

THE WORK OF FRIEDMAN

Friedman (1950b) summarized some results of his study of the Oedipus complex in the *American Psychologist*. This report was, in fact, part of his doctoral dissertation (Friedman, 1950a) and it was more comprehensively written up in a later paper (Friedman, 1952). These three reports will therefore not receive separate treatment.

For his sample he used 305 normal children, 5-16 years old. Age-groups were formed of two years' span. In each group there were twenty-six male and twenty-six female children.

Castration complex

Hypothesis. At the age of 5 years fears of castration will be great. During latency these fears will subside but by puberty they will be great again.

Method. Three unfinished 'castration fables' were presented to the children to complete. It was hypothesized that there would be *fewer* mentions of loss of tails, etc., at 5 years and 13 years than at other ages. Fewer castration stories were expected when castration anxiety was high because it had previously been shown that reaction-time to stories with no cutting in them was longer.

The fables used by Friedman (1952) were those originally used by Duss (1940), and translated by Despert (1946). The castration-complex fable is known as 'The Elephant'. In this a child comes into a playroom and finds his favourite toy, an elephant, broken. The subject is asked to say what he thinks is wrong with it.

Results

Boys. Significantly more had stories without cutting at ages of 5 and 13 years than at other ages. Freudian theory was, therefore, supported.

Girls. There was no difference between Oedipal ages and latency. Overall 75 per cent of children had castration fears. This is interesting in the light of Sears' (1943) claim that Freud grossly overestimated the incidence of castration fears.

The Oedipus complex

Friedman reviewed the earlier studies of the Oedipus complex, many of which have been discussed by Sears (1943) who concluded that Freud's notion of the Oedipus complex was a grotesquerie. Most of these studies simply asked the children which parent they preferred. As has already been pointed out, these questions are irrelevant to the Freudian concept of the Oedipus complex which is repressed and therefore unconscious. The fact that the majority of these investigations failed to support the theory is, therefore, irrelevant.

Method

1. There were two fables for the children to complete: a child enjoys himself with one parent then meets the other. Why does the face of 'at home' parent look different? Then the same fable, with parental roles reversed, has to be completed by the children.
2. Three TAT-like pictures were shown:
    (a) *Boys*: father and son are standng by the stairs and near them is a toy waggon. *Girls*: father and daughter by stairs, with a toy doll.
    (b) Mother and child.
    (c) Father and mother.

Data

1. Direct questions as to parental preference, as in other investigations.
2. Analysis of themes to pictures.
3. Analysis of movement tendencies and reactions to common psychoanalytic symbols.

Results

1. *Direct questions*. There were no significant differences between the sexes. Each sex liked each parent equally. This, therefore, follows the results of other similar investigations and fails to 'support' Freudian theory.
2. *Incomplete fables*. There were more negative endings to the fable where a child met the parent of his own sex than to the other fable. This fits Freudian theory in that the child would be expected to project his own feelings on to the parent. The difference was significant at the 0.05 level. Method 2 therefore supports Freudian theory.
3. *Themes*
    (a) Boys had more conflict themes to father figures as did girls to mother figures. The difference was significant at the 0.001 level. Freudian theory is again supported.
    (b) More girls fantasize that father figure takes some positive action to toy than boys. The difference was significant at the 0.001 level and confirms Freudian theory.
    (c) More girls than boys (sig. 0.001 level) fantasize that the male figure mounts

the stairs and enters the room. Again this strongly supports Freudian theory in that mounting stairs in psychoanalytic theory symbolizes sexual intercourse and entering a room symbolizes inserting the penis into the vagina. (See Chapter 9 for the evidence concerning symbolism and dream theory.)

As Friedman (1952) points out, all methods other than the one most commonly used, which has been shown to be faulty, support the Freudian theory of the Oedipus complex.

Comments and conclusions

These results are so clear-cut and the hypotheses tested are so clearly derivable from the psychoanalytic theory that little comment is necessary. The large sample, 307, means that the investigation cannot be attacked on grounds of sample size. The fact that the pictures and fables constitute a projective technique does not mean that the results must be regarded as untrustworthy. Certainly, throughout this book, the Rorschach and similar tests have been eschewed. But the projective techniques used here, as is the case with the Blacky Pictures, have a clear rationale rooted in psychoanalytic theory. The results hypothesized depend upon this theory, not on the theory of the test itself as is the case with the Rorschach and the Szondi. The last finding concerning the mounting of the staircase is the most extraordinary. Only on Freudian Oedipal theory could such a finding have been predicted. This result supports, also, Freudian claims about symbolization.

It must be concluded therefore that this study by Friedman (1952) has made three main points:

1. It has empirically demonstrated the inadequacy of the questionnaire approach to investigations of the Oedipus and castration complexes.
2. It has provided good evidence for the existence of a castration complex in boys.
3. It has provided good evidence for the existence of the Oedipus complex (grotesquerie or not) in boys and girls.

THE WORK OF MICHAL-SMITH, HAMMER AND SPITZ (1951)

This was a case-study of a Negro boy whose Oedipal desires were very close to consciousness. The Oedipal dimension of the Blacky Pictures (see p. 110) agreed with the psychiatric diagnosis and showed him to be highly disturbed about such conflicts. This is, at least, an objective verification of clinical data and as such supports the existence of the Oedipus complex.

SURVEY BY ROHEIM (1952)

Roheim reviewed some anthropological evidence concerning the Oedipus complex, in an attempt to show that the Oedipus complex occurs even in those societies where free sexual play is allowed for children. Although the evidence quoted is not objective in that no standardized measurements were used, the data are pertinent to the Oedipus complex, being myths, dreams and characteristic doll-play. Thus according to Berndt and Berndt (1951) there is a myth among the Alaiva in Arnhem Land about Kadjari, who killed his son because the boy wanted to lie with his mother. Both now live on in a heavenly constellation. Yet among this tribe children are given complete sexual freedom. Among the Lesu in New Ireland (Powdermaker, 1933) Oedipal dreams, of which the men are much ashamed, are common. Henry and Henry (1944), in their study of the Pilaga Indians, claimed that the doll-play of the children showed clear indications of the Oedipus complex. Finally the Fan of West Africa (Trilles, 1912) have a myth of Crocodile, son of Crocodile, who kills his crocodile father. Yet in these three societies there is freedom of sexual play for the children.

Now it is not argued that these anthropological findings are objective evidence for the existence of an Oedipus complex. However, it would be wrong to ignore them totally, because the power of a theory depends upon its ability to comprehend a wide variety of evidence and it is in this that psychoanalytic theory is outstanding. These anthropological findings are examples of such a comprehensive power.

THE WORK OF SCHWARTZ

Schwartz (1955) developed from the TAT and validated a measure of castration anxiety. Using this measure, Schwartz (1956) then carried out an empirical study of two Freudian hypotheses concerning castration anxiety.

The measure of castration anxiety (Schwartz, 1955)

Method and sample. Three groups of students, eighteen in each group. There were three treatments — different films were shown. *The castration group* were shown a film of sub-incision rites. *The anxiety group* were shown a film about Negro deprivation. *The control group* saw a Chaplin comedy film.

The TAT variables. The TAT cards were subjected to a content-analysis. Inter-rate correlation was high, 0.80. Ten variables were extracted and examined. Validation was demonstrated if the castration group was discriminated from the other two groups. A list of the variables is set out in Table 6.1: whether they were valid or not is also indicated.

TABLE 6.1. *TAT variables and results*

Variables	Valid
1. Genital injury or loss	No
2. Loss or damage to other parts of the body	No

Variables	Valid
3. Damage to body image or symbols (e.g. guns)	Yes
4. Sexual inadequacy	No
5. Personal inadequacy	Yes
6. Repetitive attempts at mastery (e.g. risk-taking)	Yes
7. Intrapsychic threat: guilt, expectation of punishment	Yes
8. Extrapsychic threat: retaliation from external sources	Yes
9. Loss of cathected objects	Yes
10. Total score 1-9	Yes

As was pointed out by Schwartz (1955), Variables 1, 2 and 4 probably failed because they were simply too obvious for normal subjects.

Comments and conclusions

The fact that these variables, derived from the TAT, can discriminate the castration group from the other two groups is good evidence for their validity as measures of castration anxiety. Since one of the groups was an anxiety group, this discriminative ability cannot be due to their being made anxious by pictures of sub-incision. This validity is, on its own, support for the Freudian concept of castration anxiety. If no such anxiety existed the first two groups would not score differently.

Schwartz (1956)

With this TAT measure of castration anxiety, Schwartz (1956) made further investigations of the castration complex.

Sample. Twenty homosexual male students compared with a control group of twenty normal students, matched for age, education and socio-economic status.

Tests. Variables as in the previous study.

Results. Variables: 4 — sexual inadequacy, 7 — intrapsychic threat, 8 — extrapsychic threat and 11 — a new variable based on the formal characteristics of the story (misspelling and discontinuity for example) discriminated the groups in the predicted direction at the 1 per cent level by Chi-square — as did the total score. Variable 5, personal inadequacy, discriminated at the 5 per cent level by Chi-square. Similar but less significant results were obtained using the Link—Wallace statistic (Lindzey, 1954). Variables 6, 2, 3 and 9 failed to discriminate. Schwartz (1956) argues that these results support the psychoanalytic claim that castration anxiety can create homosexuality.

Comments and conclusions

Four of the variables fail to support the Freudian theory. Furthermore variables 4 and 11, which discriminate the homosexuals, were not, in the previous study

(Schwartz, 1955), related to castration anxiety. Thus only three of the original scores discriminate the groups. This cannot be regarded as good support for Freudian theory. Clearly a replication of this study is needed with more substantial samples. Nevertheless it is slight evidence for the psychoanalytic hypothesis that homosexuality is linked with castration anxiety. It is to be noted that such evidence as this inherently cannot demonstrate a *causal* link.

Schwartz (1956) also investigated sex differences in castration anxiety.
Hypothesis. Men have greater castration anxiety than women.
Sample. Twenty matched pairs of males and females.
Results. Variables 5 and 6 — personal inadequacy and repetitive attempts at mastery — discriminated the groups at the 5 per cent level, as did the total score. The other differences were non-significant.

Comments and conclusions

The Freudian hypothesis receives some support although it is clear that there is a considerable overlap of distributions. It is interesting that variable 5, which failed to discriminate before, was this time successful. From this study the Freudian theory that men have greater castration anxiety than women is supported to a limited extent.

Conclusions from the studies by Schwartz (1955, 1956)

These studies provide good evidence for the existence of castration anxiety and a useful measure of it. However the investigations with this TAT device give only limited support to the notion that homosexuality is linked with castration anxiety and that men have greater castration anxiety than women. Clearly more studies are needed with these variables and a factor-analysis of them would enable weighted scores from each to be used, perhaps allowing for greater discriminative power. In brief the results may be thus summarized:

1. The existence of castration anxiety: good support.
2. The link between homosexuality and castration anxiety: limited support.
3. Greater castration anxiety among men than women: limited support.

Findings 2 and 3 will be discussed again in Chapter 10.

THE WORK OF BIDDLE (1957)

Biddle regressed 100 subjects back to three years old under hypnosis and then investigated their Oedipal fantasies. The major finding was that all children strive for union with both parents. The conclusion, therefore, was that the Oedipus complex was not supported.

Comments and conclusions

This is an interesting study in that hypnosis was the original technique by which unconscious mental activity was uncovered in the beginnings of psychoanalysis. Only later was free association preferred, partly because Freud found difficulty in hypnotizing patients. However the assumption that hypnotic regression to any age gives a true representation of what in fact occurred at that age is by no means proven. Furthermore the choice of three years of age to investigate the Oedipus complex is curious. Yet another objection to the study involves the lack of quantification of the data and its interpretative nature. Thus the assertion that the concept of the Oedipus complex was not confirmed by this study is not considered of great importance in the empirical study of the problem. This investigation is best ignored.

THE WORK OF RABIN (1958a and b)

Rabin investigated some psychosexual differences between Kibbutz and non-Kibbutz Israeli boys.

Sample. Twenty-seven boys reared in a Kibbutz: mean age, 10 years 2 months. Twenty-seven boys reared in their families: mean age, 10 years 2 months.

Test. The Blacky Pictures (Blum, 1949).

Hypotheses

1. Fewer Kibbutz-reared children will exhibit Oedipal intensity compared with the family children.
2. Less identification with the father will be noted among the Kibbutz children compared with the family children.

Result. These hypotheses were supported. Among the Kibbutz boys there was less Oedipal intensity and less identification with the father.

Comments and conclusions

In the Kibbutz, children are reared by a nurse, live communally, and see their parents only for a short time during the day (usually in the evening). Thus these hypotheses follow naturally from such a regime. The fact that they were supported fits psychoanalytic theory but can hardly be regarded as very powerful evidence. It means little other than that the less you see your parents, the smaller will be the emotional attachments to them. This study is useful only in the context of other studies of the Oedipus complex, where it may be used as one small piece of evidence.

THE WORK OF LASKY AND BERGER (1959)

Lasky and Berger administered the Blacky Pictures to patients before and after genito-urinary surgery in a study relevant to the castration complex.

Sample. Thirty adult male patients. Age-range 20-67 years, median 48.

Tests. The Blacky Pictures were given seven days before the operation and six days after it.

Results. Phi-correlations were worked out for all the dimensions of the Blacky Pictures (see pp. 109-10 for description of this projective test). The most affected dimensions (the smallest correlations) were: *masturbation guilt*, *castration anxiety* and *narcissistic love-object*. These findings certainly support the hypothesis that genito-urinary surgery would produce castration anxiety.

Comments and conclusions

Although these results support Freudian theory, it must be remembered that the test—retest reliability of the Blacky Pictures is not high (Charen, 1956a). This investigation by Charen has been discussed (p. 111), where it was pointed out that he only used the multiple-choice questions. Nevertheless the fact that the two dimensions most affected were those related to castration discounts to some extent the effects of low test-reliability. It must be concluded, therefore, that this study supports the concept of castration anxiety.

THE WORK OF HAMMER (1953)

Relevant to the study by Lasky and Berger (1959) is the study of symbolism among a sample of prisoners who had been eugenically sterilized (for sexual offences). This investigation by Hammer has been fully described in the chapter on symbolism (p. 268). Suffice it to say here, therefore, that these sterilized prisoners showed evidence of castration fear in their drawings on the House—Tree—Person Test. Chimneys were affected as were the branches of trees. Similar changes were not noted among a control group of surgical patients. Thus, in a manner similar to that of Lasky and Berger, although only incidental to the study of symbolism, Hammer also provides evidence for the existence of the castration complex.

THE WORK OF SARNOFF AND CORWIN (1959)

This was an experimental study of castration anxiety and the fear of death.

Rationale. Repressed castration anxiety is likely to be manifested as a fear of death. It therefore follows that individuals with severe castration anxiety should have a very considerable fear of death. Subjects with severe castration anxiety should show a greater fear of death than subjects with low castration anxiety after this castration anxiety has been aroused.

The following abbreviations will be used to describe this experiment since otherwise, as can be seen from the rationale, the repetitious language becomes too cumbersome:

HCA	High castration anxiety	MS	Morality scale
LCA	Low castration anxiety	HSA	High sexual arousal
FDS	Fear of death scale	LSA	Low sexual arousal

Hypothesis. HCA subjects will show greater fear of death than LCA subjects after being exposed to sexually arousing stimuli.

Design. A before-and-after design was used. There were two treatments (levels of sexual arousal) and two levels of castration anxiety which was measured in a pre-experimental session.

Sample. Fifty-six male undergraduates.

Method

A. *The pre-tests*
   1. Five-item FDS
   2. Five-item MS
   3. Blacky Castration Picture used to test for castration anxiety. On this variable, *36 LCA* and *20 HCA* subjects were selected.

B. A four-week time-gap was allowed.

C. *The experimental sessions.* Two experimental conditions to which half of each group went. HSA: four pictures of nude women to which subjects wrote aesthetic responses. LSA: four pictures of fully-clothed models. Again aesthetic responses were recorded.

D. *The post-tests.* MS scale and FDS scale were again completed. In addition a questionnaire to assess degree of sexual stimulation was filled in.

Results

1. The HSA group were, in fact, more sexually aroused by the nude women than were the other group by the models.
2. HCA group showed a significantly greater increase in score on the FDS in the HSA condition than did the LCA group.
3. In the LAS condition, there were no significant differences.
4. To test whether it was guilt causing the shift of scores, high and low subjects on the morality scale were compared on the FDS under both conditions. The difference was not significant.

Finding 2, that under conditions of high sexual arousal the fear of death score of those with great castration anxiety increased, while under low conditions it did not, is very strong support for the Freudian concept of the castration complex.

Comments and conclusions

As should be clear, this is an elegant and clear design. Any failures in the tests used would spoil the results so that it can hardly be argued that the tests were invalid. If they were these results are even more remarkable. The fact that those with strong castration anxiety should, when sexually aroused, show a greater fear of death than those low on castration anxiety, can only be understood in terms of the whole Freudian concept of the castration complex. Finding 4 makes it clear that the results were not due to feelings of guilt.

Unlike correlational studies where the correlations can be due to errors common to both tests, e.g. response-sets, and where the validity of the test must be proven beyond doubt, experimental studies, where conditions are manipulated according to a rationale and mean scores predicted, are more difficult to fault. They provide a far more rigorous test of any theory than do non-experimental studies, provided that, as in this case, the experimental rationale is relevant to the theory.

It must be noted that the castration complex is different from castration anxiety. It embraces much more: for example it is related to fear of death and other symbolic injuries. Castration anxiety on the other hand is more specific, as in the study by Lasky and Berger (1959), where it refers simply to fear of genital injury. The complex refers to all the associated repressed material. This study by Sarnoff and Corwin provides strong support for the Freudian concept of the castration complex.

In respect of castration anxiety, Fisher and Greenberg (1977) cite three interesting unpublished doctoral dissertations. Lane (1966) found that the dreams of male surgical patients showed more castration-anxiety material than did those of female patients. However, the objective analysis of the dream material only refers to the manifest dream content rather than the latent content so that the implications of this finding are by no means clear. Schneider (1960) carried out a similar study of child surgical patients, using the Thematic Apperception Test, story completions and figure drawings and found more castration themes among boys than girls. However, whether such themes relate to the castration complex is unproven since the validity of such measures has never been demonstrated. Finally, Lewis (1969) found that male subjects produced more castration themes than did females after seeing a film of sub-incision rites.

From all these findings Fisher and Greenberg conclude that males probably are more concerned with 'body damage (castration) than are females'. We should like to point out here that while these results probably do indicate that males are more concerned with body damage than are females, this *per se* is not evidence of castration anxiety in the Freudian sense. After all the penis is an appendage that can more easily be cut off than the clitoris. This is a far cry from an unconscious fear that one's father will castrate one in talion revenge. Such studies in our view cannot confirm psychoanalytic theory.

Three other doctoral dissertations, relevant to the castration complex, are cited by Fisher and Greenberg, this time dealing with the effects of sexual arousal on castration anxiety. Brener (1969) found no effects when measuring castration anxiety with the Rorschach and the Thematic Apperception Test. This study cannot be taken too seriously since the validity of these tests is dubious. Bromberg (1967) found anxiety was increased after sexual arousal among those high on a questionnaire measure of castration anxiety. Even if the castration-anxiety questionnaire were valid (highly unlikely since there is no accepted measure of this variable), the result may mean little more than that anxiety tends to be a common factor. Certainly this research could not be used as confirmation of psychoanalytic theory. Finally, Saltztein (1971) found that exposure to an Oedipal story increased castration anxiety (as measured by the Blacky Pictures) among boys who had suffered trauma between the ages of three to six years. Since the validity of the Blacky Pictures castration picture is by no means validated, no conclusions can be drawn from this study.

Thus we disagree with Fisher and Greenberg on the value of this work. They write 'we cannot envisage any other existing theory ... that would hypothesize males would respond to sexual arousal with imagery related to getting hurt and damaged and to a degree greater than that observed in females.' While it is true that such derivations can be drawn from the castration complex, we should like to make two points:

1. These are only derivations. They are not the castration complex itself as described by Freud.

2. The castration complex may not be necessary to account for the findings. As we have stated before, there may be more objective danger to having a penis injured (especially an aroused one) than a clitoris. Furthermore, since it is not necessary to invoke Freudian theory to account for the high valuation of the penis, male worries over injuries to the penis are perhaps more simply explained.

That is why to us these experiments seem far less than objective evidence for psychoanalytic theory. There is one further objection that can be raised. This kind of evidence is very similar to the data of psychoanalysis, i.e. it is inferential in nature. Our search is really more towards clear, unequivocal findings which require a minimum of interpretation.

THE WORK OF STEPHENS

Stephens (1961) carried out a cross-cultural study of menstrual taboo using the method of Whiting and Child (1953) which has been fully described and discussed on p. 78. This study is also to be found in Stephens (1962).

Rationale. In 'Totem and Taboo' Freud (1913b) argued that in the taboos, myths, superstitions and ceremonies of primitive societies could be seen phenomena which in our society are usually deeply hidden. For example totemism was considered to be an institutionalized neurotic symptom caused by the Oedipus complex.

Hypothesis of the present study. The extensiveness of menstrual taboos in any society is determined by the intensity of castration anxiety felt by the men of that society.

Measures. Stephens (1961) argued that because there was no measure of castration anxiety *per se*, it would be necessary to measure the *antecedents* of castration anxiety. These are, according to Freudian theory, child-rearing procedures, especially those connected with the Oedipal situation. In addition he used three measures of the hypothesized *consequences* of castration anxiety — in this case castration-like incidents in folk lore. Finally a menstrual-taboo scale was used. Thus fifteen measures were used in all:

Ten measures of antecedent child-rearing procedures.
The total scores derived from these measures.
Three measures of the consequences of castration-like anxiety.
One menstrual-taboo scale.

Data on which measures were based. The anthropological reports of seventy-two primitive societies, as used by Whiting and Child (1953). Ratings were made for each of the variables.
Results. These are best set out as in Table 6.2.

TABLE 6.2. *Menstrual taboo and castration anxiety*

Child-rearing antecedent	Relation to taboo scale in expected direction	Probability of chance occurrence
1. Diffusion of nurturance	Yes	0.27
2. Post-partum sex taboo	Yes	0.01
3. Severity of masturbation punishment	Yes	0.01
4. Overall severity of sex training	Yes	0.05
5. Severity of aggression training	Yes	0.18
6. General pressure for obedience	No	0.65
7. Severity of punishment for disobedience	Yes	0.19
8. Strictness of father's obedience commands	Yes	0.20
9. Whether or not father is main disciplinarian	Yes	0.02
10. Importance of physical punishment as discipline	Yes	0.07
11. Total of variables 1 to 10	Yes	0.000001

The folk-lore incidents were not related to the menstrual-taboo scale.

Comments and conclusions

It is clear from the results that the hypothesis is very strongly confirmed. This means, as Stephens (1961) points out, that menstrual taboos are affected by the castration complex, that there is a widespread phenomenon (seventy-two societies) of castration anxiety and that it does originate in the Oedipal situation. It also implies that there is a widespread phenomenon of the Oedipus complex. All this is powerful evidence for the Freudian theory.

Careful scrutiny of the table of results, from the viewpoint of psychoanalytic theory, makes the evidence even more impressive. Thus the antecedent child-rearing procedures which would appear to be less relevant to castration anxiety are supportive of the hypothesis but to a lesser degree (e.g. variables 1 and 8) than those which are clearly most pertinent (e.g. variables 3 and 10). The enormously high statistical significance of the total score with the menstrual-taboo scale is remarkable.

The fact that the folk-lore incidents did not also confirm psychoanalytic theory is curious but may only be due to the fact that other influences than castration anxiety affect the incidence of genital injury, severing and other kinds of physical injury in folk-tales. There must, for example, as in Hammer, be historical antecedents as well as psychological.

This study by Stephens (1961) seems to us to constitute most impressive and powerful evidence for the Freudian concept of the castration complex.

THE WORK OF WHITING, KLUCKHOHN AND ANTHONY (1958)

Whiting et al., using the technique of rating societies, studied the function of male initiation ceremonies at puberty. In so doing they examined certain hypotheses concerning the Oedipus complex.

Rationale and hypothesis. The rationale for this study was derived from the anthropological speculations in 'Totem and Taboo'. It was assumed that the ideal antecedent for the development of the Oedipus complex was a long *post-partum sexual taboo*. This, of course, enables the child to sleep with its mother. Similarly a short post-partum sexual taboo will tend to inhibit development of the Oedipus complex. Thus, by selecting societies with long post-partum sexual taboos and those with short taboos, the effects of the Oedipus complex should become apparent. The following hypothesis was formulated:

> Societies with a long post-partum sexual taboo (high on the Oedipus complex) will be more likely to have initiation rites (which are symptomatic of the Oedipus complex in psychoanalytic theory (Fenichel, 1945)) than will societies with a short taboo.

Sample. Fifty-six societies, representing forty-five of the sixty culture areas designated by Murdock (1957).

Measures. The ethnographic literature relevant to these fifty-six societies was searched and ratings made.

Results. *80 per cent of the tribes with long taboos had initiation ceremonies*. The Chi-square (sig. at 0.001 level) is hard to interpret in that through known historical connections the societies may not have been entirely independent cases.

Comments and conclusions

In this paper Whiting et al. concentrate on a careful examination of the background of various tribes in the sample, whose child-rearing procedures do not accord with their initiation rites, so that they are less interested than Stephens (1961) in testing the psychoanalytic theory. Nevertheless these results do support psychoanalytic theory concerning the Oedipus complex and its acting out in ceremony.

FURTHER ANTHROPOLOGICAL STUDIES

Since we are now dealing with anthropological studies, two recent survey papers should now be examined since they are relevant to the factual basis for some aspects of the Oedipus complex and to the interpretation of anthropological results.

In 'Totem and Taboo' (Freud, 1913b), as we have pointed out, Freud argued that the incest taboo (which lies at the heart of the Oedipus complex) arises because unconsciously we all desire our parents. However, much of the frankly speculative theorizing of 'Totem and Taboo' is not taken seriously by modern analysts and Fenichel (1945) is content to argue that the Oedipus complex results from the particular family constellation that is found in the west. Thus the failure of Malinowsky (1927) to identify an Oedipus complex among the Trobriand islanders is not held by Fenichel to be fatal to the theory, although it does, of course, mean that the Oedipus complex cannot arise from a primordial memory of the patricide of the primal horde (Freud, 1913b), an outstanding example of speculation. Similar arguments apply to the similar work of Anne Parsons (Parsons, 1969) in Naples, who described a Madonna complex in place of the familiar Oedipal variety.

The work of Parker

An anthropological study by Parker (1976) of the incest taboo is helpful in clarifying the anthropological position on this topic, the factual basis, as it were, for any theory in which incest taboo plays an important part. He concluded that (a) in almost all societies incest is taboo (a finding which is congruent with psychoanalytic theorizing); (b) even among primates such a taboo may be found and (c) in children reared together as in the Kibbutz or in Chinese minor marriages sexual relations are not found (again not incongruent with psychoanalytic theory). His final conclusions was that the taboo had the social function of propelling individuals into new territories and hence into new relationships. This study by Parker (1976) at least indicates that the facts of incest taboo do not *preclude* psychoanalytic theorizing from being true. If, for example, societies were found with no incest taboo and no other social features such as would make a direct expression of the Oedipus complex likely or possible, then this would constitute powerful evidence against psychoanalytic theory.

Comments of Spiro

Incidentally this study by Parker (1976) illustrates the point made by Spiro (1979), namely that there is a tendency in anthropology to deny the biological or sexual nature of culture. Especially noteworthy here is Douglas (1966) who argues that beliefs concerning the polluting qualities of the vagina and its contents symbolize not relationships between the sexes but the social system itself, without ample argument that this is, in fact, the case.

THE WORK OF BLOCK AND VENTUR (1963)

This was an investigation of castration anxiety in a sample of amputees (symbolic castrates).

Test. The Blacky Pictures — the castration dimension.

Sample. Twenty amputees were compared with twenty surgical controls.

Results. The amputees were more disturbed on the castration dimension than the controls. Block and Ventur argue that this is support for the psychoanalytic theory of the castration complex and *ipso facto* for the validity of the Blacky Pictures.

Comments and conclusions

Although it is true that Freudian theory would predict an increase in castration anxiety among amputees, this study cannot be regarded as powerful support for the theory. This is because a simpler explanation of the findings is available. The castration card of the Blacky Pictures shows Blacky, blindfolded, with a knife suspended over his extended tail. It is not surprising that patients whose limbs have recently been cut off should be more upset at this picture than other surgical patients. This is not to impugn the Blacky Pictures. If, for example, homosexuals were higher scorers on this picture than normals, as Freudian theory predicts, a simple explanation would not be available.

This study, therefore, cannot rank high as supporting evidence for the Freudian theory of the castration complex.

THE WORK OF LEVIN (1966)

Levin investigated the Freudian concept of the female castration complex.

Sample. Twenty-six career women (mean IQ 129) and twenty-five homemakers (mean IQ 122).

Tests. Eight independent scores from the Rorschach test and the total of these scores.

Results. The unmarried, career women scored significantly more highly on the total measure of the castration complex than did the homemakers. This difference was not attributable to a general neurotic disturbance. However since five of these eight scores failed to discriminate the groups (Chi-square test), Levin questions the use of the word 'complex'. It appears from this evidence that it is not a unitary variable (not all scores discriminated) and that the construct of the castration complex is unnecessary.

Comments and conclusions

The dubious validity of the Rorschach test makes these results of doubtful value. Until the study is replicated, using different measures of castration anxiety or the castration complex, or using an experimental procedure as did Sarnoff and Corwin (1959), little weight can be placed on these results.

Ellman (1970) in a thesis cited by Fisher and Greenberg followed up the work of Levin (1966) by comparing forty high-penis-envy subjects with forty low on this variable using the same Rorschach measure as Levin (1966), a measure which is of unknown validity. The high group, as measured by the TAT, were more hostile to men and more depressed than the others. Such results neither confirm nor refute the concept of penis envy.

In addition, Ellman examined the effect of a subliminal stimulus 'women menstruating' on the subjects. This stimulus in the high subjects was claimed to increase the defence of denial as measured by responses to the TAT, typified by errors in labelling the sex of the subjects in the TAT cards.

Fisher and Greenberg (1977) claim that these results are supportive of Freudian notions concerning penis envy. However, none of the measures used are of proven validity and in view of the results this doctoral dissertation, although interesting and suggestive, cannot be regarded as objective scientific evidence for penis envy.

THE WORK OF KREITLER AND KREITLER (1966)

Kreitler and Kreitler investigated children's concepts of sexuality and birth.

Method. Twenty-five kindergarten workers interviewed the children. They were trained to do this during a course at the university.

Sample. Sixty western boys, sixty western girls, thirty-five oriental boys and thirty-five oriental girls. Age-range 4-5½ years.

Freudian hypotheses tested

1. Boys believe in the universality of the penis.
2. The sexual act is considered to be aggressive.
3. Children are believed to be born through the anus.

Results

1. There was no hint of castration of girls in any of the sample. The majority of the western and over half of the eastern sample knew that boys were different from girls. Therefore Freudian theory must be rejected, according to the authors.

2. 95 per cent of the sample said anal birth was an impossibility. Again Freudian theory is rejected.

3. Father's role in the production of children was not grasped and only 30 per cent of the children thought that their parents were different from other parents.

According to Kreitler and Kreitler the universality of the penis, a view which, in Freudian theory, was held by children, is refuted by these results. As a result a new basis for the castration complex is required.

Comments and conclusions

There are several points about this study which merit attention before the conclusions of the Kreitlers can be assessed. The first of these concerns the interviewers, who were not fully trained social scientists but kindergarten teachers. Their level of skill remains therefore an important yet unknown factor. The next point concerns the validity of the children's responses. It has long been, for example, a criticism of Piaget's work on animism among children that the very form of the questions may have suggested answers to the child, a view which receives some support from similar work carried out in non-European languages where the structure of the language is very different (Munn, 1961). In the present investigation, children who had been formally acquainted with the anatomical differences between the sexes might well be unwilling to tell an interviewer what they really thought in case it seemed silly. This is a similar response-set to that of social desirability. Only very sensitive and skilful interviewing can overcome this. As Newson and Newson (1963) found even among adults, telling the interviewer what he seems to want is also an extraneous variable affecting the veracity of interview data. Thus the skill of the interviewers and the accuracy of the data are not unquestionable.

However even if we accept the results the basis of the castration complex is not swept away as is claimed by Kreitler and Kreitler (1966). Thus Fenichel (1945) argues that 'Only the high narcissistic cathexis of the penis at this period (around 5 years) explains the efficacy of castration anxiety.' This high narcissistic evaluation is due to the fact that at the phallic stage the penis becomes rich in sensation. Freud (1909a), in the case of Little Hans, also points out that castration fear can be induced by the sight of the female genitalia which cause the boy to take a joking castration threat seriously. Thus the part of the psychoanalytic theory which the Kreitlers claim to be the cause of the castration complex and which their findings refute, namely the belief that women once had a penis, is merely *one* of the causes, not the *sole* cause.

Thus their results by no means cast doubt on the concept of the castration complex even if they are accepted. Nevertheless the difficulties of interview data, and the fact that the interviewers were not highly trained, makes the results questionable. Rational knowledge does not so easily move fantasy. Since, too, the castration complex depends in psychoanalytic theory on factors other than a belief in the universal penis, indeed it is partly due to Oedipal guilt, this study does not appear to us, as it does to Kreitler and Kreitler, to undermine Freudian theory.

STUDIES OF THE OEDIPUS AND CASTRATION COMPLEXES THROUGH THE COLLECTION OF DREAM MATERIAL

Hall and his associates at the Institute of Dream Research have conducted some large-scale studies of dream content. These investigations have been fully described and discussed in the chapter on dreams (pp. 288 et seq.). However a very short summary of the findings will be given here because many of these studies were concerned with the Oedipus and castration complexes.

Hall (1955) studied the dream of being attacked (see p. 288). He concluded that it was symbolic of being castrated rather than of castration anxiety. One of his reasons for this conclusion was that it was usually associated with feelings of weakness and impotence. Despite the ingenuity of the arguments this particular study, on its own, cannot be regarded as very convincing evidence for the castration complex.

Hall and Van De Castle (*1963*) formed the hypothesis, from psychoanalytic theory, that males would have more dreams of castration anxiety than would females who, in their turn, would dream more of castration wish and penis envy (see p. 293). Examples of dream material regarded as symbolic of castration anxiety were the inability of the dreamer to use his penis or a penis-symbol such as a gun or spear. If this happened to another person, the dream was classified as symbolic of castration-wish. Finally, if a dreamer acquired a penis or symbol in the dream or changed into a man, this was regarded as a penis-envy dream. With such criteria as these the content of the dreams of 120 college students was examined. The hypothesis was strongly supported. This study by Hall and Van De Castle is impressive support for the Freudian concept of the castration complex, as indeed it is for psychoanalytic dream theory.

Hall and Domhoff (*1963*) investigated some sex differences in dreams (see p. 290). They found that in the dreams of males there were significantly more encounters with males than there were in the dreams of females. These authors interpreted this sex difference as positive evidence for the Oedipus complex. Certainly such a difference would be predicted from Freudian Oedipal theory, but clearly on its own it is not very strong support.

Hall and Domhoff (*1962a, b*) studied aggression in dreams (see p. 291). In the dreams of men there were significantly more aggressive encounters with males than with females. In the dreams of women, however, aggressive encounters were evenly split between men and women. As with the previous study these findings are in accord with Freudian theory since hostility to males is a reflection of the old Oedipal hatred of the father. Nevertheless the findings are only corroborative evidence, not definitive proof.

Hall (*1963*) carried out a further investigation of the Oedipus complex in dreams (see p. 291). There were four hypotheses:

1. that in all dreams there would be more male than female strangers,
2. that there would be more male strangers in male than in female dreams,
3. that there would be more aggressive encounters in dreams with male strangers, and
4. that such encounters would be more common in male than in female dreams.

The basic assumption of these hypotheses is, of course, that a male stranger represents the father. Even for a girl this is true since the castration complex for girls does not entirely wipe out the fantasy of the good mother.

All these hypotheses were supported, a finding which strongly confirms Freudian Oedipal theory, in that other hypotheses to account for the results, even of the *ad hoc* variety, are not easy to develop.

Conclusions from the dream studies

If the results of all these dream studies are considered together, they constitute impressive support for the concepts of the Oedipus and castration complexes. To account for all these results, a large number of *ad hoc* hypotheses would have to be pressed into service — a less parsimonious procedure than the invocation of Freudian theory by which they were predicted.

THE WORK OF ALLEN (A STUDY OF EGO STRENGTH)

Allen (1957) investigated the effects of childhood experience on adult personality, using the cross-cultural methods of Whiting and Child (1953). However, this research differs from the others discussed in this chapter in that it is concerned with the more general psychoanalytic proposition that such experiences affect ego strength. It is not concerned with the effects of specific experiences on specific personality patterns.

Rationale. Indulgence or deprivation should result, in Freudian theory, in low ego strength. Psychoanalysis thus produces a curvilinear prediction.

Measures. As developed by Whiting and Child, a rating for a society of *initial satisfaction* was based on such variables as amount of freedom for child to perform the initial habit, encouragement of such habits and the amount of concurrent anxiety aroused by the habit.

Similarly a seven-point rating scale of societies for *ego strength* was developed. At one extreme were societies characterized by passive acceptance of, and rigid approaches to, problems where defensive processes seemed visible, at the other were those societies where there was evident a flexible approach to difficulties and a tolerance of frustration. The reliability of this measure (independent markers) was 0.74.

Finally a measure of the environment was taken where climatic factors, food supplies and soil fertility were taken into account along with other similar variables.

Sample. Fifty-eight societies which had been rated by Whiting and Child for initial satisfaction.

Results. Correlations with ego strength were as set out in Table 6.3.

TABLE 6.3. *Correlation of variables with ego strength*

Variables		Sig.
Average satisfaction (oral, anal, sexual, dependent aggression)	+0.34	0.05
Average anxiety	−0.54	0.001
Erogenous satisfaction (oral, anal, sexual)	+0.32	0.02
Erogenous anxiety	−0.44	0.001

Of the individual variables, sexual satisfaction and sexual anxiety had the highest correlations with ego strength, being $+0.4$ and -0.44 respectively. Severity of the environment had no significant correlations with any of these scores. All these regressions were linear, *not* curvilinear as predicted from psychoanalytic theory.

Comments and conclusions

The psychoanalytic claim that excessive satisfaction is as fixating as deprivation is not supported by the linearity of these results. However, although it could be argued from these findings that psychoanalytic theory is wrong on this point, Allen (1957) suggests that there may not have been sufficient numbers in the sample with very high or very low scores on indulgence or deprivation of satisfactions. This is, of course, because societies as a whole are not as extreme as individuals within a society with whom psychoanalytic theory is concerned.

Nevertheless, the general finding that these childhood experiences of satisfaction and frustration were related to ego strength is support for Freudian theory. Objections to the validity of these societal measures will not be considered here (see p. 78 for a full discussion of this cross-cultural method), but in view of the positive correlations reported which would be lowered by metric error it must be concluded that this study of Allen supports in general rather than in detail the Freudian claim that child-rearing experiences affect the balance of the adult personality.

TWO LIGHT-HEARTED STUDIES

The work of Johnson (1966)

Johnson, in a report which, perhaps, should not be taken wholly seriously, found that significantly more men than women in a sample of 300 undergraduates taking an exam returned their pencils. This, he claimed, *could* be taken as evidence of penis envy. It could, of course, also indicate that women need pencils more than men or are more dishonest than men or more flustered by the rigours of examination. Readers can put their own value on this study.

The work of Landy (1967)

Landy also investigated the Freudian theory of penis envy and castration anxiety in a study which the present writer considers to be a satire of experimental studies of psychoanalytic theory. He hypothesized that women would open an American pack of cigarettes by lifting flaps to form a cavity, thus expelling the cigarette from the bottom. Men, on the other hand, due to castration anxiety, would tend to castrate the pack and get the cigarette by thumping the bottom so that, like an ejaculation, it leaps out. Sixty-five men and sixty-one women were observed through a one-way mirror when a heavily bandaged experimenter asked them to get him a cigarette from a new pack. A Chi-square analysis of the methods of opening the pack supported the hypotheses derived somewhat tenuously from Freudian theory. Neither of these two studies can be considered as powerful support for psychoanalytic theory.

THE WORK OF SILVERMAN AND COLLEAGUES

This group has conducted some of the most interesting studies of psychoanalytic theory, especially those aspects of it concerned with defences (work which is fully described in our chapter concerned with defence mechanisms). Silverman et al. (1978) used their techniques in a study relevant to the Oedipus complex.

Essentially, pictures were presented tachistoscopically with five different sentences below the threshold of perception. The effects of these subliminal perceptions on dart-throwing ability were examined.

The five sentences were:

(a) Beating dad is wrong. This was considered as an Oedipal stimulus and likely to impair ability.
(b) Beating dad is OK. This was also regarded as Oedipal but likely to enhance ability.
(c) People are working. (d) Mommy and I are one. (c) Daddy and I are one. For the purposes of this discussion these three stimuli are not important.

In all, four experiments with thirty subjects were carried out, this number to ensure that any results were not simply artefacts of light levels or other experimental conditions. In fact, as predicted and in accord with psychoanalytic theory, according to the authors, stimulus (a) did impair performance while stimulus (b) improved it, but this occurred only in low-illumination conditions with all but two subjects showing the pattern. Silverman et al. (1978) argue that these results support the psychoanalytic concept of the Oedipus complex.

Discussion of results

The first point to note is the psychoanalytic assumption built into these results — namely that ability to play darts is related to Oedipal conflict. Inasmuch as the results support the prediction, it is clearly not unreasonable unless there is some more simple explanation. Thus the question becomes Is there another explanation of the findings? In fact it seems to us there is not. Only Oedipal theory would predict that 'beating dad is OK' and 'is wrong' would, when shown subliminally, affect dart-throwing ability. It should be pointed out that dart-throwing ability is a simple skill. The argument is that Oedipal anxiety would destroy motor control rather than that dart-playing is a skill specially likely to be affected by Oedipal conflict, although the sexual symbolism of the dart game is probably a factor that should not be entirely ignored.

Conclusions

This experiment does provide support for psychoanalytic theory, for it is an unlikely result. However, much more work would have to be done before the Oedipus complex could be said to be supported unequivocally.

STUDY OF PENIS ENVY BY TOUHEY

Touhey (1977) carried out one of the few studies of penis envy, administering the castration-complex card of the Blacky Pictures (see p. 110 for a full description), which shows a dog with a knife impending over its tail, to eighty-seven female undergraduates. The top 48 per cent scorers were labelled high on penis envy, the rest low. An anthropological film of female sub-incision rites was then shown to all subjects of whom half were told that it was a fairly painless initiation ceremony, while the others were informed that it was powerful and long-lasting punishment. The high-penis-envy group, who were told that the film was a punishment, compared with the others, approved of the procedures, thought that females should see the film and wanted to see it again.

These results can be thought of as supporting psychoanalytic theory since those with penis envy could perhaps be expected to approve of punishing sub-incision more than should controls. Thus in conclusion this study offers some support for the concept of penis envy but far more extensive research is required before penis envy can be regarded as properly substantiated.

THE WORK OF BARTON ET AL. (1977)

These authors carried out a factorial study of 333 mothers and 307 fathers who completed a child-rearing practice questionnaire (CRPQ). Factor scores derived from this test were then used to predict the HSPQ scores of the children of these subjects. The variables of the HSPQ are fully described in Chapter 4.

From the viewpoint of the need to gather evidence for the concept of the Oedipus complex factor G of the HSPQ, super-ego, is obviously critical. In fact G loaded on two family environment factors. One was a factor defining a rather cold family background, low on punishment, warmth and praise, with lack of affection and inadequate behavioural control; the other was a factor which stressed reasoning in the family and also high punishment.

Neither of these two factors is really what would have been predicted from Freudian theory although it is interesting that the effects of high and low punishment are so similar — a bipolarity which Freud often stressed in his developmental theories and one abhorred by experimental psychologists.

Generally this research is not particularly useful for elucidating the Oedipus complex because no true measure of it was used. However, as a model of how environmental determinants of personality can be empirically scrutinized, it is an excellent study.

FURTHER STUDIES

Finally, it is interesting to examine some of the experimental evidence cited by Fisher and Greenberg (1977) which we ignored in our previous edition, in some cases due to less efficient research procedures than those of these authors, but usually because they cite evidence which in our view is not properly pertinent to the Oedipus complex. In certain cases the work which they cite is discussed in our chapter on mental provinces, a subject which they do not separately treat. Their work falls under several headings and we shall scrutinize these.

Evidence of pre-Oedipal closeness to mother

However, whether an infant is closer to the same or opposite sex parent cannot be regarded as evidence for or against the Oedipal complex. First the Oedipus complex does not develop until the phallic stage, around the age of four years. Furthermore, the Oedipus complex refers to sexual feelings towards the mother and these are not necessarily the same as overt feelings of attraction or repulsion. The characteristically *Freudian* aspect of the Oedipus complex is its sexualization and it is this which demands evidence.

Attitudes at Oedipal stage to parents

Many of the same arguments apply to this work. Overt attitudes may or may not be correlated with sexualized feelings if these exist. Some of the studies employed doll-play as a projective technique. This, however, is evidence similar to that used by psychoanalysts, albeit not identical. The reliability and validity of doll-play tests is not such as could allow them to be used as objective evidence (e.g. Vernon, 1964). Again, therefore, we do not regard most of this work as worthy of detailed study.

The work of Imber (1969). However, Fisher and Greenberg (1977) do describe one highly pertinent research — a doctoral dissertation by Imber (1969) which however must be treated with extreme caution. Imber grouped male subjects into high and low Oedipal-conflict categories by means of the Blacky Pictures (Blum, 1949). These subjects were then conditioned by mild shock into classifying words as either benevolent or threatening. At this point subjects had to classify the words father and mother. High Oedipal subjects had more difficulty responding to father than did low Oedipal subjects. There was no difference for mother.

Imber and Fisher and Greenberg all claim that this result confirms Oedipal theory (without incidentally adducing reasons). Now, in our view, this result by no means is confirmatory. It surely could be argued that there should be equal disturbance over mother. Since in a later part of this study this was also found (using heart-rate) and since this finding which did not apply to father is also used as support for Oedipal theory, it seems to us that in this research any result could be said to support the theory other than no differences between the groups. For this reason we cannot accept Fisher and Greenberg's claim that this experiment confirms Freudian theory. It seems to us to confirm that Fisher and Greenberg are not sufficiently critical in their analysis of experiments, and confirms, again, that unpublished theses are not usually worthy of scrutiny.

Loss of love

Fisher and Greenberg argue that females should be characterized by a greater

concern than males about loss of love (a derivation from the Electra com
While this derivation may be possible, it seems to us that even if females
shown to be so characterized, this could not be used as confirmation of the f
Oedipus complex. After all, it could be a simple social phenomenon that fe
are more concerned, a role-expectation of current western culture. To invoke
concepts as curious as the Oedipus complex to account for the results is far from
parsimonious not to say tenuous. For this reason we shall not discuss researches of
this sort.

Vaginal—clitoral erotogenicity

Fisher and Greenberg (1977) argue that in Oedipal theory the psychosexually
mature woman should experience vaginal rather than clitoral erotogenicity. In the
first edition of this book we did not touch upon this topic because there was
simply no research relevant to it. This lacuna has to some extent been filled by
Fisher (1973).

The work of Fisher (1973). Fisher, in his study of the female orgasm,
questioned a sample of women concerning their sexual preferences. Those that
preferred vaginal rather than clitoral stimulation appeared to be more rather than
less well-adapted (using everyday indices of adjustment, such as visits to doctors
and descriptions of their relationships with family and friends rather than
validated measures of anxiety). In addition the vaginal women described their
fathers as cold and aloof.

Even if this evidence is not fully quantified as ideally as it should be if we are to
regard it as fully objective, there can be no doubt that these results are actually
contrary to psychoanalytic theory. There is also a further, perhaps more
important, point (which is surprisingly not mentioned by Fisher and Greenberg).
This concerns the doubt whether there is any difference between clitoral and
vaginal orgasm. Masters and Johnson (1966) in their study of female sexuality
claimed that physiologically there was no distinction, hence the shift from clitoral
to vaginal erotogenicity cannot be meaningful. However, even if the orgasm is
physiologically identical, it could still remain an important psychological fact that
the clitoris or vagina is the preferred source of excitation. Thus the force of
Masters and Johnson's findings for psychoanalytic theory is uncertain, in our
view. However, it indubitably deserves careful consideration.

Maladjustment

Fisher and Greenberg (1977) argue quite correctly that maladjustment should be
related to the possession of an unresolved Oedipal conflict. For this reason they
proceed to scrutinize investigations concerned with the effects of losing a father
during the Oedipal period.

The problem here is that any effects on psychological adjustment or neurotic
behaviour, even if found, while in accord with Oedipal theory, can be explicated,
and would be by most psychologists, without reference to the Oedipus complex.
Thus if fathers play any part in enabling children to develop fully, then their

absence will affect this development. Only if precise and valid measures of the Oedipus complex were available (and they are not) would studies of children who have suffered the loss of a father be useful for testing the theory.

An example of this lack of precision can be seen in Fisher and Greenberg who cite as evidence in favour of the Oedipus complex a study which showed that children who had lost fathers during the Oedipal period manifested 'significant disturbances in their identification with father' (*sic*). Now surely we do not need an Oedipus complex to explain the fact that children without fathers to identify with do not identify with them as clearly as controls.

Such investigations, therefore, in our view cannot constitute objective evidence for psychoanalytic theory although, to be fair, if it turned out that children whose fathers had died were better adjusted as adults, they could refute it. No such refutatory investigations, however, have been reported.

CONCLUSIONS FROM ALL THE STUDIES OF THE CASTRATION AND OEDIPUS COMPLEXES

The conclusions to be drawn from these studies may be briefly summarized:

1. Direct questions of parental preference are not relevant to the Oedipus complex (Friedman, 1952; Kuppuswamy, 1949).
2. There is good evidence for the Oedipus complex (Friedman, 1950a, b; Hall, 1963).
3. There is good evidence for the castration complex (Friendman, 1950a, b; Schwartz, 1956; Sarnoff and Corwin, 1959; Stephens, 1961; Hall and Van De Castle, 1963).

TABLE 6.4. *Summary of findings on the castration complex and Oedipus complex*

Investigation	Result	Comments
Kuppuswamy (1949)	No support	Inadequate methodology
Friedman (1952)	Support for O anc C	Large sample, projective measures
Miller (1968)	Support for O	Preference for pictures
Michal-Smith et al. (1951)	Some support for O	Case study with Blacky Pictures
Schwartz (1955, 1956)	Support for C	Projective measures
Biddle (1957)	No support for O	Hypnotic regression used of questionable validity
Silverman et al. (1978)	Support for O	Subliminal technique
Lasky and Berger (1959)	Some support for C	Blacky Pictures with surgical patients

Investigation	Result	Comments
Hammer (1953)	Some support for C	HTP projective test
Sarnoff and Corwin (1959)	Support for C	Experimental technique used. Very powerful evidence
Stephens (1961)	Support for C	Cross-cultural study. Very powerful evidence
Whiting et al. (1958)	Some support for O	Cross-cultural study
Block and Ventur (1963)	Some support for C	Blacky Pictures used with amputees
Touhey (1977)	Support for penis envy	Experimental method and Blacky Pictures
Levin (1966)	No support for C	Rorschach used, of dubious validity
Kreitler and Kreitler (1966)	No support for C	Interview data, of unknown validity
Dream studies by Hall and associates (1955-63)	Support for O and C	Based on analysis of dream content

PSYCHOANALYTIC THEORY AND STUDIES OF MATERNAL DEPRIVATION

Since psychoanalytic developmental theory stresses the importance of early infantile experience on later adult personality and since the mother is clearly, in western child-rearing procedures at least, a key figure in such experiences, it is generally assumed that studies of maternal deprivation are of great relevance to psychoanalytic theory. This view is reinforced by the fact that many of the investigations of the effects of maternal deprivation have been carried out by researchers with psychoanalytic orientations, for example Bowlby (1944) and Anna Freud and Burlingham (1944).

Before it is possible to interpret the results of these studies, a number of points need clarification and certain methodological problems need to be understood.

THE MEANNG OF MATERNAL DEPRIVATION

Yarrow (1961) points out that 'the concept of maternal deprivation is a rather muddled one.' Thus in the literature the term has been used to encompass such different events as institutionalization, separation from the mother or mother substitute, multiple mothering and distortions in the quality of maternal care. A major problem of research in this area is that, for obvious reasons, it is often difficult to find samples where only one of these events has occurred. Institutionalization often takes place just because there are severe distortions in the quality of maternal care or because the child has perforce been separated from his mother. Where separation is due to death the traumatic nature of death itself may produce effects independent of the separation.

THE RELEVANCE OF STUDIES OF MATERNAL DEPRIVATION TO PSYCHOANALYTIC THEORY

Of course it must be pointed out, before discussing the consequences of maternal deprivation in the light of Freudian theory, that Bowlby himself is in the English rather than the classical tradition of psychoanalysis. This means his interest in maternal deprivation is not the same as that of an orthodox Freudian. Thus he explicitly states (1969) that he has abandoned the psychical energy model of Freudian theory which only a few psychoanalysts have done. He has done this for a number of reasons, chief of which is his claim that the model is unrelated to the concepts that 'Freud, and everyone since, regards as truly central to psychoanalysis — the role of unconscious mental processes, repression as a process actually keeping them unconscious, transference as a main determinant of behaviour, the origin of neurosis in childhood trauma'.

The psychical energy model

In 'The neuro-psychoses of defence' Freud (1894) drew up the model, arguing that in mental activity a quota of affect or a sum of excitation can be distinguished. This is capable of increase, diminution, displacement and discharge and is analogous to an electric current. Furthermore he claimed that two principles, inertia and constancy, govern the mental apparatus. The principle of inertia tends to keep the quantity of excitation within the system as low as possible, whereas the principle of constancy attempts to keep it constant. These last properties are more elaborately described in *A Project for Scientific Psychology* (1895a).

The object-relations model

In place of this Bowlby (1969) has used the *object-relations model*. He states that unlike the psychical energy model that was taken from current scientific thought and was not implicit in the clinical data gathered by Freud, the object-relations model is derived from clinical experience and from the data obtained during analysis of patients. From the viewpoint adopted in this book this is, of course, no recommendation! For the whole point of this book is to attempt to underpin Freudian theory with observations and data more satisfactory by the criteria of science than of clinical experience and analysis of patients, on which most of Freudian theory is based.

Since this model is a product of clinical data, cannot be regarded as scientific and is a long way removed from orthodox theory, a brief description must suffice. Bowlby uses his own version of the model although he admits to being strongly influenced by the work of Melanie Klein, Balint, Winnicott and Fairbairn. His model employs a view of instinctive behaviour similar to that of ethology. The central concepts are 'those of behavioural systems and their control, of information, negative feedback and a behavioural form of homeostasis'. Complex behaviour is supposed to depend on the execution of plans initiated on the receipt of certain information and guided and terminated by the continuous reception of more information originating from the results of the actions already taken (feedback). The use of this model means that Freudian instinct theory, the pleasure principle and defence mechanisms are no longer employed.

This means that Bowlby cannot be considered a traditional psychoanalyst. His work, therefore, is not strictly relevant to Freudian theory. Furthermore his theory is based on data no more sound, except that they involve the observation of children, than those of psychoanalysis. However, since his work concerns a field that is obviously important in orthodox, psychoanalytic theory — maternal deprivation — his studies will be evaluated for the light they throw on the theory. They will not be considered with reference to object-relation theory.

Even if we accept the fact that Freudian theory lays such emphasis on the importance of early experience, it is still pertinent to ask exactly what hypotheses would be adduced from psychoanalytic theory concerning the effects of maternal deprivation, at least in perhaps its most important meaning of maternal separation. As our descriptions of psychoanalytic developmental theory have made clear, by around the age of four or five years the Oedipus complex has developed. This is repressed by the castration complex and this in turn becomes quiescent through the development of the super-ego. While this applies to boys, in girls the castration complex (penis envy) comes first and brings about the Electra complex which in turn is gradually superseded as the super-ego develops. (See pp. 130 and 131 for the Freudian theories.) From this outline of developmental theory it is clear that for boys, maternal deprivation in all its forms, but especially maternal separation, should produce disturbances in the Oedipus complex, the castration complex and super-ego development. The Freudian concept of identification may also be invoked (see p. 181 for the theory). Since identification with the mother can normally be expected, disturbances in this area would also be hypothesized. In addition the age at time of separation could be expected to be important. Thus children who were separated from their mother at the oral phase might develop symptoms typical of oral fixation whereas those separated later, at the anal stage, might develop correspondingly different symptoms.

The effects of maternal deprivation according to psychoanalytic theory may be summarized as follows:

1. Disturbance in super-ego development due to prior disturbances of the Oedipal and castration complexes.
2. Disturbances of identification.
3. Psychosexual fixations depending upon the age of the child at separation.

PROBLEMS OF EMPIRICAL RESEARCH

As should now be clear to readers of the previous chapters, the empirical validation of these hypotheses is beset by grievous problems.

1. There are no fully adequate, well-validated measures of the Oedipal or castration complexes. The Dynamic Personality Inventory (Grygier, 1961a) does not appear to be valid (see p. 31) though the Blacky Pictures (Blum, 1949) are at least worth using in an exploratory manner (see p. 113).

2. Super-ego functions might be equated, for the purposes of testing, with moral behaviour. This means, for example, that murderers may be regarded as a group with faulty super-ego development.

3. Measures of identification are difficult to develop — but see the section on identification (p. 181).

4. Measures of psychosexual fixation are to some extent validated, e.g. the Blacky Pictures (which incidentally contain measures of super-ego and identification), the DPI anal scales (Grygier, 1961a) and the Goldman-Eisler (1951) oral scale.

These last two psychometric measures are, of course, only suitable for use with adults.

There are thus very considerable problems of measurement in the validation of psychoanalytic hypotheses concerning maternal deprivation. In addition there are further difficulties in research into this area.

5. The meaning of maternal deprivation has already been mentioned and four meanings were distinguished (Yarrow, 1961). However from the viewpoint of the empirical validation of psychoanalytic theory these four meanings are still likely to have deleterious effects, in that they all represent disturbances of the mother—child relationship. However the institutionalized child lives in an institution and here differences in institutional regimes are likely to confound results. Furthermore normal control groups, by definition, do not live in institutions. This means that an analysis of variance design using types of institution as a factor has to be drawn up. Again the traumatic experience of parental death can confound results.

6. Immediate or retrospective studies. Retrospective studies of delinquents or neurotics suffer from the difficulty of accurately assessing the infantile history. This is particularly important in the case of maternal separation. This maternal separation may be complete or partial, it may vary in length and it may have occurred once, or on many occasions, as with the unfortunate foster-child shifted from home to home or the child whose parent suffers a succession of serious operations or is himself subjected to intermittent hospitalization. If maternal separation has any effects whatever, it is apparent that such variations in maternal separation are important. It is also essential to the third hypothesis (psychosexual fixations result from maternal separation) that the age at which separations occurred must be known.

Immediate studies, on the other hand, of infants who have been maternally deprived in any of the senses distinguished above, are not of so great a relevance to psychoanalytic theory. Thus we do not need psychoanalytic theory to understand the anxiety of the infant who has just come to hospital and left his mother. What is distinctive about psychoanalytic theory is that it postulates long-term effects on personality of such experiences. Here, then, longitudinal studies appear the best answer to this problem.

In summary, the problems of validating psychoanalytic developmental theory by studying the effects of maternal deprivation are manifold. The main ones are:

1. Problems of measurement.
2. Problems arising from the fact that the inevitable concomitants of maternal deprivation may have confounding effects.
3. Problems of obtaining the deprivation data.

DESIGN OF INVESTIGATIONS

Control groups

Control groups appear to be an essential ingredient of any research into the effects of maternal deprivation and they constitute a great difficulty in this type of research. Thus institutionalized children have no equivalents — i.e. there are no children in institutions who are not separated from their mothers. In many cases (e.g. Bowlby, 1944) there is the added complication of mental disease in the family. This may even have been the cause of the child's separation. Thus it may be difficult to find control children with schizophrenic mothers who are not separated from them. Again if hospitalized children are the object of study, then to find controls without hospitalization but the same disease is hard. Yet without a control group the finding that a high percentage of neurotics suffered maternal deprivation is of no value as evidence for a causal link between deprivation and neurosis.

Longitudinal studies

Longitudinal studies of infants with known histories of maternal deprivation up to adulthood are clearly best. Retrospective studies can at least deal with adult personality but are weak as regards their deprivation data. The reverse is true of direct studies of infants but direct studies are not very relevant to psychoanalytic theory.

Measures

Replicable, reliable and valid measures are essential. This means that tests must be used. Psychiatric diagnosis, even if made by more than one psychiatrist based on a clinical interview, cannot be regarded as scientific data.

Beck (1962) and Beck et al. (1962) have summarized the case against psychiatric diagnosis as a useful research method. In the first paper Beck reviews a number of studies of the reliability of psychiatric diagnosis among different psychiatrists. A few examples of the results of the best-designed studies make the point quite clear. Thus Masserman and Carmichael (1938) followed up 100 patients. In 40 per cent of these subjects diagnosis required a major revision one year after discharge from hospital. In fact it is clear that these patients had changed so that the low degree of agreement is, rather, a comment on the instability of the nomenclature. But, if these psychiatric classifications have so little temporal stability, it is pertinent to question their value.

Mehlman (1952), in a most convincing investigation, studied the frequency distribution of diagnosis among a number of psychiatrists to whom a total of 4036 patients had been assigned in the course of their work. There was a statistically significant difference in the frequencies with which each psychiatrist used the various diagnostic labels in categorizing their patients. This is very powerful evidence that psychiatrist rather than patient variance is important in psychiatric diagnosis. Schmidt and Fonda (1956) studied agreement between two psychiatrists in the diagnostic classification of 426 patients. Excluding organic cases the percentage agreement was only 42. Finally Pasamanick et al. (1959) conducted an investigation similar to that of Mehlman (1952). As previously, they found that individual psychiatrists significantly favoured certain diagnostic classifications. They were forced to conclude that 'psychiatric diagnosis is at present so unreliable as to merit very serious question when classifying, studying and treating patients' behaviour and outcomes.'

Beck et al. (1962), in a further study of the reliability of clinical judgements and ratings, studied the agreement in diagnostic classification of four psychiatrists with a total of 153 patients. These psychiatrists, although their classifications were quite independent, had previously discussed beforehand and reached consensus concerning the specific criteria for each category. In this study the overall agreement was higher than that in most others — 54 per cent. However, this agreement varied for the different nosological categories, ranging from 63 per cent for neurotic depressive down to only 38 per cent for personality-trait disturbance. This last figure is of particular interest as regards the study of the effects of maternal deprivation, since it is likely that many of the psychiatric assessments will fall under this head. In any case Beck et al. conclude that, although this overall rate of agreement — 54 per cent — was higher than in other investigations, it is still *not adequate for research purposes*.

From the evidence discussed above it must, therefore, be concluded that psychiatric ratings and diagnoses cannot be regarded as objective evidence for the scientific study of our psychoanalytic hypotheses.

The validity of measures of the Oedipus and castration complexes is not high. Thus it might be better to use more generally acceptable tests of neurosis, e.g. the 16PF or MMPI rather than the more risky Dynamic Personality Inventory.

Statistical analysis

If defined groups are compared with control groups an analysis of variance design would appear to be the most suitable. In this way the effects of different types of institutional regime might be taken into account.

In the light of this discussion of the problems involved in the testing of hypotheses concerning the effects of maternal deprivation, of the empirical propositions derivable from psychoanalytic theory and of possible research designs, it is now fitting to examine the objective investigations. For convenience, the categorization of researches used by Yarrow (1961) will be followed: investigations of institutionalized children and maternal separation will be examined separately. Where appropriate a subdivision of retrospective and immediate studies will be made. Finally studies of other aspects of maternal deprivation will be reviewed.

STUDIES OF MATERNAL SEPARATION

As has been indicated, studies of maternal separation represent perhaps the best method of studying the hypotheses derived from Freudian theory because there is likely to be less confounding effect from the regimes of the foster home or institution than in the case of institutionalized children.

Retrospective or longitudinal studies

These are the studies most relevant to Freudian developmental theory which predicts long-term effects on personality from maternal separation. Studies at the time of separation are not of such great importance (from the viewpoint of psychoanalytic validation).

Bowlby (1944) in his study of forty-four juvenile thieves and controls, Lewis (1954) who examined 500 children in a reception centre, Bowlby et al. (1956) who studied sixty children in a tuberculosis sanatorium and controls, and Berg and Cohen (1959) who investigated forty schizophrenic and forty neurotic women, are the only studies where *long-term effects* of maternal separation are investigated. All these are retrospective.

Method of obtaining separation data

In all these studies the separation data were obtained by interviews with subjects and their parents and guardians and by details recorded from case histories and files. Thus for each subject in each study the data clearly varied in accuracy.

Measurement techniques

Bowlby (1944) used psychiatric diagnoses. He classified subjects into types, e.g. affectionless character, schizoid character. Since he also carried out the rest of the examination, there is a risk of contamination on the diagnosis. Lewis (1954) followed up a number of his sample: the data consisted of case reports by psychiatrists and social workers. Bowlby et al. (1956) used intelligence tests (which are irrelevant to Freudian theory) and clinical evaluations from a number of sources. Berg and Cohen (1959) examined the case histories of their samples.

From this it is clear that none of these studies contains basic data from which it is possible to draw any objective conclusions. None of the studies is replicable except by the investigators making the original judgements, the validity and reliability of which are quite unknown. These deficiencies are so serious that the fact that control groups were used by Bowlby (1944) and Bowlby et al. (1956) makes them no more admissible.

Conclusions

Clearly, therefore, no conclusions can be based on such inadequate data and it is not surprising that the outcome of these studies was so diverse. Bowlby (1944) found maternal deprivation was linked to the affectionless character but Bowlby et al. (1956) were forced to admit that such a link was an overstatement of the case. Lewis (1954) found a great variety of effects and Berg and Cohen (1959) found separation important in schizophrenia. The only firm conclusion we can draw from these studies is that they were inadequate to give objective validation to the psychoanalytic hypotheses.

Direct or immediate studies

These are not so relevant to psychoanalytic theory. In all cases the data, apart from intelligence (e.g. Schaffer, 1958), are from clinical observation. Thus studies of maternal separation have not been sufficiently rigorous to support or refute psychoanalytic theory.

STUDIES OF INSTITUTIONALIZED CHILDREN

With studies of institutionalized children, whether retrospective or current, a major problem lies in the variance of child-rearing regimes among different institutions and the fact that institution life differs from family life in more ways than just mother-separation.

Retrospective studies

Goldfarb (1943, 1944, 1945, 1947, 1949) carried out a series of famous studies of institutionalized children. Although most of the children in these studies were pre-pubertal and therefore, perhaps, too young to test adequately the Freudian hypotheses, Goldfarb (1947) did test two samples of adolescent boys. However in none of the studies were there valid or reliable measures of personality. Examples of the instruments used make this clear — the Newell Checklist (1943) and the Rorschach (1949). In other instances, except in his measures of intellectual capacity which are not relevant to psychoanalytic theory, clinical assessments only were used. Thus these investigations by Goldfarb cannot be used to provide objective evidence for psychoanalytic theory.

Beres and Obers (1950), in another well-known study, examined thirty-seven clinical cases who had been in institutions when children. These authors questioned the long-term effects of such institutionalization on overt adjustment.

Again, however, little weight can be put on their conclusions since psychiatric diagnoses were the source of their data.

The present writer can find in the literature no retrospective study of institutionalized children in which any acceptable personality measures have been used. Thus, despite the fact that Goldfarb's work is much quoted, it must be concluded that no objective validation or refutation of psychoanalytic theory can be obtained from such studies.

Current studies

These are of far less interest to psychoanalytic theory unless they contain specific measures of Oedipal or castration conflict or problems of identification and psychosexual fixation. In fact no such studies have been conducted.

As was the case with the investigations of separation from the mother, it must be concluded that no objective evidence relevant to psychoanalytic theory has come from studies of institutionalized children. This is partly because the investigators have not been, in the main, concerned with hypotheses drawn from classical psychoanalytic theory and, perhaps more importantly, because they have relied on clinical assessments and psychiatric classifications when dealing with personality variables.

RESEARCH ON MULTIPLE MOTHERING

Rabin (1957, 1958a and 1958b) has studied Kibbutz children and controls in a number of studies using a variety of tests. Since the personality assessment in the first two investigations was by means of the Rorschach which is not regarded by the present writer as being capable of providing objective evidence, these studies may be ignored. In the final investigation, however, he used the Blacky Pictures in order to assess differences in Oedipal strength. This study has been fully discussed on p. 140 in the section on the Oedipus and castration complexes. His main finding was that, as expected, Kibbutz children had less Oedipal intensity and a more diffuse identification than their controls. This provided, therefore, some support for Freudian theory.

THE WORK OF HINDE

Although, in general, we have eschewed animal experiments as usually having little relevance to psychoanalytic theory, we shall now mention some animal work, that of Hinde and his colleagues in Cambridge, which is pertinent to the problem of infant—mother separation and hence, ultimately, to the Oedipus complex, although this was probably far from Hinde's intention in conducting his investigations.

Hinde, who has published extensively on this topic (e.g. Hinde and McGinnis, 1977; White and Hinde, 1975), found that with rhesus monkeys (so extrapolation to other species, let alone to man, must be cautious) where the infant—mother relationship had been good, separation produced no lasting effect. Where, however, it had been poor, then disruptive effects were seen. It is to be noted that his measures of the infant—parent relationship were objective: a good relationship was one in which infants' approaches to mothers were accepted; a bad relationship was one where such approaches were rejected or ignored.

We do not want to go into detail over these experiments because (Darwin notwithstanding) rhesus monkeys are rhesus monkeys and human beings are human beings. Nevertheless this finding would explain disparate results of research if it were true of human beings: deprivation only disrupts later behaviour where the original relationship is poor. Since the Oedipus complex is a description of the essence of this relationship, it can be argued that these findings imply that the effects of maternal deprivation on behaviour, as predicted in psychoanalytic theory, are likely to be found only where this original infant—mother relationship is bad.

It could indeed be argued that what is meant by a bad relationship as here objectively defined is perhaps the actual dyadic interaction which produces an Oedipus complex — hence the consequences of maternal deprivation. This however is a tenuous argument.

Rather, it seems to us, the relevance of these Hinde studies is to the equivocal research on matenial deprivation rather than to psychoanalytic theory *per se*.

CONCLUSIONS FROM ALL STUDIES OF MATERNAL DEPRIVATION

1. Current studies of infants, unless they concentrate on specific Freudian concepts such as the Oedipus complex, are not really relevant to psychoanalytic theory.

2. The retrospective studies carried out so far are vitiated by their measurement techniques. Psychiatric classifications, clinical assessments and case-study reports cannot be regarded as objective data.

3. Only one study, that by Rabin (1958b), is therefore relevant to the scientific validation of psychoanalytic theory. This has been previously discussed in the section on the Oedipus complex, which it supports to some extent.

7

The structure of the mind

For the brief summary of the theory that follows three main papers were used:

(a) 'The question of lay analysis' (Freud, 1926),
(b) *New Introductory Lectures in Psychoanalysis* (Freud, 1933),
(c) 'An outline of psychoanalysis' (Freud, 1940).

SUMMARY OF THE THEORY

According to Freud the mental apparatus is divided into three parts: id, ego and super-ego.

The id

'To the oldest of these mental provinces or agencies we give the name of id. It contains everything that is inherited, that is present at birth, that is fixed in the constitution — above all therefore the instincts' (Freud, 1940). Freud likens it to a cauldron of seething excitement. It is the core of our being within which the instincts operate and their sole endeavour is to seek satisfaction regardless of consequences, situation or logic.

Thus the id obeys *the pleasure principle*. Its mental processes, subject to no laws of logic, are regarded as *primary processes* and are *unconscious*.

The ego

'The ego was developed out of the cortical layer of the id, which, being adapted for the reception and exclusion of stimuli, is in direct contact with the external world' (Freud, 1940). Its function consists of interposing, between id demands and satisfying actions, intellectual activity aimed at calculating the consequences of any proposed behaviour. Thus the ego must decide whether the satisfaction may be carried out or postponed or whether the demand of the instinct should be altogether suppressed. *This is the reality principle.* If the main aim of the id is pleasure the main aim of the ego is safety. Some ego activities are *conscious*, some *preconscious* (defined as capable of becoming conscious), and others unconscious.

An example of conscious ego activity obeying the reality principle is the idea that there is a suitable time and place for everything. Preconscious ego activity is only too obvious in the examination hall when the vital facts refuse to come to mind often until the very moment the exam is over. Unconscious ego activity, on the other hand, is best exemplified in the defence mechanisms, e.g. rationalization

— the finding of good reasons for what we want to do. The processes of the ego and the preconscious are referred to as *secondary processes*.

The super-ego

'The long period of childhood ... leaves behind it a precipitate which forms within the ego a special agency in which the parental influence is prolonged. It has received the name of super-ego.' This super-ego is regarded in Freudian theory as the heir of the Oedipus complex. It internalizes what had been part of the external world (the parents) and continues to carry on their functions: 'it observes the ego, gives it orders, corrects it and threatens it with punishments exactly like the parents whose place it has taken' (Freud, 1940). We are, of course, aware of it as our conscience. Often it is more severe than the parents ever were.

From this outline of the mental structure, as hypothesized in psychoanalytic theory, it is clear that mental activity has a dynamic quality. The ego has to satisfy the instinctual demands of the id and the moral dictates of the super-ego. Indeed this is the aim of psychoanalytic therapy — to strengthen the ego and to make it more independent of the super-ego. Where id was there shall ego be (Freud, 1933).

Finally, since id activity is wholly unconscious, as is part of ego and super-ego activity, it may be justly asked how psychoanalysis can make any claims about it. The evidence for this mental structure comes from free associations and dream material. In dreams, for example — 'the royal road to the unconscious' — it is hypothesized that the ego is relaxed and that id material, although distorted by the censor, is nearer the surface. By dream-analysis it is possible to learn and understand the workings of the unconscious mind. The objective evidence for this part of Freudian theory will be examined in a later chapter in this book.

IMPORTANCE OF THE THEORY

It should be clear from the outline description of the theory that the concepts of id, super-ego and ego are crucial to psychoanalytic theory as a whole. These structures are basic to one of the most important findings of psychoanalysis — that behaviour has unconscious motivation. They are also vital in the Freudian theory of neurosis and psychosis. Indeed it is their dynamic balance that accounts for all behaviour.

PROBLEMS IN THE OBJECTIVE VERIFICATION OF THE THEORY

Any attempt to provide objective, scientifically acceptable evidence for these structures is beset with difficulties. Perhaps the most profound problem is that scientific methods, as traditionally conceived, eschew the study of mental processes on the justifiable grounds that they are not public events open to precise observation. This view finds reinforcement in the behaviouristic claim that in the study of behaviour the concept of mind is irrelevant, as stressed by Miles (1965).

Nevertheless since Freudian theory *is* concerned with mental processes objective study of it demands that they be investigated.

The scientific investigation of the Freudian theory of mental structure necessitates a clear statement of just what empirical hypotheses and statements are implicit in the theory. One hypothesis is plain: there are three kinds of mental activity — conscious, preconscious and unconscious.

The empirical consequences of the actual tripartite division of the mind are, however, far more difficult to state. Nevertheless they may be discussed under two heads — physiological and behavioural.

Physiological hypothesis

If three physiological systems in the brain could be isolated with functions similar to those required by the Freudian structures this would provide good evidence for the theory. Nevertheless, as Alexander (1950) points out, this would mean stricter localization of brain function than is justified by evidence. A possible hypothesis, therefore, is that there are brain structures corresponding in function to the ego, super-ego and id.

Functional hypothesis

This hypothesis would stress the essentially *functional* nature of the structural theory. That is these divisions are divisions of function. Consequently the hypothesis would be that in certain behaviours three strands can be distinguished — rational (ego), moral (super-ego) and wishing (id). This would have to be the case in that behaviour is mediated by the dynamic balance of ego, super-ego and id. In essence it is a three-factor theory of motivation.

In summary three empirical hypotheses have been extracted from the structural theory:

1. that there are conscious, preconscious and unconscious mental events,
2. that there are brain structures corresponding in function to the ego, super-ego and id, and
3. that behaviour may be defined in terms of these three factors.

It is to be noted that hypothesis 2, the physiological hypothesis, is not implicit in Freudian theory but would provide very strong support for it if shown to be true.

Before examining the evidence for these three hypotheses it must be stated that there are other empirical statements implicit in the structural theory which will not be considered in this chapter. Thus, for example, the ego defences or defence mechanisms — one of the major functions of the ego — will be discussed in a separate chapter. So too will the nature of the id processes. These are claimed to be revealed in dreams and the objective evidence relevant to them will be examined in a further chapter. Indeed most of the theory of psychoanalysis consists of a detailed study of the functions of these three divisions of the mind so that in a sense the whole book is relevant to this problem.

There are, too, what may be regarded as quasi-empirical statements, e.g. the

super-ego is the heir to the Oedipus complex. However such a statement is very
hard to put in precisely testable form other than that moral behaviour is not to be
expected in the under-fives. Were this found to be true it would not constitute
impressive evidence for the super-ego! Readers can easily furnish more parsimonious hypotheses.

Consequently this chapter will be devoted to the evidence for the three
hypotheses outlined above. It must be remembered however that many of the
later chapters are also relevant to it although in a more indirect way.

EVIDENCE FOR THE HYPOTHESES

THAT THERE ARE CONSCIOUS, PRECONSCIOUS AND UNCONSCIOUS MENTAL PROCESSES

As these terms were defined by Freud there can be little doubt that it is indeed the
case. Some mental processes and memory content are conscious, i.e. we are aware
of them. As was shown in the outline, other material is preconscious in the sense
of capable of becoming conscious, e.g. the forgotten telephone number. As for
unconscious mental processes, ones of which we are not aware, from the time of
James these have been accepted and were demonstrated in the work on
suggestibility and hypnosis by Charcot and Janet. Thus the Freudian postulate of
an unconscious was not new (see Whyte, 1968). What was new, however, was the
emphasis he placed on it and his description of its nature, the primary processes,
based on dream-analysis and free association. Thus it can be seen that, as defined
by Freud, there are indeed three kinds of mental process — conscious, preconscious and unconscious. There is, however, little of psychological interest
in this hypothesis and it will not be further discussed.

THE PHYSIOLOGICAL HYPOTHESIS: THAT THERE EXIST THREE PHYSIOLOGICAL STRUCTURES IN THE BRAIN CORRESPONDING TO THE EGO, ID AND SUPER-EGO IN FUNCTION

It must be stated that this is not implicit in the Freudian structural theory
although Freud (1895a) did indicate that ultimately he thought all brain functions
would be tied down to brain mechanisms. Nevertheless it is clear that were three
such structures or systems discovered, they would constitute very strong, if not
irrefutable, evidence for the Freudian theory. It is therefore necessary to consider
the physiological evidence.

Studies testing the physiological hypothesis

In a study of the influence of Darwin on the work of Pavlov, Freud and Hughlings
Jackson, Magoun pointed out certain similarities in the concepts of these writers.
Thus the three levels of Jackson correspond to the id, ego and super-ego of Freud
and to the reflex, conditioned reflex and second signalling system of Pavlov. This

paper, without delineating any of the possible structures involved in the Freudian model, at least suggests that physiological correlates are possible.

It is, of course, tempting, and Grey-Walter (1961) succumbs, to attempt to locate these Freudian structures. Grey-Walter tentatively suggests the mid-brain for the id, and the sensory cortex for the ego. A brief examination of the physiological evidence reveals, however, that it is not possible to postulate structures corresponding to the Freudian provinces with any confidence. Indeed it is probably true to say that the precise function of almost no part of the brain can be stated, so that any attempt to relate neurophysiological concepts to the Freudian model is futile in our present state of knowledge. Grossman (1967), discussing the role of the cortex in emotion, is forced to conclude that so far the role of the central nervous system in the regulation of emotional behaviour is poorly understood. Thus the Papez (1937) theory of emotion which suggested that emotional experience was a function of the cingulate gyrus, which has connections with the hypothalamus — itself certainly concerned with the expression (if not the experience) of emotions — does not fully fit the data. Nor indeed does Maclean's (1949) revision of this theory in which the hippocampal formation was substituted for the cingulate gyrus. This is particularly unfortunate since both the hippocampus and the cingulate gyrus were tempting sites to locate the id.

Similarly the super-ego, at the height of the popularity for lobotomy, might have been postulated to reside in the frontal lobes — i.e. the frontal lobes were responsible for super-ego control. Moniz (1936), for example, claimed that mental diseases characterized by severe inhibition (super-ego) such as obsessional and anxiety states were considerably improved by lobotomy. However, as Grossman (1967) points out, results with this procedure have not been clear-cut and in some cases intellectual deficits outweigh any other advangages.

Arnold (1950) has proposed that the frontal lobes are concerned with the sympathetic aspects of emotion, which accounts for their regulatory function in anxiety. However, with our present knowledge it would be quite foolhardy to attempt to argue that the function of the super-ego was attributable to the frontal lobes.

Conclusion

There is no firm support from neurophysiological studies of brain function for the Freudian tripartite division of the mind. Brain function is not sufficiently well understood for this to be possible.

THE FUNCTIONAL HYPOTHESIS: THAT ID, EGO AND SUPER-EGO FACTORS OCCUR IN CERTAIN BEHAVIOUR

Clearly in some responses, e.g. adding $2+2$, ego functions predominate — hence the restriction to 'certain' behaviours.

The work of Cattell (1957)

The researches relevant to this third hypothesis are embodied in Cattell's studies of attitudes and interests, work that is far less known than his personality studies. An attitude is defined as a tendency to act in a particular way to a situation. Cattell is careful to stress that his definition embraces far more than the 'sociologists'' approach embodied in most attitude scales, of being for or against something. It will be seen that this definition of attitude used by Cattell embraces interests, in that interest in particular courses of action strongly affects tendencies to enact them or not. Indeed Cattell considers that these studies of attitude and interest are best subsumed under the label of motivation.

Attitudes and interests studied

(a) A major professional job attitude.
(b) A respectable hobby interest.
(c) A somewhat disreputable interest.
(d) An attitude with relatively strong unconscious roots.
(e) Another with a marked moral component.

Sample. 374 adult males.

Tests and scoring. The tests used were all objective devices using T data. The principles behind their construction were ingenious as a few examples indicate. Where interest has been strong in a field, a high level of information and perceptual skill was expected. Where new material is presented, memory will be best for topics of greatest interest. Motivation sharpens attention so that in the presentation of competing stimuli there will be selective attention in areas of interest. In addition physiological measures were used, e.g. GSR, muscle tension, blood pressure. These are only a selection of the measures used to indicate their nature. Scoring was *ipsative*. Thus the scores did not represent individual differences in level, but of changes within each individual. For each person the scores are standard scores from his own mean. This is of great importance in the interpretation of the rotated factors emerging from the intercorrelations of all these variables.

Results. The following factors emerged:

Motivation factor alpha: the id component in interests. Cattell describes this factor as characterized by autism — believing that what one wants is true or practicable — by high emphasis on stated preference, by rapid decisions, by fluency on cues, means and ends to desired goals and by rationalization. It has almost no cognitive content or physiological loadings.

'Clearly it represents a component in interest most nearly corresponding to the psychoanalytic concept of the id, though we must be definite that we are redefining this as conscious id' (Cattell, 1957). It appears to be an 'I desire' component, of which the individual is partly conscious but which he has not tested against reality.

Although this factor alpha, with its emphasis on desire and lack of reality, is not unconscious, it yet appears to be not unlike the id component as defined by Freud.

Motivation factor beta: the realized ego. This is considered to be the component realized, integrated interest: an ego component adjusted to super-ego and reality demands. The motivational elements loading on this factor include high informational content relevant to the field of interest, some perceptual skills and good capacity to learn in the interests of the activity together with a regard for remote but realistic rewards. Cattell hypothesizes that this factor is interests acquired through habit and duty, fully conscious and well-integrated into the daily habits of the self. 'It corresponds pretty closely to the psychoanalytic concept of ego forces — of habits acquired under the constraint of the super-ego and reality testing' (Cattell, 1957). Ipsatizing the scores rules out the possibility of the factor being interpreted as one of intelligence.

Again, as Cattell points out, there is a considerable resemblance to the ego functions as defined by Freud. Nevertheless before the identification of this factor could become entirely convincing the negative loadings of the PGR response would have to be studied further.

Factor gamma: component of the ideal, desired self, or unrealized super-ego. This factor, according to Cattell, is the most difficult to fit into existing psychoanalytic concepts because it overlaps with the alpha factor (negatively correlated) and with the beta factor. It shows autism, fantasy, some conscious preference for an activity and a complete absence of information about it.

There is no defensiveness about and no fluency on cues, means and ends. It is identified, albeit very tentatively, as the desired ideal self.

Super-ego is perhaps the nearest existing concept (in any psychology) to this factor, but it is clearly difficult to identify the factor with any confidence.

The other factors contributed much less to the variance and were not so well replicated from matrix to matrix. These will, therefore, receive much briefer treatment:

Factor delta: unconscious symphathetic system and circulatory sensitivity or biological interest. Cattell tentatively suggests that this factor delta is the entirely unconscious id contrasted with the preconscious id, factor alpha, with its wishful cognitive loadings.

Factor epsilon: interest component from repressed complexes. Although there are no preferences or overt verbal interests loading on this factor there are memory effects and PGR effects, such as have long been noted in word-association studies, e.g. the Kent—Rosanoff list. From this evidence Cattell hypothesizes that this component of interest arises from successful repression.

Cattell concludes by arguing that it is up to further research to find out whether these five factors have opened up methods for accurate quantitative assessment of the parts played by the Freudian mental provinces in motivation.

One final point must be made about this research. Since these five factors are oblique Cattell carried out a factorization of their inter-correlations. Two second-order factors emerged.

1. *Integrated self-sentiment interests*: beta and gamma, relevant to reality-oriented and morality-recognizing habit organizations, load on this.

2. *Unintegrated unconscious interests*: on this load delta, epsilon and alpha, the factors which have in common unintegrated desires and untested wishes and aspirations. Lack of integration with self is preferred to unconscious as the identification because the id factor, at least as measured here, is not unconscious.

Comments on the whole factor-analysis

It will be remembered that this study was invoked to investigate the hypothesis, derived from the structural theory, that there would be three motivational factors corresponding to ego, super-ego and id. Cattell certainly attempts to identify the primary factors with these Freudian concepts and the second-order analysis supports the dynamic analysis of human behaviour, ego and super-ego (reality principle) *v.* id (pleasure principle).

However it must be stated that any such identification of factors, as stated above, is tentative and provisional on further research. This is mainly due to the nature of the objective test variables.

As was discussed in the chapter on personality development, these objective tests have not been fully validated. Since face-validity is almost entirely irrelevant to their actual validity, a description of them would hardly be useful. Indeed their complexity and number is such as to make any kind of adequate discussion of them here out of place. For a full description, rationale and survey of the evidence, the reader is referred to Cattell and Warburton's compendium of objective tests (1967).

Conclusion

This study of motivation supports a three-factor theory, as demanded by the Freudian theory. The nature of the factors is not a bad fit to the hypothesis. However, the experimental nature of the variables makes definite identification risky. This study cannot therefore be regarded as strong support for the psychoanalytic theory. It is however possible to consider it as positive support which urgently needs further clarification. In its present state, for example, this factor-analysis supports equally well the Platonic tripartite concept of the mind, as propounded in the *Republic* or the *Phaedrus*.

It will be noted by readers that this basic research into motivation was carried out around twenty-five years ago. Although Cattell and his colleagues have published more recent surveys of this work on motivation (e.g. Cattell and Child, 1975; Cattell and Kline, 1977), there has been surprisingly a dearth of research into this aspect of it, so that our original description is not out-dated.

This is partly because much of the motivational research has concentrated upon the number and nature of the drives rather than the strength of interest components relevant to this chapter. It also reflects the unwillingness of workers in the fields of applied psychology to use the tests on which these factors depend, and without widespread practical application the necessary research data will not be accumulated.

The work of Pawlik and Cattell (1964)

Another similar approach to the three-factor hypothesis of motivation was used by Pawlik and Cattell who subjected a battery of objective personality variables to third-order factor-analysis.

Sample. Three samples were used, two consisting each of 86 college undergraduates, the other of 315 Navy Submarine School candidates. These three studies have been described previously (when second-order factors were extracted) by Cattell et al. (1961).

Tests. Objective test devices UI16-UI36 were used. For a description of these see p. 50 and, in more detail, Cattell and Warburton (1967).

Method. The correlations between the second-order factors were subjected to two oblique rotated factor-analyses — Oblimax and Maxplane (Pinzka and Saunders, 1954; Cattell and Muerle, 1960.)

Results. Three main factors emerged:

1. *Immature self-centred temperament*. Its principal loadings were on temperamental ardour, low self-consciousness and narcissistic development.
2. *Restrained acceptance of external norms*: tied socialization, low self-consciousness and history of restraining environment.
3. *High self-assertion*: this factor loaded most highly on expansive ego and tension to achieve. Here the two rotations gave results which were not identical. This solution, preferred by Cattell, is the Maxplane solution.

Interpretation and comments. This is best left to Pawlik and Cattell (1964). They write 'Although we did not start our studies with any predilections for psychoanalytic theory, it is a striking fact that the psychoanalytic descriptions of ego, id and super-ego would fit very well the three major patterns found in this research.'

Conclusions

Pawlik and Cattell admit that this identification with ego, super-ego and id is tentative and premature and that further replication is needed. Even more important, the validity of the original objective tests on which this study is based remains far from proven. Nevertheless these results may be regarded as tentative support for the functional hypothesis implicit in the Freudian theory of mental provinces.

Warburton (1968) submitted second-order factors from Gorsuch and Cattell (1967) — in this case derived from Cattell's 16PF questionnaire — to third- and fourth-order factor-analysis. Two factors finally emerged, *integration* and *morality*. Integration appears to be related to adaptation to the environment and changing it where adaptation is unsuitable. This research does not, therefore, support the three-factor theory. Nevertheless these two factors are again not unlike the ego and super-ego of Freudian theory.

To sum up, it is clear that these two studies illustrate the potential of higher-order factor-analysis to illuminate the functional hypothesis of psychoanalytic theory.

The IES test — a direct approach to the measurement of ego, super-ego and id behaviour

As was mentioned at the beginning of the chapter, one approach to the investigation of the Freudian concept of the mental apparatus is to investigate by means of tests the kinds of behaviour hypothesized in psychoanalytic theory to be subsumed by ego, id and super-ego. In this method obsessional neurotics would be expected to be dominated by their super-ego in contrast to, for example, psychopaths who would be dominated by their id. Careful examination of Freudian theory would allow many such hypotheses to be set up and investigated. Dombrose and Slobin (1958) have adopted this approach and developed what appears to be the only test of this type — the IES test.

The IES is designed to measure the relative strength of impulses (id), ego and super-ego. It consists of a number of sub-tests as described below.

1. *Picture-title test*

'This consists of 12 drawings, each showing activities and objects which may be classified into impulse and super-ego categories' (Dombrose and Slobin, 1958). Subjects simply have to give a title to each picture.

Scoring. An impulse score is given to a title referring to an impulse activity or area. Similarly a super-ego score is given if reference is made to a super-ego activity or area. An ego score is made where both these factors are fully integrated by the title. Finally there is a defensive category where the title is claimed to put great psychological distance between subject and picture. There is an appendix to this test to facilitate scoring.

2. *Picture story completion test*

Thirteen sets of cartoons, each set consisting of two or three cartoons, have to be completed by the subject. Each set may be completed by three cartoons, one of which is chosen by the subject. Thus for each story, depending on his choice, a subject scores on ego, impulses or super-ego. Scoring is, therefore, objective.

3. *Photo-analysis test*

This test consists of the photographs of nine men. Two multiple-choice (three possibilities) questions are posed to the subject about each of the men. Each multiple-choice response indicates an ego, super-ego or impulse score. The rationale is that by projection the responses indicate how the subject would like to function. Again scoring is objective.

4. *The arrow—dot test*

This is a performance test where the subject has to draw the shortest possible line from an arrow to a dot between which are barriers of solid lines which must not be crossed. In addition dashed lines and bars, not mentioned in the instructions, provide the subject with limitations 'as determined by self-needs' (Dombrose and Slobin, 1958). There are twenty-three of these problems. An appendix scores the majority of possible solutions in terms of EI or S. For example, lines going straight through forbidden barriers are scored I. An E score is obtained by the shortest and therefore most realistic path to the goal. An S score is obtained when subjects create their own barriers out of the dashed lines and refuse to go through the parallel bars.

Such then is the IES test. The reliability and validity of the test must now be briefly scrutinized. First the evidence presented by Dombrose and Slobin will be considered.

Reliability of the IES test

(a) *Test—retest reliability coefficients* for the three scores derived from the four tests were computed for a sample of thirty men under out-patient therapy. These ranged from 0.35 to 0.83. The median value was 0.62.

(b) *Internal-consistency reliability*. The Kuder—Richardson formula 20 (Richardson and Kuder, 1939) was used to compute these on three different small samples. The median value was 0.55, overestimated, since in six scores no figure was quoted because it was below 0.2.

(c) *Inter-scorer reliability*. Only the picture-title test demands judgements by the scorer. Here there was 91 per cent agreement by raters.

Comments

These reliabilities are too low to allow the test to be used with any confidence for individuals. For purposes of research with groups they are probably sufficiently high.

Validity of the IES test

The studies of the validity of the IES test quoted by Dombrose and Slobin are based on a number of doctoral dissertations presented at Western Reserve University (Alexander, 1954; Charnes, 1953; Dombrose and Slobin, 1951; Golden, 1954; Ritz, 1954). However, as Katkovsky (1965) points out, the description of these investigations is far too short for the construct-validity of the test to be accurately assessed. The basic method in all these validity studies has been to compare small samples of neurotics and psychotics, aged subjects in different environments, or latents and adolescents. Scores on the tests of all these groups are presented. Dombrose and Slobin (1958) claim that these results supported a high proportion of the psychoanalytically derived hypotheses. However they do not say which hypotheses, so that their adequacy is impossible to estimate. In addition, as Crowne (1965) emphasizes, there is no evidence as to what the IES does *not* measure (e.g. intelligence or social desirability) — a vital feature of any construct-validity study. Thus, although the scores in these doctoral investigations look sensible in the light of psychoanalytic theory, they cannot be considered as good evidence for the validity of the test which still needs to be taken on trust. Equally, however, these results do not *destroy* the test validity.

The norms of this test are clearly inadequate. All the samples used are far too small for normative purposes, e.g. fifty-seven aged subjects in three groups, thirty normals, fifteen neurotics, fifteen paranoids.

Later studies of the validity of the IES

Verrill and Costanza (1962) found no agreement between ratings for I, E and S by a psychiatric nurse of patients and test scores. It is not, of course, possible to say whether test, rater or both were wrong. Gilbert and Levee (1963) found no differences between young and menopausal women whom they predicted would show weaker ego and greater super-ego and id conflict. On what part of psychoanalytic theory this prediction was based is not clear. These two studies, therefore, do not support the validity of the test. On the other hand they are not rigorously enough designed to refute it.

Of the other published studies of the IES the only one which seems to bear on its validity is that of Herron (1962) who found that children institutionalized for parental neglect had lower ego and higher impulse scores than children reared in a family. To some extent, therefore, this study does support the validity of the I and E scores.

Crowne (1965) indeed concluded that given the lack of evidence for the validity of the IES, its low reliability and the crudity of the test materials, it was not surprising that rigorous researchers had not used the test — one reason indeed for the lack of evidence of validity.

More recent work has not really changed this position. Kline and Trejdosiewicz (1971) did carry out a pilot study of this test by administering it individually to a small sample of undergraduates together with the Blacky Pictures. There were no correlations between the Blacky Pictures and IES test where they would be predicted from the variables the test purported to measure. Even worse from the viewpoint of the validity of the IES test the scores of the British sample were significantly different from those of comparable American samples, but inconsistently. For example, scores were both larger and smaller than the American norms depending upon from which IES test they were derived. All this renders the validity of the IES test dubious in the extreme.

More recently Ammons and Ammons (1978) have published a bibliography of the IES test up to 1977. The published papers quoted do little more than use the test and the totality of results cannot be built up into a convincing case for the construct validity of the IES test.

Conclusions concerning the IES test

It must be concluded that results with the IES test cannot be used as objective evidence pertinent to psychoanalytic theory. It is not that the validity of the test has been refuted. Rather it is the case that there is no evidence supporting its validity and in view of its other poor psychometric qualities, the results should be ignored until such evidence is adduced.

Conclusions concerning the functional hypothesis

The studies of motivation by Cattell (1957) and of third-order objective test factors by Pawlik and Cattell (1964) support, in general, the psychoanalytic hypothesis. To a lesser extent the fourth-order factorization of questionnaire scores by Warburton (1968) confirms the theory. However, as has been pointed out, at the moment all these interpretations must remain speculative because of the question of the validity of the objective tests. Until Cattell has managed to demonstrate that these test devices measure what they purport to do, it is impossible to put much weight on these results.

The IES test has even less demonstrated validity than these objective measures. Again, until such validity is demonstrated little reliance can be placed on any findings achieved with it.

What has clearly emerged from these studies, however, is that factor-analysis is a suitable technique for investigating the functional hypothesis and that, contrary to first appearances, it is a formulation capable of scientific verification.

After this examination of the physiological and functional hypotheses implicit in the Freudian theory of ego, super-ego and id, we shall examine the objective evidence for identification — the process by which in Freudian theory the super-ego is acquired.

IDENTIFICATION

As we saw from our description of the development of the super-ego, identification plays an important part in that process. In psychoanalytic theory identification can come about from two causes — fear of loss of love (known as anaclitic identification) and fear of aggression, identification with the aggressor. This last concept is often used as a defence mechanism and has been extensively described by Anna Freud in her *The Ego and the Mechanisms of Defence* (1946).

Since the psychoanalytic concept of identification is clearly a vital process in the socialization of children it has received considerable attention from psychologists, especially those concerned with learning-theory models of behaviour. This, of course, is hardly surprising since identification is essentially a learning process — learning to be like the particular model.

To review in detail all the research evidence that has accrued from these investigations would be quite inappropriate to the importance of the concept in Freudian theory. Furthermore it would be inordinately long, so that in the section that follows all that will be attempted is a brief summary and discussion of some of the main empirical approaches.

DEFINITION OF IDENTIFICATION AND IMITATION

Kohlberg (1963a, b) points out that in the research literature it is usual to distinguish between identification and imitation on the grounds that the former implies some structural change within the personality. He suggests the following criteria for this distinction (Kohlberg, 1969a):

1. In identification, modelling is generalized and trans-situational. A variety of behaviours and roles are reproduced in a variety of situations. In imitation, modelling is of specific behaviours in specific situations.

2. In identification, modelling is persistent and occurs in the absence of the model.

3. In identification, performance of the modelled behaviour appears to be motivated intrinsically. It persists in the absence of any obvious reinforcement to which it is instrumental.

4. In identification, performance of the modelled behaviour is relatively irreversible or non-extinguishable even when it is non-reinforced or punished.

For psychoanalytic theory this distinction between identification and imitation is essential. Bronfenbrenner (1960), in his study of the development of the concept in psychoanalytic theory, claims that there it is regarded as a sweeping and powerful phenomenon in which the entire personality of the parent is taken over *en bloc* with considerable emotional intensity.

If this view of identification — the psychoanalytic view — is adopted, as it must be in the empirical study of psychoanalysis, then as Kohlberg (1969a) argues, many of the gibes of the learning theorists at the theory are shown to be irrelevant. Thus Bandura (1969) claims that if psychoanalytic theory were correct a young boy, to imitate a worshipped sportsman, would have to develop incestuous desires towards the hero's wife. This is a confusion between identification and imitation. On the other hand it must be admitted that psychoanalytic theory does not explicitly attempt to explain such everyday imitation (inevitable in view of its neglect of ego psychology) and examples of identification given by Freud (1946) are sometimes, by this definition, imitation. Indeed those researchers who analyse identification in terms of theories of learning do not allow this distinction between identification and imitation but regard them rather as on a continuum, the difference lying in the amount of stimulus-generalization and resistence to extinction (e.g. Bandura, 1969; Aronfreed, 1969; Gewirtz, 1969). However, it does seem that there is an important qualitative difference, as Bronfenbrenner (1960) argues, between the Freudian concept of identification as it occurs in the development of a child, and the imitation of a model adult whether absent or present, which is frequently the object of empirical study.

RELEVANCE OF EMPIRICAL STUDIES TO FREUDIAN THEORY

From the viewpoint of the validation of psychoanalytic theory the essential questions are whether identification occurs and under what conditions. Thus by

Freudian theory we would predict that identification would be likely to occur with aggressive fathers or parents whose love the children were afraid to lose. The most important postulate, however, is the very existence of identification. If it could be shown, for example, that children in no sense imitated their parents the whole aetiology of the super-ego in Freudian theory would have to be abandoned. Actually the interpretation of identification in terms of learning theories, as has been attempted by Bandura and colleagues, for example, is by no means inimical to Freudian theory. For as is argued in the last chapter of this book, it seems likely that psychoanalysis has been concerned with the study of the learning processes in human development, examining what events act as reinforcers and conditioned stimuli.

A further point concerning the relevance of empirical studies of identification has already been mentioned. Learning theorists regard imitation and identification as essentially similar so that they set up controlled laboratory experiments using adult models with which children may identify. However, identifying with such a model seems a far cry from identifying with the father through fear of castration. A psychoanalyst would not consider the laboratory experiment a satisfactory analogue except to understand imitation.

THE EMPIRICAL STUDIES OF IDENTIFICATION

A brief discussion of some of the most important empirical studies of this concept appears below. It is not intended to be comprehensive but to illustrate the different approaches and the general consensus of opinion, as was stated earlier.

The work of Sears, Rau and Alpert (1965)

Sears et al. studied, not the process of identification itself, but the hypothesized consequences of identification and their relation to child-rearing procedures. Thus, according to these writers sex-role behaviour, pro-social agression, adult attitudes and conduct, resistance to deviation and feelings of guilt if transgressions occur, are all consequent upon identification. These variables were therefore studied in a sample of children and linked to child-rearing procedures as ascertained from a structured interview with the parents. The measures of identification were behavioural observations in structured situations, projective tests and questions to parents.

One result, which is important, was that these indices of identification were not positively correlated to any important extent among themselves. This means that it is unlikely that they are all simply the result of one simple process of identification.

However, there are methodological problems in researches of this design which, as claimed by Bandura (1969), make it unlikely that this study by Sears et al. is an adequate test of identification. If identification is the taking over of the whole pattern of the parent (see Bronfenbrenner, 1960) then it is essential to know this parental pattern for each individual subject. Thus a child showing little guilt could well have identified with his father if he too showed little guilt. As Bandura succinctly writes, 'identificatory behaviour has no intrinsic defining properties and consequently it cannot be measured or identified independently of the behaviour of the persons who have been emulated' (1969, p. 217).

Of course even similarities between parent and son, for example, especially in the case of behaviour common in the culture, are not necessarily evidence for identification since they could have been learned from some other source. However the fact that identification can only be demonstrated by comparing subject and model means that the work of Sears et al. (1965), although yielding information about child behaviour and its child-rearing antecedents, is not really relevant to identification.

Psychometric studies of identification

This method is open to a similar objection to that against the previous study. Thus Helper (1955) compared the scores of subjects on a personality questionnaire with the scores of their models for identification. Even had marked similarities been found there would have been no way of assessing whether such similarity was due to identification or to culturally common characteristics. In fact there were no greater similarities to parents than to other figures. In addition to this the common problems of personality questionnaires, especially response-sets (which have been fully discussed in the section on psychosexual personality development, see pp. 14-45), are peculiarly important in this type of study since they tend to make scores homogeneous and thus artificially create identification-like similarities. In addition the most valid types of personality questionnaire are those developed by factor-analysis (see pp. 23-6) and typically these deal with variables not relevant to studies of identification. The self-descriptive type of questionnaire concerned with attitudes, usually used in the study of identification, has little other than face-validity and thus may be vitiated by inadequacy of self-knowledge and the lack of relation of responses to items and actual behaviour (Cronbach, 1955; Bronfenbrenner, 1958). Thus psychometric studies of identification can carry but little weight.

Studies of moral behaviour

These, again, are subject to the same objection that the absence of moral behaviour may not mean that identification has not taken place, unless comparable measures of super-ego activity are made of the parental figures. Thus Brown (1965) is not strictly justified in using the findings of MacKinnon (1938) to relate identification to child-rearing procedures. Similarly the famous studies of moral behaviour by Hartshorne and May (1930) are not really relevant to the Freudian concept of the super-ego. They tell us a good deal about moral behaviour in children of various ages. This behaviour could, however, be mediated by the ego; it fails to show how it came about and is thus not a critical test of the Freudian tripartite division of the mind. As has already been said, for this purpose factor-analysis is necessary.

Identification as observational learning — the work of Bandura

Bandura (1969) presents a succinct account of his view of identification and the experimental work supporting it. This paper forms the basis of the summary and discussion of his research which is of especial interest in that he has explicitly tested some of the Freudian formulations concerning anaclitic and defensive identification. Furthermore these investigations do not suffer from the defects of the other types of study previously discussed because identification is always related to the behaviour both of subject and model.

Bandura regards identification, imitation, introjection, incorporation, internalization, copying and role-taking as essentially the same, all referring to behavioural modifications resulting from exposure to models. It must be noted, however, that this view, although parsimonious, means that laboratory studies of the effects of models on behaviour may not be relevant to the psychoanalytic concept of identification.

Observational learning is the basic learning process underlying identification and this involves imaginal and verbal representional systems based on contiguity learning. Bandura, Grusec and Menlove (1966) showed, for example, that children watching a model on film who were allowed to verbalize the model's behaviour acquired more matching responses than children who were not so allowed.

Anaclitic identification

Bandura and Huston (1961), Henker (1964) and Mischel and Grusec (1966) have studied the effects of differential amounts of rewards, given by models, on imitative behaviour. In laboratory studies of this kind, all subjects have equal exposure to the models and the reinforcement of the models' behaviour by children is eliminated — variables which can distort naturalistic studies of child-rearing in that, for example, warm nurturant mothers are likely to see more of their children and thus give greater opportunity for identification than would cold mothers. This would support the Freudian theory of anaclitic identification but merely because the children of nurturant mothers had more time to learn. The results of these laboratory studies support the Freudian claim that there is more identification with warm and nurturant models. However these studies also showed that the warmth of the model did not increase the propensity to produce aversive responses whereas aggressive responses were imitated eagerly from all types of model. In addition a further study by Bandura, Grusec and Menlove (1967) showed that in some conditions nurturance may in fact diminish identification. Bandura (1969) also argues that the generality of these experiments may be impugned on the grounds that they concern dyadic interactions. In a study involving triads, Bandura, Ross and Ross (1963) found that the addition of other social variables affected the relationship between the nurturance of the model and the imitation of the subject.

Bandura (1969) concludes that these studies support in general terms the theory of anaclitic identification proposed in Freudian theory but suggests that it is valid only in certain conditions.

These studies have not been discussed in detail because it seems questionable to us to what extent they are really testing the Freudian theory. Anaclitic identification is said to occur through fear of loss of love. Therefore, it is supposed that warm rather than cold parents should be expected to produce identification in their children. However in these experiments there is no fear of loss of love. The imitation of the model is in no way intended to replace the model, as it is in Freudian theory. Furthermore loving and nurturance cannot be identical: if they were the problem of substitute mother-figures for orphan children (see Bowlby, 1962, and pp. 160-1) would not be so considerable. If, too, as Bandura (1969) suggests, the addition of other social factors affects the relationships, to extrapolate to the natural family situation seems absurd.

On the other hand, the general tenor of the findings supports the Freudian claim that identification is related to affection. It seems to us that the main interest of these studies lies in the fact that the Freudian hypothesis is perfectly acceptable in terms of learning theory which in time may be able to define more precisely the conditions under which anaclitic identification occurs.

Identification with the aggressor

Bandura, Ross and Ross (1963) tested the Freudian theory of defensive identification together with Whiting's status-envy theory (Whiting, 1960) and a theory of identification based on social power (Parsons, 1955). From the Parsons theory it would be predicted that the person controlling rewarding resources, not consuming them, would be the model adopted. From the theory of status envy it would be predicted that the person consuming most of the desired resources would be the model. By resources Whiting means such things as food, love, attention and care.

There were two conditions:

(a) One adult was a controller of resources (magnificent toys and food), another adult was the recipient of these while the child watched the events.
(b) One adult controlled the resources of which the child was the recipient while the other adult was neglected.

For half the boys and girls in each condition the male model controlled resources, for the other half the female model.

After the distribution of resources the two adult models performed various actions which later the children had to imitate.

The results showed that children identified with the source of rewarding power rather than the envied competitor for rewards. Furthermore there was cross-sex identification. Thus Whiting was not supported.

Since Bandura (1969) regards Whiting's status-envy theory as an extension of Freudian theory, he regards the result of this experiment as evidence against the Freudian theory of defensive identification. However if it is recalled that defensive identification occurs at the threat of castration it is clear that this experiment is an inadequate test of the Freudian theory. Furthermore the imitation of certain dramatic actions of the model does not seem to be a satisfactory measure of identification. This study by Bandura et al. (1963) cannot be considered as evidence against the Freudian theory. Further studies of identification with the aggressor as a defence mechanism can be found in the chapter devoted to them (see p. 245).

Such a study seems to be a clear example of the kind of psychological research that is not relevant to psychoanalytic theory. As Bronfenbrenner (1960) points out, there is a qualitative difference between the Freudian concept of identification, especially as used in the development of the super-ego, and this kind of imitative behaviour. Unfortunately from the viewpoint of the validation of psychoanalytic theory most of the research of Bandura has been devoted to a study of imitative behaviour and the conditions influencing its acquisition.

Conclusions to the work of Bandura

Thus because Bandura admits no essential differences between identification and imitation much of his work cannot be considered relevant to the psychoanalytic theory. What is missing from these laboratory analogues is the close relationship between model and subject which is usually present in the family situation. That such factors may be important is evidenced by his admission that results with dyads may not be extrapolated to triads. Indeed he argues (1969) that attentional processes are important to identification, since subjects will not pay equal attention to all models and behaviours. It is easy to argue that it could be the relationship which the child has with its parents which compels it to pay more attention to them as models regardless of the variables which are of importance in a non-emotional situation.

In conclusion there can be little doubt that the work of Bandura has cast much light on the role of imitation in social learning. It does not appear so relevant to the special form of this learning conceptualized in psychoanalytic theory as identification.

The work of Kohlberg

Kohlberg (1969a) reviews what he calls his cognitive developmental approach to socialization. Over a number of years Kohlberg (1958, 1963a, 1963b, 1964, 1966a, 1966b, 1967, 1968 and 1969b), to mention only the publications of which he is the single author, has studied the development of moral thought in children. His work was influenced by the work of Piaget (1948) in this field. Kohlberg (1969a) considers that the two stages of moral judgement proposed by Piaget, the heteronomous and the autonomous, do not stand the test of logical scrutiny or further empirical study. In their place Kohlberg (1967) proposed three levels of moral judgement each of which embraced two stages of moral development. These levels and stages were based upon the responses to moral dilemmas of children aged between seven and seventeen years. Rest (1968) gives excellent examples of responses characterizing the different stages of moral development in the case of a husband who stole a drug to save the life of his wife. At stage 1, for example, the focus is on irrelevant consequences of the act — 'He shouldn't steal the drug ... he did a lot of damage ... breaking up the store too.' At stage 6 on the other hand, there is full appreciation of the fact that good motives do not alone justify an act and that moral principles, as legal rules, do not allow exceptions.

Brown (1965) considers that this work of Kohlberg, which indicates that moral judgement continues development until later adolescence, would surprise Freudians who believe that the super-ego is the heir of the Oedipus complex and consequently that moral development is complete by five. This argument seems to us completely false. The kind of moral development dealt with by Piaget and Kohlberg is a complex intellectual and philosophical activity, and this falls within the realm of the ego, in psychoanalytic terms, not the unconscious super-ego. Consider, for example, the complex chain of arguments by which Plato justifies the existence of The Good as the basis of all morality. These are some of the profoundest products of the ego known to the west and no Freudian would claim that these were the products of super-ego activity. The super-ego governs feeling that this act is good, this one bad regardless of the intellectual arguments we can adduce against them. Hence, for example, the guilt felt by many adolescents at masturbation despite explanations by enlightened educators (Kinsey et al., 1948).

From this it is argued that the work of Kohlberg and Piaget is not really relevant to the problem of the introjection of the super-ego. This is not, of course, to minimize its importance in the study of the acquisition of morality.

Kohlberg (1969a) does not, however, reject the concept of identification. Like Bandura (1969) he regards imitation and identification as essentially similar processes and objects to psychoanalytic theory in that there identification is a special event linked to particular effective family ties. Unlike Bandura however, as was stated earlier, Kohlberg considers there are structural differences between identification and imitation (see p. 182). The cognitive developmental view of identification differs from the Freudian one in the following respects:

1. Identification is viewed as a cognitive structural stage of more general imitative or social sharing processes.
2. Accordingly it is not uniquely dependent upon particular motives and ties only present in the early parent—child relationship.
3. Identifications are not totally fixed, irreversible or 'internalized'.

Identifications are 'solutions' to developmental tasks which may change in object or nature with new developmental tasks (Kohlberg, 1969a, p. 426). According to this theory, imitation in the young child occurs because the things imitated are interesting in the sense of arousing (Berlyne, 1961), and only afterwards does imitation come into the control of the kind of social reinforcers discussed by Bandura.

Before concluding our discussion of Kohlberg's work, the work of Kurtines and Greif (1974) merits mention. They argued in a closely reasoned survey of Kohlberg's work that the measuring instrument devised by Kohlberg and on which the findings are based was open to question on a variety of grounds: the derivation of the items, the objectivity of the administration, the scoring procedures, and the reliability and validity of the resulting scores. Furthermore, they pointed out that not only was there considerable lack of evidence concerning the assumptions of the model, in addition up to that point its utility had not been demonstrated.

More recently Thornton (1980) has shown that prisoners compared with controls score low on Kohlberg's moral-reasoning measures. They have not reached the highest developmental stage and there were interesting differences between offenders convicted of different offences. However, while this may show that the scales are useful, such findings in no way overcome our original objection that they are concerned with the ego rather than super-ego components of moral behaviour.

Conclusions of the work of Kohlberg

This summary of the work of Kohlberg has been brief because as has been argued the bulk of his research has concerned an aspect of moral development that is irrelevant to the Freudian theory of the super-ego.

Furthermore his view of identification as only one kind of social learning means that he has not concentrated on the Freudian postulate of parental identification at the Oedipal stage. The assumption that there is no difference between identification and imitation, while in Freudian theory there clearly is such a distinction, means, as was the case with Bandura, that much of the evidence cited does not seem truly relevant to the psychoanalytic concept.

Fisher and Greenberg (1978) have criticized our approach to identification and to the work of Kohlberg. They do not accept our argument that the results bear more on the psychology of the ego than the super-ego. They cite, in support, for example, the work of Hartshorne and May (1930) and the fact that many of the studies of identification which they cite use doll-play technique and other projective tests which, they feel, are likely to tap deeper (i.e. non-ego) aspects of mental functioning than questionnaires.

There are really two separate points in reply to this case. The work on identification which they cite, using doll-play techniques and projective materials, is not by the standards of experimental rigour and statistical analysis adopted in this book (see our first chapter) considered adequate as objective evidence for psychoanalytic theory. There is no evidence that such projective test behaviour is related to the variables they purport to tap. In other words there is no evidence of validity. Certainly it is possible in psychoanalytic theory to make inferences about the test results but it is this very theory that we are trying to test. Such studies add little to the original psychoanalytic data. It is to be noted that these objections do not apply to projective techniques *per se*, since some can be objectively scored and validated. That is why in some cases we have been prepared to examine (but not to take on face value) results with the Blacky Pictures or the PN test (see Chapter 5).

Kohlberg's work is generally based on questions tapping moral reasoning. Hence the objection to it that it is ego rather than super-ego controlled still stands. Hartshorne and May's (1930) work on cheating, where they showed that cheating in one task was not necessarily related to cheating in a different task, cannot be objected to on the same grounds. However, the objection to this work is that the tasks were essentially trivial and cheating on them would be regarded as a peccadillo rather than a sin. That is, it is arguable whether, in experimental tasks which were essentially trivial, to cheat would disturb the super-ego. Thus the inconsistency noted may not reflect on the inconsistency of the super-ego (which in Freudian theory according to Fisher and Greenberg is unitary and should not be inconsistent) but on the ego which of course, taking into account realistic environmental factors, need not be consistent.

Actually, even the super-ego need not be consistent, if the father-figure interjected was not itself consistent, so even the consistency argument (assuming Hartshorne and May's work taps the super-ego) breaks down.

In conclusion, therefore, we do not consider Fisher and Greenberg's arguments to be forceful. In addition much of their experimental evidence (being based on projective measures) is considered unsatisfactory.

OTHER APPROACHES

The work of Mowrer (1950) and Foss (1964)

Mowrer studied the imitation of the human voice in the budgerigar. He argued that the bird only learned to talk when it had grown to like the trainer. In terms of learning theory the sound of the trainer's voice had acquired reinforcement value through pairing with primary reinforcers. Hence imitation through stimulus-generalization could be similarly reinforcing. Mowrer suggested that a similar mechanism could underlie identification. Foss investigated this hypothesis with the mynah bird. He found that the mynah learned whistles associated with a reinforcer no more quickly than whistles alone. Thus the Mowrer (1950) hypothesis had to be rejected.

The work of Argyle

The studies by Argyle and his colleagues deserve mention if only because they have attempted to put the psychoanalytic theory of anaclitic identification to the test. Argyle (1964) regards introjection as a form of learning with special characteristics.

(a) The response tendencies learned are seen to be in conflict with the rest of the personality. As evidence for this he cites the externalized conscience of the authoritarian personality (Adorno et al., 1950): the feeling that one 'ought' rather than one 'wants' to do a certain thing.

(b) There is an internalization of the responses learned so that they occur in all situations not only in the presence of the original source of influence. This is similar to the distinction between imitation and identification, already discussed, which was proposed by Kohlberg (1969a).

(c) The effects of introjection do not seem to decay with time. This, however, Argyle supports only by anecdotal evidence from psychoanalysis (the very point we are attempting to confirm in this chapter).

The work of Argyle and Robinson (1962)

These authors gave measures of need-achievement to samples of grammar-school boys. They found, using the semantic differential, that high need-achievement was related to high reported demands by the parents for such achievement. Argyle and Robinson consider this as evidence for introjection. If this is accepted, however, it is difficult to see how introjection differs from ordinary learning.

The work of Argyle (1964)

Tests. Q technique: children had to put it rank order sixteen cards on which examples of being naughty were printed, e.g. being greedy. There were four rankings:

Things that would make you
1. feel silly,
2. feel guilty,
3. feel failure,
4. be cross with yourself.

Parents had to rank these cards for the antecedents of these feelings — laughs at child, indicates child has failed, withdraws love and uses physical punishment.

Sample. Twenty 9-10 year old children and their parents.

Results. All rankings by children and parents were correlated for each child separately. The overall hypothesis that self-reactions would be related to the type of discipline (e.g. self-aggression to physical punishment) was slightly supported. But the average correlation for all subjects in all areas with the parent of the same sex was only 0.17. The highest figures indeed were only 0.22 failure and 0.19 guilt, which, though significant, are very small. There is thus little evidence to support introjection from this study. Six children, however, showed a much higher relationship (labelled by Argyle, 1964, as introjectors). To extract subjects in this way seems quite inadmissible, however, since in any sample with any variables, some subjects would show such an agreement by chance.

Argyle concludes that 'introjection works on average for these twenty subjects over four areas ... but it works in particular for six of those subjects.'

These conclusions are quite unacceptable from this data. To single out subjects in this way is truly to capitalize on chance and the correlations, though significant, are very small. Even if similarity between self-reaction and mode of discipline is evidence of introjection, this study, on a very small sample, gives only the slightest support for the concept.

Another investigation is reported by Argyle (1964) in which subjects completed semantic differentials to include the sort of person one ought to be and the sort of person one's father thinks one ought to be.

Sample. 80 students and 500 grammar-school children.

Results. Clearly similarity of scales indicates (or is intended to indicate) the extent to which the super-ego is modelled on the parents and hence the degree of introjection.

For 160 male subjects the super-ego was more similar to the father's than the mother's demands. For the girls there was a non-significant tendency to be nearer the mother's demands than the father's. Factor scores based on these semantic differentials corresponded to the parental demand scores in the range 0.35-0.70 (Mean ρ 0.5). These data, Argyle argues, clearly illustrate the phenomenon of introjection in the formation of the super-ego.

Verbal evidence of this sort based on the semantic differential can hardly be regarded as relevant to the super-ego which is, in part at least, unconscious. This means that the extent to which such verbalizations of behaviour reflect the feelings of guilt and moral obligation which, in psychoanalytic theory, the super-ego is thought to subsume, is likely to be slight. Every schoolboy knows his Ovid: *video meliora proboque, deteriora sequor*. This investigation seems to show only that verbal statements of moral obligation are related to statements about parental ideas on these topics.

Conclusions

Both parts of this study, therefore, despite the claim of Argyle (1964) to be testing and demonstrating anaclitic introjection as described by Freud, seem to be of dubious validity. Neither part, it seems to us, convincingly demonstrates the phenomenon of introjection. Finally it should be noted that whereas we have followed Bandura (1969) and conceived introjection and identification as essentially the same process, Argyle attempts to draw distinctions between the terms. Nevertheless his definition of introjection, based on Freud's description, seems to us essentially similar to identification as it has been used in this discussion. In brief, then, the work of Argyle (1964) and Argyle and Robinson (1962) cannot be held to confirm Freudian theory.

Gewirtz (1969) takes an operant learning-theory approach to identification which he regards as synonymous with imitation and other related terms. He reanalyses the work of Bandura (1962, 1965, 1969), which stresses that identification is learned by observational learning without instrumental reinforcement, and the work of Aronfreed (1969), in terms of orthodox operant learning.

THE RELATION OF THE PSYCHOANALYTIC THEORY TO THESE IDENTIFICATION STUDIES

It is now necessary to examine the status of the psychoanalytic theory of identification in the light of all these findings: in effect to summarize this section.

Most of these theorists consider that identification is essentially no different from other forms of imitation. This has therefore led them to study, often most elegantly, forms of imitation far removed from the Freudian phenomenon. As was pointed out in the discussion of the work of Bandura, it seems improbable that a study of the variables influencing the imitation of a few spectacular gestures is closely relevant to the identification of the Oedipal child with his father. It could well be, and evidence not logic must be adduced to eliminate the possibility, that the close affectional familial bonds produced in the family situation, and the particular developmental stage reached by the child, mean that to identify with the parent is particularly reinforcing and hence likely to occur even in the absence of the reinforcers found effective in the laboratory situation. In addition, laboratory studies of modelling do not include the threat of loss of love which is, in Freudian theory, the precipitating cause of identification. It must be concluded, therefore, that the studies by Bandura and his colleagues, whether or not the claims of observational learning or operant conditioning are accepted, are not truly relevant to the Freudian concept of identification.

Similarly, the work of Kohlberg (1969a, b) cannot be considered relevant to the Freudian concept of the super-ego. His work is concerned with the part of moral behaviour that is the concern of the ego. The super-ego is concerned with feeling and it is highly unlikely, in view of all that is known about response-sets, and the fact that the super-ego is unconscious, that simple questionnaires assessing the degree of guilt following transgression will adequately tap that feeling. In addition, a further problem involved in the study of moral behaviour in relation to the super-ego is the simple one, that if the subject has identified with a parent with weak super-ego, it will appear that he has failed to identify at all. A final objection to studies of moral behaviour lies in the fact that in Freudian theory behaviour is dependent on the dynamic balance between ego, id and super-ego. Unless measures of these other variables are included, super-ego strength in terms of identification cannot be assessed.

One clear fact, however, seems to emerge from all these investigations. There seems to be no doubt that, however interpreted, identification does occur. In this respect Freud seems to be supported by the evidence — children do take adults for their models. Furthermore this act of identification can be accommodated by learning theory. Thus Mowrer (1950) fits it into classical conditioning, Gewirtz (1969) into operant conditioning and Bandura (e.g. Bandura and Walters, 1963) into observational learning — a special type of learning.

The disagreement with the psychoanalytic theory lies in the importance attached to this identification. To Bandura, identification can occur with any model depending upon such variables as the reinforcement instrumental on the behaviour or the status of the model. There is relatively little support for the Freudian claim that loss of love or fear of aggression are the important variables. From this it follows that other models than the parent will be important sources of identification whereas in psychoanalytic theory this parental identification is of crucial importance.

In conclusion it appears to us that the Freudian notion of identification has not been adequately tested because of the assumption that all forms of imitation are the same. There seems little doubt, however, that identification occurs and that the process can be embraced within learning theories.

Summary

The structural theory of the mind, ego, super-ego and id, was outlined. Three verifiable hypotheses were derived from it:

1. that there are conscious, unconscious and preconscious mental processes (this was shown to be acceptable but of little interest),
2. that there exist three physiological structures similar in function to those of the ego, super-ego and id (this was shown to be, in the present state of physiological knowledge, wholly speculative),
3. that in all behaviour there are three major motivational factors corresponding to ego, super-ego and id (this was shown to have tenuous support in the work of Cattell).

It was concluded that the objective evidence for this structural theory was slight. Finally the empirical studies of identification were examined.

TABLE 7.1 *Summary of results*

Hypothesis 1 Conscious—unconscious processes	Generally accepted
Hypothesis 2 Physiological structures	No support
Hypothesis 3 Three-factor theory of motivation	Slight support (Cattell, 1957; Pawlik and Cattell, 1964)

8

The mechanisms of defence

In 'The ego and the id' Freud (1923) states that the neurotic conflict takes place between the ego and the id. The ego seeks to bar the expression of certain instinctual impulses and to do this employs characteristic procedures known in psychoanalytic theory as mechanisms of defence. These defences have been carefully described and a brief description of each will be givn below. In psychoanalytic theory (e.g. Fenichel, 1945) it is common to distinguish between successful and unsuccessful defences. Successful defences allow expression for the instinctual drive, unsuccessful ones, on the other hand, fail to do this thus necessitating their continuous repetition.

Sublimation

Strictly this refers to successful defences and is not in itself a defence mechanism. Under sublimation are embraced various defences.

Reversal into opposites (Freud, 1915). This itself involves two processes of which examples will be given:

(a) *Change from active to passive.* Sadism becomes masochism.
(b) *Reversal of content.* Love becomes hate.

Turning round on subject. Masochism equals sadism directed onto self. Exhibitionism is voyeurism turned onto the self. Freud (1916-17) summarized the general concept of sublimation.

> It (sublimation) consists in the sexual trend abandoning its aim of obtaining a component or a reproductive pleasure and taking on another which is related genetically to the abandoned one but which is no longer sexual.

Painting is an example of this. Handling paint is regarded in Freudian theory as a sublimation of anal erotism (handling faeces). This concept of sublimation, the deflection of aims, is perhaps the commonest in psychoanalytic theory as the general definition, quoted above, indicates.

Repression

Freud (1915) in his paper on repression said that 'the essence of repression lies simply in the function of rejecting and keeping something out of consciousness.' This makes the impulse inoperative. There are two types of repression:

(a) *Primal repression*. This is the first phase of repression and refers to 'the denial of entry into consciousness to the mental presentation of the instinct' (1915). This is accompanied by fixation — the mental presentation persists unaltered and the instinct remains attached to it.

(b) *Repression proper*. This concerns the mental derivatives and associations of the repressed presentation. These associations suffer the same fate as the objects of the primal repression. 'Repression proper is, therefore, after expulsion' (1915). The mental energy which belongs to repressed instincts is transformed into affects — especially anxiety. It is this that makes repression a pathogenic or unsuccessful mechanism of defence.

Use of the term repression in the writing of Freud

To avoid confusion in readers who have read some Freud it is necessary to examine Freud's use of the term repression since its meaning gradually changed over a number of years. What follows is a summary of Appendix A to 'Inhibition, symptoms and anxiety' (Freud, 1925a, in the standard edition of his works).

In 'Inhibition, symptoms and anxiety' it is clearly stated that repression is a special kind of defence. It typifies hysteria rather as isolation (see p. 197) typifies obsessional neurosis. As is pointed out in Appendix A, this concept of repression as one kind of defence was not how Freud originally used the word. Repression first appears in 'Preliminary communication' (1893). Defence is first used in 'Neuropsychoses of defence' (1894) where repression refers to the process and defence to the motive. However, in a second paper entitled 'Further observations on the neuropsychoses of defence' (1896a) both terms are equated. By the time of 'Three essays on sexuality' (1905a) repression alone is used.

It is to be noted that the later concept of repression — as one kind of defence mechanism (1925a) — is the one adopted in this book. It clearly represents the mature Freudian view.

Denial

The nature of the defence mechanism denial can, perhaps, be illustrated best by an example. Freud (1925b) in his paper 'Negation' gives a clear instance: 'You ask who the person in this dream can have been. It was *not* my mother. We amend this: so it *was* his mother.' In a description of denial he writes: 'The ego has to ward off some claim from the external world which it feels as painful and . . . this is effected by denying the perceptions that bring to knowledge such a demand on the part of reality' (1940).

Projection

As was the case with denial an example of this defence mechanism is clearer than a definition. Freud (1911) in his paper on the mechanism of paranoia (a neurosis which in psychoanalytic theory is characterized by projection) describes the mechanism of projection thus: the proposition 'I (a man) love him' is contradicted by delusions of persecution: for it loudly asserts 'I do not love him — I hate him'.

This proposition 'I hate him' becomes transformed *by projection* into 'He hates (persecutes) me'. Projection, therefore, is the attribution of one's own unacceptable impulses and ideas onto others.

Reaction-formation

In 'Character and anal erotism' (1908a) Freud claims that during latency

Reaction-formations such as shame, disgust and morality are formed in the mental economy at the expense of the excitations proceeding from the erotogenic zones and these reaction-formations erect themselves as barriers against the later activity of the sexual instinct.

As can be seen from this example, reaction-formations create attitudes opposite to those being defended against. Thus, to continue the example quoted, disgust is a reaction-formation against pleasure in handling faeces. It is to be noted that this kind of concept gives a bad reputation to psychoanalysis. Thus even if the observed behaviour is quite opposed to prediction it can always be interpreted as a reaction-formation.

Undoing

This is a defence mechanism characteristic of obsessional neurosis and is referred to in Freud's discussion of the Rat-Man (1909b). It is there described as negative magic which endeavours by means of motor symbolism to 'blow away' not merely the consequences of some event but the event itself. Undoing may be observed in the diphasic symptoms of obsessional neurosis. Fenichel (1945) describes undoing as a process in which something is done which actually or magically is the opposite of something which again either actually or in the imagination was done. Indeed, according to Fenichel, all acts of expiation are really a form of undoing.

Isolation

This mechanism was defined for the first time in 'Inhibitions, symptoms and anxiety' (Freud, 1925a) and is peculiar to obsessional neurosis. If something unpleasant happens the patient interpolates an interval during which nothing must happen. Experiences are not forgotten but are separated from their associations and emotions. Thus isolation can make psychoanalytic therapy difficult. In 'Three contributions to the psychology of love', Freud (1910a) described the separation of the tender and the sensual components of sexuality. Thus some men cannot have satisfactory physical relations with women whom they respect but only with women whom they despise. This isolation of sexuality from the rest of life is, according to Fenichel (1945), an outstanding example of the defence mechanism of isolation — it allows such men to express their sexual drives without guilt.

Regression

This has already been described (see pp. 7-8) in the chapter on psychosexual development. However Freud (1925a) has argued that the process can be used as a mechanism of defence, citing as an example of this his case study of the Wolf-Man. In enforcing the regression the ego scores its first success in the defensive struggle. In the obsessional neurosis typically the defensive regression is to the anal sadistic level.

IMPORTANCE OF THE THEORY

These defence mechanisms are of major importance in the understanding of behaviour. The curious rituals of the obsessional neurotic, for example, may be understood in the light of *undoing*. Constant handwashing 'undoes' a previous dirtying action. The concept of sublimation gives insight into the creativity of the artist who in psychoanalytic theory is sublimating anal expulsive tendencies. Thus, then, an understanding of an individual's defence mechanisms gives insight into basic and unconscious attitudes and drives. They are also crucial to the understanding of the symptoms of neurosis and psychosis as is evident from the brief description of the mechanisms given above.

EMPIRICAL HYPOTHESES

As must be plain to the reader, these defence mechanisms are not easy to put to the empirical examination. The main reason for this is that, as yet, no measures exist for unconscious attitudes and processes, whereas essentially all these defence mechanisms postulate that a response X is due to or related to unconscious attitude Y. For example, cleanliness is due to unconscious anal erotism. As will be seen in the survey of the experimental evidence relating to defensive processes most investigators test inferences drawn from the theory rather than making direct observations. Nevertheless, these descriptions of the defence mechanisms do contain some empirical and testable statements.

1. Highly unpleasant events will be forgotten (repression).
2. Highly unpleasant stimuli will not be perceived (denial).
3. People will impute to others their own undesirable traits (projection).

These three defence mechanisms, repression, denial and projection, seem to be the only ones which can be directly investigated. The obvious problems involved in these hypotheses, for example, what is meant by unpleasant in the statement that unpleasant stimuli will be forgotten, will be discussed when the relevant experimental evidence is examined.

DEFENCES AGAINST AFFECT

The defence mechanisms outlined above were defences against instinctual impulses. Although these are of crucial importance in understanding human behaviour there are other mechanisms of defence — defences against affects.

These latter will not be described in so much detail both because they are not so important in psychoanalytic theory and because to a large extent they are identical with those already described. The defence mechanisms are turned against affects rather than impulses.

Repression of affects

In his paper 'Repression' Freud (1915) argues that repression of affects is accessible only from its results: substitute-formations (animals instead of the father in animal phobias), symptoms (the rituals of an obsessional neurosis) and an excessive innervation of spirit and body. The methods of bringing repression about have been described by Freud in various papers and a brief summary of the more important of these is given below.

Postponement of affects

This may be clearly seen in the study of grief. Freud (1918) in 'From the history of an infantile neurosis' gives a clear example of this mechanism. His patient had felt no grief at his sister's death although he had considerable depth of feeling for her. However a few month's later he had visited the grave of Pushkin and, inexplicably, had been overwhelmed by grief. This grief for the poet was a postponement of affect.

Displacement of affect

The example quoted above is a special instance of displacement of affect. Often there is displacement of object. The example of postponement of affects also exemplifies displacement of object — from sister to poet. In 'Analysis of a phobia in a five-year-old-boy' Freud (1909a) showed how fear of animals was fear displayed from his father.

Displacement of affect is the main defence mechanism against affect in psychoanalytic theory. The other mechanisms will receive a brief mention. *Affect equivalents* were described in Freud's paper on anxiety, 'On the right to separate from neurasthenia a definite symptom complex as anxiety neurosis' (1894). In this work it was claimed that sexual excitement and anxiety could be experienced as irregularities of breathing and heart rhythm — i.e. sexual excitement was displaced to these areas. In addition there is the defence known as *change of quality of affects*. An example of this would be the Freudian claim that anxiety is in fact transformed sexual energy, an argument put forward in his paper 'My views on the part played by sexuality in the aetiology of the neuroses' (1906), where he states 'the symptoms represent the patient's sexual activity.' Fenichel (1945) points out that this has never been refuted. The other defences against affects are identical with those against instinctual impulses — isolation, projection and reaction-formation. Anna Freud (1946) mentions a form of defence known as *identification with the aggressor*. Although not strictly Freudian, it is brought closely into touch with classical psychoanalytical theory by Fenichel who says it is nothing else than introjection of the object against whom the affect was directed.

Identification with the aggressor has been briefly introduced because, as the review of the experimental literature will make clear, it has been subject to empirical testing. An example of this defence mechanism from everyday life is the well known anti-semitism of certain Jews (Sarnoff, 1962). Identification with the aggressor as a developmental process involved in the formation of the super-ego has been discussed in the previous chapter (p. 18).

SUMMARY OF THE THEORY

The basis of the theory of defence mechanisms is that the ego seeks to avoid pain. Instinctual drives are warded off to avoid anxiety or guilt by certain characteristic processes (defence mechanisms). In addition the ego attempts to avoid feelings of guilt and anxiety (defences against affects).

EMPIRICAL HYPOTHESES IN DEFENCES AGAINST AFFECTS

1. Grief or aggression known to be caused by or directed at one object may be expressed towards another (displacement).
2. Persons suffering from anxiety should have severe sexual problems (change of quality of affects).
3. Subjects who have suffered severe aggression should show considerable approval of the aggressors.

THE EVIDENCE FOR REPRESSION

In his paper 'Repression' Freud (1915) distinguishes two types of repression:

1. *Primal repression.* This refers to the denial of entry into consciousness of unacceptable material, e.g. Oedipal wishes.
2. *After-repression.* This is concerned with the expulsion from consciousness of material associated with repressed impulses.

In addition there is a third manifestation of repression — one attendant upon its failure. This is the return of repressed material into consciousness — characteristic of psychotic behaviour. Studies of this manifestation of repression are concerned with disturbances of thought and behaviour (symptoms of the return) and are not relevant to this chapter. These are included in studies of Freudian theories of neuroses and psychosis. However there is one type of study of the return of the repressed which will receive brief discussion here — work done with word-association tests.

As MacKinnon and Dukes (1962) point out, the concepts of primal and after-repression require different experimental designs for proper investigation. Primal repression of its nature implies disturbance in perception; after-repression, disturbances of memory. In the first part of this chapter we shall examine the evidence for *after-repression*.

STUDIES OF AFTER-REPRESSION

As Eriksen and Pierce (1968) in their summary of the empirical studies of after-repression make clear, the normal experimental method of investigation involves the study of the *learning rate* for emotional and neutral material. Such studies may be further subdivided into those where the anxiety and repression are experimentally induced and those where it is assumed that the repression has been already learned in the everyday experience of the subjects.

PROBLEMS IN THE EXPERIMENTAL DESIGNS

These basic experimental designs are plagued by a number of problems which are best discussed before any examination of individual studies is made. These problems are set out below.

1. *In the second type of experiment is the assumption of repression justified?* This is a major difficulty in the study of repression. Since life-experiences obviously vary considerably, so, if Freudian theory is correct, must repressions — both in strength and in the subject-matter repressed. This also affects, perhaps even more, the selection of neutral material. Apparently neutral stimuli may, for individuals, be intimately related to repressed material.

2. *In the first type of experiment, is the experimental induction of repression successful?* One common method of inducing anxiety and hence repression is to make subjects think that they have failed on intelligence tests. In the case of students this is, in all probability, anxiety-provoking but to argue that any consequent decrement in learning is therefore due to repression is not necessarily justified. The disrupting effects of failure could be due to motivation (knowledge of good results is a known reinforcer) differences compared with the control group. In addition Eriksen and Pierce (1968) suggest that subjects in the failing group are probably still thinking about their failure, its consequences and reasons and are simply distracted from the subsequent learning task. In any case the kind of repression thus induced experimentally seems a long way removed from the clinical Freudian concept of repression — normally concentrated on Oedipal desires, castration wishes and other profound and basic impulses.

A further method of inducing anxiety has been to capitalize on the Zeigarnik effect. Zeigarnik (1927), in the course of investigating the Gestalt psychologists' claim that a 'good' gestalt was formed of things completed, found that subjects tended to remember tasks in which they were not ego-involved better if they were interrupted than if they were completed. If, however, subjects became ego-involved, completed tasks were remembered better than incompleted. This Zeigarnik effect has been utilized in the study of repression. However, as Sears (1950) claims, the Zeigarnik effect is so complex that to attempt to attribute the effects to repression is purely speculative. Again it may be questioned to what extent, if at all, such experimentally produced repression resembles the Freudian concept.

Perhaps the most telling point against studies where the experimental induction of repression has been attempted is that made by Eriksen and Pierce (1968). In fact, they argue, such studies are not even tests of repression because the repressing behaviour (failure to remember failed material) is not anxiety-reducing — indeed it may even be anxiety-provoking in that it represents another failure.

3. *Both neutral and emotive material must be equally difficult to learn.* This is an obvious point but, clearly, if the emotive material contains rare words little known to the subjects, differences in retention could be expected on those grounds alone.

4. *Repression not suppression.* If the experiment requires subjects to verbalize sexual or taboo words in front of an experimenter, responses may be voluntarily suppressed rather than repressed. Care must be taken in the design of the experiment, therefore, lest suppression confound the results.

5. *Individual differences.* Not all subjects use repression as a defence mechanism to the same extent. This is a variable that could clearly affect experimental results.

STUDIES OF REPRESSION USING THE ZEIGARNIK EFFECT

As mentioned above, the Zeigarnik effect — worse memory for incompleted tasks — has been used in the experimental study of repression. It is not intended to discuss any of these experiments in detail because the view of Sears (1943 and 1950), that such studies were not proper tests of the Freudian concept of repression, seems to us incontrovertibly true. Thus in the typical Zeigarnik experiment, activities are interrupted before subjects can have had the chance to complete them: later they are asked to recall these activities and others not similarly disturbed. Glixman (1949) is a good example of this approach in that he analysed the effects of interruption under three degrees of stress. In the non-stressful situation subjects thought a test was being tried out, in the moderately stressful situation subjects felt their ability was being evaluated whereas in the highly stressful condition great emphasis was placed on the performance of subjects. After subjecting his results to an extremely sophisticated analysis of co-variance where the number of completions was held constant, Glixman found that, as stress increased, non-recall of incompleted tasks decreased. There was no significant difference for completed tasks.

If we could regard this study as an analogue of Freudian repression, here indeed would be impressive experimental support for it, as in fact would be the majority of earlier studies of this type (Rosenzweig, 1933, 1934, 1938). However if we examine carefully the paper on repression (Freud, 1915) it becomes obvious that the Zeigarnik effect is a pale adumbration of what Freud intended by the term repression — so pale that it bears but little resemblance. Thus Freud refers to

a primal repression, a first-phase repression which consists in a denial of entry into consciousness to the mental presentation of the instinct. This is accompanied by fixation: the ideational presentation in question persists unaltered from then onward and the instinct remains attached to it.

Again he writes 'repression proper concerns mental derivatives of the repressed instinct — presentation.' A little later we find 'the instinct presentation develops in a more unchecked and luxuriant fashion if it is withdrawn by repression from conscious influence. It ramifies like a fungus.' This description of what Freudian repression truly is, is surely evidence enough that interruption of a task cannot be said to be the same thing. What instinct has to be repressed, or what association of instinct, in the Zeigarnik task? Is it credible that such interruption can produce repressed material that will ramify like a fungus? We are forced to agree with Sears (1943, 1950) who considered the situations and problems created in the Zeigarnik experiments so trivial as to be useless. It is clear from this Freudian description of repression that it is concerned with basic and essential drives and conflicts.

In conclusion, therefore, it must be stated that studies of repression involving the Zeigarnik effect are irrelevant to the Freudian concept. This is particularly unfortunate, since there is apparent support for the theory in carefully designed experiments.

STUDIES IN WHICH ANXIETY IS EXPERIMENTALLY INDUCED

These experiments, of which the Zeigarnik type really constitute a specific sub-class are, of course, open to the same theoretical objection that the experimentally induced anxiety, intended to create the repression, is not similar to the kind of anxiety thought to cause repression in psychoanalytic theory. Unfortunately this type of study is favoured by academic psychologists because it follows so closely the hallowed cannons of scientific method. Eriksen and Pierce (1968) regard it as superior to the type of experiment where the repression is assumed to be created in life 'when the experiment contains adequate operations for attaching anxiety to specific cues of stimuli'. With this last proviso, Eriksen and Pierce are undoubtedly correct. However the problem remains as to the best way of inducing a satisfactory measure of anxiety.

As has been mentioned, in this type of experiment a common method of inducing anxiety has been to make subjects feel they have grievously failed in an intelligence test and then have them recall the items in comparison with a control group. A much-quoted experiment of this type often held to support the Freudian notion of repression is that of Zeller (1950b).

Zeller had two groups of subjects learn nonsense syllables. They then underwent a tapping test. One group were told they had done well, the other that they had failed. On retest the group who had failed the tapping were significantly worse at recalling the nonsense syllables than the control group. However, when the purpose of the test was explained (removing the repression) the two groups became equal. It could be objected that this difference was not due to repression but due to motivation in that they lost interest in the whole procedure due to failure. Zeller therefore ran a further experiment which included a group whose failure on tapping was understood to be specific to tapping and a group who were told they had failed on both nonsense syllables and tapping, as well as the previous experimental group and a successful control group. On this occasion the experimental group who failed the tapping and the group who were told they had failed both tests were significantly worse at recall than the other groups. Thus specific task anxiety did not worsen performance. Again when repression was removed all groups became equal. From these two experiments Zeller claimed that an experimental analogue of repression had been created.

There are several points that must be made about these two experiments.

1. The fact that anxiety concerning one task (tapping) created repression of another (nonsense syllables) means that the design is not really analogous to the Freudian concept. The test should have been of the tapping.

2. This means that the anxiety itself is far more likely to have disrupted the performance through its effects on motivation or interest or simply by distracting the subjects from the recall task. Certainly there is no evidence that this is *not* the case.

3. Zeller makes the point that no experimental test of repression is complete unless it is demonstrated that removal of repression (revealing to the subject the purpose of the anxiety-creating procedures) restores performance in the recall tests. And Zeller (1950) does demonstrate this. However, it can be argued that if the repression can be so easily removed then this in itself is evidence that no true analogue of Freudian repression has been created. Typically, repression is most difficult to remove — hence the length of psychoanalytic treatment.

4. Even if it is admitted that Zeller did create anxiety in his students under conditions of failure it is still doubtful whether such anxiety is similar to that causing repression in Freudian theory. No instinctual impulses are involved, no fixation seems possible. Again, as in the case of the Zeigarnik effect, we must agree with Sears (1943, 1950) that this type of experiment is too trivial to be a proper test of Freudian theory.

All these four criticisms mean that the work of Zeller (1950), although it appears to support the Freudian concept of repression, cannot be regarded as constituting a proper test of the theory. Indeed, it is hard to see how, experimentally, a truly repression-causing situation can be created. Ethically the kind of procedures likely to produce it — Oedipal incest, patricide, sexual behaviour involving pregenital zones — are entirely inadmissible and obviously have not been attempted.

To conclude, therefore, it is argued that experimentally induced anxiety is too trivial to form an analogue of Freudian repression. This means that the only design likely to demonstrate the existence of the defence mechanism is that one which is concerned with repressions that have been developed already in the past experience of subjects.

Holmes (1974) has also criticized this work of Zeller and similar experiments. He argues that repression is a process and that the results of these experiments could be due to a process other than repression. As we argue later in our study of projection, Holmes is a psychologist devoted with Eysenckian zeal to refuting Freudian theory. In this case, however, we are in agreement with him.

Holmes also cites evidence from his own studies (e.g. Holmes, 1972) that the experimental conditions of the Zeller-type experiments interfere with performance rather than learning. Hence they are not studies of repression at all, which is why we shall not review them here.

STUDIES USING READY-MADE REPRESSION

As has been mentioned, the main difficulty with this kind of study involves the assumption of repression concerning the emotive material. This is particularly the case where negative results are reported. Here, obviously, it could be due to the fact that the neutral material was emotive or the emotive material had not been subjected to repression. A method of avoiding this pitfall is to select words which have been demonstrated for each subject to be either neutral or emotive on the criterion of a word-association test.

An early study by Flanagan (1930) showed that paired associates with a sexual connotation were less well-recalled than neutral paired associates. This can hardly be regarded as a demonstration of repression since subjects had to utter sexual taboo words in the presence of the experimenter. The detrimental performance could therefore be attributed to voluntary suppression. A similar study by Williams (1951), which is not open to the same objection of suppression, showed that words pertaining to violence were less well-recalled than non-violent words. However, to attribute this difference to repression is perhaps speculative although the result is certainly of interest.

The work of Wilkinson and Carghill (1955)

Wilkinson and Carghill, however, carried out a study of recalling stories, one with an Oedipal theme (and likely, therefore, to be subjected to repression) and one with a neutral theme. This deserves careful scrutiny.

Sample. Fifty male and fifty female subjects.

Stories. Two stories of a dream theme: one was an Oedipal dream sequence; the other was a similar sequence but non-Oedipal. Both stories were very similar except in the crucial Oedipal scenes, and used in many places identical vocabulary.

Procedure. Twenty-five men and twenty-five women read either the Oedipal or the control story. Fifteen minutes afterwards subjects were required to recall the stories.

Results. Recall for the Oedipal theme was significantly worse.

Comments and conclusions

Eriksen and Pierce (1968) argue that this result is likely to be due to the fact that both stories were not equally difficult to learn, a point reiterated by Holmes (1974). They write 'one can reasonably question whether the content of the Oedipal stories was equivalent to the neutral stories in interest value, difficulty and other variables determining retention.' First, it is to be noted that Eriksen and Pierce refer to Oedipal stories (plural). In the Wilkinson and Carghill study there was only one Oedipal story and one neutral story. As indicated both stories were very similar dream sequences. The Oedipal content was not so overtly sexual as to be likely to arouse voluntary suppression, but was symbolic in nature. Thus interest value was very similar for both themes (many of the sentences were the same) and difficulty of learning appeared to be equal. In the light of the actual dream sequences used these objections appear quite unfounded and unconvincing. If this be the case the only viable hypothesis to account for the results is that of repression. Furthermore this was indeed material where true Freudian repression would be expected to occur.

It must be concluded therefore that this study by Wilkinson and Carghill (1955) is impressive support for the Freudian concept of repression. It shows up clearly the advantages of allowing life experiences to create repression (what Freud was actually concerned with) rather than attempting experimentally to create it — and succeeding in provoking but a trivial anxiety.

The work of Laffal (1952 and 1955)

In an effort to ensure that the emotive stimuli were truly emotive and consequently liable to repression, Laffal (1952) first gave his subjects a 100-word word-association test.

Sample. Eighty college males.

Words used. Ten words with association disturbances (long-reaction time, GSR, etc.), and ten without, were chosen individually for each subject.

Procedure. Each subject learned to say the word in response to a picture. Then separate groups (N = 20) were brought back at the following time intervals: 15 minutes, 2 days, 4 days, 7 days. The recall task was to remember as many of the learned words as possible in five minutes. Then subjects had to relearn the paired associate task.

Results

1. Emotive words took significantly more trials to learn than neutral words.
2. There were no differences in retention of disturbing and neutral words.

Comments and conclusions

The first finding appears to support the Freudian concept of repression. The second fails to support it. Laffal (1952) argued that this failure could be due to the fact either that the anxiety was reduced by learning or that the original difficulty in learning disturbing words was not caused by anxiety at all but by competing responses. For it was observed that there was a far greater variety of associations to disturbing words. Since this factor of number of associations to neutral and disturbing words was not controlled, it cannot be held that the results of this experiment (finding one) support the Freudian concept of repression. Laffal (1955) suggested that the disturbance indications on word-association tests (particularly long-reaction time) were indicative not so much of disturbance but of the availability to the subject of a large number of (and therefore competing) responses. Hence the selection of such words for testing repression apparently produces a repression effect because these conflicting responses also make learning and recall more difficult.

This problem of conflicting responses (response-entropy) means that the work of Laffal (1952) does not constitute evidence in favour of the Freudian theory of repression.

The work of Levinger and Clark (1961)

An impressive study by Levinger and Clark has gone a long way towards solving the problems encountered by Laffal.

Sample. Thirty-four female undergraduates.

Procedure. Reaction times and GSRs were taken to thirty emotive and thirty neutral words balanced for frequency. Subjects were then asked to repeat their associations.

Results

(a) Forgotten associations were those accompanied by a higher GSR. Associations to emotive words were forgotten more than those to neutral words. Associations to words which the subjects had rated high on emotionality were forgotten more than those to words rated low.

(b) In the light of the work of Laffal (1952, 1955) reported above, these results were analysed in relation to response competition of which two indices were developed:

1. *Population variability* — number of responses given to each word by sample on first testing.
2. *Retest variability* — number of different responses given to each word on second test.

It was found that forgetting associations was equally related to both indices of response suppression.

Comments. So far this study is no different from those of Laffal. The results equally well support the hypothesis that forgetting is a function of response competition as the Freudian hypothesis that associations to emotive words would be repressed. Levinger and Clark (1961), however, went on to conduct further analyses of the results which discriminate between the two hypotheses.

Further analysis. Correlations and rotated factor-analysis of all variables derived from the sixty words.

Results

(a) Zero recall of associations correlated with all variables except GSR. Partial correlations (holding the two measures of response competition constant) between zero recall and mean emotionality were 0.44 and 0.50. Thus failure to recall is related to the emotionality of the words even when response competition is controlled.

(b) A rotated factor-analysis of the variables showed clearly that there were two factors involved in the forgetting of word-associations — *emotionality* and *response variability*.

Comments and conclusions

Factor 1 and the partial correlations show conclusively that forgetting associations is related to the emotionality of the stimuli. This, therefore, is a clear example of Freudian repression. Factor 2, response variability, also affects forgetting, as Laffal (1952, 1955) found. However, this in no way refutes Freudian theory. That this factor affects forgetting is equivalent to what Cattell and Warburton (1967) call instrument factors. That is, in this particular experimental procedure there is a factor influencing forgetting — response competition. With another procedure this factor would not occur and is, *once its influence is estimated*, of little importance.

This study by Levinger and Clark (1961) provides irrefutable evidence for the Freudian concept of repression. Their use of multivariate statistical techniques nicely exemplifies their advantages over the univariate analyses of single variables.

Eysenck (1973) objected to our interpretation of these results as support for Freudian theory on the grounds that the results could be as well predicted from Walker's (1958) theory of decrements of learning. However this theory is itself highly speculative, discussing unknown physiological entities such as reverberating circuits in the cortex and chemical engrams in the cells. If Walker's theory is in fact able to predict the same phenomena as can the concept of repression, then a critical experiment to choose between the two is required. However, without considerable further evidence there would be little reason to cite the Walker theory at all. In effect this is an *ad hoc* explanation and as such it is unparsimonious to invoke it. We do not regard Walker's theory as a serious objection to our interpretation.

SUMMARY OF STUDIES OF AFTER-REPRESSION

It has been argued in this section that the experimental approach which is most elegant in design — that of experimentally creating repression — cannot really provide a laboratory analogue of the Freudian concept of repression. The anxiety created is too trivial. For this reason only a few typical studies have been described. The second approach, on the other hand, where repression based on previous experience is assured has been shown to yield clear evidence of repression. The studies held to have demonstrated repression were:

1. Wilkinson and Carghill (1955) — poor recall of Oedipal themes.
2. Levinger and Clark (1961) — poor recall of disturbing words with the confounding variable of response competition controlled.

STUDIES OF THE RETURN OF THE REPRESSED

As was indicated earlier, studies of the return of the repressed are not really relevant to this chapter but are better found in the chapter on Freudian theories of neurosis and psychosis. This is because the return of the repressed is usually symptomized by hallucination and disorders of thought. That is, the return of the repressed material distinguishes, in psychoanalytic theory, the neurotic and the psychotic (Fenichel, 1945).

MacKinnon and Dukes (1962), however, consider that Jung's studies (1918) in word-association constitute sound evidence for the theory of repression. Thus Jung noticed that subjects, if asked to repeat a list of word-associations, were sometimes unable to associate again to certain words, changed their responses, were reduced to silence or responded only with great effort. These disturbances of association, indeed, may occur on the first occasion of going through the list. In addition GSR for such responses is greater than for normal responses. These observations have been instituted into a type of standardized test — the Kent—Rosanoff word-association list (Kent and Rosanoff, 1910). As will have been already noted by the observant reader these indicants of disturbed response have been used in some of the studies already discussed in this chapter in an effort to choose genuinely emotive stimuli for each subject in the investigation.

However, the evidence that such indications of disturbance in word-association do in fact indicate areas of disturbance is mainly clinical, although the fact that words so selected are harder to learn than neutral words supports the claim. Thus these indicators of emotionality may, perhaps, as Jung (1918) believed, be regarded as evidence for the return of the repressed.

At this point a brief mention must be made of Byrne's (Byrne, 1964) Repression—Sensitization scale. As we have previously argued (Kline, 1973), this Repression—Sensitization scale is made up from items in the MMPI and is based on the work of Altrocchi, Parsons and Pickoff (1961). It also clearly resembles, to the extent of sharing half the items, Ullman's (1962) Facilitation—Inhibition scale, with which it correlates (not unnaturally) extremely highly. Byrne (1964) quotes figures ranging from 0.76 to 0.94. Since its internal-consistency reliability is 0.94 and its test—retest reliability 0.82, the repression scale may be regarded, as Byrne (1964) points out, as an alternative form of the facilitation scale.

However, despite the large number of studies carried out with the test, certain findings quoted by Byrne (1964), notably those of Joy (1963) and Endler (1963), throw such doubts on its validity as to make the use of the test dubious. Thus Joy found very substantial correlations with many of the MMPI clinical scales, findings which do not support its clinical validity. For example, the R—S scale correlates 0.72 with the repression scale, 0.84 with the social introversion and 0.91 with the K scale. The same writer found a negative correlation of 0.91 with the Edwards Social Desirability scale (Edwards, 1957).

In view of the reliabilities of these tests, these correlations are astonishingly high. Endler in general supported these findings and he found a correlation of 0.92 with the Psychasthenia scale. The final nail in the coffin of this test lies in the finding that repressors come from permissive backgrounds (Byrne, 1964). This is not in accord with the Freudian notion of repression and renders the scale invalid. For this reason, then, the results with the R—S scale will not be examined.

STUDIES OF PERCEPTUAL DEFENCE

Since 1947 when Bruner and Postman first used the term there has been a vast outpouring of research into perceptual defence, a term defined by Brown (1962) as referring to any systematic relationship found to hold between stimulus emotionality and the ease of recognition of stimuli. There have been some excellent reviews of this literature, especially by Brown (1962), MacKinnon and Dukes (1962) and Eriksen and Pierce (1968), and more recently Erdelyi (1974).

DEFINITION OF PERCEPTUAL DEFENCE

Bruner and Postman (1947) found that words of an emotionally disturbing character were more difficult to recognize than were neutral words. This raising of the perceptual threshold was termed by them 'perceptual defence'. In addition they found that some emotionally disturbing words were less difficult to recognize than other less disturbing words — a process they referred to as 'perceptual sensitization'. Both concepts are important in the objective study of Freudian defence mechanisms as will be seen below. For the moment, however, we must turn our attention to the first finding, perceptual defence — the raising of the perceptual threshold — although the term is now used to embrace both raising and lowering perceptual thresholds.

RELATION OF PERCEPTUAL DEFENCE TO THE FREUDIAN CONCEPT OF REPRESSION

Since in Freudian theory, as stated at the beginning of this chapter (p. 195), repression is defined as denial of entry into consciousness, it can be seen that perceptual defence as used by Bruner and Postman (1947) is precisely the same. The raising of the perceptual threshold to the emotionally loaded stimulus word is simply an example of repression at work. Thus if it could be demonstrated that perceptual thresholds were in fact raised to stimuli that subjects desired to repress and that results were not an artefact of the experimental design (for example that the emotional words were very rare), there would indeed be experimental and unequivocal evidence for the Freudian concept of repression. That perceptual defence, if shown to occur, is an example of repression is fully supported by Fenichel (1945) who makes it clear that the defence mechanism applies to external perceptions of the real world and not just to mental events.

RESEARCH DESIGN IN EXPERIMENTS IN PERCEPTUAL DEFENCE

MacKinnon and Dukes (1962) conclude their review of studies in perceptual defence thus:

> Those who are concerned that repression serves as a shield in perception (i.e. that perceptual defence experiments are demonstrations of Freudian repression) have discovered ample evidence to justify their belief, while those who reject that notion have found no convincing data to support it.

That such a statement can be made indicates that the research designs used in many of the experiments are not sufficiently tight to allow only one interpretation of the results. However, as will be seen below it is possible to design researches such that alternative explanations other than repression are not convincing.

Eriksen and Pierce (1968) lay down the following criteria for an adequate experiment in perceptual defence:

1. *Stimuli must be shown to be anxiety-provoking for students.* Sears (1936) pointed out that many of the early experiments on repression failed in this respect. These investigated memory for pleasant compared with unpleasant words on the assumption that pleasantness was equated with non-anxiety provoking. The classic example of this fault is the study of whether quinine is less well remembered than sugar (Hilgard, 1952)!

2. *Avoidance, inhibition or distortion of the anxiety-provoking covert cue must be effective* — i.e. prevent anxiety. Thus in an experiment where electric shocks are coupled with the responses, if non-recall does not reduce shock there is no point in repression and it cannot, therefore, logically be expected to occur.

3. *The use of repression must not provoke more anxiety than its non-use.* According to Eriksen and Pierce this is frequently overlooked in otherwise good research designs. For example, if a study requires a subject to utter a taboo word, e.g. whore, not to utter it may provoke more anxiety than to do so. Not to say it may make him anxious about his sanity or his ability, especially if he is a college student fulfilling course requirements.

4. *Individual differences in responses must be taken into account*

(a) Some subjects have difference defences. A *regressive* response is different from a *projection* response. Thus in Freudian theory the paranoid typically projects his unacceptable impulses on to others (see p. 329), the hysteric represses them.

(b) The differential effectiveness of the experiment in arousing anxiety in different subjects. It need hardly be said that, for example, patricide is likely to have a different arousal effect on subjects who have never known their fathers, subjects who hate their fathers, and, presumably, those rare individuals who have killed their fathers.

(c) Subjects may differ in the amount of anxiety which is required to trigger their defences. Thus Inglis (1961) has argued that introverts need far less anxiety-provoking stimuli to bring their defences into play than do extroverts. If, however, stress is increased, defence mechanisms may collapse at this point, while on the other hand, extraverts may just begin to show their defensive processes. The work of Byrne (1964), who has studied the relationship between personality and defence behaviour, supports this claim.

These then are the four essential factors that must be taken into account in the design of adequate experiments into perceptual defence, according to Eriksen and Pierce (1968). As has been suggested previously, many of these experiments have been discounted for a number of reasons. Chief amongst these are the confounding effects of certain stimulus variables which also need to be designed out of the experiment. Eriksen and Pierce do not specifically mention these since they fall under the first heading — the selection of stimuli. However, they should be made explicit. Since the essence of perceptual defence experiments lies in the difference in recognition time between emotional and neutral stimuli, it is clear that variables likely to influence recognition differentially are important. Thus it is somewhat surprising to find that Brown (1962) discusses variables that affect the recognition of all stimuli equally. These appear to be irrelevant. The main confounding variables which affect recognition differentially are set out below.

Frequency of previous experience of the words

Howes and Solomon (1950) argued that taboo words, often used in perceptual defence experiments, had higher recognition thresholds because they were rarer than their neutral controls. The measure of word-frequency most commonly used, however, is the Thorndike—Lorge word-list (1944). The frequencies there quoted are based on a search of literary evidence and it is highly likely that taboo words such as 'whore' and 'bugger' are more commonly known than would be expected from their literary frequency (unless much modern literature were included). Indeed, Eriksen and Pierce argue that to use the Thorndike—Lorge list to balance taboo and control words is therefore to weight the experiment against getting any perceptual defence effect. Sprague (1959) showed with nonsense syllables that previous experience did affect the threshold — the greater the experience, the lower the threshold, if experience and test were in the same modality.

However, an experiment by Wiener (1955) demonstrates clearly that even if frequency is a confounding variable, as the study by Sprague shows it must be, it does not account for all the threshold variances observed in experiments into perceptual defence. With great ingenuity Wiener inserted four words, e.g. fairy — which had both a neutral and a threatening meaning — into lists of words which stressed either one or the other meaning. The four words in the threat list had lower thresholds than the same words in the neutral list (perceptual sensitization or vigilance). Thus the emotional connotation affected the thresholds. From this it is fair to conclude that while every care must be taken to ensure that word frequencies do not vary between groups of words, the perceptual defence effect cannot be imputed to word-frequency alone.

Word-length

McGinnies et al. (1952) investigated the effects of word-length on perceptual thresholds by using words of known frequency (Thorndike—Lorge word-count, 1944) but of different length. They concluded that word-length was a significant factor in recognition thresholds. Brown (1962), however, in his discussion of this experiment points out that this conclusion ignores the fact that word-length and frequency are themselves interrelated. Brown claims that only where frequency is itself an important variable (and this is only when it is rather low) does the length of word affect thresholds. It must be concluded that in any study the word-length of the emotional and neutral words should be matched. Slight differences, however, would not appear to be important.

Set

It could be that the threshold differences noted for emotional and neutral words are due to the effects of set — i.e. if a subject expects a certain type of stimulus, his expectation of such stimuli will increase and his recognition thresholds will, for those words, drop. Conversely, for other words they will rise. Wylie (1957) and Neisser (1954) found this to be the case — words for which a set had been induced did have a lower recognition threshold than control words.

Luchins (1950) has attempted to attribute all the perceptual-defence effects to set. However if the experimenter is careful not to induce sets in his subject by his instructions and if the design of the experiment is such that the subject is not likely to form any of his own, the effects of set are probably not important. Ideally, research designs should be used such that no kind of set can be built up. Later in this chapter we shall discuss some work of this kind — that of Dixon (1958 et seq.).

Brown (1962) mentions further variables which might confound results — the reward value of previous experience of the words, familiarity with the words, meaningfulness of the stimuli, recency of the experience of the words, and the organic need—state of the subjects. None of these, however, as his discussion makes clear, are of very great importance.

There is one further confounding factor which, although not a stimulus-variable, as were the ones already examined, needs discussion.

Suppression or repression

McGinnies (1949) in his experiment on perceptual defence had used taboo words as the emotional stimuli and had found the recognition threshold raised in their case. As has been discussed in the section on frequency, Howes and Solomon

(1950) had objected to the perceptual-defence hypothesis as an explanation of the results on the grounds that his taboo words were less frequent and therefore less easily recognized than the control words. In addition, however, Howes and Solomon (1950) invoked the concept of suppression rather than repression. They argued that the raised threshold could have been due to the fact that the subject recognizes the words but does not immediately say so to the experimenter. This, of course, is particularly likely to occur in the case of taboo words and where the experimenter is in a position of authority relative to the subject. This conscious suppression is quite different from repression. Repression in Freudian theory is an *unconscious* defence mechanism.

Wiener (1955), in an experiment already discussed for its relevance to the confounding factor of frequency, embedded, it will be remembered, four words in two different lists — one threatening, the other neutral. There was a lower threshold of recognition for these words in the threatening list. This disposed of frequency as the sole cause of different thresholds of recognition. In addition, however, Wiener found that subjects who were aware of the taboo meaning had *lower* not higher thresholds than those who were unaware. This disposes of suppression as the cause of raised thresholds.

Whittaker et al. (1952) found that response-suppression was admitted by Negroes with a Negro experimenter to stimuli generally regarded as derogatory to Negroes, e.g. 'Darky', although it was not admitted by subjects with a white experimenter. Many studies (e.g. Cowen and Beier, 1954) have attempted to counteract the effects of suppression by telling the subjects to expect taboo words. Fulkerson (1957) found that such a technique only affected the first taboo word. Brown (1962) likens this effect to habituation to taboo words.

The work of Wiener suggests that response suppression is probably not of great importance. Certainly it seems likely to occur only in experiments where taboo responses are used. After all, in the particular instance the stimuli of Whittaker et al. were in effect taboo words. A good design, therefore, would make no use of taboo words so that any results could not be impugned on the grounds of conscious suppression. This problem is a specific example of Eriksen and Pierce's (1968) third criterion.

Summary

What are needed, therefore, in studies of perceptual defence, if they are to be relevant to the psychoanalytic concept of repression, are research designs such that threshold differences between neutral and emotive stimuli cannot be imputed to the effects of *differential word-frequency* or *familiarity, word-length, set* or *response-suppression*. The criteria laid down by Eriksen and Pierce (1968) are important for different reasons: these criteria are designed to ensure that negative results can refute the theory. This means that stimuli must be shown to be *anxiety-provoking* (so that a psychoanalyst cannot retort that repression did not occur because anxiety was not aroused), *repression must be effective and non-anxiety-provoking and individual differences in response must be taken into account.*

EMPIRICAL STUDIES OF PERCEPTUAL DEFENCE

Blum (1955) stated that perceptual defence as a subject for experiment had obtained a dizzy popularity. This is undoubtedly true and the result is a huge volume of investigations. It is not proposed to review them all in this section for a number of reasons. First, a complete review would be inordinately long and irritatingly repetitious. In the second place many of the investigations are not strictly relevant to psychoanalysis. Thus many researches have concentrated on the problems which we have already discussed — elucidating the effects of frequency and word-length on thresholds. Thirdly, many investigations do not fulfil the criteria of good research-design. Thus when experimenters choose their emotional words on *a priori* grounds, a negative result cannot refute the concept of repression. A positive result, on the other hand, can support it. This problem — that positive results can support psychoanalytic theory, whereas negative results do not refute it — has already occurred in other chapters in this book. Finally, as was pointed out in the beginning of this chapter, there are already in existence some excellent and lengthy reviews of perceptual-defence studies.

Rationale for including studies

Investigations of the following kinds have therefore been examined.

1. All those which bear on the essential basis of perceptual defence and repression and which fulfil the criteria of adequate research-design.
2. Those which show results in favour of the theory and which in spite of their inadequate design can be held to support it. Remember experiments of this type with negative results are irrelevant to psychoanalytic theory.
3. Well-known experiments which have been cited in opposition to perceptual defence and which do not fall under category 1.

The work of Dixon

The studies of perceptual defence by Dixon differ in experimental procedure from the majority of studies in this area. Since his method avoids the problems bedevilling the interpretation of results, these investigations deserve careful scrutiny. It is all the more surprising, therefore, that the majority of reviews of perceptual defence pay little or no attention to them.

Study 1. Dixon (1958b)

In this first pilot investigation, Dixon studied the phenomenon of perceptual defence by noting changes in the visual threshold of one eye, while the other was subjected to subliminal stimulation by words of neutral and emotive connotation.

Experimental technique. A continuous recording of the visual threshold for one eye, while the other eye is presented with subliminal stimuli, is made. The method, known as closed-loop control, has been fully described by Oldfield (1955) while the apparatus itself is described by Dixon (1958a). Briefly, subjects look through a stereoscope at a screen apparently divided into two, each half visible to one eye only. On the left-eye screen are two spots of light — one brighter than the other. The brightness of both of these is controlled by the subject who during the experiment has to operate the control continuously so that 'you can just see the brighter of the two spots but never the dimmer one'. Kymograph records of all threshold differences are taken. On the right-hand screen appear subliminally the stimulus words. Thus if the visual threshold of a subject rises on the appearance of a stimulus word he increase the brightness of the spot, if the threshold falls he lowers it.

As Dixon (1958a) points out, this method has the advantage that since the subject is never aware of the stimulus material (presented subliminally) and is not required to make a verbal response, the question of voluntary suppression does not arise. In addition the results cannot be attributed to set.

Sample. Two groups of ten males and ten females. The words were presented in a different order for each group.

Words. Whore and penis were the emotional words. Rider and weave were the neutral.

Results. The results supported the perceptual-defence hypothesis:

(a) Significantly more subjects gave higher thresholds for the emotional words.
(b) The direction of threshold change tended to be consistent for any one subject.
(c) For women only, 'whore' resulted in a steep fall in threshold, followed by a rise to that above neutral words.

Comments and conclusions. This experiment certainly appears to support the concept of perceptual defence and *ipso facto* the Freudian concept of repression. As Dixon (1958b) points out, this is a pilot study, and hence there are no controls for word-familiarity or frequency of word-length. Nevertheless the sex difference in response noted to 'whore' is difficult to explain in terms other than of repression.

Despite its imperfections the ingenuity of the experimental technique makes these results difficult to interpret, if perceptual defence or repression is not accepted. This study by Dixon must, therefore, be regarded as support for the Freudian concept of repression.

Study 2. Dixon and Haider (1961)

Dixon and Haider studied this same problem again with a more refined methodology. Their results were consistent with those of the previous research and provide even surer confirmation of the phenomenon of perceptual defence.

Experimental technique. As in the previous study, closed-loop control was the method chosen.

Aim. They wanted to establish that the threshold changes observed in the previous investigation were not due either to differential familiarity with the stimulus material or to the quantity of light transmitted with the words in the closed-loop method, but were in fact due to anxiety engendered by the stimulus material.

Sample. Six male and six female subjects.

Words. Cancer, breast, recant, stance. These words were equated for brightness, length and letter content (as far as possible).

Procedure. Subjects were divided into two groups with different order of presentation of stimuli. In addition to words, in some trials a rectangle of light of the same size and intensity as the words was subliminally presented.

Results

(a) *Familiarity.* There was no relationship between the familiarity of the words (judged from the Thorndike—Lorge word-count) and the threshold recorded during their presentation. It must be noted that since the emotive words were not taboo words, frequency can probably be accurately measured by the Thorndike—Lorge list.

(b) *Light intensity.* The subliminal verbal stimuli produced a significant rise in threshold. The light stimuli produced an insignificant drop. Thus the previous results (Dixon, 1958b) could not have been due to differential light intensities.

(c) *Differences between verbal stimuli.* In the first run, for eight subjects only the word 'cancer' produced significantly higher thresholds than those recorded in the adjacent no-stimulus presentations. In this trial the stimulus 'cancer' was significantly different from the two neutral words. In the second run there were no differences between words.

(d) The words were ranked by fifty-six subjects for the degree to which they were productive of unpleasant emotion. The mean rank was cancer 1.2, recant 2.5, breast 2.9 and stance 3.4.

Comments and conclusions. These results, especially those with cancer, support the claim for the phenomenon of perceptual defence. The fact that on the second run the results were less marked suggests perhaps a generalization of anxiety (breast is a common site for cancer), for all the thresholds were increased. Certainly the recognition-threshold differences were not due to differential frequency of words, or light intensity. It should be pointed out that had Dixon and Haider first investigated the anxiety-arousing potential of their stimuli for the subjects, as suggested by Eriksen and Pierce (1968), it is highly likely that a far more striking illustration of repression would have been obtained. Only cancer was rated, afterwards, as anxiety-provoking. Again it must be concluded that Dixon and Haider have demonstrated perceptual defence taking place and provided us with an example of Freudian repression.

Study 3. Dixon (1960)

Dixon now turned his attention to investigating whether the changes in visual threshold noted in the two investigations previously discussed were dependent on peripheral or central mechanisms. From the viewpoint of psychoanalytic theory this is most important since repression is an unconscious ego-defence mechanism against, in the main, instinctual impulses. Hence if perceptual defence is in fact an illustration of repression it must be mediated centrally not peripherally.

Rationale and experimental technique. Using, again, the closed-loop method, Dixon compared threshold changes for complementary colours, during subliminal stimulation, with changes in the ratio of these colours needed to produce an achromatic patch. Dixon argued that if the thresholds changed for either of the colours (red and blue—green) and there were no corresponding changes either in the other colour or in the achromatic ratio, then threshold changes must be central not peripheral in origin.

Stimulus word. Cancer: also an inverted mirror image of cancer.

Sample. Eight males, four females.

Results. When the subliminal stimulus was red the red threshold changed (the threshold fell), when it was green, the green threshold changed (it rose). This anomaly Dixon explains by reference to the work of Krafkov (1941) who found that adrenaline decreased visual sensitivity to red but increased it to green. A further experiment reported in this paper, where cancer and stance were used as stimuli, produced similar anomalous findings.

From these results Dixon (1960) argues that the determinant of threshold change must be a central mechanism. Thus observed changes were greater for the colour with which the subject was subliminally stimulated. If the changes were peripheral in origin then any threshold change should have produced an equal change in the complementary threshold. Dixon concludes that the weight of the evidence suggests the changes are in fact central rather than peripheral, although this is a very tentative conclusion.

Comments and conclusions. This is an extremely interesting experiment with a subtle and complex rationale. Unfortunately the results, as Dixon admits, were not sufficiently clear-cut to allow a firm conclusion. Clearly with more subjects and more words (perhaps previously tested for emotional impact) this method might demonstrate the neural origins of these perceptual defence phenomena. As has been mentioned, if central in origin these threshold changes would indeed be support for Freudian theory.

In conclusion this experiment by Dixon is more impressive in rationale and method than in any firm results.

Study 4. Dixon and Lear (1962)

Dixon and Lear approached the problem of central regulation of perceptual defence effects by comparing perceptual defence in three groups — a normal control group, depressives and schizophrenics.

Rationale and experimental procedure. The closed-loop method was used in two separate experiments. In the first the subject had had to increase, by holding a lever, the brightness of a dark spot until it disappeared — i.e. was equal in intensity to the background. In the second subjects had to make it disappear then reappear — by increasing its brightness. In both experiments, unknown to the subject, all increases in intensity of the spot were accompanied by increases in the intensity of a subliminal stimulus word to the other eye. Both neutral and emotive stimuli were used. If the subject showed a rise in threshold to anxiety words he would be less able to discriminate a difference between the spot and the background. Thus in experiment 1 he would let go of the lever earlier, and later in the second experiment. If he were responding to the fact that holding the lever increased the intensity of the anxiety stimulus, he would let go of the lever earlier in both experiments.

Sample. Thirty normals, nine depressives, nine paranoid schizophrenics.

Words. Cancer was the emotive word for normals: for a patient it was a word critical for his psychopathology.

Results. The normals responded in a manner consistent with the hypothesis that they were reacting to the increasing intensity of the stimulus — their behaviour in both parts of the experiment was the same. This was not the case with the patient groups: the depressives showed evidence of a raised threshold, the schizophrenics of a lowered threshold.

Discussion and conclusions. Dixon and Lear argue that the normals seemed to be using a process under voluntary control to avoid or prolong the emotive stimulus. Thus their mode of perceptual regulation differed from that of the patients. These differed among themselves in that with depressives the threshold was raised whereas it was lowered in the case of schizophrenics. It is to be noted, however, that both patient groups were under drug treatment which itself could have influenced the results.

Dixon and Lear believe that these results show that two regulatory mechanisms are present.

(a) A system mediated by the voluntary nervous system, e.g. focusing attention, turning the head and in this experiment holding a lever.

(b) An automatic feedback mechanism operating entirely below the level of awareness of the subject.

Again, as with the previous study, this is a highly interesting piece of work which must be carefully replicated on larger samples. Again however, in the case of the patients, we can see a clear example of perceptual defence in operation. As Dixon (1960) points out, there is already in existence sufficient information concerning the working of the nervous system to make just such a central mechanism underlying perceptual defence a physiological possibility. Clearly more research needs to be done.

Study 5. Dixon and Lear (1963)

Dixon and Lear made a further attempt to investigate the neurophysiology of perceptual defence by examining the EEG correlates of threshold regulation. They implicate, by reference to the work of Samuels (1959), the reticular activating system. Their admittedly speculative model of the central regulation of perceptual defence phenomena allows certain hypotheses to be made concerning EEG and perceptual thresholds.

Hypothesis. Raised thresholds to emotive material would follow a lack of desynchronization in the pre-recognition EEG. Lowered thresholds would follow a typical desynchronous activation pattern.

Sample. Seven normal subjects.

Stimuli. Four neutral and four emotional words — chosen for each subject on the basis of a word-association test.

Method. Stimuli were presented with gradually increasing intensity until the subject signalled recognition. EEG records were obtained during this experimental procedure.

Results

1. Differences in alpha for the two types of stimuli (recorded for first 6 seconds of onset of stimulus) are correlated ($e = 0.857$) with the awareness-threshold differences for the two types of material.
2. During these first 6 seconds there was a fall in alpha for the perceptual defenders and a sharp rise for the perceptual sensitizers.
3. During the next two epochs (12 seconds) these trends were reversed.

Discussion. If lack of alpha is taken as an index of activation then perceptual sensitization for emotional stimuli is preceded and followed by cortical activation, while perceptual defence is preceded and followed by increasing inhibition of the activating response.

Comments and conclusions. As has been the case with the previous experiments by Dixon and his colleagues, this study is not conclusive. Nevertheless the results are at least in accord with the hypotheses that the reticular system is an important component in the neurophysiology of perceptual defence. It does seem clear, however, that if studies 3, 4 and 5 are considered together there is fair evidence that perceptual defence is centrally regulated. Thus although none of these investigations is powerful support on its own, the fact that each of them represents a different approach to the problem and each supports the central theory, makes them in total more impressive.

Conclusions from all studies by Dixon

In all these five studies there has been a clear demonstration of the phenomenon of perceptual defence. Since it has already been shown that perceptual defence is simply an example of Freudian repression it follows that Dixon has produced an experimental demonstration of repression. The beauty of these investigations lies in their experimental technique — the closed-loop method. This has ensured from the outset that many of the objections to the interpretation of perceptual defence phenomena as examples of repression have been overcome. Thus the results cannot be attributed to voluntary control or suppression since subjects were unaware of the subliminal stimuli. Neither could the results be attributed to the differential frequency of the emotive and neutral stimuli. The attempts to link the regulations of perceptual thresholds to central rather than peripheral mechanisms are suggestive rather than definitive.

However it must be admitted that all these studies were conducted on small numbers of patients and with few stimuli. Clearly, therefore, it is necessary to replicate and extend them. In brief, despite this limitation these experiments are regarded as firm evidence for the Freudian concept of repression.

The work of Blum and associates

Blum and his research workers have contributed much to the empirical study of Freudian defence mechanisms. In many of their investigations they have used the Defence Preference Inquiry which is a special form of the Blacky Pictures. This test and the results achieved with it have both been discussed and described in a later section of this chapter (see p. 238). Some of their researches, however, have used perceptual defence as their method and these investigations will now be examined. Needless to say, they are of especial interest and relevance to this chapter because they have been explicitly designed to test the Freudian concept of repression and have not been primarily concerned with what, in respect of this chapter, are irrelevant variables.

The work of Blum (1954)

Blum made the start. He hypothesized from Freudian theory that perceptual vigilance was essentially the *unconscious* striving for expression of underlying repressed impulses and that perceptual defence was the warding off of these threatening impulses as they began to approach *conscious awareness*. In operational terms this meant that at very fast tachistoscopic exposure rates perceptual vigilance would occur but at slower rates, approaching the recognition threshold, perceptual defence would take over.

Sample. Seven males and seven female subjects ignorant of the Blacky Pictures (see p. 110 for a description).

Procedure

1. First, to establish a base-line of the subjects' choice based on the physical properties of the pictures, four pictures, one in each corner of a card, were exposed fast (0.03 secs) for fifty-four trials in the tachistoscope. Subjects had to select the one which stood out the most. Positions of pictures were randomized.

2. Then subjects were subjected to a *sensitization procedure*. For males the masturbation card was made traumatic and attention was drawn to the sexual nature of the picture — whereas the oral sadism card was made neutral. The opposite procedure was adopted with the females.

3. Subjects were again given fifty-four trials at 0.03 secs. At this speed perceptual vigilance should ensure that each sex picked out the traumatic picture.

4. To emphasize the nearness to conscious awareness, subjects were asked to select the traumatic picture which was shown at a much slower speed. Here perceptual defence should ensure that subjects failed in this task.

Results. The vigilance hypothesis was supported in eleven of the fourteen subjects (P = 0.05). The defence hypothesis was supported in twelve of the subjects (P = 0.006).

Before discussing this study it will be better to review some similar investigations.

The work of Nelson (1955)

Nelson used these same experimental procedures for eliciting perceptual vigilance and defence with a sample of forty-four male undergraduates. In addition, however, he knew the characteristic modes of defence adopted by these subjects who had been tested on the Defence Preference Inquiry.

Results. The perceptual vigilance hypothesis was confirmed. High-conflict subjects were more vigilant than low-conflict subjects. The defence hypothesis was also confirmed in that subjects who had been classified as repressors on the Defence Preference Inquiry did show evidence of perceptual defence concerning the pictures relevant to their conflicts. Projectors, on the other hand, still showed vigilance. Subjects who were classified as favouring reaction-formation or regression as their mechanism of defence showed evidence of neither vigilance nor defence.

Comments. These two studies by Blum and Nelson would appear to support most strongly the Freudian concept of repression were it not for a study by Smock (1956) which must now be examined.

The work of Smock (1956)

Smock attempted to replicate the study of Blum (1954) but found that the perceptual-defence part of the procedures was spoiled by the fact that the males could not pick out the oral sadism picture because they were distracted by the similarity of the identification stimulus. This was attributed to the fact that although a similar stimulus to the others at the fast speed, 0.03 seconds, at the slow speed, 0.20 seconds, its stimulus properties change. Smock then ran a second experiment to study this confounding variable of stimulus similarity. In this experiment a new control card A was used, judged very similar to the oral sadism card. When the subjects were looking for the oral sadism card, card A was called more than the other neutral cards, whereas when the subjects were looking for the masturbation card, the oral erotism card, which had been altered to be like the masturbation card, was also called significantly more than the other neutral stimuli. Thus Smock argued that Blum's results with perceptual defence were confounded by stimulus similarity for which there was no control.

Comments. If the identification picture were so similar to the oral sadism picture that males were distracted by it, this, as Smock found, would reduce the likelihood of any perceptual-defence results. Thus the fact that Blum (1954) and Nelson (1955) both obtained perceptual defence effects despite this unfortunate stimulus similarity makes their evidence even stronger for the defence phenomenon. Smock's second experiment which shows that response similarity can offset results is hardly surprising. That two similar stimuli are difficult to distinguish when presented subliminally cannot be regarded as a striking result. To impugn the Blum and Nelson studies on the grounds of differential stimulus similarity is in fact impossible since for half the sample a different stimulus is critical and thus must differentially, for each half, be similar to a neutral stimulus. Stimulus similarity can only spoil the results (by distracting half the sample), as Smock found; it cannot improve them. Consequently the conclusions from this study by Smock (1956) must be that the results of Blum (1954) and Nelson (1955) still stand.

Mention here should be made of the work of Jennings and George (1975) who attempted a partial replication of Blum's (1954) perceptual-defence study. They failed to obtain results which supported either perceptual defence or vigilance. However, their sample of seven males and nine females is small (though larger than Blum's) and they used written rather than oral responses. The greater implication of the ego in writing compared with speaking is a possible reason for failure. Written responses, in general, are unlikely to be useful in tapping unconscious mental processes. We would not like to dismiss Blum's work on the strength of this investigation for this reason alone.

The study by Blum (1954) seems to provide incontrovertible evidence for perceptual defence and hence the Freudian concept of repression. It is to be noted that it does not suffer from any of the confounding variables discussed earlier in this chapter which mar so many studies of perceptual defence. Thus the results cannot be attributed to differential frequency or knowledge of the stimuli for all cards received the same number of exposures. Nor, indeed, can the variables of set or suppression be invoked to explain the results. As regards set, the subjects were looking for the pictures but could not find them, and there is no reason to think that suppression should have had any influence. Furthermore the experimental procedure, the sensitization session, ensured that the stimuli were truly anxiety-provoking and the use of repression was not more anxiety-provoking than the original stimulus. Thus two of the criteria for adequate perceptual-defence studies, as suggested by Eriksen and Pierce (1968), are fulfilled. Perhaps even more important than any of these points is the fact that the anxiety provoked (that concerning psychosexual development) in this experiment is actually that typically repressed in psychoanalytic theory and is a far cry from the use of taboo words such as bitch or belly (Rosenstock, 1951) or the use of nonsense syllables followed by electric shock. In brief, therefore, this experiment by Blum is regarded as impressive support for perceptual vigilance and defence and consequently for the Freudian concept of repression.

The investigation by Nelson (1955) which replicates the Blum (1954) study has one refinement which fulfils yet another of the criteria of Eriksen and Pierce (1968). This takes into account individual differences among the subjects in defence preference. Thus the finding that repressors (as judged by the Blacky Defence Preference Inquiry) showed perceptual defence, whereas subjects preferring other types of defence mechanism did not do so, is even more impressive evidence than the earlier investigation for perceptual defence as an analogue of repression and for the concept of repression. It also supports the validity of the repression score of the Defence Preference Inquiry.

These two studies, therefore, by Blum (1954) and Nelson (1955) are impressive support for repression.

The work of Blum (1955)

Blum carried out a yet more refined study of perceptual defence. He was very keen to answer the critics of perceptual-defence studies who had attempted to argue that the results so far observed were in no way attributable to the effects of inhibition. Postman et al. (1953), for example, attributed the experimental results to the effects of differential familiarity with the stimuli and set — the two confounding variables which we have discussed earlier in this section and which do, indeed, spoil many experiments. Postman (1953) in a more theoretical discussion of perceptual defence had argued that in the interests of parsimony results could be better understood in terms of *interference among competing hypotheses*. Thus when subjects have only partial information, as is the case in the perceptual-defence experiment, strong hypotheses incompatible with the threatening stimulus may be evoked.

In an attempt to answer these criticisms, Blum (1955) set up an experiment implicitly designed to show that perceptual defence was traceable to the perceptual process. The hypothesis was: subjects predisposed to use the mechanism of repression in conjunction with a given conflict will, when confronted subliminally with a conflict-relevant stimulus, show defensive behaviour directly traceable to the perceptual process itself. If Blum achieves this aim, it will, of course, be a clear example of Freudian repression.

Sample. Seventeen graduate clinical psychologists well-versed in the Blacky Pictures.

Indices of psychosexual disturbance. Subjects were asked to recall the Blacky Pictures freely and then in a timed session. In addition they were asked to rate the pictures as problems for themselves. This they did twice. Indices of psychosexual disturbance were: errors of recall, slips, over-detailed or very brief description, the wrong order of cards, comments and asides, and differences of placing on the two ranking procedures. Normal Blacky Pictures scoring could not be used with these very sophisticated subjects.

Index of repression. Failure in the recall task.

Experimental procedure. As in the previous perceptual-defence experiments with the Blacky Pictures, four Blacky Pictures, oral erotism, oral sadism, masturbation guilt and identification were simultaneously exposed at a subliminal speed in a tachistoscope. This was repeated for forty-eight trials during which subjects had to name the pictures. The subjects were unaware that in each trial the four pictures were always the same although their positions were randomly rotated. This procedure yielded four conditions:

Picture present: conflict + repression in subjects   1

Picture present: subjects neutral   2
Picture absent: conflict + repression in subjects   3
Picture absent: subjects neutral   4

On the perceptual-defence hypothesis pictures in condition 1 would be named less than in condition 2. Pictures in conditions 3 and 4 would be equally named.

Blum (1955) singles out three points of great importance in this procedure regarding experimental controls:

(a) The antecedents of the situation are closely tied down in the prior assessment of conflict and repression. Furthermore for all conditions these antecedents are the same.
(b) All stimulus differentials are controlled because they are the same in all conditions.
(c) Selective report cannot be a variable since conditions 1 and 3 as well as conditions 2 and 4 require the same report.

Results. As predicted the mean number of calls for conditions 3 and 4 was not significantly different. On the other hand, there was a significant difference ($P = 0.001$) in the mean number of calls for conditions 1 and 2. There were far fewer calls for condition 1. Thus where conflict and repression occurred together, so perceptual defence was noted. It was also noted that fourteen subjects who had conflicts about the pictures but no repression did not produce perceptual defence.

Comments and conclusions. In this ingenious experiment familiarity with the stimulus, set, selective verbal report and individual differences in defence have all been controlled. Furthermore the antecedent conditions (conflict and repression) were known. It seems, therefore, that perceptual defence must be a form of perceptual repression. Postman's (1953) concept of an alternative competing hypothesis is not tenable — what hypothesis could it be? The fact that conflict alone did not create perceptual defence but that repression also was necessary is further evidence for the claim that perceptual defence is an illustration of the Freudian concept of repression in action.

In summary this study by Blum is impressive support for the psychoanalytic concept of repression.

The work of Perloe (1960)

Lastly in this series of studies of perceptual defence by Blum and his associates we come to the investigation by Perloe into the inhibition hypothesis for perceptual defence.

Sample. Thirty males and thirty-one females.

Materials. The Blacky Pictures.

Experimental procedure. An anxiety score for each picture was computed for each subject — similar to the anxiety index used by Blum (1955) but validated in a factor-analytic study reported in Perloe's (1958) doctoral dissertation. A repression score, based on the recall of the Blacky Pictures, was also computed for each subject on each dimension. The perceptual task consisted of attempting to recognize the Blacky Pictures presented tachistoscopically at such a speed that for each subject 50 per cent recognition was possible.

Hypothesis. If perceptual defence is in fact the result of inhibition, subjects ought to be less accurate with the Blacky Pictures which provoked anxiety and were repressed.

Results. Since only the masturbation card provoked anxiety this was the only card where perceptual defence was to be expected. In fact the fourteen repressors had a lower accuracy score to this card than the sixteen non-repressors (sig. 0.01 level). This result could not be attributed to set since the cards were shown in groups of three and the subjects were told this card was in the group. Nor could the result be due to response suppression because the error score to this card was not different for the two groups (the error score was the number of wrong responses to this card divided by the total number of wrong responses).

Comments and conclusions. This study needs little comment. It is further support for the findings of Blum (1955). Extraneous stimulus variables are controlled, individual differences in defence mechanism are taken into account, and it seems difficult to attribute the perceptual-defence effects to anything other than the repression caused by anxiety in those who habitually use repression as a defence. This study by Perloe seems a clear example of Freudian repression.

Conclusions from the work of Dixon, Blum and associates

These investigations by Dixon and Blum and their associates seem to us to demonstrate clearly the phenomenon of perceptual defence as defined by Brown (1962) — changes in perceptual threshold due to the emotional nature of the stimuli. These experiments have been so designed that they are free from the confounding variables of stimulus frequency, response suppression, or set. If they really are examples of perceptual defence, then it follows from our definition of repression that they are examples of repression. These experiments, therefore, are laboratory demonstrations of the Freudian defence mechanism of repression which must be regarded as proven.

Since these experiments adequately demonstrate the mechanism of repression and thus support the Freudian theory it is not proposed to examine further any other experiments in perceptual defence since these are all extremely similar. As has been indicated, long reviews of such studies already exist. From the point of view of this book, the work of Blum and Dixon is sufficient: perceptual-defence studies have shown that there is a defence mechanism of repression.

FURTHER METHODS RELATED TO PERCEPTUAL DEFENCE

The work of Silverman and colleagues

We have already referred to one study by Silverman and his colleagues (Silverman et al., 1978) in our examination of the objective evidence concerning the Oedipus complex. However, at this juncture it is necessary to discuss their general approach to testing psychoanalytic theory, since they have evolved an experimental method which is particularly relevant to the empirical analysis of the mechanisms of defence and which is also specially designed to test the essentials of psychoanalytic theory.

The approach adopted in a variety of studies by Silverman, relevant to schizophrenia and suicide for example, as well as defences, is well explicated in Silverman (1971) and our description is derived from that paper. Our description here will enable us in reviewing the experiments in other parts of the book to concentrate on the results and not repetitiously explain the somewhat complex rationale and method.

Psychoanalytic rationale

The psychoanalytic proposition at the heart of Silverman's work is that psychopathology occurs in reaction to the pressure of unacceptable drive-derivatives. These threaten the individual by arousing traumatic anxiety and as a result defensive operations are adopted to ward off the derivatives. Sometimes the defences are successful in which case there is no psychopathology; where they are not, anxiety and/or the drive-derivatives emerge, or in their place phobias or obsessions. Silverman's work is aimed at investigating these drive-derivatives and unconscious conflicts. From this description it is clear that his methods, if successful, must be powerful in the study of defence mechanisms as well as psychopathology.

The technique

The aim of the technique is to stir up these drive-derivatives without 'disturbing their status as unconscious phenomena', since if they become conscious, in psychoanalytic theory, they would cease to be linked to psychopathology.

Essentially, drive-related stimuli are present subliminally through a tachistoscope thus allowing drive-derivatives to be stimulated below the level of awareness. The method is therefore in the tradition of perceptual-defence studies but much more closely tied to psychoanalytic theorizing. As Silverman (1971) points out, the technique is strongly supported by the results in that such presentation did produce pathology whereas a subliminal neutral stimulus and the drive-related stimulus presented above threshold did not.

Examples of the drive-eliciting subliminal stimuli are: a snarling man with a dagger in his upraised hand; a growling tiger chasing a monkey; a roaring lion charging; a man with teeth bared attacking a woman. Subjects have to describe these and neutral stimuli. The protocols are then examined for evidence of pathology.

Results

In fact most of the results with this technique bear upon the affects of unconscious conflicts over aggression on primary-process ego psychology among schizo-phrenics and of the effects on male homosexuals of arousing unconscious conflicts over aggression. These researches will be described in our chapter on psychopathology. Their relevance to this chapter on defences, inasmuch as the results supported psychoanalytic therapy, is this. Since such psychopathology is seen as defensive behaviour, the experimental arousal of such behaviour is *ipso facto* evidence for defences. Thus these studies may be regarded as evidence for the basic concept of the defensive process rather than for the specific defence mechanisms outlined in the beginning of the chapter.

Conclusions

Our conclusions from this set of studies by Silverman and his colleagues is that they offer support for the basic concept of defence and for some of the specific hypotheses concerning such defences and psychopathology, although there must be some doubt on the validity of the measures used.

This last point, it should be noted, was raised by Watson (1975) who had various objections to these studies by Silverman. He argues that there is no evidence that the tests in these investigations are valid, for example word-association tests, scales of sexual arousal and Rorschach indices, and that in addition the variables are all inferential in nature. While all this is true, so that we indeed do have some doubts concerning these studies as indicated above, it must be remembered that the inferences are tied in with psychoanalytic theory and that the predictions made from the theory were supported. This point Watson also deals with by arguing that the results could as well be explicated in terms of information-processing. While this may be true of defensive procedures themselves, the subliminal thresholds, it can hardly be argued that information-processing could be used, as was psychoanalytic theory, to select the stimuli and draw up the hypotheses. Given the hypotheses with these materials, then an information-processing model might be adequate.

The final point raised by Watson (1975) is to question the identity of the unconscious defined in terms of tachistoscopic thresholds and the psychoanalytic unconscious. In reply to this point we should like to cite all the results discussed in this chapter in our section on perceptual defence and the findings from the percept-genetic studies. All these results, often diverse in the extreme in terms of materials, taken *en masse* strongly suggest that the unconscious as tapped by the subliminal presentation of stimuli tachistoscopically is that, or part of that, described in psychoanalytic theory. This, we feel, refutes Watson's points although we agree with him concerning the lack of evidence for the validity of the measures used by Silverman, doubts which make us cautious in accepting the results.

This work by Silverman is clearly a special form of perceptual-defence study extended so that a wide variety of psychoanalytic phenomena can be scrutinized experimentally. We shall now examine a massive research effort into perception and personality, originating in Scandanavia, mainly at Lund and Oslo. This too can be seen as related to perceptual-defence studies but it is work of far broader scope and with a complex philosophical and theoretical basis. We refer, of course, to percept-genetics.

PERCEPT-GENETICS

Kragh and Smith (1970) have developed a theoretical approach to perception as it bears upon behaviour and a number of associated measurement techniques, work called by them percept-genetics. Since they claim that defence mechanisms can be observed and measured in the study of percept-genetics, it is clear that we must briefly describe the theory and methods so that we can properly assess the results obtained with it. Unfortunately, this work is largely Scandanavian and is little known either in Great Britain or in America.

PERCEPT-GENETIC THEORY: DESCRIPTION

Percept-genetics is the study of the development of perception carried out generally by investigating subjects' reports of stimuli presented tachistoscopically in series at gradually decreasing speeds. Our description is culled from the main sources: Kragh and Smith (1970), Kragh (1955), Sjoback (1967), Sharma (1977) and Westerlundh (1976).

1. The name percept-genetics refers to the fact that the theory is concerned with how a percept is built up. Perception is conceived of not as a reflection of objects in the outer world but as a process between the individual and the stimulus.

2. This process is investigated by the special techniques developed in percept-genetics. Basically these involve fragmentation of a stimulus (a series of tachisto-scopic presentations) such that this process (between individual and world) can be investigated. This process is held not to differ from everyday perception. To quote Westerlundh (1976):

> the searchlight of consciousness is directed towards parts of the process which normally — due to automatization — are preconscious and eliminated from the end-product of perception.

For example, as illustrated in Kragh and Smith (1970) a picture of three baskets was seen first as a monster or a gaping mouth, then as three sandbags and a column, then as three baskets and a dark wall and finally as three baskets accurately portrayed. In brief, then, percept-genetics is concerned with the usually instantaneous constructive process of perception, artificially extending it and making it visible.

3. Kragh and Smith (1970) describe five determinants of the percept which account for the relationship between personality and perception, the relationship which can be clearly seen in percept-genetics.

(a) *The stimulus* defined in terms of physical and psychological attributes. This latter refers to the consensual meaning of the stimulus to the individual. For example, psychosomatic patients have been shown figures where inner organs can be seen. In general most of the stimuli used in percept-genetic techniques are anxiety-arousing.

(b) *Reconstruction*. This is the process of making the constructed material conscious — how the individual selects and reports the relevant cognitive scheme.

This reconstruction is itself determined by two factors: defence mechanisms and set. This set may be created by the experimenter. Thus, if subjects are told to concentrate on veridical descriptions, verbal reports may be vague and brief. Set, too, may reflect the conceptualization of reality of the particular subject, say an anxiety hysteric, such that defences are provoked by the experimental situation itself.

(c) *Cumulative and eliminative transformations*. Personal meanings of a developing percept accumulate into modified percepts, other meanings are eliminated. These transformations provide an opportunity to study the self-experience through the percepts.

This is one of the most important claims of percept-genetic theory, since according to Kragh and Smith (1970) this consideration of meanings—events within the genesis of a single percept makes possible the representation of historical personality in present time. Indeed the past becomes directly available to reliable experimental investigation. An example of this given by Kragh and Smith (1970) is the description of a face as a mask by an anxiety hysteric. When it was pointed out to the subject with a prolonged exposure that a man's head was portrayed, the subject saw a white spot at the same place thus eliminating all contours which had been determined by the reconstruction.

(d) *Emerging transformations*. New formations often emerge which can be understood only by reference to an individual's life history. These emergent transformations suggest that there is a correspondence between the life history of an individual and the sequence of reports to the tachistoscopic stimuli. Kragh and Smith (1970) actually claim that 'experiences are actualized in the present micro-process (percept-genetic) in the same order as they appeared in the macro-process of life.' This claim of course is startling and surprising.

(e) *Extrapolated determinants*. These refer to the hereditary and physiological factors, drives and their derivatives which influence behaviour. These are held to be observable at the pre-threshold level. This is clearly a difficult point to summarize briefly and readers must be referred to the original papers. However, Smith (1949) in his study of twins found, interestingly enough, greater similarities in the early phases among monozygotic than dizygotic twins.

In brief, then, percept-genetic theory claims, as Sharma (1977) argues, that the perceptual processes studied in the technique yield information concerning the individual's personality, and events and life experiences of crucial emotional significance. In respect of personality, defence mechanisms are laid bare together with drives and their associated complexes.

Clearly all these claims, if verified, would render percept-genetics a most important place in experimental psychology, especially, as we have argued, the one stating that life events and experiences can be uncovered. From the viewpoint of this book obviously the critical point is the claim that defence mechanisms can be laid bare.

PERCEPT-GENETIC TECHNIQUES

The best general description of these techniques is to be found in Kragh and Smith (1970), the originators of the theory and method. Detailed descriptions are set out in the manuals to the tests, especially Kragh (1969) for the Defence Mechanism Test (DMT) which together with the Meta-Contrast technique (Kragh and Smith, 1970) typifies the percept-genetic methods. Our description will concentrate on the essentials of the methods and is not intended to enable readers to use the tests but to grasp their significance.

Serial increases in stimulus-intensity

Percept-genetic techniques study the relation between perception and personality by examining *descriptions of the same stimulus presented in series at gradually increasing levels of stimulus-intensity.* As we made clear in our description of the theory, normal perception is seen as a development proceeding from stimulus-distal to stimulus-proximal stages. Most projective personality tests, the Rorschach for example, are concerned with the stimulus-proximal stages alone and thus cannot yield much information according to this theory concerning personality. Percept-genetic techniques are designed to test the stimulus-distal stages of perception and do this by protracting the perception with a tachistoscopic presentation of the stimulus through a series with increasing exposure-time. A number of points here require some amplification.

Exposure-times. These are serially increased from sub-threshold awareness of the stimulus to the level which enables full recognition to occur. Kragh (1955) in fact specifies precise exposure-times at a given fixed ambient-light level: normally ten seconds in geometric progression to two seconds.

Stimuli. A wide variety of stimuli might be useful in percept-genetics. In fact, most of the work has concentrated upon two sets; those used in the DMT and the MCT, and these will be described.

The DMT cards

These consist of two pictures which differ in detail. Each has three elements; a central figure, the hero (a boy/girl, young man/woman), the hero's attribute (gun, car or violin), and a threat figure — a man or woman with a threatening face. There are parallel forms of these two pictures with male and female figures for male and female subjects respectively.

(a) *Response.* These cards are shown successively as described above, and subjects draw and describe what they saw after each exposure.

(b) *Scoring Protocols.* As the name suggests the DMT was designed to investigate a subject's defences. Hence, to quote Kragh and Smith (1970), scoring proceeds thus:

1. Type, intensity and frequency of the pre-cognitive defensive organization.
2. Place in the series of this organization — early, intermediate or late.

3. The succession of phases in the series.

(c) *Variables obtained from DMT with rough indication of scoring criteria*

Repression: the hero or the threat figure are living but not human; or they are objects.

Isolation: The hero and the secondary figure are separated or isolated; one may not be seen.

Denial: The threat is emphatically denied.

Reaction-formation: The threat is turned into its opposite.

Identification with aggressor: The hero becomes the aggressor.

Turning against self: The hero or his attribute is damaged, worthless or a threat to the hero.

All these variables can be measured with high inter-rater reliability.

Apropos of the DMT materials Kragh and Smith (1970) argue that other stimuli can be used although they point out that great care must be taken to select materials that are not visually too complex. Combinations of young and older people are usually effective in teasing out conflicts and problems concerning parent—child relationships. It can thus be seen that if valid the DMT results are *ipso facto* support for Freudian theory.

The MCT technique

In the MCT, pairs of tachistoscopic stimuli are presented separately in immediate succession. The last stimulus, B, of a pair represents a constant frame of reference to which subjects are accustomed. Then the first stimulus, A, is introduced, A being incongruent or threatening to B, in a series of presentations of increasing intensity, as with the DMT.

(a) *MCT stimuli*. Two pairs of pictures are usually used in an experimental version. In the original MCT test A_1 is a car and B_1 a living room. A_1 is flashed into the lower part of the room. A_2 is an ugly, threatening man's face which is introduced into B_2 — a boy sitting against a wall with a window in the upper right corner (where the face appears).

(b) *Subjects' responses*. The incongruence of the MCT which has no counterpart in the DMT is useful in identifying projection and psychotic tendencies in subjects. Furthermore, since the B percept, owing to the MCT procedure, is inevitably more stable than the hero-figure of the DMT, changes in B can be regarded as pathognomic. The MCT is less sensitive than the DMT among normals and has been used mainly among psychiatric groups. For all these reasons the MCT dimensions differ from those of the DMT. Before we set out the dimensions, it should be noted that some refer to defensive processes or principles (in Kragh and Smith's 1970 terminology) rather than specific psychoanalytic defence mechanisms and thus give us additional, experimentally derived, information about such processes. In scoring the protocols, attention is directed to changes in B and changes in A (their quality and place in the series), the control serving as a base-level for scoring.

Variables scored are:

Repression (mainly in threat-series): A is reported as stiff or lifeless, or disguised, for example.

Isolation: for example, A is painted white, is separated from hero by a barrier.

Sensitivity: absorption of A in B (at least two changes in light or perspective) before A is seen as independent.

Projection: absorption of A and B, with pronounced change.

Stereotype: repetitions (at least five in succession) of a split in B, of uninterpreted reports of A.

Depression (mainly in threat-series): repetitions (at least three) of reports of a statue or mask. A, correctly reported, disappears, or is never interpreted, or remains sick or old till end of the series.

Instability: a less pathological form of discontinuity. The structure of B changes although continuity is not endangered.

Discontinuity: At least two reports of nothing or only chaos of lines. B changes completely; reports of colour; all these are typical examples of this category.

Psychosis and abnormality: these are scored from overall impressions of the protocols.

All the variables can be measured reliably and validity studies indicate that psychiatric groups can be discriminated with this test.

Other stimuli

Kragh and Smith (1970) describe variations of this MCT which their colleagues at Lund have developed for special purposes. For example, for the study of psychosomatic disturbances, A is a figure where the internal organs are laid bare.

Similarly, serial presentation techniques have been used in the study of negative after-images and the special after-effect work discussed by Andersson et al. (1972). In addition, a special adaptation of the Stroop test, the serial colour—word test, has been used.

We have described sufficiently the rationale and methods of percept-genetics for readers to see what goes on. However, some further points require discussion before we turn to the results achieved with percept-genetic methods.

DISCUSSION OF PERCEPT-GENETICS

There are three crucial issues in percept-genetics which we shall briefly discuss: 1. the parallel between the emergence of the percept and life-experience; 2. the claim that defence mechanisms can be measured by the techniques (the most important point for this chapter); 3. the claim that discriminations can be made, by means of the percept-genetic techniques, between different psychiatric groups.

These issues are essentially empirical; in this chapter all the considerable mass of evidence cannot be examined in detail. Obviously we shall concentrate on the second point concerning defence mechanisms. However a summary of the evidence is perhaps useful at this stage.

The first point (parallelism) is not well supported. The third point (psychiatric discrimination) appears essentially correct. Whether the second point is acceptable, that defence mechanisms are exposed by these methods, as we shall see depends to some extent on interpretation. What is clear, however, is that these claims are not nonsensical nor entirely unconfirmed.

THE VALIDITY OF THE DMT

Regrettably the only evidence for the validity of the DMT and MCT defence-mechanism variables is effectively face-validity. That is if one examines what behaviour is actually entailed in obtaining a score for a given mechanism, one makes a value judgement that the behaviour resembles closely what Freud described as the appropriate defence mechanism. An example will make this clear.

DMT Isolation. A response would be labelled isolation where, as commonly occurs, a heavy bar is drawn between the threatening face in the corner and the rest of the picture. There is nothing in the stimulus to provoke such a drawing. Thus what the subject has done is to create a barrier between threat and picture, i.e. he has isolated it. It is in this sense that we argued percept-genetic techniques enabled one to see defence mechanisms in action.

None of the supporting evidence which shows that these tests can discriminate psychiatric groups (Kragh and Smith, 1970) or occupational groups bears effectively on the validity of the scores, since it is by no means clear that certain psychiatric groups should or should not show certain patterns of response except perhaps in the case of paranoids who should show reaction-formation and projection (Freud, 1911).

Thus the validity of these percept-genetic techniques for the objective study of psychoanalytic defence mechanisms depends upon the value judgement of how accurately the behaviours scored as defences in fact resemble the psychoanalytic defences. In our view, the resemblance is so striking that Kragh's claim that defences may actually be observed is by no means exaggerated, as our earlier descriptions indicated. It seems to us, therefore, that the DMT and to a lesser extent the MCT do provide experimental support for psychoanalytic defence mechanisms.

Of course further research is needed so that as far as is possible the subjective element in the identification of these defence mechanisms is removed. Furthermore, it would be useful to have the results verified in laboratories outside Norway and Sweden by independent workers.

Many of the results achieved with percept-genetics concerned with psychiatric disorders and their classifications are relevant to our chapter on neurosis and psychosis, although sometimes they are not pertinent to psychoanalytic theory, and these will be discussed there. In brief it is the very existence of the DMT, the fact that such defences can be observed, that supports the psychoanalytic position, rather than any particular set of results, for as we have argued there is no further evidence for the validity of these variables.

The work of Kline and Cooper (1977)

Finally, in connection with the validity of the defences elicited by percept-genetic techniques, we want briefly to examine a pilot study conducted by Kline and Cooper (1977) in which percept-genetic techniques were applied to the oral card of the PN test (Corman, 1969) which shows a suckling pig (see Chapter 5 for a full description of this test). Using percept-genetic methods, eight subjects were shown two slides: (a) the suckling pig of the PN test, and (b) a standard pig taken from an advertisement for bacon.

Examination of the protocols revealed in the case of the PN test-card clear defence mechanisms which we shall let speak for themselves. No such distortions were observed in the case of the control pictures.

Subjects II and III illustrate our point (Table 8.1).

TABLE 8.1   *Typical protocols*

Subject II (male). This subject seems to show a clear example of denial. By exposure 5 a good description is reached. This is then denied, asserted and denied again:

5. Pig with black spots and piglet feeding from her.

6. Pig with spots and udders, but little pig may not be feeding but talking.

7. Mother pig with piglet feeding.

8. Mother pig, but uncertain whether piglet is feeding or merely vocalizing.

9. Again two pigs; one large and one small; are close together, but relationship unclear.

10. Mother pig with infant feeding from her.

11. Mother and child pigs.

12. Mother and child pig in close physical contact.

Subject III (female). This subject seems to show a variety of defences: repression, for suckling is not mentioned and existence of piglet is questioned; displacement, for feeding at a trough (!) is described, perhaps also reaction-formation (12) mother looks happy. Oral sadism may also be shown in 4, where the suckling act is seen as aggressive 'rearing up and over'. This subject we should expect to bottle-feed her children. All twelve responses for this interesting subject are set out.

1. Black circle in middle of light background.

2. Ant with antennae in the air rearing up.

3. Big black blob in air suspended from sky, and a black crane (bird) standing by it.

4. Big white animal with patch on left rearing up and over some little white thing on right maybe a mouse.

5. Big white pig with black patch standing on hind legs. Little pig? beside it.

6. Pig doing something but not sure what. Is there another animal there?

7. Little pig on right with a feeding trough. Big pig facing this way looking at little pig, etc.

8. Big, big (pig?) with black patch looking round to see little pig which is standing next to back leg and feeding.

9. Big pig looks as if its hind legs are in the air, little pig is trying to feed from its mother.

10. Big pig is sticking its tongue out at little pig which is feeding from it.

11. Same as before, mother pig looking round at baby pig which is feeding.

12. Mummy pig looking ahead quite happy and baby pig trying to get some milk.

CONCLUSIONS

In brief we argue that, as Kragh and Smith (1970) claim, the DMT and the MCT do allow defence mechanisms to be observed and some of these appear to resemble closely the Freudian varieties: repression, isolation, denial, reaction-formation, identification with the aggressor and turning against the self. These defences, therefore, we regard as having some objective verification.

Finally we should like to make two further points. First, as Dixon (1971) has well stated, if psychologists feel too threatened to use the Freudian terminology it does not matter. What is important is the fact that these phenomena, these distortions of perception, occur. Second, the regularity of the distortions, the fact that protocols readily fall into the scoring categories used by Kragh and his associates, requires explanation. That is to say, if an alternative hypothesis to account for the findings, other than psychoanalytic defences, is to be found it must allow for this fact. There is, it seems to us, no more parsimonious explanation. Defences can be observed through percept-genetic methods.

A highly interesting pilot study of the power of the DMT to elicit defences was carried out by Sharma and Haas (1974), who administered the DMT to two patients and compared their interpretations of the protocols with the assessments of the psychiatrist. In fact there was 90 per cent agreement between test and psychiatrist regarding general aspects of personality, e.g. need for warmth and the preoccupation with violence, as well as defences. Of course not too much must be made of this investigation since two subjects and one psychiatrist represents a very small sample and there is no way of assessing the validity of the psychiatric ratings. However it does *illustrate* (as distinct from prove) the potential of the DMT.

Fontana (1978) in the thesis already discussed in our chapter on psychosexual syndromes carried out a study of reaction-formation that was heavily indebted to percept-genetic theory. In the first experiment thirty-eight paired words were compiled, e.g. wild—tame, and presented singly in random order to subjects tachistoscopically at 'threshold speed', i.e. the speed at which neutral words could be recognized within four exposures. Subjects had to indicate like or dislike to each word. Then the same words were exposed at a slow speed and subjects were asked to express their deliberate like or dislike, taking as long as they wished. It was argued that the first response was likely to be unconscious feeling and thus changes in response in the two experiments were indicative of reaction-formation since the slow, deliberate response is likely to reflect the ego.

Since subjects had been grouped on the Sandler—Hazari symptom—trait inventory of obsessionality (fully discussed in Chapter 4), it was also argued from psychoanalytic theory that subjects high on obsessional traits and symptoms would show the most reaction-formation followed by (b) those high on symptoms, (c) those high on traits and (d) those low on both variables.

In the second experiment a threatening picture was shown at a fast tachistoscopic speed and this, following percept-genetic theory, was expected to produce reaction-formations, e.g. benevolent descriptions, compared with a control picture (a man knifing another, and a man giving another a cake).

Results. In experiment 1 the hypotheses were confirmed and reaction-formations were differentially shown by the four groups. There was a Kendal coefficient of concordance between hypotheses and results of 0.784 (sig. 0.01 level). In experiment 2 there were similar but less clear-cut results.

Although the results could be interpreted in terms of cognitive dissonance or simply of indecision which is naturally higher in the obsessional groups, these explanations are merely descriptions and are only semantic variants of reaction-formation, which attempts to describe a process. These results must be regarded as some support for the notion of reaction-formation and further support our claim that percept-genetic methods are capable of elucidating psychoanalytic theory.

DISPLACEMENT

We do not intend to devote much space to the evidence for this Freudian defence mechanism because it was demonstrated to occur beyond all reasonable doubt more than thirty years ago (Dollard et al., 1939) in the case of aggression. Thus in this study of frustration and aggression, an experiment was reported where subjects were deliberately deprived of sleep, tobacco, food and any way to pass the time by what appeared to be (to the subjects) a series of accidents. Subjects did not express their feelings directly to the psychologists for obvious social reasons. One subject, however, whom the authors clearly regard as using displacement, produced a series of drawings of hideous and mutilated bodies which he labelled psychologists.

Another experiment reported in this book (see also Miller and Bugelski, 1948) describes how the attitude scores towards Japanese and Mexican groups of boys at a summer camp were changed by considerable frustration. In this study the boys had to take examinations rather than enjoy themselves playing. The attitudes of the sample towards both ethnic groups were significantly more unfavourable after the examination than before. Sarnoff (1962) regards this displacement of aggression from examiners (authorities) to minority groups as one of the mechanisms responsible for anti-semitism, a specific form of scapegoating.

In this book we have for the most part eschewed animal studies, especially conditioning studies, on the grounds that generalization beyond the species and the experimental conditions is of doubtful validity. However as regards displacement, it is noteworthy that the ethologists have described a similar mechanism, under the name 'redirection activities' — *not* displacement, which for them is somewhat different (Hinde, 1966). Redirection activities, according to Hinde, are often seen in winter flocks of birds where an individual, if prevented by a superior from obtaining food, attacks an inferior bird instead of retaliating. Tinbergen (1959) describes herring gulls who displace their aggression against other gulls onto objects in the environment. If we can trust these ethological observations, there seems little doubt that there are here natural examples of Freudian displacement amongst birds.

Miller (1948) has constructed an elaborate model based on Hullian learning theory to account for displacement in terms of stimulus- and response-generalization. However the adequacy of learning theories to accommodate the validated observations of psychoanalysis is discussed in the final chapter of this book.

CONCLUSIONS

Displacement was one of the first Freudian concepts to receive experimental confirmation. It is now a generally accepted mental mechanism with considerable anecdotal support (the clerk ticked off by his boss is quick to kick the cat at home) in everyday life. It seems also to occur among birds.

STUDIES WITH THE DEFENCE PREFERENCE INQUIRY

A number of empirical studies of defence mechanisms have been carried out with the Defence Preference Inquiry. This, therefore, must be described.

THE TEST

The Defence Preference Inquiry is, in effect, a special form of the Blacky Pictures which have already been fully described (pp. 110 et seq.). Subjects have to rank a series of alternative descriptions of thoughts and actions in terms of how well each represents the way Blacky seems to be feeling or acting in a particular picture. Each of the descriptions is, in fact, an operational definition of typical Freudian defence may be easily calculated, from the mean ranking it receives over each of formation and regression. Thus at the end of the test a subject's preferred mode of defence may be easily calculated, from the mean ranking it receives over each of the eleven Blacky dimensions. In addition it is possible to see how a subject deals with problems in a particular psychosexual area. For example Oedipal desires may be handled by sublimation, oral longings by reaction-formation.

VALIDITY OF THE DEFENCE PREFERENCE INQUIRY

Unfortunately no studies of the validity of this technique have been carried out.

Most researches, where it has been used, are content to report the results (as if they were of proven validity) discussing them as 'facts'. Unfortunately most of these researches are not such that it is possible to draw any inferences concerning the validity of the test or to use them as evidence for construct-validity. The only evidence, therefore, that can be said to support the validity of any of the measures of the Defence Preference Inquiry is that from the studies of perceptual defence where it has sometimes been used. In these investigations (e.g. Blum, 1955, 1957; Nelson, 1955) subjects classified as repressors on the test have shown repressing behaviour in the perceptual defence experiments in that they have taken longer to recognize emotional stimuli. Thus, to some extent at least, there is evidence that the Inquiry does measure repression validly.

EMPIRICAL INVESTIGATIONS WITH THE DEFENCE PREFERENCE INQUIRY

As has been mentioned above, the published researches in which this test was used cannot be used to support or refute the Freudian concept of defence mechanisms. This is simply because the authors are content to report the scores of various samples. Thus Blum (1956b, 1964) applied the test in altogether eight countries: male students in Italy, England, the Netherlands and the USA (1956b); Denmark, France, Germany and Israel (1964). Since the validity of the test is unknown and the aetiology of defence mechanisms in psychoanalytic theory unclearly defined, it is obviously not possible to draw any firm conclusions concerning Freudian theory from these results. Similarly the study by Cohen (1956) of ego-defence preference on interpersonal relations and the work of Thelen (1965) concerned with similar defence preferences among parents and children has no bearing on the correctness of the Freudian concepts of ego-defences.

CONCLUSIONS

Thus nothing relevant to psychoanalytic theory can be deduced from any of the investigations which have used the Defence Preference Inquiry. Nevertheless it remains a useful research tool: for example if paranoids (who are supposed to favour projection) were compared on the test with hysterics (who are held to use repression) this would constitute a real test of psychoanalytic theory.

In summary then the Defence Preference Inquiry is considered to be a test whose real potential for the study of psychoanalytic theory has unfortunately not been realized.

PROJECTION

The work of Sears (1936, 1937) and Wells and Goldstein (1964)

Sears (1936, 1937) carried out what appears to have been the first experimental studies of projection. He got students to rate themselves and each other for the anal traits of stinginess, obstinacy, bashfulness and disorderliness. The 'true' amount of each of these traits was the mean rating (on a seven-point scale) received by each subject. The projection score was the mean of his ratings for others. Sears (1936) argued that if Freudian projection were correct there should be a positive correlation between the two scores. In fact the correlation was small and negative. This finding, therefore, appears to refute Freudian theory.

Sears (1937), however, made a further examination of these data. He attempted to take the factor of insight into account. If a subject's self-rating was congruent with his rating of others, the subject was deemed insightful. Then it was found that non-insightful subjects did tend to attribute their traits to others. This therefore appears to confirm Freudian theory, although desirable traits were also projected.

There is of course a logical problem inherent in this method of investigating projection. If projection occurs there is no reason to think that the ratings given by others have much validity. Rather they must represent the raters as well as the ratees. Hence the mean of assessments for an individual will not necessarily be accurate.

Wells and Goldstein (1964) replicated this study by Sears on two samples of students. As with Sears' (1936 and 1937) studies, each subject rated himself on a seven-point scale for stinginess, obstinacy, disorderliness and bashfulness. According to Wells and Goldstein, the results of Sears (1937) did not prove that projection took place — rather they were an artefact of the definition of insightful. Thus they claim that in the Sears study 'insightful' was attributed to those whose average rating of others was lower than their self-rating, while 'non-insightful' was attributed to those whose average rating of others was *higher* than their self-rating. Hence *by definition* the non-insightful project their traits since projection is defined as seeing in others traits in oneself. However in fact Sears (1937) defined 'non-insightful' by the *incongruence* of ratings. If self-rating and average rating by others were in the same half of the distribution a subject was regarded as insightful. Thus Wells and Goldstein's methodological examination does not seem to be fair.

Wells and Goldstein (1964) analysed their data by a method similar to that of Sears. A subject was insightful if more than half the raters agreed with his self-rating of 123 or 567 on the rating scale. They found no evidence for the projection of traits, contrary to the finding of Sears (1937), among either the insightful or the non-insightful.

Comments and conclusions

If we ignore the methodological point raised by Wells and Goldstein we are left with the fact that Sears' study gave slight support for the concept of projection while that of Wells and Goldstein failed to do so. However neither of these investigations has been examined in detail because it seems to us that the design used is incapable of putting the Freudian concept of projection to the test. Stinginess is not repressed into the unconscious. Stinginess itself in Freudian theory is a defence against anal retention. It is nonsense to say that a defence must itself be repressed. It is of course true that stinginess is less socially desirable (in the response-set sense) than say generosity but the defence mechanisms are postulated by Freud to be defences against id material. Thus the attribution of traits to others does not seem an adequate test of projection. Hence neither of these experiments seem relevant to the Freudian notion of projection and cannot therefore be regarded as either confirmation or refutation of the theory.

A more general point applies to the method of comparing self-ratings and ratings by others. If in fact projection does occur the validity of ratings by others cannot be used to compare with self-ratings. Indeed the test of projection might be to compare the *variance* of each individual's ratings of a sample (which should be small if projection occurs) with the variance of the overall ratings of the class.

It must therefore be concluded that neither of these studies is relevant to projection and that the comparison of rating scales is a dubious procedure.

The work of Blumberg and Maher (1965)

Blumberg and Maher attempted to test the Freudian theory of projection in a small sample of psychotic patients.

Sample. Thirty-three psychotic patients.

Test. Forty-item adjective check-list (twenty desirable and twenty undesirable traits).

Method. Subjects had to

(a) check traits describing themselves,
(b) check traits describing twelve people whom they knew, and
(c) check traits descriptive of twelve anonymous photographs (faces).

The subjects themselves were rated by nursing aides.

Results. There was no significant association (X^2) between having any knid of trait and perceiving it in others. Nor was there any significant difference between paranoids (believed in Freudian theory to favour the defence mechanism of projection: see p. 329 for the theory and pp. 330-41 for the objective evidence) and the others. There was, therefore, no support for the defence mechanism of projection.

Comments

This failure to support Freudian theory could be due to the defects of the theory or the test. In this case, however, the experiment was clearly defective. The unreliability of ratings by any but highly trained observers is considerable. In this study the ratings were done by nurses' aides and psychotic patients. It would therefore be wise to conclude nothing from this investigation.

The work of Price-Williams (1965)

Price-Williams carried out a highly interesting and imaginative study of projection among the Tiv of Northern Nigeria combining the quantitative methods pioneered by Whiting and Child (1953) (see p. 78 for a description) with actual field data, rather than the colourful but possibly unreliable observations of anthropologists — for example Rattray's (1923) description of the Ashanti — used by these latter authors.

Rationale of the study. Severe or protracted illness is attributed by the Tiv to the fact of akombo, a supernatural agency, being offended or to the sick person being assailed by *mbatsav*, a class of supernatural beings generally malevolent. Spiro (1961) has argued that the postulation of the existence of malevolent supernaturals to account for illness or disaster is an example of a culturally constituted defence mechanism — to permit the gratification of repressed impulses by projection and displacement. Since Tiv witchcraft, as mentioned above, exhibits this cultural defence mechanism (against aggression), it should be possible, if the theory is correct, to trace the path of repression or aggression in childhood to projection in folk-tales. Folk-tales are considered by some anthropologists as projective systems (e.g. Kardiner, 1945) or tests and, as is well-known, they have been thus used in the study of achievement-motivation by McClelland and Friedman (1952).

Method

1. Field observations of child-rearing procedures were rated by students for severity of independence-training and indulgence of aggression (the relevant variables).

N.B. There was considerable unreliability of rating.

2. Stories and folk-tales of the culture were also rated for the occurrence of various behaviour systems, e.g. succorance, nurturance and aggression (see Whiting, 1963).

Results. In these stories aggression was by far the commonest theme — as judged by all raters. Furthermore, despite the unreliability of the judges, it does appear that aggression is suppressed as far as possible in the child-rearing procedures of this tribe.

Comments and conclusions

Price-Williams (1965), in a complex interpretation of these results demanding considerable knowledge and insight into the background of this tribe, argues that these findings support the claim of Spiro (1961) that such witchcraft practices, as attributing illness to outside agencies, are a cultural defence mechanism of projection or displacement. Although this particular paper is too speculative to be regarded as firm objective evidence for projection, it does nevertheless illustrate, as did Whiting and Child (1953), the possibilities inherent in their method for the cross-cultural study of psychoanalytic phenomena. Nevertheless, as was stated earlier in the cross-cultural study of personality (see p. 74), this investigation could be regarded as more evidence for the claim that such studies are a dangerous chimera.

The work of Halpern (1977)

Halpern (1977) carried out an extremely ingenious experiment using nearly 200 students who were first given an eleven-item scale to tap their admission of sexuality: a typical item was 'I never have sexual dreams.' Subjects then rated for degree of liking six photographs of people. The experimental manipulation then followed in which pornographic pictures were shown. Finally the most disliked photograph had to be rated for twenty traits.

Results. Those subjects in the experimental condition (pornographic pictures) who did not admit their sexuality denied being sexually aroused by the pornography and rated their photograph as 'lustful'.

This is a clever experiment in that powerful feelings were aroused and a measure of projection was used which was objective in the Cattellian sense of the term, i.e. it was unlikely to be spotted by subjects and thus deliberately distorted. The fact that it was possible to predict which subjects would project (the sexually defensive ones) is also confirmation of the defence mechanism at work. This experiment must be regarded as clear evidence for projection.

The work of Holmes (1968)

Since we have now cited a study which seems to us to provide clear evidence of projection, we must now examine the theoretical paper by Holmes (1968), who is a psychologist determined to demonstrate, as Freud predicted would happen, that psychoanalytic theory cannot be true. In this paper he examines the defence of projection and looks at some of the experimental studies.

Holmes (1968) concluded from a similar study that persons only project traits that resemble or are related to traits that the projecting persons think they possess. Recent work has not changed Holmes's view and this of course is not projection in the Freudian sense since projection is of traits unacceptable to the conscious (and thus unknown). Thus Holmes argues that experiments in projection only show that subjects project traits they know they possess although they may be unaware that they are doing so. Hence there is no evidence for the psychoanalytic concept.

Holmes, indeed, likes to distinguish two senses of projection: (a) attributive projection, where a subject's traits are projected on to others and (b) complementary projection, where the cause of feelings is projected on to others.

Even if we were to accept Holmes's points, it is to be noted that projection does occur, so to this extent Freud was correct, and that subjects are or may be unaware of their projecting. Thus the point at issue between Holmes and psychoanalytic theory is the *defensive function* of projection which Holmes attempts to deny.

Holmes draws a number of conclusions:

1. There is no evidence that projection of an undesirable trait helps to keep from awareness the fact that a person possesses this trait. Certainly the evidence which we review fails to treat this point. However, the studies of paranoia discussed in a later chapter of this book do suggest that the paranoid's projection of homosexuality has this function.

2. Holmes argues that the experiments show that subjects project traits on to desirable persons as well as undesirable and that this latter is inconsistent with the theory and that, therefore, projection cannot have a defensive function. We fail to

see why in fact the projection of traits on to undesirable persons is contrary to theory. It is a perfectly acceptable defence to say he is bad not I. That is all that is required of projection and projection of traits on to undesirable persons allows this. Holmes's argument seems quite unsound.

3. Holmes claims that once traits are projected they are not then thought of as less desirable and that they should be according to psychoanalytic theory. Again we fail to take this argument. A trait in another person can be regarded as bad without threat to the ego. Thus there is no necessity for their desirability to change.

4. Holmes argues that there is no evidence that projection of traits reduces stress as assessed by self-report, physiological or performance measures. While this is so, there is no reason in psychoanalytic theory why it should do so. Defence is an ongoing process. Only when threats are serious and almost breaking into consciousness should we expect changes in anxiety after projection. It is certain that no experimental study could present this degree of physical threat.

Thus despite the complexity and detail of Holmes's paper, the basic arguments, it seems to us, are not strong and it appears that Holmes, like Eysenck, is keen to infirm the theory. This is unfortunate since there is no need to adduce weak arguments over the evidence for projection, which as we have seen is not convincing, other than the work of Halpern (1977).

The work of Kreines and Bogart (1974)

Kreines and Bogart (1974) obtained self-ratings and ratings of others from 100 subjects for the following traits: stinginess, stubborness, messiness and bashfulness. Depending upon the agreement of the two rating sets, individuals were put into insightful and not-insightful groups. Subjects were then given their true scores so that for those without insight the information was dissonant. Ratings were then again obtained and dissonant subjects (i.e. those without insight) increased projection of traits to others including good traits such as generosity. Projection, they therefore concluded, was a function of low insight.

This conclusion does not hold water since the experimental conditions confound insight and dissonance. If the insightful subjects had been fed dissonant information (i.e. fake) they might have projected traits also. Thus without this control it could be argued that projection is a function of dissonance.

This type of experiment also invokes a logical difficulty. If subjects are insightful because of agreement between self-ratings and others' ratings, and if others' ratings contain projections, then the agreement implies inaccurate self-ratings, i.e. lack of insight.

In our view this is not a powerful experiment and its results are not to be used as support for Freudian theory.

CONCLUSIONS CONCERNING PROJECTION

Only one of these empirical objective studies supports the mechanism of projection. It may be that methodological difficulties account for this but never-theless, despite the intuitive attraction of the notion, there is as yet little firm evidence in its favour — but see the objective studies of paranoia (p. 330).

IDENTIFICATION WITH THE AGGRESSOR

In our discussion of identification as a developmental process in the formation of the super-ego (see p. 181), it was pointed out that in Freudian theory identifica-tion is thought to occur through fear of the castrating father. Bandura (1969) pours scorn on this concept on the grounds that in everyday life imitation cer-tainly takes place without this fear. The laboratory studies of imitative behaviour carried out by Bandura and colleagues have not, however, specifically tested this hypothesis of aggressive identification as a defence. Anna Freud (1946) regards it as an important defence mechanism, quoting clinical examples of children identifying with dentists and other threatening figures. It is to be noted that the examples of identification used by Bandura and Anna Freud differ in one important respect: in Bandura's examples there is no defensive purpose in the imitative behaviour.

Clinical evidence for the concept of identification is not hard to find. Bettel-heim (1943) regards the behaviour of the inmates of concentration camps as examples of this mechanism while Sarnoff (1962) considers that Jewish anti-semitism is an illustration of it. Objective evidence is scanty. Sarnoff (1951) has, however, conducted one such study of Jewish anti-semitism.

The work of Sarnoff

Sample. Forty-five highly anti-semitic Jewish students and fifty-five neutral Jewish students were selected by means of an anti-semitism questionnaire. This was the measure of identification with the aggressor.

Hypotheses

1. Anti-semites should have negative feelings to parents. This is, according to Sarnoff (1951), because such feelings are an antecedent to the development of this defence mechanism.

This hypothesis is faulty in that *by definition* Jewish anti-semites (unless converts to the religion) would be hostile to their parents.

2. Anti-semites should be insecure and anxious. This is because anxiety feelings are the cause of the identification with a source of strength.

3. Anti-semites should be more passive in the face of hostility. This follows from the notion of identification. A person who resists hostility is unlikely to identify with hostile or aggressive people.

Method. Personality questionnaires were used to assess anxiety, insecurity, feelings to parents and attitudes towards aggression.

Results. All these hypotheses, derived from psychoanalytic theory, were supported.

Comments and conclusions

The fact that these hypotheses were supported must be regarded as confirmation of psychoanalytic theory. Nevertheless it must be admitted that the hypotheses are rather distant from the actual identificatory process itself as studied by Bandura in the laboratory. Thus, just as hypothesis 1 could be predicted without the notion of identification with the aggressor so it can be argued that hypothesis 2, for example, could be interpreted differently. Thus if insecurity and anxiety are regarded as symptoms of neuroticism it could be inferred that anti-semitism is itself a sign — being, presumably, irrational. The concept of identification is one explanation of these observed correlations, but equally it could be argued that anit-semitism is the result of a neurotic projection of feelings (as in paranoia) — hence its relation with anxiety.

REACTION-FORMATION

The work of Sarnoff (1960)

Sarnoff has also carried out a study of reaction-formation — a notoriously difficult concept to verify objectively.

Rationale of study. Cynicism, it was argued by Sarnoff, is a reaction-formation against feelings of affection. If other people are unpleasant then negative behaviour towards them is permissible. On this assumption, people with strong reaction-formations against affection, i.e. cynics, should become anxious when they are confronted by stimuli evoking affectionate responses. To reduce anxiety by increased reaction-formation cynics should become more cynical.

Hypothesis. Subjects with a strong reaction-formation (HRF) should become more cynical than subjects with a weak reaction-formation (LRF) after affection has been aroused.

Sample. Eighty-one male undergraduates.

Method. A cynicism scale (CS) and a measure of reaction-formation (RF) were administered to the subjects. These were then assigned at random to two treatments. One group saw a play which was chosen to arouse affection (HA). The low-arousal group heard a tape-recording of the same piece. Then subjects again filled in the cynicism scale.

Results. Both HRF and LRF groups tended to become less cynical after both conditions — a finding contrary to hypothesis. However the high group did shift less than the low group in the aroused condition. There was a small correlation between the reaction-formation score and the cynicism score.

Comments

Sarnoff (1962) in discussing this experiment claims that the shift in scores and the correlation between reaction-formation and cynicism supports Freudian theory. However, it cannot be denied that the main hypothesis was not supported. This seems hardly surprising in that the original assumption of this study, that cynicism is a reaction-formation against affection, may well be false. This experiment shows considerable experimental ingenuity and dialectical skill in deriving hypotheses. However it seems too far removed from psychoanalytic theory to be an adequate test of it.

SUBLIMATION

Wallach (1960) and Wallach and Greenberg (1960) have published two studies pertaining to the defence mechanism of sublimation as it affects liking for music. Since both these investigations used the same sample they cannot be considered to be independent.

FREUDIAN THEORY OF SUBLIMATION IN MUSIC

Very simply, in psychoanalytic theory listening to music can provide an outlet for repressed sexuality. Hence liking for music is a sublimation of sexuality.

The study of Wallach and Greenberg (1960)

Rationale. If the Freudian theory be correct, anxious introverts should express more sexuality by listening to music than anxious extroverts. This is because the anxiety of the introvert indicates that his introversion is not a good defence and introverts cannot express their sexuality alone. On the other hand, non-anxious introverts should express very little sexuality in listening to music since their non-anxiety indicates their defences are sound.

Hypotheses

1. Highly anxious introverts should show greater symbolic sexual arousal to music than highly anxious extroverts.
2. The opposite should be the case for low anxious introverts and extroverts.

Sample. Seventy-three female students.

Method. These subjects wrote stories in response to three pieces of jazz which had been previously rated for their ability to arouse the listener sexually. They then stated their preference for the music and completed the Maudsley Personality Inventory and the Minnesota TSE Test (Evans and McConnell, 1951).

Scoring. These stories were scored for sexual symbolic arousal, using the method of Clark and Sensibar (1956) and Beardslee and Fogelson (1958). This involves counting the incidence in the stories of motion, peak, penetration, rhythm and symbolic content. The validity of these indices of sexual arousal is derived from Clark and Sensibar who found them related to gazing on pictures of nude women in a sample of men. Wallach and Greenberg themselves support the validity of these scores by showing that they are all inter-correlated. In addition the incidence of sexual events was noted.

Results. Both hypotheses were supported. Introverts who were anxious were more strongly sexually aroused by jazz than extroverts.

The research of Wallach (1960)

Sample. As in the previous study.

Music. Three classical pieces, two by Ravel, one by Debussy.

Method. As above, these subjects had to write stories in response to each piece of music. One month later subjects had to choose which of these three pieces they liked best and to rate them on a seven-point rating scale for preference. In addition the MPI was administered to the students.

Scoring. The stories in response to this serious music were again scored for symbolic sexual arousal and manifest sexual content.

Results. An analysis of variance on the symbolic sexuality scores showed degree of preference and degree of anxiety to be significant factors. Thus sexual arousal was related to both these variables. Correlations were also computed between sexual arousal and these variables: sexual arousal and anxiety correlated 0.3, sexual arousal and preference correlated 0.32.

Comments on both studies

Taken together these investigations support the Freudian claim that liking for music is a sublimation of sexuality. The fact that the relationship is not higher between sexual arousal and preference is not an argument against Freudian theory. As Waelder (1965) points out, the fact that there are ego components in appreciation of the arts (understanding of harmony, contrapuntal devices, for example) is the bribe for the super-ego to allow listening to proceed. It is these complex intellectual skills that make a liking for music respectable. An illustration of the point is the generally accepted difference between pornography and high art.

Spiegel and Zelin (1973) carried out a study of sublimation. Twenty-one subjects were frustrated, after which a five-minute story had to be written in response to one of three TAT-like pictures (of which one portrayed the experimenter). Frustration produced no more aggression than was seen in the twenty-one controls who were not frustrated. There is thus here no support for catharsis or sublimation.

While there is no confirmation of Freudian theory, small experiments of this kind in which the psychological implications of the frustration are (for ethical reasons) necessarily slight cannot be used to refute the theory.

CONCLUSIONS

These investigations by Walach could not be held, on their own, to prove that sublimation of sexuality accounts for pleasure in music. Nevertheless they have shown that symbolic sexual arousal and preference are linked as would be expected from the psychoanalytic theory. These investigations may be regarded, therefore, as support for the concept of sublimation and also for the Freudian theory of art (see p. 259). The work of Spiegel and Zelin is probably not useful.

THE WORK OF GLESER AND IHILEVICH (1969)

Gleser and Ihilevich have developed what they claim to be an objective measure of defence mechanisms. If this were shown to be valid it would be a most important advance in the elucidation of psychoanalytic theory.

Rationale of the test: the Defence Mechanism Inventory

Having scrutinized the descriptions of defence mechanisms the authors decided that five categories would embrace them all and it is these five basic defences that the test purports to measure:

1. *Turning against object* (TAO), e.g. identification with the aggressor, displacement.
2. *Projection* (PRO).
3. *Principalization* (PRN), e.g. intellectualization, isolation, rationalization.
4. *Turning against self* (TAS), e.g. masochism.
5. *Reversal* (REV), e.g. denial, repression, reaction-formation.

Description of the test

Ten stories are included, two per conflict-area. The conflict-areas are:

(a) authority,
(b) independence,
(c) competition,
(d) situational, and
(e) masculinity (for males) or femininity (for females).

For each story there are four questions tapping actual behaviour, fantasy behaviour, thoughts and feelings. For each of these questions there are five possible responses tapping the five defences to which subjects have to indicate the most and least liked.

Scoring rationale. Three psychologists and seven social workers only agreed 60 per cent of the time as to what defence a response indicated on TAS, REV and PRN. There was even less agreement on the other scales.

Comments and conclusions

The fact that there was so little agreement as to what defence a response indicated means that in its present form the test cannot be considered useful. Nevertheless it may provide an objective measure of defence mechanisms on further development. *A priori* it seems an ingenious scheme. Ideally, instead of classifying defences subjectively, an objective classification based on a factor-analysis of correlations between items tapping individual defences would have been preferable. This could overcome the lack of agreement as to what defences a response was tapping since reference to its factor-loadings would make this clear.

Clearly, evidence of its validity must be presented and disagreements between scorers as to the implications of responses removed, before the test can be used seriously. Nevertheless it does appear to be a potentially useful measure of defence mechanisms.

STUDIES WITH THE DEFENCE MECHANISM INVENTORY

A number of studies have been conducted with the DMI despite the problems over its reliability and validity. Dudley (1978) investigated the effects of sex, birth order, and social desirability on the DMI scores using a sample of sixty subjects. He found that it was possible to create a good impression in respect of most of the variables, i.e. they were affected by social desirability. This being the case, it is even less likely that the scores could be valid.

Gleser and Sachs (1973) carried out what they regard as a validation study of the DMI using forty-five female and forty male Introductory Psychology students. In part 1 of this experiment DMI scores were obtained. Then the students were made to feel they had suffered severe academic failure. After this mood-scales (friendliness, anger, depression and anxiety) were completed together with rating scales of performance on the test which they thought they had failed (these were compared with previous estimates). Subjects were also allowed to criticize the test and the whole investigation (perhaps no difficult task). From the original defence scores, as a test of their validity, predictions were made concerning changes in ratings and criticisms. In males some variables were successfully predicted but this was not the case for females. This study is not powerful in our view. Not only is the sampling dubious, but in addition all the other measures and rating scales are of unknown validity. Thus the failure to validate the DMI may reflect the errors in the other scales. What is certain, however, is that this study does not support the validity of the DMI.

Martin (1977) showed that in Oklahoma, Indian adolescents turned aggression outwards less than did the whites. However, this study simply assumed the validity of the test, and moreover ignored the possible cultural determinants of responses. It cannot be regarded as evidence for or against the validity of the test.

Blacker and Farcher (1977) had raters examine the DMI items for defences and threats to the ego. The raters showed little agreement. These authors regard this as a content-validity study. In fact it is simply a study of face-validity and the opinion of judges is irrelevant to test validity, which is a purely empirical matter. This study is certainly best ignored. Content-validity properly refers to studies of items where the item population can be defined, as in vocabulary or music tests.

Gordon and Brackney (1979) gave the DMI and the MMPI to more than 100 students and computed correlations between the two tests. However, the correlations were small, making interpretation difficult and little light is thrown upon the validity of the DMI scores by this study.

Clum and Clum (1973a) reported a study in which moods were related to the DMI variables. Again, however, little can be inferred about the validity of the scales from a study such as this.

In the last three studies, one notable feature was that the significant correlations between the DMI scales and other tests were fewer in number among females than males. This suggests that the scales may work more efficiently with males than females but its significance for the validity of the DMI is not high.

In brief these more recent studies do little to attest to the validity of the DMI. As with so many clinical psychological tests, many researchers simply assume them to be valid.

Conclusions concerning the DMI

It still remains true that there is little evidence attesting to the validity of the DMI variables. It is indubitably an interesting test but it is not such that results with it can be taken on trust. Nor can the scales be used as objective measures of defences. Its validity does, however, deserve investigation.

CONCLUSIONS CONCERNING ALL STUDIES OF DEFENCE MECHANISMS OTHER THAN REPRESSION

Generally speaking, most of the researches (other than the percept-genetic) reviewed in this chapter are not well enough designed to allow of either refutation or confirmation of Freudian theory. The basic difficulty is, of course, that defence mechanisms are internal processes which have to be inferred from behaviour rather than observed. However, percept-genetic techniques do allow such observations to be made, and as we have argued the DMI confirms a number of Freudian defence mechanisms: especially isolation, projection, denial and reaction-formation or processes which closely resemble them. Clearly much more research should be carried out in percept-genetics with the aim of validating these defence-mechanism scores. Silverman's techniques also support the general notion of defences and both these approaches are apparently powerful for the study of unconscious processes.

Of the individual researches not within the methods of Silverman or percept-genetics, only those of Wallach (1960) and Wallach and Greenberg (1960) are satisfactory and these support the notions of sublimation in music.

SOME OTHER RELATED PSYCHOANALYTIC HYPOTHESES

In this chapter, studies of the Freudian theory of slips of the tongue, wit and humour and artistic creativity will also be reviewed. Their position here is not arbitrary for each, as will be seen, represents a breach of defence mechanisms and hence a glimpse into the unconscious. They therefore constitute a link between the major portion of this chapter and the next which is concerned with dreams, which constitute in Freudian theory as complete a breakdown of ego defences as may be observed outside psychosis.

SLIPS OF THE TONGUE

Freudian theory

In *The Psychopathology of Everyday Life*, Freud (1901) devotes considerable attention to slips of the tongue. He does not consider these errors to be random or due to the similarities between adjoining words but believes such slips to be due to unconscious mental activity. Careful analysis of the errors by free association would reveal their unconscious determination in each case. An unconscious thought striving to emerge distorts the conscious intent. Freud gives an example: Brill told a patient she was incompetent (his true opinion) to run her own affairs when he intended to say competent. In psychoanalytic theory, therefore, slips of the tongue are evidence of the failure of defence mechanisms, brief glimpses of the unconscious. They are examined here, under defence mechanisms of which they constitute a breach not an example, as has been discussed above. Strictly, perhaps, they are better included under dreams but this huge subject deserves separate treatment.

The work of Veness (1962)

Veness carried out an experimental investigation into this theory although on a small and restricted sample.

Sample. Thirty-two females. These were acquaintances of the author, secretaries and lecturers in the university. Female subjects were used to ease the embarrassment of a female experimenter.

Words. Eight lists of words, matched for frequency in the Thorndike—Lorge word-list (Thorndike and Lorge, 1944) and for ease of pronunciation, were used. Half the words were neutral, half emotive, as rated independently by three judges.

Method. The eight typed lists were presented to each subject who had to speak one word, then utter an association to it, speak the next word, and so on to the end, in time with a metronome set to beat sixty times a minute. Two judges scored the experiment as it went on.

Scores. Missed beats, slips of the tongue and delayed reactions (faults) were recorded for each subject.

Results

(a) *Slips.* Only forty-one slips were made in all — almost equally divided between emotional and neutral words. Furthermore over half of these were made by five subjects. This was too small a number to provide an adequate sample for statistical analysis. There were more slips to emotional words than neutral and to the associations to neutral than emotional words.

(b) *Missed beats.* Although there were more missed beats (sig. 0.01 level) for the emotional words there was also a high correlation for missed beats between the lists.

(c) *Faults.* Here the variance was attributed by analysis of variance to differences between both subjects and lists.

From this Veness concludes that the Freudian theory underlying slips of the tongue was not confirmed.

Comments and conclusions

Veness recognizes the problem that emotional words may not be emotional to some subjects and that neutral words may be emotional to others. Nevertheless, this aside, the experiment may not provide an adequate test of the theory. According to the theory the unconscious breaks out and overcomes our defences, hence the more errors when we are tired or thinking of something else. In this study, by virtue of the experimental conditions subjects are concentrating on the words. Thus errors will be likely to be reduced, an argument which accounts for the low number recorded. However if the theory were correct more errors would still be expected to occur with the emotional words.

This experiment entirely fails to support Freudian theory. However, as was discussed in our study of repression (see p. 201), it would have been better to have selected words which were relevant to the problems of each subject to test the theory adequately.

WIT AND HUMOUR

Outline of the psychoanalytic theory

In *Jokes and their Relation to the Unconscious* (1905b), and also in the paper 'Humour' (1927b), Freud proposed the psychoanalytic theory of wit and humour. It is somewhat akin to the theory of parapraxis (Freud, 1901) in that the joke allows material to pass the super-ego (or censor, as at this state of psychoanalysis it was known), which in an ordinary situation it would not do. The explosive quality of the laughter is related to the strength of the unconscious impulses being satisfied through the content of the joke. In addition Freud attempts to distinguish between wit and humour. Humour is defined as the situation where the principal character reacts to intolerable problems with a verbal jest rather than resignation or hostility. Humour is the characteristic response of well-adjusted individuals. Wit, on the other hand, especially hostile wit, is favoured by maladjusted individuals. Typically hostile wit deals with people in a highly derogatory fashion, the wit concealing the true hostility. Thus wit and humour allow the expression of repressed wishes and other material of the id.

Importance of the theory

This theory of humour is not an important part of psychoanalysis from the viewpoint of theory. It could be proven entirely false in every detail and the basic structure of Freudian theory could remain unshaken. For this reason the description given above has been abbreviated. It has been included in this book because, from the point of view of understanding an interesting portion of human behaviour and for the light it throws on literature and verbal skills, it is of considerable importance.

Empirical hypotheses of the theory

There appears to be a large number of testable hypotheses which can be drawn from this theory. The hypotheses set out below are not considered to be the total number of possible deductions but are rather examples to which the reader can add his own.

1. Individuals finding aggressive jokes the funniest will be those whose aggression is normally repressed.
2. Similarly those who find sexual jokes the most amusing will be those whose sexuality is normally repressed.
3. Highly repressed individuals (with a very strong super-ego) will be humour-less (they will not dare to laugh at jokes).
4. Psychopaths, similarly, will not find jokes amusing (they have no need to express their repressions in this way).
5. Witty people will have strong unconscious aggression.
6. Wits will be more neurotic than the normal population.

The work of Cattell — the IPAT Humour Test

The IPAT Humour Test of personality has been developed by Cattell and his associates from a series of empirical studies of humour. (Cattell and Luborsky, 1947; Luborsky and Cattell, 1947; Cattell and Luborsky, 1952). Originally (Cattell and Luborsky, 1952) there were two forms to this test: in form A subjects have to choose from pairs of jokes which they think is the funnier, while in form B the subjects rate jokes for humour on a two-point scale. Since both forms do not correlate highly the authors suggest that in any application of the test both forms be used. 91 pairs of jokes are used in form A, 112 jokes in form B.

Measures derived from the test

From a study of the inter-correlations between jokes on around 100 subjects thirteen clusters were isolated. A cluster was defined such that the jokes within it had to correlate more than 0.17 with each other and less than this with jokes outside it. These clusters of jokes were then related to scores on the Guilford—Martin test (see p. 57) (Luborsky and Cattell, 1947). Ten of these clusters were identified and used as the test variables — debonair sexual uninhibitedness, good-natured play, tough self-composure, gruesomeness, hostile derogation, resignation, cold realism, ponderous humour, whimsical retort and mistreatment humour.

Cattell and Luborsky (1947) found that jokes could not be rated reliably for their underlying impulses (e.g. aggression or masochism) but that once these dimensions had been empirically defined jokes could be assigned to them with some accuracy.

Both these early forms of the test were vitiated by a lack of clear evidence of validity. The manual to the test (Cattell and Luborsky, 1952) refers constantly to the articles by Cattell and Luborsky (1947) and Luborsky and Cattell (1947) which however refer only to sixty-nine of the items in the two forms of the test (Lubin and Loos, 1953). Furthermore their references to correlations with the 16PF test are too vague to be useful. Wittenborn (1953) also points to a possible logical flaw in the test, namely that if custom stales the humour of a joke subjects are likely to find unfunny the very jokes they characteristically use!

Cattell (1957) reports briefly some later findings with this test, findings which still have not been fully reported in the literature. The research discussed above was unusual for Cattell in that it was based on cluster-analysis rather than his beloved factor-analysis, and was beset with the problem of instability from population to population. Form A and form B have therefore been subjected to a full factor-analysis and a new C form was constructed. This work has resulted in ten factors which seem reasonably stable — the ten described above (see p. 254). However as Cattell (1957) points out even these are not stable with extreme samples, as Pichot (1954) found with paranoids.

Comments and conclusions

Neither the handbook to the test, the articles cited in it, nor the description of the factorial studies with the IPAT Humour Test give sufficient detail for an accurate assessment of the validity of these factors to be made, so that the test must be regarded as purely experimental. The rationale of this test has been examined because in the handbook to it Cattell and Luborsky (1952) claim that the results support the Freudian hypotheses concerning humour. However we are forced to agree with Lubin and Loos (1953) that there is no factual evidence to support this assertion. Indeed the only relation this test would seem to have with the Freudian theory of humour is the basic assumption that humour is in some way related to personality.

It must, therefore, be concluded that despite the claims of the authors this test is not really relevant to the psychoanalytic theory of humour.

The work of O'Connell

O'Connell (1960, 1962, 1964) has investigated the psychology of humour with a scale developed to test certain psychoanalytic hypotheses. This is known as the Wit and Humour Appreciation Test (WHAT).

O'Connell (1960) had 332 subjects complete the Worchel (1957) Self-Concept Inventory (for predicting maladjustment) in which self and ideal adjustment is rated. A number of these subjects was then put in a stressful situation where they were made to feel failure and insulted. All the sample then completed the WHAT in which jokes have to be rated on a four-point like—dislike scale.

Hypotheses and results. Men preferred hostile wit more than did women. Women, however, showed a greater preference for nonsense wit than did men. O'Connell (1960) admits that the derivation of this finding from psychoanalytic theory is not clear. However such a hypothesis is in fact made by Grotjan (1957). To test further Freudian hypotheses an analysis of variance of the WHAT scores was computed with the following main factors: high and low self—ideal discrepancy on the Worchel (1957) test, sex, and stress, no stress. The main findings from this analysis were:

(a) In the non-stressful situation the maladjusted men appreciated hostile wit more than did the well-adjusted men. However in the stressful situation this was reversed and the maladjusted did not favour hostile wit.

This supports Freudian theory. It has already been noted that a liking for hostile wit is symptomatic of maladjustment in psychoanalytic theory and it could be expected that in a stressful situation the maladjusted would repress everything.

(b) This finding did not hold for women. Adjusted women preferred hostile wit on both occasions.

(c) The well-adjusted subjects preferred humour.

This finding supports Freudian theory.

(d) There was no confirmation that well-adjusted subjects preferred nonsense to hostile wit.

O'Connell (1960) argues that these results support the Freudian distinction between wit and humour and that, in accord with psychoanalytic theory, in some circumstances wit does reduce tension.

To what extent this study by O'Connell supports Freudian theory depends heavily on the validity of the WHAT. Are the categories of wit and humour, for example, really distinct? O'Connell (1962) describes the rationale and construction of the test so that it is possible to evaluate these results.

Construction of the WHAT

Sixty-five jokes were independently classified on the criteria of psychoanalysis by eleven clinical psychologists into humour, hostile wit and nonsense wit. Thirty-two of these jokes were reliably classified so that, when two were rejected at random, ten jokes were left in each of these categories.

The split-half reliability was 0.84 and the test—retest reliability was 0.8.

These are very impressive reliability coefficients for a personality test and compare well with those of the well-established measures. It is certainly a more reliable test than the IPAT Humour Test discussed above. It is extremely interesting that the psychologists in the O'Connell (1962) study were able to classify the jokes with such accuracy, because Cattell and Luborsky (1947) found that their raters were unable to do so although these latter used content rather than categories of humour and wit.

Using a Chi-square analysis (sex and adjusted or maladjusted), O'Connell (1962) examined the individual items of his test. This analysis supported the claim in the psychoanalytic theory that adjusted subjects preferred humour and that men preferred hostile wit. However, his sample in this study was the same as in the earlier research.

The fact that the WHAT is so reliable is impressive. However O'Connell has presented no evidence, other than that eleven psychologists agree, that these three categories of jokes are in fact separate and valid measures. Without this, the support for Freudian theory that the results appear to give cannot be upheld. In any case the only clear findings confirming the theory were that maladjusted subjects did not enjoy humour as much as adjusted ones.

The study by O'Connell (1964)

In this investigation O'Connell had six clinical psychologists choose, from a pool of forty-nine items purporting to be either wit or humour, those items which they regarded as humour (in the Freudian sense). Ten of these humorous items were used in a multi-dimensional study of the Freudian concept of humour with 100 undergraduates. These subjects compared each joke with every other (eighty comparisons in all) and the ratings were subjected to factor-analysis, following the procedures suggested by Messick and Abelson (1956).

Results. Four factors underlying liking for humorous jokes were revealed — loss of face, gallows humour, being pursued, and non-fatal loss.

O'Connell concluded that Freudian theories of humour were supported in that gallows humour emerged as a factor. However he regarded this study as evidence that the theory needed elaboration since there were three other factors.

These conclusions do not appear to be warranted by this evidence. After all, the original six judges used psychoanalytic criteria (gallows humour) to select the items. The emergence, therefore, of a factor of gallows humour supports the accuracy of their subjective judgements. In effect the factor confirms the claim that there is a class of jokes with gallows-humour content. Psychoanalytic theory is not needed to discover this. What would be needed to demonstrate the Freudian theory by this method would be a factor-analysis of a large sample of jokes. If a clear factor emerged loading on jokes with gallows humour, orthogonal to jokes pertaining to wit, and if it could be further shown that different people liked these two types of jokes and neurotics favoured wit, then support would be adduced for Freudian theory.

Conclusions to the work of O'Connell

These investigations by O'Connell are worthy of note in that they demonstrate that the psychoanalytic theory of wit and humour can be investigated objectively. Nevertheless, as yet they have not given sound confirmation for the theory apart from the finding that maladjusted men do prefer wit to humour. Thus this research must be praised because it is pregnant with possibilities rather than for the fruits of its labours.

The work of Gollob and Levine (1967)

These authors investigated the effects of distraction in the enjoyment of aggressive humour.

Rationale of the study. As we have seen in our description of the Freudian theory of wit and humour, there are ego and id components in the enjoyment of jokes. Thus the technique of the joke is enjoyed by the ego whereas the id appreciates the expression of forbidden aggressive or sexual impulses. However if the impulses expressed in the joke are too obvious enjoyment ceases. Thus a good joke must distract the ego and super-ego from the fact that impulses are being expressed. Remember that it is a cardinal point of Freudian theory (Freud, 1925a) that anxiety is a signal that id material is approaching consciousness and anxiety is antithetical to the enjoyment of jokes. Gollob and Levine tested the Freudian claim that distraction is important in enjoyment of humour by having subjects rate cartoons for humour before and after concentrating on their content. Aggressive cartoons should be more affected by this procedure than non-aggressive ones.

Sample. Fourteen female college students.

Cartoons. Eight very aggressive, eight least aggressive and eight nonsense cartoons.

Method. These cartoons were rated on an eight-point scale for humour and four from each group were selected on the basis of their mean humour rating score. Ten days later subjects had to say what was funny about each cartoon (thus destroying any distracting qualities) and they re-rated them for humour.

Results. In accord with the Freudian hypothesis, after studying the contents, the ratings for the aggressive cartoons dropped more than for the others. This result was repeated in a second study where the twelve cartoons were used in both presentations.

Comments and conclusions

The hypothesis drawn from Freudian theory that distraction is an important factor in the enjoyment of aggressive humour is certainly supported by these results. It is possible to argue, without recourse to psychoanalytic theory, that aggressive humour seems less funny than other types of joke on analysis. However, the question as to why this should be is still left unanswered. This study by Gollob and Levine supports one aspect of the Freudian theory of humour — the importance of distraction from the 'real' content of the joke in the enjoyment of a joke.

The work of Lamb (1968)

Lamb investigated the personality correlates of humour enjoyment following the arousal of sexual feelings.

Sample. Forty males saw photographs of nude women; forty controls saw neutral photographs.

Measures. After arousal subjects rated cartoons for humour.

Results. The experimental, aroused group enjoyed the cartoons more than the control group. Among the aroused subjects those who were high on a questionnaire measure of feelings of guilt about sex rated the cartoons more highly than did the control group. From this it was argued that sex guilt is an important factor in the enjoyment of humour.

Comments and conclusions

The relevance of this study to the Freudian theory of wit and humour is equivocal. Thus as Gollob and Levine (1967) have shown, distraction is important in the enjoyment of jokes. Now it could be argued that by arousing sexual feelings, Lamb was increasing vigilance against sexual themes and that the aroused group would, therefore, enjoy the jokes less. On the other hand the fact that this group enjoyed the jokes more supports the broad Freudian notion that the enjoyment of humour is related to the repression of forbidden wishes. However, excessive reliance should not be placed on the results concerning sex guilt since the validity of the test of sexual anxiety is unknown. Since this subject is highly contaminated by social desirability, it is not easy to accept a measure on face-validity alone. In conclusion this study by Lamb supports slightly the Freudian theory that humour is an expression of repressed wishes.

THE PSYCHOANALYTIC THEORY OF THE ARTS

Outline of the theory

'Before the problem of the creative artist analysis must, alas, lay down its arms.' Thus wrote Freud discussing the personality of Dostoevsky (Freud, 1928). Despite this modest disclaimer, psychoanalytic theory does in fact purport to embrace the creation of artistic works — visual, literary and musical. It has no especial theory of art but merely applies its usual analytic technique to the work of art much as is done in the study of dreams or wit and humour.

Thus in an early paper on poetry and daydreaming Freud (1908b) makes the basic psychoanalytic position quite clear. Daydreams express the private fantasy wishes of the dreamers which most people normally strive to keep hidden because they are ashamed of them and because, even if communicated, they would tend to repel the audience. The man of literary talent however, by his *ars poetica*, expresses his fantasies in such a way that the audience takes great pleasure in them. Thus the poetic art is this ability to overcome our repulsion. Freud argues that the aesthetic pleasure of the formal structure of the work acts as a 'bribe' for us to enjoy the deeper pleasure of seeing basic, impulsive wishes acted out in the content. We can enjoy our own wishes without shame. In brief then, just as slips of the tongue and dreams express basic wishes, so too do the arts. Here the super-ego is quieted not only by disguise, as in dreams, but by the formal nature of the work. In this way we can vicariously and guiltlessly express our repressions.

Naturally the nature of these wishes underlying great art is no different from the nature of the wishes underlying all human behaviour. Freud (1928) points out that it is unlikely to be accidental that three of the great literary masterpieces of the world are concerned with the Oedipus complex — *Oedipus Rex*, *Hamlet* and *The Brothers Karamazov*.

The visual arts, too, are easily encompassed in this theory. Freud (1908b) has attempted to link the actual desire to use paint with sublimated anal erotism. Fairbairn (1938) and Rickman (1940) have attempted to relate the symbolism of art, which they call art-work, to dream-work, i.e. both represent disguises for repressed material. Fairbairn, indeed, attempted to correlate the quality of a work of art with the amount of art-work in it. Pickford (1969) however has convincingly demonstrated, by using examples of psychiatric art where the art-work was remarkably clear, that no such correlation with aesthetic excellence can be true.

This relatively simple theory has been much developed, especially in this country, by Stokes and Ehrenzweig who are virtually psychoanalytic aestheticians and by Waelder in America. Thus in their view the weakness of orthodox psychoanalytic theory lies in its inability to deal with the formal aspects of art. As Waelder (1965) and Ehrenzweig (1967) point out, the original Freudian theory can account for the content of the art but not the form and, an even more serious defect, it cannot distinguish between a mediocre work and an excellent one (if the content be the same). This is what Freud (1928) means when he says that the problem of the creative artist remains unsolved. Even his point that the aesthetic pleasure is a bribe for the super-ego does not explain the nature of this aesthetic pleasure. In brief then orthodox Freudian theory can account for the content of great art but not its essence.

Ehrenzweig (1967) attempts in psychoanalytic terms to account for the very essence of art. For him great art is characterized by the syncretic vision of its author. Syncretic vision is undifferentiated, unconscious perception for the existence of which Ehrenzweig cites as evidence the work on perceptual defence and the Poetzl phenomenon (see p. 308). This unconscious vision, independent of logic and reason and to be observed in children's art, is what distinguishes the great works from the lesser, gives them their universal appeal. Sometimes this unconscious syncretic perception imposes on the work of art an apparent superficial chaos — the Ninth Symphony by Beethoven is regarded by Ehren-zweig as an outstanding example of the problems of order (disorder) caused by powerful unconscious creative processes. *The Hidden Order of Art* (Ehrenzweig, 1967) fully discusses the import of this view. Great art, then, in this view, is the untrammelled expression of the most profoundly unconscious drives and impulses, combined with, not stifled by, ego-controlled techniques. Only to very few individuals is such a combination possible. Stokes (1965) also attempts to account for form within a psychoanalytic framework. His work, however, deserves only brief mention in this book since his theories have departed far from Freudian theory. His avowed mistress is Melanie Klein (see p. 416). His view of art is that it reflects the inner world of the artist — an inner world, dominated as in Kleinian theory, by introjections and introjected projections of the parent and the good and the bad breast.

Testability of the theory

So far no evidence for any part of this Freudian theory of art has been adduced. No studies have been carried out. The only investigation of even marginal relevance was that of Kline (1967c) which has been fully discussed earlier in this book (p . 38). He found that a sample of painters had a lower score on a test of anal characteristics than other comparable groups — a result which supports the claim that painting is a sublimation of the desire to handle the faeces.

However the orthodox Freudian theory concerning the content of art is, at least in part, amenable to test. For example psychosexual testing of painters should reveal anal, oral and, say, Oedipal painters. Their paintings could then be surveyed for evidence of these fixations. The same technique could be applied to novelists. *Couples* (Updike, 1968) seems overtly concerned with oral erotism. We should hypothesize, therefore, that Updike would score high on oral measures. Readers can no doubt think up similar hypotheses for writers of their choice. Of course, it remains a fact that the judgement of what fixations a picture or story reveals is subjective. Nevertheless a number of independent judges to some extent overcomes this subjective element.

It is certainly clear in the paintings of Hieronymus Bosch or the etchings of Goya that processes are at work in these fantasies akin to dream-work and related to psychosexual fixations. Oral sadistic and anal sadistic images are common — consider, for example, the monstrous hooked beaks of many of these denizens of hell. However, studies of this type, of the content of art-works, unrelated to accurate measures of the personality and/or background of the artist cannot be considered as evidence for the Freudian theory. These constitute but the data of the theory.

The second part of the theory, as proposed by Ehrenzweig (1967), does not seem amenable to test. Apart from the difficulty of deciding what is or is not great art — a quite different problem from that of the subjective nature of the assessment of orality in a picture — there is no way of proving that a picture is typical of unconscious as distinct from conscious perception. This is not because the statement that X is a product of the unconscious is non-empirical and thus not a subject of scientific study, in the way that the statement X is a great work of art is non-empirical and thus a subject for philosophy rather than science. It is because as yet we have no measure of whether a percept is conscious or unconscious. Nor in the near future are we likely to develop one. Yet the statement is not meaningless. If we accept the assumption made by Ehrenzweig, certain consequences follow — for example teaching methods in the arts will be radically different from the Victorian approach based on careful life-drawings and development of techniques. Furthermore, if we accept it, our appreciation of modern abstract art, and also more formal styles, becomes changed. Nevertheless we must accept that Ehrenzweig's theories, and thus psychoanalytic theory in a developed form, is quite unscientific because it cannot be tested.

Summary

The orthodox Freudian theory of art applies only to the content of artistic productions rather than their form: it fails to establish the essential difference between a great work of art and a mundane production. Although it is a testable theory it has never been put to the test. Freudian theory, as developed by Ehrenzweig, can account for the essence of art. It cannot however be tested. For the entire psychoanalytic theory of art there exists no objective evidence whatever. However, in that it gives insight into art, for some writers at least, it should not be abandoned. Here, indeed, is a field where research should be developed, for unlike many contemporary psychological theories psychoanalysis can embrace the arts.

9

Freudian dream theory

INTRODUCTION

Freudian dream theory has been most extensively developed especially in *The Interpretation of Dreams* (Freud, 1900) and in the 'Introductory lectures on psychoanalysis' (Freud, 1916-17). This means that any outline of the theory must do it scant justice. Because of this complexity the outline itself will be analytic — categorized under various headings.

OUTLINE OF THE THEORY

'Every dream is an attempt to put aside disturbance of sleep by means of a wish fulfilment. The dream is thus the Guardian of Sleep' (Freud, 1940).

FORMATION OF DREAMS

Dreams may be provoked in two different ways:

1. An instinctual impulse which is as a rule suppressed (i.e. *an unconscious wish*) finds expression during sleep.
2. A desire left over from waking life obtains reinforcement during sleep from an unconscious element.

Dreams therefore may arise from the id or the ego (Freud, 1940).

NATURE OF THE DREAM CONTENT

Manifest dream material

This is the overt dream content as remembered by the dreamer. However in Freudian dream theory this manifest content is relatively trivial. What is important are the processes concealed behind it. This is known as *latent dream thought*. The process by which the manifest dream material is derived from the latent dream thoughts is the *dream-work*.

> The study of dream-work affords us an excellent example of the way in which unconscious material from the id forces itself upon the ego, becomes preconscious and owing to the efforts of the ego, undergoes the modifications which we call *dream distortion*. (Freud, 1940)

Dream-work, then, is an example of the unconscious working-over of preconscious mental processes, i.e. an example of primary processes at work.

Several mechanisms of dream-work have been described:

1. *Condensation* — the formation of unities from things which we keep separate in our working thoughts.
2. *Displacement* — the most important thing in the manifest content may be trivial in the dream thoughts and vice versa.
3. Thoughts are transformed into visual images (Freud, 1916-17).
4. *Opposites* — the manifest dream may express a latent dream thought by its opposite (!). Freud tries to support this claim by recourse to linguistic examples, e.g. *altus* means high or deep, *sacer* means sacred or accursed.
5. *Secondary elaboration* — the attempt to give a coherent overall picture of the dream on recounting it.

All these mechanisms, indeed the latent dream thought itself, were discovered by getting the subject to free-associate to the manifest dream content. However, it frequently happens that there are certain 'silent' elements in the manifest dream content to which no associations are possible (Freud, 1916-17). These 'silent' elements are the *symbols*.

Dream symbols

'The number of things which are represented symbolically in dreams is not great. The human body as a whole, parents, children, brothers and sisters, birth, death, nakedness and one thing more' (Freud, 1916-17).

TABLE 9.1. *Examples of dream symbols*

Object (in latent dream)	Manifest symbol
Human body	House
Male body	Smooth-fronted house
Female body	House with ledges and balconies
Parents	Emperor, empress, king and queen
Children	Little animals or vermin
Birth	Some reference to water
Dying	Setting out on a journey, travelling by train
Nakedness	Clothes and uniforms

However, the overwhelming majority of symbols in dreams are sexual symbols (Freud, 1916-17):

Whole male genitalia	Number three
Penis	Sticks, umbrellas, poles, trees, knives, daggers, lances, sabres, guns, pistols, revolvers, taps, watering cans, springs, pulley lamps, pencils, penholders, nail files, hammers, reptiles, fishes, serpents, hats and cloaks, machinery

Object (in latent dream)	Manifest symbol
Erection	Balloons, aeroplanes, the sensation of flying
Female genitalia	Pits, hollows, caves, jars, bottles, bones, chests, coffers, pockets, slips, landscapes, jewel cases
The womb	Cupboards, stores, rooms
Genital opening — female	Doors, gates, mouth
Woman	Wood, paper, tables, books, snails and mussels, churches and chapels
Breasts	Apples, peaches, fruit in general
Pubic hair	Woods and thickets
Sexual pleasures	Sweetmeats
Auto erotism	Play
Masturbation	Sliding, gliding, pulling off a branch
Castration fear	Falling out or extraction of teeth

WHY IS THERE DREAM-WORK AT ALL?

With the help of the unconscious every dream in the process of formation makes a demand upon the ego for the satisfaction of an instinct (if it originates from the id) or for the removal of a conflict . . . (if it originates from a residue of preconscious activity in the working life).

The sleeping ego desires to sleep, it regards the demand as a disturbance, and to remove the disturbance by replacing the demand by a fulfilment of a wish. 'This *replacement of a demand by the fulfilment of a wish remains the essential function of dream-work*' (Freud, 1940).

Freud admits that in the case of dreams arising from residues of the previous day it is often hard to detect the unconscious motive force and the wish fulfilment 'but we may assume it is always there'. For wish fulfilment is the motivation of dreams (Freud, 1916-17).

ANXIETY DREAMS AS WISH FULFILMENTS

Freud (1916-17) accounts for anxiety dreams in a number of ways.

1. The dream-work may not be entirely successful in creating a wish fulfilment so that a part of the painful latent thought enters the manifest content of the dream.

2. The very fulfilment of the wish may provoke anxiety.

3. Anxiety dreams often have a content in which there is no distortion: it has escaped the censorship. Thus the anxiety dream is the open fulfilment of a

repressed wish. The anxiety indicates that the repressed wish was too strong for the censor. If the wish is only too likely to break through we wake up — in considerable anxiety — and the dream has failed to protect our sleep.

Every dream is an attempt to put aside a disturbance of sleep by means of a wish fulfilment. The dream is thus the guardian of sleep.

THE HYPOTHESES OF FREUDIAN DREAM THEORY

(a) *Symbolism*. Certain objects, especially sexual organs, are represented by other objects in dreams and in primary, unconscious, thought-processes. Since dream contents are primary processes symbolism can be observed outside dreams and, as we shall see, symbolism is best investigated outside dreams. This is because there is no reliable way of inducing dreams except by hypnosis, so that dream content could be predicted. Unfortunately, as Tart (1965) makes clear, the process of hypnosis is not sufficiently well understood for hypnotically induced dreams to be equated with normal, nocturnal dreaming.

If, however, other parts of Freudian theory are assumed to be true such as the Oedipus complex or castration complex the content of dreams may be predicted — sex differences in content would be expected. Symbolism in dreams can be checked this way. For example a sex difference would be expected from psycho-analytic theory in the dreams of kings and queens.

(b) *Dreams fulfil wishes*. This part of Freudian theory can be tested, in theory at least, by comparing the dreams of subjects whose repressed wishes have been independently assessed. Similarly dream-deprivation would be expected to produce disorders of waking behaviour.

From this it is clear that it is exceedingly difficult to put Freudian dream theory to an adequate test. One of the major problems lies in the fact that psychoanalytic theory is derived from the *interpretation* of dreams. There seems to be, except in the case of symbolism, no other method of reaching similar conclusions. Hence an independent check not based on interpretation is hard to carry out. The most hopeful procedure probably lies in the study of criterion groups whose dreams may, from the nature of their problems and background, be predicted (in terms of psychoanalytic theory).

IMPORTANCE OF THE THEORY

Freud (1909a) claims that the 'interpretation of dreams is in fact the royal road to a knowledge of the unconscious: it is the securest foundation of psychoanalysis and the field in which every, worker must acquire his convictions and seek his training.' Although this is an early statement, Freud clearly holds broadly to this position. Much of the data of psychoanalysis on which Freudian theory was based was dream material. Dreams give us a chance to see primary processes at work. Since Freud (1940) has argued that unconscious mechanisms discovered from dreams help us to understand the neuroses and psychoses it is clear that dream theory is a fundamental part of psychoanalytic theory as a whole. If it be shown to be false, considerable doubt must be cast on much of psychoanalytic theory.

SYMBOLISM

As is clear from the psychoanalytic theory of dreams, an important element in interpretation is the claim that certain objects represent or are symbols for others. In the outline of the theory various examples of these were given. This part of the theory contains an obvious testable question: are certain objects represented by others as Freudian theory states? Although symbolism was originally derived from the analysis of dreams, to test the theory it is not necessary to consider only dream material. This is, of course, because dream material reflects the workings of the unconscious mind, the primary processes, which may be evinced in all behaviour even if less clearly (dreams being the royal road to the unconscious).

THE EMPIRICAL EVIDENCE CONCERNING SYMBOLS

In this review of the objective evidence for the psychoanalytic theory of symbols, those studies not concerned with dreams will be first considered. The arrangement will be broadly chronological unless a research sparked off a series of other investigations; these will be examined together.

The work of Krout (1950) — the Symbol Elaboration Test (SET)

In this investigation Krout administered twelve symbolic drawings to a sample of 169 subjects aged 6-69 years of whom 12 were Indians. To give examples of the symbols used a semi-circle represented femaleness, two counter-opposed semi-circles stood for female society, a single straight line represented maleness and a diffuse mass was a symbol for anxiety. The subjects had to make drawings from these symbols and they were then questioned about them. There were thus three sources of data — the manner of drawing, the content of drawings and verbal associations. Based on purely subjective judgements of this data Krout concluded that these symbols were universal. As regards the sample, apart from the twelve Indian children there were thirty normal American white children, two small groups of normal adults (N24 and 30), thirteen children with behaviour problems and sixty adults undergoing psychotherapy.

Comments and conclusions

Clearly with such a small sample it is not possible, whatever the results, to claim that these symbols were universal: to do that, representative samples from all cultures would be necessary. Furthermore, the extremely subjective and interpretative nature of the scoring of the responses robs this study of real objectivity. Indeed, this investigation has only been discussed because it is an early forerunner of the kind of approach possible with the investigation of symbolism. Again, many of the symbols, combinations of lines and semi-circles, stem more from the author's clinical experience and skill than from psychoanalytic theory.

This study cannot be regarded as support for the Freudian theory of symbols — it is far too subjective for that. It is, none the less, an interesting approach to the problem.

The work of Hammer (1953)

Hammer studied the Freudian theory of genital symbolism in a group of male patients who had been sterilized and a group of controls who had undergone other operations.

Test used. Hammer employed the HTP projective test (Buck, 1948). In this the subject is required to make a drawing of a house, a tree and a person. It yields a measure of genital symbolism, and hence castration anxiety, directly. From Freudian theory, for example, it would be predicted that those suffering from castration anxiety would in their pictures of the house omit the chimney (penis) or draw it billowing smoke. The tree might well be cut down or the head of the person cut off.

Experimental design. Since the sterilized subjects were prisoners, HTP protocols were obtained from them on admission to prison, on admission to hospital, on the day of operation, and the day after operation. A similar sequence was obtained from the control group. Matching of the groups (twenty in each) was not perfect — the experimental group were of lower intelligence.

Analysis of results. The Fisher Exact Probability Test was applied. The operation scores of the experimental group were compared with their original scores (obtained in the prison) and the operation scores of the surgical control group.

Results. The results strongly support the Freudian theory of genital symbolism. Examples of items differentiating the experimental group from the controls and their original scores at the 0.05 level, or better, were: chimney missing, tree cut through, penis-like feet and the admission on interview that the house needed a chimney.

Comments and conclusions

The assumption upon which this study rests is that patients undergoing sterilization will feel fears of castration. This is the rationale for comparing them with surgical controls. The results support this claim. In doing so, as has been indicated, the Freudian theory of sexual symbolism has been strongly supported. The theory predicts certain differences in drawings between the groups and these were found. It is to be noted that the experimental design, comparing operation protocols with previous scores and a control group, is very neat. It seems unlikely that imperfect matching of the groups on intelligence and psychopathy (more in the experimental group) could have contributed to these predicted differences.

This study must be regarded as good evidence for the psychoanalytic theory of genital symbolism.

The work of McElroy (1954) and Jahoda (1956)

On the Freudian hypothesis that rounded shapes represent the female genital organs and pointed shapes the male, McElroy presented a twelve-item test (each item consisting of one rounded and one pointed shape) to 380 boys and 399 girls. Subjects had to indicate for each item which of the two drawings they preferred.

As predicted from the Freudian theory, males preferred female shapes and females preferred male shapes, a preference which increased with age.

Although this study appears to confirm the Freudian theory it is not entirely satisfactory for a number of reasons as, indeed, McElroy himself admits. In the first place other hypotheses are possible to account for the results. It is possible that in some items the shapes had different associations for boys and girls which would account for the differential preference. Item 2, for example, portrayed a shield and a fleur de lys. It is also possible, if unconvincing, to account for the findings in terms of stimulus-generalization. So Jahoda, in an attempt to overcome these problems and to make a more critical test of the Freudian hypothesis (and also because he claimed there was an error in the computations), replicated this study in an alien culture — Ghana.

Owing to the nature of the society in Ghana, a far more critical test of the psychoanalytic hypotheses was possible since the alternative hypotheses were not tenable. Among the Ga, the tribe who constituted his sample of 858 middle-school children (age-range approximately 12-15 years) and 278 similar subjects in a further subsidiary experiment, there is far less repression of childhood sexual activity (e.g. Field, 1940) than is usual among Scottish children (McElroy's sample). Therefore sex differences in preference for shapes would be expected to be less pronounced.

In fact there were sex differences on only five of the twelve items. The Accra boys (town dwellers) did not change with age whereas the girls converged towards the boys' preference patterns. In the subsidiary experiment, where the children were afterwards questioned, it emerged that the preferred drawings were those that could be named. This, however, fails to account for the sex difference noted. Furthermore, the girls' preferences were not attributable to the quality of drawings as McElroy had suggested they might be. From this evidence Jahoda argued that only the psychoanalytic theory of symbolism had not been eliminated as being responsible for the sex differences in preferences. McElroy's other hypotheses had been shown to be false. As regards the older girls' decline in preference for male shapes, Jahoda argues that this is due to the fact that by this age the Ghanaian girl has had far more sexual experience than the boy.

Conclusions

These two experiments taken together must be regarded as support for the Freudian theory of symbolism, specifically that rounded shapes represent the female and pointed shapes the male sexual organs. The cross-cultural study in Ghana seems to rule out other alternative explanations accounting for the sex preferences observed. In general, therefore, Freudian theory is upheld.

Of the four studies so far examined, it will have been noted that three support the psychoanalytic theory while one (Krout, 1950) is neutral in this respect. Now an investigation must be discussed which claims to show that the theory is false. Apart from the interest of the results this study also sparked off other similar investigations.

The work of Levy (1954)

Levy put the theory of genital symbolism to the test in a sample of around sixty ten-year-old children. Two methods were used. In the first, children had to allocate names to figures symbolic of female or male sexual organs. The hypothesis was that were the theory correct female names should be given to rounded objects and male names to pointed ones. In the second method the sample was divided into two groups. One was given a paired-associate learning task — the male names with the male symbols and the feminine names with the female symbols. The other was given the same task but with the genders reversed — female names and male objects. It was hypothesized that the first group would remember their material significantly better since, according to the theory, there ought already to be unconscious connections.

Results and conclusions

(a) *Method* 1. Contrary to the Freudian hypothesis, male and female names were not matched to their respective symbols. Levy concluded from this that the Freudian theory was disproved.
(b) *Method* 2. There was no significant difference in memory for the paired associates between the two groups.

From the results of this investigation Levy concluded that the Freudian theory of genital symbols was disproved.

Comments

At this point in the discussion it will suffice to say that on the face of it this study looks like convincing proof that in this sample of children, at least, there is no evidence whatever of symbolism. Certain objections have been made to the study and these will be taken up as they appear in the investigations stimulated by this work. Nevertheless the fact remains that this is evidence contrary to Freudian theory.

The work of Jacobs (1954)

Jacobs gave a list of symbols for the male and female sexual organs to a sample of ninety-nine mental-hospital patients, twenty-seven student nurses and twelve hospital attendants, and asked them to assign a gender to each of the words.

Results and conclusions

The correct (in psychoanalytic theory) gender was assigned to the symbols far beyond the chance level. Normals were superior in this to his patient population.
Jacobs regarded these results as supporting Freudian theory.

Comments

As Moos and Mussen (1959) point out, it is wrong to assume from these results that symbolism is impaired in psychotics. This is because psychotics often suffer from a general intellectual deficit which would of itself account for the results. In addition small samples of student nurses and hospital attendants are hardly sufficient as normal control groups. Nevertheless the overall result that there was a better than chance matching of gender to symbol does provide support for the Freudian theory.

The work of Starer (1955)

Starer replicated the work of Levy (1954) asking subjects to match names to rounded or pointed figures. He used a substantial sample of psychotics, mainly schizophrenics, and a control group of the inevitable student nurses.

Results

Contrary to the findings of Levy these patients matched figures to names significantly better than chance (by Chi-square) thus providing more evidence in favour of psychoanalytic theory. Starer also claimed that he had the *impression* that inability to match names was increased by psychotic confusion.

Comments

These results directly support Freudian theory and are entirely opposed to those of Levy. In addition the clinical impression that the degree of psychotism impaired matching bears out the work of Jacobs (1954) already discussed. This investigation constitutes yet more evidence for the Freudian theory of symbolism.

The work of Mosak (1955)

Mosak adopted an entirely different and novel approach to the question of symbolism. He examined the gender of the words for the Freudian symbols in French, Spanish and German.

Results and conclusions

In French, fifteen of thirty-two male symbols are feminine and twelve of the twenty-six female symbols are masculine. In Spanish the respective figures are nineteen and twelve while in German these figures fall to eleven and nine.

Mosak concluded that these results threw considerable doubt on the veracity of the Freudian theory.

Comments

It is difficult to know what interpretation to place on this finding that the gender of sexual symbols in a number of European languages is not in accord with the psychoanalytic theory of symbols. Since the psychological origins of language are not well understood it may be presumptuous to expect such an accordance. Indeed it is not clear whether, from psychoanalytic theory, matching would be predicted. It is true that had the gender of words fitted the sexual symbols psychoanalytic investigators would have claimed it as support for the theory — on the grounds that it indicated the unconscious origins of language.

However, if the unconscious origins of language are the basis for the claim that male sexual symbols should be masculine then the gender of words derived from the same language, as French and Spanish are derived from Latin, should be the same. The fact that they are not is evidence that there are other factors in the acquisition of gender in the development of languages. Such an argument of course suggests a further more fundamental investigation: if unconscious factors are important in the origins of language, then symbols in the original languages, e.g. Sanskrit and Basque, ought to be the same. However, since it is evident that there are other factors than unconscious ones in the development of languages, Mosak's failure to find agreement between the theory of sexual symbolism and the gender of words cannot seriously be considered as disproof of the Freudian theory.

The work of Minturn (1965)

Minturn, in a rather more extensive investigation, also studied the gender of various symbolic words in a variety of languages.

Rationale. Minturn accepts that the gender of words is not likely to be entirely determined by their symbolic referents and therefore he subjected the Freudian theory to the test by examining the direction of gender classification of symbol words in *several* languages rather than the *magnitude* of this relationship in one language.

Symbols. Symbol words were selected from the studies by Hall (1966 for example, see pp. 288-95) rather than from orthodox psychoanalytic writings, because Hall's symbols were derived from normals not neurotics and reflected modern dreams rather than those early in the century. Hall's list, of course, very largely overlaps that of the psychoanalysts. Fifty-four male and sixty female symbols were used — those rated by judges as unambiguously masculine or feminine.

Languages. From each branch of the Indo-European languages only one language was used in this study since in related languages, for example, French and Italian, gender classification is not independent in that in both are derived from Latin. Since four non-Indo-European languages were also used, the language sample was as shown in Table 9.2.

TABLE 9.2 *Minturn's language sample*

French (Romance), German (Germanic) Russian (Slavic), Greek (Hellenic) Irish (Celtic), Maharata (Indic)	} Indo-European
Arabic (Semitic), Tunica (American Indian) Nama (Khoisan), Hausa (Uad-Hamitic)	} non-Indo-European

Method. Fluent speakers of these ten languages translated the symbols. In addition stratified random samples of nouns in each of the languages were classified for gender.

Results

Test 1. The expected frequencies for gender classification based on the random sample were compared with the observed frequencies for the classification of the symbolic words, and the probabilities of these differences were computed by the sign test. Four tests had high probabilities in the expected direction, the Tunican sample being significant at the 1 per cent level (males). Only three female differences and one male difference were in the wrong direction.

Test 2. A Chi-square analysis was computed to test the association between symbolic classification and actual gender. In eight out of ten cases the results were in the predicted direction (probability of such a result is 5 per cent).

The Tunican sample is again significant at the 1 per cent level.

Since it has been admitted that other variables affect gender than the symbolic significance of the words, constancy of results across languages is the crucial test. For female symbols the difference between observed and expected frequencies is correct only five out of eight times (NS) but for male symbols it is correct seven out of eight times (sig. 3 per cent level).

Thus it can be concluded that masculine symbols do tend to be classified as male in a wide variety of languages (not just the Germanic of Freud's original data) but also in non-Indo-European languages, while female symbols are classified with less consistency as feminine.

Test 3. A Chi-square analysis was performed comparing the gender of symbolic words with the expected frequency of neuter words in the language. Here the results were more equivocal since in some languages there was a greater frequency, in others less, of symbolic neutral words. The interpretation of this is complicated by the fact that neuter words, as symbolic words, are often the commonest in the languages.

Conclusions

The data presented in this study support the hypothesis derived from Freudian theory that symbolic words in a wide variety of languages do tend to be put into the gender appropriate to their sexual referent. This evidence therefore supports the notion of dream symbolism and the claim that such symbolism represents primary mental processes common to all men regardless of their linguistic background. That the evidence is not statistically more definitive must be attributed to the fact that gender in languages is influenced by other factors linguistic and non-linguistic.

The work of Mullen (1968)

Mullen attempted to investigate the universality (and by implication the validity) of Freudian and Jungian sexual symbols. This study suffers from the logical difficulty already mentioned in connection with the method of examining the gender of symbolic words in various languages — namely that since the gender of words in languages derived from a common source is often different, some external influences must be affecting gender. Thus Mullen's finding that the gender of words symbolic in both Jungian and Freudian theory cannot be correctly predicted from either theory in French, German or Spanish cannot be regarded as refuting either theory. To use languages as a test of the theory, investigators must examine basic root languages. Here communality of gender would be not definitive proof but highly suggestive evidence. This study by Mullen cannot therefore be regarded as a true test of symbolism.

The work of Jones (1956)

Jones extended the work of Levy (1954) in a very sophisticated analysis-of-variance study aimed to eradicate certain faults in the previous work. First Jones claimed that failure of the Levy study could have been due to the fact that the names used were not equated for all their stimulus attributes. In addition it was pointed out that the children in Levy's investigation were not sexually mature, a fact which could be of some importance.

Design of the experiment. Ten male and ten female students were used together with ten male and ten female psychotics. The main factors examined in the analysis of variance were sex, psychiatric classification and type of sexual symbol. Between-symbol differences were also examined.

Results. There were four main findings:

(a) Symbolism did occur — there was better-than-chance matching of names to symbols.
(b) The psychiatric groups matched less well than the students.
(c) Males were better than females. This finding was linked by Jones to the fact that males are more easily aroused by a variety of sexual stimuli than are females (Kinsey et al., 1948).
(d) Although there was significant variation between symbols (not in accord with Freudian theory), this was due to the influence of one symbol alone — a box — a fact which cannot be held to invalidate the theory.

Comments

Again this study gives results, contrary to those of Levy (1954). Freudian genital symbolism is indubitably supported. Clearly the age variable in symbolism needs further investigation. The findings concerning psychotics confirm those of Jacobs (1954) and Starer (1955), although as with those studies the warning of Moos and Mussen (1959) must be borne in mind — that the observed differences reflect the general intellectual impairment of psychotics rather than a specific disability to use symbols. In conclusion the work of Jones must be regarded as confirming Freudian theory.

The work of Winter and Prescott (1957)

Starer (1955), as has been discussed above, had a clinical impression that psychotics matched names to symbolic objects less well than normals. Winter and Prescott, using the same technique as Starer, attempted to validate these findings.

Method. Fifty-five female and fifty-two male hospitalized mental patients were administered the Starer (1955) test of symbolism and the MMPI.

Results. These psychotics matched names to objects significantly better than chance and Freudian theory was thus supported. However, correct matching was quite unrelated to any of the scores on the MMPI clinical scales. In addition the female psychotics in this study matched symbols to names as well as the normal females in the Starer study. Winter and Prescott concluded, therefore, that there was no relationship between the ability to match symbols and psychotic confusion.

Comments and conclusions

Although the fact that the matching of symbols to names was better than chance supports Freudian theory, the main finding that psychotism is unrelated to the ability to form symbols is not really supported by this evidence for two reasons:

(a) The fact that all the samples were psychotic means that it was very homogeneous thus depressing any correlations with the MMPI scales.
(b) The inadequacy of Starer's (1955) normal sample has already been mentioned (p. 271) so that any comparison with it, as in this study, is not meaningful.

Despite this, however, the study does support the Freudian theory of genital symbolism.

The work of Stennett and Thurlow (1958)

Stennett and Thurlow were interested in the discrepancy between the work of Starer (1955) and that of Levy (1954). They therefore investigated the question of whether the difference in results was due to the figures used by Levy differing in some unknown way from those of Starer.

Method. Both sets of figures were given to a group of thirty-seven nurses.

Results. With both sets of stimuli matching was better than chance, Freudian theory was supported, and the failure of Levy to confirm the theory could not be laid at the door of the pictures he used. The authors concluded from this study that the age variable in matching names to symbols must be examined.

Comments and conclusions

This study does suggest that the reason for the discrepancy of the results of Levy (1954) might lie in the age of the sample. It must be remembered that all the other studies so far reviewed in this section confirm the theory. Furthermore, as Stennett and Thurlow point out, the cause of the discrepancy cannot be the normality of the sample (e.g. Jones, 1956). The nature of the stimulus material cannot be the cause and the only other difference (group rather than individual testing) is unlikely to be important.

This study supports Freudian theory and demonstrates that the age of the subjects may be a crucial factor in the development of the ability to symbolize.

The work of Accord (1962)

The influence of age on the ability to symbolize was studied by Accord. He administered the usual matching test to a total of 305 subjects divided into five groups by age. The groups were grades 3, 6, 9 and 12 plus an adult sample.

Results. Only the last two groups (i.e. those of seventeen years and above) were able to put the name that first came to their mind to ten designs better than chance. The younger children, as was the case with Levy, were not able to match name and symbol.

Comments

This finding, that maturity is related to the ability to make the Freudian symbolic connections, neatly accounts for the discrepancy noted between the results of Levy (1954) and other investigators. This result still supports Freudian theory although, were it confirmed in further experiments, it would be necessary to make Freudian theory quite explicit on this point of age.

The work of Lessler (1962)

Lessler, using three groups of twenty males and twenty females with respective mean ages of 9.4, 14.4 and 20.2 years, also investigated age as an influence on symbolism.

Method. Twenty Freudian symbols were presented to the subjects to be sorted into two piles as masculine or feminine. In addition twenty other symbols were presented, varying in texture (rough or smooth) but the results from this part of the investigation are not relevant to this book.

Results. Contrary to the work of Levy (1954) and Accord (1962) although more fully in accord with psychoanalytic theory, all three groups did significantly better than chance at assigning gender to these objects.

Comments

Clearly it is necessary to attempt to account for the discrepancy from the other result with children.

Cameron (1967) explains these results in terms of the fact that in this experiment the subjects did not have to match names from a list or name symbols themselves, procedures which alert subjects' defences. The procedure of merely sorting into two piles, being less disturbing, is more effective. If this hypothesis were correct it still does not convincingly account for the fact that the 'disturbing' technique works with adults. However, whatever the explanation for the fact that with the children in this sample genital symbolism appears to have been present, the experiment as a whole is further confirmation of psychoanalytic theory.

The work of Meissner (1958)

All but one of the investigations so far discussed have restricted themselves to but one aspect of the psychoanalytic theory of symbolism — genital symbolism. As an important extension of the work in this area Meissner studied psychoanalytic death symbols.

Method. Twenty words regarded in psychoanalytic theory as symbols of death, for example a bird, a journey across a bridge and an old man, together with thirty random control words from the Kent—Rosanoff list were presented to forty Roman Catholic seminarians. Their GSR response to each word was collected and in addition they were asked to group all fifty words under common headings.

Results. There were more references to the symbol words under the heading of death than to the control words. Unfortunately no statistical test of this difference was made. More importantly there was a significantly greater amplitude of GSR to the death words than to the controls. Meissner regarded these results as confirming the Freudian theory.

Comments and conclusions

These GSR responses must be considered as good evidence for the Freudian death symbols, for they are difficult to fake or bring under rational control. It could be argued that some of the psychoanalytic death symbols take on their disturbing quality because they are, in everyday life, symbols of or connected with death — for example, black or the silent one. On the other hand it can be argued that this is in itself support for the Freudian theory. As regards the finding that the symbols were more frequently classified under death than their controls little can be inferred without a statistical test.

This study is further support for the Freudian theory.

The work of Moos and Mussen (1959)

As has been previously pointed out, Moos and Mussen have objected to previous studies of symbolism among psychotics (e.g. Jacobs, 1954) because they consider that any deficit in ability to symbolize was due to a more general intellectual dysfunctioning. To put this to the test Moos and Mussen had three groups — of psychotics, neurotics and surgical controls respectively (ten males in each) — indicate masculine or feminine to a number of psychoanalytic sexual symbols.

Results. All three groups matched symbol and gender better than chance. Moos and Mussen considered that this supported their claim because all groups were matched on age, education and, the crucial point, intellectual functioning as measured by the forty-word vocabulary test of the Shipley Institute for Living Test.

Comments

This study, despite the size of the samples which would have only revealed large differences, does seem to support their claims regarding the inferior performance of psychotics. It also fully supports Freudian theory.

The work of Glotter and Reece (1962)

Glotter and Reece made a study of tactility and sexual symbolism in which four stimulus objects were presented to thirty students. There was one straight and one spherical object made of wood and a similar pair made of rubber. After feeling each object students responded on twenty scales of the semantic differential. The hard/soft dimension was highly significant for the concept of masculinity and femininity but the effects of form were confounded by weight and flexibility.

Comments and conclusions

In that the hard/soft dimension was relevant to the concept of masculinity it could be argued that this study supports Freudian theory. Nevertheless these two terms are related to the concept in everyday life and psychoanalytic theory is not the parsimonious explanation of these results. Furthermore the fact that the effect of form was confounded by weight and flexibility means that the most important dimension of Freudian symbolism was confounded.

Although on the surface, at least, this study appears to confirm psychoanalytic theory it does not stand close scrutiny. Little relevant to Freudian theory may be concluded from it.

The work of Cameron (1967)

Cameron, in a study which has already been mentioned, carried out a most extensive study of symbolism in more than 2000 children of age from three to seventeen years.

Method. Children had to choose male or female symbols presented in pairs. The shapes were those used by McElroy (1954) and Jahoda (1956). Forty-two interviewers, randomly selected within areas, were used.

Hypotheses. Psychoanalytic theory predicts, as Fenichel (1945) emphasizes, that individuals tend to prefer shapes representative of the sexual organs of the opposite sex. This, therefore, was the basic hypothesis investigated in this study. However in the light of Freudian psychosexual theory it was modified according to age, as set out below:

(a) Children below four years of age, being oral or anal, will show no preference for male or female symbols.

(b) Children four to six years of age, being at the phallic stage, will prefer shapes symbolic of the opposite sex.

(c) Children from seven to twelve years of age, being at the latency period, will prefer shapes representative of the same sex.

(d) Children of twelve years and upwards, at the genital stage, will prefer symbols representative of the opposite sex.

One further hypothesis was made, namely that girls of thirteen and more would tend to have a greater preference for masculine shapes after latency because of the masculine orientation of the culture which younger phallic children would not perceive.

Results. The preference for symbols when tested by Chi-square all fitted the Freudian hypotheses. Nevertheless it must be noted that the Chi-squares although significant were small.

Comments

This investigation fully supports the Freudian theory of genital symbolism and, indirectly, psychosexual theory. Cameron attributes the failure of Levy (1954) and Accord (1962) to demonstrate symbolism in their samples of children to the fact that in their experiments the children were required to match symbols with names — a rational procedure. In this ego defences could easily override the more primitive secondary processes of symbolization. Preference on the other hand as used in this experiment is non-rational. Cameron points out that the other successful investigation with children, that of Lessler (1964), also required a non-rational procedure — sorting into piles.

Conclusions

From this experiment, carried out on very large samples of children, it can be argued that genital symbolism occurs in children of all ages. The failure of earlier investigations with children seems to be attributable to method. As a whole therefore Freudian theory is again supported. But it must be pointed out that the results with the youngest children who showed no preference while fitting psychoanalytic theory are also consonant with the hypothesis that no symbolism occurs in young pre-school children.

Mention should be made here of the work of Forster and Ross (1976) who replicated Cameron's work on sixty-one 12-grade students (a very small sample). They found that both sexes preferred female symbols. This discrepancy is hard to account for although some new symbols were used. It shows that caution must be exercised in interpreting Cameron's findings.

Munroe et al. also found that spherical candy (not cylindrical as predicted by psychoanalytic theory) was preferred by girls between the ages of four and twelve years. Perhaps these were symbolic of testicles! Again Cameron is not supported.

OTHER DETERMINANTS OF GENDER

As we have seen from the attempts to examine the Freudian theory of symbolism by a study of the gender of symbolic words in various languages, there are clearly extra-symbolic determinants of gender. We finally turn to a number of studies which have investigated some of these factors.

The work of Lessler

Lessler (1964) and Lessler and Eriksen (1968) studied this problem among a sample of college students (1964) and school children (1968).

Lessler (1964)

Sample. 169 college students.

Symbols. They were chosen such that they could be classified as masculine or feminine in Freudian theory and as maculine or feminine through cultural influences. Thus Schonbar and Davitz (1960) in a study of the connotative meaning of sexual symbols found that choice of gender was determined by cultural factors: for example baseball bats were considered to be masculine because men exclusively played with them. To test this cultural hypothesis, Lessler developed a list of forty symbols with obvious cultural content:

(a) Masculine in Freudian theory and by cultural content, e.g. baseball bat.
(b) Feminine in Freudian theory and by cultural content, e.g. powder puff.
(c) Masculine in Freudian theory but feminine by cultural content, e.g. rolling pin.
(d) Feminine in Freudian theory but masculine by cultural content, e.g. baseball.

He also devised forty symbols where the cultural gender was more ambiguous (as rated by judges).

Finally he chose twenty symbols where there was no cultural bias.

Method. Subjects had to assign gender to these symbols.

Results

(a) Where the symbols had a cultural referrent, that was used to assign gender to the word.
(b) Where there was no cultural bias, the symbols were sorted in accord with Freudian theory.

Comments and conclusions. Lessler argues that these findings may account for the disparity of results that we have already noted in the study of symbolism. Thus where in previous studies symbols were chosen which had cultural biases contrary to Freudian theory, that theory would not be supported. He argues that cultural factors were used to assign gender because it was more socially acceptable to do so, less threatening and more rational. The fact that in normals, at least, ego processes (cultural influence) override primary processes (selection of gender by symbols) is in no way contrary to psychoanalytic theory. Indeed, these results of Lessler are strong support for the Freudian theory of symbolism, which states that in the unconscious certain objects represent the sexual organs. These primary unconscious processes are usually only noticeable in psychosis, dreaming and in free association. Thus if Lessler had found that cultural factors did not influence the choice of gender then psychoanalytic theory would not be so well supported. In conclusion this study strongly confirms Freudian theory.

Lessler and Ericksen (1968)

Lessler and Ericksen repeated this study on a sample of school children.

Sample. 142 boys, 164 girls in grades 1-6.

Symbols. As in previous study, but only half the numbers in each group were used.

Results were essentially similar to those reported for students. Thus where there was a clear cultural sex-role, that was used to assign gender. Otherwise Freudian symbolism was used. However female symbols were not correctly classified.

Comments and conclusions. This study fails to support the Freudian theory of sexual symbolism as regards the female sexual organs. It is difficult to produce a convincing reason for this particular finding in the light of the previous study.

Relevant here is the work of Solway (1971) who carried out a study similar to that of Lessler but with subjects in various different age groups. He found that the psychoanalytic theory of symbolism was confirmed only in subjects of seventeen years of age and upwards.

The work of Jones and Lepson (1967)

Jones and Lepson carried out a similar test of the Freudian theory of symbolism using colour as the alternative classificatory cue.

Sample. Twenty male and twenty female students and twenty male and twenty female psychiatric patients.

Symbols. Five pointed and five rounded figures (masculine and feminine). There was a black (strong colour and therefore masculine) and a grey series of each. Thus each system (shape or colour) could mediate a sexual response and in one half of each series there would be opposition of the two systems.

Method. Subjects had to assign gender to the shapes.

Results. Each system showed itself capable of mediating a choice of gender. Neither system appeared stronger than the other. These authors conclude that Freud was wrong to stress the primary generalization features in his theory of symbolism.

Comments and conclusions

As was pointed out in our discussion of the work of Lessler, the fact that ego processes can account for the assignment of gender is not contrary to psychoanalytic theory. Thus this study which shows that symbolic sorting can occur does support Freudian theory. The claim of Jones and Lepson that Freud overstressed symbolization is not confirmed by this study since symbolization is a primary process. The influence of colour is probably, by association of strong and masculine, best regarded as preconscious. This investigation is further support for the Freudian theory of symbolism and demonstrates yet another determinant of the assignment of gender — colour association.

The work of Worthy and Craddick (1969)

Worthy and Craddick investigated the gender of Freudian sexual symbols using the semantic differential.

Sample. Thirty-six male and thirty-six female undergraduates.

Symbols. Typical Freudian symbolic words, e.g. umbrella and oven.

Measure. Subjects had to rate these for masculinity and femininity using the semantic differential.

Results. Some symbols were rated in accord with psychoanalytic theory but others were not.

Comments and conclusions

This study is difficult to interpret in that the precise significance of rating on the semantic differential is not known. Since this involves rating objects on a seven-point scale for masculinity or femininity, in effect it is little different from assigning gender to words. However two points are worthy of note. First, rating on a seven-point scale involves considerable thought compared with the forced choice decision about gender. As Cameron (1967) points out (see p. 276), this conscious ratiocination is liable to bring defensive processes into play. Hence the equivocal results. Again, as will be discussed below, there was no control in this study for the cultural components of the attribution of gender to words — a failing which could account for these findings (see Lessler, 1964). The conclusion must be, therefore, that the failure of this study to give complete support to the Freudian theory may be due to methodological problems.

Similar objections can be launched at all studies of symbolism which require subjects to use the semantic differential. Hence we shall not deal with these in any detail. Thus the fact that Althouse (1970) failed to find that sixty-eight Freudian symbols and seventy-seven Jungian symbols were allocated gender in accord with either of these theories may simply reflect this difficulty with the semantic differential rather than the failure of the theory. Similarly, Archer and Burgess (1970) who replicated the study of Worthy and Craddick (1969) failed to confirm psychoanalytic theory but the use of the semantic differential makes the results equivocal.

Brar (1973) used the semantic differential as a rating measure for Freudian symbols and failed to confirm the theory in a small sample of psychotics.

COMMENTS ON ALL THESE STUDIES

Since the methodology and rationale of all the studies of symbolism reviewed have been similar there are a number of points of discussion common to all of them. These will now be considered.

1. To what extent were the symbols in these investigations an accurate reflection of psychoanalytic theory?

Freudian dream theory, as may be seen from the outline of the theory at the beginning of this chapter, is absolutely explicit as regards symbolism: lists of symbols and what they represent are given as well as general principles such as pointed things representing the male genitalia. Not surprisingly, therefore, examination of the symbols in these investigations shows that most of them cannot be impugned on that account. The Krout (1950) Symbol Elaboration Test seems to deviate fairly strongly away from classical Freudian theory (although not unwittingly) as do the textural symbols of Glotter and Reece (1962). It can safely be assumed that in the majority of experiments the symbols are psychoanalytic.

2. Is it a fair prediction from the psychoanalytic theory of genital symbolism that subjects should be able (in some form or other) to assign gender to the symbols?

As Hall (1953) has made explicit in psychoanalytic theory, there are really two distinct accounts of why symbolism occurs. In one of them symbols are regarded as disguises for the objects they represent. In this way ideas and principally wishes can find conscious expression (as in dreams according to the Freudian theory) because symbolically disguised they can avoid the censor — the super-ego. In the other account symbols are regarded as visual means to express abstract ideas, e.g. chastity represented as a lily. On both these accounts there is therefore a link in the unconscious between the symbol and the object. If the objects claimed to be sexual symbols really are so then it does seem a fair prediction that subjects should be able to assign gender to them better than by chance. It therefore does not seem reasonable to attempt to argue that the type of experiment reviewed in this section of the book is not a fair test of the psychoanalytic theory. It is of interest to note that the procedure of Levy (1954) where the prediction was made that masculine names and masculine symbols would be better remembered than feminine names and the same symbols appears to be a good test of this unconscious link, despite its failure to confirm the Freudian theory.

The more specific point of just how this assigning of gender should be carried out has already been discussed in respect of each of the studies individually. Suffice it to say here that it appears that the less rational the procedure is the more likely it is that the Freudian theory will be confirmed. In short it is argued that these experiments are a fair test of the psychoanalytic theory of symbolism.

CONCLUSIONS

Since it can be accepted that these experiments are a fair test of the theory what conclusions may be drawn from them? The main finding is satisfactorily clear.

1. Among adults sexual symbolism occurs

All the studies with adult subjects have demonstrated genital symbolism. There have been no findings contrary to theory.

1a. Sexual symbolism does not seem to be different from normal among psychotics

This is an important area of research since in Freudian theory (Freud, 1924b) psychotics are characterized by the emergence of repressed material and primary processes into the conscious. Whereas earlier workers (Jacobs, 1954; Starer, 1955) had found differences, Moos and Mussen (1959) showed that it was due to a general mental dysfunction rather than a specific disability that psychotics were inferior. In any case if primary processes are nearer consciousness in psychotics it could be argued that psychotics should be superior at symbolism, itself a primary process.

1b. Sexual symbolism probably does occur in prepubescent children

The work of Cameron (1967) with large samples of children appears to show that even among young children sexual symbolism occurs. Nevertheless it must be stated that his findings are bound up with psychoanalytic psychosexual theory and if the predictions made from this are not acceptable the Cameron study shows only that sexual symbolism occurs with adults (conclusion 1 — which is not in doubt). Levy (1954) had failed to confirm Freudian theory with children and Accord (1962), in a study of the age-variable, also found that prepubescent children failed to symbolize. Lessler (1962) found the opposite result, however, as did Jones (1961). This discrepancy was imputed to method: matching names — a rational procedure — was thought to invoke defences, while sorting into piles (Lessler) and preference (Cameron) were considered not to do so — hence the successful results. Thus owing to these disparate results, the problems of methodology and the fact that the work of Cameron (1967) is bound up in other parts of Freudian theory, conclusion 1b may be stated only tentatively. This is particularly so since the more recent but small-scale studies of symbolism in children have not confirmed Freudian theory.

2. Symbolism of death occurs

This conclusion is based on one study only — that of Meissner (1958) which concerned only a small sample of students. The fact that GSRs to death symbols were larger than to neutral words is at least evidence that they provoked anxiety. Clearly conclusion 2 must remain tentative until further work is carried out.

FURTHER POINTS

It is to be noted that these studies of symbolism deal mainly with one aspect of it (albeit a very important one) — sexual symbolism. One further study deals with death symbols. Thus other aspects of Freudian symbolism remain unproven. It can be argued, however, that since the whole of the theory was derived from the same original data — the dreams of patients undergoing analysis — the fact that one part of it has been substantially validated makes it unlikely that the other parts would not be correct. Nevertheless it is clear much work remains to be done. It should also be noted that symbolism in art and literature had been recognized long before Freud, and is a commonplace of literary and artistic aesthetic appreciation.

Thus the first part of the study of symbolism, based on material not collected from dreams, has supported Freudian theory. It is now necessary to consider work based on the study of dreams. In this section symbolism will not be studied on its own but rather as one part of the phenomenology of dreams.

SUMMARY CONCERNING SYMBOLISM

In this section some objective studies of the psychoanalytic theory of symbolism have been reviewed. In this section only investigations not directly concerned with dreams were examined. The basic methodology of most of the researches was to get subjects to assign gender to Freudian symbols for male and female genitalia. Although there were certain problems inherent in this method, notably that the more rational the procedure the more ego-defences seemed to be involved, it was considered that such experiments constituted a good test of the Freudian theory. The basic conclusion to emerge from these studies was that among adults Freudian sexual symbolism does, in fact, occur and that it probably does so among children as well. It was noted that only one study attempted to examine symbolism other than sexual — death symbolism. There can be no doubt that these studies strongly support the Freudian theory of sexual symbolism.

TABLE 9.3. *Summary of positive conclusions concerning symbolism*

Hypothesis	Support	Investigation
Sexual symbolism in adults	Strong	Hammer (1953) McElroy (1954) Jahoda (1956) Jacobs (1954) Starer (1955) Jones (1956) Winter and Prescott (1957) Stennett and Thurlow (1958) Accord (1962) Lessler (1962) Moos and Mussen (1959) Cameron (1967)
Sexual symbolism not different in psychotics	Strong	Moos and Mussen (1959)
Sexual symbolism in children	Strong	Lessler (1962, 1964) Cameron (1967)
Death symbolism in adults	Fair	Meissner (1958)

REMs AND EGG

To help the reader unacquainted with the concept of rapid eye movement (REM) sleep, a brief description of the main findings from the electro encephalograph (EEG) study of sleep now follows. Two approaches have been used in the empirical study of dream content (apart from psychoanalytic free association):

1. Subjects on awakening in the morning are required to fill in report forms about their dreams.
2. Subjects are awoken during REM sleep and dream reports are then obtained.

EEG STUDIES OF SLEEP AND DREAMING

A full and detailed discussion would be out of place both because much of it would not be relevant to psychoanalytic theory and because, since Aserinsky and Kleitman (1955) first linked rapid eye movements with dreaming, there has been such an outpouring of research in this area.

Stages of sleep

1. As a subject falls asleep the EEG record shows increasing desynchrony with occasional waves of less than 8 cycles per second. There are low-amplitude high-frequency waves and fast frequencies. *1-REM*. This shows the same characteristic EEG pattern as above but is accompanied by *rapid eye movements* and *loss of muscle tone*. Aserinsky and Kleitman (1955) also found associated with these REM periods increased heart rate and changes in the pattern of breathing. Snyder (1963) claims that the truly distinctive feature of REM periods are the 'saw-tooth' shaped waves overlapping the rapid eye movements. Although there can be no doubt that dreaming occurs during REM periods as was pointed out by Aserinsky and Kleitman, as a result of later research, there is also no doubt that mentation, though of a less bizarre and dream-like character, does occur at other stages of sleep; see, for example, the study by Foulkes (1964).

2. Stage 2 is characterized by 'sleep spindles' — pointed waves of 14-16 cycles per second which occur against a background of low-voltage activity, in frequent bursts.

3. In this are found high-amplitude waves of 1-2 cycles per second together with the sleep spindles of stage 2.

4. This stage is typified by large-amplitude waves of 1-3 cycles per second.

Stages 1 to 4 excluding REM sleep may be regarded as on a depth-continuum. Characteristically, changes from stage to stage are in sequential order when moving towards stage 4 (although REM periods usually emerge from stage 2 sleep) but are abrupt when returning from stage 4. Stages are usually less than fifteen minutes in length except for REM sleep. Usually most of stage 4 sleep occurs in the early part of the night whereas much of the REM sleep occurs late (Webb, 1968).

Thus then EEG studies have shown the cyclic nature of the sleep process and the fact that dreaming is largely associated with one particular stage of sleep, the REM stage, although mentation occurs at other stages.

It is hoped that this brief and inevitably simplified summary will give the reader sufficient background to appreciate the implications of the EEG studies of dreaming that are to be reviewed later in the chapter.

DISADVANTAGES OF METHOD 1 (RECORDING DREAMS IN THE MORNING)

A disadvantage of the first method is simply one of memory: it is sometimes impossible to remember the content of any dream in the morning even though one can remember dreaming. Furthermore, since in normal sleep there are several REM periods the common occurrence of apparently having had no dreams is unlikely to be true. It is more likely that there has been complete forgetting. Again the fact that there are several REM periods each night implies the strong possibility of several dreams each night so that any dream report recorded in the morning is likely to be either a composite of these dreams or the recall of only one REM period. In addition to all these problems, one of the actual Freudian mechanisms it would be hoped to investigate with such studies could well effect reports — secondary elaboration (see p. 264). A final disadvantage of this method lies in human weakness. The possibility must be faced that subjects will not bother to complete their dream reports or will fill them in much later than they should, possibly even inventing data.

ADVANTAGES OF METHOD 1

It is possible to build up very large samples of dreams both from special groups and the general population. There are two strategies: large numbers of dreams may be obtained from the same individuals or one dream may be recorded from each of a very large sample.

DISADVANTAGES OF METHOD 2 (EEG STUDIES)

For this method an EEG laboratory with sleeping facilities for subjects is necessary. The whole procedure of recording EEGs for eight-hour periods is extremely costly and laborious. The amount of paper on which the EEG is recorded over an eight-hour period is huge. There are, therefore, storage and marking problems. These difficulties and the fact that each EEG machine can only deal with a small number of subjects, if there is to be simultaneous recording, means that only very small samples may be used. Few studies use more than twenty subjects. There are other obvious administrative difficulties in this second method. There must be comfortable sleeping facilities for the subjects. Many subjects are, of course, unwilling to spend their nights in the sleeping laboratory and it is arguable that volunteers for this procedure do not constitute a normal sample. Equally it is not easy for psychologists, especially those employed as university teachers, to spend their nights in sleep research and their days in normal work. Nor do night hours appeal to those engaged purely on research. Webb (1968) contains an eloquent account of the personal difficulties of those engaged on sleep research.

ADVANTAGES OF METHOD 2

Dream reports elicited during an REM period are usually fuller and more dream-like (in Freudian terms less affected by secondary elaboration) than those obtained after a full night's sleep. In addition it is possible to obtain dream reports from all the REM periods. It is also possible to study experimentally the effects of external stimuli on dream content as in, for example, the work of Berger (1963). In addition, it is possible to induce dream deprivation by wakening subjects immediately an REM period begins — a method in some ways superior to the use of drugs where any effects are inevitably confused by possible side-effects of the drug itself.

We will next examine the results of dream studies relevant to Freudian theory. First those investigations in which the first method was used will be discussed. Since Hall at the Institute of Dream Research has launched a truly massive attack on the phenomenology of dreams, in which more than 10,000 dreams have been subjected to detailed content-analysis, it is fitting to deal with his work first.

THE WORK OF HALL (FROM 1953)

Undoubtedly the most extensive investigations into the phenomenology of dreams have been carried out by Hall and his associates, now at the Institute of Dream Research. Their basic technique is to have subjects recall their dreams on specially prepared dream-report forms as soon as possible on waking. This has enabled them to analyse for manifest content more than 10,000 dreams from a very large number of subjects. Hall (1953 and 1966), in *The Meaning of Dreams*, has presented his main conclusions in an entertaining and easily readable form. Unfortunately, however, he does not refer in detail to any of the original data so that for the purposes of this chapter it is necessary to examine some of the individual research papers of which the book was a summary.

Before any of these studies is reviewed in detail a number of points need to be made clear. First, Hall studies only the manifest content of the dream, i.e. the reported dream material. He does not seek to uncover the latent content. Nevertheless he does attempt to 'understand' the dream, for to Hall the dream is a key to understanding the dreamer's conflicts. For example, in 1966 he writes 'This, above all, is what dreams are, an authentic record of a mind made anxious by conflict.' For Hall the interpretation of dreams is largely carried out by examining not one of a subject's dreams but a whole series. He writes 'From a single dream we may learn a few things about the dreamer but not until we have studied a number of his dreams are we able to paint a valid picture of his essential character.' Essentially the understanding of a dream is based on a hunch and if the intuitions resulting from interpretation of each of a series of dreams are internally consistent and sensible, then the dreams are considered to be correctly understood.

For the purpose of this book, what is interesting about the work of Hall is not so much the interpretation (for which there is little objective validity) but the fact that he has collected so many dreams from a large normal sample and that he has, in some cases, specifically tested hypotheses directly derived from Freudian theory. The normality of his sample means that the results may be more widely generalized without injury to scientific rigour than may, for example, the observations of analysts upon their patients. The immense number of dreams collected means that statistical tests may be employed to elucidate any differences in dream-content observed between groups, and thus to test hypotheses.

Results from studies of Freudian hypotheses

A. *The dream of being attacked — Hall (1955)*

Hall (1955) investigated the significance of the dream of being attacked. In two previous studies Harris (1948, 1951) had attempted to test the Freudian hypothesis that dreams of being attacked represented a fear of castration by the father and that the dream of falling was a fear of losing maternal love. This was done with a small number of subjects by hypothesizing that those who had the first dream would find difficulty in expressing aggression to their fathers whereas those who had the second would have difficulty in expressing aggression towards their mothers. Harris, in fact, despite the size of his sample, found support for these hypotheses and thus, indirectly, the Freudian hypothesis. Hall (1955) put these hypotheses to a more stringent test.

517 subjects were asked whether they had ever had either of the two dreams (being attacked and falling), which was the more unpleasant, and with which parent they found it easier to argue. The first results were contrary to Freudian theory in that females who had only one kind of dream were more likely to dream of being attacked, while males with only one dream were more likely to dream of falling. Yet castration fear is characteristically male, a fear of loss of love, female (Freud, 1933).

Again contrary to the Freudian hypothesis was the fact that females found the dream of being attacked significantly more unpleasant than the dream of falling while for males there was no significant difference. Furthermore, and again contrary to the psychoanalytic hypothesis, for both sexes the mother was more easy to argue with than the father. The hypothesis that those who can argue more easily with the father will be dreamers of falling (predominantly) was supported at the 0.05 level for males but not for females. Though significant the difference was not large. To sum up, these results do not support the claim that the dream of being attacked symbolizes fear of castration.

Hall then made a content-analysis of 106 dreams of being attacked. Typically, the dreamer responds in a passive way to an unprovoked attack by a male or a group of men. From this Hall concludes that the dream of being attacked is equivalent to *being castrated*, not fear of castration — hence the feeling, in the content-analysis, of being weak and impotent. This hypothesis fits the data far better since for women castration has already taken place (Freud, 1926) — hence women would dream this more. Indeed Hall develops the theme that the dream of being attacked symbolizes *being castrated* (the attack itself) and femininity — the passivity of the dreamer. Femininity is characterized in Freudian theory by

(a) passive aims (Freud, 1931),
(b) a sense of inferiority (Freud, 1926),
(c) masochism (Freud, 1931).

All these points are typified in the inability of the dreamer to fight back his attackers. Thus a content-analysis of dreams of being attacked supports the claim that for both sexes it embodies the psychoanalytic concept of femininity and that the attack itself represents being castrated rather than fear of castration.

Conclusions. This study by Hall (1955) is a good example of how predictions of dream content may be made from Freudian theory using both dream theory and other parts of psychoanalysis — in this case the theory of femininity. The findings support the theory. However, it must be pointed out that, in this case at least, the links between femininity and the dream content are not obvious but a tribute rather to the skill of Hall in seeing relationships and educing correlates! Hall has shown the results can be seen as congruent with theory. They do not disprove it but they are not sufficient to support it with any degree of confidence.

B.1. Evidence relevant to the Oedipus complex

Hall and Domhoff (1963) pooled the results of eleven investigations and reported a ubiquitous sex difference in the dreams of 1399 men and 1418 women. 64 per cent of the characters in the dream narratives of the men (3874 in number) were male, whereas in the dream narratives of the women (3065 in number) only 52 per cent were male. Similar findings have been made for the Hopi of the south-west United States and for the Yiv Yoront of Australia.

As a supplement to this study, a small sample of students was asked to write the initials of persons they liked and disliked (one minute). For males the percentage of male names was far greater than for females. In addition it was noted that in short stories by men 75 per cent of the characters were male — a figure which fell to only 54 per cent in stories by women.

Similarly, Hall and Domhoff (1962a, b) found that aggression in the dreams of men was more directed against males than females, whereas in the dreams of women aggression was directed equally against both sexes. The reverse (Hall and Domhoff, 1962b) was true of friendly acts. Here in the dreams of men they were directed significantly more towards females than males. In the case of the dreams of women, there was again an even split.

As with the previous study it is difficult to draw precise conclusions from these findings. The fact that male aggression is directed towards males and friendliness towards females could be regarded as evidence for the Oedipus complex — characterized by jealousy and hatred of the father by the son. Hall and Domhoff interpret the ubiquitous sex difference of more males in male dreams as support for the Oedipus complex because they follow Hall's theory (1966) that dreams reveal conflict. But there is some circularity here — men dream more of males — males have conflict with their fathers through the Oedipus complex — dreams show conflicts. Thus it would not be fair to invoke this sex difference as support for the Oedipus complex.

Conclusions. The finding that male dreams are characterized by aggression against males does appear to confirm Oedipal theory — although this is only manifest content. The ubiquitous sex difference confirms Oedipal theory only if dreams are regarded as evidence of conflict (Hall, 1966), a theory which needs further verification. These studies, therefore, provide only modest support for Freudian theory.

B.2. Further evidence relevant to the Oedipus complex — Hall (1963)

Hall (1963) made a further study relevant to the Oedipus complex in an investigation of the incidence of male strangers in dreams. The psychoanalytic hypotheses underlying the paper are clearly stated and are embodied in the central part of psychoanalytic theory:

(a) that in girls the fantasy of a 'good' mother and a 'bad' father is not altogether obliterated by the castration complex (for the Freudian theory, see p. 131).
(b) that for the boy, father is 'bad' — the Oedipus complex.

Thus the early concept of father, in psychoanalytic terms, is of a feared stranger. Therefore, if dreams reflect early conflicts (Hall, 1966) he will be represented in the dream by a male stranger unknown to the dreamer.

From these psychoanalytic hypotheses four empirical hypotheses were drawn. There will be:

1. More male strangers in dreams than female.
2. More male strangers in male dreams than in female dreams.
3. More aggressive encounters with male strangers than female strangers.
4. Higher proportion of such encounters in male than female dreams.
5. To male strangers in dreams more free associations of fathers and authority figures.

It is to be noticed that this investigation is a model of how from general psychoanalytic theory (Oedipus and castration complex) testable hypotheses concerning dream content may be drawn. The only other assumption made is that dreams are concerned with early conflict — a theory which is not contrary, though not specific, to psychoanalytic theory.

Samples. Various samples were used. There were two samples of children. One, 2-12 years of age, the other 13-18 years. Three samples of young adults and one of mature people, 30-80 years old, were also included. From most samples one dream per subject was examined, and sample sizes were all greater than 200, many more than 400, evenly split by sex. One sample consisting of twenty-seven men from whom 492 dreams were analysed and twenty-eight women who supplied 525 dreams was also included.

Results. In most of these groups the first four hypotheses were confirmed at beyond the 0.05 level. Hypothesis 3 was significant in only fifteen of the thirty-six comparisons, but, since the numbers of aggressions were small and the direction of difference was always correct, Hall is satisfied that the hypothesis was confirmed.

Hypothesis 4 was confirmed clearly only in group six with the largest number of dream reports where the difference was highly significant — beyond the 0.001 level. As regards the last hypothesis concerning free association, Hall cites Rees (1959) who collected free associations to ten dreams of twelve male and twelve female students. While the numbers were too small to reach significance, more father and authority-free associations than any other were in fact given to male strangers.

From these findings Hall concludes that four hypotheses were confirmed — the first four — while hypothesis 5 received marginal confirmation. He argues that it is irrelevant to ask whether any other theory could have predicted these results — the fact is that psychoanalytic theory *did* predict them. The education of *ad hoc* theories is usually unsatisfactory. If all studies of psychoanalytic hypotheses were considered together, the collection of *ad hoc* hypotheses would not be parsimonious either. Thus, while for any one experiment the psychoanalytic hypothesis may defy the law of Occam's razor, for a number of experiments this would not necessarily be the case since their explication might well involve an equal number of *ad hoc* hypotheses.

Comments and conclusions. This study, as has been mentioned, is a good example of how clear, testable hypotheses may be derived from psychoanalytic theory. The fact that they were largely confirmed is not only support for Oedipal theory but for Freudian dream theory. If these results are accepted it would be impossible to argue, for example, that the mental content while dreaming is the result of random firing or stimulation of the brain during the REM period while protein is being synthesized (Oswald, 1969). On the contrary, the dream content appears to conform to a meaningful pattern. As suggested in the outline of Freudian dream theory, the dream allows normally repressed impulses expression (in this case Oedipal aggression towards the father). In this instance the Hall theory that old childhood-conflicts are re-enacted in dreams is not far different from the orthodox psychoanalytic claim that the dream allows expression of a repressed wish. These findings, therefore, must be regarded as good evidence for psychoanalytic dream theory and as evidence for the Oedipus complex.

C. Further evidence relevant to the castration complex

Hall and Van De Castle (1963) made a further investigation (see Hall, 1955, p. 289) of the evidence from dreams for the castration complex. The hypothesis derived from the psychoanalytic theory of the Oedipus complex and castration complex (see pp. 130 et seq.) was that male dreamers would report more dreams expressive of castration anxiety than of castration wishes or penis envy: for females the pattern would be reversed. This hypothesis is easily deduced from the Freudian theory and would appear from that point of view to be quite un-exceptional.

Sample. 120 college students in three groups of forty (twenty male and twenty female). A total of 953 dreams was analysed.

Measures. Clearly the validity of the measures used for castration anxiety, castration wish and penis envy is crucial to evaluating this study. The dream reports were searched for evidence of any of these three states. Examination of the criteria used shows them to be well in accord with psychoanalytic dream theory (dream-work). Examples of the criteria are given below.

(a) *Castration anxiety*

    1. Actual or threatened loss, removal or injury to a specific part of the dreamer's body. Similarly threatened, or actual, stabbing or cutting.
    2. Any defect of a part of dreamer's body.
    3. Loss or injury or defect of any animal or object belonging to dreamer.
    4. Inability of dreamer to use penis or symbol of penis.
    5. Male dreamer is female in any way, e.g. clothes.

(b) *Castration wish.* As above but to another person *not* dreamer.

(c) *Criteria for penis envy*

    1. Acquisition by dreamer of penis or phallic symbol.
    2. Dreamer envies or admires a man's physical characteristic or performance.
    3. Female dreamer becomes male in some way.

It will be noticed that most of these criteria embody phallic symbolism.

Inter-marker reliability of scoring. 87-96 per cent. This is a satisfactory figure.

Results. X^2 was used to test the hypothesis which was supported beyond the 0.001 level ($X^2 = 24$). 50 per cent of females had no castration-anxiety score, for example, compared with only 8 per cent of males in this position.

Two further small studies were carried out which should be mentioned.

Freud (1916-17) argued that the penis wish implicit in penis envy becomes a wish for a baby, then a wish for a man. Hall, therefore, put the hypothesis derived from this — that girls have more dreams of babies and getting married than do men — to the test. Although it was strongly confirmed in this case, as Hall points out, other alternative hypotheses are possible. Finally a further study showed that the incidence of castration anxiety, castration wishes and penis envy in the dreams of older men was very similar to that among college students.

Comments and conclusions. The major finding of this study strongly supports Freudian theory and the existence of male castration anxiety. As in the previous investigation (1963), Hall is careful to point out that it is possible to produce *ad hoc* theories to account for these results. Nevertheless, what more can be expected of a theory than that it predict correctly? For example, he points out that injury can be expected to be a more frequent part of male dreams in that in their everyday life and even hobbies men undertake more dangerous things than women. In short, it must be accepted that these findings support Freudian theory — both dream theory and developmental hypotheses. It is also to be noted that these results are sound evidence for symbolism.

D. Evidence relevant to the development of the super-ego

The psychoanalytic theory of the development of the super-ego in men and women (see p. 131) strongly implies that women develop a less severe and less well-internalized super-ego (e.g. Freud, 1931). From this Hall (1964) derived the hypothesis that more women would be the victims of aggression in dreams than men (their super-ego being external) whereas men would more often suffer a misfortune. This he tested by examining, as usual, the dream reports of men and women.

Sample. Around 1500 male dreams and 1500 female dreams were subjected to content-analysis.

Results. The hypothesis was supported at the 0.01 level.

Conclusions. As Hall indicates in the title to this paper, these results may be regarded as *modest* confirmation of the differential development of the super-ego in men and women. Confirmation is justified in that the prediction was supported but it is not powerful enough to support the whole theory. This finding is but one tile in the mosaic of construct-validation.

Conclusions from Hall's empirical studies

Taken together these studies illustrate the problems of testing Freudian theory. Thus Hall's 1955 investigation of the dream of being attacked involves Freudian attributes of femininity and attempts to show that these are present in the mani-fest content of the dreams. This is only a subjective judgement, however, and although ingenious cannot be regarded as strong or objective evidence in favour of the theory. The 1963 study of the Oedipus complex, on the other hand, derives precise testable hypotheses from Oedipal theory concerning the objective content of dreams — e.g. either strangers are in the dream or they are not. Thus confirmation of this hypothesis must be considered as good evidence for both developmental and dream theory in psychoanalysis.

On the criteria, therefore, of clearly defined hypotheses capable of clear and objective measurement two of these studies may be regarded as supporting Freudian theory:

1. Hall (1963). Strangers in dreams: an empirical confirmation of the Oedipus complex.
2. Hall and Van De Castle (1963). An empirical demonstration of the castration complex in dreams.

The other dream studies reported in the previous section cannot be held to be strong support for the theory. Either the hypotheses are too tenuous or the subjective element in measurement too great to stand close scrutiny. Nevertheless, the fact that the results, as they stand, do support the theory cannot be ignored. These studies may be regarded as slender support — useful in the total consideration of all the evidence but unsatisfactory on their own.

Relevance to dream theory of Hall's studies

The fact that Freudian phenomena such as the Oedipus complex can be observed in the content of dreams indicates that there is psychological meaning in them — that they are not the results of random firing in certain areas of the brain. Since, in psychoanalytic dream theory, wishes normally repressed find expression in dreams together with other repressed material, the occurrence of Oedipal aggression and penis envy would be expected. Thus these studies by Hall support the Freudian claim that the dream is the royal road to the unconscious. In addition, they support the concepts of the Oedipus and castration complexes. Further study of these investigations may be found in the chapter on these complexes (pp. 150-2).

THE WORK OF LEE (1958)

Lee studied the dreams of 600 Zulu subjects (120 of these in great detail) and provided some powerful evidence in favour of Freudian dream theory. An interesting point about this cross-cultural study is the fact that it is not possible to argue that these subjects were influenced in reporting or remembering their dreams by Freudian or Jungian dream theory! — a common jibe at psychoanalytic clinical case studies. If influenced at all in this way it would be by the Zulu dream diviners who interpret dreams, which in their culture are regarded as of great importance (Callaway, 1868, quoted by Lee, 1958).

Sample. 600 rural Zulus. Of these 120 female subjects were subjected to further interview.

Method. The 600 subjects were asked how much they dreamed and the content of their dreaming. In the more intensive interviews of the sub-sample, the women were asked to describe in detail two dreams. Other information was also obtained from these subjects. Thus manifest content, in Freudian terms, was the subject of the study.

Results

Many dreams had an apparent lack of latent content — i.e. the manifest content of the dream appeared to express the wish.

Lee shows that Freudian dream theory can accommodate such a finding. Thus Freud (1935) in 'An autobiographical study' argues that young children often have such undistorted dreams because repressions are not yet fully developed. Adults too can have such infantile dreams if the need is imperative. Thus a crucial test of Lee's interpretation of these Zulu dreams is to establish to what extent the dream wishes did in fact reflect imperative needs.

To test the relationship between dream material and imperative needs, the dream content was related to the obstetric history of the subjects (more than 400 women).

(a) Dreamers of 'a baby' had much the worst record of married infertility. Those who had borne children had lost more than half of them and these were the youngest group (if the eldest, the deaths of their children would not have been so surprising).

Lee shows that in Zulu society there is a powerful psychological need for a baby. Failure to produce one brings contempt. Eysenck (1953a) has tried to argue that the Freudian claim that dreams represent wishes is disproved by the fact that hungry people do not produce hunger dreams. However, as Lee neatly argues, this evidence tests the hypothesis that dreams reflect all wishes, which is *not* the Freudian theory. This study by Lee shows that in the case of these young Zulu girls, dreams of a baby do indeed reflect an imperative need. This finding must be regarded, therefore, as support for the Freudian claim that dreams represent wishes.

(b) Sufferers from pseudocyesis (false pregnancy), which was common in the area, also tended to have the direct baby dream which again supports the Freudian notion.

(c) Nine of the twenty-one subjects who had 'baby' dreams said a baby was their main wish, and four said children were their main desire. Of the ninety-seven others only eighteen gave either baby or children as their wish. This difference is significant at the 1 per cent level. Thus further support for Freudian theory comes from this finding.

(d) Lee presents further data linking dreams of still water and flooding to conflicting desires for more children (a cultural norm) among those who already have sufficient of their own. Since this interpretation is largely speculative it will not be examined in further detail. Nor indeed will his other findings relating dreams of snakes and toholoske (a kind of Priapic river god) since they suffer to some extent from the same fault as orthodox psychoanalytic dream interpretations, being speculative and essentially untestable.

Comments and conclusions

This study by Lee is powerful evidence that in a sample of Zulu women certain common dreams do reflect wishes, in accordance with psychoanalytic theory. It also supports the Freudian claim that certain imperative needs may be directly expressed in the manifest content of the dream. In this sample there can be little fear that the results were biased by the subjects' knowledge of Freudian theory.

THE PHYSIOLOGY OF DREAMING

Snyder (1963, 1965) has claimed that dreaming, in man, is the subjective con-comitant of a pervasive and distinctive physiological state. This state, most obviously typified by rapid eye movements, is according to Snyder as qualitatively different from sleep as is waking from sleep. There are, therefore, three biological states in man, and indeed mammals. Dement (1963) makes this point with complete clarity.

(a) *Awakeness*. This enables the organism to act on the environment.
(b) *Sleep* (slow-wave sleep, stages 2, 3, 4). This very probably enables the organism to recuperate.
(c) *REM*. Function not truly known.

CHARACTERISTICS OF THIS THIRD STATE — REMs

Since our interest in REMs stems from the fact that dreaming in its most typical, bizarre form occurs in them, a brief description of the major physiological characteristics of REMs must suffice. Snyder (1965) has an excellent summary. *The eyes* are in intermittent frantic activity, first related to dreaming by Aserinsky and Kleitman (1955). *Breathing* is shallow, rapid and irregular. In the face and hands there are twitch-like, muscular movements. This twitching occurs in animals also (e.g. in the opossum) as a constant twitching of ears, snout muscles and digits. Pet lovers have all observed similar things in their dogs and cats. The pulse tends to increase in man (Aserinsky and Kleitman, 1955) as does systolic blood pressure (Snyder et al., 1963). In man there is an EEG pattern of 2-3 per second 'saw-toothed' shaped waves preceding or overlapping the clusters of eye movements. This EEG pattern is never seen outside REMs. Furthermore, there is almost complete loss of muscle-tone — i.e. the organism is paralysed. In men 85 per cent of these REMs are accompanied by penile erection (Fisher, 1965; Karacan et al., 1966).

OCCURRENCE OF REMs IN ANIMALS AND MAN

In organisms lower in the phylogenetic scale than mammals it is unlikely that REMs occur. Klein (1963) found no REMs in the tortoise (reptile) although a very brief period has been seen in a bird. Among mammals, however, REMs have been found: cats, dogs, rabbits, rats, sheep, monkeys and chimpanzees (Klein, 1963). Even the marsupial opossum (Snyder, 1964), low in the mammalian scale, has REMs. Based on an examination of many investigations, Fisher (1965) shows that in man there is a decided age-trend in the amount of REM sleep per night. Thus a premature (30-week) infant spent 80 per cent of its sleep time in REM sleep. Between 33-5 weeks this fell to 67 per cent. The neonate typically spends 50 per cent of its sleep in REM sleep, a figure which drops to 35 per cent at one year, 30 per cent at three years to 20 per cent at five years. This 20 per cent appears reasonably constant until late in life. At 50-70 years the figure falls again to 13-18 per cent and one 100-year-old man spent only 13 per cent of his sleep time in REM sleep.

These figures and the fact that mammals undergo REM sleep are of great importance in appreciating the significance of REM sleep for the psychoanalytic theory of dreaming. This will be discussed later (see pp. 317 et seq.).

PHYSIOLOGICAL MECHANISMS INVOLVED IN REMs

Jouvet has carried out much research on the physiology of sleep and REMs. He claims (1967) that the overall results of his experiments

> reveal that the structures *sufficient* for the periodical appearance of the major behavioural and EEG signs of PS [paradoxical sleep — the term favoured by Jouvet but to be equated with REMs] are located at the level of the pons. Another series of experiments shows that some pontine structures are equally necessary.

Dement et al. (1967) and Jouvet (1967) both argue from the complex mass of evidence that in some way during REMs a neurochemical substance, a mono-amine, is being metabolized. This chemical, which piles up during REM deprivation, is thought to underlie the effects of such deprivation. Some evidence for this comes from the fact that cerebro-spinal fluid from a cat deprived of REM sleep, when injected into a normal cat, produces an increase in REM sleep (Dement et al., 1967).

RELATION OF REMs TO DREAMING

From the viewpoint of psychoanalytic dream theory, the importance of the discovery by Aserinsky and Kleitman (1955) that REMs were associated with dreaming cannot be too strongly emphasized: for the first time it enabled some kind of objectivity to be brought into the study of dreaming since it indicated when a subject was and was not dreaming.

Dement and Kleitman (1957)

Dement and Kleitman made a rigorous examination of this relationship. Seven male subjects and two females participated in the study. Three approaches were used:

1. Dream recall from REM and NREM periods was elicited without direct contact between the experimenter and subject.
2. A subjective estimate of the length of the dream was correlated with the length of the REM period before awakening, and
3. The pattern of eye movements was related to dream content.

Results

As Dement and Kleitman had previously found, REMs and the characteristic EEG were associated in all subjects. REMs had a mean duration of twenty minutes (range 3-50) and REMs late at night tended to be longer. For every individual there was a regular cycle of REMs, on average every ninety-two minutes.

The main findings in relation to the three problems examined in this paper were:

1. Very high recall in REM awakenings, very little in NREM.

1b. This recall dropped precipitately on cessation of REMs.

2. Positive relationship between estimated length of dream and whether waking was after five or fifteen minutes. Also a positive relationship between length of dream narrative and length of REM (0.71 to 0.40 with five subjects).

3. There was a relationship between eye movements and content of dream reports. Examples will best make this clear. Subjects were woken after one minute of continuous eye movement in either the vertical or the horizontal plane. Alternatively they were awoken after one minute's fixation. In fact there was only one period of horizontal movement observed. In the dream report immediately elicited people had been throwing tomatoes at each other. In two cases there was a period of inactivity followed by large movements and in each of these the subject was driving a car. On the basis of these results Dement and Kleitman (1957) concluded that REMs were so closely related to dreaming that it was possible to use them as objective measures of dreaming.

There can be little doubt that this experiment is solid evidence for the relationship between REMs and dreaming and there is little point, therefore, in examining earlier or merely confirmatory experiments. Nevertheless further studies have shown these findings to be somewhat over-simplified and the more recent elaborations will now be considered, although it must be stressed at this point that these further studies are elaborations and that the broad findings have been confirmed.

Dement and Wolpert (1958)

Dement and Wolpert investigated the relationship of eye movements, bodily motility and external stimuli to the content of dreams using as raw data 204 dream reports from fourteen men and two women.

Results

Chi-square analyses showed that there was little bodily movement associated with continuous dreaming whereas for fragmented dreams there was much movement. The amount of eye movement was related to the activity or passivity of the dream and, as was reported by Dement and Kleitman (1957), the direction of eye movement, whether it was horizontal or vertical, was related to the dream content. Finally it was found that some stimuli were incorporated into dreams: a water spray 42 per cent of the time, a tone only 9 per cent of the time and the arousing stimulus, a bell, not at all.

Conclusions

This study is further support for the fact that eye movements and muscular activity of the REMs are not random activations of the central nervous system but, on the contrary, are related to the processes of dreaming.

DREAM REPORTS FROM REM AND NREM PERIODS OF SLEEP

The work of Foulkes (1960, 1962)

Foulkes (1960) in his doctoral dissertation investigated the question of when dreams occur in three subjects over twenty-five nights. In this study he found that dreaming occurred outside REM periods but was of a qualitatively different kind: REM dreaming was mainly perceptual, NREM dreaming conceptual. Foulkes (1962) extended this study using eight male subjects who were awoken at various stages of sleep over a period of fifty-seven nights. They were asked to classify their dreams into 'thoughts' or 'dreams', the criterion for dreams being the presence of sensory imagery.

Results

There was recall from NREMs in 74 per cent of awakenings and in 87 per cent of awakenings from REMs. From NREMs there was 'thinking' rather than dreaming. Foulkes attempts to align his findings with those of Dement and Kleitman (1957), discussed above, by claiming that these writers had a more stringent criterion for dreaming than his. When he asked his subjects for dreams rather than reports of what was 'going through their minds' much less material was elicited.

Conclusions

Thus it appears that dreaming as normally defined — bizarre and hallucinatory mental events — does occur during the REM periods but that, in addition, a more mundane kind of mentation also takes place during NREM periods.

A number of studies have investigated the relatedness of the mental activity occurring during sleep. Thus, for example, Dement and Wolpert (1958) examined the dreams from eight subjects over thirty-eight nights. On any night dreams were not duplicated and there was not a truly continuous series of dreams. Nevertheless, the manifest content of dreams on the same night was related and in seven out of thirty-eight sequences all dreams were united by a common theme. In fact, these authors likened the dreams to the different chapters of a book. This tendency for there to be some kind of relationship between dreams of the same night is generally confirmed by the other researches in this field (e.g. Trosman et al., 1960; Offenkrantz and Rechtschaffen, 1963; Rechtschaffen, Verdone and Wheaton, 1963; Kramer et al., 1976).

The work of Rechtschaffen, Vogel and Shaikun (1963)

In the light of these findings concerning the relatedness of dream material during the same night and the work of Foulkes (1960 and 1962) concerning REM and NREM mentation, which has already been discussed, Rechtschaffen, Vogel and Shaikun (1963) made a further and most interesting investigation of this problem. They examined three questions:

(a) The relationship of NREM mentation of the same night (for the other studies had concentrated on REM dream reports), and
(b) the relation of REM and NREM material of the same night.
   Finally,
(c) they were interested in investigating the nature of any such relationships.

As is the case with almost all these EEG studies of dreaming, for reasons of objectivity the manifest content of dreams, not the latent content, was investigated.

Sample. There were two samples:

1. Two subjects for three nights were subjected to awakenings every thirty or ninety minutes. The time interval was chosen at random.
2. Seventeen subjects from whom, in all, the dreams of thirty nights were investigated. Since the results from both these samples were similar the results will be discussed together.

Results

(a) Identical or almost identical manifest elements are repeated in reports of NREM awakenings.
(b) NREM and REM elements are also similar.
(c) In each report the elements have different contents. There is no continuous narrative.
(d) The manifest element appears in the first NREM report. Therefore the report cannot be a hangover from the first REM period — i.e. a memory of a previous dream.

Conclusions

There is an obvious problem in this study that the actual dream-reporting early on in the night could influence later dream reports. Nevertheless, as will be discussed more fully in the section on the implications of these studies for psychoanalytic dream theory, NREM mentation is not unlike the Freudian day-residues of dreaming which are secondary or preconscious processes and REM mentation is precisely what would be considered a primary process. This relationship of common elements in REM and NREM mentation is again similar to the relation between day-residues and dreaming proper suggested by Freud in 'A metapsychological supplement to the theory of dreams' (Freud, 1917c).

It should be noted that in addition to the studies by Foulkes (1960, 1962) and

Rechtschaffen, Vogel and Shaikun (1963) where NREM mentation was observed, other researches have confirmed this finding, notably Rechtschaffen, Verdone and Wheaton (1963), Foulkes and Rechtschaffen (1964) and Kamija (1961). Although the subjects in the second Rechtschaffen (1963) study were the same, in part, as those of the first (1963), there can be no doubt that mentation is not, as was first thought, restricted to REM periods.

Foulkes (1964) in an attempt to summarize the findings and implications of all these studies emphasizes the resemblance already referred to between NREM mentation and day-residues and REM dreams and secondary processes. REM dreams, he argues, are distortions of NREM dreams.

EYE MOVEMENT AND DREAM CONTENT

Of major importance in a study of the relation between REM periods and dreaming is clearly the relationship between eye movements and dream content. In the original investigations by Dement and Kleitman (1957) it was shown that vertical eye movements corresponded to reports of vertical activity in dreams, as did horizontal eye movements. This was confirmed by Dement and Wolpert (1958). Even more impressive evidence for the fact that REMs are associated with the hallucinatory imagery of dreaming was offered by Roffwarg et al. (1962). These authors elicited dream reports from REM periods of sleep. Where the dreamer felt that his recall was good an independent reader of the dream report was able to predict what the pattern of REMs would be. In one case eye movements compensated for an hallucinatory head movement — where a subject was climbing stairs holding a cat. If eye movements in dreams do in fact scan visual imagery, the question of REMs in the blind, especially the congenitally blind, is clearly relevant evidence.

REMs IN THE BLIND

Berger et al. (1962) carried out an investigation of just this point. They found no evidence of REMs in their sample of congenitally blind subjects. Amadeo and Gomez (1964) on the other hand found exactly the opposite in a study of subjects with life-long blindness. Fisher (1965) accounts for this apparent contradiction in terms of method. He cites a study he carried out with Gross and Feldman (Fisher, Gross and Feldman, 1965) with subjects suffering from retrolental fibrophasia. These subjects showed no REMs when tested by the usual method. This is because in this disease the retina is destroyed and there is no corneo-retinal potential. By using a different method REM activity was observed.

Conclusions

The conclusion must be drawn, therefore, that REMs occur in the congenitally blind. This does not contradict the previous findings that REMs are scanning hallucinatory images, especially when the findings of infant REMs and mammalian REMs are taken into account. REMs are presumably, as Fisher (1965) argues, a phylogenetically ancient mechanism which has been taken over by the phylogenetically more recent visual dreaming.

DREAM-DEPRIVATION AND THE NEED TO DREAM

If, as psychoanalytic dream theory claims, every dream expresses a wish which replaces some instinctual demand, unable in waking life to find expression but in dreaming able to evade the censoring super-ego, then dream-deprivation should produce on waking what could be regarded as substitute symptoms. Demands unexpressed at night should, therefore, force themselves through in other ways.

When Dement and Kleitman (1957) apparently showed that dreaming was synchronous with REM sleep and did not occur at other stages of sleep, an obvious method of testing Freudian hypotheses by dream-deprivation was suggested. Subjects could be selectively deprived of REM sleep alone: the effects of fatigue or simple sleep-deprivation could be controlled for by, at a later stage, selectively depriving subjects of NREM sleep and comparing the effects. Dement (1960, 1963), Dement et al. (1967), Berger and Oswald (1962) have carried out such procedures with human subjects while Jouvet (1960, 1965) has made extensive studies of REM sleep (rather than dream) deprivation in cats. Since the papers of Dement (1963) and Dement et al. (1967) are, in part, reviews of past work in the field, it is simplest to examine these rather than review in detail earlier work to which later findings have tended to run counter.

Dement (1960), in a study where twenty subjects were deprived first of REM sleep and then of NREM sleep, noted that deprivation of REM sleep produced a tendency for REM sleep to appear more frequently. On the recovery night the amount of REM sleep was greater than the subject's normal amount. In addition, compared with controls moderate psychological disturbances were observed in those deprived of REM sleep — anxiety, irritability and difficulty in concentration. Dement interpreted these results as a need to dream. Fisher and Dement (1963) attempted to fit these results into the psychoanalytic theory of dreaming. They argued REM sleep was concomitant with instinctual id-drive discharge processes which would lead to hallucinatory dreams. Sufficient dream-deprivation therefore should produce psychotic symptoms, delusions and hallucinations. However, thirteen nights' REM-deprivation (in the case of one subject) did not produce any such symptoms. In fact he was becoming fatigued and could not be awakened for REM-deprivation.

Dement (1963), in the review paper already referred to, argues that the simple interpretation of this early work as showing a *need to dream* cannot stand scrutiny

(a) because REM sleep has been shown to occur in sub-humans,
(b) because of the emergence of the concept of a third biologic state (Snyder, 1963 and 1965, see p. 297) of which REMs are but one indication, and
(c) because mentation has been shown to occur in NREM periods (see p. 300).

Thus any results can only be interpreted as due to *REM-* not *dream*-deprivation.

In addition Dement (1963) points to a methodological weakness in these studies — namely that small amounts of REM sleep could have occurred in that subjects were woken when the characteristic EEG pattern and eye movements had begun. However, in cats at least Jouvet and Mounier (1960) have shown that even a little paradoxical or REM sleep reduces their hyper-excitability (the main effects of REM-deprivation in cats). However, Berger (1961) had noted that EMG suppression took place a few seconds before REM activation and Dement (1963), using this EMG suppression (measured from neck muscles) as a signal for waking subjects to induce REM-deprivation, quotes three case studies to illustrate its effects:

1. In one case 95 per cent REM-deprivation for eight nights produced almost no effect except slight drowsiness.

2. In his second subject dexedrine was also used to reduce REMs chemically. This was necessary because of habituation to the arousing stimulus and the greater press for REM sleep on deprivation which means that long periods of deprivation become difficult to produce. After night 14 there was a sudden dramatic change in the personality of the subject. A taciturn, moral man became garrulous, expressed annoyance and anger and impulsively wanted to do things, such as go to a night club and cheat the waitress, that he otherwise would not contemplate.

3. Dexedrine was again used with this subject whose NREM sleep time was equal to or above normal — a fact which makes fatigue unlikely as a cause of these results. He endured sixteen nights' REM-deprivation. Again after the fourteenth night there was an abrupt change. He became paranoid and thought his friends were disparaging him.

On the recovery night in all cases REM sleep showed a great increase in frequency. Dement (1963) argues that it is unlikely that these changes in the last two subjects were due to the dexedrine, they must be imputed to REM-deprivation. Clearly, the slight changes noted in earlier experiments were due to the small amounts of REM-deprivation — fourteen days of 95 per cent deprivation seems critical.

The conclusions to be drawn from this paper will be discussed after the work of Dement et al. (1967) has been examined. This paper reviews all the animal and human REM-deprivation studies up to this date and provides an excellent summary of the work done. According to these authors the main results of REM-deprivation in both animals and men are:

1. *REM increases in frequency*: as deprivation goes on more arousals become necessary and when left there is a long period of REM. This was found in the work of Dement (1960, 1963) which has already been discussed by Kales et al. (1964) and by Sampson (1965). This increase in REM time on recovery has also been found with animals. For example, Jouvet et al. (1964), in their study of cats, found that after thirty days' or more deprivation the recovery curves remain the

same. In addition the intensity of the REM state appears to increase (great increase in brain temperature and blood flow).

The next three findings are not important from the viewpoint of relevance to psychoanalytic theory so they will simply be listed.

2. More rapid recovery of potential evoked by the second of a pair of clicks in the cat.

3. Drop in the seizure threshold, for rats.

4. Rise in heart rate for cats (with lesions in nucleus pontis caudalis).

5. In cats, up to as long as seventy days' deprivation produced no impairment of motor performance and no fatigue.

6. In cats the eating drive was increased.

7. In cats, compulsive mounting of anaesthetized cats. In rats 80 per cent of REM-deprived animals (only 14 per cent in control group) attempted to mount a female.

8. On six subjects, there were some changes on TAT scores, but deprivation was only six days and Dement's (1963) data imply that a longer period is needed to be effective.

9. In cats, seizures seemed to compensate for REM periods. For nine human subjects similar results were observed although the data were less consistent. Furthermore, an epileptic patient who was also REM-deprived for four nights showed an increase in the number of seizure discharges in his EEG.

Dement et al. (1967) conclude from these results that REM-deprivation leads to increased excitability in the organism. As was mentioned in the section on the physiology of REMs these authors link the findings to a neurochemical theory involving the build-up of monoamines in the organism when REM-deprived. It is noteworthy that the concept of hyper-excitability hypothesized to account for the findings is insufficient to explicate the two case studies quoted by Dement (1963).

Conclusions from REM-deprivation studies

The fact that REM is but an indicant of a biological state means that REM-deprivation studies deprive organisms of being in that state. This means that REM-deprivation studies are *more* than just dream-deprivation studies. The fact that organisms low (relatively) in the phylogenetic scale such as the opossum have REM states almost certainly implies that their function is more than that of dreaming but is orginally at any rate biological. This, coupled with the finding that there is a relationship between REM-deprivation in man and epileptic seizure, also means that even for man there is a basic physiological necessity for undergoing REM periods. Since, too, it has been shown that mentation does occur outside REM periods in other stages of sleep REM-deprivation must not be equated with dream-deprivation. Thus it must be argued that REM-deprivation studies are not adequate tests of psychoanalytic theories of dreaming. This is disappointing in view of the interesting and suggestive data obtained by Dement (1963) with his prolonged deprivation studies of human subjects.

However this irrelevance to Freudian theory certainly only applies to the REM-*deprivation* studies. There is no doubt that study of dream reports elicited during REM periods, when clearly the most striking dreaming takes place, is relevant and this will be discussed later in this chapter. What is stressed now is that neither the positive nor the negative (e.g. Kales et al., 1964) results of REM-deprivation studies are in fact relevant to Freudian dream theory.

Mention should be made of a paper by Giora (1972) who argued that in REM sleep the brain is processing information (as always) and it is therefore not sensible to ask its function, since we take it for granted during waking hours. This seems to us an absurd argument which confuses two universes of discourse, the physiological and psychological. We do want to know its psychological function, if any, and it is irrelevant whether we wish to know or not any particular diurnal functions. This paper is best ignored.

PENILE ERECTION DURING REM PERIODS

If Freudian dream theory were correct in assuming that instinctual demands were expressed in dreaming, then the observation that penile erections accompanied REM periods deserves careful scrutiny especially since it would be hypothesized, from the study of psychoanalytic theory, that sexual demands would be very common at least in western society.

Ohlmeyer et al. (1944 and 1947) reported cyclic erection during sleep. This was done before Aserinsky and Kleitman (1955) had noted the crucial link between REMs and sleep so that there was no attempt in either of these papers to relate such cyclic erections to dreaming or REM. Fisher et al. (1965), however, found that full or partial erections accompanied 95 per cent of REM periods observed. Furthermore, erections very rarely occurred outside REM periods in other NREM phases of sleep. Various methods of penile measurement were used — this was done because of the problems involved in placing anything on the penis without affecting its size — including observations of some of the sleepers in the nude. In fact, erection took place two minutes before the REM period began and detumescence set in about one minute before the end of the REM period.

Karacan et al. (1966)

Karacan et al. carried out a highly interesting study of these nightly penile erections — an investigation which has an important bearing on the question as to whether such erections are evidence for sexual impulses during REM periods or rather for a more generalized physiological excitement. Since, in waking life, anxiety can cause temporary impotence, in sleep anxiety in the dream experience could well inhibit or prevent erection. The following hypothesis was, therefore, put to the test: *Less anxious dreams would be reported by subjects awoken from REM periods with full erection than by subjects awoken with irregular or no erection.*

Sample. Sixteen paid volunteer students. Each spent six nights in the laboratory.

Measures

1. *The Nowlis Check-list (Nowlis, 1963)*

   This is an adjective check-list which has been factored into seven dimensions, of which anxiety is one. To use the Nowlis measure the dreamer rates his dream 1 to 3 for each word of the list.

2. *The Gottschalk rating scale*

   This is a scale used for rating the anxiety of the dream content.

These were the two measures of anxiety used in this investigation — in an attempt to lessen the subjectivity of the dream judgements.

3. *Measurements of the penis*. Three categories were employed:

   (a) *Regular erection* — this was when the penis reached its maximum extent and continued thus until awakening. 42 per cent of REM periods (N = 100) were thus classified.

   (b) *Irregular erection* — this was when the amplitude of the penis fluctuated or detumescence had begun before awakening. 37 per cent (N = 91) of REMs were thus classified.

   (c) *No erection* — 20 per cent (N = 46) of REMs were thus classified.

There were thus 237 REM periods examined of which 80 per cent were accompanied by penile erection. It was noteworthy that there were only nineteen NREM erections.

Results

1. The anxiety score for A dreams (regular erection) as measured by the Gottschalk test was significantly higher than the anxiety score for other dreams.

2. There was no significant difference on the Nowlis test.

The erection cycle did not appear to be affected by coitus — in that subjects who came to the laboratory having just performed coitus showed the usual erection cycle. Nor did nocturnal emissions produce detumescence.

Conclusions

In view of the problems of attempting to score dreams for anxiety, the fact that one such objective measure is related to penile erection may be taken as evidence for the relationship of dream content to penile erection.

Implications for Freudian theory

This study appears indicate that the penile erections are related to the dream content, a finding which supports the idea that instinctual impulses are expressed in dreaming, as Freudian theory suggests. This view is endorsed by Fisher (1965) who stated that rapid erection has been found to accompany erotic dream content while detumescence was associated with dreams having castration anxiety content. Although this study by Karacan et al. must be held to support Freudian theory, the evidence will be considered again in the section on the implications of all these REM studies for psychoanalytic dream theory (p. 319) where other material concerning erection must be considered.

EXTERNAL INFLUENCE ON DREAM CONTENT AND REMs (OTHER THAN DRUGS)

The effects of drugs on REMs and dream content is not considered relevant to the psychoanalytic theory of dreaming. This is because it is fully accepted that all behaviour must have its neurological and biochemical correlates. However to know what these are tells us nothing about the behaviour. Consequently the fact that drug A can or cannot affect the process of dreaming is quite irrelevant to *any psychological theory* of dreaming. No doubt while dreaming certain neurochemical processes are going on, and no doubt these may be interrupted by chemical interference.

The relevance to Freudian theory of experiments showing the influence of external stimuli on dream content is also not entirely straightforward. This is, of course, because the wish which is substituted for the gratification of the instinctual impulse is expressed through the *latent* rather than the *manifest* content of the dreams. Most dream investigators have not been committed to Freudian theory and, in the interests of precision and objectivity, have deliberately restricted themselves to the manifest content. For this reason studies of this type will be given only brief consideration.

Ramsey (1953) has an excellent survey of the work on the dreams up to the time of his paper. Most of the findings, however, are vitiated by the fact that they all depend on dream reports on awakening in the morning — inevitably since the relationship between REM and dreaming was not then known. This means that it is unclear as to whether the reports refer to REM or NREM mentation and also, inevitably, that a large number of dreams never get reported. However Maury (1861) reported that stimuli, such as perfumes and water drops on his forehead, did influence the manifest content of his dreams. Poetzl (1917) found that subjects to whom pictures were presented tachistoscopically dreamed of details which they had been unable to report immediately after seeing the picture. This curious finding is known as *the Poetzl phenomenon*.

Studies of the Poetzl phenomenon

Shevrin and Luborsky (1958) investigated the Poetzl phenomenon with twenty-seven subjects. After seeing the picture (1/5 second) subjects had to report the dreams of the night. From those who offered no dreams an 'image' of the picture was obtained. The number of new elements (compared with their original description) in either the dream or the image was regarded as a measure of preconscious perception. Poetzl's claim that dream imagery excludes conscious perception in favour of preconscious was supported.

Shevrin and Luborsky regard this Poetzl phenomenon as support for Freudian dream theory in that the 'neutral' nature of this preconscious perception allows it to be used as a cover for unconscious ideas that would otherwise be suppressed. Thus a correlation was observed of 0.57 between preconscious recall and peak unpleasantness as rated by a judge. Fisher (1954, 1960) has also found evidence for the Poetzl phenomenon.

Waxenberg et al. (1962), however, have considerable doubts about the occurrence of the Poetzl phenomenon. First they note that although Fisher (1954) claimed that he had confirmed the phenomenon in thirty experiments, he gave no details of the experimental procedures used. Furthermore, they point out that Shevrin and Luborsky (1958), despite their claim to have supported Poetzl, in fact did not do so. Thus in his original paper Poetzl (1917) showed that it was the unreported parts of stimuli which had been presented tachistoscopically which tended to occur in dreams, whereas Shevrin and Luborsky found that the more subjects saw initially, the more was seen in the dream. Waxenberg et al. (1962) therefore put the Poetzl phenomenon to further test on a sample of twenty-four medical students who at weekly intervals were shown a different picture tachisto-scopically and asked to draw it. It was suggested that they might later dream about it and thirty-four dream experiences were collected.

Five judges working independently failed to support the Poetzl hypothesis in that they were unable to match dreams to drawings better than by chance using either the complementary hypothesis or trying to match by similarity. Waxenberg et al. (1962) thus conclude that the existence of the Poetzl phenomenon is doubtful.

Actually, an earlier study by Johnson and Eriksen (1961) had also put the existence of the Poetzl phenomenon into some doubt. These authors had found that the daydreams of subjects were conceptually similar to their descriptions of tachistoscopic stimuli — a finding which was considered confirmatory of the Poetzl pheonmenon (N.B. the objection of Waxenberg et al., 1962, to this for-mulation). However, the daydreams of subjects who had not seen the stimuli were not different from the experimental group as regards the presence of related items! This finding means, in simple terms, that the judgement of conceptual similarity was too general or too ingenious.

Tart (1965), however, thinks that these results may be due to 'the demand-characteristic' of the situation. The concept of demand-characteristic (Orne, 1962) according to Tart vitiates many studies of dreaming in that the very nature of the experimental procedures and the questions asked by the experimenter, suggests answers to the subjects. It is thus a specific form of experimental bias.

Erdelyi (1972) found that guessing rather than fantasizing about tachisto-scopically shown stimuli recovered more material, but this study is a long remove from the original Poetzl phenomenon.

Conclusions from studies of the Poetzl phenomenon

Despite the claims of Fisher (1954) and Shevrin and Luborsky (1958) much more firm evidence needs to be provided before the Poetzl phenomenon may be accepted. Thus interesting support for preconscious perception in dreaming must be abandoned.

The work of Dement and Wolpert (1958)

In a study already discussed (p. 299) Dement and Wolpert presented stimuli during REM sleep. A pure tone was incorporated into 9 per cent of the trials, a light into 23 per cent of the trials and drops of water into 42 per cent of the trials. There was no effect if stimuli were presented during NREM sleep.

Conclusions

This study illustrates clearly the faults and problems of work on the influence upon dreams done without EEG monitoring of sleep — i.e. all work before 1955. Clearly, even stimuli which have a profound effect when presented in REM sleep would produce no effect when presented during other phases. In addition, since recall of dreams after the REM period is finished is slight, dream reports on awakening in the morning are not sound evidence. This means that since stimuli presented in NREM periods produce no effect, dreams must be regarded only as the guardians of REM sleep, not, as Freud stated, of sleep. In addition, since dreams occur every night and since, in normal life, stimuli during REM periods are few in number, the generality of experiments such as this must be regarded as slight.

Berger (1963b), however, conducted an experiment into the effects of external stimuli on dreaming which has far more implications for Freudian theory and it will be examined, therefore, in greater detail.

The work of Berger (1963)

Berger (1963b) in his doctoral dissertation on the psychophysiology of sleep and dreaming noticed, *en passant*, that words and phrases spoken below the threshold of waking were incorporated into dreams elicited soon after. He decided to investigate more systematically what was little more than a clinical impression. The results and description of the study are set out below.

Sample. Four male and four female students. Their past girl- or boy-friends were known as was the type of relationship each subject had with them.

Stimuli. The names of two friends + two neutral names (neutrality previously determined by the criterion of GSR response). These names were uttered below the threshold of waking during an REM period. Twenty seconds afterwards a dream was elicited.

Treatment of data. Subjects were asked to match dreams to stimuli as was one independent judge.

Hypotheses

(a) Potentially arousing stimuli (names associated with dreamer) will be experienced as belonging to the dream or distorted to fit in with it.

(b) Names should be matched to dreams better than by chance (both by dreamer and judge).

(c) Names with emotional significance will be matched more frequently.

Results. Subjects and judge both matched names to dreams better than chance. The sex of the subject and the emotional quality of the stimulus did not affect the matching.

Of the forty-eight dreams influenced by a stimulus, thirty-one worked through *assonance*, six by *association*, eight *directly* and three by *representation*. The examples given by Berger (1963b), some of which are set out below, may perhaps be regarded as experimental illustrations of Freudian dreamwork.

Assonance. Jenny became 'Jemmy', Edward became 'Out a Gourd'. Naomi became 'An aim to ski', Gillian became 'A woman from Chile' — i.e. a Chilian.

Assocation. Richard became 'Had been to a shop for a sale'. Association: Richards was the name of a shop to which the subject had recently been for a sale.

Direct. A background voice utters the name in the dream.

Representation. The person appears directly or disguised in the dream.

Discussion. Berger argues that these results support the Freudian view that dreams are the guardian of sleep. However, as was the case with the Dement and Wolpert (1958) study, these results can only be interpreted as showing that dreams are the guardians of REM sleep. For stimuli presented during NREM periods do not influence dreams. However, it is clear that the external stimulus is woven into the dream. It does not provoke it. According to Berger the stimuli are incorporated into the dream to rob them of reality: for example, the dream that names are being whispered to them or that they even wake up. This last is very reminiscent of Freud's example of the nursemaid's dream to illustrate its function as guardian of sleep.

Sexual symbolism. A few of the dreams where the symbol was incorporated contained Freudian sexual symbols (see p. 285). This only occurred to an emotional stimulus — usually the current boy- or girl-friend.

Examples. Eileen and *a big lamp*: *A snake of fairy lights, snaking in and* out: digging out *a gourd like a round cucumber*. Smoking a *cigar*: the *cigarette*, frayed and burnt, *I inhaled*. These are clear examples of sexual symbolism and it is very interesting to note that none occurred to non-emotional stimuli.

Discussion and conclusions

The distortions noted seem characteristic of dream-work and the fact that the stimuli were incorporated into the dreams supports the Freudian claim that dreams are the guardian of (REM) sleep. The symbolism is also good support for Freudian theory especially because it was found only with emotional names — where sexual impulses were more probable. Nevertheless, the fact that such stimuli are effective only if presented during REM periods seems to limit, as was the case with Dement and Wolpert (1958), the generality of the findings. Surely pre-sleep or diurnal influences must be more relevant. Nevertheless, with that proviso this study must be regarded as good evidence for certain aspects of the psychoanalytic theory of dreaming.

The work of Foulkes and Rechtschaffen (1964)

These authors studied the pre-sleep determinants of dream content on a sample of twenty-four subjects. One night, subjects saw a violent episode of a TV film: on another night they saw a non-violent episode: dream periods were identified by REMs and reports of a dream were immediately elicited. In addition to this these subjects completed the TAT and the MMPI and rating scales concerning their dreams.

Results

After the violent film, dream reports were significantly longer, clearer, more imaginative and more emotional than after the peaceful episode. They were not more unpleasant or more violent. Imagination as measured by the TAT had a correlation of 0.4 with dream recall. There was also a significant correlation between some of the clinical scales of the MMPI and the dream-like quality of the dreams. There was little direct incorporation of the content of either film into any of the dream reports. Finally there was little similarity between TAT and dream fantasy material concerning instinctual impulses.

Discussion

Foulkes and Rechtschaffen argue that the violent film was more arousing (since the dream reports were more brilliant) although, somehow, the film content was disassociated from the arousal it produced. However if NREM reports are combined with the REM dreams there is no difference between the dreams produced by the two films. They also argue that the MMPI correlations are consistent with Freudian theory in that dream experience helps the expression of affect, which becomes more important with increasing pathology. Since these correlations could be interpreted as evidence that dream *reports* are correlated with psychopathology, the eye-movement activity itself was correlated with the MMPI scales. No correlation was found, however. It should be pointed out that REMs have been related to content and activity and passivity (see pp. 302-3) but not to dream-like quality so that no correlation should, perhaps, have been expected.

Comments and conclusions

This investigation is worthy of study because it deals with a problem which may be generalized to normal life. Clearly we are all subject to environmental stimulation before sleep yet its effects on dreams are not known. It thus differs from other studies so far examined which have concentrated on the effects of stimuli presented during REM periods. First of all these results are implicitly in flat contradiction to the Poetzl phenomenon. Foulkes and Rechtschaffen (1964) are aware of this but by no means regard the Poetzl phenomenon as a proven fact. They follow Johnson and Eriksen (1961) who review a number of studies of the Poetzl phenomenon and discredit it on the grounds of methodology.

It should be pointed out that the correlations between the MMPI, the TAT and the dream-rating scales should be interpreted with the utmost caution on a sample as small as this in view of the low reliability of these personality tests.

The correlation between the bizarre quality of the dreams and the MMPI clinical scales is some support for Freudian theory. The failure to confirm the Poetzl phenomenon is, however, really contrary to psychoanalytic theory since dreams 'use' preconscious material to evade the super-ego. To be really relevant to the theory these dreams need examination from the viewpoint of *latent* content — where no differences would be expected between groups since latent content reflects personality rather than environment. This study has been carefully examined because it illustrates the problems of testing Freudian dream theory without first having precise predictions derived from it in terms of manifest content (as does Hall) or without examining the latent content.

Hypnotic suggestion and dream content

Fisher (1953) and Tart (1965) have both shown that post-hypnotic suggestion can influence the content of dreams. Tart (1965) claims, indeed, that for some subjects (a minority) it is the most powerful and precise method of affecting dreams. For others, however, it has no effect. These studies will not be further discussed since their relevance to psychoanalytic theory is enigmatic — in view of the fact that hypnotic suggestion is not itself well understood psychologically.

Other variables influencing dream content and REM

A number of other variables has been shown to influence dream content or REM itself. However, a brief list of these will suffice since the relevance of these findings to Freudian dream theory is small.

(a) *Social isolation.* Wood (1962), quoted by Tart (1965), showed in his doctoral thesis that the social isolation of subjects before sleep produced dreams in which more than usual social intercourses took place.

(b) *The dream laboratory.* It is now an established fact of REM and EEG research into dreams that the first laboratory night is affected by the experimental situation: both the content of the dreams, which tend to be about the laboratory (e.g. Dement, Kahn and Roffwarg, 1965), and the process of REM sleep itself, the first cycle of which is usually missed out (e.g. Dement and Kleitman, 1955; Snyder, 1963). As a result of this, data from the first experimental night should not be used in investigations. Except for the fact that these findings indicate that anxiety (presumably) can affect the overt content of dreams and inhibit dreaming itself, as was stated earlier, it is difficult to demonstrate their relevance to Freudian theory. Altshuler (1966), however, regards the fact that anxious subjects (Dement, 1963) tend to miss more REM sleep on the first night than do non-anxious subjects as evidence *against* the psychoanalytic theory of dreams. Increased anxiety should lead to increased dreaming.

Internal stimuli and dreaming — thirst and hunger

Dement and Wolpert (1958), in a study already discussed (see p. 299), subjected some of their subjects to water and food deprivation because of its relevance to the relationship between REMs and dreaming. This had no effect on either REM time or content. A similar finding was reported by Rechtschaffen (1964).

Comments and conclusions

These studies are not convincing since the amount of deprivation for ethical and practical reasons (subjects are likely to be needed for further experiments) was not considerable. If Freudian theory were correct, hunger and thirst motifs should have been noted in the dreams, provided deprivation was effective. Anecdotal evidence quoted by Hall (1966) concerning the Himalayan expedition of Hunt and the reports of other explorers (e.g. Cherry-Garrard, 1970) suggest that dreams are affected by the absence of pleasant rather than nutritious food. O'Neil (1964), on the other hand, did find that dream reports of four groups differing in food and drink customs and nutritional state revealed differences in accordance with psychoanalytic theory. These were not, however, REM dream reports. Clearly more research needs to be done in this area.

THE INFLUENCE OF A CONSCIOUS WISH ON DREAMS

The work of Cartwright (1974)

Cartwright (1974) carried out a highly ingenious study of meaning and function of dreams in relation to a conscious wish among seventeen student subjects. These subjects had to sort some descriptive adjectives in respect of the person they would most like to be and least like to be, as well as using them as self-descriptors. For each subject one adjective was chosen which was three points lower on their ideal than their self-description. Then before sleep subjects were asked to say 'I wish I was not so X' (X being the discrepant adjective). Dream reports were then taken during REM episodes. As a control there was a word for each subject with the same discrepancy but they were not asked to wish they were not like it and in addition there was a further control word with no discrepancy.

Dream reports were then rated for these words by independent raters who had no knowledge of the experimental conditions. The results were clear. The first word was incorporated into a significant number of the subjects' dreams, which was not the case for the two control words. However, Cartwright points out that the function was not simply a wish fulfilment, there was a review of all the emotional implications associated with the being X.

This study certainly shows that conscious wishes are incorporated into dreams although it does not demonstrate that this is the function of the dream.

CREATIVITY AND DREAM REPORTS

Domino (1976) compared the dream reports of thirty-eight subjects who were classified as creative using the Remote Associations Test and the Guilford Alternate Uses tests, standard tests of divergent thinking, with the reports of thirty-eight controls. The creative students showed more primary process thinking, i.e. symbolism, contradiction, condensation and unlikely combinations. If we accept the psychoanalytic argument that creativity is to some extent dependent on primary process activity (e.g. Freud, 1928) and that divergent thinking is related to creativity, as claimed by Guilford (1967), then this finding is support for Freudian dream theory, dream-work being primary processing.

More recently, Holmes (1977) working with Oswald and Hudson in Edinburgh found that divergers and convergers had characteristically different dream reports in REM dreams, but in NREM dream reports this was not so, suggesting that the REM dream reports of divergers did indicate primary-process thinking rather than just superior verbal fluency compared with the convergers.

These two researches give some confirmation, albeit modest, of some of the psychoanalytic claims concerning creativity, primary-process thinking and dreaming.

Fisher and Greenberg (1977) cogently make the point that the physiological basis of REM sleep periods, their regularity and periodicity, makes it highly unlikely that dreams are the guardians of sleep. Challenges to sleep, if there were any, would also have to have such regularity. REM studies, they conclude, and we agree with them here, suggest that dreams are not the guardians of sleep.

SUMMARY OF FINDINGS IN THE EEG AND REM STUDY OF SLEEP AND DREAMING

To facilitate comprehension of the discussion of the implications of all these findings for psychoanalytic theory a summary of the main results will be found in Table 9.4.

IMPLICATIONS FOR FREUDIAN THEORY

Findings 3 and 4

The fact that REM states occur in mammals and in infants more frequently and as a greater proportion of the total sleep time than in adults, implies inevitably that REMs are not psychogenically caused. In Freudian theory, there is no psychic structure at birth. REMs are therefore one symptom of a basic physiological process. However we must be careful not to confuse REMs with dreaming. REMs may be a physiological correlate of dreaming but dreaming itself is a psychological event. It is a self-evident fact that psychological events have such physiological processes. Thus, for example, vision implies physiological activity in the retina, the optic chiasma and the visual cortex. But the study of such neural activity tells us nothing about the experience, what was seen and the implications of it for the observer. Thus it is with REMs: the fact alone that they occur in lower organisms is not in itself contrary to Freudian theory.

TABLE 9.4. *Summary of findings in EEG and REM studies*

Results	Investigator	Comments
1. REM a distinct biologic state distinct from sleep and wakefulness	Snyder (1963, 1965)	Based on review of literature
2. REM associated with dream reports	Aserinsky and Kleitman (1955)	The first of many such observations
3. REM occurs in many other animals	Klein (1963)	
4. The younger the organism the greater the proportion of REM sleep	Fisher (1965)	Based on review of literature
5. Positive mechanism involved in REM	Jouvet (e.g. 1967)	Based on animal studies
6. Relation between eye movements and dream content	Roffwarg et al. (1962)	
7. Thought-like mentation from NREM sleep Dream-like mentation from REM sleep	Foulkes (1962)	
8. Dream material of same night related	Rechtschaffen et al. (1963)	
9. REM-deprivation produces psychotic-like effects	Dement (1963)	Not necessarily dream-deprivation
10. REM-deprivation produces increased attempts at REM	Dement (1963)	
11. Penile erection associated with REM sleep	Fisher (1965)	
12. Penile erection can be affected by dream content	Karacan et al. (1966)	
13. The Poetzl phenomenon	Poetzl (1917)	Methodological problems may vitiate results
14. Stimuli presented during REM sleep may be incorporated into dreams	Berger (1963a)	Examples of Freudian dream-work
15. Effects of the first laboratory night	Dement et al. (1965)	
16. Influence of conscious wish	Cartwright (1974)	
17. Primary processing and creativity	Domino (1976)	Interesting for theories of dreaming and creativity
18. Dreams not the guardian of sleep	Fisher and Greenberg (1977)	General inference from REM studies

Finding 2

The fact that REMs are associated with reports of 'dreaming' rather than 'thinking' is of great methodological importance for the scientific study of dreams. It means that very full dream reports may be obtained. This is especially important since waking after the REMs have finished produces, usually, very poor memory of dreams. This means that the dreams which Freud was able to analyse are but fragments of the total dreaming experience of his patients — often of the last REM period. The use of REM awakenings should allow the relationship between dream content and the personality and life of the dreamer to be examined more accurately.

Finding 6

Eye movements are related to dream content. If then it is accepted that REMs are a symptom of a basic physiological process, and are not caused by the act of dreaming, then findings 2 and 6, which hint at an intimate relationship between dreaming and REM periods, remain to be explained. Fisher (1965) proposes that REMs are a prepared mechanism ready at birth which is later taken over for the visual scanning of hallucinations.

Finding 5

The implication of the caudal pontile nucleus in REM sleep, a structure which is part of the pontile reticular formation (the reason why Jouvet, 1967, also used the term mid-brain sleep) is of some interest for Freudian theory. In the earlier chapter on the evidence for the hypothesized psychic structure of ego, id and super-ego (pp. 172-3), some very tentative physiological bases of such a division were examined. It is to be noted, therefore, that this pontile nucleus is connected to the hypothalmus which has been suggested as the possible neural correlate of the id (see p. 173). In Freudian theory of course the drive for dreaming originates there. Consequently while it is in no way claimed that the physiological work on REM states by Jouvet and his collaborators confirms Freudian dream theory, it is contended that such work in no way runs counter to the theories, and fits in with what little is so far known.

Findings 7, 8, 9 and 1

From these findings there are several points which are of great relevance to the elucidation of Freudian theory. Since it has been shown that mentation or dreaming (even if not of a bizarre or hallucinatory nature) occurs in NREM periods, it cannot really be argued that deprivation of REM sleep is dream-deprivation. At most it is deprivation of 'dream-like' dreams. Thus finding 7 considerably nullifies the results of Dement (1963) whose subjects after fifteen days' deprivation of REM sleep began to develop psychotic-like symptoms.

Needless to say, attempts to deprive subjects of all dream time in both REM and NREM periods could not be used to assess the effects of dream-deprivation since any such effects would be inextricably confounded with fatigue due to sleep loss.

Finding 1, that REMs are really a third distinct biologic state, also means that REM deprivation studies are not good dream-deprivation studies. If REMs are a symptom of a basic physiological process of which dreaming is a concomitant, then the effects of REM dreaming cannot by any logical process be accounted for by dream-deprivation. To do this (ignoring for a moment the fact of NREM mentation) would require, for example, a drug which abolished dreaming without abolishing REMs and the other physiological processes.

From these two arguments, therefore, based on the occurrence of NREM mentation and the fact of the biologic state of REM, current dream-deprivation studies may not be regarded as adequate tests of psychoanalytic dream theory.

Findings 7 and 8, however, which suggest that REM and NREM mentation of the same night is related, are important as regards Freudian theory. In addition all these studies show that REM dreaming is typically dream-like whereas NREM dreaming is quite mundane and often referred to by subjects as thinking rather than dreaming. In fact, therefore, empirical observation has yielded two distinct types of dream. Psychoanalytic dream theory is certainly not upset by this result since in 'The interpretation of dreams' Freud (1900) distinguishes between day-residues and dreams. Furthermore the distinction is very similar to that between the 'thinking' and 'dreaming' of the two stages of sleep.

Rechtschaffen et al. (1963) have clearly shown that NREM and REM dream material is related. This fits the Freudian claim that internal processes (NREM mentation) can instigate dreams. For in dream theory preconscious day-residues can form the point of contact for unconscious dream thoughts. NREM mentation may therefore be the conscious representation of such day-residues. This would certainly fit the thought-like character of NREM mentation. Foulkes (1964) and Rechtschaffen et al. (1963) both incline to this view. Of course it follows, as Foulkes points out, that the collection of NREM dream material, the raw data, as it were, for the dream-work, would facilitate the Freudian interpretation of dreams.

In summary, therefore, it may be said that findings 7 and 8 accord well with the Freudian concepts of day-residues and dreaming.

Finding 10

It has already been shown in the last section that the need for REM sleep cannot be equated with a need for dreaming. Snyder (1963, 1965) interprets the need for REM sleep in physiological terms — there is a need for a physiological process which occurs during REM periods. This is also the view of Dement et al. (1967). It is assumed that under REM-deprivation there is a build up of some neuro-chemical substance which would otherwise be metabolized. However, it has been pointed out that REM studies and Freudian dream theory are really separate universes of discourse and in this case we must guard against confusion. This finding, once REM and dreaming deprivation have been separated is not, in fact, relevant to Freudian theory.

Findings 11 and 12

These two results dealing with penile erection and REM periods are, superficially at least, powerfully in accord with psychoanalytic theory. Berger and Oswald (1962), indeed, remark that had psychoanalysts read the journals in which the early results were announced, they would most certainly have used them as ammunition for the cause. Fisher (1965), who has carried out research in this area, has examined the implications of the results for Freudian theory in considerable detail. Broadly he regards the erection, which starts just before the REM period, *not simply as a symptom of sexual excitement but as an index of activation in the limbic area*. (The limbic area has been discussed in the section on ego, super-ego and id — see p. 173; it is part of the mid-brain and includes the hypothalmus.) To support the possibility of non-sexual erection, Fisher cites the work of Ramsey (1943) who showed that non-sexual stimuli could produce erection in boys, and also the Kinsey report (Kinsey et al., 1948) in which similar observations may be found. In addition Fisher (1965) argues that the morning erection, which is often thought to be caused by a full bladder, is, in fact, the final REM erection. This is important since such morning erections are often experienced as non-erotic, and impotent men can have such erections (Kinsey et al., 1948). Thus Fisher supports the claim that erection during REM periods is not necessarily proof positive of the sexual aetiology of all dreaming.

Against this, rapid erection has been observed where the erotic nature of the dream was very strong and detumescence where there was castration anxiety, and Karacan et al. (1966) reported that anxiety in dreams affected erection (although very recent sexual intercourse did not appear to do so).

Perhaps the best conclusion concerning penile erection and REM periods is to admit, along with Fisher (1965), that originally it may be but an index of limbic activity (a description which could also be applied to it during sexual excitement), but that as with the rapid eye movements it can be affected by dream content. It is probably the case that erection *per se* does not imply the sexual aetiology of dreaming. The fact that it can be affected by some dreams certainly imputes psychological significance to dream content and to this extent the phenomenon is in accord with psychoanalytic theory.

Findings 13 and 14

The finding that stimuli presented during REM sleep may be incorporated into the dream whereas at other stages of sleep they either have no effect or wake the sleeper is in fact relevant to Freudian theory. As has already been pointed out this means that dreams are the guardians of REM sleep, not sleep in general. However Altshuler (1966) says that even in this they are inefficient since up to 50 per cent (Dement, 1963) of REM periods include occasions in which the subject is awake. Berger's (1963a) study does appear to illustrate experimentally the very process of dream-work and must be regarded, therefore, as good evidence for Freudian theory. The examples of symbolism were also impressive.

The importance of the Poetzl phenomenon is more enigmatic. If the methodological problems of the studies could be ignored and the results accepted, it does mean that there is some objective evidence for the claim that preconscious perception is the basis of dream imagery. It does not, however, bear on the aetiology in the Freudian theory — that preconscious imagery helps the avoidance of repression. However, in view of the problems associated with it it is probably wise not to put too much reliance on the results.

Finding 15

As was discussed in the paragraph on the first laboratory night, the fact that anxiety appears to inhibit REM sleep is contrary to Freudian theory in that anxiety should lead to more rather than less REM sleep.

Finding 16

Cartwright's study which demonstrated the influence of a conscious wish on a dream is interesting in the light of the psychoanalytic claims concerning wish fulfilment. Furthermore, it is in line with the research of Lee with the Zulu. However this finding is not to be regarded as definitive evidence that wish fulfilment is the purpose of the dream.

Finding 17

The work on creativity and dreaming is highly pertinent not only to dreaming but to the relationship of fluency and primary-process thinking. It is not so much objective evidence for psychoanalytic theory (although to some extent it is), rather it is support for psychoanalytic theorizing on the aetiology of creativity given the implicit assumptions of the theory, i.e. that dreams reflect primary processes as do creative writing and art. This is an aspect of dream study which merits further research.

Finding 18

This needs little further comment. We have already discussed the arguments (with which we agree) that in general REM sleep studies suggest that dreams cannot be the guardians of sleep.

CONCLUSIONS FROM STUDIES OF REM SLEEP

In considering the implications of REM sleep studies for the psychoanalytic theory of dreams, great care must be taken not to confuse the two universes of discourse — the psychological and the physiological. Studies of REM and NREM mentation indicate that dream material during REM periods does appear to be worked over in a manner similar to Freud's description of primary processes. Dream-deprivation studies (based on REM-deprivation) must be treated with great caution since REM-deprivation clearly involves far more than just dream-deprivation.

Perhaps the greatest value of REM studies for psychoanalytic theory lies in the fact that they offer a technique for obtaining access to a far greater proportion of dream material and with greater accuracy than was ever possible with recall on the succeeding day. They also offer up hope of experimental study of factors affecting dream content. Clearly the most exciting work in this area still remains to be done.

AN EXAMINATION OF SOME POINTS OF DIFFERENCE BETWEEN OUR FINDINGS AND THOSE OF FISHER AND GREENBERG (1977)

Obviously in as huge and complex a subject as dream interpretation there is a variety of ways of approach to the question. Fisher and Greenberg (1977), whose conclusions are broadly in agreement with those in our book, adopt an approach which to some extent cuts across that adopted here and raises some interesting questions which we should like to comment upon because in some cases we feel that their arguments are unsound, although in others they add new and valuable information.

First they deal with a question which we have ignored, i.e. the relation of manifest and latent content. They review a number of investigations which show that ratings by judges of dreams based simply on the manifest content are correlated with ratings based upon their interpretation — their latent content (e.g. Reiss, 1951; Proctor and Briggs, 1964).

From this evidence (and the work of Hall, 1966, which we have fully discussed and which also supports this point) they argue correctly that Freud put too much emphasis on the latent content of the dream since the manifest content is also important in that it reflects current conflicts and interests. This is a point well taken.

However, Fisher and Greenberg (1977) then develop this argument making assumptions that not all psychologists would be prepared to make. Thus they write that projective tests can detect feelings 'in sectors corresponding to what Freud called the unconscious' (p. 35). 'Many studies may be found that demonstrate significant correlations between projective test indices and measures that bypass surface defences (for example, responses to tachistoscopically presented pictures of symbols' (ibid.).

There are a number of objections against this line of reasoning and implicit and questionable assumptions that we should like to discuss.

1. The evidence that projective tests can detect unconscious feelings is by no means strong. Vernon (1964) clearly demonstrates that projective-test scores are influenced by extraneous variables such as the rapport of the tester and subject, the sex of the tester, the opinion of the projective test held by the subject. Furthermore, as Eysenck (1959a) has cogently pointed out, the reliability and demonstrated validity of projective techniques is low. Again the evidence that projective tests measure unconscious conflicts is only assessment of this by

psychiatrists or clinical psychologists and it is this very criterion which is highly questionable and for which in this book we are seeking objective evidence. Thus we cannot accept the claim that projective tests do measure unconscious conflicts. Indeed, as we have pointed out elsewhere (Kline, 1979a), we are only prepared to accept projective-test results as objective evidence when they have been objectively scored and the scores subjected to a proper statistical analysis (e.g. Holley, 1973), in which case the variables are empirical, and depth-interpretations are avoided.

2. The notion of surface defences is vague. If anything it is a psychoanalytic assumption and not one we should make in trying to find evidence for other parts of Freudian theory. Again it is a concept for which we are seeking evidence.

3. Even if the conceptualization of surface defences is held to be allowable, then it is a further assumption that the tachistoscope can bypass these. Certainly in our examination of percept-genetics (Chapter 8) we argued that in a series of tachistoscopic presentations defences could be observed. However, the originators of percept-genetics (Kragh and Smith, 1970) argue that the subliminal presentation by tachistoscope cannot do this as cannot projective techniques. It is the series of presentations, gradually brighter, that allow the observation of defences.

Thus this second assumption is by no means acceptable even to specialists in this field of research.

Furthermore the fact that there are correlations between projective-test responses and responses to tachistoscopically presented stimuli is open to a wide variety of interpretations — an obvious one being that the correlations reflect the verbal style of the individual and the content of his thoughts at any one time — an interpretation that would also account for the relationship of dream reports to projective-test indices and responses to tachistoscopically presented stimuli.

Thus Fisher and Greenberg, having reviewed the evidence, are satisfied that manifest dream content is related to projective-test responses. However, their conclusion that therefore manifest dreams reflect basic personality vectors is unsound. We cannot accept that projective tests do measure these basic personality vectors.

Incidentally, the verbal jump from 'unconscious conflicts' to 'basic personality vectors' should be noted. Vectors if used here with any meaning are dimensions and projective tests even by their adherents are held to be not nomothetic but idiographic.

In conclusion we argue that this review of work relating dream themes to projective-test responses is not capable of providing objective evidence relevant to psychoanalytic theory.

Fisher and Greenberg attach great significance to all the work which shows that the manifest content of dreams bears on issues important to the dreamer on the grounds that in Freudian theory only the latent content is important, the manifest content being defensive in function. For example, an Oedipally conflicted subject is likely, in psychoanalytic theory, to have serious dilemmas over his real-life relationships with women. If he dreams of these, and the evidence suggests he may, then the defensive function can still be served since through such a dream the latent Oedipal wishes could be expressed. In other words there is no necessary antithesis between dreaming of dilemmas and dreams having a defensive function.

In our discussion of REM sleep and its significance for the psychoanalytic theory of dreaming we have dealt with the phenomenon of the incorporation into dreams of various events in the subject's environment including intra- and pre-sleep stimuli. Fisher and Greenberg (1977) seem to feel that the fact that these things occur is contrary to psychoanalytic theory. This, however, seems to us to take too narrow a view of it. All these incorporations may be seen essentially as day-residues which are used by the dream to express wishes. Thus the fact that such events are or are not incorporated into dreams is not really relevant to Freudian dream theory.

Fisher and Greenberg (1977) also cite a good deal of evidence that scores on various personality questionnaires, such as the Minnesota Multiphasic Personality Inventory, the Authoritarian Personality Scales and the Edwards Personal Preference Schedule, are related to the manifest content of dreams. This they consider contrary to Freudian theory: 'If the manifest content of dreams in individuals were a defensive shell, there would be little reason for expecting it to contain solid information about the sort of person he is' (p. 43).

In our view there is considerable confusion in this argument and when clarified it can be seen to be weak if not absolutely erroneous. Personality variables of the kind measured by tests such as the MMPI and EPPS are not those described in Freudian theory. Thus the fact that dreams reflect such variables is truly not pertinent to psychoanalytic theory. Psychoanalytic personality variables such as Oedipus complex, castration complex or oral personality traits are the aspects of personality that would be expected to be disguised in dreams and evident in the latent content not the manifest content. Thus the fact that EPPS scores are related to dream content tells us nothing about psychoanalytic personality manifestations.

This problem can be looked at from another angle. All the work on dreams (including psychoanalytic theory) suggests that dreams are not random, i.e. they reflect some aspect of the dreamer's life (conscious or unconscious). Psycho-analytic theory suggests the dream material is utilized by the unconscious or the censor to express unfulfilled wishes. The question then becomes (in respect of manifest content) how does this dream material arise? Now surely it would not be unexpected if the kind of person one was — neat, orderly, reliable, for example — reflected itself in manifest dream content. Just as in waking life all our behaviour reflects our personality, what we say, how we say it, so it is likely to be (unless shown otherwise) in dreams. Thus the manifest content is indeed likely to reflect such personality variables.

What is distinctly Freudian, however, is the claim that beneath the dream lie disguised unfulfilled wishes. Thus the style of the dream may well indeed reflect personality variables of the non-Freudian variety without thereby contradicting Freudian theoretic emphasis on the disguised wish. All this evidence, therefore, adduced by Fisher and Greenberg in respect of the relation of dream content and personality does not contradict or seem relevant to psychoanalytic theory. If the personality variables involved had been distinctly Freudian, then of course the theory would have been, in that aspect at least, refuted.

In conclusion therefore we would argue that much of Fisher and Greenberg's survey of objective work on dreams is not strictly relevant to psychoanalytic theory. The personality variables they have examined are in addition of dubious validity, as is the case with projective tests, or are concerned with aspects of personality not considered important in psychoanalytic theory. This leads to one important issue which requires examination.

Their conclusions differ from ours in one respect: they regard the evidence as supporting the Freudian claim that dreams provide an outlet for drives and impulses whereas we can find no good relevant evidence either way.

Once again the difference lies in the rigour of the evidence they are prepared to accept. Thus (a) they use the REM-deprivation studies which we have argued cannot test the effects of dream-deprivation; (b) they utilize studies where the indices of disturbance are derived from the Rorschach, a test which we do not regard as objective evidence, and from TAT responses which are similarly lacking in validity. Since, as they argue, it is only the balance of studies that lie in favour of the Freudian hypothesis, the reasons for the disagreement are clear. By the criteria adopted in this book, this aspect of Freudian theory remains unsupported.

10

Psychoanalytic theory of neurosis, psychosis and other emotional and psychogenic disturbances

INTRODUCTION

Empirical study of Freudian theory in this area, it must be frankly admitted at the outset, is extremely difficult. For example, Freud (1923) in 'The ego and the id' claims that the neurotic conflict takes place between the id and the ego. Again, in 'Neurosis and psychosis' (1924b) he argues that the neurotic obeys the external world and represses the instinct whereas the psychotic denies the external world and obeys the instinct. Since, as was made clear in the discussion of they dynamic view of the mind (p. 181), there are at present no adequate measures of either ego or id, and since there are not as yet any satisfactory classifications of behaviours into either of these categories, it is obvious that the broad molar psychoanalytic approach to emotional disturbances is not readily put to the empirical test. In one sense, therefore, the theory must be regarded as unscientific — testable hypotheses are not derivable from it.

The whole basis of psychoanalytic theory was discovered from the study of patients with hysteria, a major psychiatric nosological category, so that it is perhaps surprising that examination of this field should yield so little in the way of testable hypotheses. The paucity of clear-cut material is, however, more apparent than real. The fact is that the basis of psychoanalytic theory *was* derived from studies of neurosis and psychosis and this basis has already been empirically examined in the earlier sections of this book. Furthermore a very careful study of the work of Freud, aided by the indefatigable Fenichel (1945), does in fact reveal a number of clear testable propositions concerning various types of emotional disturbance, neurosis and psychosis. As is to be expected in so sexually oriented a theory, there is a large number of such hypotheses concerning sexual anomalies.

In the next section a list of testable Freudian hypotheses will be given. They will be grouped according to widely used psychiatric classifications and the source of each will be stated. Where necessary, some brief comments will be given to indicate how the hypothesis fits into the broader Freudian theory. In this chapter, therefore, we have departed from the regular format of 'outline of theory' followed by 'hypotheses'. This is because an outline of theory section would be very cumbrous (Fenichel runs to 500 pages!) and because the hypotheses would not be self-evident from the theory.

THE HYPOTHESES

A. Neuroses and psychoses

A.1.   *Coitus interruptus is a major precipitating factor in anxiety neurosis.*
         Source: 'Sexuality in the aetiology of the neuroses' (Freud, 1898). 'On the grounds for detaching a particular syndrome from neurasthenia under the description anxiety neurosis' (Freud, 1895c).

A.2.   *Neurasthenia due to excessive masturbation.*
         Source: 'My views on the part played by sexuality in the aetiology of the neuroses' (Freud, 1906).

A.3.   *Oedipus complex very important in conversion hysteria.*
         Source: 'Further observations on the neuropsychoses of defence' (Freud, 1896a).

A.4.   *Regression to anal sadistic level typical in obsessional neurosis.*
         Source: 'Notes upon a case of obsessional neurosis' (Freud, 1909b). 'The predisposition to obsessional neurosis' (Freud, 1913b).

A.5.   *Oedipus complex central to obsessional neurosis.*
         Source: See A.4.

A.6.   *Oral fixation always evidenced in depression.*
         Source: 'Mourning and melancholia' (Freud, 1917b).

A.7.   *Narcissism also found in depression.*
         Source: See A.6.

A.8.   *Paranoid delusions caused by projection of homosexual feelings.*
         Source: 'Psychoanalytic notes on an autobiographical account of a case of paranoia (dementia paranoides)' (Freud, 1911).

Comments

There is no need of explanatory notes for the hypotheses concerning neuroses and psychoses since all the psychoanalytic concepts invoked have already been discussed earlier in the book and the evidence for them has also been examined. Some of these hypotheses are among the earliest speculations of psychoanalysis. Brief descriptions of the psychiatric categories used in this section are given below.

Since the problems of psychiatric classification are so great and since there is considerable disparity between for example the Freudian classifications used in the hypotheses given above and the Schneiderian phenomenological school (Schneider, 1958), the brief clinical descriptions must, of necessity, be taken from psychoanalytic workers. In fact these descriptions are based on the work of Glover (1949).

A.1.   *Anxiety neurosis.* 'The characteristic feature is a great increase in anxiety readiness' (Glover, 1949). Anxiety reaching even to panic develops for no apparent reason. Often, in addition, there is irritability, moodiness, restless sleep and anxious dreaming. There are frequently cardiovascular, respiratory and gastro-intestinal disturbances.

A.2. *Neurasthenia*. The two main features are chronic fatigue and fatigue readiness. There is lack of interest, inability to concentrate and no initiative — a combination of apathy, weakness and indifference. Sleep is disturbed and there is marked hypochondria.

A.3. *Hysteria (conversion)*. The typical symptoms of conversion hysterias are somatic. They can affect any organ and can vary in intensity from mild cramps to complete paralysis. The symptoms may be translated — i.e. they have a psychic meaning and represent a body language (Freud, *The Aetiology of Hysteria*, 1896b). This distinguishes them from psychosomatic symptoms. It is to be noted that this particular psychoanalytic hypothesis was not considered empirical and testable. Conversion hysterias must be carefully distinguished from *anxiety hysterias* which are often expressed as phobias of particular objects or situations.

A.4. *Obsessional neuroses*. Typical symptoms are thoughts or actions which the patient feels compelled to consider or carry out against his will. Housewives may spend hours cleaning and recleaning the stairs, others are forced to consider again and again the precise meaning of a word or phrase. Sometimes before a particular action, e.g. going to bed, obsessive rituals must be carried out which often are long and complex. Care must be taken to distinguish these ego-dystonic *symptoms* which the patient knows to be absurd with ego-syntonic obsessional traits of which the patient is often proud, e.g. the orderliness of an efficient clerk. This distinction has been fully examined by Sandler and Hazari, 1960; Kline, 1967b; and Pichot and Perse, 1967.

A.6. *Depression*. Depression quite often alternates in manic—depressive patients with mania. The symptoms are an exaggerated form of the normal feeling. Listlessness, indolence, sadness, a feeling of complete unworthiness, that everything is useless, are typical symptoms of depression and attempted suicide is common.

A.8. *Paranoia*. This is a chronic state, characterized by fixed delusional symptoms usually of persecution with or without hallucination and often separated from the rest of the personality which may be unaffected and otherwise normal. The delusions often create a desire for litigation and literally at any cost.

B. Sexual anomalies

B.9. *Impotence is based on the unconscious sexual attachment to the mother* (the Oedipus complex).
Source: 'Three essays on sexuality' (Freud, 1905a).

B.10. *The castration complex is a major factor in male homosexuality.*
Source: 'Analysis of a phobia in a five-year-old boy' (Freud, 1909a).

B.11.   *Homosexuals identify with their mothers.*
        Source: 'The ego and the id' (Freud, 1923).
B.12.   *Homosexuals are hypothesized to have weak fathers.*
        Source: See B.11.

Identification in psychoanalytic theory is likely to occur with the major frustrating figure in the child's life — identification through fear of loss of love. Hence if B.11 is true, B.12 follows since strong domineering mothers are likely to create the identification noticed, and this domination implies weak fathers. A similar argument applies to hypothesis B.15 set out below — as regards its first part. The empirical studies of identification have been discussed in Chapter 7, pp. 181-92.

B.13.   *Homosexuals who choose young boys are fixated at the phallic level.*
        Source: 'Three essays on sexuality' (Freud, 1905a).
B.14.   *Homosexuals (who express their anal erotism directly) should have few anal traits.*
        Source: 'Character and anal erotism' (Freud, 1908a).
B.15.   *Identification with the father and the castration complex are major factors in female homosexuality.*
        Source: 'Female sexuality' (Freud, 1931).
B.16.   *Two factors are basic to fetishism: the castration complex and denial.*
        Source: 'Fetishism' (Freud, 1927a).
B.17.   *Pyromaniacs (and firemen) fixated at the phallic level.*
        Source: 'The acquisition of control over fire' (Freud, 1932).

In psychoanalytic theory there is an association between fire and urethral and phallic erotism, hence the pyromaniacs of the B.17 hypothesis. The present author has, somewhat gratuitously perhaps, added firemen to it. But surely a glance at the brazen helmets and the clanging bells, the dazzling red of the vehicles, the remarkable contrivance in place of stairs in the fire station, the hoses and ladders and the obvious fascination with heights, is sufficient to make the insertion worthy of test?

C. Psychogenic and other disturbances

C.18.   *Peptic ulcer reflects oral conflicts.*
C.19.   *Ulcerative colitis reflects anal conflicts.*

These two hypotheses, C.18 and C.19, although easily derivable from Freudian theory, were not explicitly thus stated by Frued. They are the results of long study of the problems by the Chicago school of psychoanalysis, notably Alexander (1934). They are directly in the classical Freudian tradition however in that, if shown to be true, they would directly support Freudian theory.

C.20.   *Stutterers have an anal fixation.*
        Source: The Psychoanalytic Theory of Neurosis (Fenichel, 1945).

C.21. *Tics are related to anal and narcissistic fixations.*
    Source: Fenichel, ibid.

As with C.18 and C.19, hypotheses C.20 and C.21 are not explicitly stated by Freud but are easily derived from Freudian theory. In the case of the stutterers, it is the 'retentive' tendency of the anally fixated that stops words coming out.

C.22. *Psychogenic disturbances of vision are symptoms of repressed impulses to look at or be looked at (exhibitionism and voyeurism).*
    Source: 'The psychoanalytic view of psychogenic disturbance of vision' (Freud, 1910b).
C.23. *Passion for gambling related to masturbation conflicts.*
    Source: Fenichel, op. cit.

Hypothesis C.23 is a somewhat wild assertion based on a small number of case studies. Put in for interest only and as an example of the problems of attempting to validate the more extreme positions of the followers of Freud.

STUDIES OF THE FREUDIAN THEORY OF PARANOID SCHIZOPHRENIA

DEFINITION OF PARANOID SCHIZOPHRENIA

Of all the schizophrenias, which are characterized by disturbances of thinking, the blunting and incongruity of emotions, disturbances of volition — e.g. negativism, catatonic symptoms, delusions and hallucinations, paranoid schizophrenia is the most homogeneous (Mayer-Gross et al., 1961). The leading symptoms are *primary delusions, secondary delusional interpretations* and, in some cases, *hallucinations*. These, indeed, may be the only symptoms. These delusions and their interpretations are *persecutory in nature*.

FREUDIAN THEORY

The psychoanalytic theory of paranoid schizophrenia is derived from Freud's study of the autobiography of Dr Schreber (Freud, 1911). According to his interpretation of this case material, the persecutory delusions are due to *repressed homosexuality* and the defence mechanism of *projection*. The thought-process of the paranoid schizophrenic may, therefore, be stated thus: 'I love him' becomes by a reaction-formation as a defence against homosexuality, 'I hate him' which by projection becomes 'he hates me'.

EMPIRICAL PROPOSITIONS AND CONSEQUENCES OF THE PSYCHOANALYTIC THEORY

From the psychoanalytic theory of paranoid schizophrenia a number of testable hypotheses may be derived.

1. Paranoid schizophrenics should show evidence of repressed homosexuality.
2. Male paranoid schizophrenics should have male persecutors.
3. Female paranoid schizophrenics should have female persecutors.

EMPIRICAL STUDIES OF PARANOID SCHIZOPHRENIA

The work of Norman (1948)

Norman carried out a clinical study of schizophrenic and paranoid schizophrenic patients, in an attempt to establish the incidence of homosexuality in the two groups.

Sample. Seventy-five paranoid schizophrenics and twenty-five non-paranoid schizophrenics.

Method. The patients were given a clinical examination under sodium amytal, followed by a further interview the next day 'to eliminate fantasy'. Sodium amytal, it is to be noted, is one of the so-called 'truth' drugs.

Results. Of the paranoid patients, 24 per cent were consciously homosexual and 31 per cent gave evidence of symbolic homosexuality during the clinical examination. The corresponding figures were 12 per cent and 16 per cent respectively for the control group. Norman considers these results support the Freudian theory although they do not prove the aetiology.

Comments

Clinical studies of this kind may only just be regarded as objective evidence. They are not replicable since no tests or fixed interview schedules were used. The validity of results obtained with sodium amytal, especially when fantasies had afterwards to be rejected, is also open to doubt. The only claim to respectability of this study is that it deals with a large number of specified cases. It has been quoted, therefore, to illustrate the difficulties of obtaining clinical evidence of a reputable kind. If the data are trustworthy the fact that not all paranoid patients were homosexual and that some non-paranoid patients were homosexual casts doubt on the Freudian claim that homosexuality is causative in paranoid schizophrenia. It does, however, support the claim that homosexuality is an important factor in it. A further point arises as to whether the incidence of *actual expressed* homosexuality is relevant to the psychoanalytic theory which is concerned with *repressed* homosexuality. It could be argued that it is possible to repress and express homosexuality, i.e. not express it completely, but strictly the theory demands the investigation of repressed homosexuality only.

Conclusions

The unobjective data of this study make firm conclusions difficult to draw. To attempt to support or refute theory from such data would be hazardous. Nevertheless compared with controls paranoid schizophrenics do show more signs of homosexuality. To this extent psychoanalytic theory is supported. Such homosexuality however cannot, from this study, cause the paranoia.

In brief, as far as clinical studies can, this work by Norman (1948) supports the implication of homosexuality in paranoid schizophrenia, but it is weak evidence.

The work of Klein and Horwitz (1949)

Since this is another clinical study where the data are of an unobjective kind it may be very briefly discussed. Case material from forty female and forty male paranoid schizophrenics was examined for evidence of homosexuality. In 20 per cent of cases this was discovered. However in the absence of a control group of any kind the significance of this figure is unknown.

Conclusions

Without a control group and with data of unknown validity and replicability the fact that this study implicates homosexuality in paranoid schizophrenia is only the very slightest support for Freudian theory. More objective evidence than that supplied by these two relatively large clinical studies is necessary.

The work of Aronson (1953)

Aronson used the Blacky Pictures (Blum, 1949) in a study of the Freudian theory of paranoia.

Sample. Thirty paranoid schizophrenics, thirty non-paranoid schizophrenics and thirty normals.

Test. The Blacky Pictures.

Results. The paranoid schizophrenics were more disturbed than the *normals*, on the following dimensions of the Blacky Pictures: oral erotism, oral sadism, anal retentiveness, masturbation guilt, castration anxiety, identification processes, internalization of guilt, narcissistic love-object and anaclitic love-object. They were more disturbed than the non-paranoid schizophrenics on anal erotism and the internalization of guilt.

Comments

The validity and reliability of the Blacky Pictures have already been discussed in Chapter 5 (see p. 110), and will therefore not be examined again now. There is some evidence for their validity, of which this study is an important part, in that it shows that the Blacky Pictures can discriminate, as measures of psychosexual fixation should do, normals from neurotics.

The Blacky Pictures themselves contain no direct measure of homosexuality. However it is possible to argue from the Freudian theory of homosexuality (Freud, 1909a) that homosexuals would be more disturbed in the dimensions of *castration anxiety*, especially as this is the most important factor in becoming homosexual — the refusal to face the fact that there are beings without a penis — *Oedipal intensity* and *identification*. Aronson (1953), in a series of extremely involved arguments, puts the case for even more differences on other dimensions. However, Freudian theory is so diffuse that such tenuous logical convolutions are not convincing: indeed it might well be possible to demonstrate the opposite. Thus it is very significant from the point of view of Freudian theory that the paranoid schizophrenics were not higher on the dimensions which are clearly related to the psychoanalytic theory of homosexuality than the non-paranoid schizophrenics. On the evidence of their being higher on anal retentiveness and internalization of guilt it could not be argued that the paranoids were more homosexual than the non-paranoids. Thus Freudian theory is not supported. It is also interesting to note that Oedipal intensity did not differentiate the neurotics (or psychotics) from the normals although, according to psychoanalytic theory, the Oedipus complex is the kernel of neurosis (Freud, 1916-17).

Conclusions

Although this investigation supports in general the discriminative power of the Blacky Pictures with normals and neurotics and hence the importance of psychosexual development in psychological disorders, it cannot be said to support the Freudian theory of paranoia. If paranoid schizophrenics were to be distinguished from non-paranoid schizophrenics by being homosexual, differences on castration anxiety would be expected from the Blacky Pictures. These differences were not found.

　　Therefore this study by Aronson fails to support the Freudian theory of paranoid schizophrenia. Indeed, if the Blacky Pictures are valid this investigation refutes the theory.

The work of Zeichner (1955)

Zeichner tested two hypotheses derivable from the Freudian theory of paranoid schizophrenia:

1. that paranoids would be more confused over sexual identification than normals or non-paranoid schizophrenics, and
2. that paranoids would identify more with females than either of the two control groups.

Sample. Fifteen paranoid, fifteen non-paranoid schizophrenics, fifteen normals.

Tests. Rorschach and TAT. All statistical comparisons were done by Chi-square.

Results. The paranoids were more confused than the other two groups as regards sexual identification. However, although the experimental group were more feminine than the normal controls, they were only more feminine than the schizophrenics at the 0.06 level — just below the usual significance level.

Comments and conclusions

These results support the Freudian theory. However, the small size of the samples and the dubious, unproven validity of both the Rorschach and the TAT make it difficult to put much weight on the findings.

The work of Daston (1956)

Daston used an experimental technique — the perception of homosexual words presented tachistoscopically — to test the psychoanalytic theory. The hypothesis he derived was that paranoids should recognize homosexual words more quickly than controls because, according to theory, they should have a greater awareness and sensitivity to such stimuli.

Sample. Twenty-five paranoid, twenty-five non-paranoid schizophrenics, twenty-five normal controls.

Method. Homosexual, heterosexual and non-sexual words with pleasant, unpleasant or neutral connotations, as rated by judges, were shown to the subjects through a tachistoscope. Recognition times were then subjected to analysis of variance and co-variance (with baseline recognition times held constant).

Words used. Homosexual words were: fruit, fairy, pansy, homos, blown, rectum, sissy, sucked, queer. Their heterosexual equivalents were: caress, bosom, breast, piece, pick-up, screw, fucked, whore, rapist. Some non-sexual, neutral words were also shown.

Results. The paranoid schizophrenics were significantly quicker than normals or non-paranoid schizophrenics on the recognition of homosexual words. There was no difference between schizophrenics and normals.

Comments

This experiment is similar in conception to many of the studies of perceptual defence which have already been discussed in the chapter on defence mechanisms (see p. 210). Many of the objections to those studies are not applicable here however because of the finding that there was no difference between schizophrenics and normals. Thus it cannot be argued that the slowness of recognition be due to the sexual or socially undesirable nature of the response, which normals were loth to put down. If this were the case the non-paranoid schizophrenics would have been quicker as well. Again the argument that the rarity of the non-neutral words accounts for the results cannot be adduced. This rarity would equally affect all groups: indeed *both* the neurotic groups, if this were a factor, would be expected to be slower, for it may be the case (e.g. Moos and Mussen, 1959) that schizophrenia dulls general cognitive efficiency.

Since, therefore, it is not possible to explain the results as artefacts of the experimental technique, this result must be considered to be powerful evidence for the implication of homosexuality in paranoid schizophrenia. Since too the non-paranoid schizophrenics were not different from the normals the homosexuality cannot be linked to schizophrenia in general.

Conclusions

In this investigation Daston (1956) has provided good evidence for the psychoanalytic claim that homosexuality is an important factor in paranoid schizophrenia — for the results could not be explained on any other hypothesis. It must be noted, however, that this experiment does not bear on the aetiological significance of homosexuality in paranoia. In brief this experiment is strong support for one aspect of Freudian theory.

The work of Zamansky (1958)

Zamansky carried out what is probably the best-known objective investigation into homosexuality and paranoia. The experimental technique was clever and the derivation of the hypotheses from the psychoanalytic theory subtle yet precise.

Sample. Twenty male psychotic paranoids and twenty non-paranoid schizoid psychotics. Both groups were hospitalized.

Experimental measure. Time spent looking at pictures presented in pairs of males and females (time on male minus time on female).

Hypotheses. Since it had been previously shown by Zamansky that homosexuals did spend longer looking at male than female pictures, it could be hypothesized *that paranoids would spend more time looking at male pictures than a control group.* Freudian ego-defence theory states that defence mechanisms prevent the emergence of unacceptable impulses into consciousness. Two further hypotheses were therefore drawn up:

1. Paranoids would fixate less on threatening pairs of pictures, and
2. Paranoids when asked to select liked pictures, a process in which ego-defence would be involved, would select fewer male pictures than when their liking was measured by time of fixation.

In addition the experiment attempted to answer the question of whether the homosexuality was due to the rejection of women (the Freudian theory — castration anxiety) or the attraction of men. If it were attraction, the hypothesis was set up that *paranoids would spend longer looking at males if a male and neutral pair of pictures was presented.* If it were rejection, *paranoids would fixate longer on the neutral of a female and neutral pair.*

Pairs of pictures. Nine male—female pairs, four male—neutral pairs, four female—neutral pairs, four threatening male (e.g. two men kissing) and four threatening female pairs and four neutral—neutral pairs. There was high agreement among raters for the threat-value of the pictures.

Results

(a) Male *v.* female pairs. The paranoids fixated significantly longer (t = 5.34 sig. 0.01 level). The hypothesis was supported.
(b) Threatening male *v.* female. No significant difference. Hypothesis not supported.
(c) Attraction score of paranoids would be greater than their stated preference. Hypothesis supported t = 4.40. No difference in controls.
(d) Male *v.* neutral pairs. Paranoids fixated significantly longer on males (t = 2.18 sig. 0.05 level). Hypothesis supported.
(e) Female *v.* neutral pairs. No significant difference.

Comments

The fact that paranoids fixated longer on the male pictures than did the controls is impressive evidence that homosexuality is implicated in paranoia, especially since homosexuals have been shown to thus fixate. Results of this kind cannot, as with tests such as the Rorschach or Blacky Pictures, be impugned on grounds of dubious validity. Furthermore no other theory could predict such a finding. This result is, therefore, powerful support for the psychoanalytic theory. Result (c), that the attraction score was greater for paranoids — but not for schizophrenics — than the stated preference for pictures, is also good evidence for the work of ego-defences and the claim of Freudian theory that in paranoia the homosexuality is repressed. This experimental evidence is a far more precise test of the theory than the clinical surveys of the incidence of homosexual activity among paranoid schizophrenics. Finding (b) on the other hand fails to confirm the notion of ego-defence in that no differences were found between the groups. It is possible, of course, that the pictures were not as threatening to homosexuals as they appeared to the clinical psychologists. Clearly more research is needed into this type of measure of ego-defence. The last two findings (d) and (e) support the claim that homosexuals are attracted to men rather than repelled by women. However, it is arguable that this part of the experiment is less well-designed to test psychoanalytic theory than the earlier part of it. In Freudian theory, rejection of women comes about in homosexuality through castration anxiety — the rejection of the idea of beings without a penis. This fear is only likely to be effective in the case of a sexual object. Since the neutral pictures were designed specifically not to arouse sexual desire, the female pictures may well not have provoked castration anxiety in this context.

Eysenck and Wilson (1973) commenting upon this study do not regard it as good support for psychoanalytic theory. However, their arguments do not stand scrutiny. For example they cite as counter-evidence a study by Rossi, Delmonte and Terracciano (1971) who claimed that 'clinical assessments' of unconscious homosexuality in paranoid schizophrenics do not support Freudian theory. If we in our book had dared to quote clinical evidence, Eysenck and Wilson (quite rightly, for this is what we are trying to find objective evidence for) would have torn it to shreds.

However Eysenck and Wilson explain these results not by a theory (no indeed!) but by the claim that paranoids are suspicious and hence are more suspicious of men who pose a greater threat. This apparently explains their looking longer at pictures of men. In addition the paranoids are alert to the 'shrink's' attempting to label them homosexual and this explains their caution in showing preference for male pictures.

We do not consider this *ad hoc* speculation about the results as explanatory of anything except Eysenck and Wilson's desire to deny any aspect of psychoanalytic theory. These comments seem worthless to us, although if readers prefer this explanation to the psychoanalytic hypothesis they are, of course, free to adopt it.

Conclusion

Zamansky (1958) has provided powerful support for the psychoanalytic theory of paranoia. He has produced good evidence for the importance of homosexuality in this form of psychosis and for the fact that this homosexuality is repressed (despite the failure of one of his measures of this). The evidence that homosexuals do not reject women is perhaps not quite so watertight. However Zamansky notes that this finding fits the work of Knight (1940) who argued that the homosexuality of paranoids was due to reaction-formation against hostile Oedipal wishes against the father. This, however, is a departure from orthodox Freudian theory.

In brief, therefore, Zamansky may be regarded as having offered good support for the psychoanalytic theory that repressed homosexuality lies behind paranoid schizophrenia.

The work of Klaf and Davis (1960)

Since this is a clinical study it may be briefly examined. It is worthy of note, however, in that it uses statistical techniques to evaluate the data and tests one hypothesis which is not generally investigated.

Sample. 150 paranoid schizophrenics and 150 non-paranoid controls.

Data. Case records of the sample groups.

Statistical analysis. Chi-square tests between the groups.

Results. Significantly more of the paranoids had revealed homosexual preoccupation during therapeutic sessions (41 per cent compared with 9 per cent). Homosexual experiences were also twice as frequent (X^2 sig.). In addition 82 per cent of the paranoids had male persecutors. Only 26 per cent had delusions with sexual content. The control group, being non-psychotic, had no delusions.

Comments and conclusions

The non-schizophrenic controls are unsatisfactory in that differences could be due to being either paranoid or schizophrenic. The case file data too are of unknown validity and reliability. Nevertheless the fact of homosexual preoccupations and male persecutors does support Freudian theory. Whether or not incidence of overt homosexuality is evidence of the *repressed* homosexuality demanded by Freudian theory has already been discussed. If homosexuality is repressed the sexual content of delusions might not be high. This study, despite its shortcomings, does offer some support for Freudian theory.

The work of Klaf (1961)

Klaf approached the problem of paranoid homosexuality by conducting a clinical study of overt homosexuals to determine the extent of their paranoid ideation.

Sample and data. The case-files of 100 homosexuals were examined.

Results. Paranoid ideation was found in 24 per cent of males and 18 per cent of females.

Comments and conclusions

This study appears to bear on the question of paranoia and homosexuality. However, it is illogical to argue that if paranoids are homosexual, homosexuals should be paranoid. In addition the difference between repressed and overt sexuality has been ignored. Furthermore paranoid ideation among homosexuals is more parsimoniously explained in the light of the social problems of being homosexual in a heterosexual society. It is, therefore, concluded that this study is valueless for any light it can shed on the psychoanalytic theory of paranoia.

The work of Moore and Selzer (1963)

Moore and Selzer, in another clinical study, attempted to remedy the deficiency of the control group of Klaf and Davis (1960) by using as controls non-paranoid schizophrenics.

Sample. 128 paranoid and 177 non-paranoid schizophrenics.

Data. Case-files of the two groups.

Results. To a significantly greater degree than controls, the paranoid sample showed a greater incidence of homosexuality, a greater preoccupation with homosexuality during the therapeutic sessions and were more often judged by psychiatrists and psychologists to be latently homosexual.

Comments and conclusions

Within the limits of this kind of clinical survey, Freudian theory is supported by these findings. However, it must be noted that *some* non-paranoid schizophrenics had similar homosexual backgrounds. Moore and Selzer conclude from this that homosexuality cannot therefore be aetiological in paranoia. This however is an inadmissible case. If *projection* is not the chosen defence mechanism, by theory paranoia will not develop. Thus the incidence of homosexuality in some non-paranoid schizophrenics does not weaken the Freudian theory. This study therefore gives very limited clinical support for the psychoanalytic theory of paranoia.

The work of Watson (1965)

Watson, aware of the weakness of the clinical studies — they were concerned with *overt* homosexuality — investigated the incidence of repressed homosexuality among a small sample of paranoid schizophrenics.

Hypotheses. Since, in Freudian theory, homosexuality in paranoids is repressed, the following hypotheses may be drawn up:

(a) Paranoids should be lower than controls on a true—false, face-valid aware-ness-of-homosexuality scale.

(b) Paranoids should have response latencies to TAT-like pictures, with and without homosexual content, different from those of controls.

(c) Paranoids should be higher than controls on the MMPI Mf scale (whose items are unthreatening).

Sample. Twenty-seven paranoid, twenty-three non-paranoid schizophrenics.

Tests. MMPI, L, F, K and Mf scales, some TAT-like pictures and a homo-sexual-awareness scale.

Method. The L, F, and K scales of the MMPI were used to select out from the sample those subjects whose attitudes to test-taking, for example defensiveness and putting the socially desirable response, were likely to distort the results.

Results

(a) The paranoids were lower (t = 2.85 sig. at 0.01 level) on the homosexual-awareness scale.

(b) Paranoids had a higher latency ratio for homosexual pictures (t = 2.28 sig. at 0.05 level).

(c) Paranoids were lower on the Mf scale of the MMPI than the controls (diff. not sig.).

Thus the first two findings confirmed the hypothesis: the third finding was contrary to prediction.

Comments and conclusions

The confirmation of hypotheses (a) and (b) is again powerful support for the psychoanalytic theory of repressed homosexuality being linked with paranoid schizophrenia. The failure of the third hypothesis to stand investigation could be due to the invalidity of the Mf scale. Indeed, as Grygier (1957a) points out in a survey of the psychometric techniques available for the assessment of person-ality, despite its construction by empirical methods (criterion keying) the Mf scale reads suspiciously like a mid-west stereotype of a real man and a good woman. A simpler explanation could be that the MMPI Mf scale is in fact threatening to repressed (as distinct from overt) homosexuals — hence the low score.

Despite the problem of the failure of the third hypothesis to receive support, this study by Watson (1965) must be regarded as good evidence for the Freudian theory.

The work of Wolowitz (1965)

In an interesting study Wolowitz investigated a conflict theory of homosexuality in male paranoids. However, it assumed that that approach involves a wish to be dependent on powerful men and to appropriate their power through magical sexual aggression whereas avoidance involves castration fear by powerful males. This theory seems too far removed from classical psychoanalysis to be relevant. None the less, he tried to compare predictions from this theory and from the orthodox theory by having a sample of paranoids and controls move photographs of men and women, whose power had been previously rated in a tube-like apparatus until they looked 'best'. On classical theory men should always be placed nearer than women regardless of power-rating: on the conflict theory male photographs should be displaced further away as their power increases. The results supported the conflict theory and Wolowitz concluded that attraction to men was based on power.

Comments and conclusions

This study has been only briefly summarized because of the curious nature of the theory it sought to prove and because of the unknown validity of the measurement technique. How valid was the 'power-rating'? How do we know that such a rating was not inversely related to the sexual attractiveness of the men? Is placing a picture near or far a measure of sexual attraction?

Without further research on the techniques, especially the power-rating, these results can be regarded only as ingenious and interesting, not as evidence against the Freudian theory.

DISCUSSION AND CONCLUSIONS FROM EMPIRICAL STUDIES OF PARANOID SCHIZOPHRENIA

A. Clinical studies

Even where large samples of patients are used and statistical analysis of the results carried out, it is clear that clinical studies are beset by problems:

1. The reliability and validity of the case material.
2. The reliability and validity of the interpretations of these data, e.g. evidence for 'latent homosexuality'.
3. The relevance of homosexual activity to the Freudian claim that *repressed* homosexuality is important in the development of paranoia.
4. The contaminating effects of the fact that, in some cases at least, the investigators had also carried out the psychotherapy.

These difficulties inevitably mean that all results must be treated with very great caution. The one good point of the studies resides in the large samples used. Nevertheless it is of interest that in general these clinical studies do support the psychoanalytic theory inasmuch as homosexuality appears to be an important factor in paranoid schizophrenia. The fact that, albeit to a much smaller degree, homosexuality was implicated in schizophrenia does not disprove the Freudian theory. What is clearly needed is a study of the defence mechanisms used against it. If it could be shown that paranoids characteristically employed projection as a means of defence whereas the non-paranoid schizophrenics did not, there would be support for the theory, or if this was not the case, refutation. The final conclusion, therefore, from these clinical studies must be *that to a very limited extent, they support the psychoanalytic theory of paranoid schizophrenia.*

B.1. Objective studies using tests

With this type of investigation all depends upon the samples and the validity of the tests used. In all the three researches examined the samples were small and the validity of the tests by no means well proven. Thus the Rorschach and TAT as used by Zeichner (1955) are not universally accepted, a statement which must also apply to the projective pictures used by Watson (1965). The Blacky Pictures (Aronson, 1953) do not even contain a direct measure of homosexuality, repressed or overt. The psychometric measures such as the MMPI are also open to question especially in the light of the problems of response-sets (e.g. Cronbach, 1946 and 1950). As with the clinical studies, therefore, the results must be regarded with caution.

In fact two studies do support the theory (Zeichner, 1955; Watson, 1965) while the work of Aronson (1953) fails to confirm it. Of all these the research by Watson is the most persuasive in that his hypothesis embraced the concept of repressed, not overt, homosexuality and his measure of homosexuality — reaction-time to pictures — would appear to be valid since reaction-time is generally considered a fair indicator of emotional involvement (e.g. Jung, 1918; and the Kent—Rosanoff word-association list).

Thus from these studies with tests, it may generally be concluded *that psychoanalytic theory is confirmed but that great weight cannot be put upon the results.*

B.2. Objective experimental studies

If the sampling is acceptable, experimental studies must provide the most powerful evidence, provided only that the experimental procedures are good derivations from the psychoanalytic theory. If this is the case the results must either confirm or refute the theory. Thus the fact that Daston (1956) found that paranoids recognized homosexual words more quickly than controls must be regarded as powerful evidence that homosexuality is implicated in paranoia. The results cannot be interpreted in any other way. Similarly the work of Zamansky (1958) is impressive support. Thus his finding that paranoids fixate longer than controls on homosexual pictures agrees with Daston (1956). However, his finding that an attraction score was higher than a stated preference score for homosexual partners is evidence that the homosexuality is repressed. The work of Wolowitz (1965), on the other hand, illustrates the problems in the experimental method in that the hypotheses he tested do not seem very close or relevant to the underlying theory.

In summary, then, *two of the experimental studies are impressive support for psychoanalytic theory.*

Summary

Clinical studies of paranoid schizophrenia and objective studies using tests give support for the Freudian theory but need to be treated with caution. The experimental studies, however, provide good evidence for the psychoanalytic theory. In brief the Freudian theory of paranoid schizophrenia is confirmed.

TABLE 10.1 *Summary of studies of paranoid schizophrenia*

Investigation	Comments	Result
Norman (1948)	Clinical: case-records	Some support
Klein and Horwitz (1949)	Clinical: case-records and no control group Methodologically weak	No support

Investigation	Comments	Result
Aronson (1953)	Blacky Pictures used	No support
Zeichner (1955)	TAT and Rorschach	Some support
Daston (1956)	Experimental: reaction-times	Strong support
Zamansky (1958)	Experimental	Strong support
Klaf and Davis (1960)	Clinical: poor control group	Some support
Klaf (1961)	Clinical: illogical hypothesis	No support
Moore and Selzer (1963)	Clinical	Some support
Watson (1965)	TAT, MMPI and reaction-times	Support
Wolowitz (1965)	Experimental: complex derivation of hypotheses	No support

ORAL CONFLICT AND SCHIZOPHRENIA

The work of Bergman et al.

Bergman et al. (1968) studied the strength of oral conflict among schizophrenics. These authors claim that oral conflict is an important factor in schizophrenia in psychoanalytic theory, although Fenichel (1945) clearly indicates that regression is seen as the main feature of this disease. However since regression to a narcissistic stage implies regression to an oral stage, oral conflict can be implicated in schizophrenia. Nevertheless it must be admitted that oral conflict is not a central issue in the development of schizophrenia in Freudian theory.

Sample

Study 1. Twenty-six male and twenty-nine female schizophrenics and normal controls.

Study 2. Thirty-three male and twenty-seven female schizophrenics, sixteen neurotics, twenty-three depressives, twelve co-twins, twenty-seven biological parents and fourteen adoptive parents.

Measures. The authors reasoned that oral conflict would show itself in impairment in oral behaviour. Thus three measures of oral behaviour were used, which in a previous study (Bergman et al., 1967) had shown themselves to be related negatively to the MMPI R scale which may be considered to be a measure of repression. These oral tests were:

Sucking. Strength of suck on a pipe.

Swallowing. Four sizes of pill were presented — the biggest one that could be swallowed was noted.

Biting. Time taken to bite through a hose.

Vital capacity, i.e. lung capacity, was also measured, as was *manual strength*.

Results. In the first study, male schizophrenics had a significant deficit in sucking strength compared with normals, a deficit which was not so marked in the second study. Female schizophrenics showed this deficit in both studies. The second investigation showed that neurotics, depressives and the familial blood relatives of schizophrenics did not differ from normals in sucking strength. The authors conclude that oral conflict is a factor in schizophrenia.

Comments and conclusions

A nice feature of this study is the measure of oral conflict. As must now be only too evident to the reader of this book, a major weakness of so many investigations into psychoanalytic hypotheses is the validity of the tests, especially when these consist of questionnaire items. In this case the validity cannot be impugned. The test is an example of the required behaviour and if oral conflict has any behavioural implications, i.e. is a useful concept, it must evince itself in decrements of oral behaviour. Of course it could be that other factors such as embarrassment (which the authors discount) influenced the sucking of schizophrenics. However, it is still pertinent to ask, if this be the case, why schizophrenics and not others are thus affected. Thus these results may be taken as evidence of oral conflict in schizophrenia.

In psychoanalytic theory (see p. 326) oral fixation is strongly implicated in depression. The finding, therefore, that depressives were no different from normals and less conflicted than schizophrenics is not really in accord with psychoanalytic theory. It is also curious that other oral behaviours were not similarly affected. The sex difference, which was evident in their previous study (Bergman et al., 1967), where sucking strength was related to personality variables in females but physical variables in males, is also an inexplicable feature for an oral test.

These difficulties and problems mentioned in the last paragraph mean that although the results may be regarded as evidence for oral conflict in schizophrenia, they must be treated as suggestive rather than definitive. In addition it must be remembered that oral conflict is not a major point in the Freudian theory of schizophrenia. It seems to us, in conclusion, that this study is memorable more for the ingenuity of its measures than the power of its results. The work of Silverman, which covers a variety of clinical topics, also deals with orality and schizophrenia.

STUDIES OF THE FREUDIAN THEORY OF HOMOSEXUALITY

THE THEORY

The basis of the Freudian theory may be found in the castration complex. The homosexual male refuses to admit that there are beings without a penis and devotes his attention, therefore, to males. According to Fenichel (1945), the female homosexual has a similar castration fear. In addition cross-sex identification aids homosexual object choice.

Empirically, then, homosexuals suffer from castration anxiety and identify with the opposite sexual parent.

INVESTIGATIONS OF THE FREUDIAN THEORY

The work of Grygier

In three publications (Carstairs and Grygier, 1957; Grygier, 1957a; Grygier, 1958) Grygier has discussed problems inherent in the empirical study of homosexuality and reported some preliminary results with his own personality test, the Dynamic Personality Inventory (1961). In a previous chapter on Freudian psychosexual theory the construction and validity of this test have been fully discussed (see p. 20). The conclusion was reached, it will be remembered, based on a study by Kline (1968b) that the validity of the Dynamic Personality Inventory was open to doubt. Nevertheless it is one of the few instruments capable of testing psychoanalytic theory and the results obtained with it deserve scrutiny.

Carstairs and Grygier (1957); Grygier (1957a)

In the study reported in these two papers a small group of homosexuals was compared with normals on the DPI scales.

Sample. 203 normals and 30 neurotic homosexuals.

Test. DPI.

Results. The homosexuals were significantly higher on narcissism and feminine identification. Half the homosexual sample showed a reversal of sexual identification.

Comments and conclusions. This study was unsatisfactory because the experimental group was both homosexual and neurotic. It is obvious, therefore, that any differences from the normal group could be attributed to either neurosis or homosexuality. Although the results — that homosexuals were more narcissistic and identified with women rather than men — support Freudian theory (indeed narcissistic fixation is an element in the psychoanalytic theory) the main theoretical claim relating to castration anxiety was not supported. This is important since it is this anxiety that leads to the feminine identification and hence the homosexuality. Thus even if the error of the non-neurotic control group is ignored this study by Grygier cannot be said to confirm the Freudian theory. It does, however, indicate that the DPI may be a useful test for discriminating homosexuals.

Grygier (1958)

In an attempt to improve his control group, Grygier compared neurotic homosexuals with neurotic heterosexuals. Thus any differences were now attributable to homosexuality.

Sample. Twenty homosexual neurotics and twenty-two heterosexual neurotics.

Results. The homosexuals were high (significantly higher than the control group) on *need for warmth* (Wp). They were significantly higher than controls and normals, indeed as high as women, on *narcissism* and *feminine identification*.

Comments and conclusions. These results with the DPI confirm the findings from the earlier study. Again they support the utility of this personality test as a measure of homosexuality. They do not, however, confirm the psychoanalytic theory that castration anxiety is fundamental to homosexuality.

Conclusions from the three studies by Grygier

Although the DPI seems capable of discriminating homosexuals from heterosexuals, psychoanalytic theory is not entirely supported. Whether this be due to the invalidity of the test or the failure of the theory cannot be determined from this work. Nevertheless psychoanalytic theory cannot be said to be supported by these investigations.

The work of Lindner (1953)

Lindner made a psychological study of sixty-seven prisoners guilty of sexual offences.

Sample. Sixty-seven prisoners convicted for offences of: homosexuality (37), sodomy (10), rape (9), paedophilia (8), exhibitionism (1), carnal knowledge (1) and contributing to the delinquency of minors (1). Controls were used matched for age, race, IQ, marital status, number of crimes and length of sentence.

Test. The Blacky Pictures.

Results. The sex criminals were differentiated by the Chi-square test from the controls on nine of the thirteen variables. The sexual offenders were higher on: oral erotism, Oedipus complex, masturbation guilt, castration complex, sibling rivalry and guilt feelings (0.001 level), oral sadism and narcissistic love-object (0.01 level) and anaclitic love-object (0.05 level). However the Blacky Pictures were unable to differentiate any of the sub-groups within the sex offenders nor could they discriminate between the homosexual (homosexuals and sodomites) offenders and the others.

Comments and conclusions

Although in the most general terms this study by Lindner supports psychoanalytic theory in that sexual offenders were more disturbed in psychosexual development than non-sexual offenders, in specific terms it fails to do so. The fact that homosexuals were not differentiated from heterosexuals certainly on the castration-anxiety card, is contrary to theory. Whether this failure be due to the test or the theory is difficult to determine. However some positive results have been obtained with the Blacky Pictures and there is, as has been discussed in an earlier chapter (see p. 113), some evidence for their construct-validity.

It must be concluded, therefore, that this study by Lindner (1953) fails to support the psychoanalytic theory of homosexuality. It is of interest to note here that Thomas (1951), in an unpublished doctoral dissertation cited by Taulbee and

Stenmark (1968), also failed to support the psychoanalytic theory of homosexuality in a study with the Blacky Pictures.

In a research already fully discussed in our study of the evidence for the castration complex (see p. 137), Schwartz (1956) compared a sample of twenty homosexuals with a normal control group on indices of the castration complex derived from the TAT test. The validity and reliability of these measures is not considerable so that the fact that three of the scores differentiated the groups cannot be considered as anything but very limited support for the Freudian claim that castration anxiety is an important factor in homosexuality.

The work of Bieber et al. (1962)

Bieber et al. carried out a large clinical study of 106 homosexuals and controls. All subjects were undergoing analysis which varied from strictly Freudian to 'cultural' — a term applied to those psychiatrists who regard the Oedipus complex as pathological rather than the inevitable result of the nuclear family constellation.

The main body of results will not, however, be discussed here since it was derived from data which cannot be held to be scientific despite the fact that they were subjected to very detailed statistical analysis.

Data. Seventy-seven psychoanalysts of whom fifty-eight contributed data on the homosexual group took part in this investigation. They filled in three questionnaires about homosexual patients and controls.

Examples of questions. Did patient regard his father as an admirable person? Did mother humiliate patient?

Comments and conclusions

From this brief description of the methodology it appears that the data refer only to the analysts' clinical impressions of the patients. All these responses must be inferred from the therapeutic session. The statistical results therefore refer, in truth, to analysts' conceptions of homosexual patients contrasted with controls. Furthermore, since the data were contributed by so large a number of analysts comparability between protocols is suspect. Thus in our view Bieber's study cannot be regarded as objective evidence of homosexual behaviour, despite the statistical analysis and the control group: rather it is a study of analytic views of homosexuals and controls.

However, the final part of the study was concerned with the therapeutic outcome of these 106 homosexual patients. This part does constitute an objective test of the psychoanalytic treatment of homosexuality and is discussed in the next chapter (see p. 398).

The work of Goldberg and Milstein (1965)

Goldberg and Milstein carried out a perceptual investigation into the psychoanalytic theory of latent homosexuality in women.

Sample. Fifteen low-latent homosexual women and ten high-latent homosexual women. These groups were selected by the MMPI.

Method. Six pictures were shown to the groups by tachistoscope. Three pictures were rated as non-threatening to both groups — a clothed male, a clothed female and an ambiguous figure. Three pictures were rated on psychoanalytic theory as threatening to the high group — a nude male (fear of female genitalia), a nude female and two nude females.

Hypothesis. By *selective vigilance* (Blum, 1954, see p. 223) people should be sensitive to cues relevant to repressed impulses. However, when impulses begin to approach consciousness, a second process occurs — *ego-defence* — and at this point individuals try not to perceive the impulses. With these two concepts (related to psychoanalytic theory) the hypothesis was formed that the high-homo-sexual group would show *longer latencies for the highly threatening pictures (perceptual defence) but shorter latencies for the low-threat pictures (selective vigilance)*.

Results. The hypothesis was confirmed.

Comments and conclusions

Psychoanalytic theory concerning the defensive processes in homosexuality in women was supported by this study. It also supports the claim that castration anxiety (the unclothed male) is important in female homosexuality. The design of the experiment precludes sexual anxiety from being the source of variance since this would have equally affected both groups. This study supports, therefore, the psychoanalytic theory of the role of the ego-defences in female homosexuality.

The work of Kline (1967c)

Kline studied the Freudian claim (Freud, 1908a) that as homosexuals express their anal erotism directly, they should therefore possess few anal traits.

Sample. Thirteen homosexual men referred to a clinic for treatment.

Test. Ai3, a measure of the anal character.

Results. The mean score of the homosexuals was not significantly different from that of comparable student groups. The non-significant differences were also in the wrong direction.

Comments and conclusions

The validity of Ai3 as a measure of the anal character has already been fully discussed (p. 38) and it appears to be a valid test. The sample of homosexuals was small but all were rated by the psychologist in charge of them as Kinsey 3 or more. The Kinsey scale of homosexuality (Kinsey et al., 1948), which attempts to measure the amount of homosexual behaviour and feeling within individuals, has 3 as its middle ranking. It means that 50 per cent of sexual outlets and feelings are homosexual. Thus the homosexuality of the sample can hardly be impugned. It must be concluded that this study entirely fails to support the Freudian hypo-thesis.

The work of De Luca (1967)

De Luca attempted to examine the psychosexual constitution of male homo-sexuals by means of the Blacky Pictures.

Sample. Twenty male homosexuals and forty male controls.

Test. The Blacky Pictures (Blum, 1949).

Scoring system. Blum's (1962) factor-analytic scoring system was used (see p. 112).

Results. The homosexuals were differentiated on only one of the thirty factors.

Comments and conclusions

Since, according to psychoanalytic theory, as we have seen, a number of psycho-sexual differences would be predicted between homosexuals and normals — for example, differences in castration anxiety, Oedipal conflict and parental identi-fication — the fact that only one of the thirty factors discriminated significantly certainly fails to support the theory. Since also, in our discussion of the Blacky Pictures (see p. 113), it appeared that there is some evidence for the validity of this projective technique, it is difficult in this case to impute the failure to confirm psychoanalytic theory to the test rather than the theory.

Thus this study by De Luca certainly fails to confirm Freudian developmental hypotheses concerning male homosexuality.

The work of Silverman (1973)

We have already fully discussed in our chapter on defence mechanisms the highly interesting subliminal-perception method developed by Silverman and his colleagues for the investigation of psychoanalytic phenomena. We shall, therefore, say no more here about its rationale and justification. In the study which we shall now examine Silverman et al. (1973) used their method to investigate the role of the mother in the aetiology of male homosexuality.

Thirty-six male homosexuals were compared with thirty-six heterosexuals. Each subject was seen in three sessions. The incest session, the symbiotic session and the control session. In each session baseline measures were taken and compared with the same measures after stimulation.

(a) *The incest session.* Subliminal stimulus of 'Fuck Mommy' together with a nude man and woman in a sexually suggestive position.

(b) *The symbiosis session.* Subliminal stimulus of 'Mommy and I are one' with a man and woman standing merged together (like Siamese twins).

(c) *Control session.* Subliminal stimulus of 'Person thinking' with a bland picture of a man. In addition there were three baseline neutral stimuli: 'person looking, person walking and person talking', each accompanied by a bland male figure.

The measures. Three Rorschach cards, Rorschach 1, Harrower 2 and Zulliger 8.

Sexual-feelings assessment. Ten females and ten males (pictures) were rated on a twenty-point scale for sexual attraction.

The critical scores were the changes on these measures before and after each session.

Results. Homosexuals increased their homosexual attraction score after the incest-conflict stimulation. This was not the case for the control stimulus or for the control heterosexual group.

Conclusions

This study does support the psychoanalytic claim that Oedipal incestuous wishes are involved in male homosexuality. It is difficult to account for the findings in terms of any other theory. We have not discussed the Rorschach results because, as we have indicated previously, we do not accept the validity of Rorschach indices and do not regard such scores as objective evidence of the kind we are searching for. This study by Silverman et al. (1973) must be regarded as confirmatory of the implication of Oedipal conflicts in homosexuality.

The work of Freund et al. (1974)

These authors carried out a study of the aversion to women that homosexuals should show if psychoanalytic theory were correct. Nude pictures of women were shown to homosexuals who, however, exhibited no aversion (as measured by detumescence). Certainly if the castration complex were a determinant of homosexuality, nude women should fuel the castration conflict (being penisless beings) and thus produce aversion. However, pictures of women are not the same as women and it is possible that pictures of women are bearable, while real women in the flesh are not. Despite these caveats, this study certainly runs counter to psychoanalytic theory.

The work of Maussakalian, Blanchard, Abel and Barlow (1975)

These writers provided a similar test to that of Freund et al. (1974) of the psycho-analytic claim that the castration complex is implicated in homosexuality by examining the responses of homosexuals and heterosexuals to erotic pictures. While heterosexuals showed aversion to homosexual pictures, homosexuals did not thus respond (as they should by theory have) to pictures of the vulva. Thus this study does not support psychoanalytic notions of the castration complex being a determinant of homosexuality. The validity of aversion to vulvas as a measure of the castration complex is, of course, unknown (although it is intuitively attractive). This study, therefore, needs to be accepted with caution.

The work of Freund et al. (1974)

Freund and colleagues administered a questionnaire concerning parent—child relations to 52 homosexuals who wanted surgery to change their sex, 206 volunteer homosexual subjects and 193 heterosexual controls. The first two groups were not significantly different for the variable 'unreplaced loss of father in childhood and father—son relationship'. The homosexuals, however, did have a poorer relationship with their fathers than heterosexuals and were closer than that group to their mothers.

We shall say no more about this study for it is one of those quoted by Fisher and Greenberg as supporting psychoanalytic theory and falls into that group which we have categorized in our study of their evidence as failing to match the criteria for an objective scientific study, the problem being that of the validity of questionnaire data from adults about the events of an inevitably distant childhood.

CONCLUSIONS FROM STUDIES OF HOMOSEXUALITY

One of these studies, that of Goldberg and Milstein (1965), supports psychoanalytic theory regarding homosexuality and that was concerned more perhaps with its concomitant defensive mechanisms for which good evidence exists (see Chapter 8). For the main Freudian hypothesis that homosexuality is a result of the castration complex and Oedipal conflict only the work of Silverman (1973) and colleagues confirms the theory. The other studies fail to support the Freudian theory of homosexuality. Silverman's work which we discuss later in this chapter (for it bears on a variety of clinical topics) is highly impressive but before giving it full affirmation we should like to see it replicated in laboratories uninfluenced by Silverman, as is the case with percept-genetics. In fact we have such work under way in Exeter but at the time of writing results are not available. In summary then, the Freudian theory is in general not supported except by the work of Silverman and colleagues.

FISHER AND GREENBERG ON THE AETIOLOGY OF HOMOSEXUALITY

As has been evident from earlier chapters, Fisher and Greenberg (1977) drew conclusions from their survey that were broadly in agreement with those in the first edition of this book. However, we now come to an issue where there was a totally different conclusion in the two books. This is the psychoanalytic theory of the origins of homosexuality. In our first edition it was concluded that there was little objective support for psychoanalytic theories. Fisher and Greenberg (1977), however, consider that some of the psychoanalytic claims are supported and in commenting on the previous edition they write that on this issue our review 'was grossly incomplete and overlooked many positive findings'.

The hypotheses examined by Fisher and Greenberg in relation to the aetiology of homosexuality are: 1. that the homosexual male is intensely involved with his mother and for this reason tends to choose as lover an individual like himself; 2. that his relationship with his father is cold and hostile; and 3. that the homosexual male characteristically has a severe castration complex. It is broadly the evidence for these hypotheses that Fisher and Greenberg (1977) consider that we failed to scrutinize. We shall examine the evidence that Fisher and Greenberg (1977) cite on behalf of these hypotheses.

Do homosexuals have close relationships with their mothers but hostile ones with their fathers? First of all Fisher and Greenberg classify the numerous studies of these hypotheses into two kinds — (a) those based upon interview and clinical appraisal and (b) those using a 'more controlled questionnaire-type methodology'. This classification immediately indicates why Fisher and Greenberg claim that we have failed to examine considerable amounts of evidence. For according to the criteria of objective evidence adopted in this book, clinical appraisals and interviews would not thus be classified. Normally we have not examined studies where this is the data-base since essentially this is no different from the original psychoanalytic data which are not regarded as sound. In certain instances such material, if shown to be reliable and quantified precisely, can be used, but this is rarely the case and is certainly not so in the studies cited by Fisher and Greenberg. Thus their first group of studies we would exclude on the grounds that they cannot provide objective quantified evidence. This, of course, was also the case with some of the studies of dreaming cited by Fisher and Greenberg but ignored by us, as discussed in the last chapter.

It is of course possible to argue that our criterion is too rigid and that to exclude interview data is to exclude a useful source of evidence. While it is true that it is difficult to find alternatives to interviews and questionnaires with respect to investigating parent—child relationships, the fact remains that there are considerable doubts about the validity of such data. Factors such as social desirability, the reinforcement by interviewers of the desired response and the fact that many subjects have imperfect insight into and memory for experiences of this kind, all render the veracity and validity of these data dubious. In addition, for homosexual patients, often the subjects in this first group of studies, many of their views on their feelings for their parents and similar matters may have been influenced by the very questions asked in treatments by psychiatrists and in group discussions. All these influences are such as to render interview and questionnaire data far from objective, attractive though they appear, and we cannot regard them as objective scientific evidence for or against psychoanalytic theory. In addition, as we have pointed out, they resemble too closely the original psychoanalytic data which they are trying to confirm.

The second group of studies relevant to these hypotheses which are cited by Fisher and Greenberg (1977) are based upon 'systematic questionnaires or psychological tests' (ibid., p. 235). Since much of our book is concerned with the results from psychological tests, it is clear that this second category of studies cannot be dismissed as not according with the criteria of objectivity which we have suggested.

However, when these experiments are examined many of them fall far short of the standards of design necessary to obtain results from which any conclusions can be drawn, and/or use tests (often projective tests) of, to say the least, uncertain validity.

For example, the first study quoted compared homosexuals with psychiatric records and non-homosexual controls without such records. Thus no conclusions about homosexuality can be made. The second study had subjects rate their parents. The validity of such rating scales is unknown and in any case the ratings for fathers did not fit Freudian theory. The third study had homosexuals choose adjectives to describe themselves and their parents, a technique again of unknown validity. Thus these three studies which we did not review do not meet adequate standards for scientific work and no conclusions could be based upon them.

Next Fisher and Greenberg (1977) cite two investigations which we have already discussed — those of Bieber et al. (1962) and McCord et al. (1959), a study which we examined in relation to alcoholism. As we have shown, the Bieber et al. (1962) work cannot be regarded as scientific evidence since it pertains only to analysts' views of homosexuals (see p. 345), the very matter under scrutiny. The McCord et al. study is better and their observational data suggest that those with overt or latent homosexuality came from a repressive, disordered familial atmosphere. This description is derived from ratings of the family made earlier in the Summerville Youth Study (Witmer and Powers, 1951). Thus this investigation cannot be impugned on grounds of poor methodology. However, the results are contrary to Freudian theory, although the fact that the father was rejecting and absent does fit psychoanalytic theory better.

So far the studies quoted by Fisher and Greenberg (1977) are not such as we would wish to include in our book (where they have not been included) for the reasons given, and a number of the other investigations which they cite suffer from the same faults of using inadequate measures or imperfectly matched controls.

However, there is one group of investigations cited by Fisher and Greenberg which does need to be considered and which we feel should have been discussed in our first edition. Some researchers have followed up the work of Bieber et al. (1962) which as we have argued consists only of impressions about homosexuals by analysts by having homosexuals and controls complete detailed questionnaires about their families and their relationships with their parents.

The overall picture that emerges from studies of this kind, according to Fisher and Greenberg (1977), is that Freud was basically correct in arguing that the homosexual had a close relationship with his mother and rivalrous feelings with a cold and hostile father. However, we cannot accept these retrospective questionnaire studies of family attitudes as sound scientific evidence. In our studies of the effects of pot-training we quoted the observational studies of child-rearing carried out by Newson and Newson (1963). There it was found that after only a year parents were unable to remember quite important events in their children's development, nor were they able to recall accurately how they had felt about their children (accuracy being judged by the observations made at the time). These findings of the problems of the recall of such events make retrospective data about family attitudes extremely dubious. Furthermore, in a culture where Freudian ideas have become widely spread among the population, watered down perhaps though they be, responses to a questionnaire on family attitudes are likely to reflect popularly received opinions. This applies to both homosexuals and non-homosexuals, thus tending to make differences significant. Thus an example of this contaminating influence can be found in the popular American novel *The Women's Room* (French, 1977); a father enters a room where his wife is dandling their small boy on her knee, and says severely, 'Do you want to turn him into a queer?'

For all these reasons we do not consider such studies as Fisher and Greenberg quote in this section constitute scientific evidence for psychoanalytic theory. We feel, therefore, that their conclusions that Freud is here supported by the evidence are correct but that this evidence is not objective or scientific. We still maintain the position that these aetiological hypotheses are not confirmed by objective evidence.

Fisher and Greenberg (1977) deal more briefly with the other aetiological hypotheses — that concerned with identification with the mother, and the claim that the castration complex is an important determinant of homosexuality.

As regards identification, Fisher and Greenberg are far more cautious than with the previous work. Here they admit that methods of measuring identification are weak, although they cite with cautious approval studies conducted with the Masculinity—Feminity scale of the MMPI which show that homosexuals are more feminine (hence probably more identified with mother than non-homosexuals). Here we must comment on the hopeless circularity of this MMPI research which cannot even be cautiously admitted as support for Freudian theory or, indeed, for any other theory. The MMPI, as we have fully discussed in Chapter 4, is a criterion-keyed test. This means that the items of the M—F scale were selected because they could discriminate homosexuals from controls. The point of the items is simply that they can discriminate. Scores on the M—F scale, therefore, can be said to measure resemblance to homosexuals. Thus it is hardly surprising, given that the MMPI was a well-constructed test, that homosexuals score differently from controls on the M—F scale. It is not admissible, however, to use this as evidence that homosexuals are more feminine or more identified with their mothers.

It is this problem of psychological meaning that makes criterion-keyed scales of less value than scales measuring unitary factors (see Kline, 1979a, for a full discussion of this issue). Certainly, as regards this first hypothesis, there is no evidence cited by Fisher and Greenberg which merits inclusion here.

In respect of the work on the castration complex, Fisher and Greenberg cite no work (other than that which we have cited and discussed) which meets the rigorous criteria adopted in this book. Certainly their conclusions do not differ from ours.

Conclusions

This important issue of the origins of homosexuality was the one point on which there was clear disagreement between our first edition and the work of Fisher and Greenberg (1977). They argued that our difference lay in our failure to review all the studies supporting the Freudian claims. However, examination of the evidence cited by them indicates that it falls woefully short of scientific precision being based on interviews, ratings, questionnaires and projective techniques, almost all of which are of unproven validity. Our difference, therefore, lies in the quality of evidence which we are prepared to accept. Fisher and Greenberg, in this chapter at least, are willing to utilize work of a standard too low for us to use. Thus on this issue we would still argue that there is no sound evidence in support of psychoanalytic theory, other than the special work of Silverman, on which we have already commented.

PSYCHOSOMATIC DISORDERS

Alexander (1950) and Alexander and French (1948), at the Chicago Institute of Psychoanalysis, have concentrated on developing Freudian theory to give a specific understanding of certain diseases or disorders which are known to be affected by psychological events. The diseases subjected to special study have been asthma, peptic ulcer and ulcerative colitis. Although, strictly, a development of orthodox Freudian theory it is such an easily taken step which introduces little new into the theory, that objective study of their claims must lead to a better appreciation of the orthodox Freudian concepts involved. This application of psychoanalytic theory to psychosomatic disorders has not gone uncriticized by non-analytic psychiatrists. Thus, for example, Mayer-Gross, Slater and Roth (1961) write that 'The Psychoanalytic interpretation of psychosomatic disorders is, of all applications of Freudian theory, the least satisfactory.'

OBJECTIVE STUDIES OF THE PSYCHOANALYTIC THEORY OF ASTHMA

The work of Stein and Ottenberg (1958)

Stein and Ottenberg investigated the role of odours in asthma.

Samples. Two methods were used. For method 1 the sample was twenty-five asthmatics, for method 2, twenty asthmatics and twenty controls were studied.

Methods

1. Asthmatics were interviewed about the role of odours in their attacks. Judges then classified substances which were mentioned as oral or anal.

2. Nineteen odorous substances were presented to asthmatics and controls. Free associations were then elicited to the smells.

Results

Method 1. In this sample 5 per cent of attacks were provoked by smells of food; 75 per cent of attacks were provoked by smells on a continuum clean—unclean; 13 per cent of attacks by substances such as perfume or flowers. From this Stein and Ottenberg concluded that the majority of attacks were provoked by smells which could be classified as anal derivative.

Method 2. The free associations to smells of the asthmatic group were significantly more blocked than were the free associations of the controls. From this it was argued by the authors that such smells were a source of conflict for the asthmatic group.

From both these results Stein and Ottenberg (1958) concluded that asthma was a psychological defence against activation of childhood conflicts (anal) by odours. Hence the anal phase of development was implicated in asthma.

Comments and conclusions

If the anal significance of clean—unclean smells is accepted, then this investigation does implicate anality in asthma. It cannot be the case that such smells naturally create chronic bronchial disturbances since a control group was used in the experiment. This study, therefore, supports the psychoanalytic anal aetiology of asthmatics.

Eysenck and Wilson (1973) disagree with this conclusion. They think that asthma represents an effort to avoid taking in 'unpleasant' rather than anal smells. It fits well, they argue, with the hypersensitivity theory of asthma. However, as Freudian psychosexual theory states (e.g. Abraham, 1921), the notion of unpleasant smells is 'anal', e.g. the anal character resembles in appearance one who is smelling an unpleasant smell. That smells are called unpleasant is itself a function of fixated anality. Thus this reinterpretation by Eysenck and Wilson does not affect the relevance of the study to Freudian theory.

Their second point that the blocking of free associations to the smells may result from the unpleasant nature of the asthmatic attack is reasonable, but overall this study does constitute, it seems to us, modest confirmation of psychoanalytic theory.

The work of Margolis (1961)

Margolis investigated the mother—child relationship in bronchial asthma.

Samples. Twenty-five mothers of asthmatic children, twenty-five mothers of children suffering from rheumatic fever, and twenty-five mothers of normal children.

Tests. The mothers were given the Blacky Pictures and a test of parent—child relationships.

Results. The 'asthmatic' mothers were higher than the other groups on Oedipal conflict and oral erotism.

Comments and conclusions

This study sought explicitly to test the hypothesis of French and Alexander (1941) that behind the asthmatic attack lies excessive dependence on anal longing for the mother. It would appear a better strategy to examine such a claim by testing the children rather than the mothers. The fact that the asthmatic mothers were more Oedipal gives only very slight confirmation of the hypothesis. This study cannot be held to support psychoanalytic theory.

The work of Pollie (1964)

Pollie carried out a projective study of conflict and defence in both bronchial asthmatics and patients suffering from peptic ulcers.

Sample. Sixty-one patients with duodenal ulcer, forty-six asthma patients, fifty-two patients with gastro-intestinal symptoms and twenty normal controls (medical students).

Tests. The Blacky Pictures and the related Defence Preference Inquiry.

Results. The asthmatics were less defensive than ulcer patients: avoidance rather than reaction-formation was their preferred mode of defence. Over-attachment to the mother was also noted.

Comments and conclusions

The validity of the Defence Preference Inventory is not well established so that the conclusions concerning defensive processes cannot be accepted uncritically. The authors claim that these results support French and Alexander (1941) — especially the finding concerning the mother—child relationship. However they cannot be regarded as good evidence for classical psychoanalytic theory since this mother relationship is usually associated with oral fixation (Fenichel, 1945). Thus differences on Blacky anal and oral cards would be expected. In brief this study supports the psychoanalytic claim that the mother—child relationship is disturbed in asthma but does not confirm the pregenital fixation which is a part of such disturbance.

The work of Seiden (1965)

Seiden administered the Blacky Pictures to a sample of asthmatic children to determine whether the age of onset of the attacks was related to the level of fixation. Unfortunately, this is a very brief report in the *American Psychologist* so it is difficult to evaluate the study.

Sample. Forty-five asthmatic children. Three groups, defined by age of onset as oral, anal and phallic.

Test. Blacky Pictures (old scoring system).

Results. Freudian theory, that asthma is related to pregenital fixation, was supported in that each group showed the strongest conflict in the area related to the age of onset of attacks.

Comments and conclusions

This study by Seiden indicates that onset of asthma is related to problems associated with the period. Pregenital fixations are, therefore, implicated. However without a control group of normals and, for preference, other psychosomatic groups, further conclusions cannot be drawn.

Conclusions from all the studies of the psychoanalytic theory of asthma

The general tenor of these studies implicates psychosexual developmental factors in asthma. This certainly fits psychoanalytic theory. However, as Fenichel (1945) admits, what differentiates the development of a pregenital conversion neurosis (e.g. asthma) or a compulsion neurosis is not fully understood. Furthermore pregenital fixation is a factor in a large number of abnormalities in psychoanalytic theory. Thus the objective findings reported here can only be regarded as very tenuous support for Freudian theory which is by no means explicit. French and Alexander (1941) argue that the asthmatic attack is a reaction to the danger of separation from the mother, an equivalent of a cry of rage, and that mastery of fear of being left alone governs the asthmatic's life. This however is a long way from orthodox Freudian theory. In summary, therefore, these objective studies of asthma give only vague support for psychoanalytic theory which on this point is itself vague.

PEPTIC ULCER AND ULCERATIVE COLITIS

Psychoanalytic theory, in the case of peptic ulcer at least, is certainly better defined than is the case with asthma. Fenichel (1945), summarizing Freudian beliefs, argues that the peptic ulcer patient is hungry for love. This hunger causes the mucous membrane of the stomach to secrete — hence the ulcer — and is related to repressed oral erotism.

Similarly ulcerative colitis represents the result of anal (rather than oral) conflicts. Fenichel (1945) points out that colitis may be the result of the organism's being constantly under eliminative and retentive pressure, just as the peptic ulcer results from receptive pressure. This relationship between peptic ulcers and ulcerative colitis, reception and retention or elimination, was powerfully developed to embrace all the neuroses by Alexander (1935) in the concept of vector-analysis. Vector-analysis is, however, a long way from orthodox psychoanalytic theory and its investigation is beyond the scope of this chapter.

What is clear, therefore, from this brief discussion of the psychoanalytic theory of peptic ulcer and ulcerative colitis is that oral and anal influences are to be expected in these disorders.

OBJECTIVE STUDIES OF PEPTIC ULCER AND ULCERATIVE COLITIS

Studies using the Blacky Pictures

A series of studies of peptic ulcer patients was carried out beginning with Blum and Kaufmann (1952) and ending with an investigation by Berger (1959). Since each of these studies is related the discussion and conclusions will be common to all of them.

The work of Blum and Kaufmann (1952)

Sample. Fourteen male peptic ulcer patients + controls.

Results. All fourteen patients were disturbed for oral eroticism — on the criterion of the spontaneous story. However on the multiple-choice questions two trends were found:

1. Half the sample put, as expected, the disturbed response.
2. Half the sample put the conflict-free response.

Blum and Kaufmann argued from these findings that there were two patterns of dynamics in ulcer patients: *primary*, where the oral conflict is close to conscious, and *reactive*, where there is an attempt at denial of dependency.

The work of Marquis, Sinnett and Winter (1952)

Sample. Sixteen male ulcer patients.

Results. These authors report similar results to those of Blum and Kaufmann (1952). The peptic ulcer patients were characterized by oral disturbances. Again a reactive type where the dependency was denied and a primary type were recognized. No control group was used, however, so that the importance of the oral conflict is difficult to gauge.

The work of Streitfield (1954)

Sample. Twenty ulcer patients and twenty non-gastro-intestinal psychosomatic controls.

Results. Oral eroticism scores on the Blacky Test did not distinguish the ulcer group from the control group, as would be expected from psychoanalytic theory. There were however, from the Rorschach test, stronger oral aggressive wishes in the ulcer patients.

The work of Winter (1955)

Winter developed further the findings already reported.

Sample. Sixty-eight peptic ulcer patients.

Results. Two separate scales for measuring the primary and reactive ulcer patients were constructed from responses to the Blacky Pictures. The primary pattern was one of overt, immature dependency. The reactive pattern was self-sufficient, high-achieving and determinedly independent. These two Blacky scales were validated against the Rorschach test. Winter concluded that the Blacky Pictures could discriminate two patterns of ulcer dynamics, the primary and the reactive, this last being the typical ulcer personality. This study therefore confirms the findings of Blum and Kaufmann (1952) and Marquis et al. (1952).

The work of Bernstein and Chase (1955)

Bernstein and Chase objected to the study of Blum and Kaufmann on the grounds that the half of the sample who made neutral choices on the enquiry items had not in fact been diagnosed as reactive by any independent judge or criterion: they were reactive because they chose the neutral items. It is, therefore, circular to use neutral items to discriminate reactive ulcer patients. They therefore further investigated the problem.

Sample. Twenty peptic ulcer patients, twenty psychosomatic non-ulcer patients, twenty surgical patients.

Results. Contrary to the majority of findings but in agreement with Streitfield (1954), the ulcer patients could not be discriminated from the others on the Blacky Pictures. Furthermore, Bernstein and Chase could find no evidence for differentiating a primary or a reactive pattern.

The work of Berger (1959)

Berger points out that the primary and reactive patterns described by Blum and Kaufmann and Marquis et al. (1952) were worked out from the same small group of subjects. Furthermore, although Winter (1955) cross-validated the Blacky indices of primary and reactive patterns on sixty-eight ulcer patients, no control group was used. Berger therefore administered these scales to a control group and compared the results with those of Winter.

Sample. Thirty surgical, non-ulcer patients.

Results. On the original primary scale of Winter this surgical control group differed to some extent from Winter's ulcer patients: on the reactive scale there was even better discrimination. However, on the revised scales, as developed by Winter, the surgical controls were not significantly different from Winter's ulcer patients. Berger therefore concluded that Winter's claim of two personality patterns in patients suffering from peptic ulcer was correct, but that these patterns were also to be found in non-ulcer cases.

Conclusions from these studies using the Blacky Pictures

The position is that three investigators, Streitfield (1954), Bernstein and Chase (1955) and Berger (1959) fail to support the psychoanalytic theory of peptic ulcers and fail to find either a prominent position for oral fixation or two distinctive personality patterns. Blum and Kaufmann (1952), Marquis et al. (1952), using the same sample, and Winter (1955) do however support the theory. The fact that Berger found patterns in surgical controls similar to those of Winter, who had no control group, rather discounts the work of Winter. Such patterns are of little value if they are not peculiar to ulcer patients. This only leaves the studies by Blum and Kaufmann and Marquis et al. on sixteen patients, to support the theory. Thus the weight of the evidence from these studies of ulcer patients with the Blacky Pictures does not support psychoanalytic theory. Only two early studies (with the same sample) favour Freud. Later studies fail to replicate the findings.

Other studies

The work of Mednick, Garner and Stone (1959)

Mednick et al. carried out an ingenious investigation of Alexander's specificity theory. The study is relevant to this chapter in that this theory was derived from psychoanalytic theory, but it deserves only brief mention because it is not truly testing Freudian theory. Ulcerative colitis patients, it was hypothesized, on a complex task would *initially show a devil-may-care attitude, produce a fantastic performance or give up entirely*, and afterwards would *show projection* in explaining their performance. Ulcer patients, on the other hand, would *be initially optimistic*, would *persist in the task until it was completed*, and would afterwards *deny any dependence* on the help of the experimenters.

Experimental task. Amidst a complex mass of electronic machinery a pursuit-rotor task had to be performed.

Measures. Questionnaire measures of initial attitude and post-task defences were taken.

Results. None of these hypotheses was confirmed.

Discussion and comments. To the extent that Alexander's themes are dependent on psychoanalytic theories this failure to confirm the theories fails to confirm psychoanalytic theory. Even if the initial and post-task measures were not valid, the actual behaviour during the task did not support the theory. This study certainly runs counter to psychoanalytic psychosomatic theory.

The work of Pollie (1964)

This investigation with the Blacky Pictures has already been reviewed in our discussion of the studies of bronchial asthma. The experimental details may be found on p. 355.

Sample. Sixty-one patients with duodenal ulcers.

Results. Compared with control groups of asthma patients, gastro-intestinal patients and a small group of normal controls, the ulcer patients showed great defensiveness in almost all conflict areas. They were not, however, differentiated from the other groups on oral erotism.

Comments and conclusions. The fact that the ulcer patients were not higher than the controls on oral erotism is certainly contrary to Freudian theory. However, the fact that they were so defensive could account for this low score. Thus it will be remembered that in those studies where the primary and reactive patterns of ulcer dynamics were noted (e.g. Marquis et al., 1952), the reactive type was characterized by just this fact: he picked neutral choices on the questions attached to the oral card. Thus his overall oral-erotism score, using the orthodox scoring manual, would not be high. This defensiveness could account for the low scores obtained for ulcer patients in this study by Pollie. On the other hand, as we have seen, the validity of such reactive scores is strongly open to doubt. It must be concluded, therefore, that this study fails to support the Freudian theory of gastric ulceration.

The work of Wolowitz

Wolowitz (1967) and Wolowitz and Wagonfeld (1968) have produced two studies of the psychoanalytic theory of peptic ulcer, as explicitly formulated by Alexander (1950). Unlike the majority of empirical investigations in this area, they used not the Blacky Pictures but the Food Preference Inventory (Wolowitz, 1964). This test which, it is claimed, taps oral passive or oral sadistic involvement consists of a number of forced-choice items concerning food preferences where the subject has to choose a hot, sweet liquid food (passive) or a sharp, sour dry one (sadistic) — rice pudding or pickles. It is thus, in content at least, not unlike the corresponding scales of the Dynamic Personality Inventory (Grygier, 1961a) which is not well validated (e.g. Kline, 1968b; Stringer, 1970). The validity of the FPI rests on the fact that it discriminated alcoholics from controls (Story, 1963; see p. 370).

Rationale of the studies. Since peptic ulcer is a symptom of oral fixation, the hypothesis can be made that peptic ulcer patients will score more highly on the oral passive scale of the FPI than comparable controls.

Sample in study 1 (Wolowitz, 1967). Twenty male peptic ulcer patients and twenty-three psychiatric controls.

Results. Seventeen of the ulcer patients were above the median on the FPI and eighteen controls below the median — a difference significant at the 0.005 level.

The psychiatric controls were an obvious objection to this study. To improve the experimental design the second investigation was carried out by Wolowitz and Wagonfeld (1968).

Sample. Thirty-eight peptic ulcer patients and sixty-two patients with gastro-intestinal complaints other than peptic ulcer.

Results. Again the peptic ulcer patients were higher on the oral passive scale than the controls (t = 4.01, sig. at the 0.01 level).

Comments (*both studies*). The results of the first study are probably better ignored, not merely because the control group were psychiatric rather than normal, but because they were not also suffering from gastro-intestinal complaints. It is well known that ulcer sufferers are frequently recommended to milky diets in an effort to prevent the ulcer worsening, and indeed preference for such foods on the part of ulcer patients could merely indicate the fact that they tend to cause less discomfort than other foods. Such an explanation could easily account for the findings of the first study, especially since the onset of peptic ulcer is frequently insidious rather than acute.

This interpretation of the observed differences on the FPI is less applicable to the second study where the controls were also suffering from gastro-intestinal complaints, especially where these were also insidious. However the results only indicate that peptic ulcer patients prefer soft, pappy foods rather than sour, spicy food. Whether this indicates oral passivity is another question. We cannot really just assume it does since this link is a part of the psychoanalytic theory we are attempting to verify.

Conclusions

Nevertheless the fact remains that from psychoanalytic theory we should hypothesize peptic ulcer patients as oral passive and by a further theoretical jump as liking soft foods. This prediction has been clearly confirmed — a prediction unlikely to be made from any other theory. Thus these studies by Wolowitz, especially the second by Wolowitz and Wagonfeld (1968), must be held to confirm the psychoanalytic theory of peptic ulcer.

Eysenck and Wilson (1973) in their attempt to find an alternative explanation for the results suggest that the control group were suffering from acute rather than chronic complaints, such that dietary preferences were hardly likely to be affected. However, functional constipation, chronic gastritis, diverticulitis, polycystic kidney, haemorrhoids, cancer, chronic regional enteritis, functional bowel disorders and ileocolitis are certainly not acute, and this is far more than half the control group. The description of the complaints of the rest of the group is such that it is unclear whether they are acute or chronic. Thus this explanation is not powerful.

Another explanation suggested by Eysenck is that soft, sweet, rich foods are more effective as reducers of anxiety through reciprocal inhibition. This, however, is the Freudian psychosexual theory cast in the language of learning theory and, as we argue in the final chapter of this book, this is a happy outcome for the experimental study of psychoanalytic theory which may well be able to specify the nature of reinforcers and the particular conditioning processes which occur in the development of abnormalities.

The final possibility suggested by Eysenck and Wilson seems absurd in that it suggests that preference for such foods (soft and sweet) causes ulceration, the opposite of their first explanation.

In brief we would still argue that this second investigation by Wolowitz and Wagonfield is some support for psychoanalytic theory.

The work of Bellini and Tansella (1976)

Psychoanalytic theory (Fenichel, 1945) states that ulceration is a function of psychosexual fixation: thus oral fixation produces duodenal ulcers; anal fixation, ulceration of the bowel (ulcerative colitis) — hypotheses put to the test by Bellini and Tansella (1976). These authors administered the Leyton Obsessional Inventory (Cooper, 1970) and forty-six items from the Cornell Medical Inventory which is a useful symptom list, to thirty disordered ulcer and thirty colitis patients.

As we saw from our discussion of the anal character in Chapters 3 and 4, anal traits and obsessional traits are essentially similar, so that in psychoanalytic theory the colitis patients would be expected to be higher on the Leyton Obsessional Inventory. In fact it turned out that colitis patients were more worried about their obsessional traits than were the duodenals and analyses of the obsessional items showed that the colitis patients were more indecisive, morose, rigid and punctual.

This study provides some confirmation of the hypothesis and link between anal fixation (as measured by obsessional traits) and ulcerative colitis, although this link can only be maintained if the relationship between obsessional traits and anal erotism is accepted, an aspect of Freudian theory for which we found very little objective evidence. Nevertheless the deduction from the theory is supported by this study. A note should be added concerning the Leyton Obsessional Inventory. This test has become popular as a measure of obsessionality in psychiatric circles, although psychometrically in terms of norms and evidence for validity it is by no means perfect. (However, some evidence for its validity is attested by the agreement between scores derived from it and ratings of obsessional behaviour.) Thus although not an ideal measuring instrument, the results cannot be dismissed simply on the ground that the test is not valid.

In summary then this study provides modest support for psychoanalytic theorizing about colitis.

Conclusions from all studies of peptic ulcer and ulcerative colitis

The majority of the investigations discussed in this section fail to support psychoanalytic theory. Those that do depend on ignoring the normal scoring system for the Blacky Pictures and counting neutral responses as reactive. Blum (1962), in his factor-analytic study of the Blacky Pictures, provides a rationale for this procedure in that a 'defensive' factor loaded on such neutral items can be observed. On the other hand Berger's (1959) study does not lend empirical support to scales derived from this approach to scoring.

It must be concluded, therefore, that in the case of peptic ulcers and ulcerative colitis the evidence does not confirm psychoanalytic theory, except for the studies of Wolowitz using a food-preference inventory and, to a lesser extent, the work of Bellini and Tansella.

INVESTIGATIONS OF THE PSYCHOANALYTIC THEORY OF STUTTERING

Theory

Fenichel (1945) claims that the psychoanalysis of stutterers reveals the anal sadistic universe of wishes as the basis for the symptom. Speaking has an anal sadistic significance. In addition phallic, oral and exhibionistic impulses play a part, though minor to that of the anal components.

The work of Merchant (1952)

Blum and Hunt (1952), in their study of the validity of the Blacky Pictures, cite this unpublished study of stuttering by Merchant.

Sample. Twenty stutterers and twenty controls.

Results. Stutterers were significantly higher on the following scores of the Blacky Pictures: oral erotism, oral sadism, castration anxiety and penis envy, identification, guilt feelings and anaclitic love-object. They were lower on anal expulsiveness.

Comments and conclusions

This study supports the implication of the minor components (oral and phallic erotism) in stuttering. It is reasonable to take scores on the castration-complex and penis-envy card as indicative of phallic fixation. It does not, however, confirm the most important psychoanalytic claim — that relating to anal sadism. This investigation cannot therefore be regarded as support, except in a very minor way, for Freudian theory.

The work of Carp (1962)

Carp also used the Blacky Pictures to investigate the psychosexual development of stutterers.

Sample. Twenty stutterers and twenty student controls at a midwestern college.

Results. The experimental group were higher on oral sadism, the spontaneous story of the oral erotic card, and phallic erotism. On anal retentiveness there was no difference, while they were lower on anal expulsiveness.

Comments and conclusions

This study is very similar to that of Merchant. It again fails to support the main psychoanalytic hypothesis, although oral and phallic components do appear to play a part in stuttering.

Conclusions from both studies

These studies fail to support the major psychoanalytic propositions concerning stuttering. Obviously further study is required with the oral pictures to see whether stutterers can be separated from, for example, ulcer patients. The final conclusion concerning stuttering must be 'no support'.

The work of Silverman

Later in this chapter we deal *en bloc* with the studies of Silverman and colleagues using his libidinal wish-activation method. One of these investigations was concerned with stuttering and it was demonstrated that the subliminal stimulus 'go shit' produced in stutterers an increase in stuttering while control stimuli did not do so. This anal stimulus did not produce an increase in psychopathology in other clinical groups. This study, which needs to be taken in the whole context of such studies, is support however for the psychoanalytic theory of stuttering. The paper is Silverman et al. (1972).

APPENDICITIS

The work of Eylon (1967)

As Eylon points out, most writers on psychosomatic medicine, for example Alexander (1950), Alexander and French (1948), Lief et al. (1963), contain no reference to appendicitis. However, Dunbar (1954) does discuss pseudo-appendicitis and, in connection with this, Eylon draws attention to the fact that pathologists regard chronic inflammation of the appendix as rare (e.g. Robbins, 1962).

Hypothesis. The basic hypothesis tested by Eylon was that 'some event in real life gives rise to birth fantasies which initiate acute pain in the right iliac fossa, leading to the diagnosis of acute appendicitis and appendectomy.' Such real-life events are: childbirth, forthcoming childbirth or weddings among people who are psychologically close to the patient.

These hypotheses were derived partially from the few case studies of appendicitis and birth fantasy by Inman (1958, 1962), who did not, however, have any pathologists' findings on the appendices to support his speculative theories.

Freud (1905c), in the case history of Dora, related appendicitis to birth fantasy. Eylon supplies the precise quotation 'Her supposed attack of appendicitis had thus enabled the patient . . . to realize a fantasy of childbirth.'

Sample. Thirty-five appendectomy patients where both pre- and post-operative diagnosis was appendicitis. A matched group of thirty-five controls was used.

Birth data. Obtained by interview based on an open-ended questionnaire.

Results

1. There was a significant association (P < 0.005) between birth events and appendectomy.
1b. No such relationship existed between birth events and other operations.
2. Proportion of normal appendices in patients with and without birth events was the same. However this was an artefact of the sampling in that post- and pre-operative diagnosis had to be appendicitis.
3. Young females did not have more appendectomies than other operations.

Comments and conclusions

The main finding, that birth events were related to appendectomy as distinct from other surgical operations, suggests strongly that psychogenic factors influence appendicitis. This is striking support for the Freudian claim. It is difficult to think of any other theory that could predict such results. This study must be regarded, therefore, as good evidence for this aspect of Freudian theory. As was pointed out under result 2, the sampling precluded, to a large extent, patients with normal appendices. It would have been interesting to see to what extent birth events were related to such appendectomies. Thus Eylon supports the Freudian theory relating birth fantasy to the onset of appendicitis.

Eysenck and Wilson (1973) argue that this relationship between birth events and appendectomy can be explained by the nature of appendicitis and differences between the experimental and the control groups. Thus, in their view, appendicitis being acute does not interfere with social life, while other diseases being chronic do so. Hence appendectomy patients go to weddings, the controls do not. This argument seems patently absurd. Examination of Eylon's control group implies that patients with the following problems cannot go to weddings within three months either side of their treatment: haemorrhoids, nasal operations, ligation of leg veins, hysterectomy, ovarian cyst, rectal fissures, elbow drainage, operations on toes, excision of ingrowing toenail. This argument seems weak in the extreme and in the absence of empirical evidence about medical problems in wedding guests is not worthy of mention. Freudian theory may be fantastic, but this counter-argument is worse. Our conclusions cannot be changed on these grounds.

ANOREXIA NERVOSA

A case study by Beech (1959)

Beech carried out an experimental case study on a woman of twenty-seven suffering from anorexia nervosa. This investigation is examined because it is entirely replicable and because the data are objective. Obviously, however, further cases will have to be tested before any firm conclusions can be drawn.

Experimental technique. Twenty-five neutral and five sexual words were presented below the threshold of hearing. An audible signal was sounded just before each word to which the subject had to free-associate.

Sex words. The five sex words were unequivocal: vagina, penis, breast, intercourse, sexual.

Hypothesis. There would be a greater possibility of food associations to sexual than neutral stimuli.

Results. This hypothesis was supported by the Chi-square test. Three normals to whom the technique was also administered produced no food responses at all. Of course such a result, it could be argued, might be due to the link between sex and anxiety so that the chain of events was sex, anxiety, food. Again the link between sex and food could have been learned by the patient during previous psychotherapy.

Conclusions

In psychoanalytic theory oral problems naturally play a large part in the understanding of eating difficulties. Nevertheless the sexualization of oral activity, as suggested in this study, would fit in well with Freudian theory. Oral fixation can lead to the oral expression of any kind of instinctual conflict (Fenichel, 1945). This study by Beech clearly cannot confirm psychoanalytic theory. However, further studies of this kind could perhaps produce some interesting support for the psychoanalytic theory of anorexia nervosa. This investigation must be regarded as highly suggestive.

Perhaps of relevance here is the study of food preferences and oral-personality traits (Kline and Storey, 1978b) conducted as part of our extensive study of the oral character discussed in Chapters 3 and 5. Here it was found in a sample of students that oral optimistic traits were related to preferences for soft milky foods, the highest correlation being with fruit fools. Oral pessimistic traits were related to preference for hot pickles. This study clearly requires replication before much reliance is placed upon it.

ALCOHOLISM

Psychoanalytic theory

The psychoanalytic theory of alcoholism is clear. Fenichel (1945) writes 'The unconscious impulses in alcoholics typically are not only oral but homosexual in nature.' The orality, since drinking is involved, is logical enough. The homosexuality is not so obvious. Fenichel claims that the all-male heartiness and back slapping of the typical drinking man is everyday evidence for the latent homosexuality.

The work of Botwinick and Machover (1951)

These writers carried out a psychometric examination of latent homosexuality on a small sample of alcholics.

Sample. Thirty-nine male alcoholics: age-range 30-49 years.

Tests. MMPI Mf Scale and Form A of the Terman and Miles Attitudes and Interests analysis test.

Results. The alcoholics were not higher than non-alcoholics on these scales.

Comments and conclusions

Grygier (1957a), in a survey of all the then-current measures of homosexuality, came to the conclusion that none of them was satisfactory. In an earlier section of this chapter — that concerned with the claimed link between paranoid schizophrenia and repressed homosexuality — it will be recalled that we found one of the major problems to be the assessment of *repressed* homosexuality. Indeed if the items of the Mf scale of the MMPI are too overtly homosexual, latent homosexuals would be expected to score lower and not higher than normals. Thus the failure of this study to confirm Freudian theory could have been due to the invalidity of the measures of homosexuality. Nevertheless this study by Botwinick and Machover clearly offers no support for Freudian theory.

The work of Scott (1958)

Scott investigated the role of homosexuality in alcoholism by examining the case records of 267 male and 33 female alcoholics. A very brief review of this study will be sufficient in view of the subjective nature of the data. As evidence for homosexuality, divorce and marriage rates were studied. Scott concluded that immaturity rather than homosexuality characterized their sexual relationships.

Conclusions

Despite the impressive number in its sample this study cannot be regarded as a serious refutation of Freudian theory. Again the problem turns round an adequate measure of homosexuality, particularly *latent* homosexuality.

The work of Machover, Puzzo and colleagues (1959)

Machover et al. conducted a number of studies of alcoholism of which two are relevant to the Freudian theory.

A. Study of the alcoholic personality by Machover and Puzzo (1959)

Sample. Twenty-three remitted alcoholics and twenty-three non-remitted subjects. Mean age was 41.9 years and the mean WISC IQ was 119. All were male.

Measures. A large battery of projective and psychometric techniques was employed amongst which were the Blacky Pictures, the Rorschach and the TAT.

Statistical analysis. If a trait as measured by any of these tests occurred in 60 per cent or more of the sample it was deemed typical of the alcoholic personality.

Results. Oral dependence and castration anxiety (variables relevant to psychoanalytic theory) were typical of these alcoholics.

Comments and conclusions. These results are regarded by Blum (1966) as supporting Freudian theory. However, the fact that there was no matched control group vitiates the results to a large extent.

B. *Study of latent homosexuality by Machover* et al. (*1959*)

Sample. As above, a homosexual control group and a normal control group.

Tests. Rorschach, Machover Figure-Drawing Test and the MMPI Mf scale.

Results. With these tests the alcoholics (both groups) did not show greater homosexuality than the normal controls though remitted alcoholics were higher than the drinking alcoholics.

Comments and conclusions. These results cannot be held to refute Freudian theory in that none of these tests is regarded as a highly valid measure of repressed homosexuality.

Conclusions from both studies

The implication of orality and homosexuality in alcoholism has not been confirmed by this study. Also, the reliance on projective techniques and the MMPI Mf scale makes the results of this investigation of dubious validity.

The work of McCord et al. (1959)

These authors examined various theories of alcoholism in the light of evidence from a longitudinal study of young people.

Sample. 29 alcoholics and 158 men (not neurotics or criminals), the attenuated sample from the Cambridge—Somerville Youth Study (Witmer and Powers, 1951), all of whom had been investigated in great detail.

Measures

(a) *Orality*: thumb-sucking after infancy, excessive early smoking, eating orgies, playing with the mouth.
(b) *Latent homosexuality*: feminine tendencies, doll-playing, dressing up as girls. Overt homosexuality was also noted.

Results

(a) *Orality.* Fifty-nine boys were classified as oral on these measures. Of these 12 per cent became alcoholic. 18 per cent of the 128 non-oral boys became alcoholics. Freudian theory is not supported.

(b) *Homosexuality*. Of boys thus classified only 4 per cent became alcoholics whereas 16 per cent of the normals fell into this category. Two of the six overt homosexuals became alcoholics. Again Freudian theory was not supported.

Comments and conclusions

There can be no doubt that McCord et al. have cast the strongest doubt on the psychoanalytic theory of drinking. Certainly these indices of latent homosexuality and orality seem good: it is probably fair to say that had the results supported the theory Freudians would not have disputed them. However, it could be argued that, although thumb-sucking is an index of orality, fixation at the oral level is more likely to result where thumb-sucking was *prevented* when it was desired. A mere counting of thumbs is not on its own sufficient. Furthermore the omission of neurotics and delinquents who might have also been alcoholics could have affected these results. The conclusion must be that Freudian theory is not supported and would be refuted were the indices used a little more sensitive.

The work of Gibbins and Walters (1960)

Gibbins and Walters used a perceptual-defence technique (see pp. 210 et seq.) to investigate homosexuality as a factor in alcoholism, as Daston (1956) did in the case of paranoia (see p. 333). Three experiments were reported in this paper.

First experiment

Sample. Fifteen alcoholics, fifteen controls and ten homosexuals.

Method. Homosexual words and control words were exposed tachistoscopically to the subjects.

Score. The difference in recognition threshold between control and experimental words.

Results. There were no significant differences between the groups although, as predicted by psychoanalytic theory, the alcoholics were midway between the homosexual and normal groups.

Second experiment

Sample. The same numbers in groups were used but composed of new subjects.

Method. As in the first experiment, but this time the sexual words were unequivocal — breast, bowel, etc.

Results. There were significant differences between the groups but these were unrelated to the homosexuality of the words.

Third experiment

Sample. Thirteen drinkers, twenty controls and sixteen homosexuals.

Stimuli. Symbolic pictures were shown (male and female sex symbols).

Results. Homosexuals and drinkers selected more male pictures than did the controls.

Conclusions from all these studies by Gibbins and Walters

Only the last experiment supports homosexuality as being a factor in alcoholism. However, in both the other experiments the drinkers were more homosexual than the normals. If we take into account the problems with this type of perceptual-defence experiment, which we fully discussed in the chapter on repression (control words may be emotive, for example the greater frequency of sexual words in reality than is apparent from a word-list), then it is hardly surprising that only the symbolic picture test produced significant results. Daston (1956), however, did show a difference with words in the case of paranoid schizophrenics.

We must conclude that these results support to a slight degree the implication of homosexuality with alcoholism. It would not appear to be as important here as in paranoia.

The work of Engeset et al. (1963)

These authors studied the incidence of peptic ulcer among abusers and non-abusers of alcohol in Norway.

Sample. 251 alcoholics and a random sample of 329 males.

Rationale. Since in psychoanalytic theory peptic ulcers and alcoholism are both related to oral fixation, more gastric ulcers would be expected among alcoholics than among normals.

Results. Significantly more (19.1 per cent) abusers than non-abusers (13.1 per cent) suffered or had suffered from ulcers. The difference was restricted to gastric ulcers and did not apply to duodenal ulcers.

Comments and conclusions

This study points to a relationship between the two phenomena — as predicted from Freudian theory. It does not, of course, demonstrate that the common factor is oral fixation. This study could be one piece of evidence in the construct validation of the Freudian theory.

The work of Bacon et al. (1965) — cross-cultural studies of drinking

Bacon et al. produced a series of related papers on drinking habits in a large sample of societies, using the cross-cultural methods of Whiting and Child (1953) which we have described in an earlier chapter (see p. 78). Their second paper contains the findings relevant to this chapter.

Sample. 139 societies.

Measures. Anthropological descriptions of these societies were rated for indulgence or severity of child-training practices. The measures of drinking were the presence and extent of ceremonial drinking, the general consumption of the society and the frequency of drunkenness.

Results. The correlations between these variables (ratings) showed that indulgence of dependency needs during infancy, childhood and adulthood and the diffusion of nurturance were each related to a low degree of drinking and insobriety.

Comments and conclusions

Since dependency is an aspect of the orally fixated personality, it should follow from Freudian theory that orally fixated persons whose dependency was not indulged would seek other oral gratifications — hence the correlation noted. This study is again one small piece of evidence supporting psychoanalytic theory.

Orality and alcoholism

The work of Story (1968)

Story examined the scores of alcoholics on a number of indices of orality.
   Sample. Thirty alcoholics and thirty normals.

Measures:

1. *Chain-association test.* Five oral and five non-oral words are presented to the subject who has to make fifteen associations to each word. The time for this is noted as is the number of oral responses.
2. Seven oral and seven non-oral proverbs are presented to the subject who has to explain the meaning (from which an abstraction score is taken) and indicate agreement or otherwise.

   Results. There were highly significant differences between the groups on the oral stimuli and the alcoholics were considerably worse at the oral tasks than at the non-oral tasks.

   Comments. This study no doubt implicates problems over oral responses (e.g. eating, drinking, biting) among alcoholics. In a normal group we could postulate that responses did indicate orality in the Freudian sense of an over-concern with oral behaviour. However, we know such problems exist in an alcoholic group (drinking *is* the problem), and such responses tell us little new about the patients. To demonstrate orality in alcoholics we need a measure (e.g. of oral character) not overtly concerned with oral behaviour. This study, therefore, demonstrates that alcoholics have oral problems which Freudian theory predicts. It can only be regarded as slight support for Freudian theory, however, in that it fails to implicate other aspects of orality.

Nevertheless in fairness to the author, he did relate these scores to oral personality traits as part of his doctoral dissertation (1963). As reported by Wolowitz (1964), Story found that this same sample of alcoholics scored significantly higher on the Goldman-Eisler scales of orality (Goldman-Eisler, 1951) which have already been fully described and discussed (see p. 14).

   If we take these two findings together we can argue that Story (1963, 1968) has truly implicated orality in alcoholism.

The work of Wolowitz and Barker (1968)

Wolowitz and Barker replicated the work of Story (1963) — who reported that alcoholics scored higher than controls on the FPI — by using a non-patient alcoholic sample.

Sample. One extended family of twenty-three members: fourteen alcoholics and nine controls.

Rationale of Sample. This curious sample was chosen because the authors claim that the role of being a patient tends to make subjects dependent and affects their responses on the FPI as used by Story (1963).

Test. The FPI (Wolowitz, 1964), which is described on p. 359.

Results. The whole family were significantly higher than other samples tested by Wolowitz and reported in this book (see his work on ulcer patients, p. 360). By the median test, the alcoholics of the family were significantly higher than the others.

Comments and conclusions. These findings support the previous study by Story (1963). Wolowitz and Barker have shown the results cannot be attributed to the dependent patient role. However, as with the study by Story (1968), the result only implicates food preferences in alcoholics even though such interests have been related to oral personality traits by Story (1963). Thus this investigation implicates orality in alcoholism if it is taken together with previous findings.

The work of Bertrand and Masling (1969)

These writers studied the incidence of orality in the Rorschach responses of heavy drinkers.

Sample. Twenty heavy drinkers matched for age, education, intelligence and diagnosis with twenty other patients.

Measures. The Rorschach orality indices described by Schafer (1954). There are references to:

(a) *oral dependence*: e.g. foods, food sources, food objects, supplicants.

(b) *oral sadism*: e.g. oral assaults, destruction, aggression.

Results. The drinkers were significantly more oral dependent than the controls.

Comments. We have not usually considered the Rorschach as coming under the category of scientific evidence but this study differs somewhat in that the indices are, for oral dependency at least, unequivocally oral responses (in the main). Indeed Masling et al. (1968) found that such imagery in the Rorschach was related to the tendency to conform in the Asch experiment, where subjects are asked to make perceptual judgements clearly against the evidence but in conformity with other stooge subjects in the experiment. Hence the fact that drinkers make more food-reponses than controls is of relevance to the Freudian claim that drinkers are fixated at the oral level.

Maletzky and Klotter (1974) investigated smoking and drinking in fifty alcoholics and fifty controls. They found that there was a high correlation (0.74) between smoking and drinking among the alcoholics and that this fell to 0.29 among the controls. This might seem evidence for a high oral drive among the alcoholics, a view contradicted by the fact that on cessation of drinking, smoking did not increase.

This study is therefore not in accord with the psychoanalytic hypothesis that smoking and drinking are symptomatic of oral fixation. The only way to maintain the psychoanalytic claim in the face of this evidence would be to argue that the treatment involved in stopping drinking in some way affected the underlying orality. For example, it would be interesting to know whether they ate more or talked more or indulged in more oral sex. Nevertheless, as it stands, this study certainly fails to support psychoanalytic theory.

Conclusions from all studies of alcoholism

Of the ten studies just reviewed three run contrary to the theory (Botwinick and Machover, 1951; Scott, 1958; McCord et al., 1959). The others give some degree of support although in most cases only slight. Of the three refutatory studies the first two are not good methodologically but the longitudinal study by McCord et al. is hard to fault despite the insensitivity of the measures. Of the supporting studies the best appears to be that of Gibbins and Walters (1960) whose perceptual-defence technique had proved useful with paranoid schizophrenics. Yet even this gave only limited confirmation. As is so often the case with cross-cultural studies of Freudian concepts, the work of Bacon et al. (1965) promised more than it achieved.

Thus with slight confirmation from some studies, though with different kinds of data (experimental, psychometric and cross-cultural), and definite disconfirmation from the longitudinal study, the final conclusion must be that there is only very slight support for the Freudian theory of alcoholism.

ORALITY AND SMOKING

The work of McArthur et al. (1958)

These authors studied the psychology of smoking using as a sample 252 Harvard alumni who had been selected in their sophomore year as suitable for forming a panel of normals for research purposes.

Results. Most of the variables investigated were not relevant to the psychoanalytic theory of smoking. However, in their investigation of the ability to stop smoking, one finding stands out and we can do no better than quote their words: 'A signal fact is this: ability to stop smoking is directly proportional to the number of months our subjects were fed from their mother's breast!' (p. 272). Thus light smokers who could stop were weaned at 8 months, heavy smokers who could stop, at 6-8 months. Smokers (mainly heavy) who do not try to stop were weaned at 5 months, and a similar group, who were unable to stop, at 4-8 months.

Comments and conclusions

These findings are powerful support for the implication of orality in smoking and they are certainly in full accord with psychoanalytic predictions from the concept of orality. Incidentally they run counter to the learning-theory account of thumb-sucking (Sears and Wise, 1950; see p. 105) from which an opposite result would be expected — the more sucking subjects had during infancy the more sucking they would need later.

One argument against this study is that the weaning data were retrospective and as we have shown, such recollected data are not accurate. However, inaccuracy would be expected to blur the results so that these findings are even more striking.

This study must be regarded as confirming the Freudian theory that orality is linked with smoking.

The work of Jacobs et al. (1965, 1966)

Jacobs et al. carried out two studies into the personality of smokers which are relevant in part to this chapter in that one of the variables studied was orality. Both these investigations will be examined together since the second was to some extent a replication of the first.

Method. Questionnaires were constructed to measure maternal over-control, maternal harshness and maternal coldness, danger-seeking, impetuousness, defiance, emotional lability and orality. This last was measured by oral habits such as nail-biting.

Results and samples. In the first investigation, reported in the first paper, the sample consisted of ninety-seven adult male electronic engineers. Heavy smokers (20+ per day) were higher on all variables except danger-seeking and significantly higher on orality.

In the second investigation of this first paper, where the sample was 136 factory workers, the results were not so clear-cut. Indeed the categories of 'heavy smoker' and 'moderate smoker' had to be combined to produce any differences compared with non-smokers. In their second paper Jacobs et al. (1966) studied a sample of 134 males and produced essentially similar results to the previous findings except that maternal malevolence was not implicated as a factor.

Comments and conclusions

These two papers have merited only brief discussion since the validity and reliability of the questionnaire measures is highly dubious. It will be recalled by readers how, in our earlier chapter on the influence of child-training procedure on adult personality (see pp. 68-70), the difficulty of obtaining accurate measures of such procedures was discussed. Jacobs et al. are content, however, to rely on adult recollection of maternal attitudes! Similarly their measure of orality lacks good evidence of validity (indeed any evidence). Certainly there was no check on social desirability as a response-set.

Thus the fact that psychoanalytic theory is supported and heavy smokers were more oral than non-smokers cannot be regarded as evidence in favour of the theory, until evidence is forthcoming pertaining to the validity of these scales. Actually even this Freudian hypothesis is doubtful: if smokers express their orality by smoking we might predict them to be *less* not more oral than their non-smoking controls.

The work of Kimeldorf and Gewitz (1966)

Kimeldorf and Gewitz carried out a small-scale study of smoking among students.

Sample. Fifteen non-smokers and seven smokers (more than 20 cigarettes a day).

Test. The Blacky Pictures — oral cards.

Scoring system. Blum's (1962) scoring system based on a factor-analysis of the responses (see p. 112) was used.

Results. Smokers were higher than their controls on Blum's first two factors, oral craving and playfulness, a factor which was interpreted by Blum (1962) as defensive avoidance of hostility to the mother.

Comments and conclusions

The validity of the Blacky Pictures has already been fully discussed in this book (see pp. 112-13). There is probably more evidence for their validity as measures of psychosexual fixation than for any other test. Nevertheless results with the Blacky Pictures have to be accepted cautiously. The small size of the sample and the restricted population from which it was drawn both necessitate that these findings be regarded as only limited support for the Freudian theory.

The work of Veldman and Bown (1969)

Veldman and Bown studied the characteristics of smokers and non-smokers in a large sample of college freshmen.

Sample. 401 cigarette smokers were compared with 401 non-smokers. These two groups were matched for education, social background and ability.

Measures. Seventy variables in all were used, although only the one relevant to our needs is the orality score.

Orality score. This was derived from thirty-six sentence completions which were administered to the subjects. The orality score comprised any reference to food, eating, drinking, and smoking. Veldman and Brown point out that the inclusion of this last item 'smoking' did not bias the results because in fact there were very few such sentence completions.

Results. Smokers were significantly higher on the orality score than were the control group. Males too scored significantly higher than females on this variable.

Comments and conclusions

As with the two studies by Jacobs et al. (1965, 1966), great caution must be shown in interpreting these results which appear to confirm psychoanalytic theory in that they link orality and smoking. Again it is the dubious nature of the oral scale which calls the findings into question. The authors admit that scoring food responses to the sentence completions as indices of orality was purely *a priori*: there is no evidence for validity and the reliability is unknown. Furthermore the discovery of a sex difference on this scale is not hopeful from the viewpoint of construct-validity. Thus these findings may be regarded as only slight support for psychoanalytic theory. In fairness to the theory, however, it is noteworthy that three investigations have found a positive correlation between orality and smoking which if the scales were not valid is a surprising coincidence. Clearly what is needed above all is a well-validated and reliable oral scale.

Alone, this study by Veldman and Bown is modest confirmation of Freudian theory. Together with the investigations of Jacobs, however, it amounts to a somewhat more solid support.

The work of Fisher and Fisher (1975)

These researchers divided a group of heavy smokers (30 + cigarettes a day) into an experimental and a control group and took baseline measures of orality using Rorschach indices (mentions of food and drink, for example). The experimental group then underwent a two-hour smoking-deprivation. In this group correlations were found between the orality scores and symptoms and body-image distortion. This was not the case in the control group. This study is highly interesting but its meaning is unclear because the validity of these Rorschach indices is unknown. If these indices were acceptable as evidence, the study would constitute some support for the implication of orality and smoking.

The work of Kline and Storey (1978b)

Kline and Storey (1978b) in their extensive study of the oral character which has been fully discussed in Chapters 3 and 5 of this book carried out an investigation into orality and smoking. Our two tests of the oral character, OOQ measuring oral optimistic traits and OPQ measuring oral pessimistic traits (see Chapter 3 for a description and for evidence of validity), were administered to two separate university-student samples. In the first sample there was a significant point biserial correlation of 0.38 between smoking and OPQ. In the second sample heavy smokers (20 + a day) scored significantly higher on OPQ than light smokers.

Although the results in the two samples are not the same, both support the Freudian hypothesis that smoking is related to oral fixation due to insufficient sucking in infancy. Smoking is therefore a compensatory oral activity, the assumption here being that oral pessimistic traits, as measured by OPQ, are related to such oral fixation. In connection with these results it should be pointed out that in neither of these samples were Eysenck's E or N related to smoking. This study must be regarded as modest confirmation of the implication of orality in smoking but not too much should be made of it, since these oral traits are only theoretically not empirically related to oral erotism.

The work of Howe and Summerfield (1979)

Howe and Summerfield investigated the relationship between cigarette smoking and other mouth habits among ninety-seven students of whom fifty-four were smokers. They developed a fifty-item face-valid questionnaire about oral habits and found that continuous smokers were high on pencil-sucking and nail-biting. This finding could support the psychoanalytic notion of orality that was expressed in these three ways (smoking, nail-biting and pencil-sucking).

However, all three could be symptoms of an underlying factor such as neuroticism. In addition, it could be argued that smokers express their orality through smoking and hence should have fewer other mouth habits than non-smokers. This study is unable to sort out these different hypotheses and hence cannot be regarded as well-designed for the elucidation of psychoanalytic theory.

In addition a Varimax analysis of the questionnaire was carried out which might have revealed an oral factor. However, the factor-analytic side of this investigation is technically poor. Nunnally (1978) argues that for a reliable factor-analysis ten times the number of variables to subjects is necessary and the lowest factor quoted by any reputable worker is two (Guilford, 1956). Thus even on this simple criterion the Varimax is suspect. Since there was no test of simple structure (to show otherwise) the likelihood of the orthogonal Varimax reaching simple structure rather than an oblique rotation is not high. Thus the results from the factor-analysis cannot be taken seriously.

In summary, an interesting investigation but too deficient in method and design to draw firm conclusions.

Conclusions from all studies of smoking

In brief there is modest support from the work of Jacobs, Veldman and Bown and Kline and Storey. However, not too much should be made of these findings. Clearly larger-scale studies with many categories of smokers should be used if definitive results are to be obtained.

BRUXISM

To non-psychoanalytic psychologists, the psychoanalytic claim that bruxism (teeth-grinding) is related to oral sadism is one of the more outlandish hypotheses. Although, in principle, this is a hypothesis that is relatively easy to put to the empirical test, there are few relevant investigations. Glaros and Rao (1977) have carried out a useful survey of research examining relationships between bruxism and a variety of psychological variables. They make the point (one with which we fully agree and where we disagree most with Fisher and Greenberg, 1977) that most of the studies are weak because the measures which are used are of dubious or unknown validity (usually, in fact, projective tests). Their work indicates clearly that no links between orality and bruxism have been demonstrated.

One of the few studies which attempted to provide evidence for this link is that of Vernallis (1955) who compared forty bruxic students and matched (sex, intelligence, age and educational status) controls on the Blacky Pictures (Blum, 1949). There were no differences between the groups on the two oral cards. However, even had there been so, we would have had to treat the result with great caution since the Blacky Pictures themselves, though more reliable than many projective tests, are not well validated.

This work by Glaros and Rao makes it clear that, as yet, the psychoanalytic hypothesis concerning bruxism and orality is unconfirmed.

ENURESIS

The work of De Luca (1968)

De Luca investigated the psychosexual constitution of a sample of adolescent enuretics drawn from army trainees.

Sample. Twenty enuretics and forty controls.

Test. Blacky Pictures (Blum, 1949).

Scoring system. The factor-analytic system of Blum (1962).

Results. There were no significant differences on any of the thirty factors.

Comments and conclusions

In psychoanalytic theory enuresis is linked (see Fenichel, 1945) to unresolved Oedipal conflicts, castration fears and fixation at the phallic stage. Thus this failure of the Blacky Pictures — of which there is some evidence for validity (see pp. 112-13) — to discriminate enuretics from controls is certainly contrary to psychoanalytic theory. Whether the Blacky Pictures are sufficiently robust for this finding to constitute a refutation of psychoanalytic theory is, however, less certain. Nevertheless, this study by De Luca clearly fails to substantiate Freudian claims concerning the aetiology of enuresis.

THE PHOBIAS

The work of Dixon et al. (1957)

This investigation was a psychometric study of phobia in a sample of patients at the Tavistock Clinic.

Sample. 125 men and 125 women patients at the Tavistock Clinic.

Test. The Tavistock Self-Assessment Inventory (Sandler, 1954). Items referring to phobias were used.

Statistical analysis. Phi-coefficients of correlations were computed between the test items. The resulting correlation matrix was then subjected to a centroid factor-analysis.

Results. Seven factors emerged accounting for just under 37 per cent of the variance. The first two factors, a general factor and a bipolar factor, accounted for 22 per cent of the variance. Dixon et al. argued that these findings showed that within a general framework of phobias there were two distinct groups of fears:

1. A fear of being left alone, of being helpless and lonely.
2. A fear of pain, operations, the dentist and accidental injury.

These two groups were differentiated by the second bipolar factor. Their relationship was demonstrated by the first general factor on which all items had positive loadings.

The separation phobia was characterized by items pertaining to fears about being left alone, crossing a bridge or street, open spaces, water, trains and the dark. The second part of the bipolar factor was concerned with accidental pain and injury, fears about the dentist, surgical operations and the like.

Comments and conclusions

Dixon et al. argue that this pattern of phobias, revealed by the factor-analysis, closely fits the Freudian theory of anxiety. Thus Freud (1925a), in 'Inhibition, symptoms and anxiety', contrasts the anxiety with loss of love (the first group of phobias) with castration anxiety (the second group in this study). Thus according to Dixon et al. the separation phobias in the first group are symbolic forms of anxiety about separation from the mother, just as the other phobias are symbolic forms of castration anxiety. If their conclusions and interpretations of this factor-analysis were acceptable, this study would constitute powerful and compelling evidence for psychoanalytic theory. However, such an interpretation ignores some important methodological difficulties.

(a) *The validity of the test.* The items were selected from the Tavistock Self-Assessment inventory originally because they were face-valid, that is they appeared to be relevant to phobias. However, as has been earlier discussed in the section on the psychometric study of personality (p. 14), face-validity is not a good guide to true validity. Furthermore all items were keyed 'Yes' which could easily confound the true variance with the response-set of acquiescence. In addition there was no check on the other main response-set — the tendency to put, in questionnaires, the socially desirable response. Thus these two response-sets could have considerably lowered the validity of the test (see Cronbach, 1946 and 1950) which rests alone on face-validity.

(b) *Phi-coefficients.* Phi-coefficients of correlation, which are highly affected by the ratio of the two responses, were computed between all the items. Thus limits are set to the phi as soon as the dichotomy becomes uneven, e.g. 75 per cent put 'Yes', 25 per cent 'No'. Phi is at its most accurate when the response is evenly split — 50 per cent put 'Yes', 50 per cent 'No' to an item. Guilford (1956) contains a full discussion of this problem. It is particularly important when the resulting matrix of correlations is factored, as in the present study. Some writers indeed argue that the factorization of a matrix of phi-coefficients yields merely 'difficulty' factors (Cattell, 1957). This means that the factors are comprised of items of similar difficulty or with a similar ratio of responses.

(c) *The centroid factor-analysis.* As Harman (1976) demonstrates, with a matrix of positive correlations a centroid factor-analysis always yields a general factor followed by bipolar factors. Thus to claim that such a pattern, a statistical artefact, supports a theory is not acceptable. Clearly 'blind' rotation to simple structure would overcome this difficulty in that it can then be argued that the rotated solution is not a product of the method but the most simple fit to the data. If this then fits the theory, support for that theory is justified.

These three problems which are common to the factor-analytic approach to personality measurement make the interpretation by Dixon et al. (1957) appear rather too disingenuous. Nevertheless they do not entirely discount it. After all, the items loading on the bipolar factor do fit the theory — i.e. fall into two recognizable and predicted groups (even though less than one-quarter of the variance of the items is accounted for).

It is thus concluded in the light of this discussion that this study by Dixon et al. gives qualified support to the psychoanalytic theory of phobias.

DEPRESSION

The work of Leckie and Withers (1967)

These authors carried out a psychometric study of depression of particular interest because they attempted to distinguish between liability to depressive illness and actual depressive symptoms. Psychoanalytic theory was the basis of the items in the questionnaires.

Tests used. 150 items were tried out from which 58 were selected mainly by item-analysis. The items fall into three scales:

A.　*Eleven direct depressive items.* In themselves these items could indicate prevailing moods of patients.

　　Examples　5. I seldom worry about my health.
　　　　　　　23. I work under a great deal of tension.

The remaining scales were designed to test the psychoanalytic theory of depression.

B.　*Nine threshold items.* These items were negatively correlated with the direct depressive scale.

　　Examples 18. Deep down I regard myself as rather a poor specimen.
　　　　　　　46. I hardly ever feel envious.

C.　*Thirty-two indirect depressive items or unconcious items.*

　　Examples 34. I very often get a gnawing feeling.
　　　　　　　52. I do not feel that any part of me is bad.

In addition six unscored items were included to lighten the depressing effects of reading the items.

Validity test of the three scales. The scales were given to thirty-one depressives and thirty-one matched controls. All three scales and the total score discriminated the two groups.

Test—retest reliability of the scales. For each scale this was around 0.90 which is very satisfactory.

Cross-validation study. Sixty-seven psychiatric cases filled in these scales. The inventory was then scored to give a blind diagnosis. The scoring rationale constituted a test of psychoanalytic theory.

Rationale of scoring

(a) *The unconscious items.* A high score on these items indicates an underlying tendency to depressive illness.

(b) *The threshold items* indicate whether this tendency might materialize as depressive illness.

A high score on the threshold items will lead to symptomatic depression. A low score on the threshold items + a high score on the direct depressive items may reflect a *mood* of depression. However if such a patient had a low unconscious depression score, the overt depression would be considered a mood.

(c) *The direct depressive items.* A high score on these items reflects a prevailing depression.

Thus then the crucial scale is the *threshold scale.* A high score on this indicates endogenous or reactive depression. The unconscious items then discriminate the endogenous (high) from the reactive (low).

Results. There was a 73 per cent agreement between the blind diagnoses and psychiatric ratings based on five-months' clinical experience with the patients. Endogenous depressives had the highest total scale of any of the nosological categories.

Discussion

Leckie and Withers (1967) argue that these results support the Freudian theory. For example, in reference to the unconscious scale they claim that item 6 'I sometimes get the feeling that I was terribly let down as a child' and item 12 'I wonder whether something terrible must have been done to me when I was too young to remember it' tap primary narcissistic injury as defined in 'Mourning and melancholia' (Freud, 1917b). Similarly items 11 'I find it difficult to remember the things I have read' and 34 'I very often get a gnawing feeling' are intended to tap object-loss through oral incorporation (Freud, 1917b). Other items attempt to tap the part played by anal sadism in the destruction of the internalized loved objects. Thus the scales go a long way in measuring apparently unmeasurable unconscious factors.

In the opinion of Leckie and Withers the threshold items determine whether a person will suffer from depression or not, despite his liability to depression as measured by the unconscious scale, because a low score on them indicates an ability to deal with the self-denigration which is so destructive a factor in depression.

The extent to which the three scales (tapping liability to depression, actual depressive symptoms and ability to handle some of the aggression denigration) support Freudian theory by discriminating depressives from normals and other psychiatric cases, must now be considered. The fact that the items of the unconscious depression scale were drawn from Freudian theory and that the scale can discriminate depressives must be regarded as good evidence for the theory — especially since the scale is distinct from a description of depressive *symptoms* (which could otherwise account for the discrimination of the scale). However, whether an item such as 'I very often get a gnawing feeling' taps loss of orally incorporated objects as unproven. Clearly therefore much more work needs to be done with these scales to establish their construct-validity.

Conclusions

These scales can discriminate depressives from normals and other neurotics. Their construction was based on the psychoanalytic theory of depression. This study, therefore, must be considered as supporting Freudian theory, although until further work is done with the scales the theory cannot be regarded as proven.

The work of Manchanda et al. (1979)

These authors studied thirty obsessional neurotics and thirty neurotic depressed controls, approximately half being males. These subjects were administered certain TAT pictures (1, 2, 3BM, 4, 6BM, 8BM and 13) together with Foulds' (Foulds et al., 1960) five punitive scales in a Hindi translation.

On the Foulds' scales, acting-out-hostility scales were higher among the obsessionals as they were on the TAT.

We do not wish to make too much of this study simply because the validity of the Hindi version of the Foulds' scales is as yet unproven and the TAT in India is certainly not a well-validated test. Despite these difficulties, the result is consonant with the psychoanalytic claim of underlying hostility in obsessional neurosis (Fenichel, 1945). This study cannot be taken as objective evidence for Freudian theory but it does suggest that a larger-scale, British replication could prove illuminating.

MALE PREGNANCY SYMPTOMS

The work of Munroe

Our description of this work is taken from Kline (1977) where the force of cross-cultural studies in the elucidation of psychoanalytic theory is fully discussed.

Munroe and colleagues have carried out a series of experiments into cross-sex identity. The research concerned the phenomenon of male pregnancy symptoms and its relation to cross-sex identification — positive in Freudian theory. Munroe and Munroe (1971) compared males with symptoms and controls in three societies — Boston in the United States, the Black Caribs of British Honduras and the Logoli of Kenya. The hypothesis was that males with symptoms would show, on measures of sex identity, female or ex-aggeratedly male responses. It was also considered likely that the symptom group would have had less contact with males (as models) during childhood. The hypotheses were supported in the Boston group (twenty-six with symptoms and thirty controls) where measures of sexual identity were: Franck drawing-completion test, Gough brief scale of femininity, semantic-differential descriptions of family roles, concealed-figures test and a questionnaire on interest, activities and early background. On overt measures the experimental group was exaggeratedly masculine but feminine on the covert measures.

In the Black Carib different experimental procedures had to be adopted. In this group couvade is common, a custom which would apparently reflect strong cross-sex identity in itself. Certainly, as confirmation of the hypothesis, pregnancy symptoms among males are more common among the Caribs (90 per cent). Since the Franck test was not suitable for this sample and since so high a proportion of the sample showed symptoms, rhos were computed between intensity of symptoms and couvade practices, baby care, family-role description, sex-role preferences, early experience and exaggerated masculinity as measured in ratings for bravery, drinking and wife-beating. In fact the symptoms were associated with indices of exaggerated masculinity — cursing, wife-beating, drinking and gambling. Practising the couvade was also related. Similar findings were obtained in the third society, the Logoli, where thirteen of the twenty males examined showed symptoms. These findings were replicated in a small sample of the Luo (Kenya) and the Gusii (Munroe and Munroe, 1973).

This link in five societies of male pregnancy symptoms (and couvade where appropriate) with cross-sex identity would be good evidence for psychoanalytic theory which was derived from a Viennese neurotic sample if the validity of the measures were better attested. Of course, although the validity of the tests is not overwhelming, the results still have to be explained and even on an intuitive basis alone the results are not unconvincing. These studies seem to us to offer reasonable support for psychoanalytic theory, for it must be remembered that many of the variables are factual, e.g. wife-beating and drinking, and the test variables are by no means as subjective in nature as Rorschach or TAT responses. In brief these investigations are reasonable, albeit imperfect, support for the psychoanalytic theory relating to couvade and the symptoms of male pregnancy.

THE WORK OF SILVERMAN AND COLLEAGUES

In our chapter on defence mechanisms we described the experimental technique used by Silverman in some detail. As we there pointed out it was a variant of perceptual-defence studies, one specially adapted for the investigation of psychoanalytic dynamic hypotheses.

The basis of the method, it will be recalled, is the manipulation of an unconscious wish followed by the observation of the consequences of the manipulation on psychopathology. Great care is taken to ensure that the wish does not become conscious because if it does, in psychoanalytic theory, very different consequences would ensue and, of course, unconscious wishes are at the root of much psychopathology according to Freudian theory. While this method is ideally suited to the study of defences, it has in fact been most widely used by Silverman in the study of psychopathology and we shall now review the results of his experiments. Our discussion is based upon Silverman's (1976) paper entitled 'Psychoanalytic Theory: "The reports of my death are greatly exaggerated"', together with a few more recent studies.

Silverman divides the experiments into two groups: (a) those designed to stir up unconscious conflict and thereby increase psychopathology, and (b) those designed to diminish unconscious conflict and decrease psychopathology.

Experiments that increase pathology

1. *Primary-process ego pathology* — illogical, loose or unrealistic thinking, inappropriate or intensive overt behaviour. In sixteen experiments with a total sample of more than 400 schizophrenic subjects, aggressive subliminal stimuli produced an intensification of ego pathology as measured on a variety of psychological tests. Typical stimuli were a lion charging, a snarling man with a dagger or a message, cannibal eats person. Neutral control stimuli, e.g. a man reading a paper, produced no effect. It has also been shown by Lomangiro (1969) that among schizophrenics it is orally aggressive stimuli that produce the effects as distinct from simply aggressive stimuli.

2. *Depression*. Here the studies investigated the claim that depression involved turning unconscious aggressive wishes against the self. Three studies investigated this claim (on depressed women patients) on college students with depressive trends and on a group of young adults who had lost a parent in childhood. In all cases depression, as measured by self-ratings on mood and affect-rating scales, was increased by stimuli designed to stir up aggressive wishes. Neutral stimuli produced no effects.

3. *Homosexuality*. We have already described this study (Silverman et al., 1973) in which an incest-related stimulus produced an increase in homosexual feelings as measured by a rating scale in two samples of homosexuals.

4. *Stuttering*. Here stutterers were shown a subliminal anal stimulus as well as control stimuli and in accord with psychoanalytic theory the anal stimulation produced an increase in stuttering as judged by raters who listened (ignorant of the experimental conditions) to samples of speech.

A final important point about these studies is made by Silverman (1976), namely that while these results support psychoanalytic theorizing it could be argued that it is not their specific content producing the changes rather the generally negative affective quality of the stimuli. However, a recent study is quoted by Silverman who shows that while incest increased psychopathology for homosexuals it did not do so for the groups for whom incest was an irrelevant stimulus. Similar stimulus-specific results were found for schizophrenics, stutterers and depressives.

Comments on these experiments

These experiments do demonstrate that the activation of an unconscious wish increases psychopathology and that the wish is as specific as is hypothesized in psychoanalytic theory. Thus the whole set must constitute striking evidence for aspects of the Freudian theory of neurosis that would appear to be extremely difficult to test. However we have two reservations about these experiments.

(a) *The activation of the unconscious wish.* It is still only an assumption that the subliminal stimuli did activate an unconscious wish. Certainly compared with the neutral stimuli the effect expected was noted. However suppose instead of 'Fuck Mommy' just 'Fuck' or 'Fuck Daddy' had been exposed, what then would the results have been? Even if this objection is accepted, the results are still impressive inasmuch as only psychoanalytic theory would link the subliminal perception of such stimuli to such specific psychopathology.

(b) *Measurement of psychopathology.* This is, in our view, the weakest aspect of these experiments, especially those concerned with psychopathology in the schizophrenic where the Rorschach, word-associations and story-recall tests are used (Silverman, 1971). These tests are of dubious validity as we have argued throughout this book. The rating scales and mood scales have greater face-validity and are not as problematic, although their validity is far from certain. The stuttering measure is, however, impeccable.

Despite these reservations, this set of experiments must be regarded as impressive evidence for the claim that the unconscious wish affects psychopathology.

Experiments that decrease pathology

In this work, the clinical hypothesis of analysts that the unconscious fantasy of symbiotic gratification reduces psychopathology in schizophrenics (e.g. Searles, 1965) was put to the test. In seven investigations where a total of more than 200 schizophrenics was tested, this hypothesis has been confirmed, the method being identical to that previously described and the symbiotic subliminal stimulus being 'Mommy and I are one', together with a picture of them merged as Siamese twins. A neutral subliminal stimulus and a supraliminal presentation of the symbiotic stimulus produced no effect.

Again these experiments support psychoanalytic notions implicating unconscious libidinal wishes in psychopathology, although similar reservations about the measurement of such psychopathology to those mentioned in connection with the first group of experiments apply here.

One of the purposes of this book, reviewing attempts to put psychoanalytic theory to the experimental test, is not only to demonstrate that this can be done and that some parts of the theory do have experimental support, in addition it is hoped that psychoanalytic theory can be extended and amplified by experiment, a point made by Silverman in connection with these experiments. The psychodynamic activation method can be used to explore and modify some of these psychoanalytic hypotheses. As an example, Silverman cites the work of Kaye (1975) who examined the effects not only of 'Mommy and I are one' compared with a neutral stimulus but also of 'Daddy and I are one' and 'My girl and I are one'. Interestingly, this last subliminal stimulus decreased pathology to a greater extent than the original, while 'Daddy and I are one' had no effect. This result is interpreted by Silverman thus: it is less threatening to merge with a mother-figure (my girl) than mother herself because the latter threatens incest and engulfment. Whether this be so or not, this study by Kaye (1975) exemplifies how Silverman's technique can be used to extend and modify experimentally these psychoanalytic hypotheses.

In summary then the work of Silverman and colleagues supports the implication of libidinal wishes in schizophrenia, depression, homosexuality and stuttering, such as is hypothesized in psychoanalytic theory. There is little doubt, furthermore, that the method has wide application in the experimental verification and modification of psychoanalytic theory.

Finally, in connection with this work it should be pointed out that Silverman (1980) has collated fifty-three studies done in laboratories other than his own in which his subliminal activation technique was used. All but seven confirmed psychoanalytic theory. Readers must be referred to this paper for detailed references to this work, most of which are unpublished theses. Nevertheless, such confirmation is hopeful even though, as yet, most of the investigators are not well-established figures.

The work of Reyher and colleagues (e.g. Reyher, 1967)

In his 1976 paper Silverman also describes the work of Reyher and colleagues at Michigan University which is complementary to his own and we shall scrutinize these experiments.

Reyher uses normal subjects and activates unconscious libidinal wishes by the implanting of false memories through hypnosis (paramnesia). Then the post-hypnotic suggestion is made that sexual or aggressive feelings related to the paramnesia will become aroused, when words associated with the paramnesia are mentioned, followed by an impulse to express these feelings. Subjects are awakened, presented with a series of words (of which some are paramnesiac) and asked after each word 'How are you doing?' Reactions to this are scored for appearance, type and intensity of symptoms.

Results

In each of the seven studies reported by Reyher and colleagues, a large number of symptoms were reported by the great majority of hypnotized subjects (> 75 per cent) in whom paramnesias were implanted. Symptoms include: ANS disturbances (e.g. nausea, sweating), disturbances of somatic and muscular structures (e.g. tremors, pains), disturbances of affect (guilt, disgust), states of confusion and dissociative reactions (e.g. limbs feeling detached).

Control subjects who either responded to non-paramnesiac words or went through the same procedures but were not hypnotized produced far fewer symptoms than the experimental subjects.

Comments

Silverman argues that these studies complement his own in that by a different method the same results have been discovered, namely that libidinal wishes that are unconscious do produce psychopathology. It is noteworthy that guilt seems to be an important component or concomitant of the libidinal wish for in those few studies where the paramnesia did not also stir up guilt, then few symptoms were found. Of course a control experiment is necessary here to investigate whether guilt alone, rather than wishes plus guilt, could produce increased symptomatology.

These results fit psychoanalytic theory in that various additional implications of the theory were supported. For example, where the wishes become conscious (as they did by verbal report in six subjects) symptoms disappeared.

Furthermore, subjects who responded to the question 'How are you doing?' with poor defences, i.e. gave many wish-derivatives, also showed more symptoms. Of course we must point out here that those who responded thus actually produced more words and thus were likely to produce more symptoms perhaps for this reason alone. This claim by Silverman, therefore, that poor defences thus measured were correlated with symptomatology must be treated cautiously.

Finally, since the psychoanalytic theory claims that unconscious libidinal wishes can generate symptoms, it is to be noted that these Michigan studies used normal subjects who in the main had never shown such symptoms before.

In brief then these hypnotic induction studies would seem to support the central formulation of psychoanalytic theory implicating unconscious libidinal wishes and guilt in psychopathology.

Before leaving the work of Reyher, there is one aspect of the experimental design that seems to us less than satisfactory, although Silverman does not mention it. This concerns the post-hypnotic suggestion that the patient will become aroused. Since he does become aroused, it is fair to attribute the arousal to the suggestion rather than the paramnesia. What seems to be required here is an experiment in which post-hypnotic suggestions are made without previous implantation of paramnesias. Without these, this work seems to us still somewhat equivocal, although the control condition of the non-paramnesiac word goes some way to meet this objection.

Conclusions

The work of Silverman and colleagues does give confirmation of a central tenet of psychoanalytic theory implicating unconscious libidinal wishes in psychopathology. The work of Reyher also provides confirmation although here the results are still open to other possible, if less likely, interpretations.

For ease of continuity we have not referred separately to all the studies of Silverman and Reyher. However, references to these are to be found in the full list of references at the end of the book.

PERCEPT-GENETIC STUDIES RELEVANT TO MENTAL DISTURBANCES AND PSYCHOSOMATIC PROBLEMS

Although percept-genetic methods have been widely used with neurotic and other clinical psychiatric groups, often the results have been of no great import for the validation of psychoanalytic hypotheses, being rather designed as tests of the adequacy of the perceptual genetic methods. Inasmuch as the results have supported the operationalization of, say, defence mechanisms, as in the DMT, they must be regarded as confirmation of psychoanalytic theory, but often the samples are too small for broad generalizations to be made from them (e.g. Westerlundh, 1976). Rather, then, such results confirm psychoanalytic theorizing about defence mechanisms (which is why our main discussion of percept-genetics may be found in that chapter). Some investigations, however, are more relevant to neuroses and other disturbances and we shall examine these below. We shall not describe the percept-genetic method, its rationale or its justification, since that has already been done in Chapter 8. Here we shall concentrate on the relevant substantive findings.

Kragh and Smith (1970) report a study using the Meta-contrast technique and the serial Colour—Word Test together with some questionnaire measures with twenty-four student subjects showing symptoms of obsession, phobia, anxiety neurosis and sensitivity. The percept-genetic methods were able to discriminate between the groups in terms of the defences hypothesized as likely to do so in psychoanalytic theory. However, the validity of these measures of defence is attested by precisely this evidence that they can discriminate nosological groups. Hence it is somewhat circular to use the same evidence as support for the psycho-analytic claims about such groups. Nevertheless this study is at least no refutation of psychoanalytic postulates concerning the typical defences used by subjects with different kinds of mental disturbances.

Similar results were obtained with endogenous and exogenous depressive patients and between patients classified as character or symptom neurotics by the psychiatrist in charge of them. Again, however, the same objection applies here that independent evidence other than this discrimination of the validity of the MCT and CTW defence measures is required.

In general there is little objective support for psychoanalytic theories of neurosis and psychoses from these clinical studies. There are several reasons for this:

1. The fact that percept-genetics is relatively new and a massive body of research has not yet been built up.

2. The tests have proved so useful in practice with their powerful discrimination of neurotic groups that for diagnostic purposes it is sufficient that they work.

Thus this lack of evidence is not attributable to the failure of percept-genetic techniques but to their utility in practice. Clearly studies are required deliberately to test specific psychoanalytic hypotheses and in general these have not yet been done.

CONCLUSIONS FROM ALL STUDIES OF FREUDIAN THEORIES OF NEUROSIS AND OTHER EMOTIONAL ABNORMALITIES

TABLE 10.2. *Summary of findings reported in this chapter*

Paranoid schizophrenia	*Support* for link with repressed homosexuality
Homosexuality	*No support* for importance of castration anxiety, except in the work of Silverman which was concerned more with Oedipal conflict
Asthma	*Almost no support*: vague implication of developmental difficulties
Peptic ulcer and colitis	*No support* for importance of oral and anal fixation
Stuttering	*No support* for importance of anal fixation except in the work of Silverman
Appendicitis	*Support* for relationship with birth fantasies
Anorexia nervosa	*Slight support* based on an experimental case study
Alcoholism	*Slight support* for importance of repressed homosexuality and orality
Smoking	*Slight support* for importance of orality
Phobias	*Some support* for separation and castration phobias
Depression	*Some support*

This summary makes it clear that attempts to impugn psychoanalytic theory in general are useless. Parts are supported, others are not. As should be clear from the discussions contained under the relevant headings, failure to find objective support may only mean that inadequate methods have been applied. Thus in paranoid schizophrenia experimental techniques have implicated repressed homosexuality. This has not been demonstrated in alcoholism where only questionnaire measures have been used.

The final conclusion is that more research must be devoted, in these areas, to explicit psychoanalytic hypotheses. At present, however, about half of those tested have been supported. The work of Silverman, percept-genetic methods and the hypnotic studies of Reyher seem particularly hopeful.

11

The effects of psychoanalytic therapy

Problems involved in the assessment of psychotherapeutic success

Since the study of the effects of any kind of psychotherapy involves considerable methodological problems and a large number of variables, it will be convenient to list these briefly before turning to a consideration of the empirical studies.

1. *Patient variables*. There is a tendency to consider patients as essentially homogeneous. Kiesler (1966) considers that the fallacy of patient-uniformity undermines the validity of many studies of the outcome of psychotherapeutic procedures.

2. *Therapist variables*. Meehl (1955) has pointed out the problems involved in assuming homogeneity among therapists just because they belong to the same school. These problems are essentially the same as those confronting educational research into the efficacy of different teaching methods. Clearly, in evaluating the outcome of any method of psychotherapy, a large number of practitioners must be used or else an analysis of variance-design accounting for differences between therapists should be drawn up. Possible solutions to the problems here discussed will be found below (p. 390).

3. *Criterion for success*. In psychological disorders there is no generally agreed fixed criterion for success — i.e. recovery of the patient. In medicine, for example, there would be a high reliability for assessing recovery from measles; in the case of obsessionality, on the other hand, there is no such agreement. This is particularly important in evaluating the success of psychoanalysis, especially as compared with therapies purportedly based on learning theory. In these, by theory, removal of the symptom is the aim. For psychoanalysts this could not in any way be regarded as a cure. Hence measurement of recovery is a vital problem in this area.

4. *The use of control groups*. Most researchers in this area regard a control group as a methodological *sine qua non* (e.g. Eysenck, 1960a, b; Cross 1964). This is obviously true when attempting to attribute the outcome of any procedure to that procedure. Normally a control group receives no treatment. Nevertheless the problems of matching control groups are well known and are especially acute in the matching of patients when psychiatric diagnosis is itself unreliable.

5. *Spontaneous remission*. Eysenck (1952, 1960a, b and 1965b), in view of the problems involving control groups, has used the concept of spontaneous remission from neurosis to form a baseline from which to judge the success of therapies. He points out (1952) that the studies of Landis (1937), who followed up

patients discharged from a custodial hospital where they received no psychotherapy, and of Denker (1947), who investigated patients treated by their own doctors, indicate that 70 per cent of neurotic patients get better of their own accord. Therefore therapists must show a significantly higher success rate than 70 per cent to claim success. Kiesler (1966), however, has denied the validity of this concept of spontaneous remission, as have numerous other writers. This will be fully discussed below (see p. 391).

In evaluating the outcome of psychotherapy the most basic of these problems is the *criterion for success*. As Malan (1959) points out, subjective methods of assessment such as improved/not improved are poor because they fail to do justice to quantitative differences. On the other hand many quantitative assessments fail to do justice to qualitative differences. In addition it should be stressed that the use of tests for assessing improvements due to treatment where scores before and after therapy are employed demands tests of very high test—retest reliability. This quality is notably lacking from the most popular clinical tests — the TAT and the Rorschach among projective tests (see Zubin et al., 1965), and the MMPI among psychometric tests.

Possible solutions

Kiesler (1966) makes explicit the implications of these problems — the solution by analysis of variance-design. *Main* factors would therefore be *types of patient* (hysterical, obsessional, etc.) and *school of therapy* (psychoanalysis, Rogerian, control group, etc.). However, account would be taken of individual differences between therapists within schools and between individuals. Such a design would yield interactions between types of patient and school of therapy.

However, such a design means that adequate measures of success, more sensitive than a rating scale, would have to be devised since the scores subjected to the analysis of variance would be 'improvement' scores on a number of criterion measures. In addition this solution needs, in toto, a number of adequately matched patients of each nosological category for each therapist in the study. The *practical* problems of this theoretically elegant solution are therefore considerable. Consideration of outcome or criterion scores alone without control of these factors is clearly inadequate, however. On account of these problems of sampling and measurement another approach has been adopted — examination of the therapeutic process itself.

STUDIES OF THE THERAPEUTIC PROCESS

Truax and his associates (e.g. Truax, 1963; Truax and Carkhuff, 1964), working with the concept of Constructive Personality Change (Rogers, 1957) which is the intended outcome of Rogerian psychotherapy, have been energetic workers in this field of examining the effects of the therapeutic process itself. Their work will be reviewed only briefly since it is mainly concerned with the work of Rogers. However it is relevant to psychoanalytic therapy in that as a *method* it can be applied to any psychotherapeutic procedure.

Constructive personality change — the intended outcome

This is measured by conventional psychological tests such as the F scale of the Authoritarian Personality (Adorno et al., 1950), the MMPI, the Rorschach and the TAT. This part of their approach is identical with the outcome studies and is subject to the same weaknesses of both unreliability and validity.

Therapist variables

Truax has measured, the *therapist's self-congruence, his unconditional positive regard for the patient,* and *his accurate empathy*. These measures were blind ratings from four main samples of taped therapeutic sessions. Again this involves the measurement problem of rating scales (e.g. Vernon, 1953).

Patient variables

From the same tape the patient's *depth of self-examination* is rated. All scores are then related to the criterion outcome scores.

From this it can be seen that although these particular variables are relevant to Rogerian rather than Freudian theory there is no intrinsic reason why a similar method could not be applied to psychoanalytic sessions. In addition this method also comes closer to the analysis-of-variance method of examining the outcome of therapy, which was suggested by Kiesler (1966) as an ideal solution in that the effects of therapist and patient differences are not assumed to be randomly distributed.

With this brief outline of the problems and advantages of both methods it will now be possible to evaluate the empirical studies which bear on the effectiveness of psychoanalytic therapy.

STUDIES OF THE OUTCOME OF PSYCHOANALYTIC THERAPY

THE WORK OF EYSENCK

Eysenck (1952, 1960a and 1965b) has launched three savage attacks on the effectiveness of all types of psychotherapy in general, except that based on learning theory. He is particularly severe on psychoanalytic therapy which he regards as worse than useless — in fact definitely deleterious to a patient's well-being. Since this view has become accepted in some quarters, the evidence quoted by Eysenck (1952) must be carefully examined.

Spontaneous remission

Eysenck, as has been previously noted, claimed that 70 per cent of the patients discharged from custodial care without treatment recovered. This figure was based on the study of Landis (1937). Denker (1947), following up patients on insurance company lists and treated by their own physicians (who were not, of course, psychiatrists), found a similar recovery rate. From these two studies Eysenck (1952) argued that 70 per cent of neurotic disorders therefore got better without treatment — spontaneous remission. Effective psychotherapy, therefore, must needs better this figure. This baseline of 70 per cent recovery was used because at this time there were no studies of psychotherapeutic success using control groups.

Eysenck's (1952) figures for the success of psychoanalytic therapy were based on five studies — Fenichel (1930), who reported on 484 cases; Kessel and Hyman (1933), who used 34 subjects; Jones (1936), 59 subjects; Alexander (1937), 141 subjects and Knight (1941), who used 42 cases. Eysenck thus had psychoanalytic success rates on a total sample of 760 cases — a not unimpressive figure. Of these 760 patients, 335 were rated by these authors as either cured, greatly improved or slightly improved — a 44 per cent success rate. In comparison with this, 64 per cent of patients treated eclectically were regarded as successes. The precise baseline rate was 72 per cent. Thus the more treatment given (for psychoanalytic treatment is the longest), the worse the results. The very low figure for psychoanalytic treatment is partly due to the fact that patients who broke off the lengthy treatment before completion were regarded as failures. If these are ignored, the success rate for psychoanalysis rises to 66 per cent or about the same as eclectic treatment.

Conclusions

Even if the improved rate for psychoanalysis (66 per cent) is accepted it is still worse than no treatment and the argument that the more prolonged the treatment the worse the result still holds. In addition, since there is a good chance that a patient will not complete his psychoanalytic therapy, on these figures it would not be possible to recommend psychoanalytic therapy. It could, indeed, be regarded as positively harmful.

Comments

This paper produced a flood of enraged protest from psychotherapists of all persuasions. If, as Eysenck (1965b) later claimed, the case was overstated to provoke research it must be considered a very successful paper. It would not be relevant to examine all the attempts to refute Eysenck and show that psychotherapy was effective. Two papers, however, those of Luborsky (1954) and Rosenzweig (1954) challenge the data for spontaneous remission and the consequent baseline for success. Since Rosenzweig's paper also contains many of the other objections raised in the refutatory papers, it must be carefully considered.

The comments on Eysenck's (1952) paper by Rosenzweig (1954)

Definition of neurosis and interpretation of results

In his 1952 paper Eysenck, for purposes of comparison, was forced to classify results under headings on a scale running from cured to discontinued and failed. Furthermore he only concerned himself with psychoneuroses. He therefore had to interpret the results given in the reports. Rosenzweig argues that this interpretation was idiosyncratic. For example, while Eysenck claims that there were 484 cases, the total number of cases in Fenichel's (1930) paper was, in fact, 604 — which is not a small discrepancy. Again, while Eysenck's interpretation of this report led to a success figure of only 39 per cent Landis (1937) interpreted the same results as a 58 per cent rate of success. In brief Rosenzweig considers that Eysenck has completely ignored the problem of the definition of a psychoneurosis.

Spontaneous remission

Rosenzweig argues that there is no evidence to gauge precisely how ill were the patients on the insurance company lists examined by Denker (1947). But he also suggests, with some justice, that in view of the fact that they only saw their own doctors and did not require hospitalization, they were probably less ill than the psychoanalytic patients. The patients studied by Landis, on the other hand, were probably more ill. However, their discharge from hospital was on totally different criteria from those employed by a psychoanalyst. Thus Landis (1937) writes that hospitalization yields 'sufficient improvement for favourable discharge' (quoted by Rosenzweig, 1954) whereas for Fenichel (1945) recovery was defined as a change entirely explicable by the psychoanalyst in terms of Freudian theory. Rosenzweig therefore claims that comparisons between the 'success' rates of two such groups, where success is so differently defined, is meaningless.

In addition, it is doubtful whether Denker's or Landis's patients were in fact untreated. Denker (1947) even admits that the patients were not so well treated as they would have been by expert eclectic psychiatrists.

Conclusions

The conclusions that follow from this paper are that the base rate of spontaneous remission so ingeniously derived by Eysenck is by no means so clear-cut as he would have us believe. This is due to the problems of working out a comparable figure for successful treatment by psychoanalysts and to the fact that the so-called 'untreated' patients were in fact treated. In addition, the criterion for recovery is so different from school to school of psychotherapy that comparison is not meaningful.

Comments

Even if, therefore, we agree with Kiesler (1966) that spontaneous remission is a myth propagated mainly by Eysenck, this in no way demonstrates the efficacy of psychoanalytic therapy. In summary, therefore, Eysenck (1952) has not entirely destroyed any rational belief in the efficacy of psychoanalytic therapy, although the process obviously still requires much research.

The work of Eysenck (1960a)

Eysenck (1960a) made a further review of studies of the success of psychotherapy. In this paper he concentrated on investigations which complied to some extent with the minimum requirements laid down by Meehl (1955) for the evaluation of psychotherapy. These are

(a) the use of a control group — a requirement which rules out the studies of psychoanalysis already mentioned,

(b) an objective and uncontaminated pre- and post-therapy evaluation, and

(c) follow-up evaluation.

Since, however, only one paper was thus rigorously designed he examined all those reports where control groups had been used. Because only one of the reports, that of Barron and Leary (1955), dealt with analytic therapy (psychoanalytically orientated) this paper is not as relevant to this chapter as the earlier work. Again Eysenck claimed that psychotherapy was not useful, with the exception of behaviour therapy as practised by Wolpe.

Similarly the latest review by Eysenck (1965b) is not concerned with psychoanalytic therapy. In conclusion these three papers by Eysenck demonstrate clearly that psychotherapy is by no means as efficient as its adherents would desire. They do not however, as has been stated, indicate that psychoanalytic therapy is useless.

OTHER REVIEWS OF PSYCHOANALYTIC THERAPY AND ITS OUTCOME

Because of the difficulties of matching different criteria of success, Malan (1959) has suggested that special criteria for psychoanalytic therapy should be set up — it being irrelevant that other schools of psychotherapy do not have similar objectives. He suggests nine basic principles for the evaluation of results:

1. True assessment depends on a knowledge of all the disturbances in a patient and the changes in each.

2. Disturbances may be subtle and unknown to the patient.

3. Such disturbances may be discovered only after psychodynamic hypotheses concerning the case have been drawn up.

4. The most important evidence must come from the patient's life (tests are only a supplement).

5. The point of breakdown is not usually the beginning of the illness. Therefore the baseline from which to assess recovery must be the health of the patient some time before breakdown.

6. The criteria which must be fulfilled for true resolution of the neurotic conflict must be stated.

7. These criteria should be laid down before treatment.

8. Results should be judged quantitatively in terms of these criteria.

9. Occurrences in therapy should not be allowed to override these criteria.

As Malan most fairly admits, this scheme of evaluation is similar to that advocated by Wallerstein et al. (1956). There are several points worthy of note about this method.

A scheme such as this obviates the crudity of attempting to rate recovery as successful or not, as Eysenck (1952) was compelled to do in his attempt to find overall rates of success for various schools of psychotherapy. It takes into account the patient-variable. Since, too, predictions dependent on theory are made, the therapist-variable becomes an error-variable since therapist-variance will destroy prediction. Thus some of the sources of error in outcome studies are taken into account.

On the debit side, however, it is not possible to compare any group with an untreated control group or with the therapeutic procedures of other schools. This scheme is an attempt to combine the best features of subjective assessment, since the outcome is strictly geared to each patient, and objective assessment, since quantification of results is suggested. The emphasis on life data is salutory. The example quoted by Malan refers to homosexuality in a boy, which appeared to be cured. However this could have been due merely to improved external conditions — he went to help his father in his work and thus gave up the Oedipal conflict. Only later behaviour could determine whether this was, therefore, true improvement.

Unfortunately, as with many of the studies to be examined in this chapter, the chief interest of this paper lies in its methodological possibilities rather than any practical results so far achieved with it. Yet even this is important. Up till now there have been no adequate studies of the effects of psychoanalytic therapy, perhaps indeed of any psychotherapy. Clearly, therefore, any potentially useful method of assessment deserves note, especially since psychoanalytic therapy may have been unfairly condemned as a result of inadequate methods.

Other reviews of the outcome of psychotherapy add little relevant to a study of psychoanalytic therapy mainly because of the shortage of quantified reports using control groups (e.g. Cross, 1964). Indeed, Fox (1961) makes the point that there is a strong negative correlation between the rigour of the research design in reports of the effects of psychotherapy and positive, favourable results.

Fisher and Greenberg (1977) in their study of the effectiveness of psychoanalytic therapy agree with our conclusions and like us they were unable to find any studies that could be unequivocally interpreted, because their basic design was not sound. They cite six studies which despite their flaws all show consistent results — that psychoanalytic therapy does have some effect but no firm conclusions can be drawn, except perhaps in one case (Duhrssen and Jorswiek, 1965).

Orgel (1958) found that treatment of ten ulcer patients who had long histories of the complaint produced remission as far as twenty-two years after treatment. There was, however, no control group and it is possible that remission would have occurred *sua sponte*.

Cappon (1964) followed up 200 patients twenty months after a six-month treatment. Self-ratings and patient-ratings of improvement and the loss of at least one presenting symptom showed that about 75 per cent of patients had improved. After twenty months the relapse rate was about 10 per cent. Again, however, without a control group the study is not powerful.

A similar objection can be launched at the investigation by Schjelderup (1955) and we shall not therefore discuss it here. However, Fisher and Greenberg (1977) cite a study by Duhrssen and Jorswiek which compared 125 patients undergoing psychoanalytic therapy with 100 patients on the waiting list, and 100 people selected from the records of the Berlin Department of Social Medicine. The measure used for the three groups was rate of hospitalization.

The two patient groups did not differ on this variable preceding therapy but were higher than the normal control group. Following treatment the therapy group had a significant decrease in hospitalization; there were no changes in the other groups. This study does seem to show that long-term psychoanalysis improves chronically neurotic patients and days of hospitalization is a good objective index. It is one small piece of evidence that psychoanalytic therapy can produce improvement.

Fisher and Greenberg (1977) cite a study by O'Connor et al. (1964) of ulcerative colitis patients who were compared with controls (untreated colitis patients). This investigation seems typical of the confused research in this area since the treated group consisted of patients undergoing different types of therapy and had a higher proportion of schizophrenics than the controls. In addition no statistical analyses of the results were made. The only conclusion from such a study is that no firm conclusions can be drawn.

Finally, Fisher and Greenberg cite a study by Barendregt et al. (1961) who compared the results of psychoanalysis of forty-seven patients and a control group of seventy-four patients on the waiting list or advised not to take therapy. This last means that some of the control group were not comparable with the patients.

The only change rate in a variety of measures of dubious validity (e.g. Rorschach and TAT indices) was a change in the lie scores of a personality questionnaire. This does not seem powerful evidence and, given the problem of unmatched controls and the fact that the therapists in this study were novices (it was a training institute), again no conclusions can be drawn.

These six studies cited by Fisher and Greenberg truly clarify our point that such investigations are almost worthless. Thus those studies where only one therapist was used cannot form a basis for statements about psychoanalytic therapy: strictly only the effectiveness of the therapist is measured. Without control groups nothing can be said about any changes noted after treatment. Where control groups are ill-matched the same applies. Again we have to be certain the measures are valid and relevant.

With all these points in mind, one study only emerges as of any value, that of Duhrssen and Jorswiek who have shown that psychoanalysis decreases subsequent rates of hospitalization. This is a modest confirmation that there was some effect (in this study at least) of psychoanalytic therapy.

Fisher and Greenberg (1977) also have a considerable section reviewing investigations which compare psychoanalysis with other therapies. As with the previous experiments, however, much of this research is vitiated by faults so severe as to render its scientific value low.

Cartwright (1966) compared psychoanalytic treatment with three other therapies. However, there were only four patients and four therapists. No generalizations could conceivably be drawn from this investigation which is described by Fisher and Greenberg as 'one of the most well-controlled studies in the literature'.

A study by Heine (1953) is cited by Fisher and Greenberg with eight patients in client-centred, Adlerian and psychoanalytic therapies. The measures used were statements which patients had to categorize as true of them or not. The validity of these measures is quite unknown and samples of eight are clearly insufficient. Again, this study is not powerful.

Indeed, the other researches cited by Fisher and Greenberg (1977) are little better so we shall simply list them and the faults in design which infirm their conclusions (see Table 11.1).

TABLE 11.1. *Summary of outcome studies*

Investigation	Design flaws
Cremerius (1962)	Patients in analytic treatment were different from those in other therapies
Ellis (1957)	Three different therapies compared but all conducted by Ellis himself thus making generalization impossible
Dudek (1970)	Measure of change Rorschach indices of dubious validity
Weber et al. (1966, 1967)	Patients in analysis not comparable with patients in other group
Kernberg (1973)	Patients in analysis were compared with patients in analytically oriented therapy. Measures were ratings of case material made by clinicians and are of unknown validity and patient groups were not the same
Heilbrunn (1963, 1966)	Studies of his own patients. Hence no generalizations are possible

From Table 11.1 it can be seen that Fisher and Greenberg in their detailed and extensive survey of the outcome of psychoanalytic therapy can find only one study (that of Duhrssen and Jorswiek, 1965) sufficiently soundly designed for any conclusions to be drawn.

Finally, the work of Mintz et al. (1979) should be briefly discussed, a report on the Penn psychotherapy project in which seventy-three patients were studied over five years. They found that there was some agreement even among therapists of different viewpoints about therapeutic outcome, a finding contrary to most studies of this kind. They also found that post-treatment ratings (by patients and therapists) of benefit were correlated with changes in adjustment scores after therapy. This gives some support for the use of such measures in the study of psychotherapeutic outcome, and this study may prove of methodological use for future research into the outcome of psychoanalytic therapy.

SUMMARY OF STUDIES OF THE OUTCOME OF PSYCHOANALYTIC THERAPY

Since in this book we have attempted to examine the objective scientific evidence pertaining to psychoanalysis, in this chapter we have inevitably been highly restricted in the reports that could be considered. Studies of the outcome of psychoanalytic therapy where even the minimum standards of methodology, using control groups and quantification of results (as suggested by Meehl, 1955), are satisfied simply do not exist. This is the reason why Eysenck's (1952) paper is so important: with great ingenuity he manages to impose a crude quantification on psychoanalytic results and to produce instead of a control group a baseline of minimum performance. Unfortunately, as Rosenzweig (1954) has made clear, neither the quantification nor the concept of spontaneous remission really stands critical examination. Malan's (1959) study is important in that it suggests a possible method for evaluating the outcome, which takes into account some of the variables which are known to affect it. Thus then the net result of the studies of the outcome of psychoanalytic therapy is very small and little is yet known about its efficiency.

INVESTIGATION OF THE THERAPEUTIC EFFECTS OF PSYCHOANALYSIS ON HOMOSEXUALITY

The work of Bieber et al. (1962)

This study has already been discussed (see p. 345) in connection with the psychoanalytic theory of homosexuality. The follow-up results are of great interest, since they indicate that therapy may be successful.

Results

Of the 106 patients,

(a) Twenty-nine (27 per cent) became exclusively heterosexual. 19 per cent of the exclusively homosexual patients achieved this change and 50 per cent of the bisexual patients.

(b) The longer the treatment, the more likely was this change to exclusive heterosexuality to come about.

(c) Objective factors for a favourable prognosis were: bisexuality of patient, length of analysis and early age at beginning of analysis (before thirty-five years). Important also was the desire to become heterosexual. Other favourable indicators, which can be regarded as non-objective because they reflect only the analyst's opinion (e.g. patient idolizes women), will not be discussed since the adequacy of the data based on analysts' reports is doubtful. This data problem has been discussed in the previous chapter.

(d) Factors which appeared unimportant for prognosis were the sex of the analyst, his theoretical orientation and the psychiatric diagnosis of the patient.

Comments

If we put value judgements aside and regard as a criterion of success the attainment by a homosexual of heterosexual activity, then the figure of 27 per cent is certainly larger than other comparable success rates. Thus Woodward (1958) reports that only 7 out of 113 cases at the Portman Clinic showed an absence of homosexual inclination and increased heterosexual activity while Curran and Parr (1957) present a similarly low success rate. Indeed the Wolfenden Report (1957) appeared to accept the impossibility of such changes.

It must be noted, however, that these figures were gathered by the analysts at the *end of treatment*, so this study does not tell us how long these new sexual inclinations continued. Furthermore, there was no control group for this part of the study. The control group was used only to compare the attributes of homosexuals. For the investigation of therapeutic success a different control group (consisting of untreated homosexuals of whom some wish to change) is necessary. Nevertheless this lack of control group is not as important as it might at first appear since the subjects can, to a certain extent, serve as their own controls. An examination of their previous sexual history shows that no similar exclusively heterosexual behaviour had occurred. In addition, other studies of homosexuals (e.g. Woodward, 1958) indicate that such changes in sexual orientation are not normal events.

Conclusions

This study by Bieber demonstrates that long periods of analytic therapy can change the homosexual behaviour of some patients who want to become heterosexual. The success rate at termination of therapy was higher than in comparable studies. But before any firm conclusions could be drawn, long-term evaluation and study of a comparable untreated group would be necessary.

The work of Meyer (1966)

Meyer attempted to show that the success rate achieved by Bieber et al. with their homosexual sample was superior to that with behaviour therapy — as reported by Freund (1960) in Eysenck (1960b). Meyer frankly admits, however, that there were differences in the two samples and that the method used by Freund was not perhaps the most efficient for the treatment of homosexuality. A Chi-square analysis of success and type of treatment demonstrates that psychoanalysis was significantly better than behaviour therapy. An important difference in the two samples was their motivation to become heterosexual. Freund's sample was certainly less motivated, a fact which could well account for the resulting inferiority of his therapy.

STUDIES OF THE THERAPEUTIC PROCESS ITSELF

The problems involved in making a judgement about the outcome alone of psychotherapy have already been indicated. The main one is probably the criterion of success to be adopted. This is peculiarly difficult for psychoanalysis since the criterion of change explicable in terms of Freudian theory is hardly comparable with that of other schools. It also means that control groups cannot be used for comparison. This is, of course, because untreated groups could not possibly be assessed in terms of such dynamic changes. The use of control groups is also difficult. Most psychiatrists would regard the assignment of a patient to an untreated control group as unethical although Eysenck (1960a) argues that this view presupposes (contrary to evidence) that there is some value in psychotherapy. However, the use of patients on a waiting list as controls (e.g. Rogers and Dymond, 1954) is more acceptable unless the treatment, as in psychoanalysis, is prolonged. All the normal control-group problems of matching still exist even if a group can be obtained.

For all these reasons, therefore, interest has turned among a number of investigators towards a study of the psychotherapeutic process. Very influential in research in this area is the work of Truax.

STUDIES BY TRUAX

As was stated above (p. 390), only a brief mention of this work will be made since it is specific to the psychotherapeutic concepts of Rogers (1957) in his school of non-directive therapy. That it is discussed at all is due to the fact that, in theory at least, the methodology could be applied to the study of psychoanalytic therapy.

Brief summary of findings

Truax (1963), studying recorded samples of psychotherapeutic sessions with fourteen schizophrenic patients, found that therapists who were rated high for positive regard for patients, empathy and congruence produced improvements in their patients whereas therapists rated low on these variables produced deterioration. This means that the quality of therapist is a vital matter in the psychotherapeutic process.

Comments and conclusions

The importance of this result, especially with reference to the general findings concerning the outcome of psychotherapy as propounded by Eysenck (1952, 1960a and 1965b) — that psychotherapy is not useful — cannot be missed. The failure of psychotherapy to produce results may be due to the fact that some patients improve and others deteriorate — thus cancelling out the effects; this is what occurred in Truax's study. His control group was the same as his experimental group on the criterion scores — but the variance of the experimental was significantly larger. This is a further argument against the first method of examining the overall results of psychotherapy. Bergin (1963) quotes the study of Cartwright et al. (1960) who used an own-control design where patients had matched periods of therapy and no therapy. Again there was no significant difference in mean score on the criterion-variables but the variance in the experimental sessions was greater.

It must be concluded therefore that in this type of therapy, at least, and with schizophrenic patients, the quality of the therapist is a major factor in the results. A bad therapist may do harm. Certainly studies of effects of psychotherapy with the therapist-variable uncontrolled are of doubtful value.

A weakness of these studies, from the viewpoint of their application to psychoanalytic therapy, resides in the nature of the criterion-variables which are scores on the MMPI and the TAT test (among other similar scales) none of which is suitable for the assessment of psychoanalytic therapy.

Nevertheless, this method of studying the process of the therapeutic session as well as the outcome is clearly applicable, in principle, to psychoanalytic sessions and studies of these will now be examined.

The work of Bellak (Bellak, 1958; Bellak and Smith, 1956)

These two papers will be discussed together since the 1958 article is in effect a summary of the earlier paper.

Method. Psychoanalytic sessions were recorded. Two psychoanalysts then made independent judgements on what had occurred while two other psychoanalysts made independent predictions of the next psychoanalytic hour. Statistical comparisons of agreement and disagreement were then made. In this way, according to Bellak (1958), psychoanalysis becomes a public event (in the sense that the term is used in the philosophy of science).

Patients and judges. Two patients were recorded for fifty sessions: two analysts made predictions and two analysts made judgements of the tapes. Predictors and judges were continuously swopped around. Every four weeks correlations were computed between judgements and predictions.

Results. On many variables there were good correlations (tetrachoric). This means, according to Bellak (1958), that there is good agreement as to how five analysts describe in psychoanalytic language the psychodynamics of a patient.

Examples of variables considered. Positive transference, oral striving, homosexuality, repression and projection. For each of these variables the judges had to indicate presence or absence in both conscious and unconscious form. The judges of the recorded session indicated the present status of these variables. Those predicting the analytic sessions indicated their status, for the next hour, the next week and the next month. In addition, multiple-choice questionnaires were used to elucidate the themes of the sessions.

Advantages of the method. According to Bellak there are numerous advantages in studying the psychoanalytic process by this method.

1. *There is no need of control groups.* This is clearly true since all that is being attempted is the prediction of behaviour from psychoanalytic theory. If behaviour as specific as that shown in the analytic hour can be predicted, then it must be regarded as support for the theory.

2. *No criterion needed for success.* This is again the case because the investigation involves the prediction of behaviour. At the end of the treatment it could well

be possible to say whether the outcome (predicted or not) was an improvement or deterioration, but that would not affect the study of the process itself. Thus, unlike the work of Truax (1963), which studies the process of psychotherapy in relation to the success, Bellak studies the process only — attempting to predict its course.

3. *The long duration of the investigation.* Bellak attempts to argue that this makes spontaneous remission irrelevant. However, since we have shown that spontaneous remission refers only to recovery due to treatment by non-psychiatrists this point does not seem particularly important. It could be claimed, however, that spontaneous remission, if it occurred, would be noted in the Bellak method by failure to predict behaviour in the analytic hour.

4. *One case can be the population under investigation.* This is important from the practical point of view since it is often difficult to gather sufficiently large and homogeneous samples of patients for convincing statistical analysis. Repeated observations on one case are respectable psychometrically and form the basis of P factor-analysis — the technique advocated by Cattell (1957) for the investigation of clinical and psychiatric problems.

5. *The judges are psychoanalysts.* This is important in the study of psychoanalysis, since the objective validation of psychoanalytic concepts by psychologists is frequently subjected to criticism by psychoanalysts on the grounds that the psychologists have misapplied or misunderstood the theory. Since judgements and predictions, in the Bellak method, are by psychoanalysts this argument (which is irrefutable, if unfair) no longer obtains.

6. *Whole behaviours are examined.* Tests and rating scales are usually only samples of the behaviour we wish to measure as in, say, an individual intelligence test, such as the WAIS. Sometimes indeed they are correlates of such behaviour: an example of these would be the objective tests of Cattell (Cattell and Warburton, 1967). Other tests such as the MMPI are merely self-reports of behaviour. Clearly therefore examination of the actual behaviour during the session, if quantified and specified, is superior to any of the above methods. Bellak's scheme of short-term prediction allows for this last type of observation.

7. *Such a scheme of short-term prediction can be used to evaluate any interaction.* It would be possible to compare other schools of psychotherapy in this way. Those where predictions were never verified could be dismissed as worthless.

Comments

Bellak believes that this method of short-term prediction is the best way of validating psychoanalytic therapy and theory. Indeed, this claim is reiterated in a later paper (Bellak, 1961). If the method is looked at with the problems outlined at the beginning of this chapter in mind, it will be seen that it obviates many of the difficulties. The patient and therapist variables are both taken into account. The necessity of finding adequate control groups is removed as is the problem of spontaneous remission. The criterion of success does not have to be defined in this evaluation of psychoanalysis. However, this is probably its weakest point.

After all, logically it is possible to predict an interminable number of sessions in which deterioration or no improvement occurred. In this case the method would appear to validate psychoanalytic theory in that predictions would be supported and agreement noted among judges. However, this objection is more theoretical than real since psychoanalytic theory normally predicts success, for the psychoanalytic session, as a therapeutic method, is based on psychoanalytic theory.

Is short-term prediction a method of verifying psychoanalytic theory? Bellak claims that it is possible to validate psychoanalytic theory in the true scientific fashion by using this method. His grounds are that prediction of events is the standard scientific test for theory; hence the ability to predict the content of psychoanalytic sessions must support psychoanalytic theory. This is especially true when the fact that each prediction, entered on the prediction sheet for each session, must be supported by theory — to obviate accurate guessing through insight into the particular method of the analyst conducting the case.

Certainly the results obtained by Bellak and Smith (1956) indicate that a good part of the psychoanalytic sessions could be predicted from the theory. However, to say that such predictions, even when based on theory, support the theory is to ignore other explanation of such results. For instance, if the analyst concerned were in fact reinforcing certain verbalizations of the patient (the Greenspoon effect, Greenspoon, 1955) the judges could well predict that other similar points would be reinforced. The flexibility of Freudian theory is such that experts in it would find little difficulty in using it to support their predictions. Again experts in psychoanalytic theory could use it to support insights that came from clinical intuition of the interaction recorded between patient and therapist.

Conclusions

It seems to this author, therefore, that the study by Bellak (1958) is impressive support for Freudian theory although other *ad hoc* hypotheses can be adduced to account for the results. The actual results in this study with two patients are clearly not extensive enough to accept or reject psychoanalytic therapy. As so often, therefore, it must be concluded that more research needs to be done. Nevertheless, as a method of investigating psychoanalytic therapy this seems to be most promising.

The work of Knapp (1963)

Knapp also reports the results of 600 short-term predictions of behaviour during therapy for four patients undergoing psychoanalysis, and for several patients in psychotherapy.

Method. The predictions were made by Knapp, who also carried out the psychotherapy, and by an independent collaborator. Sessions were recorded on tape. Predictions were classified as *verified, wrong* or *no evidence*.

Results. As Knapp points out, the mathematical distribution of outcomes was unclear — a fact which made statistical analysis difficult. Nevertheless he concludes that with all patients there was a better-than-chance prediction of events.

Examples of predictions

Prediction: Patient will be depressed before next session.

Outcome: Patient reports that she felt her life had been wasted. Prediction was verified.

Prediction: Patient would arrive between 10-20 minutes late for session.

Outcome: Patient arrives 12 minutes late. Prediction was again verified.

Some predictions were even made during the analytic hour and were not written down but recorded in the mind. These were, however, a minority.

Comments

This study by Knapp, although interesting, is far less rigorous than that reported by Bellak (1958) and is consequently less impressive evidence for psychoanalytic theory than the previous work. The main weakness lies in the fact that Knapp himself was taking the psychoanalytic sessions and making the predictions. This kind of experimenter-contamination can clearly lead to all kinds of experimental bias (Rosenthal, 1964) of which the Greenspoon effect, already mentioned in connection with the work of Bellak, is but one example. Furthermore, in this study it is difficult to separate predictions based on clinical insight from those derived from Freudian theory.

Conclusions

The methodology of this investigation is not rigorous enough to use it as evidence for or against Freudian theory. It is, however, worthy of note, in that it exemplifies how a study of the psychotherapeutic process itself could lead to a verification of psychoanalytic claims.

WORK ON THE PSYCHOANALYTIC PROCESS AT THE UNIVERSITY OF ULM

At Ulm there has been a considerable research effort into the psychoanalytic process under the leadership of Thoma and Grunzig. This work is far too lengthy to describe in its entirety and not all of it is relevant to our purposes. One paper, however (Grunzig, 1977), effectively summarizes the aspects of the work which bear on the problem of the validation of psychoanalytic therapy and we shall discuss this here. It should be pointed out that the interest here for us lies not in the results but the potential of the method which the research at Ulm will shortly, it is hoped, realize.

In this work, psychoanalytic sessions are subjected to content-analysis by computer. The aim is to avoid the almost hopeless task of rating clinical material using expert raters (time-consuming and not always reliable) by programming the computer to make these judgements using the text characteristics that lead the clinical rater to his judgement. It is, therefore, an automatic clinical rating procedure. What was done in these studies was to have psychoanalysts and other experts just classify forty-one patient-statements into four psychoanalytic concepts of anxiety — shame, castration, guilt and separation. Then three questions were asked:

1. Could the statements be classified into these groups by text characteristics alone?
2. If so, what are the intrinsic characteristics by which the classifications are made and how are they related to psychoanalytic theory?
3. Is it possible to validate the characteristics by applying them to a new set of statements?

It was assumed that clinical judgements are made through a linear additive model.

$$Y_j = \sum_{i=1}^{t} c_{ij} X_i + k_j$$

j Group index (j = 1, 2, 3, 4)
t Number of variables included
c_{ij} Weight for variable i in group j
X_i Observed value of variable i
k_j Constant in group j

The test of this model (essentially working out the weights the clinician applies to each variable intuitively) is to see by applying it to clinical statements whether it is possible automatically to classify the statements as do the clinicians and whether by cross-validation on new statements these weightings still allow accurate judgements to be made. In fact this has been done and it does appear possible to classify automatically extracts from psychoanalytic sessions at least into the four anxiety groups. If this system is extended, it will allow eventually detailed study of psychoanalytic sessions and patient- and therapist-variables can be related to these categories as the sessions continue. Such categories can, of course, also be related to more objective indices of therapeutic outcome so that ultimately validation of the psychoanalytic process will become possible. In addition the same automatic procedures could be applied to clinical judgements of outcome so that these also may be introduced into quantified investigations.

There can be little doubt that his work at Ulm is highly important and when fully developed will become a powerful tool for the scientific investigation of psychoanalytic therapy. For further descriptions of this work readers are referred to Kachele et al. (1979) and Thoma et al. (1976).

CONCLUSIONS FROM ALL STUDIES

The conclusions to be drawn from these studies of psychoanalytic therapeutic success may be summarized under a number of headings.

1. Studies of the outcome alone of psychoanalytic therapy are too crude because the criteria of success from school to school and of any control groups are inevitably too disparate.

2. The use of the concept of spontaneous remission to form a baseline, above which successful psychotherapy must rise, is of dubious validity.

3. Short-term prediction of behaviour during the psychoanalytic sessions, as used by Bellak (1958), seems to offer a possible method of evaluating psycho-analytic therapy. This should clearly elucidate what kinds of patient can be successfully treated by such procedures.

4. The automatic categorization of psychoanalytic sessions at Ulm seems to offer the best chance of evaluating psychoanalytic therapy.

FINAL COMMENTS

If, therefore, we are correct in arguing that the best method for evaluating the effects of psychoanalytic therapy is to examine the psychoanalytic session itself, it is disturbing to note that Crown (1968), in a paper designed to propound the merits of psychoanalysis, still argued that the psychoanalytic hour should remain inviolate — no tapes or cameras.

Thus while it is true to say that the studies reported in this chapter have done little to elucidate the value of psychoanalytic therapy, at least it may be argued that a viable research method has emerged. In addition some misconceptions about the value of psychoanalytic therapy, based on inadequate methodology and conceptualization of the problems, have been revealed.

Nevertheless it is clear that the present state of knowledge concerning the effectiveness of psychoanalytic therapy is little advanced from the days of Feni-chel (1945) who wrote — commenting on his own report (1930) from the Berlin Psychoanalytic Institute and on studies of analytic success rates by Coriat (1917), Oberndorf (1942) and Sadger (1929) — that without doubt psychoanalytic therapy leaves much to be desired.

12

The neo-Freudians and other analytic psychologists

As is well known, in the course of the development of psychoanalysis by Freud, a number of his followers of whom the most famous were Jung and Adler broke with Freud on points of psychoanalytic theory. These analysts proceeded to found their own schools or branches of psychoanalysis. Thus, centred in Zurich, Jung developed Analytical psychology while Adler expounded his Individual psychology. Other analysts again, while they formed no distinctive school, concentrated on certain aspects of psychoanalytic theory to the exclusion of others so that their brand of psychoanalysis cannot be considered part of the orthodox theory — for instance Rank, who regarded the birth trauma as of crucial importance in the psychological development. All these writers are often referred to (e.g. Brown, 1961) as early schismatics.

During the 1930s and 1940s, as psychoanalysis continued to develop, two divergent systems came into being — the continental school, representing the orthodox position and typified by the work of Anna Freud (driven by the Nazis into Britain), and the British school influenced most by the work of Melanie Klein. Furthermore in America there have grown up a number of systems of dynamic psychology which have concentrated to a greater extent than has orthodox psychoanalysis on the psychology of the ego. The main progenitors of these systems are Horney, Fromm and Sullivan. These psychiatrists are known as neo-Freudians although it has been said that, in their concentration on social factors, they are perhaps better called neo-Adlerians.

AIM OF THE CHAPTER

The complexity and volume of the works of Jung alone, quite apart from the other writers mentioned in the introduction, make any kind of detailed review of their work impossible in one chapter. However the procedure adopted has been to outline the main divergences of these writers from orthodox Freudian theory, as discussed in this book, and to scrutinize these divergences in the light of the experimental evidence relevant to the portion of Freudian theory concerned. For example, good evidence has been adduced for repression (see pp. 201-26). Thus any theorist whose divergence includes the exclusion of that concept could not be regarded as well supported. On the other hand, no study has been able to demonstrate the existence of a phallic character (see p. 46). The theorist, therefore, who rejects this concept would be supported by the empirical evidence. Inevitably, some of the theories reviewed here demand their own body of experimental studies for support or disconfirmation, but this will not be attempted here since it is irrelevant to the purpose of this book — to examine Freudian theory. Furthermore since the influence of these other theories has been less, little empirical work in fact exists.

JUNG*

THE JUNGIAN MENTAL STRUCTURE

As we have seen (p. 169), in psychoanalytic theory there is a tripartite mental structure of ego, super-ego and id. Conscious and unconscious mental activity is held to occur.

Jung postulates three mental systems:

(a) *The conscious.* This is concerned with the individual's relation to the real world around us. This is the outward appearance of the personality and is called *the persona.*

(b) *The personal unconscious.* This is, in part, the opposite of the persona. Thus the brave man is unconsciously cowardly. It consists of repressed, neglected and unrealized qualities. Thus, as Brown (1961) says, the personal unconscious is compensatory in function. Just as the conscious, seen by the world, is called the persona, so the personal unconscious, the opposite, is called *the shadow.* If too strongly repressed by social conventions, for example, the shadow is likely to burst forth and overwhelm the conscious.

(c) *The collective unconscious.* This is the deepest layer of the mind. It contains the collective beliefs and myths of the race to which an individual belongs. Even deeper down it contains the universal unconscious common to all men (Brown, 1961). These universals are called *archetypes.* One archetype that a man has is *the anima* — the archetype of woman, by which he 'apprehends the nature of woman' (Jung, 1953). A woman has a corresponding archetype of man, *the animus.* One of the aims of Jungian psychotherapy is to help a person know his anima or animus, to plumb the depths of the racial unconscious and thus to become more fully himself. Other archetypes are the wise old man and the great mother. Possession by these archetypes is called by Jung *inflation* and produces psychotic-like effects of delusions of grandeur.

BALANCE IN JUNGIAN THEORY

In Freudian theory the ideal balance of the dynamic forces in the mental struc-

* The description of Jung's system is based on the writings of Jung and summaries and discussions by Brown (1961), Lindzey and Hall (1965), Glover (1950), Fordham (1959) and Blum (1953).

ture, the aim of psychotherapy, is control by the ego: 'Where id was, there shall ego be' (Freud, 1933). In the psychopath, for example, the id has gained control, in the obsessional neurotic, the super-ego is too powerful.

In Jungian theory the ideal is a balance between conscious and unconscious. Thus the influence of reason (consciousness) is important, but so too is the influence of the unconscious. If a blend of reason and vitality can be struck, a new centre of personality emerges — *the self*. The self, as Fordham (1959) points out, is not used by Jung in its everyday sense but is used in the sense of the eastern mystics. In *The Secret of the Golden Flower* (Jung and Wilhelm, 1931) Jung develops the theme of what the self truly is. It seems to mean complete acceptance of both oneself and the world around. Fordham quotes the Jungian mystical description: 'The self is not only the centre but also the circumference that encloses consciousness and the unconscious; it is the centre of this totality as the ego is the centre of consciousness' (Jung, 1940).

Clearly this brief description of the mental apparatus as conceived by Jung must do violence to the mystical complexity of his full concept. Nevertheless the main points have been presented.

Comments

Jung's concept of the collective unconscious — the inherited racial foundation of the whole structure of personality (Hall and Lindzey, 1957) — perhaps differentiates his theories most profoundly from those of Freud. Unfortunately modern genetics cannot support the possibility of the inheritance of acquired characteristics, a necessary implication of the collective unconscious. It is to be noted that Freud (1913) also postulated inherited memory traces to account for symbolization in dreams. However, unlike Jung, Freud made no use of the concept in his general theory and the fact of symbolization may be accounted for without recourse to inherited memories. Jung, as we have seen, placed great emphasis on the collective unconscious since it contains all the 'wisdom and experience of uncounted centuries' (Jung, 1953) and is the creator of the self.

In Chapter 7, surveying the empirical evidence for the Freudian theory of ego, super-ego and id, it was noted that factor-analysis by Cattell and his associates had yielded three factors which could be identified with the Freudian constructs. Furthermore, at least the basic theory was in accord with modern concepts of the neurophysiology of the brain. In addition, a test (the IES test) had been developed to measure the behaviours relevant to each of the parts of the mental apparatus. Thus, difficult as it obviously is to provide empirical evidence for this type of theory, there is some support for the psychoanalytic concepts. Jung's concepts on the other hand cannot be put to the empirical test. Indeed the anima and animus resemble more the Platonic ἐιδη which, of their nature, can only be conceived.

In short, for the Freudian theory, which is hard enough to test but has some degree of support, Jung has substituted an untestable system which flies in the face of current genetics.

CONTENTS OF THE UNCONSCIOUS

The concept of unconscious mental activity was not invented by Freud. His contribution was to specify what such contents were, e.g. the Oedipus complex, the castration complex, repressed sexual desires and aggressions. Jung, too, has specified the contents of the unconscious. The personal unconscious contains repressed and neglected ideas and abilities, the racial or collective unconscious, the wisdom of ages in the form of *archetypes*. The archetypes identified include birth, rebirth, death, power, magic, unity, the hero, the child, God, the demon, the earth mother, the wise old man, the animal (Jung, quoted by Hall and Lindzey, 1957). As indicated, archetypes can take possession of the individual: Bertrand Russell might be thought to have been possessed by the archetype of the wise old man. Certain archetypes, such as the anima, animus, shadow and persona, operate almost as separate systems. Thus the ego frequently identifies with the persona, and the shadow (man's animal side) is frequently repressed into the personal unconscious.

Comments

Freud's theories of Oedipal and castration complexes can be subjected to empirical test; the antecedent conditions of such complexes are specified and so are the consequences. These theories of archetypes are not thus testable. All individuals must have them, being racially inherited, but the evidence for them comes from their appearance in myths and dreams and psychotic episodes. As Brown (1961) points out, the concept of archetypes depends on reasoning from the particular symbol to a generalized idea in the Platonic sense. Indeed, as is the case with dream symbols, there is no need to postulate a collective unconscious for these common themes are explicable in terms of the common experiences of men in different societies. The only evidence for archetypes is their actual occurrence in conscious behaviour.

For example, the occurrence of the Odysseus theme in various cultures is evidence for an archetype of the lost prince. No other kind of evidence can support the construct. It is therefore untestable. On the other hand the basic contents of the unconscious in Freudian theory such as the Oedipus complex and castration complex have a certain amount of empirical support, both in cross-cultural and experimental studies and from the study of dreams by Hall and his associates.

Jung (1955), in *Psychology and Alchemy*, demonstrates in a long series of dreams from one patient similarities between his dream symbolism and the symbols of mediaeval alchemy — evidence, he claims, for the racial unconscious and the existence of archetypes.

Freud's dream theories, on the other hand, claim that the dreams represent the disguised wishes of the dreamer, and that most of the dream symbols represent not archetypes but the sexual organs. In Chapter 9, where the evidence for dream theory was reviewed, we discussed a considerable amount of work supporting the

Freudian theory of symbolism (e.g. Lessler, 1962), the enormous empirical dream studies of Hall (1966) which support dream symbolism and the Oedipus and castration complexes, and finally the EEG studies of dream activity. These again, especially Berger (1963a), provide support for the Freudian theory of dreams.

Jung, however, with an untestable theory of archetypes which is inevitably contrary to modern genetics since the whole concept of the racial unconscious implies the inheritance of acquired characteristics, diverges from Freud at a point where Freudian theory is strongly supported.

From this study of two basic differences between Jung and Freud, the concept of the racial or collective unconscious and the notion of archetypes, it is clear that in place of the Freudian theory which has empirical support to some extent at least and which *can* be tested, Jung has substituted two untestable hypotheses. This is a good illustration of the reasons why this book, apart from this brief chapter, has been restricted to orthodox psychoanalytic theory. As must be clear, Freudian theory itself has little empirical support originating from psychoanalysis. Deviations from it, therefore, if based on clinical evidence would not be likely to be useful. What is needed is rather to attempt to utilize those parts of psychoanalytic theory which have been confirmed.

JUNGIAN CONCEPTS OF EXTRAVERSION AND INTROVERSION

Jung (1949) first coined the terms extraverted, to describe the person mainly interested in the external world, and introverted, which applied to the person more concerned with his internal subjective world. For Jung, most people would be classified into types in that their persona was either extraverted or introverted and the opposite tendency existed in the personal unconscious. In addition, since Jung (1949) also recognized four basic psychological functions — thinking, feeling, sensing and intuiting — the stage is set for eight basic personality types — the extraverted thinker, feeler, the introverted thinker, feeler and so on. For Jung considered that one of these functions was especially developed in each person.

Comments

This classification, in Freudian terms, is an ego psychology — a branch of psychology that was not highly developed in orthodox psychoanalytic theory. This, undoubtedly, is a part of Jungian psychology which is well supported by the empirical studies of personality reviewed in this book (see Chapter 4).

Here it will be remembered that both Cattell, Eysenck and Guilford isolated an extraversion—introversion factor, and a social introversion scale occurs in the MMPI. While these studies support the basic concept of extraversion—introversion, they do not confirm the quadruple functional division although, in point of fact, two questionnaires have been developed which purport to measure these variables — the Gray—Wheelwright Questionnaire (Gray and Wheelwright, 1946) and the Myers—Briggs Type Indicator (Myers, 1962). Our description of these tests is that found in Kline (1973a). Since the constructon of this last test was begun in 1943, neither test can be really described as new except that there have been relatively few researches using them. Indeed, the Gray—Wheelwright test has not yet been published.

Since both tests claim to identify types rather than place subjects on a continuum, a brief description of each is necessary. For whether or not these tests can thus categorize subjects is crucial for assessing their validity and for interpreting certain aspects of the psychometric data reported about the Myers—Briggs Type Indicator.

The Gray—Wheelwright Questionnaire and The Myers—Briggs Type Indicator

The Gray—Wheelwright Test. This consists of eighty-five forced-choice items. Subjects have to indicate which of two things they prefer. Each response places a subject into a category. The instructions to this test are curious in the extreme in that subjects are asked to choose the answer which best reflects 'your original inborn tendency rather than what you wish to do or what you have made of yourself'. Experience in testing educated subjects in Great Britain suggests strongly that these instructions would be insuperable obstacles to satisfactory test-completion.

The Myers—Briggs Test (form F). The first part consists of seventy-one forced-choice items as above. Part 2 contains fifty-two pairs of words. For each pair subjects have to choose the more appealing, whereas the third part is identical with part 1 in form (forty-three items).

Scoring. These inventories categorize subjects into types. If a subject has more E responses than I responses he is classified extravert. His score is the difference between extraversion and introversion. Similarly for the other scales. A continuous-scale score (like a dimension) is also available for parametric statistical analysis.

From this description it is clear that two independent tests have been constructed such that subjects, depending on their choices, can be placed into Jungian categories. Thus Jungian theory has shown itself amenable to test. A number of difficulties with these tests must be mentioned.

Although the manual to the Myers—Briggs test (Myers, 1962) quotes satisfactory reliabilities in the order of 0.7 to 0.8, these are for the continuous scores (which are not apposite to Jungian theory), not the category scores. For the category scores, Myers reports a similar figure but she used tetrachoric correlations (notoriously unreliable) corrected for length. Even if we accept the test as reliable, evidence for validity is far more difficult to come by. Is, then, the Myers—Briggs Indicator a valid test of Jungian categories?

Mendelsohn (1965) and Sundberg (1965), surveying the evidence, both agree that there is not good support for the validity of this test, a conclusion confirmed in the recent survey by Carlyn (1977). The classic study is that of Stricker and Ross (1964), who correlated the continuous scores with a large number of other tests — notably the MMPI, the Strong Interest Blank, the Edwards Social Desirability scale, the Californian Psychological inventory and the Gray—Wheelwright test. Although this kind of construct-validity study is difficult to interpret, these authors are forced to conclude that there was no strong evidence for its validity. However, there were good correlations with the Gray—Wheelwright test. Indeed, Myers (1962), correcting these correlations for the unreliability of both scales, arrives at correlations greater than $+ 1$ — i.e. the two tests' true variances are identical.

Thus from this study of the correlations with the continuous scores of the Myers—Briggs Indicator, three conclusions appear warranted: (a) that the Myers—Briggs test and the Gray—Wheelwright are measuring very similar variables; (b) that the Myers—Briggs test is of unproven validity; (c) that the Myers—Briggs test used empirically may be highly useful (as claimed by Myers, 1962, in the manual).

However, Stricker and Ross (1964) also investigated the typological side of the test. Here, by a study of the distributions, they were forced to conclude that there was little evidence for the Jungian types. Evidence in the manual from regression lines of scales on IQ which appear to change slope at the O or cutting point does not seem convincing. Indeed, the conclusion from all this would appear to be negative were it not for a study by Bradway (1964) reprinted in Vetter and Smith (1971).

Bradway (1964) overcame the problem of validity by getting Jungian analysts to put themselves into their personality groups. This is a true criterion. For the meaning of a category is only that given it by a Jungian analyst. In fact, compared with the twenty-eight analysts' self-typing both the Gray—Wheelwright and the Myers—Briggs showed full agreement for introverts and extraverts. Both tests were better than chance as regards the sensation/intuition. For thinking, feeling and perception judgement the Gray—Wheelwright also showed better than chance matching. These are sound impressive findings in support of the validity of the tests; clearly, they measure what these Jungian analysts regard as Jungian types. What we do not know, of course, is to what extent these analysts are a random sample of Jungian analysts or whether their theoretical knowledge was sound.

In conclusion, we should like to propose that both these tests merit further study and development, especially perhaps the Gray—Wheelwright. If they do measure variables similar to those implicit in Jungian theory it might be possible to use them to elucidate the theory and relate it to other theories of personality. Certainly it seems to us that both these tests offer forms of measurement applicable to Jungian theory and hence support for it.

Clearly, therefore, introversion—extraversion as a dimension of personality has been strongly confirmed and the more specifically Jungian aspects are not without some support.

CONCLUSIONS CONCERNING JUNG

As was indicated in the introduction to this chapter, to do justice to the immensity and complexity of Jungian theory in part of a chapter is not possible. Thus a few major points of Jung which differ markedly from orthodox psychoanalytic theory have been discussed. His basic theory, including the inherited racial unconscious, is harder to test empirically than that of Freud and is not in accord with modern opinions concerning genetics. On the other hand, the Freudian theory of ego, id and super-ego does have a modicum of support. As regards extraversion— introversion, for which there is no psychoanalytic equivalent, Jung is supported by the evidence although his typological notions have not been confirmed.

Before we leave the analytic psychology of Jung, one further point needs to be mentioned. It is generally accepted that Jung first split off from Freud on account of Freud's pansexualism. Jung, indeed, claimed this to be a most important reason in a personal communciation to Hall and Lindzey (Hall and Lindzey, 1957). Readers may therefore object that this point should surely have been explicitly dealt with. Implicitly it has been covered. Freud's concept of the id, repository of the Oedipus complex and repressed instinctual impulses (pansexual) has been contrasted with the Jungian concept — the collective unconscious. What evidence there is favours the Freudian version. However, in this book, as was made clear in the opening chapter, the technique used has been to break down the Freudian concepts into explicit or implicit empirical testable hypotheses. Thus such broad questions as to whether the libido is primarily sexual or not have not been considered. Nevertheless the Cattell studies of drive (ergs) do support the importance of sexual drive.

ADLER

THE INDIVIDUAL PSYCHOLOGY OF ADLER

Like Jung, Adler broke with Freud partly on account of Freud's emphasis on the importance of sexuality. In place of the Freudian struggle between ego, id and super-ego, Adler's view of man was more optimistic: basically socially oriented, man struggles to realise his creative self. An examination of some of the most important terms in Adler's psychology will demonstrate clearly his divergence from Freud.

The inferiority complex

Adler will be immortalized, if for no other reason, by this term alone. In his view the individual is always striving towards goals, realistic or unattainable. His view of men is thus held to be teleological. Constant failure to reach his goals produces in an individual feelings of inferiority — the inferiority complex. Thus Adler (1930) says 'I begin to see clearly in every psychical phenomenon *the striving for superiority*.' To Adler this feeling of inferiority is inevitable for a child — he is inferior. Often this inferiority real or imagined is met by *compensation*. Organ inferiority, a concept by which Adler tried to account for particular organic symptoms, is often thus countered by compensation. Had not Demosthenes stuttered, there would have been no *Philippics*. An example of compensation is the *masculine protest*, seen in the aggressive masculinity of the stereotypic suffragette. Thus then the striving for superiority is a basic driving force of behaviour — 'the great upward drive' (Adler, 1930).

Goals

'Individual psychology insists absolutely on the indispensability of finalism for the undertaking of all psychological phenomena. . . . The final goal alone can explain man's behaviour' (Adler, 1930). Indeed, what distinguishes neurotics from normal people is the realism of their goals. Neurotics are neurotic because they aim at the unattainable. Another feature of neurotic goals is that they are selfish or lack *social interest*. Social interest refers to the socialization of the striving for superiority. Thus the goal of becoming headmaster is, presumably, socialized, oriented to the good of society. Without social interest this goal might be transformed to that of gang-leader — oriented to selfish gain.

Style of life

This represents the *way* in which these strivings to overcome inferiority take place, and thus is the source of individual differences among people. It is formed early on in childhood and, once formed, influences our whole perception of the world. Partly it is the child's compensation for his inferiority and is closely related to the kinds of goal he has set himself (which depend upon where he feels inferior). This style of life, the personality resulting from the goals adopted and the methods of overcoming inferiority in respect of them, is what has to be changed in the neurotic personality. This is the function of psychotherapy and it may be done by either changing goals to one which the individual can attain, or changing his means of compensation for inferiority.

Comments

Although Adler broke away from Freud in 1911 his individual psychology bears little relation to psychoanalysis. In effect it is an ego psychology only. Thus although the style of life is adopted early in childhood and the goals of the individual may be unconscious, they are unconscious only in the sense that they are unverbalized.

What has been abandoned from Freudian theory, therefore, is the whole concept of the motivating power of repressed sexuality and aggression, the Oedipus and castration complexes and the importance of infantile sexuality. As we have seen from the studies discussed in this book, Adler is on safe ground in so doing to the extent that it is these unconscious elements that are so difficult to put to the empirical test. Nevertheless it must be pointed out that a limited amount of empirical evidence does exist for the castration and Oedipus complexes (see p. 158), for sexual symbolism (see p. 285), for id and super-ego (see p. 178) and for the application of these concepts to an understanding of neurosis (see p. 388) and even the arts (see p. 259).

In place of this Adler has erected a striving for superiority based on early family background and tinged, in the normal, adapted individual, with social interest which appears to be innate. Empirical and theoretical studies of personality such as those of Eysenck, Cattell and Guilford (pp. 48-57) do not in fact support the claim that striving for superiority is a major factor in personality. Cattell (1965), however, has isolated an erg of self-assertion, though this is only one among many. At this point, in fairness to Adler, a body of research conducted by McClelland and his associates on the achievement motive may also be related to Adler's ideas of striving for superiority (see for example McClelland, 1961). Cattell, however, relates this achievement motive empirically to self-assertion, self-sentiment and super-ego. A weakness of Adlerian theory, as has been discussed by Brown (1961), is that the attractive simplicity of the theory involves the defect that, in respect of neurosis, it is quite unable to explain how different symptoms develop in different people. If the goal is wrong, the style of life misdirected, there is nothing to account for obsessional rather than hysterical symptoms.

CONCLUSIONS CONCERNING ADLER

Adler's individual psychology is hardly a branch of psychoanalytic theory since it is concentrated on the psychology of the ego. For Adler, man is, therefore, essentially a rational animal. There can be no doubt that one of the most attractive features of Freudian theory — its immense explanatory power — has therefore been abandoned. Furthermore, as the evidence in this book shows, such total rejection is probably not justified. On the other hand Adler's emphasis on the social determinants of personality — for the style of life is entirely socially determined — and the importance of the ego in behaviour, were needed improvements in psychoanalysis. Indeed it is interesting to note that orthodox modern psychoanalysts are now trying to develop their own psychology of the ego, for example Anna Freud (1946) and Hartman, Kris and Lowenstein (1947). It still remains to be seen whether Adler's emphasis on the struggle for superiority is justified. In the light of the evidence, however, it must be concluded that, salutary as Adler's emphasis on ego psychology was, his theories abandoned too much of Freudian theory and robbed it, perhaps, of what was most interesting and valuable.

MELANIE KLEIN

HER THEORIES

A brief mention must now be made of the theories of Melanie Klein. These are interesting because the majority of modern developments of psychoanalytic theory have, like Adler, turned their attention to the ego and its mode of development, as an individual grows up within a culture, whereas Klein has very much concentrated on the early infantile determinants of behaviour and its instinctual basis. These developments are also important in that they have exerted a profound influence on a number of British analysts, notably Winnicott and Bowlby (see Winnicott, 1957, or Bowlby, 1969, for example). Indeed, Brown (1961) calls the analysts thus influenced the British school. Despite its influence and its intrinsic interest, however, only a bare summary of the main differences between Melanie Klein's work and that of Freud will be given because, as will become clear, her theories are inherently untestable.

The raw data on which Melanie Klein based her theories

Freudian theories of infantile development, despite the case of Little Hans (Freud, 1909a), came largely from the free associations and dream material of adults. Melanie Klein, however, analysed children, using an interpretation of their play and their verbalizations about their play. Using this play-association technique Klein was able to analyse children from two years upwards. Many orthodox analysts reject the theories derived from the play method because they do not believe it can open up the unconscious in the same way as the standard free-association technique (which was generally used with highly intelligent and articulate patients). Fenichel (1945), however, does say the method may work. If the original data obtained by Freud are regarded as of dubious reliability, then an example of a child analysis will show how much more interpretative this is. Segal (1964) quotes an example of one of her analyses of a child of five:

> she started spreading glue on the floor of the playroom and her shoes ... I interpreted that she wanted to glue herself to the floor so as not to be sent away at the end of the session. ... She confirmed this interpretation verbally and then proceeded to smear the glue in a more messy and dirty fashion, saying with great satisfaction 'But it's also a "sick" right on your floor.' I interpreted that she wanted to glue herself not only to the inside of the room, but also to the inside of my body, where new babies grew, and to mess it and dirty it with the 'sick'.

No implication is intended concerning the correctness or otherwise of this interpretation. It is quoted to show how very subjective and interpretative are the original 'data' for the theories of Melanie Klein. Such data are not sufficient to construct a theory of personality development. Yet much of Melanie Klein's theorizing concerns infantile personality development in the first six months. Since classical, free-association techniques did not normally recapture such early memories, it is difficult even to imagine how scientifically respectable techniques could get at such early memories or fantasies (if indeed they exist).

HER BASIC CONCLUSIONS

The super-ego begins its development in earliest infancy. It is not, as in Freudian theory, the heir of the Oedipus complex. In early infancy the infant is orally aggressive. This aggression, the fantasy of biting the mother, is projected on to the mother — who is therefore seen as a violent hostile figure. This in turn creates anxiety. Aggression (which is innate) is of more importance than sex in the theories of Melanie Klein. Flugel (1945), describing this portion of the theory, writes that 'He wants ("cannibalistically") to incorporate the nipple and the breast and later to consume the contents of the mother's body (this last being perhaps one of the most startling of Klein's discoveries).'

Jones (1923) regarded this fantasied aggression of the infant as a far more important determinant of that infant's development than the actual aggression of the parent in the way he handles the child.

As Flugel makes clear, this projection of aggression on to the mother is crucial to the development of the super-ego, because in Kleinian theory in addition to projection (the mental analogue of defaecation) the child also indulges in introjection (the mental analogue of eating). Originally indeed the child introjects the 'good' breast and projects the 'bad'. By introjection these violent aggressions projected on to persons or objects are incorporated into the self. These introjections constitute the beginnings of the super-ego. Hence the super-ego is developed over a long period from earliest infancy. Hence too the barbaric severity of the super-ego, noted by Freud (1933) and attributed by him to the fact that it is the parents' super-ego which is introjected. To Melanie Klein, of course, this severity is but a reflection of the child's own savage impulses projected on to others and again introjected.

Comments

The data from these play-sessions with children are not sufficient to found any respectable theory. As the example from Segal (1964) showed, there is an enormous amount of interpretation by the analyst. However, with children of this age it is difficult to see how more satisfactory data might be obtained. After all, intelligence testing, which is one of the most valid and reliable forms of assessment in psychology, is at its weakest with young children — excellent though the baby tests such as those of Griffiths (1951) and Psyche Cattell (1940) be.

Klein is, of course, a thoroughgoing psychoanalyst. She accepts most of the major tenets of psychoanalytic theory, including even the death instinct. Her divergence from classical theory lies in the developmental sphere, the fact that she attributes so much importance to the first six months of life, and claims that the super-ego has clearly begun its development. Since this occurs through the ego-defence processes of projection and introjection a further divergence from orthodox theory is implied. In orthodox theory the ego develops slowly from the id during childhood. In Kleinian theory the ego is already sufficiently developed at birth to project and introject.

MELANIE KLEIN'S THEORY AND THE EMPIRICAL EVIDENCE

By the evidence adduced in this book for the Freudian theory of the mental apparatus and the defence mechanisms of introjection and projection, it is to be noted that both theories are equally supported. This is because the evidence does not attempt to establish at what age these structures and defences appear. To choose between the theories, therefore, on rational empirical grounds would need a specific critical test. For example super-ego behaviour would be expected by Freudian theory *not* to occur in children of three years old; by Kleinian theory it could be expected. In principle, therefore, a critical test could be devised. At present however no such test can be devised in practice. This is because the precise testing of such behaviour in young children is not possible. Studies of specific moral behaviours, e.g. cheating, are not really relevant to the psycho-analytic theory since not cheating can be due to feelings of guilt (super-ego) or fear (ego). That is why factor-analytic studies of super-ego and ego activity are superior to purely observational studies. If a factor common to a large number of moralistic actions can be isolated it may be interpreted as a super-ego factor. However, this technique requires a large number of quantified variables which cannot be obtained from young children.

CONCLUSIONS CONCERNING MELANIE KLEIN

Empirical evidence gives equal support to the theories of orthodox psychoanalysis and those of Melanie Klein. At present no critical tests can be devised for the two hypotheses because it would involve the testing of young infants. The data, however, on which Melanie Klein based her theory are highly dubious even by the standards of psychoanalysis. Her theories, therefore, cannot rationally be accepted. On the evidence it is possible to argue for the construct of a super-ego. There is little evidence concerning its origins. Nevertheless regarding the theories of Klein, we must agree with Flugel (1945), who wrote of the findings of Melanie Klein: 'when described in forthright scientific language [they] are apt sometimes to appear so far-fetched, weird and sinister as to be scarcely credible'. However, it should be noted that Sharma (1977) has applied percept-genetic methods to Melanie Klein's theories and such work might perhaps elucidate her ideas experimentally.

FROMM

HIS THEORIES

Unlike Freud, whose main concern was with the psychology of the individual, Fromm was equally interested in individuals and society. At present however we shall concern ourselves with his views of man, concentrating on his points of divergence from Freud.

In *The Fear of Freedom*, Fromm (1942) outlines his debt to and his disagree-ments with Freud. Basic to Fromm's ideas are 'some of the fundamental discoveries of Freud, particularly those concerning the operation of unconscious forces in man's character and their dependence on external influence.' However, contrary to the Freudian view that man's relationship with others is always a means to an end, the satisfaction of biologically given drives, Fromm holds that 'these drives which make for the *differences* in men's characters, like love and hatred, the lust for power and the yearning for submission, the enjoyment of sensuous pleasure and the fear of it are all *products of the social process*' (our italics). He continues, 'Man's nature, his passions, and anxieties are a cultural product.' Thus, then, for Freud biological man, for Fromm social man.

The clearest exposition of Fromm's view of man is to be found in *Man for Himself* (1949). Here his divergences from Freud become quite clear.

Character

Fromm's theory of character formation follows that of Freud (see pp 7-8) quite closely, as he himself admits, but with the fundamental difference that

the basis of character is not seen in various types of libido organization (e.g. repressed anal erotism produces the anal character) but in specific kinds of a person's relatedness to the world. In the process of living, man relates himself to the world.

1. by acquiring and assimilating things, and
2. by relating himself to people (and himself).

The former I shall call the process of assimilation, the latter that of socialization. (1949)

Fromm continues,

These orientations by which the individual relates himself to the world, constitute the core of his character: character can be defined as the (relatively permanent) form in which human energy is canalized in the process of assimilation and socialization. (ibid.)

TABLE 12.1. *The various character types*

	Assimilation	Socialization	Descriptions Positive aspect	Negative aspect
1.	Non-productive orientation			
(a)	Receiving (Accepting)	Masochistic (Loyalty)	Optimistic, responsive	Wishful thinking, passive
(b)	Exploiting (Taking)	Sadistic (Authority)	Impulsive, active	Aggressive, rash
(c)	Hoarding (Preserving)	Destructive (Assertiveness)	Cautious, orderly	Pedantic, obsessional
(d)	Marketing (Exchanging)	Indifferent (Fairness)	Adequate, purposeful	Indiscriminating, opportunistic
2.	Productive orientation			
	Working	Loving, Reasoning	No similar description attached	A development of true spontaneity

[(Fromm, 1949, p. 111)]

Fromm points out that most people are blends of these orientations and that the non-productive characters are clinically similar to the pregenitaɪ character types of Freud (see p. 7). The difference lies in the hypotheses concerning their aetiology.

For example, the hoarding character of Fromm is very similar to the anal character of Freud. However, the anal character (Freud, 1908a) is the result of reaction-formation and sublimation of repressed anal erotism. To Fromm the retentive nature of the hoarding orientation is merely a reflection of his general relation to the world. He is mean with money, not as a substitute for faeces, but because he is mean with everything, including faeces.

The productive orientation is the ideal development, equivalent to the genital character of Freud. In a later work Fromm (1965) uses two further concepts to describe character. *The necrophilous character* — 'the malignant form of the character structure of which Freud's anal character is the benign form' — 'is attracted to and fascinated by all that is not alive, all that is dead; corpses, decay, faeces, dirt.' It is related to the death instinct. This is contrasted with the *biophilous orientation* to be found in the productive character and typified by a love of life.

Fromm's theories in the light of the evidence

Fromm's character typology is professedly the equivalent of the Freudian psycho-sexual theory of personality development (see pp. 7-9). There, it will be remembered, it was argued that implicit in the psychosexual theory were two hypotheses capable of empirical validation:

(a) that certain personality syndromes exist, and
(b) that these are the result of repressed pregenital erotism.

Fromm's theory of characters or orientations is therefore virtually the same as Freud's regarding the first hypothesis but quite different regarding the second.

A considerable body of evidence supports the existence of the personality syndromes: Goldman-Eisler (1953) supports the oral character, Beloff (1957) and Kline (1969a) confirm the anal character. So far there has been no confirmation of the phallic personality or Fromm's marketing orientation. This evidence equally supports, therefore, the receptive and exploiting orientations (oral dependent and sadistic), the hoarding orientation (anal character) and necrophilous character.

The second hypothesis, concerning the aetiology of these syndromes, is the point of difference. Studies such as those of Beloff and Goldman-Eisler are not helpful here since, even if child-rearing processes are implicated in the aetiology of the syndromes (thus supporting repressed pregenital erotism), Fromm has argued that the general social background of parsimony and retention makes 'anal' mothers give severe pot-training. However, the studies with the Blacky Pictures (Blum, 1949), discussed earlier in this book (pp. 113-19), where responses to a lactating and defaecating dog are related to various aspects of per-

Freud. Thus Kline's (1968a) finding that anal characteristics were related to the anal dimension of the Blacky Pictures and McNeil and Blum's (1952) research into handwriting and anal scores on the Blacky Pictures support the Freudian hypothesis. Thus although the evidence for the link between repressed pregenital erotism and personality development is slight, what little there is must favour Freud rather than Fromm.

Conclusions

Fromm's theory of character is in reality little different, other than in nomenclature, from that of Freud. The evidence for the personality syndromes gives both views equal support. There is little firm evidence, as yet, in favour of either of the hypotheses concerning the development of these personalities. What little there is supports the Freudian theory, although Beloff (1957) did find that anal traits between mother and child were correlated (as would be predicted from Fromm's theories).

The Oedipus complex

As was the case with personality development, Fromm accepts the clinical finding of Freudian theory — the existence of the Oedipus complex — but desexualizes its origins, considering it to be the result of the social forces of the typical western family structure. For Freud, the Oedipus complex was the sexual rivalry for the mother of father and son. Fear of castration by the father (as a punishment) created its repression which was finalized by the development of the super-ego (see p. 131 for the theory). Fromm admits that the discovery of fixation to the mother 'is, indeed, one of the most far-reaching discoveries in the science of Man. But in this area . . . Freud narrowed his discovery and its consequences by being compelled to couch it in terms of his libido theory' (1965, p. 95). Fromm continues, 'Incestuous (Oedipal) wishes are not primarily a result of sexual desires but constitute one of the most fundamental tendencies of man: the wish to remain, to return to where he came from, the fear of being free' (p. 107). In an earlier paper, Fromm (1948) had argued that Oedipal rivalry with the father was due to the fact that western society was patriarchal and authoritarian: the conflict was due to this harsh treatment, meted out by the father to the son. As support, anthropological evidence was quoted to show that the Oedipal complex did not occur in matriarchal societies — that it was not universal.

Comments

Because Fromm accepts the fact of the Oedipus complex but disagrees with Freud regarding its interpretation, the approach adopted in this book — to examine the objective evidence for the clinical findings of psychoanalysis — does not readily favour one or other of the two views. Nevertheless it must be stated that many psychologists do not even accept the fact of the Oedipus complex (e.g. Valentine, 1960). However certain points concerning Fromm's concepts of the Oedipus complex must be discussed. Orthodox psychoanalysis accepts the fact that the

Oedipus complex is dependent upon the typical western family constellation. Thus Fenichel (1945) says 'the sexual conflicts of children would be different if they did not live together with their parents and a few brothers and sisters, exposed to the typical family conflicts of sexual excitation and frustration. Different environments provoke different reactions' (p. 98). Consequently Fromm's (1948) argument as demonstrated by anthropological studies (e.g. Malinowsky, 1927), that the Oedipus complex is not universal, does not destroy the psychoanalytic theory. It does, of course, destroy the psychoanalytic hypothesis that the Oedipus complex originates in a phylogenetic memory of the destruction of the primal horde (Freud, 1913). However, unlike Jung, Freud makes little use of this phylogenetic hypothesis in his general theory. It must also be pointed out that although Malinowsky's findings are accepted, the evidence presented is really only clinical in nature and does not reach the standards of objectivity and reliability desirable in scientific research. However, the attempt to rebut the evidence by Jones (1925) is, equally, entirely unconvincing. Thus what Fromm has done is to stress the importance of the social (familial) influence on the Oedipus complex.

However, Fromm's denial of the sexual nature of the Oedipus complex clearly needs further examination: is rivalry of the father the result of sexual jealousy or authoritarian treatment?

The evidence we have examined supporting the Oedipus complex (see pp. 132-59), slight as it is, tends towards an aetiology based on sexual jealousy. Thus the study by Friedman (1952) was interesting because of the sexual symbolism in the responses of the children — girls indicated their fathers would mount some steps and enter a room. Certainly too, the work of Stephens (1961, 1962) stresses the sexual aetiology of the Oedipus complex.

Again the study by Whiting et al. (1958), where long post-partum sexual taboo was found to be related to totemism, which is in Freudian theory an acting-out of the Oedipus complex (Freud, 1913b), very strongly points to the sexual nature of the Oedipus complex. Thus the evidence favours a sexual interpretation of the Oedipus complex.

Conclusions

As we have seen, Fromm accepts the fact that there is such a phenomenon as the Oedipus complex. His divergence from Freud lies in the hypothesized origin, which Fromm claims is simply the family environment which in patriarchal societies causes resentment of the father by the son. Fromm (1965) claims that fixation on the mother is a symptom of an inherited tendency to be dependent. What little evidence bears on the interpretation strongly supports the Freudian view of the sexual nature of the Oedipal tie with the mother. It should be pointed out that Fromm's view of an inherited tendency to be dependent is, like all instinct theories, very circular. Behaviour A occurs due to inherited tendency A1: A also provides the evidence for A1. Finally it must be stated that the universality of the Oedipus complex is not an essential plank in psychoanalytic theory.

Thus logically Fromm's theory is inferior to that of Freud and is less supported by the empirical evidence.

Super-ego

Fromm (1949) discusses the super-ego not from Freud's topological viewpoint but from the angle of its empirical manifestations, i.e. as conscience. He recognizes two forms of conscience:

A. *Authoritarian conscience.* 'The authoritarian conscience is the voice of an internalized external authority, the parents, the state or whoever the authorities in a culture happen to be' (pp. 143-4). A little later Fromm writes 'The authoritarian conscience is what Freud has described as the super-ego; but . . . this is only one form of conscience' (p. 144).

B. *Humanistic conscience.* 'Humanistic conscience represents not only the expression of our true selves; it contains also the essence of our moral experience in life' (p. 159). Again on the same page, 'Humanistic conscience is the expression of man's self-interest and integrity.'

These two forms of conscience appear in every person. 'The problem is to distinguish their respective strength and their interrelation' (p. 165).

Comments

Once again Fromm adopts the clinical findings of Freud, but this time adds something of his own. Little can be said about the humanistic conscience because, essentially, it is extremely hard to put to the empirical test. Presumably, if all classes of moral behaviour were subjected to factor-analysis, the emergence of *two* factors rather than a general factor of conscience or super-ego would favour the theory of Fromm. The factor-analyses of Cattell and Pawlik (1964) support a Freudian theory in that only one super-ego factor was found together with an ego and id factor.

Nevertheless, apart from the Cattell studies the empirical investigations have not been such as be relevant to Fromm's theory, so that no evidence can be adduced to support or refute it.

Mechanisms of escape

Fromm (1942) describes several mechanisms of escape, which Blum (1953) considers to be the equivalent of the Freudian defence mechanisms, and which Fromm himself likens to the concept of neurotic trends utilized by Horney (1939). These mechanisms of escape result from 'the insecurity of the isolated individual'. They are attempts to overcome the aloneness of the individual, characterized by 'the more or less complete surrender of individuality and the integrity of the self. Thus it is not a solution which leads to happiness and positive freedom: it is, in principle, a solution which is to be found in all neurotic phenomena' (p. 121). Three main mechanisms are discussed by Fromm:

1. *The masochistic—sadistic striving* — a striving for submission or domination which is caused by 'unbearable aloneness'. Fromm says this defence mechanism

is different from that of Adler (striving for superiority) because Adler's is entirely conscious whereas the drive for submission and domination, is, for Fromm, unconscious — the terror of aloneness and insignificance.

2. *Destructiveness*. This mechanism too originates from feelings of 'individual powerlessness and isolation. . . . If I succeed in removing it (the world outside), I remain isolated . . . but I cannot be crushed by the overwhelming power of the objects outside myself' (p. 154). This mechanism is to be seen everywhere in action, disguised as 'Love, duty, conscience and patriotism'. However, it has to be distinguished from destructiveness which is rational — a reaction to a genuine attack. For Fromm *'destructiveness is the outcome of unlived life'* (p. 156). Thus the more constricting a society is, the more destruction will be found within it.

3. *Automaton conformity*. This is the solution that the 'majority of normal individuals find in modern society' (p. 160). The individual ceases to be himself, he adopts the kind of personality offered to him by cultural patterns. Thus for Fromm national differences are real.

Comments

Freud did not regard sadism, masochism (sadism turned towards the self) or destructiveness as defence mechanisms. For him they became emanations of the death instinct. This has not been discussed in this book since the concept is simply not open to empirical validation. However, neither destructiveness nor sadism play an important part in Freudian theory. Nor is the evidence adduced for Freudian defence mechanisms relevant to Fromm's concepts. In fact, the claim that terror of being alone is the cause of sado-masochism and destructiveness is hard to put to the empirical test. Even the consequence that more of these defensive processes would be observed in a restrictive society (ignoring problems of defining this) would not definitely prove the thesis. Essentially these are un-testable and therefore unscientific speculations. As regards automaton conform-ity, this implies that in every different society would be found different person-ality types. Cross-cultural research with the Blacky Defence Preference Inventory (discussed on p. 239) points to the dangers of assuming that such national stereo-types in fact exist. Within-nation differences may be greater than between-nation differences.

Conclusions

To regard, as Fromm does, sadism and destructiveness as due to fear of isolation (when no operational definition of this is given) is to propound untestable hypotheses. Their importance in the development of behaviour is not supported by general studies of personality such as those conducted by Cattell, although dominance is an important factor (which could equally support Adlerian theory). The evidence in favour of Freudian defence mechanisms, especially repression, is such that to abandon them is to lose concepts with considerable empirical support. Naturally the evidence for Freudian mechanisms is not relevant to these very different mechanisms proposed by Fromm. In conclusion, therefore, Fromm's concepts are not supported by evidence and are inherently untestable.

As must be clear, with the exception of his mechanisms of escape Fromm has accepted the clinical observations of Freud concerning personality types, the Oedipus complex and the super-ego. Where he differs is in his interpretation. Freud interprets the findings in terms of libido theory; Fromm in terms of social factors. Fromm however is not explicit as to how these social factors produce their effects. Since the empirical consequences of the two theories are so similar the evidence cited in this book generally equally supports both. However, where there is evidence concerning the aetiology of the phenomena, the Freudian theory has been generally favoured.

KAREN HORNEY

HER THEORIES

Like Fromm, Horney stresses the social rather than the biological determinants of personality and rejects the libido theory.

Penis envy

Freud (1933), in the 'New introductory lectures in psychoanalysis', regards penis envy as the crucial concept in the psychology of women (see p. 131 for the theory). Horney (1939) emphatically denies this. Thus she writes:

> The wish to be a man, as Alfred Adler has pointed out, may be the expression of a wish for all those qualities or privileges which, in our culture, are regarded as masculine, such as strength, courage, independence, success, sexual freedom, right to choose a partner. (p. 108)

She continues (pp. 109-10): 'In short, interpretations in terms of penis envy bar the way to an understanding of fundamental difficulties such as ambition, and of the whole personality structure linked up with them.' Here then, as Blum (1953) points out, are shades of Adler — the masculine protest and the emphasis on cultural factors.

Comments

In Freudian theory penis envy begins around the age of three at the phallic stage. It is biologically rooted in that it stems from the inferiority of the clitoris compared with the penis. However Fenichel (1945) agrees with Horney in that he accepts that the effects of this primary penis envy may be modified by social factors. Thus penis envy in our culture is reinforced by the fact that the male *does* have privileges. In other cultures where the female is the dominant sex, the psychological effects of penis envy may be cancelled out. Clearly, as Blum (1953) suggests, studies of penis envy in other cultures are needed. The major difference, therefore, between Freud and Horney is not that Freud failed to take into account social factors, rightly stressed by the neo-Freudians, but that for Horney penis envy is irrelevant to the understanding of women. If a woman wishes for a penis, it is merely symbolic of wishing for masculine privileges. Thus like Adler's concept of the masculine protest, Horney has substituted for penis envy an ego psychology of struggling for status — ambition.

Conclusions

The studies of the castration complex have been reviewed in Chapter 6 (pp. 132-59). Levin (1966) investigated penis envy in a group of career women but used the Rorschach test, the validity of which is a matter of doubt. Kreitler and Kreitler (1966) found no evidence of penis envy in their sample of children. However, the interviews were conducted by untrained personnel so that the results are again open to doubt. Nevertheless there is, at present, no firm evidence for penis envy. No studies relevant to the Adlerian-Horney concept have been conducted. Cross-cultural research using quantitative techniques and longitudinal studies are clearly called for.

The Oedipus complex

Horney does not deny that the Oedipus complex may be seen in large numbers of people. However, she rejects its biological foundation and regards it instead 'as a product of describable conditions' (1939, p. 82). 'One of them is, briefly, sexual stimulation by the parents. . . . The other series of conditions is entirely different in nature . . . it is connected . . . with its [the child's] anxiety' (ibid.). This anxiety, according to Horney, arises from the conflict in the child between its dependency on its parents and its hostile impulses. It is thus aimed at security. She claims that the 'vast majority of infantile attachments to parents, as they are retrospectively revealed in the analysis of adult neurotics, belong to this group' (ibid., p. 83).

Comments

As was the case with Fromm, Horney accepts the clinical facts of the Oedipus complex but denies its universality and to a large extent its sexual nature. The typical neurotic Oedipus complex is, for Horney, a bid for security. Only those Oedipus complexes based on parental stimulation are sexual in nature. As was made clear in the discussion of Fromm (see p. 422), psychoanalysts, e.g. Fenichel (1945), do not accept the biological phylogenetic foundation of the Oedipus complex, nor is such a Lamarckian belief necessary for Freudian theory. Thus the real point of difference between Horney and Freud lies in the interpretation of the Oedipus complex: sexuality or security.

The empirical evidence

The empirical evidence has been mainly concerned to demonstrate whether or not an Oedipus complex could be said to exist. Thus such evidence cannot bear on the relative value of the two theories. Since, however, Horney has a sexual

Oedipus complex as well as a security-oriented version, the evidence for its sexual nature (Friedman, 1952; Whiting et al., 1958) again equally supports both theories. Thus at present no rational decision can be made between them since no empirical test of Horney's concept has been carried out.

Horney's theory of neurosis

The basis of neurosis for Horney was not the Oedipus complex but *basic anxiety*. Basic anxiety is defined in *The Neurotic Personality of Our Time* (Horney, 1937) as 'a feeling of being small, insignificant, helpless, endangered in a world that is out to abuse, cheat, attack, humiliate, betray, envy'. Observant readers will notice the similarity to Adler's concept of inferiority feelings (see p. 414). This basic anxiety is unconscious — i.e. below the level of awareness of the subject. Horney (1942) describes ten neurotic trends developed in an effort to overcome this basic anxiety. The most important are:

1. The neurotic need for affection.
2. The neurotic need for power.
3. Neurotic withdrawal.
4. Neurotic submissiveness.

Horney (1945) later classifies these needs into three categories:

(a) Moving towards people — the compliant type.
(b) Moving away from people — the detached type.
(c) Moving against people — the aggressive type.

All these three attitudes are present in individuals, but the normal person handles his conflicting demands in a rational and flexible manner, the neurotic rigidly. Thus the neurotic may externalize certain attitudes by projection or he may create an idealized image of himself so that he sees only his good points. An example of idealized image, quoted by Mullahy (1948), is the large, middle-aged women who sees herself as a slender young girl. Externalization is more than projection for, as Mullahy points out, *all* one's feelings are experienced in others. Profound disturbance at political oppression (really one's own oppression) exemplifies this defence.

Comments

Basic anxiety as defined by Horney is a reinterpretation of Adler's feelings of inferiority in that both are seen to arise from marked positions of inferiority. To Adler this means that the individual strives to become superior, to Horney that he strives for security. The mechanism of externalized image again closely resembles Adler's fictive goal, an unrealistic style of life. Externalization resembles projection (in the Freudian sense). Thus with these concepts Horney has but reinterpreted the clinical findings of Adler and Freud. It is to be noted too that in orthodox psychoanalytic terms basic anxiety is oral anxiety — fear that supplies will dry up — and would be likely to produce the oral pessimist.

The character types thought by Horney to be derived from three basic defences again have much in common with the typology derived from libido theory by Freud, with Fromm's analysis of character and also with Jung. Thus the compliant type is similar to Freud's oral erotic character (see p. 10) and Fromm's receiving orientation (see p. 420), the aggressive type resembles Freud's oral sadistic character and Fromm's exploiting orientation while the detached type resembles Jung's extravert (see p. 411).

THE EVIDENCE

The evidence cited in this book has concerned itself broadly with attempting to establish the accuracy of Freud's clinical findings since it was argued that there is little point in researching into the interpretation of findings which turn out to be grossly inaccurate. Thus in the main where Freud and Horney overlap, the evidence cannot decide between them, and where they differ there is, in fact, little evidence. The evidence for the character types has been reviewed (see p. 47) and in that Horney overlaps with Freud and Jung she is supported. There is no evidence relating these types to moving away, from or towards people and it seems an unverifiable hypothesis. On the other hand, as we have shown, studies with the Blacky Pictures (Blum, 1949) do provide evidence for the libido theory. There is the further point that rejection of libido theory makes the understanding of dream material, especially sexual symbolism (for which the evidence is considerable — see p. 285), unconvincing.

Basic anxiety, often caused by maternal rejection (Horney, 1937), has perhaps been put to an empirical test in the studies of the effects of maternal separation. These studies have been reviewed (see pp. 159-68) and it was found that they were vitiated by their inadequate methodology. Nevertheless, as Bowlby et al. (1956) admit, the effects of maternal separation are not necessarily lasting. This finding militates against the importance of basic anxiety as the driving force behind neurotic behaviour.

CONCLUSIONS CONCERNING KAREN HORNEY

The conclusions concerning Horney are similar to those drawn about Fromm. Since both accept many of the clinical findings of Freud, the evidence cited in this book tends to support them equally with Freud. The denial of sexuality (not so complete in Horney as in Fromm) runs against the tide of the evidence which is not however very considerable. Perhaps the chief value of Horney lies in her concentration on the social factors — denying the universality of the Oedipus complex, for example — work which has been generally accepted in orthodox psychoanalytic theory.

CONCLUSIONS CONCERNING THE WORK OF THESE DIVERGENT ANALYSTS

From the viewpoint of the empirical evidence is the work of these divergent analysts an improvement upon orthodox theory? Jung's major contributions —

the collective unconscious and the theory of archetypes — appear to be unverifiable. They are, therefore, better considered as metaphysics and cannot be regarded as an improvement on orthodox theory. His theory of character types is, however, verifiable and in name, at least, has received support. Thus extraversion, though now rather differently defined, has turned out to be a major variable in the description of personality. This seems to be Jung's sole addition to knowledge of personality.

Adler, on the other hand, with his stress on the social influences on the development of personality — for he considers a man's style of life to be a major determinant of behaviour — and his emphasis on ego behaviour, has had a salutory influence on psychoanalysis. Thus the phylogenetic Lamarckian racial memory of the Oedipus complex has been abandoned in favour of an explanation of the Oedipus complex in terms of family life. On the other hand, Adler's major concepts that struggling for superiority is the driving force of behaviour, or that neuroses can be explained in terms of goals, have not been validated. Incidentally it should be noted that to call Adlerian psychology teleological is false since the goals are themselves determined by the style of life determined in its turn by the family situation.

The work of Melanie Klein, which is a true extension of psychoanalytic theory in that the full implications of libido theory are accepted, and which accepts the basic findings of Freud but throws them back to an earlier stage which is then subjected to detailed analysis, is by current techniques not verifiable.

Finally Horney and Fromm, who are really neo-Adlerians in that they reject libido theory and the importance of sexuality but emphasize the cultural determinants of development, accept many of the clinical findings of Freud but reject his interpretation, which however does appear to have some support.

Studies with the Blacky Pictures support in general the libido theory. Kline (1968) for example found scores on the anal dimension of the Blacky Pictures related to anal characteristics. This is confirmation for Freudian theory. Similarly the oral character was related to weaning procedures by Goldman-Eisler (1953). As explanations, the neo-Freudian accounts of the hoarding character, for example, are weak — he is mean with money because he's generally mean. This is, of course, circuitous and fails to account for other traits in the syndrome. In addition considerable evidence supports Freudian dream symbolism (see especially Berger, 1963a) and the castration complex (Sarnoff and Corwin, 1959), both of which are inexplicable in terms of a non-sexual unconscious and a non-sexual libido.

In conclusion, therefore, it must be admitted that the work of the divergent analysts is no improvement on Freud. Certainly their data are no more carefully collected or quantified. The most important of them, Adler and Fromm, present what are virtually ego psychologies. However, for this kind of psychology far better methods of data collection are available. Many of their hypotheses are unverifiable interpretations of inadequate material. Certainly there is little empirical support for their claims.

If we regard Freudian theory as valuable because of its explanatory power and its scope, then the rational procedure must be first to verify the clinical findings and then to attempt to incorporate them into a theory. To accept findings uncritically, as these neo-Freudian have done, and to reinterpret them in untestable form does not appear a useful procedure.

For Freudian theory, however, one useful theory has resulted. Psychoanalysts have examined the social determinants of development (and thus abandoned unsupportable phylogenetic hypotheses) and have attempted to develop an ego psychology. Useful for *Freudian theory*, it must be stressed, rather than psychology, for quantification and precision of data are still missing from modern psychoanalysis.

13

The status of Freudian theory in the light of the evidence

In this final chapter we shall examine the status of psychoanalytic theory in the light of the evidence from the objective studies discussed in the previous chapters. For example, if the concepts supported by these investigations are so few and so unrelated to each other that no coherent link between them can be found, it will be better, clearly, to incorporate them into the body of established psychology. If, on the other hand, sufficient Freudian theory has demonstrated validity such that academic psychology cannot easily accommodate the findings, it is equally obvious that the retention of the theory is justified.

TABLE 13.1. *Summary of verified concepts*

Concept	*Exemplar investigations and page no.*	*Comments*
1. Oral character	Goldman-Eisler (1950), p. 14; Kline and Storey (1977), p. 38	
2. Anal character	Kline (1969a), p. 38 and Kline (1979a)	
3. Oral erotism. No links between personality and child-training procedures	Levy (1928), p. 104 Kline and Storey (1980), p. 125	Severe methodological difficulties. Theoretical problem of psychosexual constitution, see p. 116
4. Oedipus complex	Friedman (1952), p. 135	
5. Castration complex	Stephens (1961), p. 144	
6. Id — ego — super-ego	Cattell and Pawlik (1964), p. 177	N.B. Validity of experimental personality variables uncertain
7. Repression and other defences	Dixon (1958b), p. 215 Percept-genetics, p. 229	
8. Sexual symbolism outside dreams	Jahoda (1956), p. 269	

Concept	Exemplar investigations and page no.	Comments
9. Psychological meaning of dreams	Hall (1966), p. 298	
10. Sexual symbolism in dreams	Berger (1963a), p. 310	
11. Sexual nature of dreams	Karacan et al. (1966), p. 306	
12. Paranoia and homosexuality	Zamansky (1958), p. 334	
13. Appendicitis and birth fantasy	Eylon (1967), p. 363	
14. Phobias	Dixon et al. (1957), p. 377	
15. Depression	Leckie and Withers (1967), p. 379	
16. Libidinal wishes and psychopathology	The work of Silverman, p. 382	

The first point to emerge from Table 13.1 is that any blanket rejection of Freudian theory as a whole (e.g. Eysenck and Wilson, 1973) simply flies in the face of the evidence. Nor can it be objected that, among the myriad observations and deductions made by Freud in the course of his studies, some were bound to be true, for the fact is that these concepts are, for the most part, cardinal points of Freudian theory. Only the hypotheses concerning neuroses cannot fall under that heading.

Nevertheless it would be wrong to assume that, because these concepts have been to some extent verified, the whole or even the majority of psychoanalytic theory must be accepted on the grounds that failure to confirm the rest is due to the methodological problems of verification. In some cases the objective evidence has severely delimited the concept so that Freudian theory needs to be modified accordingly. This indeed would be an ideal outcome of the scientific study of psychoanalysis — namely that Freudian theory became thus modified and adapted in the light of the evidence. Some of these modifications and limitations must now be discussed so that we can see more precisely just what parts of the theory are supported.

THE SUPPORT FOR FREUDIAN THEORY

THE ORAL AND ANAL CHARACTER

Miles (1954) argued that it was a mistaken strategy to study psychosexual personality syndromes only because their childhood antecedents had been hypothesized in Freudian theory. Nevertheless, the interest of these personality constellations lies in the fact that, were Freudian theory true, some powerful determinants of adult behaviour would be known. If the oral and anal character are unrelated to pregenital erotism or infant-rearing procedures, their importance would be diminished, because empirical studies of personality such as those of Cattell and Eysenck have shown that such personality constellations account for only a minor part of the variance in personality measurement. Thus it is disappointing to note that the objective studies of psychosexual theory have demonstrated only that the adult personality constellations exist and have, except for a few studies, universally failed to link them to infant-rearing procedures or pregenital erotism.

In the light of this evidence it would seem reasonable to abandon the terms oral and anal. The obsessional personality is a syndrome fully recognized in non-psychoanalytic psychiatry and is very similar to the anal character. Fenichel (1945), indeed, describes an obsessional character in terms indistinguishable from those he uses to describe the anal character. The oral character could be called the dependent personality. Nevertheless, if the psychoanalytic aetiology be abandoned, the question still remains as to why, in the anal character for example, the disparate and logically unconnected traits of obstinacy, orderliness and parsimony be found together. Here the neo-Freudians such as Horney, or Fromm (1942, 1965) with his hoarding and necrophilous characters who simply resemble their parents, are far from convincing. This failure to understand how such syndromes of personality traits come into being is a serious defect of a non-sexual concept of oral and anal characters. Eysenck (1967b, for example) accounts for his two main factors of extraversion and neuroticism in terms of excitability of the central nervous system and lability of the autonomic system.

Oral erotism

Before abandoning the anal or oral aetiology of these personality constellations it must be remembered that there does seem to be evidence for oral erotism as evinced by thumb-sucking if feeding is completed with but little sucking activity. The fact that there is, therefore, early in life a need to suck strongly supports the Freudian concept of oral erotism. As has been discussed in the relevant chapter (p. 108), there have been no comparable studies of anal erotism because of the practical rather than logical difficulties of obtaining the requisite evidence. Furthermore studies attempting to link personality characteristics with infant-rearing problems are beset with severe methodological difficulties.

The constitutional factor

A final difficulty of investigating the psychosexual theory of personality development lies in the theory itself. Freud (1905a) makes it clear that there is a constitutional factor in psychosexual development. Thus some individuals will be strongly oral erotic, others strongly anal erotic. This means, of course, that studies attempting to link pot-training procedures or methods of weaning to personality characteristics, without taking this constitutional factor into account, are not properly testing the theory. Blum (1953) refers to this aspect of the theory in a somewhat disparaging tone as the fudge factor. However, if there *is* a constitutional factor, the fact that it makes scientific testing difficult is irrelevant. Nor can it be dismissed just because it makes testing difficult.

Conclusion

Thus in the light of the evidence it would be wrong to abandon psychosexual theory. The mass of negative evidence is due largely to the problems of methodology. Some of the personality syndromes postulated by Freud have been shown to exist. Their links to repressed pregenital erotism have not been convincingly demonstrated but the theory has not yet been refuted.

OEDIPUS AND CASTRATION COMPLEXES

Freud regarded his discovery of the Oedipus complex as his supreme achievement, a discovery fit to rank beside that of electricity and the wheel. It is therefore ironic not to say tragic that, only four years after the death of Freud, Sears (1943) should write that the Oedipus complex was a grotesquerie of Freud's imagination. We have however cited some evidence (Friedman, 1952; Hall, 1963) for the Oedipus complex. Nevertheless it must be admitted that this evidence, though confirming the Freudian concept, does not establish the Oedipus complex as the central conflict of mental life or show it to be the kernel of neurosis. Far more modestly, it shows in one case that boys and girls do have sexual feelings towards the opposite sex parent of which they are largely unaware. In the other example the study of dream content indicates that the Oedipal situation is a source of psychological conflict in that it regularly appears in dreams. This, therefore, is an example of where the objective evidence so far confirms the Freudian theory but suggests that Freud may have attached too much importance to it.

Stephens' (1961) study of the castration complex is most impressive. Here the full scope of the Freudian concept as it affects the customs of whole societies has been put to the test. The fact that this cross-cultural study confirms the castration complex means that this particular concept has not been delimited.

ID, EGO AND SUPER-EGO

Presumably the perfect proof of this part of psychoanalytic theory would be the demonstration of three physiological systems in the brain which subsumed the activities characteristic of ego, super-ego and id. This has not been done. However, the empirical studies, using objective personality devices of Cattell at the IPAT laboratories, have revealed three third-order factors which resemble to some extent the tripartite division of Freud (Cattell and Pawlik, 1964).

Further support for this division comes from Cattell's studies of interests (Cattell, 1957) and the isolation of alpha, beta and gamma factors. These studies, as yet, are not definitive proof but rather are strikingly suggestive. If the validity of these objective test devices could be fully established and the results replicated on large samples, impressive support for this aspect of the theory could be mustered. Of course it must be realized that in Cattell's work the id is not unconscious as in the original theory.

REPRESSION AND OTHER DEFENCES

Little needs to be said about defence mechanisms of repression. It seems to us that the experimental studies of Dixon (1958a, b) and Blum (1955) are laboratory demonstrations of repression, as denial of entry into consciousness, in action. The other defences have not been confirmed to the same degree although the percept-genetic studies of Kragh and Smith (1970) go a long way towards doing this without entirely removing the subjective judgement of the observer in deciding that various responses are or are not defence mechanisms. Nevertheless repression is probably the most important of these defence mechanisms in Freudian theory since the whole dynamic view of mental life turns upon this concept. Thus the fact that it has been so powerfully supported means that one of the cornerstones of psychoanalytic theory as a whole still remains.

SEXUAL SYMBOLISM

This has been amply demonstrated to occur both within and outside dreams. Whether it must be regarded as a disguise to evade the censor, as Freud maintained, or whether, more simply, symbolism generally is the result of a visual transformation of abstractions, as Hall suggests, has not been decided by the empirical evidence. The fact that sexual symbolism has been verified means that the insights into art and literature offered by psychoanalytic theory need not be dismissed out of hand.

DREAM THEORY

The large-scale studies by Hall at the Institute of Dream Research make it clear that dream content has some kind of psychological meaning for the individual. Certainly Freudian theory was supported in that by using the concepts of Oedipal and castration complexes differential dream content for the two sexes was successfully predicted. Nevertheless the Freudian claim that dreams contain a wish has not been confidently verified — partly because the very subjective interpretation of dream content (to reach latent dream content) cannot, justifiably, be regarded as a scientific procedure. However, the study by Lee (1958) among the Zulu does support this claim.

Although the 'need to dream', such as it is, is clearly physiological rather than psychological — that is some essential metabolic process appears to go on during REM periods — and clearly dreams are the guardians of REM sleep rather than sleep itself, as postulated by Freud, the fact that dream content influences penile erections is evidence for the sexual nature of this type of dream. The finding, however, that REM periods are usually accompanied by penile erection cannot be regarded as evidence for the sexual nature of all dreams since penile erection is probably symptomatic of a more general subcortical stimulation, rather than specific sexual excitation.

Thus the objective study of dreams has confirmed the sexual symbolism of dreams and the psychological importance of dream content to the individual. REM study of dreaming has not yet yielded much evidence relevant to Freudian theory although as a method it offers great hopes. It must be noted that objective studies of dreaming (as Fisher and Greenberg (1977) point out) put a greater emphasis on the importance of the manifest content than did Freud.

NEUROSES

Many of the Freudian claims concerning the neuroses have simply never been put to the objective test. This is largely because until recently no adequate measuring instruments existed. Thus the hypotheses which have been put to the test are usually those where convenient measures are at hand rather than those most crucial to the theory.

It is noticeable that where experimental techniques can be used, as in the investigation of the homosexual element in paranoia, clear-cut results have been obtained in favour of the Freudian theory. This is particularly true of the work of Silverman and colleagues which allows the significance of unconscious wishes in the development of psychopathology to be tested. Some support has been adduced also for Freudian theory concerning depression, phobias and appendicitis. It is a curious fact that, although Freudian theory was developed from the study of neurotics and psychotics, there seems to be more objective evidence supporting the basic concepts of the theory than there is in favour of the particular theories underlying mental disturbances.

CONCLUSIONS

We are left from a study of the objective evidence with some confirmation of a tripartite division of mental activity into ego, super-ego and id. Developmental theory is supported in that oral erotism, Oedipus and castration complexes appear to occur. Furthermore adult personality patterns like the oral and anal character can be generally observed. There seems no doubt that the defence mechanism repression is commonly used and other defences have been observed. Sexual symbolism is a verified phenomenon both within and outside dreams which do indeed seem concerned with basic human conflicts. In addition to this certain Freudian hypotheses concerning neuroses have been supported.

From these conclusions it seems clear that far too much that is distinctively Freudian has been verified for the rejection of the whole psychoanalytic theory to be possible. Furthermore it is to be noted that there are few good experiments which actually refute the theory. For example, as has been said, the fact that no link between infant-rearing procedures and adult personality has been shown is at least in part due to severe methodological problems. Similarly many areas which have not been confirmed have not been put to the test.

The Blacky Pictures, to illustrate the point, contain a measure of the Oedipus complex. This is claimed by Freud (1916-17) to be the kernel of the neuroses, yet not one investigator has attempted the obvious check of seeing how neurotics and normals compare on this test other than the present author in a small pilot study (Kline, 1969b) which gave very limited support to the theory.

Two points must, however, be discussed before the status of Freudian theory can be evaluated. First we must consider those aspects of the theory which we have not touched on in this book. Finally we must try to establish whether or not the findings that have been verified could have been predicted from other psychological theories.

UNEXAMINED PARTS OF FREUDIAN THEORY

In the first chapter (see especially pp. 2-4), it was pointed out that the Freudian hypotheses examined in this book were the empirical and specific psychoanalytic proportions (Rapaport and Gill, 1959). However, the fact is that much of psycho-analytic theory is, in this terminology, metapsychology of which the empirical propositions are the building blocks. It is this metapsychology, of course, which is characteristically difficult to put to the empirical test and against which many of the objections on the grounds of scientific rigour have been aimed. Meta-psychology has been ignored in this book both because in many cases it cannot be tested, and because, unless the original propositions are shown to be true, even attempting to test it seems useless.

EXAMPLES OF METAPSYCHOLOGICAL THEORY

The collective unconscious

Freud (1913b) in 'Totem and taboo' put forward the tentative hypothesis that there is a kind of collective unconscious or mass psyche which accounts for the continuity of man's psychological life over the years. By means of this entity, whatever or wherever it is, man is able to inherit ideas, for example a memory of the primal horde and the original killing of the father.

Comments

As was made clear in our discussion of Jung (see p. 408), for whom the collective unconscious is an essential concept, this notion of a collective unconscious is quite untestable. The empirical consequences are not such as could ever prove the theory. For example, the similarity of the folk tales of all cultures does not necessitate such an explanatory concept. This mystical concept did not, fortunately, enter into the basic theory of psychoanalysis.

The inheritance of former experiences

Freud (1939), in his last work *Moses and Monotheism*, suggested that man brings with him into the world a heritage of ideational contents, memory traces of the experiences of former generations.

Comments

This hypothesis, related to that already discussed, is again not amenable to the scientific test. However, it is not worth testing in that modern studies of genetics indicate that the inheritance of acquired characteristics (except by interference with DNA processes) is not possible. Lysencko seems finally to have been rejected. Furthermore, to leave genetic arguments aside, even were individuals reared up without contact with others, the fact of their ignorance of their archaic heritage could be put down to the linguisitic and emotional disturbances that would inevitably, in psychoanalytic theory, result from this experimental rearing procedure. Thus the theory is not refutable.

Conclusions

Neither of these two hypotheses which are clearly quite unscientific are much used in general psychoanalytic theory. Thus they may be abandoned without loss to even the metapsychology of the general theory. It is interesting to note how closely these theories mirror early Platonic writing. Thus the notion of a collective mind occurs in the *Phaedo* and the doctrine of memnesis is 'proven' in the *Meno*, the subject of which, poor unfortunate slave, is made to recall from his collective mind a geometric proof. A further noteworthy point is that the tripartite division of the soul is also to be found in the *Phaedrus* and *The Republic*. Although Freud's notions were based on observations, as he thought, it would be informative to know how acquainted he was with these Platonic dialogues. Ellenberger (1970) has of course made the point that Freudian theory is not all that original and most of it was current in the Zeitgeist at the turn of the century.

Eros and thanatos, the life and death instincts

Freud (1923) in 'The ego and the id' claims that in man there are two instinctual forces, eros and thanatos. The association and opposition of these two forces create the very essence of life itself. The death instinct, to be found in all living matter, manifests itself as a tendency to return to the original inorganic state. Eros, on the other hand, represents the life force, the drive behind the sexual instincts.

Comments

Actually, as Fenichel (1945) states, psychoanalysts have tended to ignore this last formulation of Freud. Only Melanie Klein, indeed, seems to make any use of the concept of thanatos. These two concepts of eros and thanatos, as is the case with all instinct theories, cannot be put to any kind of empirical test. The only evidence that could be adduced in support of the death instinct is the fact that organisms die. Why do they die? Because of the death instinct for which the evidence is their death. The argument is thus circular. Even if two factors could be found to account for all human behaviour, this would not support the concept of life and death instincts. The fact is that these concepts have no empirical consequences other than life and death itself.

The only part of Freud's general theory that would appear to be affected by the rejection of eros and thanatos is the theory of sadism and masochism which are manifestations of thanatos turned, in the case of masochism, inwards to the self. Nevertheless if we wish psychoanalysis to become a scientific discipline it is necessary to abandon the concepts of life and death instincts.

The pleasure principle

Basic to Freudian theory is a concept which has not been put to the empirical test — the pleasure principle. In 'Beyond the pleasure principle' (Freud, 1920), it is made clear that the aim of mental functioning is pleasure, the reducing of tension within the nervous system.

Comments

Again this is not a testable aspect of the theory partly because Freud himself (1920) was not clear precisely how this occurred or how such tension could be measured. Nevertheless, although this principle underlies the workings of the psychical apparatus, failure to test it does not mean that Freudian theory has not really been tested because the actual workings of this mental apparatus have been examined — Oedipus complex, repression, pregenital erotism and the like.

These examples, it is hoped, make it clear that in this book we have made no attempt to demonstrate the scientific validity of what are, perhaps, the most fundamental aspects of Freudian theory. These concepts, the metapsychology of psychoanalysis, are, however, as we have shown, untestable and unscientific in that they have no empirical consequences. For this reason, therefore, it is argued that failure to test these concepts does not mean that we have not put psycho-analytic theory to the test. Indeed it emerges that these fundamental postulates can be removed without affecting the empirical propositions of the theory. Thus, for example, the finding that the castration complex is an important factor in the development of boys is not at all changed whether or not we regard the reason for this as being due to reduction of tension (the pleasure principle) or to some emanation of eros and thanatos. What is of interest is the fact of the castration complex, its antecedents and its consequences.

PREDICTION OF VERIFIED PSYCHOANALYTIC FINDINGS FROM OTHER THEORIES

Conant (1947) has made the point that theories tend to get displaced not by the discovery of dissonant facts but by the elaboration of an alternative theory. Despite the apparently large number of findings which do not neatly fit psycho-analysis, the fact remains that no alternative theory has been proposed. In the main this is because the idea of developing a theory to account for so huge a range of phenomena is not, as it was at the turn of the century, in accord with scien-tific *Zeitgeist*. Indeed, Skinner (1954) is expressly and proudly atheoretical. Nevertheless operant conditioning as developed in the work of Skinner and his associates is clearly regarded by adherents of that school as containing the key to the understanding, prediction and control of human behaviour (Bolles, 1967).

Certainly a school of behaviour therapy making use, as it claims, of operant conditioning techniques and Pavlovian conditioning has arisen, led in this country by Eysenck and Rachmann (Rachmann, 1963). Thus the question arises as to whether these verified findings of Freudian theory mean that the theory must be supported. Eysenck and Wilson (1973), as we have seen, have made a considerable but largely unsuccessful effort to reinterpret some of our experimental results using other theories and *ad hoc* hypotheses of monstrous inelegance. If, for example, these findings could be predicted from operant conditioning there is no need to invoke Freudian theory. We can simply say that Freud made certain observations which, as it turned out, were correct.

Dollard and Miller (1950) have made what is probably the most determined attempt to interpret psychoanalytic theory in terms of the findings from studies of learning although, as Breger and McGaugh (1965) point out, behaviour therapists have tended to ignore their work because the treatment derived from it is little different from psychoanalysis and also because behaviour therapists do not even accept the accuracy of the findings interpreted by Dollard and Miller. It is therefore interesting to see to what extent the findings of Freudian theory which we have shown to be verified by objective evidence can be predicted from theories of learning.

ORAL EROTISM

Dollard and Miller (1950) reject this concept on the basis of the study by Sears and Wise (1950; see p. 105). However, following Yarrow (1954) it was shown that this study did not invalidate the concept of oral erotism supported by Levy (1928; see p. 104). Hence the claim of Dollard and Miller that the 'specific desire for nursing at the breast or bottle is at least in part learned as a result of the primary reinforcement of getting food when hungry,' is not supported in the light of later evidence. Learning theory, therefore, would not predict such a concept as oral erotism.

ORAL AND ANAL CHARACTERS

Apart from the totally circular argument that these characters are the result of reinforcement schedules it would be difficult to account for them in terms of

learning. The fact that anal characters seem to have parents with similar personalities perhaps might be explained in terms of imitation (Mowrer, 1950). Thus
the talking budgerigar talks because it is then like its master, which is reinforcing.
However, were this analysis the whole truth, children would be expected to
resemble their parents to a far greater extent than in fact they do. Furthermore an
analysis of personality in terms of learning by imitation would fail to explain why
these particular syndromes rather than others occurred.

However, even if these syndromes are not satisfactorily to be understood in
terms of learning theory, it must also be remembered that the psychoanalytic
hypothesis linking them to repressed pregenital erotism and child-training
procedures were not verified. Indeed had they been so the findings could have
been interpreted in terms of learning theory also. Beloff (1957) argues that the
anal character may be regarded as the result of over-learning and subsequent
stimulus-generalization — what Eysenck (1947) hypothesizes to be typical of
introverts. The oral character could be interpreted in this way — dependency
during feeding, for example, being strongly reinforced and continuing through
life.

OEDIPUS AND CASTRATION COMPLEXES

Dollard and Miller (1950) are able to incorporate both these concepts into the
learning model. Very briefly they regard the Oedipal situation as one where overt
sexual behaviour has been suppressed yet the child, through sex-typing, has a
vague expectation of reward from the opposite sex. Similarly fear of the father is
aroused because the father is the source of discipline and has a unique relationship
with his mother which the child is not allowed to share. The specific genital
anxiety can arise from the fact that his motives are sexual (hence he fears a fitting
punishment), from stories current in childhood lore and from observed sex
differences. These fears bring about the resolution of the Oedipal conflict because
'When anxiety is greatly dominant over the approach tendencies, the conflicted
individual strays away from his goal and but few of the acquired elements in the
sexual appetite are aroused' (p. 147).

Thus, although the facts of the Oedipal and castration complex can be fitted
into models derived from learning theories, a more important question is
whether, in the absence of Freudian theory, any such predictions would have
been made from these theories. This question underlines an essential point. The
possible hypotheses to be derived from learning theories are almost as great in
number as those that may be drawn from psychoanalytic theory. Furthermore in
the absence of knowledge of just what are particular reinforcers for individual
human beings, it is not possible on the basis of learning theories alone to choose
any particular hypotheses. Indeed it can be argued that what psychoanalysis is
really concerned with, and these two concepts are good examples of it, is studying
just what elements in the environment (the family situation) act as conditioned
stimuli and reinforcers for the child's behaviour.

REPRESSION

This is, of course, one of the key concepts in psychoanalysis. If repression could not be objectively verified, many other essential concepts would themselves automatically become suspect. Thus any other theory purporting to replace psychoanalysis must also be able to fit repression into its model. Dollard and Miller (1950) are easily able to accommodate this concept. They write: 'repression is the symptom of avoiding certain thoughts; it is reinforced by drive-reduction' (p. 201). The actual response that is reinforced by drive-reduction (anxiety-reduction) is stopping thinking. These formulations are the basis of their analysis of repression in terms of drive-reduction theory and although they proceed to develop it in some detail this is unnecessary for our purpose. There can be little doubt that the mechanism of repression fits easily into learning theories of human behaviour, more easily indeed than the other Freudian concepts so far discussed.

SEXUAL SYMBOLISM

The fact of sexual symbolism fits easily into a learning-theory analysis of behaviour. Clearly, it is a simple example of stimulus-generalization. On its own, stimulus-generalisation fails to explain why it should be that the sexual organs are favourite objects of symbolization. After all, on this theory a gun could represent a penis or a penis a gun — not the usual psychoanalytic interpretation! However if sexual symbolism is taken together with repression as it is in psychoanalytic theory, similar predictions about symbolism could be made from both learning theory and psychoanalysis. Thus there is no problem concerning sexual symbolism if learning theory models are preferred to Freudian theory.

SYMBOLISM IN DREAMS

The phenomenology of dreams is, however, a subject outside the bounds of learning theory. Here only the clinical dynamic psychologies such as those of Freud or Jung attempt to account for the content of dreams and the reason for their occurrence for individual subjects. Jungian theory involving archetypes of the collective unconscious appears even less testable than Freudian hypotheses. Hall (1966) has postulated a theory of dreaming in which the content is related to the most basic conflicts and hence the most important events in men's lives. This, however, unlike the psychoanalytic theory of dreaming which is conceived as an expression of the unconscious — particularly clear because in sleep the super-ego is somewhat relaxed — is an *ad hoc* theory. It fails to explain why conflicts should be thus acted out in dreams. It is therefore probably still true to say that for all its inadequacies the psychoanalytic theory of dreaming is the most coherent. Learning theory is ill at ease in this field.

PARANOIA AND HOMOSEXUALITY

In Freudian theory the paranoid projects his repressed homosexuality (changed by reaction-formation into hatred) on to his fellow men. Hence come his persecutory delusions. Dollard and Miller (1950) explain this in terms of learning theory with the following example: the homosexual thoughts create anxiety and are repressed (see their rationale for repression). Because of this conflict the subject feels miserable in the presence of a particular colleague. This is rationalized as a dislike for the man which is regarded as mutual. This logical explanation reduces anxiety, caused by the fact that previously his feelings had been inexplicable. In addition the idea of dislike eliminates thoughts of love and is thus another source of reinforcement. From this it appears that the psychoanalytic formulation linking homosexuality and paranoia can be explained in terms of learning theory. However it is very much a *post-hoc* explanation. Given the facts of a paranoid's persecutory delusions, learning theory would not of itself *predict* repressed homosexuality and projection as a cause. Thus this example strengthens the case already put forward that psychoanalysis is concerned with the study of reinforcement. Learning theory, without a knowledge of what does and does not act as reinforcement for human beings, is quite inadequate for an understanding of human behaviour. Hence in this instance psychoanalysis may be regarded as completing the (*all-important*) details of the learning process in this particular form of mental illness. Without this psychoanalytic knowledge learning theory would not be invoked. Thus it can be argued that in this instance Freudian theory is superior to learning theory.

APPENDICITIS AND BIRTH FANTASIES

This relationship, postulated by Freud and supported by Eylon (1967), must be regarded as one of the more surprising claims in psychoanalytic theory of the sort which has led to outright ridicule and disbelief. Suffice it to say that learning theory (as almost all other theories) would not be able to predict this finding.

PHOBIAS

Freud (1925a) tries to discriminate between separation anxiety and castration anxiety. To some extent (see p. 377) Dixon et al. (1957) were able to support such a dichotomy with a factor-analysis of certain questionnaire items from the Tavistock Self-Assessment Inventory (Sandler, 1954). Phobias, of course, are the very meat and drink of the behaviour-therapy school and it is with these complaints that their greatest successes are gained. Phobias, in terms of the learning-theory model, are avoidance-responses (reinforced by reduction in fear) often to quite inappropriate stimuli. The fact that such stimuli elicit these responses is, in part, a function of stimulus-generalization and higher-order conditioning.

The typical behaviour-therapy treatment of phobias, in which by desensitization the fear is gradually extinguished and then more appropriate responses are reinforced, again highlights the point previously made about psychoanalysis that it concentrates on the nature and origins of reinforcers and conditioned stimuli. Thus, pragmatically, behaviour therapy is interested only in the fact that maladaptive responses have been learned to, say, snakes and in the extinction of these responses. Freudian theory on the other hand, in the spirit of enquiry, is concerned implicitly with the question of how snakes can elicit such responses; it is concerned with the study of the nature of the stimulus-generalization (perhaps snakes to penis) and the reasons why there is fear-reduction (perhaps the castration complex) and hence reinforcement. Thus while it is not denied that the learning-theory model fits phobias well, it seems to us that psychoanalytic theory is concerned with the far more important and interesting task of examining the fundamental nature of the learning process in particular phobias.

DEPRESSION

Some support has been demonstrated for the psychoanalytic theory linking orality and narcissism with depression. In this area psychoanalytic theory is superior to learning-theory models which seem unable to accommodate it. Dollard and Miller (1950) mention it on only one page, Eysenck and Rachmann (1965) have two references to it, in neither of which is the learning-theory analysis mentioned. Franks (1969), in a book devoted to the appraisal and status of behaviour therapy, does not even contain one reference to it. Learning theorists simply relate depression to a lack of reinforcers.

ID, EGO, AND SUPER-EGO

Dollard and Miller (1950) find no problem with the super-ego. They write 'Anxiety reactions, never labelled, are attached to stimuli, also unlabelled. When these stimuli recur later, the anxiety actions automatically occur. The resulting affect, Freud has called "super-ego".' They regard the ego as higher mental processes, e.g. thinking, planning and organizing and make no explicit mention of the id. However, they do talk about the unconscious which, they argue, means the unverbalized in Freudian theory. This unconscious includes the super-ego, of course, as well as the id. Nevertheless, for these writers the unconscious is characterized by its lack of verbal responses and cue-producing responses (e.g. counting) which are the essence of the higher mental processes or the ego. Hence the importance in the unconscious of childhood experiences before such responses could be made. As Dollard and Miller point out, these definitions demand a somewhat extended concept of cue and response.

From this brief outline of one attempt to integrate the psychoanalytic theory of mental structure into a learning-theory model, it will be clear that, even if vague, it is not entirely impossible. Of course it cannot be too strongly emphasized that this is a process which most learning theorists would not even attempt, since it is not in their view a profitable exercise. Mental structure is a field which theories of learning would not seek to embrace, with the exception of the super-ego. The super-ego is of relevance because in psychoanalytic theory it comes about through identification with the father by the child. Even if identification is not clearly defined it is clearly some sort of learning process. Mowrer (1950), in his interesting discussion of the concept of identification and its lack of clarity in orthodox Freudian formulations, makes the point that identification with the father may not come about as the result of the castration complex and the Oedipal conflict but that the identification may come first, through love of the father, and that this brings about the object-choice of mother.

Thus although with the exception of the super-ego the Freudian concepts of mental structure are inherently foreign and irrelevant to theories of learning, as Dollard and Miller demonstrate, it is not impossible to fit them into such a theory.

CONCLUSIONS AND FINALE

Three points have been emphasized in this chapter. Much of the metapsychology of psychoanalytic theory, it has been agreed, is unscientific in that it cannot be subjected to any kind of empirical test and so be refuted. Such concepts as the death instinct and the pleasure principle fall under this head. On the other hand we have shown much of psychoanalytic theory to consist of empirical propositions which can, logically at least, be tested. Most of this book has been concerned with sifting the objective evidence relevant to these propositions. Many of the Freudian concepts most important to psychoanalytic theory have been supported, for example repression and the Oedipus complex. We should make it clear that we have not examined psychoanalytic theory as a *theory*; that is to examine whether it is coherent, consistent and meaningful in the Wittgenstein sense.

This is a valuable task and has been excellently done by those with philosophical training such as Farrell (1964) and Cheshire (1975). This is an important topic from the viewpoint of the scientific value of Freudian theory but one beyond the scope of the author and of this book which concentrates on the logical positivistic aspect of the theory alone — are the propositions refutable or not?

Finally we have raised the fundamental question as to whether the verification of these Freudian concepts means that psychoanalytic theory should be retained. To this end, for those psychoanalytic propositions that were verified we examined the predictions made from theories of learning. Here it was found that in most cases the Freudian phenomena could be fitted into a model derived from theories of learning but that these theories on their own could not have predicted the clinical observations.

So, far from regarding learning-theory models and psychoanalytic theory as opposed, we consider them to be closely related — the Freudian theory supplying the details of the learning procedures. The status of psychoanalytic theory must now be clear. It must be retained not as a whole but only after rigorous objective research has revealed what parts are correct or false or in need of modification. But, as has been shown in this book, much of it has been confirmed. Now, however, a huge task of research remains and some powerful research tools are now at hand, especially those developed in percept-genetics and by Silverman and colleagues in New York. If well done it could illuminate our understanding of human behaviour; if left undone, we shall be left to wander in a circular maze of undefined reinforcement.

Bibliography

Abert, K., Bally, C. and Schade, J.P. (eds) (1965) *Sleep Mechanisms*, Amsterdam, Elsevier.

Abraham, K. (1916) 'The first pregenital stage of the libido', in *Selected Papers of Karl Abraham* (1965), London, Hogarth Press and Institute of Psychoanalysis.

Abraham, K. (1921) 'Contributions to the theory of the anal character', in *Selected Papers of Karl Abraham* (1965), London, Hogarth Press and Institute of Psychoanalysis.

Abraham, K. (1924) 'Character-formation on the genital level of libido development', in *Selected Papers of Karl Abraham* (1965), London, Hogarth Press and Institute of Psychoanalysis.

Abramson, H. A. (1961) 'Intractable asthma: conflict of period of toilet-training', *J. Psychol.*, **52**, 223-9.

Abt, L. E. and Reiss, M. (eds) (1964) *Progress in Clinical Psychology*, New York, Grune & Stratton.

Accord, L. D. (1962) 'Sexual symbolism as a correlate of age', *J. Consult. Psychol.*, **26**, 279-81.

Adcock, C. J. (1965) 'A comparison of the concepts of Eysenck and Cattell', *Brit. J. Educ. Pyschol.*, **35**, 90-7.

Adelson, J. and Redmond, J. (1958) 'Personality differences in the capacity for verbal recall', *J. Abnorm. Soc. Psychol.*, **57**, 244-8.

Adler, A. (1930) *Individual Psychology*, in Murchison (1930).

Adorno, T. W., Frenkel-Brunswik, E., Levinson, D. J. and Sandford, R. N. (1950) *The Authoritarian Personality*, New York, Harper & Row.

Alexander, F. (1934) 'The influence of psychological factors upon gastro-intestinal disturbances', *Psychoanal. Quart.*, **3**, 501.

Alexander, F. (1935) 'The logic of emotions and its dynamic background', *Internat. J. Psychoanal.*, **16**, 399-413.

Alexander, F. (1937) *Five-Year Report of the Chicago Institute for Psychoanalysis, 1932-7.*

Alexander, F. (1950) *Psychosomatic Medicine*, New York, Norton.

Alexander, F. and French, T. M. (1948) *Studies in Psychosomatic Medicine*, New York, Ronald Press.

Alexander, W. A. (1954) 'A study of normal and psychotic subjects who deviate in their performance on the IES tests', Ph.D. thesis, Western Reserve University.

Allen, M. G. (1957) 'Childhood experience and adult personality: a cross-cultural study using the concept of ego-strength', *J. Soc. Psychol.*, **71**, 53-68.

Alper, T. G., Blane, H. T. and Abrams, B. K. (1955) 'Reactions of middle- and lower-class children to finger paints as a function of class-differences in child-training practices', *J. Abnorm. Soc. Psychol.*, **51**, 439-48.

Althouse, R. H. (1970) 'A semantic differential investigation of sexually symbolic concepts: Freud and Jung', *J. Proj. Tech.*, **34**, 507-12.

Altrocchi, J., Parsons, O. A. and Pickoff, H. (1961) 'Changes in self-ideal discrepancy in repressors and sensitizers', *J. Abnorm. Soc. Psychol.*, **61** (1), 67-72.

Altshuler, K. Z. (1966) 'Comments on recent sleep research related to psychoanalytic theory', *Arch. Gen. Psychiat.*, **15** (3), 235-9.

Amadeo, M. and Gomez, E. (1964) 'Eye movements and dreaming in subjects with life-long blindness', *Paper at Annual Meeting of Assn. Psychophysiol. Stud. Sleep*.

Ammons, R. P. and Ammons, C. H. (1978) 'Use and evaluation of the IES test', *Percept. Mot. Skills*, **47**, 1076-8.

Andersson, A., Nilsson, A., Ruuth, E. and Smith, G. (1972) *Visual After-effects and the Individual as an Adaptive System*, Lund, Gleerup.

Andrich, J. and Kline, P. (1981) 'Within and among population item-fit with the simple logistic model', *Educ. Psychol. Meas.* (in press).

Anshen, R. N. (1948) *The Family: its Function and Destiny*, vol. V, New York, Harper Bros.

Anthony, J. E. (1957) 'An experimental approach to the psychopathology of childhood: encopresis', *Brit. J. Med. Psychol.*, **30**, 146-75.

Archer, G. S. and Burgess, I. S. (1970) 'A further investigation of sexually symbolic concepts using the semantic differential technique', *J. Proj. Tech.*, **34**, 369-72.

Argyle, M. (1964) 'Introjection: a form of social learning', *Brit. J. Psychol.*, **55**, 391-402.

Argyle, M. and Robinson, P. (1962) 'Two origins of achievement motivation', *Brit. J. Soc. Clin. Psychol.*, **1**, 107-20.

Arnold, M. B. (1950) 'An excitatory theory of emotion', in Reymert, M. L. (1950).

Aronfreed, J. (1968) *Conduct and Conscience: the Socialization of Internalized Control over Behaviour*, New York, Academic Press.

Aronfreed, J. (1969) 'The concept of internalization', chapter 4 in Goslin, D. A. (1969).

Aronson, M. L. (1953) 'A study of the Freudian theory of paranoia by means of the Blacky Pictures', *J. Proj. Tech.*, **17**, 3-19.

Aserinsky, E. and Kleitman, N. (1955) 'Regularly occurring periods of eye motility, and concomitant phenomena, during sleep', *J. App. Physiol.*, **8**, 1-10.

Atkinson, J. W. (ed.) (1958) *Motives in Fantasy, Action and Society*, New York, Van Nostrand.

Bacon, M. K., Barry, H. and Child, K. (1965) 'A cross-cultural study of drinking — II: Relations to other features of culture', *Quart. J. Stud. Alcohol. Supp.*, **3**, 29-48.

Bandura, A. (1962) 'Social learning through imitation', in Jones, M. R. (1962).

Bandura, A. (1965) 'Influence of models' reinforcement-contingencies on the acquisition of imitative responses', *J. Pers. Soc. Psychol.*, **1**, 589-95.

Bandura, A. (1969) 'Social learning theory of identificatory processes', chapter 3 in Goslin, D. A. (1969).

Bandura, A., Grusec, J. E. and Menlove, F. L. (1966) 'Observational learning as a function of symbolization and incentive-set', *Child Development*, **37**, 499-506.

Bandura, A., Grusec, J. E. and Menlove, F. L. (1967) 'Some social determinants of self-monitoring reinforcement systems', *J. Pers. Soc. Psychol.*, **5**, 449-55.

Bandura, A. and Huston, A. C. (1961) 'Identification as a process of incidental learning', *J. Abnorm. Soc. Psychol.*, **63**, 311-18.

Bandura, A., Ross, C. and Ross, S. (1963) 'A comparative test of the status envy, social power, and secondary reinforcement theories of identificatory learning', *J. Abnorm. Soc. Psychol.*, **67**, 601-7.

Bandura, A. and Walters, R. H. (1963) *Social Learning and Personality Development*, New York, Holt, Rinehart & Winston.

Barendregt, J. T., Bastiaans, J. and Vermeul Van Mullen, A. W. (1961) 'A psychological study of the effects of psychoanalysis and psychotherapy', in Barendregt, J. T. (ed.) *Research in Diagnostics*, The Hague and Paris, Mouton.

Bargmann, R. (1953) 'The statistical significance of simple structure in factor-analysis', Frankfurt am Main, Hochschule Fuer Internationale Paedagogische Forschung.

Barnes, C. A. (1952) 'A statistical study of the Freudian theory of levels of psychosexual development', *Genet. Psychol. Monogr.*, **45**, 109-74.

Barret, W., Caldbeck-Meenan, J. and White, J. G. (1966) 'Questionnaire measures and psychiatrist ratings of a personality dimension', *Brit. J. Psychiat.*, **112**, 413-15.

Barrett, P. and Kline, P. (1980) 'A comparison between Rasch analysis and factor-analysis of items in the EPQ', unpublished manuscript, University of Exeter.

Barrett, P. and Kline, P. (1981) 'The observation to variable ratio in factor analysis', *Person and Group Behav.* (in press).

Barron, F. and Leary, T. F. (1955) 'Changes in psychoneurotic patients with and without psychotherapy', *J. Consult. Psychol.*, **19**, 239-45.

Barton, K. (1973) 'The relative validities of the CTS, the EPI and the Comrey Scales as measures of second-order personality source traits by questionnaire', *Advance publications no. 1*, Boulder, Institute for Research on Morality and Adjustment.

Barton, K., Dielman, T. E. and Cattell, R. B. (1977) 'Child-caring practices related to child personality', *J. Soc. Psychol*, **101**, 75-8.

Beardslee, D. C. and Fogelson, R. (1958) 'Sex-differences in sexual imagery aroused by musical stimulation', in Atkinson, J. W. (1958).

Beck, A. T. (1962) 'Reliability of psychiatric diagnoses — I: A critique of systematic studies', *Amer. J. Psychiat.*, **119**, 210-15.

Beck, A. T., Ward, G. H., Mendelsson, M., Mock, J. E. and Erbaugh, J. K. (1962) 'Reliability of psychiatric diagnoses — II: A study of the consistency of clinical judgements and ratings', *Amer. J. Psychiat.*, **119**, 351-7.

Beck, S. B., Wind-Hull, C. I. and McClean, P. M. (1976) 'Variables related to women's somatic preferences of the male and female body', *J. Pers. Soc.*, **34**, 1200-10.

Beck, S. J. (1958) 'Review of the Blacky Pictures', *J. Consult. Psychol.*, **20**, 487-8.

Beech, H. R. (1959) 'An experimental investigation of sexual symbolism in anorexia nervosa employing a subliminal stimulation technique: preliminary report', *Psychosom. Med.*, **21**, 277-80.

Bell, H. M. (1938) *The Bell Adjustment Inventory,* Stanford, University of Stanford Press.

Bellak, L. (1958) 'Studying the psychoanalytic process by the method of short-range prediction and judgement', *Brit. J. Med. Psychol.*, **31**, 249-52.

Bellak, L. (1961) 'Research in psychoanalysis', *Psychoanal. Quart.*, **30**, 519-48.

Bellak, L. and Smith, M. B. (1956) 'An experimental exploration of the psycho-analytic process', *Psychoanal. Quart.*, **25**, 385.

Bellini, M. and Tansella, M. (1976) 'Obsessional scores and subjective general psychiatric complaints of patients with duodenal ulcers or ulcerative colitis', *Psychol. Med.*, **6**, 461-7.

Beloff, H. (1957) 'The structure and origin of the anal character', *Genet. Psychol. Mongr.*, **55**, 141-72.

Beres, D. and Obers, S. (1950) 'The effects of extreme deprivation in infancy on psychic structure in adolescence', *Psychoanal. Stud. Child.*, **5**, 121-40.

Berg, M. and Cohen, B. B. (1959) 'Early separation from the mother in schizo-phrenia', *J. Nerv. Ment. Dis.*, **128**, 365-9.

Berger, L. (1959) 'Cross-validation of "primary" and "reactive" personality patterns with non-ulcer surgical patients', *J. Proj. Tech.*, **23**, 8-11.

Berger, L. and Everstine, L. (1962) 'Test—retest reliability of the Blacky Pictures Test', *J. Proj. Tech.*, **26**, 225-6.

Berger, R. J. (1961) 'Tonus of intrinsic laryngeal muscles during sleep and dreaming', *Sci.*, **134**, 840.

Berger, R. J. (1963a) 'Experimental modification of dream content by meaningful verbal stimuli', *Brit. J. Psychiat.*, **109**, 722-40.

Berger, R. J. (1963b) Ph.D. thesis, University of Edinburgh, quoted by Berger, R. J. (1963a).

Berger, R. J., Olley, P. and Oswald, I. (1962) 'The EEG, eye-movements and dreams of the blind', *Quart. J. Exp. Psychol.*, **14**, 183-6.

Berger, R. J. and Oswald, I. (1962) 'Effects of sleep-deprivation on behaviour, subsequent sleep and dreaming', *J. Ment. Sci.*, **108**, 457.

Bergin, A. E. (1963) 'Negative results revisited', *J. Consult. Psychol.*, **10**, 244-55.

Bergman, P., Malasky, C. and Zahn, T. P. (1967) 'Relation of sucking strength to personality variables', *J. Consult. Psychol.*, **31** (4), 426-8.

Bergman, P., Malasky, C. and Zahn, T. P. (1968) 'Oral functions in schizo-phrenia', *J. Nerv. Ment. Dis.*, **146**, 351-9.

Berkley-Hill, O. (1921) 'The anal erotic factor in the religion, philosophy and character of the Hindus', *Internat. J. Psychoanal.*, **2**, 306.

Berlyne, D. (1961) *Conflict Arousal and Curiosity*, New York, McGraw-Hill.

Berndt, R. and Berndt, C. (1951) *Sexual Behaviour in West Arnhem-land*, New York, Viking Fund.

Bernstein, A. (1955) 'Some relations between techniques of feeding and training during infancy and certain behaviour in childhood', *Genet. Psychol. Monogr.*, **51**, 3-44.

Bernstein, L. and Chase, P. H. (1955) 'The discriminative ability of the Blacky Pictures with ulcer patients', *J. Consult. Psychol.*, **19**, 377-80.

Berry, J. W. and Dasen, P. R. (1974) *Culture and Cognition*, London, Methuen.

Bertrand, S. and Masling, J. (1969) 'Oral imagery and alcoholism', *J. Abnorm. Psychol.*, **74**, 50-3.

Bettelheim, B. (1943) 'Individual and mass behaviour in extreme situations', *J. Abnorm. Soc. Psychol.*, **38**, 417-52.

Biddle, W. E. (1957) 'Investigation of the Oedipus fantasy by hypnosis', *Amer. J. Hypnosis*, **114**, 175.

Bieber, I. et al. (1962) *Homosexuality*, New York, Basic Books.

Biesheuvel, S. (1962) 'Personality tests for personnel selection and vocational guidance in Africa', in Taylor, A. (1962).

Bishop, F. V. (1965) 'The effects of ego-strength and stress on attitude change under conditions of forced compliance', Ph. D. thesis, New York University.

Blacker, M. and Farcher, R. E. (1977) 'A content-validity study of the Defence Mechanism Inventory', *J. Pers. Ass.*, **41**, 402-4.

Block, W. E. and Ventur, P. A. (1963) 'A study of the psychoanalytic concept of castration anxiety in symbolically castrated amputees', *Psychiat. Quart.*, **37**, 518-26.

Blum, G. S. (1949) 'A study of the psychoanalytic theory of psychosexual development', *Genet. Psychol. Monogr.*, **39**, 3-99.

Blum, G. S. (1953) *Psychoanalytic Theories of Personality*, New York, McGraw-Hill.

Blum, G. S. (1954) 'An experimental reunion of psychoanalytic theory with perceptual vigilance and defence', *J. Abnorm. Soc. Psychol.*, **49**, 94-8.

Blum, G. S. (1955) 'Perceptual defence revisited', *J. Abnorm. Soc. Psychol.*, **51**, 24-9.

Blum, G. S. (1956a) 'A reply to Charen, J.', *J. Consult. Psychol.*, **20**, 406.

Blum, G. S. (1956b) 'Defence preferences in four countries', *J. Proj. Tech. and Pers. Ass.*, **20**, 33-41.

Blum, G. S. (1957) 'An investigation of perceptual defence in Italy', *Psychol. Rep.*, **3**, 169-75.

Blum, G. S. (1962) 'A guide for the research use of the Blacky Pictures', *J. Proj. Tech. and Pers. Ass.*, **26**, 3-29.

Blum, G. S. (1964) 'Defence preferences among university students in Denmark, Germany and Israel', *J. Proj. Tech. and Pers. Ass.*, **28** (1), 13-19.

Blum, G. S. and Hunt, H. F. (1952) 'The validity of the Blacky Pictures', *Psychol. Bull.*, **49**, 238-50.

Blum, G. S. and Kaufman, J. B. (1952) 'Two patterns of personality dynamics in male ulcer patients as suggested by responses to the Blacky Pictures', *J. Clin. Psychol.*, **8**, 273-8.

Blum, G. S. and Miller, D. R. (1952) 'Exploring the psychoanalytic theory of the "oral character"', *J. Pers.*, **20**, 287-304.

Blumberg, S. and Maher, B. A. (1965) 'Trait-attribution as a study of Freudian projection', *J. Soc. Psychol.*, **65**, 311-16.

Bolles, R. C. (1967) *Theory of Motivation*, New York, Harper & Row.

Borgatta, E. F. and Lambert, W. W. (eds) (1968) *Handbook of Personality Theory and Research*, Chicago, Rand-McNally.

Botwinick, J. and Machover, S. (1951) 'A psychometric examination of latent homosexuality in alcoholism', *Quart. J. Stud. Alcohol.*, **12**, 268-72.

Bowlby, J. (1944) 'Forty-four juvenile thieves', *Int. J. Psychoanal.*, **25**, 1-57.

Bowlby, J. (ed.) (1962) *Deprivation of Maternal Care*, Geneva, World Health Organization.

Bowlby, J. (1969) *Attachment*: vol. I, *Attachment and Loss*, London, Hogarth Press and Institute of Psychoanalysis.

Bowlby, J., Ainsworth, M., Boston, M. and Rosenbluth, D. (1956) 'The effects of mother—child separation: a follow-up study', *Brit. J. Med. Psychol.*, **29**, 211-47.

Bradway, K. (1964) 'Jung's psychological types: classification by test versus classification by self', *J. Analyt. Psychol.*, **9**, 129-35.

Brar, H. S. (1973) 'Semantic differential investigation of sexually symbolic concepts using a psychiatric population', *J. Pers. Ass.*, **37**, 260-2.

Breger, L. and McGaugh, J. L. (1965) 'Critique and reformulation of "learning theory" approaches to psychotherapy and neuroses', *Psychol. Bull.*, **63**, 338-58.

Brener, E. M. (1969) 'Castration anxiety, sexual fantasy and sexual adjustment', doctoral dissertation, Boston University Graduate School, quoted by Fisher and Greenberg (1977).

Briggs, K. C. and Myers, I. B. (1962) *Manual to the Myers—Briggs Type Indicator*, Princeton, ETS.

Bromberg, P. M. (1967) 'The effects of fear and two modes of anxiety on social affiliation and phobic ideation', doctoral dissertation, New York University, quoted by Fisher and Greenberg (1977).

Bromley, E. and Lewis, L. A. (1976) 'A factor-analytic study of the Dynamic Personality Inventory using a psychiatric population', *Brit. J. Med. Psychol.*, **49**, 325-8.

Bronfenbrenner, U. (1958) 'The study of identification through interpersonal perception', in Tagiuri, R. and Petrullo, L. (1958).

Bronfenbrenner, U. (1960) 'Freudian theories of identification and their derivatives', *Child Development*, **31**, 15-40.

Brown, R. (1965) *Social Psychology*, New York, The Free Press.

Brown, W. C. (1961) *Freud and the Post-Freudians*, Harmondsworth, Penguin.

Brown, W. P. (1962) 'Conceptions of perceptual defence', *Brit. J. Psychol.*,

Monogr. Suppl., 1962, no. 35.

Browne, J. A. and Howarth, E. (1977) 'A comprehensive factor-analysis of personality questionnaire items: a test of twenty putative factor hypotheses', *Multiv. Behav. Res.*, **12**, 399-427.

Bruner, J. S. and Postman, L. (1947) 'Emotional selectivity in perception and reaction', *J. Pers.*, **16**, 69-77.

Buck, J. N. (1948) 'The HTP test', *J. Clin. Psychol.*, **4**, 151-9.

Buros, O. K. (ed.) (1959) *The Vth Mental Measurement Year Book*, New Jersey, Gryphon Press.

Buros, O. K. (ed.) (1965) *The VIth Mental Measurement Year Book*, New Jersey, Gryphon Press.

Byrne, D. (1964) 'Repression—sensitization as a dimension of personality', in Maher, B. A. (ed.) *Progress in Experimental Personality Research*, New York, Academic Press.

Caldwell, B. M. (1964) 'The effects of infant care', in Hoffman and Hoffman (1964).

Callaway, C. (1868) *The Religious System of the Amazulu*, cited in Lee (1958).

Cameron, P. (1967) 'Confirmation of the Freudian psychosexual stages utilizing sexual symbolism', *Psychol. Rep.*, **21**, 1.

Campbell, D. T. and Narroll, R. (1972) in Hsu, F. L. K. (ed.) *Psychological Anthropology*, Cambridge, Mass., Schenkman.

Cappon, D. (1964) 'Results of psychotherapy', *Brit. J. Psychiat.*, **110**, 34-45.

Carlyn, M. (1977) 'An assessment of the Myers—Briggs Type Indicator', J. Pers. Ass., **41**, 461-73.

Carp. F. M. (1962) 'Psychosexual development of stutterers', *J. Proj. Tech.*, **26** (4), 388-91.

Carstairs, G. M. (1957) *The twice-born: a study of a community of high-caste Hindus*, London, Hogarth.

Carstairs, G. M. and Grygier, T. G. (1957) 'Anthropological, psychometric and psychotherapeutic aspects of homosexuality', *Bull. Brit. Psychol. Soc.*, **32**, 46-7.

Cartwright, R. D. (1966) 'Dream and drug-induced fantasy behaviour', *Arch. Gen. Psychiat.*, **15**, 7-15.

Cartwright, R. D. (1974) 'The influence of a conscious wish on dreams — a methodological study of dream meaning and function', *J. Abnorm. Psychol.*, **83**, 387-93.

Cartwright, R. D., Dymond, R. and Vogel, J. L. (1960) 'A comparison of changes in psychoneurotic patients during matched periods of therapy and no therapy', *J. Consult. Psychol.*, **24**, 121-7.

Cattell, P. (1940) *The Measurement of Intelligence of Infants and Young Children*, New York, Psychological Corp.

Cattell, R. B. (1946) *Description and Measurement of Personality*, London, Harrap.

Cattell, R. B. (1957) *Personality and Motivation Structure and Measurement*, Yonkers, New World.

Cattell, R. B. (1965) *The Scientific Analysis of Personality*, Harmondsworth, Penguin.

Cattell, R. B. (1966a) 'The Scree Test for the number of factors', *Multiv. Behav. Res.*, **1**, 140-61.

Cattell, R. B. (1966b) *Handbook of Multivariate Experimental Psychology*, Chicago, Rand-McNally.

Cattell, R. B. (1973) *Personality and Mood by Questionnaire*, New York, Jossey-Bass.

Cattell, R. B. (1978) *The Scientific Use of Factor-Analysis in Behavioural and Life Sciences*, New York, Plenum Press.

Cattell, R. B. and Bolton, L. S. (1969) 'What pathological dimensions lie beyond the normal dimensions of the 16PF? A comparison of MMPI and 16PF factor-domains', *J. Consult. Clin. Psychol.*, **33**, 18-29.

Cattell, R. B. and Child, D. (1975) *Motivation and Dynamic Structure*, New York, Halsted Press.

Cattell, R. B., Eber, H. W. and Tatsuoka, M. M. (1970) *Handbook for the Sixteen Personality Factor Questionnaire*, Champaign, IPAT.

Cattell, R. B. and Gibbons, B. D. (1968) 'Personality factor-structure of the combined Guilford and Cattell Personality questionnaires', *J. Pers. Soc. Psychol.*, **9**, 107-20.

Cattell, R. B. and Kline, P. (1977) *The Scientific Analysis of Personality and Motivation*, London, Academic Press.

Cattell, R. B., Knapp, R. R. and Scheier, I. H. (1961) 'Second-order personality factor-structure in the objective test realm', *J. Consult. Psychol.*, **25**, 345-52.

Cattell, R. B. and Luborsky, L. (1947) 'Personality factors in response to humour', *J. Abnorm. Soc. Psychol.*, **42**, 402-21.

Cattell, R. B. and Luborsky, L. (1952) *The IPAT Humour Test of Personality*, Champaign, IPAT.

Cattell, R. B. and Muerle, J. L. (1960) 'The "Maxplane" program for factor-rotation to oblique simple structure', *Educ. Psychol. Meas.*, **20**, 569-90.

Cattell, R. B., and Nesselroade, J. R. (1965) 'Untersuchung der interkulturellen konstanz der persönlichkeitsfaktoren im 16PF-Test', *Psychologische Beiträge*, **8**, 502-15.

Cattell, R. B. and Pawlik, K. (1964) 'Third-order factors in objective personality tests', *Brit. J. Psychol.*, **55**, 1-18.

Cattell, R. B., Pichot, P. and Rennes, P. (1961) 'Constance interculturelle des facteurs de personnalité mesures par le test 16PF — II: Comparaison franco-américaine', *Rev. Psychol. App.*, **11**, 165-96.

Cattell, R. B. and Schuerger, J. M. (1978) *Personality Theory in Action*, Champaign, IPAT.

Cattell, R. B. and Warburton, F. W. (1967) *Objective Personality and Motivation Tests*, Urbana, University of Illinois Press.

Charen, J. (1956a) 'Reliability of the Blacky Tests', *J. Consult. Psychol.*, **20**, 16.

Charen, J. (1956b) 'A reply to Blum, G. S.', *J. Consult. Psychol.*, **20**, 407.

Charnes, G. (1953) 'The relative strengths of impulse, ego and super-ego in latency, adolescence and adulthood', Ph.D. thesis, Western Reserve University.

Cherry-Garrard, A. (1970) *The Worst Journey in the World*, Harmondsworth, Penguin.

Cheshire, N. M. (1975) *The Nature of Psychodynamic Interpretation*, Chichester, Wiley.

Child, I. L., Cooperman, M. and Wolowitz, H. M. (1969) 'Aesthetic preference and other correlates of active *v.* passive food preference', *J. Pers. Soc. Psychol.*, **11**, 75-84.

Childers, A. T. and Hamil, B. M. (1932) 'Emotional problems in children as related to the duration of breast-feeding in infancy', *Amer. J. Orthopsychiat.*, **2**, 134-42.

Cioffi, F. (1970) 'Freud and the idea of a pseudo-science', in Borger, M. R. and Cioffi, F. (eds) *Explanations in the Behavioural Sciences*, Cambridge, Cambridge University Press.

Clark, R. A. and Sensibar, M. R. (1956) 'The relationship between symbolic and manifest projections of sexuality with some incidental correlates', in Atkinson, J. W. (1958).

Clum, G. A. and Clum, J. (1973) 'Choice of defence mechanisms and their relationship to mood level', *Psychol. Rep.*, **32**, 910.

Cohen, A. R. (1956) 'Experimental effects of ego-defence preference on inter-personal relations', *J. Abnorm. Soc. Psychol.*, **52**, 19-27.

Comrey, A. L. (1961) 'Factored homogeneous item-dimensions in personality research', *Educ. Psychol. Meas.*, **21**, 419-31.

Comrey, A. L. (1962) 'A study of thirty-five personality dimensions', *Educ. Psychol. Meas.*, **22**, 543-52.

Comrey, A. L. (1965) 'Scales for measuring compulsion, hostility, neuroticism and shyness', *Psychol. Rep.*, **16**, 697-700.

Comrey, A. L. (1966) 'Comparison of personality and attitude variables', *Educ. Psychol. Meas.*, **26**, 853-60.

Comrey, A. L. (1970) *The Comrey Personality Scales*, San Diego, Educ. and Indus. Testing Service.

Comrey, A. L. and Jamison, K. (1966) 'Verification of six personality factors', *Educ. Psychol. Meas.*, **26**, 945-53.

Conant, J. B. (1947) *On Understanding Science*, New Haven, Yale University Press.

Cooper, J. (1970) 'Leyton obsessional inventory', *Psychol. Med.*, **1**, 48-64.

Cooperman, M. and Child, I. L. (1971) 'Differential effects of positive and negative reinforcement on two psychoanalytic character types', *J. Consult. Clin. Psychol.*, **37**, 57-9.

Coriat, I. H. (1917) 'Some statistical results of the psychoanalytic treatment of the psychoneuroses', *Psychoanal. Rev.*, **IV**, 208-16.

Corman, L. (1969) *The Test PN*, Paris, Presses Universitaires de Paris.

Cowen, E. L. and Beier, E. G. (1954) 'Threat expectancy, word frequencies and perceptual recognition hypothesis', *J. Abnorm. Soc. Psychol.*, **49**, 178-82.

Cremerius, J. (1962) *Die Beurteilung des Behandlungserfolges in der Psycho-therapie*, Berlin, Springer-Verlag.

Cronbach, L. J. (1946) 'Response-sets and test-validity', *Educ. Psychol. Meas.*, **6**, 475-94.

Cronbach, L. J. (1950) 'Further evidence on response-sets and test-design', *Educ. Psychol. Meas.*, **10**, 3-31.

Cronbach, L. J. (1955) 'Processes affecting scores on "understanding of others" and "assumed similarity"', *Psychol. Bull.*, **52**, 177-94.

Cronbach, L. J. and Meehl, P. E. (1955) 'Construct-validity in psychological tests', *Psychol. Bull.*, **52**, 281-302.

Cross, H. J. (1964) 'The outcome of psychotherapy: a selected analysis of research findings', *J. Consult. Psychol.*, **28** (5), 413-17.

Crown, S. (1968) 'Psychoanalysis and problems of scientific method', in Sutherland, J. D. (1968).

Crowne, D. P. (1965) 'Review of the IES Test in *VIth Mental Measurement Year Book*', in Buros O. K. (1965).

Curran, D. and Parr, D. (1957) 'Homosexuality: an analysis of 100 male cases seen in private practice', *Brit. Med. J.*, 797-801.

Dahlstrom, W. G. and Welsh, G. S. (1960) *An MMPI Handbook*, London, Oxford University Press.

Daston, P. G. (1956) 'Perception of homosexual words in paranoid schizo-phrenia', *Percept. Mot. Skills*, **6**, 45-55.

Davis, H. V., Sears, R. R., Miller, H. C. and Brodbeck, A. J. (1948) 'Effects of cup-, bottle- and breast-feeding on oral activities of new-born infants', *Pediatrics*, **2**, 549-58.

Davis, R. E. and Ruiz, R. A. (1965) 'Infant feeding method and adolescent per-sonality', *Amer. J. Psychiat.*, **122**, 673-8.

Davis, W. A. and Havighurst, R. J. (1946) 'Social-class and colour differences in child-rearing', *Amer. Sociol. Rev.*, **11**, 698-710.

Davis, W. A. and Havighurst, R. J. (1947) *Father of the Man*, Boston, Houghton Mifflin.

Delay, J., Pichot, P. and Perse, J. (1962) 'Personnalité obsessionelle et caractère dit obsessionel: étude clinique et psychometrique', *Rev. Psychol. App.*, **12**, 233-62.

De Luca, J. N. (1967) 'Performance of overt male homosexuals and controls on the Blacky Test', *J. Clin. Psychol.*, **23**, 497.

De Luca, J. N. (1968) 'Psychosexual conflict in adolescent enuretics', *J. Psychol.*, **68**, 145-9.

Dement, W. C. (1960) 'The effect of dream-deprivation', *Sci.*, **131**, 1705-7.

Dement, W. C. (1963) 'Perception during sleep', *Proc. Am. Psychopath. Assoc.*

Symposium on psychopathology of perception, New York.

Dement, W. C., Henry, P., Cohen, H. and Ferguson, J. (1967) 'Studies on the effects of REM-deprivation in humans and animals', in Pribram, K. H. (ed.) *Brain and Behaviour* (1967), Harmondsworth, Penguin.

Dement, W. C., Kahn, E. and Roffwarg, H. (1965) 'The influence of the laboratory situation on the dreams of the experimental subject', *J. Nerv. Ment. Dis.,* **140**, 119-31.

Dement, W. C. and Kleitman, N. (1955) 'Incidence of eye motility during sleep in relation to varying EEG pattern', *Fed. Proc.,* **14**, 216.

Dement, W. C. and Kleitman, N. (1957) 'Cyclic variations in EEG during sleep and their relation to eye movements, bodily motility and dreaming', *EEG Clin. Neurophysiol.,* **9**, 673-90.

Dement, W. C., and Wolpert, E. A. (1958) 'The relation of eye movements, bodily motility and external stimuli to dream content', *J. Exp. Psychol.,* **53**, 543-53.

Denker, P. G. (1947) 'Results of treatment of psychoneuroses by the general practitioner: a follow-up study of 500 cases', *Arch. Neurol. Psychiat.,* **57**, 504-5.

Deregowski, J. B. (1966) 'Difficulties in pictorial perception in Africa', *Inst. Soc. Res.,* University of Zambia.

Despert, J. L. (1944) 'Urinary control and enuresis', *Psychosom. Med.,* **6**, 294-307.

Despert, J. L. (1946) 'Psychosomatic study of fifty stutterers', *Amer. J. Orthopsychiat.,* **16**, 100-32.

Devereux, G. (1947) 'Mohave orality', *Psychoanal. Quart.,* **16**, 519-46.

Devereux, G. (1951) 'Cultural and characterological traits of the Mohave related to the anal stage of psychosexual development', *Psychoanal. Quart.,* **20**, 398-422.

Dixon, J. J., De Monchaux, C. and Sandler, J. (1957) 'Patterns of anxiety: the phobias', *Brit. J. Med. Psychol.,* **30**, 34-40.

Dixon, N. F. (1958a) 'Apparatus for the continuous recording of the visual threshold by the method of "closed loop control"', *Quart. J. Exp. Psychol.,* **10**, 62-3.

Dixon, N. F. (1958b) 'Apparent changes in the visual threshold as a function of subliminal stimulation', *Quart. J. Exp. Psychol.,* **10**, 211-15.

Dixon, N. F. (1960) 'Apparent changes in the visual threshold: central or peripheral', *Brit. J. Psychol.,* **51** (4), 297-309.

Dixon, N. F. (1971) *Subliminal Perception: the Nature of a Controversy,* London, McGraw-Hill.

Dixon, N. F. and Haider, M. (1961) 'Changes in the visual threshold as a function of subception', *Quart. J. Exp. Psychol.,* **13**, 229-35.

Dixon, N. F. and Lear, T. E. (1962) 'Perceptual regulation and mental disorder', *J. Ment. Sci.,* **108**, 356-61.

Dixon, N. F. and Lear, T. E. (1963) 'EEG correlates of threshold regulation', *Nature,* **198**, 870-2.

Dollard, J., Doob, L. W., Miller, N. E., Mowrer, O. H. and Sears, R. R. (1939) *Frustration and Aggression*, New Haven, Yale University Press.

Dollard, J. and Miller, N. E. (1950) *Personality and Psychotherapy*, New York, McGraw-Hill.

Dombrose, L. A. and Slobin, M. S. (1951) 'An approach to the measurement of relative strengths of impulses, ego and super-ego and the determination of the effects of impulses and super-ego upon ego functions', joint Ph.D. thesis, Western Reserve University.

Dombrose, L. A. and Slobin, M. S. (1958) 'The IES Test', *Percept. Mot. Skills*, **8**, 347-89.

Domino, D. (1976) 'Primary process thinking in dream reports as related to creative achievement', *J. Consult. Clin. Psychol.*, **44**, 929-32.

Douglas, M. (1966) *Purity and Danger*, New York, Praeger.

Dudek, S. Z. (1970) 'Effects of different types of therapy on the personality as a whole', *J. Nerv. Ment. Dis.*, **150**, 329-45.

Dudley, G. E. (1978) 'Effects of sex, social desirability and birth order on the Defence Mechanism Inventory', *J. Consult. Clin. Psychol.*, **6**, 1419-22.

Duhrssen, A. and Jorswiek, E. (1965) 'An empirical statistical investigation into the efficacy of psychoanalytic therapy', *Nervenarzt.*, **36**, 166-9.

Dunbar, H. F. (1954) *Emotions and Bodily Changes*, 4th edn, New York, Columbia University Press.

Durrett, M. (1959) 'Relationship of early infant regulation and later behaviour in play interviews', *Child Development*, **30**, 211-16.

Duss, G. (1940) 'La méthode des fables en psychoanalyse', in Despert, J. L. (1946).

Duthie, H. L. and Gairns, F. W. (1960) 'Sensory nerve-endings and sensation in the anal region of man', *Brit. J. Surg.*, **47**, 585-9.

Edwards, A. L. (1957) *The Social Desirability Variable in Personality Research*, New York, Dryden.

Ehrenzweig, A. (1967) *The Hidden Order of Art*, London, Weidenfeld & Nicolson.

Ellenberger, H. F. (1970) *The Discovery of the Unconscious*, New York, Basic Books.

Ellis, A. (1951) 'The effectiveness of psychotherapy with individuals who have severe homosexual problems', *J. Consult. Psychol.*, **20**, 191-5.

Ellis, A. (1957) 'Outcome of employing three techniques of psychotherapy', *J. Clin. Psychol.*, **13**, 344-50.

Ellman, C. S. (1970) 'An experimental study of the female castration complex', doctoral dissertation, New York University, quoted by Fisher and Greenberg (1977).

Endler, N. S. (1963), paper quoted by Byrne, D. (1964).

Engeset, A., Lygren, T. and Idsoe, R. (1963) 'The incidence of peptic ulcer among alcohol abusers and non-abusers', *Quart. J. Stud. Alcohol.*, **24**, 622-6.

Erdelyi, M. H. (1972) 'Role of phantasy in the Poetzl (emergence) phenomenon', *J. Pers. Soc. Psychol.*, **24**, 186-90.

Erdelyi, M. H. (1974) 'A new look at the new look: perceptual defence and vigilance', *Psychol. Rev.* **81**, 1-25.

Eriksen, C. W. and Pierce, J. (1968) 'Defence mechanisms', chapter 20 in Borgatta and Lambert (1968).

Evans, C. and McConnell, J. R. (1951) 'The Minnesota TSE Test', Princeton, ETS.

Eylon, Y. (1967) 'Birth events, appendicitis and appendectomy', *Brit. J. Med. Psychol.*, **40**, 317.

Eysenck, H. J. (1947) *Dimensions of Personality*, London, Routledge & Kegan Paul.

Eysenck, H. J. (1952) 'The effects of psychotherapy: an evaluation', *J. Consult. Psychol.*, **16**, 319-24.

Eysenck, H. J. (1953a) *Uses and Abuses of Psychology*, Harmondsworth, Penguin.

Eysenck, H. J. (1953b) *The Structure of Human Personality*, London, Methuen.

Eysenck, H. J. (1959a) 'Review of the Rorschach Test', in Buros, O. K. (1959).

Eysenck, H. J. (1959b) *Maudsley Personality Inventory*, London, University of London Press.

Eysenck, H. J. (1960a) 'The effects of psychotherapy', in *Handbook of Abnormal Psychology*, London, Pitman.

Eysenck, H. J. (ed.) (1960b) *Behaviour Therapy and the Neuroses*, New York, Pergamon Press.

Eysenck, H. J. (1961) *Handbook of Abnormal Psychology* (also 1960), New York, Basic Books.

Eysenck. H. J. (1964) 'Principles and methods of personality description, classification and diagnosis', *Brit. J. Psychol.*, **55**, 284-94.

Eysenck, H. J. (1965a) *Fact and Fiction in Psychology*, Harmondsworth, Penguin.

Eysenck, H. J. (1965b) 'The effects of psychotherapy', *Internat. J. Psychiat.*, **1**, 99-142.

Eysenck, H. J. (1967a) 'The logical basis of factor-analysis', in Jackson, D. N. and Messick, S. (eds) *Problems in Human Assessment* (1967), New York, McGraw-Hill.

Eysenck, H. J. (1967b) *The Biological Basis of Personality*, Springfield, C. C. Thomas.

Eysenck, H. J. (1972) 'The experimental study of Freudian concepts', *Bull. Brit. Psychol. Soc.*, **25**, 261-7.

Eysenck, H. J. (1978) *Ai3 Questionnaire*, in Buros, O. K. (ed.) *The VIIIth Mental Measurement Year Book* (1978), New Jersey, Gryphon Press.

Eysenck, H. J. and Eysenck, S. B. (1964) *The EPI*, London, University of London Press.

Eysenck, H. J. and Eysenck, S. B. (1969) *Personality Structure and Measurement*, London, Routledge & Kegan Paul.

Eysenck, H. J. and Eysenck, S. B. (1975) *The EPQ*, London, University of

London Press.

Eysenck, H. J. and Rachmann, S. (1965) *The Causes and Cures of Neurosis*, London, Routledge & Kegan Paul.

Eysenck, H. J. and Wilson, G. D. (1973) *The Experimental Study of Freudian Theories*, London, Methuen.

Fairbairn, W. R. D. (1938) 'Prolegomena to a psychology of art', *Brit. J. Psychol.*, **28**, 298-303.

Farber, M. L. (1955) 'The anal character and political aggression', *J. Abnorm. Psychol.*, **51**, 486-9.

Farber, M. L. (1958) 'Anality, political aggression, acquiescence and questionnaire construction', *J. Abnorm. Psychol.*, **56**, 278-9.

Farrell, B. A. (1951) 'The scientific testing of psychoanalytic findings and theory, III', *Brit. J. Med. Psychol.*, **24**, 35-51.

Farrell, B. A. (1961) 'Can psychoanalysis be refuted?', *Inquiry*, **4** (1), 16-36.

Farrell, B. A. (1964) 'The status of psychoanalytic theory', *Inquiry*, **7**, 104-22.

Fenichel, O. (1930) *Ten Years of the Berlin Psychoanalysis Institute*, 1920-30.

Fenichel, O. (1945) *The Psychoanalytic Theory of Neurosis*, New York, Norton.

Ferguson, G. A. (1949) 'On the theory of test development', *Psychometrica*, **14**, 61-8.

Fessard, A., Gerard, R. W. and Konorski, J. (1961) *Brain Mechanisms and Learning*, Oxford, Blackwell.

Field, M. J. (1940) *Social Organization of the Ga People*, London, Crown Agents for the Colonies.

Field, M. J. (1960) *Search for Security*, London, Faber & Faber.

Finney, J. C. (1961a) 'The MMPI as a measure of character structure as revealed by factor-analysis', *J. Consult. Psychol.*, **25**, 327-36.

Finney, J. C. (1961b) 'Some maternal influences on children's personality and character', *Genet. Psychol. Monogr.*, **63**, 199-278.

Finney, J. C. (1963) 'Maternal influences on anal or compulsive character in children', *J. Genet. Psychol.*, **103**, 351-67.

Finney, J. C. (1966) 'Relation and meaning of the new MMPI scales', *Psych.*, **18**, 459-70.

Fisher, C. (1953) 'Studies on the nature of suggestion — I: Experimental induction of dreams by direct suggestion', *J. Amer. Psychoanal. Ass.*, **1**, 222-55.

Fisher, C. (1954) 'Dreams and perception: the role of preconscious and primary modes of perception in dream formation', *J. Amer. Psychoanal. Ass.*, **2**, 389-445.

Fisher, C. (1960) 'Subliminal and supraliminal influences on dreams', *Amer. J. Psychiat.*, **116**, 1009-17.

Fisher, C. (1965) 'Psychoanalytic implications of recent research on sleep and dreaming', *J. Amer. Psychoanal. Ass.*, **13**, 197-303.

Fisher, C. and Dement, W. C. (1963) 'Studies on the psychopathology of sleep and dreams', *Amer. J. Psychiat*, **119** (12), 1160-8.

Fisher, C., Gross, J. and Feldman, M. (1965), quoted by Fisher, C. (1965).

Fisher, C., Gross, J. and Zuch, J. (1965) 'Cycle of penile erection synchronous with dreaming (REM) sleep', *Arch. Gen. Psychiat.*, **12**, 29-45.

Fisher, J. M. and Fisher, S. (1975) 'Response to cigarette-deprivation as a function of oral fantasy', *J. Pers. Ass.*, **35**, 143-5.

Fisher, S. (1970) *Body Experience in Fantasy and Behaviour*, New York, Appleton-Century-Crofts.

Fisher, S. (1973) *The Female Orgasm*, New York, Basic Books.

Fisher, S. and Greenberg, P. R. (1977) *The Scientific Credibility of Freud's Theories and Therapy*, Hassocks, Harvester Press.

Fisher, S. and Greenberg, P. R. (eds) (1978) *The Scientific Evaluation of Freud's Theories and Therapy*, Hassocks, Harvester Press.

Flanagan, D. E. (1930) 'The influence of emotional inhibition on learning and recall', Master's thesis, University of Chicago.

Flugel, J. C. (1945) *Man, Morals and Society*, London, Duckworth.

Fontana, D. (1978) *An Investigation of Reversal and Obsessionality*, Ph.D. thesis, University of Wales.

Fordham, F. (1959) *An Introduction to Jung's Psychology*, Harmondsworth, Penguin.

Forster, C. and Ross, R. J. (1976) 'References for sexual symbols in the genital stage: a replication', *Psychol. Rep.*, **37**, 1048-50.

Foss, B. M. (1964) 'Mimicry in mynas (Gracula religiosa): a test of Mowrer's theory', *Brit. J. Psychol.*, **55**, 85-8.

Foulds, G. A. (1965) *Personality and Personal Illness*, London, Tavistock Publications.

Foulds, G. A., Caine, T. M. and Creasy, M. A. (1960), 'Aspects of extra- and intro-punitive aggression in mental illness', *J. Ment. Sci.* **106**, 599-610.

Foulkes, W. D. (1960) 'Dream reports from different stages of sleep', Ph.D. thesis, University of Chicago.

Foulkes, W. D. (1962) 'Dream reports from different stages of sleep', *J. Abnorm. Soc. Psychol.*, **65** (1), 14-25.

Foulkes, W. D. (1964) 'Theories of dream formation and recent studies of sleep consciousness', *Psychol. Bull.*, **62**, 236-47.

Foulkes, W. D. and Rechtschaffen, A. (1964) 'Pre-sleep determinants of dream content: the effects of two films', *Paper read at Mid-Western Psychological Association*.

Fox, B. (1961) 'The investigation of the effects of psychiatric treatment', *J. Ment. Sci.*, **107**, 493-502.

Franks, C. M. (ed.) (1969) *Behavior Therapy Appraisal and Status*, New York, McGraw-Hill.

Freeman, P. R. (1970) 'A multivariate study of students' performance in university examinations', *J. Roy. Stat. Soc.*, Series A (General), **133**, 38-55.

French. M. (1977) *The Women's Room*, London, André Deutsch.

French, T. M. and Alexander, F. (1941) 'Psychogenic factors in bronchial asthma', *Psychosom. Med. Monogr.*, II and IV.

Freud, A. (1946) *The Ego and the Mechanisms of Defence*, London, Hogarth Press and the Institute of Psychoanalysis.

Freud, A. and Burlingham, D. T. (1944) *Infants without Families*, New York, International University Press.

Freud, S. (1966) *The Standard Edition of the Complete Psychological Works of Sigmund Freud*, London, Hogarth Press and Institute of Psychoanalysis.

Freud, S. (1893) 'On the psychical mechanism of hysterical phenomena: preliminary communication'; vol. II, 3.

Freud, S. (1894) 'The neuropsychoses of defence'; vol. III, 43.

Freud, S. (1895a) 'A project for a scientific psychology'; vol. I, 295.

Freud, S. (1895b) *Studies in Hysteria*; vol. II.

Freud, S. (1895c) 'On the grounds for detaching a particular syndrome from Neurasthenia under the description Anxiety Neurosis'; vol. III, 87.

Freud, S. (1896a) 'Further observations on the neuropsychoses of defence'; vol. III, 163.

Freud, S. (1896b) *The Aetiology of Hysteria*; vol. III.

Freud, S. (1898) 'Sexuality in the aetiology of the neuroses'; vol. III, 191.

Freud, S. (1900) *The Interpretation of Dreams*; vols IV and V.

Freud, S. (1901) *The Psychopathology of Everyday Life*; vol. VI.

Freud, S. (1905a) 'Three essays on sexuality'; vol. VII, 135-243.

Freud, S. (1905b) *Jokes and their Relation to the Unconscious*; vol. VIII.

Freud, S. (1905c) 'Fragment of an analysis of a case of hysteria'; vol. VII, 3.

Freud, S. (1906) 'My views on the part played by sexuality in the aetiology of the neuroses'; vol. VII, 271.

Freud, S. (1908a) 'Character and anal erotism'; vol. IX, 169.

Freud, S. (1908b) 'Creative writers and day-dreaming'; vol. IX, 143.

Freud, S. (1909a) 'Analysis of a phobia in a five-year-old boy'; vol. X, 3.

Freud, S. (1909b) 'Notes upon a case of obsessional neurosis'; vol. X, 153.

Freud, S. (1910a) 'Three contributions to the psychology of love'; vol. XI, 163.

Freud, S. (1910b) 'The psychoanalytic view of psychogenic disturbance of vision'; vol. XI, 211.

Freud, S. (1911) 'Psychoanalytic notes on an autobiographical account of a case of paranoia (dementia paranoides)'; vol. XII, 3.

Freud, S. (1913a) 'Totem and taboo'; vol. XIII, 1.

Freud, S. (1913b) 'The predisposition to obsessional neurosis'; vol. XII, 317.

Freud, S. (1915) 'Repression'; vol. XIV, 143.

Freud, S. (1916-17) *Introductory Lectures on Psychoanalysis*; vols XV and XVI.

Freud, S. (1917a) 'On the transformation of instincts with special reference to anal erotism'; vol. XVII, 127-33.

Freud, S. (1917b) 'Mourning and melancholia'; vol. XIV, 239.

Freud, S. (1917c) 'A metapsychological supplement to the theory of dreams'; vol. XIV, 219.

Freud, S. (1918) 'From the history of an infantile neurosis'; vol. XVII, 3.

Freud, S. (1920) 'Beyond the pleasure principle'; vol. XVIII, 7.

Freud, S. (1923) 'The ego and the id'; vol. XIX, 3.

Freud, S. (1924a) 'The dissolution of the Oedipus complex'; vol. XIX, 173.

Freud, S. (1924b) 'Neurosis and psychosis'; vol. XIX, 149.

Freud, S. (1925a) 'Inhibition, symptoms and anxiety'; vol. XX, 77.

Freud, S. (1925b) 'Negation'; vol. XIX, 235.

Freud, S. (1925c) 'Some psychical consequences of the anatomical distinction between the sexes'; vol. XIX, 243.

Freud, S. (1926) 'The question of lay analysis'; vol. XX, 179.

Freud, S. (1927a) 'Fetishism'; vol. XXI, 149.

Freud, S. (1927b) 'Humour'; vol. XXI, 161.

Freud, S. (1928) 'Dostoevsky'; vol. XXI, 175.

Freud, S. (1931) 'Female sexuality'; vol. XXI, 223.

Freud, S. (1932) 'The acquisition of control over fire'; vol. XXII, 185.

Freud, S. (1933) *New Introductory Lectures in Psychoanalysis*; vol. XXII.

Freud, S. (1935) 'An autobiographical study'; vol. XX, 7.

Freud, S. (1939) *Moses and Monotheism*; vol. XXIII.

Freud, S. (1940) 'An outline of psychoanalysis'; vol. XXIII, 141.

Freund, K. (1960) 'Some problems in the treatment of homosexuality', in Eysenck, H. J. (1960a).

Freund, K., Langerin, R., Zajac, Y., Steiner, B. and Zajac, A. (1974) 'Parent-child relations in transexual and non-transexual homosexual males', *Brit, J. Psychiat.*, **124**, 22-3.

Friedman, S. M. (1950a) 'An empirical study of certain psychoanalytic propositions', Ph.D. thesis, Western Reserve University.

Friedman, S. M. (1950b) 'An empirical study of the Oedipus complex', *Amer. Psychol.*, **5**, 304.

Friedman, S. M. (1952) 'An empirical study of the castration and Oedipus complexes', *Genet. Psychol. Monogr.*, **46**, 61-130.

Fromm, E. (1942) *The Fear of Freedom*, London, Routledge & Kegan Paul.

Fromm, E. (1948) 'The Oedipus complex and the Oedipus myth', in Anshen (1948).

Fromm, E. (1949) *Man for Himself*, London, Routledge & Kegan Paul.

Fromm, E. (1965) *The Heart of Man: its Genius for Good and Evil*, London, Routledge & Kegan Paul.

Fulkerson, F. C. (1957) 'The interaction of frequency, emotional tone and set in visual recognition', *J. Exp. Psychol.*, **54**, 188-94.

Galbraith, G. G. and Leiberman, H. (1972) 'Associative responses to double-entendre words as a function of repression—sensitization and sexual stimulation', *J. Consult. Clin. Psychol.*, **39**, 322-37.

Gewirtz, J. L. (1969) 'Mechanisms of social learning: some roles of stimulation and behaviour in early human development', chapter 2 in Goslin, D. A. (1969).

Gibbins, R. J. and Walters, R. H. (1960) 'Three preliminary studies of a psychoanalytic theory of alcohol addiction', *Quart. J. Stud. Alcohol.*, **21**, 618-41.

Gilbert, J. G. and Levee, R. F. (1963) 'A comparison of the personality structures of a group of young married and a group of middle-aged married women', *Percept. Mot. Skills*, **16**, 773-7.

Giora, Z. (1972) 'The function of the dream and reappraisal', *Amer. J. Psychiat.*, **128**, 1067-73.

Glaros, A. G. and Rao, S. M. (1977) 'Bruxism: a critical review', *Psychol. Bull.*, **84**, 767-81.

Glasberg, H. M., Bromberg, P. M., Stein, M. and Luparello, T. J. (1969) 'A personality study of asthmatic patients', *J. Psychoaom. Res.*, **13**, 197-204.

Gleser, G. C. and Ihilevich, D. (1969) 'An objective instrument for measuring defence mechanisms', *J. Consult. Clin. Psychol.*, **33**, 51-60.

Gleser, G. C. and Sachs, M. (1973) 'Ego-defences and reactions to stress', *J. Consult. Clin. Psychol.*, **40**, 181-7.

Glixman, A. F. (1949) 'Recall of completed and incompleted activities under varying degrees of stress', *J. Exp. Psychol.*, **39**, 281-95.

Glotter, A. N. and Reece, M. M. (1962) 'Tactility and sexual symbolism', *Percept. Mot. Skills*, **14**, 302.

Glover, E. (1924a) 'Notes on oral character formation', in Glover E. (1956).

Glover, E. (1924b). 'The significance of the mouth in psychoanalysis', in Glover, E. (1956).

Glover, E. (1949). *Psychoanalysis*, London, Staples Press.

Glover, E. (1950) *Freud or Jung?*, London, Allen & Unwin.

Glover, E. (1956) *On the Early Development of Mind*, London, Mayo.

Goldberg, P. A. and Milstein, J. T. (1965) 'Perceptual investigation of psycho-analytic theory concerning latent homosexuality in women', *Percept. Mot. Skills*, **21**, 645-6.

Golden, O. (1954) 'Manifestations of impulse, ego and super-ego in elementary schoolboys and girls', Ph.D. thesis, Western Reserve University.

Goldfarb, W. (1943) 'Effects of early institutional care on adolescent personality', *J. Exp. Educ.*, **12**, 106-29.

Goldfarb, W. (1944) 'Effects of early institutional care on adolescent personality: Rorschach data', *Amer. J. Orthopsychiat.*, **14**, 441-7.

Goldfarb, W. (1945) 'Psychological privation in infancy and subsequent adjust-ment', *Amer. J. Orthopsychiat.*, **15**, 247-55.

Goldfarb, W. (1947) 'Variations in adolescent adjustment of institutionally reared children', *Amer. J. Orthopsychiat.*, **17**, 449-57.

Goldfarb, W. (1949) 'Rorschach test differences between family-reared, in-stitution-reared and schizophrenic children', *Amer. J. Orthopsychiat.*, **19**, 625-33.

Goldman-Eisler, F. (1948) 'Breast-feeding and character formation — I', *J. Pers.*, **17**, 83-103.

Goldman-Eisler, F. (1950) 'Breast-feeding and character formation — II: The aetiology of the oral character in psychoanalytic theory', *J. Pers.*, **19**, 189-96.

Goldman-Eisler, F. (1951) 'The problem of "orality" and its origin in early childhood', *J. Ment. Sci.*, **97**, 765-82.

Goldman-Eisler, F. (1953) 'Breast-feeding and character formation', in Kluckhohn, C. and Murray, H. A. (1953).

Gollob, H. F. and Levine, J. (1967) 'Distraction as a factor in the enjoyment of aggressive humour', *J. Pers. Soc. Psychol.*, **5**, 368-72.

Gombrich, E. H. (1963) *Meditations on a Hobby-Horse and other Essays on the Theory of Art*, London, Phaidon Press.

Gordon, N. N. and Brackney, B. E. (1979) 'Defence mechanism preference and dimensions of psychopathology', *Psychol. Rep.*, **44**, 188-90.

Gorer, G. (1943) 'Themes in Japanese culture', *Trans. New York Acad. Sci.*, **2**, 106-24.

Gorsuch, R. L. (1974) *Factor-Analysis*, Philadelphia, W. B. Saunders.

Gorsuch, R. L. and Cattell, R. B. (1967) 'Second-stratum personality factors defined in the questionnaire realm by the 16PF', *Multiv. Behav. Res.*, **2**, 211-23.

Goslin, D. A. (1969) *Handbook of Socialization Theory and Research*, Chicago, Rand-McNally.

Gottheil, E. (1965a) 'Conceptions of orality and anality', *J. Nerv. Ment. Dis.*, **141** (2), 155-60.

Gottheil, E. (1965b) 'An empirical analysis of orality and anality', *J. Nerv. Ment. Dis.*, **141**, 308-17.

Gottheil, E. and Stone, G. C. (1968) 'Factor-analytic study of orality and anality', *J. Nerv. Ment. Dis.*, **146**, 1-17.

Gottschalk, L. A. and Gleser, G. C. (1969) *The Measurement of Psychological States Through the Content Analysis of Verbal Behaviour*, Berkeley, University of California Press.

Gough, H. G. (1957) *The Californian Psychological Inventory*, Palo Alto, Consulting Psychologists Press.

Granick, S. and Scheflin, N. A. (1958) 'Approaches to the reliability of projective tests with special reference to the Blacky Pictures Test', *J. Consult. Psychol.*, **22**, 137-41.

Gray, H. and Wheelwright, J. (1946) 'Jung's psychological types, their frequency of occurrence', *J. Genet. Psychol.*, **34**, 3-17.

Greenspoon, J. (1955) 'The reinforcing effect of two spoken sounds on the frequency of two responses', *Amer. J. Psychol.*, **68**, 409-16.

Grey-Walter, W. (1961) *The Living Brain*, Harmondsworth, Penguin.

Griffiths, R. (1951) *The Griffiths Mental Development Scale for Testing Babies from Birth to Two Years*, London, Author.

Grossman, S. P. (1967) *A Textbook of Physiological Psychology*, New York, Wiley.

Grotjan, M. (1957) *Beyond Laughter*, New York, McGraw-Hill.

Grunzig, H. J. (1977) 'Computer-aided content analysis of psychoanalytic interaction towards an operationalization of psychoanalytic anxiety concepts', Paper at the Workshop on Content-Analysis at 27th Annual Conference of International Communication Association and International Conference Congress for Communication Sciences, Berlin.

Grygier, P. (1956) 'The personality of student nurses: a pilot study using the DPI', *Int. J. Soc. Psychiat.*, **2**, 105-12.

Grygier, T. G. (1957a) 'Psychometric aspects of homosexuality', *J. Ment. Sci.*, **103**, 514-26.

Grygier, T. G. (1957b) 'A factorial study of insularity', *Psychol. Rep.*, **3**, 613-14.

Grygier, T. G. (1958) 'Homosexuality, neurosis and normality', *Brit. J. Delinq.*, **4**, 59-61.

Grygier, T. G. (1961a) *The Dynamic Personality Inventory*, Windsor, NFER.

Grygier, T. G. (1961b) *The Dynamic Personality Inventory: Manual*, London, NFER.

Grygier, T. G. (1970) *The Dynamic Personality Inventory: Experimental Manual*, Windsor, NFER.

Grygier, T. G. (1979) 'Deficiencies of the Dynamic Personality Inventory — and the limitations of factor-analysis', *Brit. J. Med. Psychol.*, **52**, 259-62.

Grygier, T. G. and Grygier, P. (1976) *Manual to the Dynamic Personality Inventory*, Windsor, NFER.

Guilford, J. P. (1956) *Psychometric Methods*, 2nd edn, New York, McGraw-Hill.

Guilford, J. P. (1958) *Fundamental Statistics in Psychology and Education*, London, McGraw-Hill.

Guilford, J. P. (1959) *Personality*, New York, McGraw-Hill.

Guilford, J. P. (1967) *The Nature of Human Intelligence*, New York, McGraw-Hill.

Guilford, J. P. (1977) 'Will the real factor of extraversion—introversion please stand up? A reply to Eysenck', *Psychol. Bull.*, **84**, 412-16.

Guilford, J. P. and Guilford, R. B. (1934) 'An analysis of the factors in a typical test of introversion—extraversion', *J. Abnorm. Soc. Psychol.*, **28**, 377-99.

Guilford, J. P. and Guilford, R. B. (1936) 'Personality factors, S, E and M, and their measurement', *J. Psychol.*, **2**, 109-27.

Guilford, J. P. and Zimmerman, W. S. (1949) 'The Guilford—Zimmerman Temperament Survey', *Manual of Instructions and Interpretations*, Beverly Hills, Sheridan.

Guilford, J. P. and Zimmerman, W. S. (1956) 'Fourteen dimensions of temperament', *Psychol. Monogr.*, **70** (10), 1-26.

Guilford, J. S., Zimmerman, W. S. and Guilford, J. P. (eds)(1976) *The Guilford—Zimmerman Temperament Survey Handbook*, San Diego, Sheridan.

Hall, C. S. (1953) *The Meaning of Dreams*, New York, Harper & Row.

Hall, C. S. (1955) 'The significance of the dream of being attacked', *J. Pers.*, **24**, 168-80.

Hall, C. S. (1963) 'Strangers in dreams: an experimental confirmation of the Oedipus complex', *J. Pers.*, **31** (3), 336-45.

Hall, C. S. (1964) 'A modest confirmation of Freud's theory of a distinction between the super-ego of men and women', *J. Abnorm. Soc. Psychol.*, **69**, 440-2.

Hall, C. S. (1966) *The Meaning of Dreams*, New York, McGraw-Hill.

Hall, C. S. and Domhoff, B. (1962a) 'Aggression in dreams', quoted by Hall and Domhoff (1963).

Hall, C. S. and Domhoff, B. (1962b) 'Friendliness in dreams', quoted by Hall and Domhoff (1963).

Hall, C. S. and Domhoff, B. (1963) 'A ubiquitous sex-difference in dreams', *J. Abnorm. Soc. Psychol.*, **66** (3), 278-80.

Hall, C. S. and Lindzey, G. (1957) *Theories of Personality*, New York, Wiley.

Hall, C. S. and Van De Castle, R. L. (1963) 'An empirical investigation of the castration complex in dreams', *J. Pers.*, **33** (1), 20-9.

Helpern, J. (1977) 'Projection and test of the psychoanalytic by patterns', *J. Abnorm. Psychol.*, **86**, 536-42.

Hammer, E. F. (1953) 'An investigation of sexual symbolism: a study of HTPs of eugenically sterilized subjects', *J. Proj. Tech.*, **17**, 401-15.

Hampson, S. and Kline, P. (1977) 'Personality dimensions differentiating certain groups of abnormal offenders from non-offenders', *Brit. J. Criminol.*, **17**, 310-31.

Harman, H. H. (1976) *Modern Factor-Analysis*, Chicago, University of Chicago Press.

Harris, I. (1948) 'Observations concerning typical anxiety dreams', *Psychiatry*, **11**, 301-9.

Harris, I. (1951) 'Characterological significance of the typical anxiety dream', *Psychiatry*, **14**, 279-94.

Hartman, H., Kris, E. and Lowenstein, R. M. (1947) 'Comments on the formation of psychic structure', *Psychoanal. Study of the Child*, **11**, 11-38.

Hartshorne, H. and May, M. A. (1930) *Studies in the Nature of Character*, New York, Macmillan.

Hathaway, S. R. and McKinley, J. C. (1951) *The Minnesota Multiphasic Personality Inventory Manual (Revised)*, New York, The Psychological Corp.

Hazari, A. (1957) 'An investigation of obsessive—compulsive character traits and symptoms in adult neurotics', Ph.D. thesis, University of London.

Heilbrunn. G. (1963) 'Results with psychoanalytic therapy: report of 211 cases', *Amer. J. Psychotherap.*, **17**, 427-35.

Heilbrunn, G. (1966) 'Results with psychoanalytic therapy and professional commitment', *Amer. J. Psychotherap.*, **20**, 89-99.

Heine, R. W. (1953) 'A comparison of patients' reports on psychotherapeutic experience with psychoanalytic, non-directive and Adlerian therapists', *Amer. J. Psychotherap.*, **7**, 16-23.

Helper, M. M. (1955) 'Learning theory and the self-concept', *J. Abnorm. Soc. Psychol.*, **51**, 184-94.

Henderson, D. K. and Gillespie, R. D. (1956) *A Text Book of Psychiatry*, 8th edn, London, Oxford University Press.

Hendrickson, A. L. and White, P. O. (1966) 'A method for the rotation of higher-order factors', *Brit. J. Math. Stat. Psychol.*, **19**, 97-103.

Henker, B. A. (1964) 'The effect of adult model relationships on children's play and task imitation', *Dissert. Abstracts*, **24**, 4797.

Henry, J. and Henry, Z. (1944) 'Doll play of Pilaga Indian children', *Assn. Inc. Res. Monogr.*, **4**.

Hernstein, M. I. (1963) 'Behavioural correlates of breast—bottle regimes under varying parent—infant relationships', *Monogr. of the Society for Research in Child Develop.*, **28**, 4.

Herron, W. G. (1962) 'IES Test patterns of accepted and rejected adolescents', *Percept. Mot. Skills*, **15**, 435-8.

Hetherington, E. M. and Brackbill, Y. (1963) 'Etiology and covariation of obstinacy, orderliness and parsimony in young children', *Child Development*, **34**, 919-43.

Hilgard, E. R. (1952) 'Experimental approaches to psychoanalysis', in Pumpian-Mindlin, E. (1952).

Hill, A. B. (1976) 'Methodological problems in the use of factor-analysis: a critical review of the experimental evidence for the anal character', *Brit. J. Med. Psychol.*, **49**, 145-9.

Hinde, R. A. (1966) *Animal Behaviour*, New York, McGraw-Hill.

Hinde, R. A. and McGinnis, L. (1977) 'Some factors influencing the effects of temporary mother—infant separation: some experiments with Rhesus monkeys', *Psychol. Med.*, **7**, 197-212.

Hinnie, L. E. (ed.) (1937) *Concepts and Problems of Psychotherapy*, New York, Columbia University Press.

Hoefer, C. and Hardy, M. (1929) 'Later development of breast-fed and artifically fed infants', *J. Amer. Med. Assoc.*, **92**, 615-19.

Hoffman, M. L. and Hoffman, L. W. (eds) (1964) *Review of Child Development Research*, vol. I, New York, Russell Sage Foundation.

Holley, J. W. (1973) 'The Rorschach' in Kline, P. (1973a).

Holley, J. W. and Guilford, J. P. (1964) 'A note on the G Index of agreement', *Educ. Psychol. Meas.*, **24**, 749-53.

Holmes, D. S. (1968) 'Dimensions of projection', *Psychol. Bull.*, **69**, 248-68.

Holmes, D. S. (1972) 'Repression or interference? A further investigation', *J. Pers. Soc. Psychol.*, **22**, 167-70.

Holmes, D. S. (1974) 'Investigations of repression: differential recall of material experimentally or naturally associated with threat', *Psychol. Bull.*, **84**, 632-48.

Holmes, D. S. (1978) 'Projection as a defence mechanism', *Psychol. Bull.*, **85**, 677-88.

Holmes, M. A. M. (1977) 'REM sleep patterning and dream recall in convergers and divergers', Ph.D. thesis, University of Edinburgh.

Holway, A. R. (1949) 'Early self-regulation in infants and later behavior in play interviews', *Amer. J. Orthopsychiat.*, **19**, 612-23.

Horney, K. (1937) *The Neurotic Personality of Our Time*, New York, Norton.

Horney, K. (1939) *New Ways in Psychoanalysis*, New York, Norton.

Horney, K. (1942) *Self-Analysis*, New York, Norton.

Horney, K. (1945) *Our Inner Conflicts*, New York, Norton.

Howarth, E. (1976) 'Were Cattell's "personality sphere" factors correctly identified in the first instance?', *Brit. J. Psychol.*, **67** (2), 217-30.

Howe, M. and Summerfield, B. (1979) 'Orality and Smoking', *Brit. J. Med. Psychol.*, **52**, 85-90.

Howes, D. H. and Solomon, R. L. (1950) 'A note on McGinnies' "Emotionality and perceptual defence"', *Psychol. Rev.*, **57**, 229-34.

Hudson, W. (1960) 'Pictorial depth perception in subcultural groups in Africa', *J. Soc. Psychol.*, **52**, 183-208.

Hudson, W. (1967) 'The study of the problem of pictorial depth perception among unacculturated groups', *Inst. J. Psychol.*, **2**, 89-107.

Huschka, M. (1942) 'The child's response to coercive bowel training', *Psychosom. Med.*, **4**, 301-28.

Hsu, F. L. K. (1961) *Psychological Anthropology: Approaches to Culture and Personality*, New York, Dorsey Press.

Hytten, F. E., Yorston, J. C. and Thomson, A. M. (1958) 'Difficulties associated with breast-feeding', *Brit. Med. J.*, **1**, 310-15.

Imber, R. (1969) 'An experimental study of the Oedipus complex', doctoral dissertation, The State University of New York, Rutgers.

Inglis, J. (1961) 'Abnormalities of motivation and "ego functions"', in Eysenck, H. J. (1961).

Inman, W. S. (1958) 'Clinical thought-reading', *Internat. J. Psychoanal.*, **38**, 299-304.

Inman, W. S. (1962) 'Ophthalmic adventure: a story of frustration and organic disease', *Brit. J. Med. Psychol.*, **35**, 299-309.

Iscoe, I. and Stevenson, H. W. (eds) (1960) *Personality Development in Children*, Austin, University of Texas Press.

Jackson, D. N. and Messick, S. (1961) 'Content and style in personality assessment', *Educ. Psychol. Meas.*, **21**, 771-90.

Jacobs, A. (1954) 'Responses of normals and mental hospital patients to Freudian sexual symbols', *J. Consult. Psychol.*, **18**, 454.

Jacobs, M. A. et al. (1965) 'Relationship of oral frustration factors with heavy cigarette smoking in males', *J. Nerv. Ment. Dis.*, **141**, 161-71.

Jacobs, M. A. et al. (1966) 'Orality, impulsivity and cigarette smoking in men — further findings in support of a theory', *J. Nerv. Ment. Dis.*, 207-9.

Jahoda, G. (1956) 'Sex-differences in preferences for shapes — a cross-cultural replication', *Brit. J. Psychol.*, **47**, 126-32.

Jennings, L. B. and George, S. G. (1975) 'Perceptual vigilance and defence revisited', *Percept. Mot. Skills*, **41**, 723-9.

Jennrich, R. J. and Sampson, P. F. (1966) 'Rotation for simple loading', *Psychometrika*, **31**, 313-23.

Jensen, A. R. (1958) *The Reliability of Projective Techniques: Review of the Literature and Methodology*, Amsterdam, North Holland.

Johnson, G. B. (1966) 'Penis envy or pencil needing?', *Psychol. Rep.*, **19**, 758.

Johnson, H. and Eriksen, C. W. (1961) 'Preconscious perception: a re-examination of the Poetzl phenomenon', *J. Abnorm. Soc. Psychol.*, **62**, 497-503.

Jones, A. (1956) 'Sexual symbolism and the variables of sex and personality integration', *J. Abnorm. Soc. Psychol.*, **53**, 187-90.

Jones, A. (1961) 'Sexual symbolic responses in prepubescent and pubescent children', *J. Consult. Psychol.*, **25**, 383-7.

Jones, A. and Lepson, D. S. (1967) 'Mediated and primary stimulus generalization basis of sexual symbolism', *J. Consult. Psychol.*, **31**, 79-82.

Jones, E. (1915) 'Urethalerotik und Ehrgeiz', *Internat. Z. Psychoanal.*, **3**, 156.

Jones, E. (1923) 'Anal erotic character traits', in *Papers on Psychoanalysis*, London, Baillière, Tindall & Cox.

Jones, E. (1925) 'Mother-right and the sexual ignorance of savages', *Internat. J. Psychoanal.*, **6**, 109-30.

Jones, E. (1933) 'The phallic phase', *Internat. J. Psychoanal.*, **14**, 1-33.

Jones, E. (1936). *Decennial Report of the London Clinic of Psychoanalysis, 1926-36.*

Jones, M. R. (ed.) (1962) *Nebraska Symposium on Motivation*, Lincoln, University of Nebraska Press.

Jouvet, D., Vimont, P., Delorme, F. and Jouvet, M. (1964) 'Etude de la privation selective de la phase paradoxale du sommeil chez le chat', *C. R. Soc. Biol. Paris*, **158**, 156-9.

Jouvet, M. (1965) 'Paradoxical sleep: a study of its nature and mechanisms', in Abert, K. et al. (1965).

Jouvet, M. (1967) 'Neurophysiology of the states of sleep', *Physiol. Rev.*, **47**, 117-77.

Jouvet, M. and Mounier, D. (1960) 'Effets des lésions de la formation réticule pontique sur le sommeil du chat', *C. R. Soc. Biol. Paris*, **154**, 2301-5.

Joy, V. L. (1963) 'Repression—sensitization personality and interpersonal behaviour', Ph.D. thesis, University of Texas.

Jung, C. G. (1918) *Studies in Word Association*, London, Heinemann.

Jung, C. G. (1940) *The Integration of the Personality*, London, Routledge & Kegan Paul.

Jung, C. G. (1949) *Psychological Types*, London, Routledge & Kegan Paul.

Jung, C. G. (1953) *Two Essays on Analytical Psychology*, London, Routledge & Kegan Paul.

Jung, C. G. (1955) *Psychology and Alchemy*, London, Routledge & Kegan Paul.

Jung, C. G. and Wilhelm, R. (1931) *The Secret of the Golden Flower*, London, Routledge & Kegan Paul.

Kachele, H., Grunzig, H. J. and Thoma, H. (1979) 'Towards a linear-additive model of clinical procedures', *Med. Psychol.*, **5**, 66-80.

Kagan, J. and Moss, H. A. (1962) *Birth to Maturity: A Study in Psychological Development*, New York, Wiley.

Kagan, J. and Phillips, W. (1964) 'The measurement of identification', *J. Abnorm. Soc. Psychol.*, **69**, 442-3.

Kales, A., Hoedemaker, F. S., Jacobson, A. et al. (1964) 'Dream-deprivation: an experimental reappraisal', *Nature*, **204**, 1337-8.

Kamija, J. (1961) 'Behavioural, subjective and physiological aspects of drowsiness and sleep', in Fiske, D. W. and Maodi, S. R. (eds) *Functions of Varied Experience*, Illinois, Dorsey Press.

Karacan, I., Goodenough, D. R., Shapiro, A. and Starker, S. (1966) 'Erection cycle during sleep in relation to dream anxiety', *Arch. Gen. Psychiat.*, **15** (2), 183-9.

Kardiner, A. (1945) *The Psychological Frontiers of Society*, New York, Columbia University Press.

Katkovksy, W. (1965) 'Review of the IES Test', in Buros, O. K. (1965).

Kaye, B. (1962). *Bringing up Children in Ghana: an Impressionistic Survey*, London, Allen & Unwin.

Kaye, M. (1975) 'The therapeutic value of three merging stimuli for male schizophrenics', Ph.D. thesis, Yeshiva University, quoted by Silverman (1976).

Kent, G. H. and Rosanoff, A. J. (1910) 'A study of association in insanity', *Amer. J. Insan.*, **67**, 37-96.

Kerlinger, F. N. (1953) 'Behaviour and personality in Japan: a critique of three studies of Japanese personality', *Soc. Forces*, **31**, 250-8.

Kernberg, D. F. (1973) Summary and conclusions of 'Psychotherapy and psychoanalysis: final report of the Menninger Foundation's psychotherapy research project', *Inst. J. Psychiat.*, **11**, 62-77.

Kessel, L. and Hyman, H. T. (1933) 'The value of psychoanalysis as a therapeutic procedure', *J. Amer. Med. Assoc.*, **19**, 1612-15.

Kiesler, D. J. (1966) 'Some myths of psychotherapy research and the search for a paradigm', *Psychol. Bull.*, **65**, 110-36.

Kilbride, P. L. and Robbins, M. C. (1969) 'Pictorial depth perception and acculturization among the Baganda', *Am. Anthropol.*, **71**, 293-301.

Kimeldorf, C. and Gewitz, P. J. (1966) 'Smoking and the Blacky orality factors', *J. Proj. Tech. and Pers. Ass.*, **30**, 167-8.

Kinsey, A. C., Pomeroy, W. B. and Martin, C. E. (1948) *Sexual Behaviour in the Human Male*, Philadelphia, Saunders.

Klackenberg, G. (1949) 'Thumb-sucking frequency and aetiology', *Pediatrics*, **4**, 418-24.

Klaf, F. S. (1961) 'Evidence of paranoid ideation in overt homosexuals', *J. Soc. Ther.*, **7**, 48-51.

Klaf, F. S. and Davis, C. (1960) 'Homosexuality and paranoid schizophrenia: a survey of 150 cases and controls', *Amer. J. Psychiat.*, **116**, 1070-5.

Klein, H. and Horwitz, W. (1949) 'Psychosexual factors in the paranoid phenomenon', *Amer. J. Psychiat.*, **105**, 697-701.

Klein, M. (1963) *Etude polygraphique et phylogénique des états de sommeil*, Lyon, Bon Frères.

Kline, P. (1967a) 'The use of Cattell's 16PF Test and Eysenck's EPI with a literate population in Ghana', *Brit. J. Soc. Clin. Psychol.*, **6**, 97-107.

Kline, P. (1967b) 'Obsessional traits, obsessional symptoms and general emotionality in a normal population', *Brit. J. Med. Psychol.*, **40**, 153-7.

Kline, P. (1967c) 'An investigation into the Freudian concept of the anal character', Ph.D. thesis, University of Manchester.

Kline, P. (1968a) 'Obsessional traits, obsessional symptoms and anal erotism', *Brit. J. Med. Psychol.*, **41**, 299-305.

Kline, P. (1968b) 'The validity of the Dynamic Personality Inventory', *Brit. J. Med. Psychol.*, **41**, 307-11.

Kline, P. (1969a) 'The anal character: a cross-cultural study in Ghana', *Brit. J. Soc. Clin. Psychol.*, **8**, 201-10.

Kline, P. (1969b) 'A study of the Oedipus complex and neurotic symptoms in a non-psychiatric population (correspondence)', *Brit. J. Med. Psychol.*, **42**, 291.

Kline, P. (1970) 'A projective and psychometric study of the oral character', *Proc. VII Internat. Conf. Soc. Rorsch. and Proj. Tech.*, Vienna, Hans Huber.

Kline, P. (1971) 'Obsessional traits and academic performance in the VIth form', *Educ. Res.*, **13**, 230-2.

Kline, P. (ed.) (1973a) *New Approaches in Psychological Measurement*, London, Wiley.

Kline, P. (1973b) 'The validity of Gottheil's oral trait scale in Great Britain', *J. Pers. Ass.*, **37**, 551-4.

Kline, P. (1975) 'The Pin-Men Test with S. Indian University students', *Psychological Studies*, **20**, 1-6.

Kline, P. (1977) 'Cross-cultural studies and Freudian theory', in Warren, N. (ed.) *Studies in Cross-Cultural Psychology*, vol. I, pp. 50-90, London, Academic Press.

Kline, P. (1978a) 'The status of the anal character: a methodological and empirical reply to Hill', *Brit. J. Med. Psychol.*, **51**, 87-90.

Kline, P. (1978b) *OOQ and OPQ Personality Tests*, Windsor, NFER.

Kline, P. (1978c) 'Freudian confusion', *Encounter*, **51**, July, letter, p. 93.

Kline, P. (1979a) *Psychometrics and Psychology*, London, Academic Press.

Kline, P. (1979b) 'Psychosexual personality traits, fixation and neuroticism', *Brit. J. Med. Psychol.*, **52**, 393-5.

Kline, P., Barrett, P. and Svaste-Xuto, B. (1980) 'The EPQ in Thailand', *J. Soc. Psychol.* (in press).

Kline, P. and Cooper, C. (1977) 'A percept-genetic study of some defence mechanisms in the test PN', *Scand. J. Psychol.*, **18** (2), 148-52.

Kline, P. and Mohan, J. (1974) 'Item endorsements in a personality test — Ai3 — in three countries', *J. Soc. Psychol.*, **94**, 137-8.

Kline, P. and Storey, R. (1977) 'A factor-analytic study of the oral character', *Brit. J. Soc. Clin. Psychol.*, **16**, 317-28.

Kline, P. and Storey, R. (1978a) 'The Dynamic Personality Inventory: what does it measure?', *Brit. J. Psychol.*, **69**, 375-83.

Kline, P. and Storey, R. (1978b) 'Oral personality traits and smoking', *Brit. J. Proj. Tech.*, **23**, 1-4.

Kline, P. and Storey, R. (1980) 'The aetiology of the oral character', *J. Genet. Psychol.*, **136**, 85-94.

Kline, P. and Trejdosiewicz, T. (1971) 'The IES and the Blacky Pictures', *Brit. J. Proj. Tech.*, **16**, 19-21.

Kluckhohn, C. and Murray, H. A. (1953) *Personality in Nature, Society and Culture,* New York, Knopf.

Knapp, P. H. (1963) 'Short-term psychoanalytic and psychosomatic predictions', *J. Amer. Psychoanal. Assoc.*, **11**, 248-80.

Knight, R. P. (1940) 'The relationship of latent homosexuality to the mechanism of paranoid delusions', *Bull. Menning. Clin.*, **4**, 149-59.

Knight, R. P. (1941) 'Evaluation of the results of psychoanalytic therapy', *Amer. J. Psychiat.*, **98**, 434-46.

Kohlberg, L. (1958) 'The development of modes of moral thinking and choice in the ten years to sixteen', Ph.D. thesis, University of Chicago.

Kohlberg, L. (1963a) 'Moral development and identification', in Stevenson, H. (1963).

Kohlberg, L. (1963b) 'The development of children's orientation towards a moral order — I: Sequence in the development of moral thought', *Vita Humana*, **6**, 11-33.

Kohlberg, L. (1964) 'Development of moral character and ideology', in Hoffman, M. L. and Hoffman, L. W. (1964).

Kohlberg, L. (1966a) 'Cognitive stages and pre-school education', *Human Development*, **9**, 5-17.

Kohlberg, L. (1966b) 'A cognitive developmental analysis of children's sex-role concepts and attitudes', in Maccoby, E. E. (1967).

Kohlberg, L. (1967) 'Moral and religious education and the public schools', in Sizer, T. (1967).

Kohlberg, L. (1968) 'Early education: a cognitive developmental view', *Child Development*, **39**, 1013-62.

Kohlberg, L. (1969a) 'Stages and sequences: the cognitive developmental approach to socialization', chapter 6 in Goslin, D. A. (1969).

Kohlberg, L. (1969b) *Stages in the Development of Moral Thought and Action,* New York, Holt, Rinehart & Winston.

Krafkov, S. V. (1941) 'Colour vision and the autonomic nervous system', *J. Opt. Soc. Amer.*, **31**, 235-7.

Kragh, U. (1955) *The Actual Genetic Model of Perception Personality,* Lund, Gleerup.

Kragh, U. (1969) *DMT Manual,* Stockholm, Scandinaviska Tesforlaget AB.

Kragh, U. and Smith, G. (1970) *Percept-Genetic Analysis,* Lund, Gleerup.

Kramer, M., Klaszy, R., Jacobs, G. and Roth, T. (1976) 'Do dreams have meaning? An empirical enquiry', *Amer. J. Psychiat.*, **133**, 778-81.

Kreines, D. C. and Bogart, K. (1974) 'Defensive projection and the reduction of dissonance', *J. Soc. Psychol.*, **92**, 103-8.

Kreitler, H. and Kreitler, S. (1966) 'Children's concepts of sexuality and birth', *Child Development*, **37**, 363-78.

Krout, M. H. and Krout, T. J. (1954) 'Measuring personality in developmental terms', *Genet. Psychol. Monogr.*, **50**, 289-335.

Krout, T. J. (1950) 'Symbol Elaboration Test (SET). The reliability and validity of a new projective technique', *Psychol. Monogr.*, **64** (4).

Kuhn, T. G. (1970) 'Logic of discovery or psychology of research?', in Latakos, I. and Musgrave, A. (eds) *Criticism and the Growth of Knowledge* (1970) Cambridge, Cambridge University Press.

Kuppuswamy, B. (1949) 'Preliminary report of a statistical study of the Oedipus complex', *Ind. J. Psychol.*, **24**, 23-5.

Kurtines, W. and Greif, W. B. (1974) 'The review and evaluation of Kohlberg's approach', *Psych. Bull.*, **81**, 453-70.

La Barre, W. (1945) 'Some observations on character structure in the orient: the Japanese', *Psychiatry*, **8**, 319-42.

Laffal, J. (1952) 'The learning and retention of words with association disturbances', *J. Abnorm. Soc. Psychol.*, **47**, 454-62.

Laffal, J. (1955) 'Application of Guttman's scaling method to the TAT', *Educ. Psychol. Meas.*, **15**, 422-35.

Lamb, C. W. (1968) 'Personality correlates of humour enjoyment following motivational arousal', *J. Pers. Soc. Psychol.*, **9**, 237-41.

Landis, C. A. (1937) 'Statistical evaluation of psychotherapeutic methods', in Hinnie, L. E. (1937).

Landy, E. E. (1967) 'Sex-differences in some aspects of smoking behaviour', *Psychol. Rep.*, **20**, 578-80.

Lane, R. W. (1966) 'The effect of pre-operative stress on dreams', Ph.D. thesis, University of Oregon, quoted by Fisher and Greenberg (1977).

Lasky, J. L. and Berger, L. (1959) 'Blacky Test scores before and after genito-urinary surgery', *J. Proj. Tech.*, **23**, 57-8.

Lazare, A., Klerman, G. L. and Armor, D. J. (1966) 'Oral, obsessive and hysterical personality patterns: an investigation of psychoanalytic concepts by means of factor analysis', *Arch. Gen. Psychiat.*, **14**, 624-30.

Lazare, A., Klerman, G. L. and Armor, D. J. (1970) 'Oral, obsessive and hysterical personality patterns: replication of factor analysis in an independent sample: *J.Psychiat. Res.*, **7**, 275-90.

Leckie, E. V. and Withers, R. F. J. (1967) 'A test of liability to depressive illness', *Brit. J. Med. Psychol.*, **40**, 273.

Lee, S. G. (1953) *TAT for African Subjects*, Pietermaritzburg, University of Natal Press.

Lee, S. G. (1958) 'Social influences in Zulu dreaming', *J. Soc. Psychol.*, **47**, 265-83.

Lerner, B. (1961) 'Auditory and visual thresholds for the perception of words of anal connotation: an evaluation of the sublimation hypothesis on philatelists', Ph.D. thesis, Yeshiva University, quoted by Fisher and Greenberg (1977).

Lessler, K. (1962) 'Sexual symbols structured and unstructured', *J. Consult. Psychol.*, **26**, 44-9.

Lessler, K. (1964) 'Cultural and Freudian dimensions of sexual symbols', *J. Consult. Psychol.*, **28** (1), 46-53.

Lessler, K. and Ericksen, M. T. (1968) 'Response to sexual symbols by elementary school children', *J. Consult. Clin. Psychol.*, **32**, 473-7.

Levin, R. B. (1966) 'An empirical test of the female castration complex', *J. Abnorm. Psychol.*, **71**, 181-8.

Levine, M. L. and Bell, A. I. (1950) 'The treatment of colic in infancy by use of the pacifier', *J. Pediat.*, **37**, 750-5.

Levinger, G. and Clark, J. (1961) 'Emotional factors in the forgetting of word associations', *J. Abnorm. Soc. Psychol.*, **62**, 99-105.

Levy, D. M. (1928) 'Finger-sucking and accessory movements in early infancy (an etiological study)', *Amer. J. Psychiat.*, **7**, 881-918.

Levy, D. M. (1934) 'Experiments on the sucking reflex and social behaviour in dogs', *Amer. J. Orthopsychiat.*, **4**, 203-24.

Levy, L. H. (1954) 'Sexual symbolism: a validity study', *J. Consult. Psychol.*, **18**, 43-6.

Lewis, G. A. (1969) 'Experimental induction of castration anxiety and anxiety over loss of love', Ph.D. thesis, University of Yeshiva, quoted by Fisher and Greenberg (1977).

Lewis, H. (1954) *Deprived Children*, London, Oxford University Press.

Lief, H. I., Lief, V. F. and Lief, N. R. (eds) (1963) *The Psychological Basis of Medical Practice*, New York, Harper & Row.

Lindner, H. (1953) 'The Blacky Pictures Test: a study of sexual and non-sexual offenders', *J. Proj. Tech.*, **17**, 79-84.

Lindzey, G. (ed.) (1954) *The Handbook of Social Psychology*, Reading, Mass., Adison Wesley.

Lindzey, G. (1961) *Projective Techniques and Cross-cultural Research*, New York, Appleton-Century-Crofts.

Lindzey, G. and Hall, C. S. (1965) *Theories of Personality: Primary Sources and Research*, New York, Wiley.

Lish, J. A. (1969) Ph.D. thesis, University of Yeshiva, quoted by Fisher and Greenberg (1977).

Littman, R. A., Nidorf, L. J. and Sundberg, N. D. (1961) 'Characteristics of a psychosexual scale', *J. Genet. Psychol.*, **98**, 19-27.

Lomangiro, L. (1969) 'The depiction of subliminally and supraliminally presented aggressive stimuli and its effect on the cognitive functioning of schizophrenics', Ph.D. thesis, Fordham University, quoted by Silverman, L. H. (1975).

Lorr, M. (1978) 'Ai3 Questionnaire', in Buros, O. K. (ed.) *The VIIIth Mental Measurement Year Book* (1978), New Jersey, Gryphon Press.

Lubin, A. and Loos, F. M. (1953) 'The IPAT Humour Test', in Buros, O. K. (ed.) *The IVth Mental Measurement Year Book* (1953), New Jersey, Gryphon Press.

Luborsky, L. (1954) 'A note on Eysenck's article "The effects of psychotherapy:

an evaluation"', *Brit. J. Psychol.*, **45**, 129-31.

Luborsky, L. and Cattell, R. B. (1947) 'The validation of personality factors in humour', *J. Pers.*, **15**, 283-91.

Luchins, A. S. (1950) 'On an approach to social perception', *J. Pers.*, **19**, 64-84.

Lystad, R. A. (1958) *The Ashanti, A Proud People*, New Brunswick, New Jersey, Rutgers University Press.

Lytton, H. (1969) 'Parent—child interaction studies: an unresolved dilemma?', *Paper at Brit. Psychol. Soc. Annual Conf. 1969.*

McArthur, C., Waldron, F. and Dickinson, J. (1958) 'The psychology of smoking', *J. Abnorm. Soc. Psychol.*, **56**, 267-75.

McClelland, D. C. (1961) *The Achieving Society*, Princeton, Van Nostrand.

McClelland, D. C. and Friedman, G. A. (1952) in Newcomb, T. M. and Hartley, E. L. (1952) *Readings in Social Psychology*, New York, Holt.

Maccoby, E. E. (ed.) (1967) *The Development of Sex-Differences*, Stanford, Stanford University Press.

Maccoby, E. E., Newcomb, T. M. and Hartley, E. L. (eds) (1958) *Readings in Social Psychology*, 3rd edn, New York, Holt, Rinehart & Winston.

McCord, W., McCord, J. and Gudeman, J. (1959) 'Some current theories of alcoholism: a longitudinal evaluation', *Quart. J. Stud. Alcohol.*, **20**, 727-49.

McElroy, W. A. (1950) 'Methods of testing the Oedipus complex hypothesis', *Quart. Bull. Brit. Psychol. Soc.*, **1**, 364-5.

McElroy, W. A. (1954) 'A sex-difference in preferences for shapes', *Brit. J. Psychol.*, **45**, 209-16.

McGinnies, E. (1949) 'Emotionality and perceptual defence', *Psychol. Rev.*, **56**, 244-51.

McGinnies, E., Comer, P. B. and Lacy, O. L. (1952) 'Visual recognition thresholds as a function of word-length and word-frequency', *J. Exp. Psychol.*, **44**, 59-65.

Machover, S. and Puzzo, F. S. (1959) 'Clinical and objective studies of personality variables in alcoholism — I: Clinical investigation of the alcoholic personality', *Quart. J. Stud. Alcohol.*, **20**, 505-27.

Machover, S., Puzzo, F. S., Machover, K. and Plumeau, F. (1959) 'Clinical and objective studies of personality variables in alcoholism', *Quart. J. Stud. Alcohol.*, **20**, 528-42.

MacKinnon, D. W. (1938) 'Violation and prohibitions', in Murray, H. A. (1938).

MacKinnon, D. W. and Dukes, W. F. (1962) 'Repression', in Postman, L. (1962).

Maclean, P. D. (1949) 'Psychosomatic disease and the "visceral brain"', *Psychosom. Med.*, **11**, 338-53.

McNeil, E. B. and Blum, G. S. (1952) 'Handwriting and psychosexual dimensions of personality', *J. Proj. Tech.*, **16**, 476-84.

Magoun, H. W. (1961) 'Darwin and concepts of brain function', in Fessard, Gerard and Konorski (1961).

Malan, D. (1959) 'On assessing the results in psychotherapy', *Brit. J. Med.*

Psychol., **32**, 86-105.

Maletzky, R. M. and Klotter, J. 'Smoking and alcoholism', *Amer. J. Psychiat.*, **131**, 445-7.

Malinowski, B. (1927) *Sex and Repression in Savage Society*, New York, Harcourt Brace.

Manchanda, R., Sethi, B. B. and Gupta, S. C. (1979) 'Hostility and guilt in obsessional neuroses', *Brit. J. Psychiat.*, **135**, 52-4.

Margolis, M. (1961) 'The mother—child relationship in bronchial asthma', *J. Abnorm. Soc. Psychol.*, **63** (2), 360-7.

Marke, S. and Nyman, E. (1960) *MNT — Skalan*, Stockholm, Skandinaviska Tesforlaget AB.

Marquis, D. F., Sinnett, E. R. and Winter, W. D. (1952) 'A psychological study of peptic ulcer patients', *J. Clin. Psychol.*, **8**, 266-72.

Martin, M. (1964) 'Mr Farrell and the refutability of psychoanalysis', *Inquiry*, **7**, 80-98.

Martin, T. C. (1977) 'Choice of defence mechanism by Indian and white adolescents', *J. Clin. Psychol.*, **33**, 1027-8.

Marx, M. H. (ed.) (1963) *Theories in Contemporary Psychology*, New York, Macmillan.

Masling, J., Rabie, L. and Blondheim, S. H. (1967) 'Obesity, level of aspiration, Rorschach and TAT measures of oral dependence', *J. Consult. Psychol.*, **31**, 233-9.

Masling, J., Weiss, L. and Rothschild, B. (1968) 'Relationships of oral imagery to yielding behaviour and birth order', *J. Consult. Clin. Psychol.*, **32**, 89-91.

Masserman, J. H. (ed.) (1964) *Science and Psychoanalysis*, vol. VII, New York, Grune & Stratton.

Masserman, J. H. and Carmichael, H. T. (1938) 'Diagnosis and prognosis in psychiatry, with a follow-up study of the results of short-term hospital therapy of psychiatric cases', *J. Ment. Sci.*, **34**, 893-946.

Masters, M. W. H. and Johnson, V. E. (1966) *Human Sexual Response*, Boston, Little, Brown.

Maury, A. (1861) *Le Sommeil et Les Rêves*, Paris, Didier.

Maussakalian, M., Blanchard, E. B., Abel, G. C. and Barlow, D. H. (1975) 'Responses to complex erotic stimuli in homosexual and heterosexual males', *Brit. J. Psychiat.*, **126**, 252-7.

Mayer-Gross, W., Slater, E. and Roth, M. (1961) *Clinical Psychiatry*, London, Cassell.

Medawar, P. B. (1969) *Induction and Intuition in Scientific Thought*, London, Methuen.

Mednick, S. A., Garner, A. M. and Stone, H. H. (1959) 'A test of some behavioural hypotheses drawn from Alexander's specificity theory', *Amer. J. Orthopsychiat.*, **29**, 592-8.

Meehl, P. H. (1955) 'Psychotherapy', *Amer. Rev. Psychol.*, **6**, 357-78.

Mehlman, B. (1952) 'The reliability of psychiatric diagnoses', *J. Abnorm, Soc.*

Psychol., **47**, 577-8.

Meissner, W. W. (1958) 'Affective response to psychoanalytic death symbols', *J. Abnorm. Soc. Psychol.*, **56**, 295-9.

Mendelsohn, G. A. (1965) 'The Myers—Briggs Type Indicator', in Buros, O. K. (1965).

Menninger, W. C. (1943) 'Characterologic and symptomatic expressions related to the anal phase of psychosexual development', *Psychoanal. Quart.*, **12**, 161-93.

Merchant, F. C. (1952) 'Psychosexual development in stutterers', unpub. Ms. quoted by Blum and Hunt (1952).

Messick, S. and Abelson, R. (1956) 'The additive constant problem in multi-dimensional scaling', *Psychom.*, **21**, 1-15.

Meyer, A. E. (1966) 'Psychoanalytic versus behaviour therapy of male homosexuals: a statistical evaluation of clinical outcome', *Comprehen. Psychiat.*, **7**, 110-17.

Michal-Smith, H., Hammer, E. and Spitz, H. (1951) 'Use of the Blacky Pictures with a child whose Oedipal desires are close to consciousness', *J. Clin. Psychol.*, **7**, 280-2.

Miles, D. W. (1954) 'The import for clinical psychology of the use of tests derived from theories about infantile sexuality and adult character', *Genet. Psychol. Monogr.*, **50**, 227-88.

Miles, T. R. (1965) *Eliminating the Unconscious* (a behaviourist's view of psychoanalysis), Oxford, Pergamon Press.

Miller, A. R. (1968) 'Analysis of the Oedipal complex', *Psychol. Prep.*, **24**, 781-2.

Miller, D. R. and Swanson, G. E. (1966) *Inner Conflict and Defence*, New York, Schocken.

Miller, N. E. (1948) 'Theory and experiment relating psychoanalytic displacement to stimulus-response generalization', *J. Abnorm. Soc. Psychol.*, **43**, 155-78.

Miller, N. E. and Bugelski, R. (1948) 'Minor studies of aggression — II: The influence of frustrations imposed by the in-group on attitudes expressed towards out-groups', *J. Psychol.*, **25**, 437-42.

Minturn, L. (1965) 'A cross-cultural linguistic analysis of Freudian symbols', *Ethnology*, **4**, 336-42.

Mintz, J., Luborsky, L. and Auerbach, A. H. (1971) 'Dimensions of psychotherapy: a factor-analytic study of ratings of psychotherapy sessions', *J. Consult. Clin. Psychol.*, **36**, 106-20.

Mintz, J., Luborsky, L. and Christoph, P. (1979) 'Measuring the outcomes of psychotherapy: findings of the Penn Psychotherapy Project', *J. Consult. Clin. Psychol.*, **47**, 319-34.

Mischel, W. and Grusec, J. (1966) 'Determinants of the rehearsal and transmission of neutral aversive behaviours', *J. Pers. Soc. Psychol.*, **2**, 197-205.

Moniz, E. (1936) *Tentatives Opérations dans le Traitement de Certaines Psychoses*, Paris, Masson.

Moore, R. A. and Selzer, M. L. (1963) 'Male homosexuality, paranoia and the schizophrenias', *Amer. J. Psychiat.*, **119**, 743-7.

Moos, R. and Mussen, P. (1959) 'Sexual symbolism, personality integration and intellectual functioning', *J. Consult. Psychol.*, **23**, 521-3.

Mosak, H. R. (1955) 'Language and the interpretation of sexual symbolism', *J. Consult. Psychol.*, **19**, 108.

Mowrer, O. H. (1950) *Learning Theory and Personality Dynamics*, New York, Ronald.

Mullahy, P. (1948) *Oedipus Myth and Complex*, New York, Hermitage Press.

Mullen, F. G. (1968) 'Estimation of the universality of Freudian and Jungian sexual symbols', *Percept. Mot. Skills*, **26**, 1041-2.

Munn, N. L. (1961) *The Evolution and Growth of Human Behaviour*, London, Harrap.

Munroe, R. H., Munroe, R. L. and Lasky, M. L. (1976) 'A sex-difference in shape preference', *J. Soc. Psychol.*, **98**, 139-40.

Munroe, R. L. and Munroe, R. H. (1971) 'Male pregnancy symptoms and cross-sex identity in three societies', *J. Soc. Psychol.*, **84**, 11-25.

Munroe, R. L. and Munroe, R. H. (1973) 'Male pregnancy symptoms and cross-sex identity: two replications', *J. Soc. Psychol.*, **89**, 147-8.

Murchison, C. (ed.) (1930) *Psychologies of 1930*, Worcester, Mass., Clarke University Press.

Murdock, G. P. (1949) *Social Structure*, New York, Macmillan.

Murdock, G. P. (1957) 'World ethnographic sample', *Am. Anthropol.*, **59**, 664-87.

Murphy, L. B. (1962) *The Widening World of Childhood*, New York, Basic Books.

Murray, H. A. (1938) *Explorations in Personality*, New York, Oxford University Press.

Mussen, P. H. and Distler, L. (1959) 'Masculinity identification and father—son relationships', *J. Abnorm. Soc. Psychol.*, **59**, 350-6.

Myers, I. B. (1962) *The Myers—Briggs Type Indicator*, Princeton, ETS.

Naroll, R. and Cohen. R. (eds) (1970) *A Handbook of Method in Cultural Anthropology*, Garden City, Natural History Press.

Neisser, U. (1954) 'An experimental distinction between perceptual processes and mental responses', *J. Exp. Psychol.*, **47**, 399-402.

Nelson, S. E. (1955) 'Psychosexual conflicts and defences in visual perception', *J. Abnorm. Psychol.*, **51**, 427-33.

Neuman, G. C. and Salvatore, J. C. (1958) 'The Blacky Test and psychoanalytic theory. A factor-analytic approach to validity', *J. Proj. Tech.*, **22**, 427-31.

Newson, J. and Newson, E. (1963) *Infant Care in an Urban Community*, London, Allen & Unwin.

Newton, N. R. (1951) 'The relation between infant-feeding experience and later behaviour', *J. Pediat.*, **38**, 28-40.

Noblin, C. D. (1962) 'Experimental analysis of psychoanalytic character types through the operant conditioning of verbal responses', *Amer. Psychol.*, **17**, 306.

Noblin, C. D., Timmons, E. O. and Kael, H. C. (1963) 'Differential effects of positive and negative verbal reinforcement on psychoanalytic character types', *Amer. Psychol.*, **18**, 412.

Noblin, C. D., Timmons, E. O. and Kael, H. C. (1966) 'Differential effects of positive and negative verbal reinforcement on psychoanalytic character types', *J. Pers. Soc. Psychol.*, **4**, 224-8.

Norman, J. P. (1948) 'Evidence and clinical significance of homosexuality in 100 unanalysed cases of dementia praecox', *J. Nerv. Ment. Dis.*, **107**, 484-9.

Nowlis, V. (1963) 'Research with the mood adjective check-list', in Tomkins, S. S. and Izard, E. C. (eds) *Affect, Cognition and Personality*, New York, Springer.

Nunnally, J. (1978) *Psychometric Theory*, 2nd edn, New York, McGraw-Hill.

Oberndorf, C. P. (1942) 'Results with psychoanalytic therapy', *Amer. J. Psychiat.*, **99**, 374.

O'Connell, W. E. (1960) 'The adaptive function of wit and humour', *J. Abnorm. Soc. Psychol.*, **61**, 263-70.

O'Connell, W. E. (1962) 'Item-analysis of the WHAT test', *J. Soc. Psychol.*, **56**, 271-6.

O'Connell, W. E. (1964) 'Multi-dimensional investigation of Freudian humour', *Psychiat. Quart.*, **38** (1), 97-108.

O'Connor, J. F., Daniels, G., Karus, A., Moses, L., Flood, C. and Stern, L. (1964) 'The effects of psychotherapy on the course of ulcerative colitis: a preliminary report', *Amer. J. Psychiat.*, **20**, 738-42.

O'Connor, N. and Franks, C. M. (1961) 'Childhood upbringing and other environmental factors', in Eysenck, H. J. (1961).

Offenkrantz, W. A. and Rechtschaffen, A. (1963) 'Clinical studies of sequential dreams', *Arch. Gen. Psychiat.*, **8**, 497-508.

Ohlmeyer, P., Brilmayer, H. and Histlstrung, H. (1944) 'Periodische Vorgänge im Schlaf', *Pflug. Arch. Ges. Physiol.*, **248**, 559.

Ohlmeyer, P., Brilmayer, H. and Histlstrung, H. (1947) 'Periodische Vorgänge im Schlaf', II Mitteilung, *Pflug. Arch. Ges. Physiol.*, **249**, 50.

Oldfield, R. C. (1955) 'Apparent fluctuations of a sensory threshold', *Quart. J. Exp. Psychol.*, **7**, 101-15.

O'Neil, C. W. (1964) 'A cross-cultural study of hunger and thirst motivation manifested in dreams', *Human Development*, **8**, 181-93.

Orgel, S. Z. (1958) 'Effects of psychoanalysis on the course of peptic ulcer', *Psychosom. Med.*, **20**, 117-23.

Orlansky, H. (1949) 'Infant care and personality', *Psychol. Bull.*, **46**, 1-48.

Orme, J. E. (1965) 'The relationship of obsessional traits to general emotional instability', *Brit. J. Med. Psychol.*, **38**, 269.

Orne, M. (1962) 'On the social psychology of the psychological experiment, with particular reference to demand characteristics and their implications', *Amer. Psychol.*, **17**, 776-83.

Oswald, I. (1969) 'Do dreams have a function?', *Paper at Ann. Conf. Brit. Psychol. Soc.*, Edinburgh.

Papez, J. W. (1937) 'A proposed mechanism of emotion', *Arch. Neurol. Psychiat.*, **38**, 725-43.

Parker, S. (1976) 'The precultural basis of the incest taboo: towards a social theory', *Am. Anthropol*, **78**, 285-305.

Parsons, A. (1969) in Muensterberger, W. (ed.) *Man and Culture*, London, Rapp & Whiting.

Parsons, T. (1955) 'Family structure and the socialization of the child', in Parsons and Bales (1955).

Parsons, T. and Bales, R. F. (1955) *Family, Socialization and Interaction Process*, New York, Free Press.

Pasamanick, B., Dinitz, S. and Lefton, M. (1959) 'Psychiatric orientation and its relation to diagnosis and treatment in a mental hospital', *Amer. J. Psychiat.*, **116**, 127-32.

Pawlik, K. and Cattell, R. B. (1964) 'Third-order factors in objective personality tests', *Brit. J. Psychol.*, **55**, 1-18.

Paykel, E. G. and Prusoff, B. A. (1973) 'Relationships between personality dimensions: neuroticism and extraversion against obsessive, hysterical and oral personality', *Brit, J. Soc. Clin. Psychol.*, **12**, 309-18.

Payne, D. E. and Mussen, P. H. (1956) 'Parent—child relations and father-identification among adolescent boys', *J. Abnorm. Soc.*, **52**, 358-62.

Pedersen, F. and Marlowe, D. (1960) 'Capacity and motivational differences in verbal recall', *J. Clin. Psychol.*, **16**, 219-22.

Peil, M. (1965) 'Ghanaian University students: the broadening base', *Brit. J. Sociol.*, **16**, 19-28.

Perloe, S. I. (1958) 'An experimental test of two theories of perceptual defence', Ph.D. thesis, University of Michigan.

Perloe, S. I. (1960) 'Inhibition as a determinant of perceptual defence', *Percept. Mot. Skills*, **11**, 59-66.

Peterson, C. H. and Spano, F. (1941) 'Breast-feeding, maternal rejection and child personality', *Char. and Personal.*, **10**, 62-6.

Pettit, T. F. (1969) 'Anality and time', *J. Consult. Clin. Psychol.*, **33**, 170-4.

Phillips, H. P. (1965) *Thai Peasant Personality*, Berkeley, University of California Press.

Piaget, J. (1948) *The Moral Judgement of the Child*, Glencoe, Free Press.

Pichot, P. (1954) quoted by Cattell, R. B. (1957).

Pichot, P. and Perse, J. (1967) 'Analyse factorielle et structure de la personnalité', *Paper in honour of Prof. Essen-Møller*, Lund, University of Lund.

Pickford, R. W. (1969) 'Dream-work, art-work and sublimation in relation to art therapy', *Paper at Ann. Conf. Brit. Psychol. Soc.*, Edinburgh.

Pinzka, C. and Saunders, D. R. (1954) 'Analytic rotation to simple structure — II: Extension to an oblique solution', *Res. Bull.*, RB-54-3, Princeton, ETS.

Poetzl, O. (1917) 'Experimentell erregte Träumbilder in ihren Beziehungen zum indirekten Sehen', *Ztschr. f.d. Neurol. und Psychiat.*, **37**, 278-349.

Pollie, D. M. (1964) 'A projective study of conflict and defence in peptic ulcers and bronchial asthma', *J. Proj. Tech. and Pers. Ass.*, **28**, 67-77.

Popper, K. (1959) *The Logic of Scientific Discovery*, New York, Basic Books.

Postman, L. (1953) 'On the problem of perceptual defence', *Psychol. Rev.*, **60**, 298-306.

Postman, L. (ed.) (1962) *Psychology in the Making*, New York, Knopf.

Postman, L., Bronson, W. and Gropper, G. L. (1953) 'Is there a mechanism of perceptual defence?', *J. Abnorm. Soc. Psychol.*, **48**, 215-24.

Powdermaker, H. (1933) *Life in Lesu*, New York, Norton.

Price-Williams, D. R. (1965) 'Displacement and orality in Tiv witchcraft', *J. Soc. Psychol.*, **65** (1), 1-15.

Proctor, J. T. and Briggs, A. G. (1964) 'The utility of dreams in the diagnostic interview with children', in E. Herns (ed.) *Problems of Sleep and Dreams in Children*, New York, MacMillan.

Prugh, D. G. (1954) 'Childhood experience and colonic disorder', *Amer. N. Y. Acad. Sci.*, **58**, 355-76.

Pumpian-Mindlin, E. (ed.) (1952) *Psychoanalysis as Science*, Stanford, Stanford University Press.

Rabin, A. I. (1957) 'Personality maturity of Kibbutz (Israeli collective settlement) children and non-Kibbutz children as reflected in Rorschach findings', *J. Proj. Tech.*, **21**, 148-53.

Rabin, A. I. (1958a) 'The Israel Kibbutz (collective settlement) as a "laboratory" for testing psychodynamic hypotheses', *Psychol. Rec.*, **7**, 111-15.

Rabin, A. I. (1958b) 'Some psychosexual differences between Kibbutz and non-Kibbutz Israeli boys', *J. Proj. Tech.*, **22**, 328-32.

Rabinowitz, W. (1957) 'Anality, aggression and acquiescence', *J. Abnorm. Psychol.*, **54**, 140-2.

Rachmann, S. (1963) *Critical Essays in Psychoanalysis*, Oxford, Pergamon.

Ramsey, G. V. (1943) 'The sexual development of boys', *Amer. J. Psychol.*, **56**, 217-33.

Ramsey, G. V. (1953) 'Studies of dreaming', *Psychol. Bull.*, **50**, 432-55.

Rapaport, D. and Gill, M. M. (1959) 'The points of view and assumptions of metapsychology', *Internat. J. Psychoanal.*, **40**, 153-62.

Rasch, G. (1960) *Probabilistic Models for Some Intelligence and Attainment Tests*, Copenhagen, Denmark Institute of Education.

Rattray, R. S. (1923) *Ashanti*, London, Oxford University Press.

Rechtschaffen, A. (1964), in Masserman, J. H. (1964).

Rechtschaffen, A., Verdone, P. and Wheaton, J. (1963) 'Reports of mental activity during sleep', *Canad. Psychiat. Assoc. J.*, **8**, 409-14.

Rechtschaffen, A., Vogel, G. and Shaikun, G. (1963) 'Interrelatedness of mental activity during sleep', *Arch. Gen. Psychiat.*, **9**, 536-47.

Rees, A. (1959) quoted by Hall, C. S. (1963).

Reich, W. (1945) *Character Analysis*, New York, Orgone Institute.

Reiss, W. (1951) 'A comparison of the interpretation of dream series with and without free association', Ph.D. thesis, Western Reserve University.

Report of the Committee on Homosexual Offences and Prostitution (Wolfenden Report) (1957) London, HMSO.

Rest, J. (1968) 'Developmental hierarchy in preference and comprehension of moral judgement', Ph.D. thesis, University of Chicago.

Reyher, J. (1967) 'Hypnosis in research on psychopathology', in J. E. Gordon (ed.) *Handbook of Clinical and Experimental Hypnosis*, New York, MacMillan.

Reymert, M. L. (ed.) (1950) *The Second International Symposium on Feelings and Emotions*, New York, McGraw-Hill.

Richardson, M. W. and Kuder, F. (1939) 'The calculation of test-reliability coefficients based upon the method of rational equivalence', *J. Educ. Psychol.*, **30**, 681-7.

Rickman, A. (1940) 'The psychology of ugliness', *Internat. J. Psychoanal.*, **21**, 294-31.

Ricoeur, P. (1970) *Freudian Philosophy: an Essay in Interpretation*, New Haven, Yale University Press.

Ritz, G. H. (1954) 'The relative strengths of impulse, ego and super-ego in three groups of aged males', Ph.D. thesis, Western Reserve University.

Robbins, L. C. (1963) 'The accuracy of parental recall of aspects of child development and of child-rearing practices', *J. Abnorm. Soc. Psychol.*, **66**, 261-70.

Robbins, S. L. (1962) *Textbook of Pathology*, 2nd edn, Philadelphia, W. B. Saunders.

Roberts, E. (1944) 'Thumb- and finger-sucking in relation to feeding in early infancy', *Amer. J. Dis.*, **68**, 7-8.

Robinson, S. A. and Hendrix, V. L. (1966) 'The Blacky Test and psychoanalytic theory: another factor-analytic approach to validity', *J. Proj. Tech. and Pers. Ass.*, **30**, 597-603.

Roffwarg, H. P., Dement, W. C., Muzzio, J. and Fisher, C. (1962) 'Dream imagery: relationship to rapid eye movements of sleep', *Arch. Gen. Psychiat.*, **7**, 235-58.

Rogers, C. R. (1957) 'The necessary and sufficient conditions of therapeutic personality change', *J. Consult. Psychol.*, **21**, 95-103.

Rogers, C. R. and Dymond, R. (1954) *Psychotherapy and Personality Change*, Chicago, University of Chicago Press.

Rogerson, B. C. F. and Rogerson, C. H. (1939) 'Feeding in infancy and subsequent psychological difficulties', *J. Ment. Sci.*, **65**, 1163-82.

Roheim, G. (1934) 'The study of character development and the ontogenetic theory of culture', in E. E. Evans-Pritchard et al. (eds) *Essays Presented to C. G. Seligman*, London, Routledge & Kegan Paul.

Roheim, G. (1952) 'The anthropological evidence and the Oedipus complex', *Psychoanal. Quart.*, **21**, 537-42.

Rokeach, M. (1960) *The Open and Closed Mind: An Investigation into the Nature of Belief Systems and Personality Systems*, New York, Basic Books.

Rosenstock, I. M. (1951) 'Perceptual aspects of repression', *J. Abnorm. Soc. Psychol.*, **41**, 304-15.

Rosenthal, R. (1964) 'Experimenter outcome-orientation and the results of the psychological experiment', *Psychol. Bull.*, **61**, 405-12.

Rosenwald, G. C. (1972) 'Effectiveness of defences against anal impulse arousal', *J. Consult. Clin. Psychol.*, **39**, 292-8.

Rosenwald, G. C., Mendelsohn, G. A., Fontana, A. and Posty, A. T. (1966) 'An action test of hypotheses concerning the anal personality', *J. Abnorm. Psychol.*, **71**, 304-9.

Rosenzweig, S. (1933) 'The recall of finished and unfinished tasks as affected by the purpose with which they were performed', *Psychol. Bull.*, **30**, 698.

Rosenzweig, S. (1934) 'Types of reaction to frustration', *J. Abnorm. Soc. Psychol.*, **29**, 298-300.

Rosenzweig, S. (1938) 'The experimental study of repression', in Murray, H. A. (1938).

Rosenzweig, S. (1954) 'A transvaluation of psychotherapy: a reply to Hans Eysenck', *J. Abnorm. Soc. Psychol.*, **49**, 298-304.

Rossi, A. M. and Solomon, P. (1961) 'A further note on female Blacky protocols', *J. Proj. Tech.*, **25**, 339-40.

Rossi, R., Delmonte, P. and Terracciano, P. (1971) 'The problem of the relationship between homosexuality and schizophrenia', *Arch. Sex. Behav.*, **1**, 357-62.

Sadger, J. (1929) 'Erfolge und Dauer der psychoanalytischen Neurosenbehandlung', *Internat. Z. Psychoanal.*, **15**, 426-34.

Saltztein, S. W. (1971) 'Relationship between Oedipal conflict and castration anxiety as a function of repressive and sensitizing defences', doctoral dissertation, New York University.

Sampson, H. (1965) 'Deprivation of dreaming sleep by two methods — I: Compensatory REM time', *Arch. Gen. Psychiat.*, **13**, 79-86.

Samuels, I. (1959) 'Reticular mechanisms and behaviour', *Psychol. Bull.*, **56**, 1-25.

Sandler, J. (1954) 'Studies in psychopathology using a self-assessment inventory', *Brit. J. Med. Psychol.*, **27**, 142-5.

Sandler, J. and Hazari, A. (1960) 'The obsessional: on the psychological classification of obsessional character traits and symptoms', *Brit. J. Med. Psychol.*, **33**, 113-21.

Sappenfield, B. R. (1965) 'Review of the Blacky Pictures', in Buros, O. K. (1965).

Sarnoff, I. (1951) 'Identification with the aggressor: some personality correlates of anti-semitism among Jews', *J. Pers.*, **20**, 199-218.

Sarnoff, I. (1960) 'Reaction-formation and cynicism', *J. Pers.*, **28**, 129-43.

Sarnoff, I. (1962) *Personality Dynamics and Development*, London, Wiley.

Sarnoff, I. and Corwin, S. M. (1959) 'Castration anxiety and the fear of death', *J. Pers.*, **27**, 374-85.

Schafer, R. (1954) *Psychoanalytic Interpretation in Rorschach Testing*, New York, Grune & Stratton.

Schaffer, H. R. (1958) 'Objective observations of personality development in early infancy', *Brit. J. Med. Psychol.*, **31**, 174-83.

Schjelderup, H. (1955) 'Lasting effects of psychoanalytic treatment', *Psychiat.*, **18**, 103-33.

Schlesinger, V. J. (1963) 'Anal personality traits and occupational choice — a study of accountants, chemical engineers and educational psychologists', Ph.D. thesis, University of Michigan.

Schmidt, H. O. and Fonda, C. P. (1956) 'The reliability of psychiatric diagnosis: a new look', *J. Abnorm. Soc. Psychol.*, **52**, 262-7.

Schneider, K. (1958) *Psychopathic Personalities*, London, Cassell.

Schneider, S. C. S. (1960) 'An analysis of pre-surgical anxiety in boys and girls', doctoral dissertation, University of Michigan.

Schonbar, R. A. and Davitz, J. R. (1960) 'The connotative meaning of sexual symbols', *J. Consult. Psychol.*, **24**, 483-7.

Schwartz, B. J. (1955) 'Measurement of castration anxiety and anxiety over the loss of love', *J. Pers.*, **24**, 204-19.

Schwartz, B. J. (1956) 'An empirical test of two Freudian hypotheses concerning castration anxiety', *J. Pers.*, **24**, 318-27.

Scodel, A. (1957) 'Heterosexual somatic preference and fantasy dependence', *J. Consult. Psychol.*, **21**, 371-4.

Scofield, R. W. and Sun, C. W. (1960) 'A comparative study of the differential effect upon personality of Chinese and American child-training practices', *J. Soc. Psychol.*, **52**, 221-4.

Scott, E. M. (1958) 'Psychosexuality of the alcoholic', *Psychol. Rep.*, **4**, 599-602.

Searles, H. F. (1965) *Collected Papers on Schizophrenia and Related Subjects*, New York, International University Press.

Sears, R. R. (1936) 'Experimental studies of projection — I: Attribution of traits', *J. Soc. Psychol.*, **7**, 151-63.

Sears, R. R. (1937) 'Initiation of the repression sequence by experienced failure', *J. Exp. Psychol.*, **20**, 570-80.

Sears, R. R. (1943) *Survey of Objective Studies of Psychoanalytic Concepts*, Bull. 51, New York, Social Science Research Council.

Sears, R. R. (1950) 'Personality', *Ann. Rev. Psychol.*, **1**, 105-18.

Sears, R. R., Maccoby, E. E. and Levin, H. (1957) *Patterns of Child-Rearing*, Evanston, Row, Peterson.

Sears, R. R., Rau, L. and Alpert, R. (1965) *Identification and Child-training*, Stanford, Stanford University Press.

Sears, R. R., Whiting, J. W. M., Nowlis, V. and Sears, P. S. (1953) 'Some child-rearing antecedents of aggression and dependency in young children', *Genet. Psychol. Monogr.*, **47**, 135-234.

Sears, R. R. and Wise, G. W. (1950) 'Relation of cup-feeding in infancy to thumb-sucking and the oral drive', *Amer. J. Orthopsychiat.*, **20**, 123-38.

Segal, H. (1964) *Introduction to the Work of Melanie Klein*, London, Heinemann.

Seiden, R. H. (1965) 'Onset, age and psychosexual conflict in bronchial asthma', *Amer. Psychol.*, **20**, 548.

Sells, S. B. (1965) 'The Dynamic Personality Inventory', in Buros, O. K. (1965).

Seward, J. P. (1950) 'Psychoanalysis, deductive method and the Blacky Test', *J. Abnorm. Soc. Psychol.*, **45**, 529-35.

Sewell, W. H. (1952) 'Infant-training and the personality of the child', *Amer. J. Soc.*, **58**, 150-9.

Sewell, W. H. and Mussen, P. H. (1952) 'The effects of feeding, weaning and scheduling procedures on childhood adjustment and the formation of oral symptoms', *Child Development*, **23**, 185-91.

Sharma, V. P. (1974) 'Identification: its relationship with the perceiver', *Brit. J. Proj. Tech. and Pers. Stud.*, **19**, 1-7.

Sharma, V. P. (1977) *Application of a Percept-Genetic Test in a Clinical Setting*, Lund, University of Lund.

Sharma, V. P. and Haas, L. (1974) 'Pre-recognition perception and personality; a pilot study (use of pre-recognition perception in a clinical context)', *Brit. J. Med. Psychol.*, **46**, 393-8.

Sherwood, M. (1969) *The Logic of Explanation in Psychoanalysis*, New York and London, Academic Press.

Shevrin, H. and Luborsky, L. (1958) 'The measurement of preconscious perception in dreams and images. An investigation of the Poetzl phenomenon', *J. Abnorm. Soc. Psychol.*, **56**, 285-94.

Silverman, L. H. (1971) 'An experimental technique for the study of unconscious conflict', *Brit. J. Med. Psychol.*, **44**, 17-25.

Silverman, L. H. (1976) 'Psychoanalytic theory: the reports of my death are greatly exaggerated', *Amer. Psychol.*, **31**.

Silverman, L. H. (1980) *A Comprehensive Report of Studies using the Subliminal Psychodynamic Activation Method*, New York, Research Center for Mental Health.

Silverman, L. H., Klinger, H., Lustbader, L., Farrell, J. and Martin, A. (1972) 'The effects of subliminal drive stimulation on the speech of stutterers', *J. New. Ment. Dis.*, **155**, 14-21.

Silverman, L. H., Kwawer, J. S., Wolitzky, C. and Coron, M. (1973) 'An experimental study of aspects of the psychoanalytic theory of male homosexuality', *J. Abnorm. Psychol.*, **82**, 178-88.

Silverman, L. H., Ross, D. L., Adler, J. M. and Lustuy, D. A. (1978) 'Simple research paradigm for demonstrating psychodynamic activation: effects of Oedipal stimuli on dart-throwing accuracy in college males', *J. Abnorm. Psychol.*, **87**, 341-57.

Simsarian, S. P. (1947) 'Case histories of five thumb-sucking children breast-fed on unscheduled regimes, without limitation of nursing time', *Child Development*, **18**, 180-4.

Sizer, T. (ed.) (1967) *Religion and Public Education*, Boston, Houghton-Mifflin.

Sjoback, H. (1967) *The Defence Mechanism Test*, Lund, The Colytographic Foundation.

Sjobring. H. (1963) *La Personnalité — Structure et Développement*, Paris, Doin.

Skinner, B. F. (1954) 'Critique of psychoanalytic concepts and theories', *Sci. Monogr.*, **79**, 300-5.

Smith, G. J. W. (1949) *Psychological Studies in Twin Differences*, Lund, University of Lund.

Smock, C. D. (1956) 'Replication and comments: an experimental reunion of psychoanalytic theory with perceptual vigilance and defence', *J. Abnorm. Soc. Psychol.*, **53**, 68-73.

Snider, M. (1959) 'On the adequacy of the Krout and Tabin Personal Preference Scale standardization group', *J. Clin. Psychol.*, **15**, 68-70.

Snyder, F. (1963) 'The new biology of dreaming', *Arch. Gen. Psychiat.*, **8**, 381-91.

Snyder, F. (1964) 'The REM state in a "living fossil"', *Paper at Ann. Meeting of Assn. Psychophysiol. Stud. Sleep*.

Snyder, F. (1965) 'Progress in the new biology of dreaming', *Amer. J. Psychiat.*, **122** (4), 377-91.

Snyder, F., Hobson, J. A. and Goldfrank, F. (1963) 'Blood pressure changes during human sleep', *Sci.*, **142**, 1313-14.

Solway, K. S. (1971) 'Freudian and cultural symbolism', *J. Clin. Psychol.*, **27**, 516-18.

Spain, D. H. (1972) in Hsu, F. L. K. (ed.) *Psychological Anthropology*, Cambridge, Mass., Schenkman.

Spiegel, S. B. and Zelin, M. (1973) 'Fantasy aggression and the catharsis phenomenon', *J. Soc. Psychol.*, **91**, 97-107.

Spiro, M. (1979) 'Whatever happened to the id?', *Am. Anthropol.*, **81**, 5-13.

Spiro, M. E. (1961) 'An overview and a suggested reorientation', in Hsu, F. L. K. (1961).

Spitzer, H. M. (1947) 'Psychoanalytic approaches to the Japanese character', *Psychoanalysis and the Social Services*, vol. I, New York, International University Press.

Sprague, R. L. (1959) 'Effects of differential training on tachistoscopic recognition thresholds', *J. Exp. Psychol.*, **58**, 227-31.

Stagner, R., Lawson, E. D. and Moffit, J. W. (1955) 'The Krout Personal Preference Scale: a factor-analytic study', *J. Clin. Psychol.*, **11**, 103-13.

Stagner, R. and Moffit, J. W. (1956) 'A statistical study of Freud's theory of personality types', *J. Clin. Psychol.*, **12**, 72-4.

Starer, E. (1955) 'Cultural symbolism: a validity study', *J. Consult. Psychol.*, **19**, 453-4.

Stein, A. (1958) 'Guilt as a composite emotion: the relation of child-rearing variables to super-ego response', Ph.D. thesis, University of Michigan.

Stein, M. and Ottenberg, P. (1958) 'Role of odours in asthma', *Psychosom. Med.*, **20**, 60-5.

Stendler, C. B. (1954) 'Possible causes of over-dependency in young children', *Child Develop.*, **25**, 125-46.

Stennett, R. G. and Thurlow, M. (1958) 'Cultural symbolism: the age variable', *J. Consult. Psychol.*, **22**, 496.

Stephens, W. N. (1961) 'A cross-cultural study of menstrual taboos', *Genet. Psychol. Monogr.*, **64**, 385-416.

Stephens, W. N. (1962) *The Oedipus Complex Hypothesis: Cross-cultural Evidence*, New York, Free Press of Glencoe.

Stevenson, H. (ed.) (1963) *Child Psychology*, Chicago, University of Chicago Press.

Stokes, A. (1965) *The Invitation in Art*, London, Tavistock Publications.

Story, I. A. (1963) 'The relationship between the effects of conflict arousal and oral thinking', Ph.D. thesis, University of Michigan.

Story, I. A. (1968) 'Effects on thinking of relationships between conflict arousal and oral fixation', *J. Abnorm. Psychol.*, **73**, 440-8.

Strassburger, F. (1966) 'The "Steeple effect": sex-differences in marginal perception and fantasy', *J. Nerv. Ment. Dis.*, **142**, 228-34.

Strauss, M. A. (1957) 'Anal and oral frustration in relation to Sinhalese personality', *Sociometry*, **20**, 21-31.

Streitfield, H. S. (1954) 'Specificity of peptic ulcer to intense oral conflicts', *Psychosom. Med.*, **16**, 315-26.

Stricker, L. J. and Ross, R. (1964) 'An assessment of some structural properties of the Jungian personality typology', *J. Abnorm. Soc. Psychol.*, **68**, 62-71.

Stringer, P. (1970) 'A note on the factorial structure of the Dynamic Personality Inventory', *Brit. J. Med. Psychol.*, **43** (1), 95-103.

Sulce, J. (1972) Ph.D. thesis in psychology, University of Paris, quoted by Grygier and Grygier (1976).

Sundberg, N. D. (1965) 'The Myers—Briggs Type Indicator', in Buros, O. K. (1965).

Sutherland. J. D. (ed.) (1968) *The Psychoanalytic Approach*, London, Hogarth Press and Institute of Psychoanalysis.

Tagiuri, R. and Petrullo, L. (eds) (1958) *Person Perception and Interpersonal Behaviour*, Stanford, Stanford University Press.

Tait, D. (1961) *The Konkomba of Northern Ghana*, London, International African Institute and University of Ghana.

Tart, C. T. (1965) 'The hypnotic dream: methodological problems and a review of the literature', *Psychol. Bull.*, **63**, 87-99.

Taulbee, E. S. and Stenmark, P. E. (1968) 'The Blacky Pictures Test: a comprehensive annotated and indexed bibliography (1949-67)', *J. Proj. Tech.*, **32**, 105-37.

Taylor, A. (ed.) (1962) *Educational and Occupational Selection in West Africa*, London, Oxford University Press.

Thelen, M. H. (1965) 'Similarities of defence preferences within families and within sex groups', *J. Proj. Tech. and Pers. Ass.*, **29** (4), 461-4.

Thoma, H., Kachele, H. and Grunzig, H. J. (1976) 'Contributions to the consensus research in psychoanalysis', translation of Ms., University of Ulm, 1976.

Thomas, R. W. (1951) 'An investigation of the psychoanalytic theory of homosexuality', Ph.D. thesis, University of Lexington.

Thorndike, E. L. and Lorge, I. (1944) *The Teacher's Word Book of 30,000 Words*, New York, Columbia University Press.

Thornton, D. (1980) 'Moral development in offenders', Ph.D. thesis, University of Exeter.

Thurston, J. R. and Mussen, P. H. (1951) 'Infant-feeding gratification and adult personality', *J. Pers.*, **19**, 449-58.

Thurstone, L. L. (1947) *Multiple Factor-Analysis: A Development and Expansion of the Mind*, Chicago, University of Chicago Press.

Timmons, E. O. and Noblin, C. D. (1963) 'The differential performance of orals and anals in a verbal conditioning paradigm', *J. Consult. Psychol.*, **27**, 383-6.

Tinbergen, N. (1959) 'Comparative studies of the behaviour of gulls (laridae): a progress report', *Behav.*, **15**, 1-70.

Touhey, J. C. (1977) 'Penis envy and attitudes towards castration — like punishment of sexual aggression', *J. Res. in Pers.*, **11**, 1-9.

Traisman, A. S. and Traisman, H. S. (1958) 'Thumb- and finger-sucking: a study of 2650 infants and children', *J. Pediat.*, **52**, 566-72.

Triandis, L. M. and Lambert, W. W. (1961) 'Pan-cultural factor-analysis of reported socialization practices', *J. Abnorm. Soc. Psychol.*, **62**, 631-9.

Trilles, R. P. H. (1912) 'Totémisme chez les Fan', *Bibliothèque Anthropos.*, **1**, 184-205.

Trosman, H., Rechtschaffen, A., Offenkrantz, W. and Wolpert, E. (1960) 'Studies in the psychophysiology of dreams — IV: Relations among dreams in sequence', *Arch. Gen. Psychiat.*, **3**, 602.

Truax, C. B. (1963) 'Effective ingredients in psychotherapy: an approach to unraveling the patient—therapist interactions', *J. Consult. Psychol.*, **10**, 256-63.

Truax, C. B. and Carkhuff, R. R. (1964) 'Significant developments in psychotherapy research', in Abt and Reiss (1964).

Tsujioka, B. and Cattell, R. B. (1965) 'Constancy and difference in personality structure and mean profile in the questionnaire medium from applying the 16PF Test in American and Japan', *Brit. J. Soc. Clin. Psychol.*, **4**, 269-86.

Ullman, L. P. (1962) 'An empirically derived MMPI scale which measures facilitation—inhibition of recognition of threatening stimuli', *J. Clin. Psychol.*, **18**, 127-32.

Updike, J. (1968) *Couples*, London, André Deutsch.

Valentine, C. W. (1960) *The Normal Child and Some of His Abnormalities*, Harmondsworth, Penguin.

Veldman, D. J. and Bown, O. H. (1969) 'Personality and performance characteristics associated with cigarette smoking among college freshmen', *J. Consult. Clin. Psychol.*, **33**, 109-19.

Velicer, W. F. (1976) 'Determining the number of components from the matrix of partial correlations', *Psychometrika*, **41**, 321-7.

Veness, T. (1962) 'An experiment on slips of the tongue and word-association faults', *Lang. and Speech*, **5** (3), 128-37.

Vernallis, F. F. (1955) 'Teeth-grinding: some relationships to anxiety, hostility and hyperactivity', *J. Clin. Psychol.*, **11**, 389-91.

Vernon, P. E. (1953) *Personality Tests and Assessments*, London, Methuen.

Vernon. P. E. (1964) *Personality Assessment*, London, Methuen.

Verrill, B. V., and Costanza, V. (1962) 'The IES Test and ward behaviour', *J. Clin. Psychol.*, **18**, 295-7.

Vetter, H. J. and Smith, B. D. (eds) (1971) *Personality Theory: A Source Book*, New York, Appleton-Century-Crofts.

Waelder, R. (1965) *Psychoanalytic Avenues to Art*, London, Hogarth Press and Institute for Psychoanalysis.

Walker, E. L. (1958) 'Action decrement and its relation to learning', *Psychol. Rev.*, **65**, 129-42.

Wallach, M. A. (1960) 'Two correlates of symbolic sexual arousal: level of anxiety and liking for aesthetic material', *J. Abnorm. Soc. Psychol.*, **61**, 396-401.

Wallach, M. A. and Greenberg, C. (1960) 'Personality functions of symbolic sexual arousal to music', *Psychol. Monogr.*, **74** (7), 494.

Wallerstein, R. S., Robbins, L. L., Sargent, H. D. and Luborsky, L. (1956) 'The psychotherapy research project of the Menninger foundation: rationale, method and sample', *Bull. Menning. Clin.*, **20**, 221.

Warburton, F. W. (1968) 'The structure of personality factors', unpub. Ms., University of Manchester.

Watson, C. G. (1965) 'A test of the relationship between repressed homosexuality and paranoid mechanisms', *J. Clin. Psychol.*, **21** (4), 380-4.

Watson, J. P. (1975) 'An experimental method for the study of unconscious conflict', *Brit. J. Med. Psychol.*, **48**, 301-2.

Waxenberg, S. E., Dickes, R. and Gottesfield, H., (1962) 'The Poetzl phenomenon re-examined experimentally', *J. Nerv. Ment. Dis.*, **135**, 387-98.

Webb, W. B. (1968) *Sleep: an Experimental Approach*, London, Macmillan.

Weber, J. J., Elinson, J. and Moss, L. M. (1966) 'The application of ego-strength scales to psychoanalytic clinical records', in Goldman, G. and Shapers, S. (eds) *Developments in Psychoanalysis at Columbia University*, New York, Haffner.

Weber, J. J., Elinson, J. and Moss, L. M. (1967) 'Psychoanalysis and change: a study of psychoanalytic clinical records, utilizing electronic data-processing techniques', *Arch. Gen. Psychiat.*, **17**, 687-709.

Wells, W. D. and Goldstein, R. L. (1964) 'Sear's study of projection: replication and critique', *J. Soc. Psychol.*, **64** (1), 169-79.

Westerlundh, B. (1976) *Aggression, Anxiety and Defence*, Lund, Gleerups.

White, L. E. and Hinde, R. E. (1975) 'Some factors affecting mother—infant relations in Rhesus monkeys', *Animal Behav.*, **23**, 527-42.

Whiting, B. B. (1963) *Six Cultures: Studies of Child Rearing*, New York, Wiley.

Whiting, J. W. M. (1960) 'Resource mediation and learning by identification', in Iscoe and Stevenson (1960).

Whiting, J. W. M. (1968) in Lindzey, G. and Aronson, E. (eds) *Handbook of Social Psychology*, vol. II, Cambridge, Mass., Addison Wesley.

Whiting, J. W. M. and Child, I. L. (1953) *Child Training and Personality*, New

Haven, Yale University Press.

Whiting, J. W. M., Kluckhohn, H. and Anthony, A. (1958) 'The function of male initiation ceremonies at puberty', in Maccoby, E. E., Newcomb, T. M. and Hartley, E. L. (1958).

Whittaker, E. M., Gilchrist, J. C., and Fischer, J. W. (1952) 'Perceptual defence or response suppression', *J. Abnorm. Soc. Psychol.*, **47**, 732-3.

Whyte, L. L. (1968) *The Unconscious Before Freud*, London, Tavistock Publications.

Wiener, D. N. (1948) 'Subtle and obvious keys for the MMPI', *J. Consult. Psychol.*, **12**, 164-70.

Wiener, M., (1955) 'Word-frequency or motivation in perceptual defence', *J. Abnorm. Soc. Psychol.*, **51**, 214-8.

Wiggins, J. S., Wiggins, N. and Conger, J. C. (1968) 'Correlates of heterosexual somatic preference', *J. Pers. Soc. Psychol.*, **10**, 82-90.

Wilkinson, F. R. and Carghill, D. W. (1955) 'Repression elicited by story material based on the Oedipus complex', *J. Soc. Psychol.*, **42**, 209-14.

Williams, M. (1951) 'Rate of learning as a function of ego-alien material', *J. Pers.*, **19**, 324-31.

Wilson, G. D. and Patterson, J. R. (1970) *The Conservatism Scale*, Windsor, NFER.

Winnicott, D. W. (1957) *The Child and the Family*, London, Tavistock Publications.

Winter, W. D. (1955) 'Two personality patterns in peptic ulcer patients', *J. Proj. Tech.*, **19**, 332-44.

Winter, W. D. and Prescott, J. W. (1957) 'A cross-validation of Starer's test of cultural symbolism', *J. Consult. Psychol.*, **21**, 22.

Witmer, H. and Powers, E. (1951) *An Experiment in the Prevention of Delinquency*, New York, Columbia University Press.

Wittenborn, J. R. (1953) 'The IPAT Humour Test', in Buros, O. K. (ed.) (1953) *IVth Mental Measurement Year Book*, New Jersey, Gryphon.

Wober, M. (1967) 'Sensotypes', *J. Soc. Psychol.*, **70**, 181-9.

Wolfenden Report. See Report of the Committee on Homosexual Offences and Prostitution.

Wolowitz, H. M. (1964) 'Food preference as an index of orality', *J. Abnorm. Soc. Psychol.*, **69** (6), 650-4.

Wolowitz, H. M. (1965) 'Attraction and aversion to power: a psychoanalytic conflict theory of homosexuality in male paranoids', *J. Abnorm. Psychol.*, **70** (5), 360-70.

Wolowitz, H. M. (1967) 'Oral involvement in peptic ulcer', *J. Consult. Psychol.*, **31**, 418-19.

Wolowitz, H. M. and Barker, M. J. (1968) 'Alcoholism and oral passivity', *Quart. J. Stud. Alcohol.*, **29**, 592-7.

Wolowitz, H. M. and Wagonfeld, S. (1968) 'Oral derivatives in the food preferences of peptic ulcer patients: an experimental test of Alexander's psychoanalytic hypothesis', *J. Nerv. Ment. Dis.*, **146**, 18-23.

Wood, P. (1962) 'Dreaming and social isolation', Ph.D. thesis, University of North Carolina, quoted by Webb, W. B. (1968).

Woodmansey, A. C. (1967) 'Emotion and the motions: an enquiry into the causes and prevention of functional disorders of defecation', *Brit. J. Med. Psychol.*, **40**, 207-23.

Woodward, M. (1958) 'The diagnosis and treatment of homosexual offenders', *Brit. J. Delinq.*, **9**, 44-58.

Woodworth, R. S. and Schlosberg, H. (1955) *Experimental Psychology*, New York, Holt, Rinehart & Winston.

Worchel, P. (1957) 'Adaptability screening of flying personnel: development of a self-concept inventory for predicting maladjustment', *USAF Schl. Aviat. Med. Rep.*

Worthy, M. and Craddick, R. A. (1969) 'Semantic differential investigation of sexually symbolic concepts', *J. Proj. Tech.*, **33**, 78-80.

Wylie, R. C. (1957) 'Cognitive set and motivational factors in the perception of neutral and threat related stimuli', *J. Abnorm. Soc. Psychol.*, **55**, 227-31.

Wyllie, R. W. (1966) 'Ghanaian students: a research note', *Brit. J. Sociol.*, **17** (3), 306-11.

Yarrow, L. J. (1954) 'The relationship between nutritive sucking experiences in infancy and non-nutritive sucking in childhood', *J. Genet. Psychol.*, **84**, 149-62.

Yarrow, L. J. (1961) 'Maternal deprivation: towards an empirical and conceptual re-evaluation', *Psychol. Bull.*, **58**, 459-90.

Zamansky, H. S. (1958) 'An investigation of the psychoanalytic theory of paranoid delusions', *J. Pers.*, **26**, 410-25.

Zeichner, A. M. (1955) 'Psychosexual identification in paranoid schizophrenia', *J. Proj. Tech.*, **19**, 67-77.

Zeigarnik, B. (1927) 'Über das Behalten von erledigten und unerleditzen Handlungen', *Psychol. Forsch.*, **9**, 1-85.

Zeller, A. F. (1950a) 'An experimental analogue of repression — I: Historical summary', *Psychol. Bull.*, **47**, 39-51.

Zeller, A. F. (1950b) 'An experimental analogue of repression — II: The effects of individual failure and success on memory measured by relearning', *J. Exp. Psychol.*, **40**, 411-22.

Zubin, J., Eron, L. D. and Schumer, F. (1965) *An Experimental Approach to Projective Techniques*, London, Wiley.

Name index

General index

APR 8 1982

DATE DUE

UC APR 2 1982